The Notebooks of Samuel Taylor Coleridge

VOLUME 2

NOTES

THE NOTEBOOKS

OF

Samuel Taylor Coleridge

Edited by Kathleen Coburn

VOLUME 2
1804–1808

NOTES

ROUTLEDGE & KEGAN PAUL

LONDON

FIRST PUBLISHED 1962
BY ROUTLEDGE & KEGAN PAUL LTD
BROADWAY HOUSE, 68–74 CARTER LANE
LONDON, E.C.4

THIS IS THE SECOND VOLUME OF

A COMPLETE EDITION OF THE NOTEBOOKS OF COLERIDGE.

THE VOLUME IS IN TWO PARTS: TEXT AND NOTES

PRINTED IN THE UNITED STATES
OF AMERICA

CONTENTS

LIST OF MAPS

ABBREVIATIONS AND CONTRACTIONS

Allston Life	*The Life and Letters of Washington Allston* J. B. Flagg (New York 1892).
ALZ	*Allgemeine Literatur-Zeitung* (Jena; Leipzig 1785–1849).
An Anthol	*The Annual Anthology* (2 vols Bristol 1799–1800).
An Reg	*Annual Register* (London 1758–).
An Rev	*Annual Review and History of Literature* (London 1803–18).
AP	*Anima Poetae from the unpublished notebooks of Samuel Taylor Coleridge* ed E. H. Coleridge (London 1895).
AP (Keats H)	A copy of *Anima Poetae* in Keats House, Hampstead, annotated by several hands.
APR	A. P. Rossiter.
AR	*Aids to Reflection in the formation of a manly character on the several grounds of prudence, morality and religion, illustrated by select passages from our elder divines, especially from Archbishop Leighton* S. T. Coleridge (London 1825).
Asra	"Coleridge and 'Asra' " T. M. Raysor *Studies in Philology* XXVI (1929) 305–24.
Bald	R. C. Bald "Coleridge and *The Ancient Mariner*" *Nineteenth Century Studies* ed Herbert Davis, W. C. De Vane, and R. C. Bald (Ithaca, N. Y. 1940).
B Critic	*The British Critic* (London May 1793–1843).
BE	*Biographia Epistolaris* S. T. Coleridge ed A. Turnbull (2 vols London 1911).
BL	*Biographia Literaria* S. T. Coleridge ed John Shawcross (2 vols Oxford 1907).
BL (1817)	*Biographia Literaria* S. T. Coleridge (2 vols London 1817).
BL (1847)	*Biographia Literaria* S. T. Coleridge ed H. N. and Sara Coleridge (2 vols London 1847).
Blackwood's	*Blackwood's Magazine* (Edinburgh and London April 1817–).
BM	British Museum.

Botanic Garden   *The Botanic Garden* Erasmus Darwin (2 vols London 1794–5).

B Poets   *The Works of the British Poets* ed Robert Anderson (13 vols Edinburgh 1792–5; vol 14 issued 1807).

Brandl   A. L. Brandl "S. T. Coleridge's Notizbuch aus den Jahren 1795–1798" in *Archiv für das Studium der neueren Sprachen und Litteraturen* xcvii (1896) 333–72.

Bristol Borrow-ings   "The Bristol Library Borrowings of Southey and Coleridge, 1793–8" George Whalley *The Library* iv (Sept 1949) 114–31.

C&S   *On the Constitution of Church and State, according to the Idea of Each with aids toward a right judgment on the late bill* S. T. Coleridge (London 1830).

C&SH   *Coleridge and Sara Hutchinson and the Asra Poems* George Whalley (London 1955).

C&S in Bristol   "Coleridge and Southey in Bristol, 1795" George Whalley *Review of English Studies* n s 1 (Oct 1950) 333.

Carlyon   Clement Carlyon *Early Years and Late Reflections* (4 vols London 1836–58).

C at Highgate   *Coleridge at Highgate* L. E. (G.) Watson (London and New York 1925).

CBEL   *The Cambridge Bibliography of English Literature* ed F. W. Bateson (5 vols Cambridge 1940–57).

C Concordance   *A Concordance to the Poetry of Samuel Taylor Coleridge* ed Sister Eugenia Logan (Saint Mary-of-the-Woods, Ind. 1940).

Chambers   E. K. Chambers *Samuel Taylor Coleridge* (Oxford 1938).

CL   *Collected Letters of Samuel Taylor Coleridge* ed E. L. Griggs (Oxford and New York 1956–).

C Life   *Samuel Taylor Coleridge; a Narrative of the Events of his Life* J. D. Campbell (London 1894).

CN   *The Notebooks of Samuel Taylor Coleridge* ed Kathleen Coburn (New York and London 1957–).

Coleorton   *Memorials of Coleorton* ed William Knight (2 vols Edinburgh 1887).

Cormorant MS   "Samuel Taylor Coleridge; Library Cormorant" George Whalley (University of London 1950).

Cornell Studies   *Some Letters of the Wordsworth Family . . . with a few unpublished letters of Coleridge and Southey and others* ed Leslie Nathan Broughton. Cornell Studies in English XXXII (Ithaca, N. Y. 1942).

Cottle (*E Rec*) Joseph Cottle *Early Recollections; chiefly relating to the late Samuel Taylor Coleridge, during his long residence in Bristol* (2 vols London 1837–39).

Cottle (*Rem*) Joseph Cottle *Reminiscences of Samuel Taylor Coleridge and Robert Southey* (London 1847).

CRBooks *H. C. Robinson on Books and their Writers* ed E. J. Morley (3 vols London 1938).

CRC *The Correspondence of Henry Crabb Robinson with the Wordsworth Circle* ed E. J. Morley (2 vols Oxford 1927).

Cr Rev *The Critical Review; or, Annals of Literature* (London 1756–1817).

C 17th C *Coleridge on the Seventeenth Century* ed R. F. Brinkley (Durham, N. C. 1955).

C Works *The Complete Works of Samuel Taylor Coleridge* ed [W. G. T.] Shedd (7 vols New York 1853).

De Q Works *The Collected Writings of Thomas De Quincey* ed David Masson (14 vols Edinburgh 1889–90).

D Life *The Life of Sir Humphry Davy* J. A. Paris (2 vols London 1831).

D Life 4º *The Life of Sir Humphry Davy* J. A. Paris (1 vol 4º London 1831).

D Memoirs *Memoirs of the Life of Sir Humphry Davy* John Davy (London 1839).

DNB *Dictionary of National Biography* (London 1885–).

D Rem *Fragmentary Remains, Literary and Scientific of Sir Humphry Davy, with a Sketch of his Life* ed John Davy (London 1858).

DW (de S) *Dorothy Wordsworth* Ernest de Selincourt (Oxford 1933).

DWJ *Journals of Dorothy Wordsworth* ed Ernest de Selincourt (2 vols Oxford 1939).

D Works *The Collected Works of Sir Humphry Davy* ed John Davy (9 vols London 1839–41).

E&S *Essays and Studies* by Members of the English Association (London 1910–).

EB   *Encyclopaedia Britannica.*

EDD   *English Dialect Dictionary* ed Joseph Wright (6 vols London and New York 1898–1905).

Ed Rev   *The Edinburgh Review* (Edinburgh and London October 1802–1929).

EHC   Ernest Hartley Coleridge.

Eng Div   *Notes on English Divines* S. T. Coleridge ed Derwent Coleridge (2 vols London 1853).

Eng Poets   *The Works of the English Poets from Chaucer to Cowper* ed Alexander Chalmers (21 vols London 1810).

EOT   *Essays on his Own Times forming a second series of The Friend* S. T. Coleridge ed Sara Coleridge (3 vols London 1850).

Estimate of WW   *Estimate of William Wordsworth by his Contemporaries* ed Elsie Smith (Oxford 1932).

Estlin   "Unpublished Letters from Samuel Taylor Coleridge to the Rev. John Prior Estlin" Philobiblon Society *Miscellanies* xv (London 1884).

Friend   *The Friend, a series of essays* S. T. Coleridge (3 vols London 1818).

Friend (1809–10)   *The Friend, a Literary, Moral and Political Weekly Paper* conducted by S. T. Coleridge (Penrith 1809–10 in numbers).

Friend (1812)   *The Friend, a series of essays* S. T. Coleridge (London 1812).

Friend (R)   *The Friend*, a critical edition of the three versions (MS) ed B. E. Rooke.

Gillman   James Gillman *Life of Samuel Taylor Coleridge* (Vol 1 [all published] London 1838).

Gillman SC   *Catalogue of a valuable collection of books, including the library of James Gillman, Esq.* (Henry Southgate, London [1843]).

Godwin (Brown)   *Life of William Godwin* F. K. Brown (London 1926).

Godwin (MS Diary)   Transcript by Dr. Lewis Patton from a microfilm in Duke University Library of the MS diary of William Godwin owned by Lord Abinger.

Godwin (Paul)   *William Godwin, his Friends and Contemporaries* C. K. Paul (London 1876).

Godwin SC (1836)	*Catalogue of the Curious Library of . . . William Godwin* (Sotheby, London 1836).
Göttingen Borrowings	"Books borrowed by Coleridge from the library of the University of Göttingen, 1799" A. D. Snyder *Modern Philology* xxv (1928) 377–80.
Green SC	*Catalogue of the Library of Joseph Henry Green which will be sold by auction* Sotheby, Wilkinson and Hodge (London July 1880).
Haney	J. L. Haney *A Bibliography of Samuel Taylor Coleridge* (Philadelphia 1903).
Hanson	Lawrence Hanson *The Life of S. T. Coleridge, the Early Years* (London 1938).
Heber	Reginald Heber (editor) *The Whole Works of Jeremy Taylor with a Life of the Author and a Critical Examination of his Writings* (10 vols London 1883).
HEHL	Henry E. Huntington Library and Art Gallery, San Marino, Calif.
HEHLB	Henry E. Huntington Library and Art Gallery, San Marino, Calif. *Huntington Library Bulletin* (11 nos Cambridge, Mass. 1931–37).
HEHLQ	*The Henry E. Huntington Library Quarterly* (San Marino, Calif. 1937–).
H Life (Howe)	*The Life of William Hazlitt* P. P. Howe (revised edition London and New York 1928).
HNC	Henry Nelson Coleridge.
House	Humphry House *Coleridge* (London 1953).
House of Letters	*A House of Letters, being excerpts from the correspondence of . . . Coleridge, Lamb, Southey . . . with Matilda Betham* ed Ernest Betham (Second edition London [1905]).
HUL	Harvard University Library, including the Houghton Library.
Hutchinson	William Hutchinson *The History of the County of Cumberland* (2 vols Carlisle 1794).
H Works	*The Complete Works of William Hazlitt* ed P. P. Howe (21 vols London 1930–4).
Inq Sp	*Inquiring Spirit; a new presentation of Coleridge from his published and unpublished prose writings* ed Kathleen Coburn (London and New York 1951).

JDC	James Dykes Campbell.
JW	John Wordsworth.
L	*Letters of Samuel Taylor Coleridge* ed E. H. Coleridge (2 vols London 1895).
LB	*Lyrical Ballads with a few other Poems* [By William Wordsworth and S. T. Coleridge] (Bristol and London 1798).
LB (1800)	*Lyrical Ballads with other Poems* William Wordsworth [and S. T. Coleridge] (Second edition 2 vols London 1800).
LCL	Loeb Classical Library.
L Letters	*The Letters of Charles Lamb to which are added those of his sister Mary Lamb* ed E. V. Lucas (3 vols London 1935).
L Life	*Life of Charles Lamb* E. V. Lucas (London 1921).
LLP	*Letters from the Lake Poets to Daniel Stuart* ed [Mary Stuart and E. H. Coleridge] (London 1889).
Logic	*Coleridge on Logic and Learning* ed A. D. Snyder (London 1929).
Logic (MS)	BM Egerton MSS 2825, 2826.
LR	*The Literary Remains of Samuel Taylor Coleridge* ed H. N. Coleridge (London 1836–9).
LS	*A Lay Sermon addressed to the higher and middle classes on the existing distresses and discontents* S. T. Coleridge (London 1817).
L Works	*The Works of Charles and Mary Lamb* ed E. V. Lucas (6 vols London 1912).
Margoliouth	H. M. Margoliouth *Wordsworth and Coleridge, 1795–1834* (London and New York 1953).
MC	*Coleridge's Miscellaneous Criticism* ed T. M. Raysor (London 1936).
M Chronicle	*The Morning Chronicle* (London 1770–1862).
Meteyard	Eliza Meteyard *A Group of Englishmen* (London 1871).
Method	*S. T. Coleridge's Treatise on Method as published in the Encyclopaedia Metropolitana* ed A. D. Snyder (London 1934).
Minnow Among Tritons	*Minnow Among Tritons; Mrs. S. T. Coleridge's letters to Thomas Poole, 1799–1834* ed Stephen Potter (London 1934).
Miscellanies	*Miscellanies, Aesthetic and Literary; to which is added "The*

	Theory of Life" S. T. Coleridge ed T. Ashe (London 1885).
MLN	*Modern Language Notes* (Baltimore 1886–).
MLR	*Modern Language Review* (Cambridge 1905–).
M Memoirs	*Memoirs of the Life of Sir James Mackintosh* ed R. J. Mackintosh (Second edition 2 vols London 1836).
Mod Philol	*Modern Philology* (Chicago 1903–).
Mon Mag	*The Monthly Magazine and British Register* (London Feb 1796–1843).
Mon Rev	*The Monthly Review; or, Literary Journal* (London 1749–1844).
M Post	*The Morning Post* (London 1772–).
MS Journal	A journal of Coleridge's visit to Germany, a foolscap MS in his holograph (intermediate between the entries in the notebooks and "Satyrane's letters", much of it used in letters to his wife, Poole, and Josiah Wedgwood. Once owned by Gabriel Wells of New York), now in the Berg Collection, NYPL.
MW	Mary (Mrs.) Wordsworth.
N	Notebook of Samuel Taylor Coleridge.
N&Q	*Notes and Queries* (London 1849–).
NBU	*Nouvelle Biographie universelle* (46 vols Paris 1852–66).
Nicholson's *Journal*	*A Journal of Natural Philosophy, Chemistry and the Arts* ed William Nicholson (London 1797–1813).
Notes Theol	*Notes, Theological, Political and Miscellaneous* S. T. Coleridge ed Derwent Coleridge (London 1853).
NYPL	New York Public Library.
OCD	*The Oxford Classical Dictionary* (Oxford 1949).
OED	*Oxford English Dictionary* (13 vols Oxford 1933).
Omniana	*Omniana* [ed Robert Southey with articles by S. T. Coleridge] (2 vols London 1812).
Omniana (Ashe)	*The Table Talk and Omniana of Samuel Taylor Coleridge* ed T. Ashe (London 1884).
Phil Lects	*The Philosophical Lectures of Samuel Taylor Coleridge* ed Kathleen Coburn (London and New York 1949).
Phil Trans	*Philosophical Transactions of the Royal Society* (London 1665–1886).

Phil Trans (*Abr*)	*The Philosophical Transactions of the Royal Society* London *Abridgement* ed C. Hutton, R. Pearson, and G. Shaw (London 1792–1809).
Philol Q	*Philological Quarterly* (Iowa City 1922–).
PML	Pierpont Morgan Library, New York City.
PMLA	*Publications of the Modern Language Association* (Baltimore 1886–).
Poems 1796	*Poems on Various Subjects* S. T. Coleridge (Bristol 1796).
Poems 1797	*Poems by S. T. Coleridge, second edition, to which are now added Poems by Charles Lamb and Charles Lloyd* (Bristol and London 1797).
Poole	*Thomas Poole and his Friends* M. E. (P.) Sandford (2 vols London 1888).
Prelude	*The Prelude or Growth of a Poet's Mind* William Wordsworth ed Ernest de Selincourt (Oxford 1926).
PW	*The Complete Poetical Works of Samuel Taylor Coleridge* ed E. H. Coleridge (2 vols Oxford 1912).
PW (JDC)	*The Poetical Works of Samuel Taylor Coleridge* ed with a biographical introduction by J. D. Campbell (London and New York 1893).
RES	*Review of English Studies* (London 1925–).
Rickman	*Lamb's Friend the Census-Taker. Life and Letters of John Rickman* Orlo Williams (London 1912).
RX	*The Road to Xanadu* J. L. Lowes (revised edition London 1930).
SCB	*Southey's Common-Place Book* ed J. W. Warter (4 vols London 1849–51).
Schneider	Elisabeth Schneider *Coleridge, Opium and Kubla Khan* (Chicago 1953).
SC Memoir	*Memoir and Letters of Sara Coleridge* [ed Edith Coleridge] (Second edition 2 vols London 1873).
Select P&P	*Select Poetry and Prose* S. T. Coleridge ed Stephen Potter (London 1933).
SH	Sara Hutchinson.
ShC	*Coleridge's Shakespearean Criticism* ed T. M. Raysor (2 vols London 1930).

SH Letters	*The Letters of Sara Hutchinson* ed Kathleen Coburn (London and Toronto 1954).
SL	*Sibylline Leaves* S. T. Coleridge (London 1817).
S Life and C	*Life and Correspondence of Robert Southey* ed C. C. Southey (6 vols London 1849–50).
SM	*The Statesman's Manual; or The Bible the Best Guide to Political Skill and Foresight; A Lay Sermon* S. T. Coleridge (London 1816).
Studies (Blunden & Griggs)	*Coleridge: Studies by Several Hands on the Hundredth Anniversary of his Death* ed Edmund Blunden and E. L. Griggs (London 1934).
Stud Philol	*Studies in Philology* (Chapel Hill, N. C. 1906–).
Tennemann	W. G. Tennemann *Geschichte der Philosophie* (12 vols Leipzig 1798–1819).
Theol Lects	Theological Lectures S. T. Coleridge (Bristol 1795 MS transcript by E. H. Coleridge, in VCL).
TL	*Hints towards the Formation of a more Comprehensive Theory of Life* S. T. Coleridge ed S. B. Watson (London 1848).
TLS	*The Times Literary Supplement* (London 1902–).
Toland	John Toland (editor) *A Complete Collection of the Historical, Political and Miscellaneous Works of Milton* (3 vols London 1694–8).
TT	*Specimens of the Table Talk of the late Samuel Taylor Coleridge* ed H. N. Coleridge (2 vols London 1835).
TT (Ashe)	*The Table Talk and Omniana of Samuel Taylor Coleridge* ed T. Ashe (London 1884).
TT (MS)	Table Talk of S. T. Coleridge (additions, in the MS of H. N. Coleridge in VCL).
UL	*Unpublished Letters of Samuel Taylor Coleridge* ed E. L. Griggs (2 vols London 1932).
UTQ	*University of Toronto Quarterly* (Toronto 1931–).
VCL	Victoria College Library, University of Toronto.
Watchman	*The Watchman* S. T. Coleridge (Bristol 1796).
Wedgwood	*Tom Wedgwood, the First Photographer* R. B. Litchfield (London 1903).
W Letters (*E*)	*The Early Letters of William and Dorothy Wordsworth* ed Ernest de Selincourt (Oxford 1935).

W Letters (L)	*Letters of William and Dorothy Wordsworth; the Later Years* ed Ernest de Selincourt (3 vols Oxford 1939).
W Letters (M)	*Letters of William and Dorothy Wordsworth; the Middle Years* ed Ernest de Selincourt (2 vols Oxford 1937).
W Life	*William Wordsworth, A Biography* Mary Moorman (Oxford 1957).
Wordsworth & Coleridge	*Wordsworth & Coleridge: Studies in honor of George McLean Harper* ed E. L. Griggs (Princeton 1939).
Wordsworth LC	Wordsworth Library Catalogue (MS).
Wordsworth SC	*Catalogue of the . . . library of . . . William Wordsworth* (Preston 1859).
W Poems (1815)	*Poems by William Wordsworth: including Lyrical Ballads . . . with additional poems, a new preface, and a supplementary essay* (2 vols London 1815).
WPW	*The Poetical Works of William Wordsworth* ed Ernest de Selincourt and Helen Darbishire (5 vols Oxford 1940–9).
WPW (Knight)	*The Poetical Works of William Wordsworth* ed W. A. Knight (8 vols London 1896).
WW	William Wordsworth.

xvi

GENERAL NOTES
ON EACH NOTEBOOK

For the General Notes on Notebooks 1, 2, 3, 3½, 4, 5, 5½, 6, 7, 8, 10, 16, 21, 22 and the Gutch Notebook, see *CN* 1: Notes xvii–xlv.

NOTEBOOK 9

BM Add MS 47,506

COVER   Brown leather with a metal clasp, a leather fold for the metallic pencil, and a round white label reading "Nº 9". In ink on the cover itself is written in another hand, "London Portsmouth/1803–4".

WATERMARK   J. RUSE 1802

SIZE AND   About 4½″ x 3″, 58 leaves of MS, part of two of
CONDITION   them torn out, two more having been torn out entirely. Pencil was chiefly used throughout.

PERIOD   The notebook was bought in Pall Mall 26 Jan 1804,
OF USE   as entry 1854 records, and was the pocketbook used during the anxious weeks in London preceding the departure on 27 March for Portsmouth and Malta. It was used again on shipboard until Gibraltar was all but in sight. Within the two-month London period some entries are difficult to place more precisely. Do the two groups of brief excerpts from the Cartwright volume, one on *ff12–12ᵛ*, the other on *ff55ᵛ–56*, with a stray on *f58*, represent notes made at one, or two, or more readings of Cartwright? In the absence of any Cartwright references anywhere to help with dating, it seemed wise to give these entries in the order in which they appear in the notebook. The sequence of entries in N 9 seems to be reasonably regular, interrupted here and there by jottings at each end of the book (which can be deduced to be out of chronological order) and by brief uses of N 21 and N 16 at Dunmow in the second week in February. The notebook was filled just as the ship approached Gibraltar, N 21 came out briefly again, and after reaching Gibraltar N 15 was the book of the voyage.

     This is a notebook of short jottings, the notebook of the journalist, the guest at dinners and breakfasts, the restless uncertain trav-

eller. There is evidence of discussions of aesthetic and social questions, of reading, of unhappiness and loneliness, but it is perhaps
of interest to notice that there are here among the London entries
none of the minute observations of his own ill-health of which the
letters at that time were full. Nor are there the long acute meditations on his mental states. This was on the whole a period of activity, in which deeper thoughts were pushed away, except as they
emerged in recollections of Wordsworth's poems, *The Ancient
Mariner,* and such poignant images as that in 1991.

NOTEBOOK 11

BM Add MS 47,508

COVER   Black leather, with a leather fold along the top for a
pencil, a metal clasp, and a pocket inside the front
cover. The label reads "N° 11. 1806".

WATERMARK   None.

SIZE AND   About 3″ x 4½″, 54 leaves of MS and about 10 pages
CONDITION   blank except for numbering in ink at the corners.
Pencil and ink are almost equally in use; unless
otherwise stated, the entries may be taken to be in pencil.

PERIOD   Dates supplied by Coleridge himself specifically fix
OF USE   the earliest use as 6 Sept 1806; three entries (11.15–
11.17) are from 11.15 dated 25 Nov 1810. Like
most of the pocketbooks, this one was used from both ends in such
a way as to make it difficult to be clear about the exact chronology
of the entries, but except for a few entries in 1810, most of them
belong to the last quarter of 1806, immediately after the return
from Malta, and the beginning of 1807. This notebook is associated with some of the most acutely unhappy moments in Coleridge's life—"that accursed Saturday, Dec. 27, 1806!" (11.15), and

the disruption of relations with Wordsworth in the autumn of 1810. It also records the resolve to separate from Mrs Coleridge. In spite of the concentration of misfortunes referred to here, the notebook also shows many signs of interest in Pindaric metres and of attempts to return to his own poems again and to write new ones for Longman's proposed two-volume edition; a good deal of reading of travel and theology and the visits to Cambridge with the Clarksons in 1806 and to Coleorton with the Wordsworths in 1806–7 provide evidence of activity, and there is as well considerable unhappy self-observation, self-denigration, and self-pity.

NOTEBOOK 12

BM Add MS 47,509

COVER   Red leather, with a leather fold along the top for a pencil, a metal clasp, and a pocket inside the front cover, like N 11, which it exactly resembles except for colour. The label reads "N° 12". In ink on the cover is written "1807". Inside is the price, 3/6.

WATERMARK   [E] & P 1801

SIZE AND   About 3″ x 4½″, 56 leaves of MS, written in pencil
CONDITION   and ink almost equally; unless otherwise stated, entries are in pencil.

PERIOD   The date of the fourth entry (3060), 28 May 1807,
OF USE   is approximately the earliest date, the notebook then being in use in a fairly straightforward way, except for some use from back to front of the book at the end, till the autumn of that year. The passages on personal miseries are fewer, though poignant and ironical enough; signs of De Quincey's first meeting and entries having to do with attempted medical conquests of opium-taking appear here. There are further evidences of efforts

to be a poet again, a good deal of reading of Nicholson's *Journal* and other scientific and theological works, probably in Poole's library, Lord Egmont's, Cottle's, and Wade's. This is a notebook of a summer in the west country, healthier than some others, but the product of a very unsettled state of mind.

In 1820 or later Coleridge went through this book and transcribed several entries on paper with an 1820 watermark, possibly a lost notebook, of which some pages are now among the fragments in BM MS Egerton 2801.

NOTEBOOK 15

BM Add MS 47,512

COVER   Black leather with a metal clasp, one half of which has now disappeared, and a fold for a pencil down the side. The price appears on the inside front cover, 6/–. The label reads "N° 15. 1804". Inside is the Hall & Co printed label; see N 4 Gen Note.

WATERMARK   B & P 1801

SIZE AND   About 6⅛" x 3¾", the second largest of the metal-
CONDITION   clasp books, with 125 leaves of MS. Some leaves have been torn or cut out, wholly or in part, as commented on in the relevant notes. This book is very rubbed and worn, and shows signs of weather—sea-water, most likely—on its pages. The pencil, chiefly used throughout, is so faint in places as to be all but non-existent. Red ink was spilt later on some pages by some transcriber or reader, perhaps by EHC, who used it at times in his transcripts from the notebooks.

PERIOD   This notebook, rather large for a pocketbook but
OF USE   apparently intended for use as such, was first taken up in April 1804 on the Malta voyage as the *Speed-*

well approached Gibraltar. On arrival in Malta it was put away, to be used again for travel notes on the Sicilian trip Aug–Nov 1804. In the spring of 1805 it came again into use, and entries appear intermittently in Malta, Sicily, and Italy until 22 June 1806, the day before Coleridge sailed for home. It was used a few times in the autumn of 1806 after he recovered his books from the custom-house in Oct 1806, again in Nov 1807, and again in the spring of 1808. More consistently than any other, it is a notebook of travels, and makes up in the richness of its contents for the unusual difficulties it presents to the transcriber. The variety of interests and pursuits suggests a very active traveller, less given to self-pity than he was to become on his return home.

NOTEBOOK 17

Add MS 47,514

COVER   Brown leather, much rubbed, similar to N 18 in shape, size, and general appearance. The leather thong has at some time been sealed down after being inserted in the loop for it. On the back cover, a sealing-wax seal; the emblem is not visible. On the front cover under the usual label, "Nº 17", is written in black ink: "S.T.C./1805/1808/& part in/1827".

WATERMARK   EDMEADS & PINE 1802

SIZE AND $4\frac{5}{8}''$ x $4\frac{1}{2}''$, 166 leaves, of which 62 are blank. This is
CONDITION   one of the thickest of the notebooks, well bound, and still in firm condition. Ink is generally used.
     A special characteristic of this notebook, more elaborately developed in N 18, is the framing of the pages with Coleridge's inscription of the names ΣAPA (in Greek capitals) and *Coleridge* in the left and right upper corners of most pages. On the inside front cover, *f1ᵛ* and *f2*, they appear at the lower corners as well. On the facing pages *f83ᵛ* and *f84* in the lower corners, there appear the

initials (*f83ᵛ*) W.W. and M:D = W, (*f84*) W.W. and M.D.
Wordsworth. These come below Grasmere entries dated 8 Sept
1809. The simpler inscriptions run on to *f129, f129ᵛ* and *f130* being
blank; some leaves preceding them have been torn out (not foli-
ated), and after them some eight leaves that had been written on
were cut out, a few of which bore the names. *Ff138ᵛ–141* have the
names, and also *ff143ᵛ–144, 146ᵛ–147, 154ᵛ–155*, and thus ir-
regularly and non-significantly, to the end. The inside back cover,
f166, and *f165ᵛ* facing it, have the same inscription as was written
in the front. It is clear that the names were not written in at one
time, but as mood and occasion dictated. Two comments on them
in confirmation of this fact, and of their real significance for Coleridge, can be seen in later entries.

PERIOD   The facts that this notebook and N 18 came into use
OF USE   in Malta in 1805, that the watermarks appear to be
                the same, and that the general appearance is similar,
suggest that Coleridge may have received them as a present from
someone in England, or Malta; or alternatively that he took them
out with him or bought them in Malta. The use of the two more
or less simultaneously would be accounted for if they were assigned
to different purposes. N 17 seems to have been the daybook from
February to mid-April, and to have been used intermittently until
Coleridge left for Sicily, Italy, and home. It was then packed up,
and did not come into use again until Jan 1808—presumably after
being recovered from Stoddart (*CL* # 664). From 1808 onwards,
the use was very intermittent indeed, with occasional entries in
1809, 1810, 1811, 1812, 1816 (?1818), and 1827, and possibly at
other times.

NOTEBOOK 18

BM Add MS 47,515

COVER   Much like that of N 17. Like it, rubbed, with a
               leather thong. In black ink on the front: "1819 its

date/& not long before 1810/Part 1805/Malta/1805/Part 1815/".
On the back cover there is an X in black ink.

WATERMARK   EDMEADS & PINE 1802

SIZE AND $4\frac{5}{8}'' \times 4\frac{1}{2}''$, the same as N 17; 174 leaves, of which
CONDITION   17 pages are blank, except for the corner inscriptions
            described below. Like N 17, this is a thick and
firmly bound notebook. The writing is in ink unless otherwise
specified.

The corners of the pages throughout are inscribed with the
names of the Grasmere circle, more elaborately than the pages of
N 17. See plate III, N 17 Gen Note, and 2624. Whereas N 17 is restricted to the names of Sara Hutchinson and Coleridge himself, in
N 18, in which the corner inscriptions were perhaps mostly written
later, probably chiefly in the period of attempted reconciliation and
work at Grasmere in 1808–10, there were even later insertions of
names in the corners, some revealing the pitifully unhappy days
after the Wordsworth quarrel. The use of the names was in itself
not exclusive to Coleridge; Dorothy Wordsworth also formed patterns of them. *DWJ* 1 148.

There is only minor variation in the arrangement of the names
up to *f22*. This far the names were written first on the pages, possibly all at one time; the entries overrun them frequently. The form
of these inscriptions can perhaps best be shown diagrammatically.
Type 1

ΣΑΡΑ	Coleridge	W+M+D=W	Coleridge
William	Dorothy	William	Mary

With minor variations, such as *Wordsworth* for *William* and the
names slightly shifted, and sometimes with the inscriptions in the
lower corners omitted, these appear on *ff1–2, 2ᵛ–22, 89ᵛ–94, 95ᵛ–
102, 160ᵛ–161, 162ᵛ–163*. A side note runs up the margin of *f96*,
ΑΣΡΑ ẅΟΝΘΙΝΤ; see Appendix C.

Type 2 includes the names of his wife and children, again probably early (Malta?) inscriptions. On *ff29ᵛ–30:*

xxv

Sara	Mary	William	Dorothy
Hartley	Derwent	Sara	S.T. + S.C.

On *ff31ᵛ–32:*

ΣAPA	Coleridge	ΣAPA	Coleridge
HARTLY	DERWENT	SARA	S.T. + S. Coleridge

Type 3 uses only

ΣAPA	Coleridge	ΣAPA	Coleridge

sometimes on the inner or outer margins. This type of inscription appears on *ff32ᵛ–55, 56ᵛ–69, 70ᵛ–89, 94ᵛ–95, 102ᵛ–138.* A variant, on *ff123ᵛ–124,* shows the names done in dots rather than strokes of the pen, and on *ff69ᵛ–70* is written apropos the dots, "Ah it is spotted!" On the next five leaves the ΣAPA on the *verso* is again written in dots, or spots. Bitterest of all, and clearly datable after March 1810, when Sara went to Wales in the midst of *The Friend,* or possibly after Oct 1810 and the quarrel (*ff55ᵛ–56*):

ΣAPA Perfidam	Coleridge Fidelis	ΣAPA Nunquam Desertam	Coleridge Desertus, Traditus
ΣAPA	Hoc eluctantis animæ suspirio ΣAPA	Coleridge	Usque adhuc ama- bam, amo!

On *ff171ᵛ–172,* his name and Sara's are given anagrammatically: Musaello Rita Gelocedri and Asra Schonthinu.

Type 4 inserts only ΣAPA in the upper corners; this is found on *ff138ᵛ–147, 153ᵛ–158.* On *f153ᵛ* there is an inserted annotation: ⟨Why alone?—Coleridge is no more! Aug. 1811.⟩

A special use was made of the names on the last opening of the notebook, ff173ᵛ–174:

ΣΑΡΑ	Coleridge S.T.C.	ΣΑΡΑ	Coleridge
W. Wordsworth	Mary	W. Wordsworth	Dorothy
Hartley, John, Derwent, Dorothy		Thomas, Sara, Catharine, & the Unseen. (a prayer)	
The Lover,		the Beloved, the Sister, the Brother!	
('Tis lonely Fancy's Bittersweet.) Close in,		dear Names! upon each other! Ah that the names alone can meet!	

The names Thomas and Catharine date these inserts after 1806; "the Unseen" probably refers to the fifth Wordsworth child, William, born 12 May 1810, whom Coleridge did not see until on his way to London through Grasmere towards the end of October. The entry must therefore be dated May–Oct 1810; Catharine, of whom Coleridge was dotingly fond, was seriously ill at the time, and died in June 1812, Thomas in December of that year. If by any curious chance Coleridge did not see the baby in Oct 1810 (and the lines of verse do seem somewhat exaggerated for a separation of but the sixteen miles between Grasmere and Keswick), the latest terminal date for the entry is the date of Catharine's death. But even before the quarrel late in Oct 1810, the sense of separation may have been strong; it had been developing since 1807, and signs of it had appeared in 1803, as hinted in 1471 and 1473n.

With the verse compare the (earlier?) version of it in 2691, possibly written in Oct 1805 at Taormina, doubtless with different thoughts and intentions.

PERIOD   If, like N 17, this notebook was first used about Feb
OF USE   1805, it was used for only a few entries, then for a
few more in July and Aug 1805, shortly before
Coleridge left Malta, but, except for 2744, not again, so far as one
may guess, until *The Friend* was in progress from 1808 to 1810.
In the beginning it was perhaps reserved for *works,* as opposed to
day-to-day jottings. 2623, 2691, and other later entries suggest this;
and possibly the leaving blank most of the notebook before the
Marino sonnets were entered and criticized was for some such purpose—perhaps for the Soother of Absence, perhaps for the projected
journal of his Sicilian tour. The book is full of signs of loneliness
and despondency and, worse, a loss of morale; a pathetic attempt
to bolster himself appears to be one function of the names in the
corners of the pages. When they failed to do that, they became a
source of bitterness.

This notebook was not packed away like N 17 on his departure
from Malta. The entry 2744 towards the back of the book was
made Nov–Dec 1805 in Italy. The separation of it from other
matter by its relegation to the rear suggests some separate intention, another category. See the note, highly conjectural, to that
entry.

Inserted in the notebook, but not related to any entry in it, possibly thrust into the book just on departure from Malta, is a letter
from a George Burgmann:

La Vallette Monday
Evening 12. o'clock
P.M. 16 Sept.

My dear Sir,

    I am just returned from an Evening Card Party with my head full of Quis-
quidity & find your heartwarming Note on my Table!—What a Contrast of
Ideas all at once! almost incredible—I thank you for it most sincerely, for
altho this sudden Revolution in me may perhaps keep me an hour or two
awake (while otherwise I would perhaps have fallen asleep from Stupidity) I
am sure I shall be much the Gainer by it.

    I thank you also for your kind offers, of which I shall certainly avail my-
self if I find occasion tho' I do not know of any at present—

    May God almighty bless you & be with you wherever you go, give you

xxviii

health & happiness, & a happy Sight of your friends & family & much Joy
among your dear Children of whom I have heard you speak with such tender
affection.

If you can ever turn me to any use here or wherever I may be, I hope I
need not say that your remembering me will ever make me happy—

How comfortable the last Expression of your good Note shall make me for
this Night!—& who knows for how many more.

Once more God bless you my dear Sir—Mrs B. who has seen your Note
has begg'd of me to say the same to you for her.

Your most faithful
& thankfull friend
& Servt
Geo Burgmann

Later entries in the notebook were made at Highgate, in
April 1816 and again in 1819, possibly also at other dates.

NOTEBOOK 19

BM Add MS 47,516

COVER   Brown leather, with a leather thong for a clasp, a
leather fold for a pencil, and a pocket containing a
receipt. The label reads "N° 19 1807".

WATERMARK   J Cripps 1806

SIZE AND $6\frac{5}{16}\frac{7}{8}''$ x 3", 30 leaves of MS and 129 pages blank.
CONDITION   The writing is largely in ink, with some suspicion
that what looks like a very pale brownish-red "ink"
in some of the first entries may be his gout medicine; see 3041n.

PERIOD   This seems to be a Stowey notebook, connected with
OF USE   intermittent visits to Poole May–Dec 1807 and perhaps left behind when Coleridge departed for Lon-
don. After the first 20 leaves were filled the notebook was turned

around for the long report of the legal case (3195), perhaps meant to be removed and given to someone else.

As well as being unusual in being largely blank, the notebook is otherwise remarkable for the development of the more elaborate of the cipher systems, and for the signs of increased and more explicit worry about health and opium, and, in general, the "path becomes daily more rugged and mazy".

The receipt in the pocket reads: "Rec^d. Augt. 11th. of Mr Coleridge from the Hands of Mr Green Nineteen Pounds, three Shillings, & 3d as per Acct deliv^d to Mr Coleridge £19.3.3. G. Monkhouse." George Monkhouse may have been one of the Wordsworth-Hutchinson connexion. Mr Green was in 1809 a clerk in the *Courier* office who handled Coleridge's accounts with Stuart (*CL* # 742, 778n, 781n, 828).

NOTEBOOK 21½

BM Add MS 47,519

COVER — Brown leather on stiff boards. There is no writing on the front cover, but on the back in black ink, "Decem. 2. 1804—1808—part 1818". The usual label bears the number "21½".

WATERMARK — PORTAL & CO 1801

SIZE AND
CONDITION — 7¼″ x 4½″, 75 leaves of MS, including one inserted leaf that shows a different watermark, RUSE & TURNER 1817. The last 10 leaves are badly stained, possibly with rain or salt water. Ink is generally used throughout.

PERIOD
OF USE — The curious chronology of this notebook is hardly to be explained. In the Christmas week of 1804, possibly at the Stoddarts', possibly at their country place at St Julian's, the book was used for the first time; then it does

not appear again in the story until about 1808, i.e. after Stoddart returned Coleridge's possessions, unpleasantly enough, at the close of 1807. It may have been in the trunk sent from Naples back to Malta (*CL* # 623) with Mr Noble, but there is no evidence one way or the other. Whatever happened physically to the book, use of it was clearly made in 1804, and not again until the spring of 1808 in London, again briefly in 1811 and 1814, and perhaps not again until about 1818 at Highgate.

The relation of Coleridge's pagination to his entries on the pages provides a useful support for other evidence as to the dating of groups of entries. The paging, normally odd numbers only, on the recto pages and centred, was done after *ff15–16* were cut out, i.e. after 21½.22, which can be dated after the "miserable Saturday morning", 27 Dec 1806, most likely in 1808 after 21½.16, which is dated "18 May 1808". When he entered the page numbers, there were already in the notebook entries 2383 (datable from 2387), 2384–2386, but not e.g. 21½.10, which is clearly later than the pagination because written in such a way as to respect the numerals; similarly the entries that follow.

At the back of the book, turning it around as it was used in Dec 1804, the inside cover and the first page from that direction were not then numbered, but on the next leaf, Coleridge's reference to "p.133" had to avoid the page numeral; i.e. this entry was made post-pagination, or later than 1808. The only 1804 entries written at the back of the book then were three, 2380–2382, although as the book was reversed, there were about 20 entries written in after that. The compressed writing at one point (on *f72*) seems to have no other reasonable explanation than that N 21½ was being reserved for something, possibly for that long-hoped-for collection of Italian poems and other materials, such as the quotation from Machiavelli in 2385, or for a diary of his travels.

In a later volume it will be shown that there are reasons for thinking that the pagination or some of it may have been much later still; that on *ff70–71* Coleridge had to avoid with his page numbers entry 21½.138 dated 2 April 1811, and at another point the pagination may have been later than that.

The use of the notebook as it pertains to this volume was slight.

xxxi

It seems to provide vindication for Coleridge's worries about being separated for a considerable length of time from some of his notebooks used in Malta.

NOTEBOOK 23

BM Add MS 47,521

COVER — Brown leather, with no clasps, thong, or fold for a pencil, a cheap little book. The usual label reads "N° 23". In the same black ink, on the cover, there is written "1807, 1808, 1822".

WATERMARK — An emblem but no date.

SIZE AND CONDITION — $6\frac{1}{4}''$ x $4\frac{1}{8}''$, 47 leaves of MS, with soft purplish interleaving, somewhat like N 3. The writing is chiefly in ink.

PERIOD OF USE — The sixth entry establishes the earliest date, Aug 1807, and the donor, Poole. The latest dated entry appears to have been made 5 May 1827, though there may have been later ones. In this wide span of years the book was used in irregular fashion, as the dated entries show—in May 1808, in June 1820, in May 1827, in April 1827, and in April 1826, and probably at other times in among these dates, as well as in the last months of 1807. It has been difficult to be at all certain of the limits of its use in the period of Volume 2. Possibly some things here may later be shown to have been assigned dates that are too early.

It seems likely that Poole gave Coleridge the book to spur him on to work, perhaps to prepare for his lectures on poetry and the fine arts for the Royal Institution. In the spring of 1808 it was used for that purpose. For the rest it is a curious hodge-podge of theology, philosophy, and science, as well as some personal entries, and some interesting linking of these with the less personal material.

NOTEBOOK 24

BM Add MS 47,522

COVER   Stiff grey-brown board, with leather corners and spine. The label reads "Nᵒ 24"; and in the same black ink is written on the cover "Dr Crompton. Part 1808 and 1810".

WATERMARK   J CRIPPS 1806

SIZE AND   About 6¼″ x 4″, 60 leaves of MS. Ink is chiefly
CONDITION   used throughout. In appearance this notebook is unlike any others.

PERIOD   Possibly this book was bought in Bristol for the pur-
OF USE   pose represented by the Dante entries at the beginning, some of them in Josiah Wade's hand. Again the exact limits of the material appropriate to the period ending Dec 1807 have been almost impossible to determine, the personal griefs of 1807 and 1810 bearing too close a resemblance to each other to admit sure distinctions. The last entry in this volume could belong to 1810, and yet it represents the mood in which 1807 began and ended.

Subsequent entries, in content not very unlike those in N 23, appear to have been made sporadically from 1808 to 1810, in 1812, 1814, and 1819, and possibly at other dates.

NOTEBOOK K

VCL MS 2

COVER   Marbled cardboard, similar to another small notebook used in 1812 (Notebook P), which has printed on the back, "Instructions/To the Storekeepers for the Transport Service at Deptford", i.e. instructions to those in charge of military stores.

WATERMARK   1804

SIZE AND   Approximately 5½″ x 3⅛″, 22 leaves of MS, 4 pages
CONDITION   being blank. Pencil was used chiefly throughout.

PERIOD   From the fact that the earliest entries appear to
OF USE   have been made on board ship between Gibraltar
and Malta in 1804, and that the little book looks like those supplied to military storekeepers, it seems fair to guess that this pocket notebook, entirely unlike any of those he had used so far, may have been acquired in Gibraltar. It was used on the outbound journey, in Malta, and again in Sicily in Aug 1804. It is a book of occasional jottings for the most part, and has the atmosphere of the immediacy of the pocket rather than the deliberation of the desk, notwithstanding the study of Italian in 2133–2136.

NOTES ON
THE NOTEBOOKS

1804–1808

Entries 1843–3231

1843 16.226   Written in ink. According to Dorothy Wordsworth in a letter to Mrs Clarkson the next day, Coleridge had Wordsworth's company "almost to Troutbeck". *W Letters* (*E*) 358. From Kendal he took the coach to Liverpool, possibly to obtain medical advice from his friends there, or possibly to go on to Bristol in order to consult Dr Beddoes and to see his west-country friends before setting out on his travels.

1845 16.228   Stage-coach conversation, with the next entry?

1847 16.230   Copied, with a lavish insinuation of capital letters, from Adam Ferguson *An Essay on the History of Civil Society* (6th ed 1793) Part v "Of the Decline of Nations" §1 "Of Supposed National Eminence, and of the Vicissitudes of Human Affairs". The page reference identifies the edition.

1848 16.231   Copied, with minor omissions, insertions, and some introduction of italic and extra capital letters, from the *Annual Review and History of Literature for 1802* (Vol 1 1803) 692. "An affectation . . . assumed" comes from the previous page, and the last phrase of the entry precedes it on the same page. The last two comments were apparently thought too good to miss.

    The correction of *M*^{r} to *Sir* Lamb was made later in ink and is surely associated with Lamb's nonsense in a letter (of 2 Jan 1810 to Manning) in which he envisages his advancement as Sir Lamb . . . Earl Lamb . . . Pope Lamb, "higher than which is nothing but the Lamb of God". *L Letters* II 90. Possibly the emendation is of about that date.

    Another point of interest is the attribution to Mrs Barbauld. The lethal review was unsigned, and Coleridge must have heard the rumour of the authorship from private sources, possibly from the Liverpool literary circle. He read it at Dr Crompton's, he said in a note to Southey, and, commenting on this review and reviewers in general, he says he "will cut her [Mrs Barbauld] to the Heart". *CL* # 538. As late as 12 April 1812 Lamb thought Mrs Barbauld his attacker, until Crabb Robinson obtained from her a flat denial. *CR Books* I 69.

Arthur Aikin (1773–1854), editor of the *Annual Review*, was the eldest son of Dr John Aikin, and Mrs Barbauld's nephew. For Coleridge's devastating opinion of him, see *CL* # 237 and *De Q Works* I 127n.

In the same number with this attack on *John Woodvil*, Coleridge's *Poems* (1803) was reviewed with a mixture of irritation and approval (*An Rev* II 556).

1849 16.232   The numerals representing the dates of his ports of call suggest a brave beginning at that diary promised to the Wordsworths (*CL* # 592), and resumed in London, on shipboard, and from time to time until he re-embarked for home. For Coleridge on the Liverpool literary circle see *CL* # 340. They were liberals and abolitionists with whom Coleridge's acquaintance went back at least to 1800, probably even to 1796, *The Watchman* period.

Dr Currie: James Currie, M.D., returned from America and settled in Liverpool, where with William Roscoe, William Rathbone, Dr Crompton, and others he founded a Literary Society that published papers with the Literary and Philosophical Society of Manchester; this group in 1800 also founded the Athenaeum Library.

Dr Crompton: see 742n.

Mr Shepherd: William Shepherd, Unitarian minister in Liverpool since 1791, a friend of Gilbert Wakefield (on whose imprisonment he took charge of his children) and of William Roscoe. In 1802 he had written a *Life of Poggio Bracciolini.*

1850 16.233   The mis-spelling of Hazlitt's name is indubitable in the MS.

If Hazlitt's severity was under discussion in Liverpool at this time it would have particular piquancy for Coleridge coming so soon after the episode of the autumn of 1803, when Hazlitt had to escape from the indignation of the country folk with the help of Southey and Coleridge. See *CL* # 1025, 1059 and Chambers 176.

1851 16.234   Friday was 19 Jan, the 20th probably the date of the entry. He was at Dr Crompton's house, Eton Hall or Eton House,

Liverpool. For other close descriptions of flocks of birds in flight (starlings) see 582, 1589, 1779.

1852 16.235   The hand of the entry is exactly like that of 1851, and there is no clear reason for disturbing the sequence here. Yet in view of the fact that Coleridge had met Dalton, the discoverer (in 1794) of colour-blindness, in London, just before going to Dunmow (*CL* # 553), it is advisable to consider this as possibly a London entry 27 Jan–7 Feb. The entries that follow on this page (1892–1894) and, except for 1853, those on the next are Dunmow entries of 7–16 Feb. Entry 1853, with which *f73* begins, was apparently an important personal entry, or at least so intimate as to be largely removed with acid by some guardian of Coleridge's reputation. I suggest that when the fresh page was used for it, more than a third of *f72ᵛ* was still blank, and a few days later filled in at Dunmow with entries 1892–1894.

1853 16.239   Most of the entry was obliterated with ink and then with acid (which also obliterates parts of the entry overleaf, 1897). Coleridge was at Dr Crompton's from 16–*c* 22 Jan; either this entry was retrospective, and should be dated, with the entries that flank it, at Dunmow 7–16 Feb, or, being of some special character, a new page was taken for it.

1854 9.5   In the letter referred to in 1862n, Mrs Segur is described as the mother of a Christ's Hospital Blue contemporary with Coleridge. Coleridge had thought he was to be Poole's guest, and on discovering that the cost of his lodging was beyond his means, he moved to Barnard's Inn with James Tobin. *CL* # 568.

1855 9.6   For a caustic description of the interview with Mackintosh, in a letter to Poole the next day, see *CL* # 540; and cf *CL* # 650. Mackintosh had been recently knighted and in a few days was to sail, 14 Feb 1804, to take up his appointment to the recorder-ship of Bombay. See also 1858 and n. It was about this interview that Coleridge later thought Tobin had gossiped to the Wedgwoods; *CL* # 650.

The phrase about Davy is used in the same letter, yet subsequently there was an affectionate exchange of letters with him. *CL* # 581 and n.

1856 9.7   *Tobin:* James W. Tobin. See 590n and 2032 and n.
Poole's Office: Poole, with eight clerks under him, had been asked by Rickman, the census-taker, at this time secretary to the Speaker of the House of Commons, to compile an abstract from the reports returned by the parish Overseers of the Poor in answer to a question-naire authorized by Parliament. *Rickman* 80–1.
    Howell: Daniel Stuart's tailor, of King St, Covent Garden, with whom Coleridge had boarded in Dec 1801. Cf 1024n and 1827.
    Sharp: Richard "Conversation" Sharp, a banker, elected two years later to Parliament, was a friend of Poole and Mackintosh. Coleridge hoped Sharp's influence would help him to get a passage, and possible employment abroad. *CL # 535.* Sharp may have been one of the persons who urged him to go to Malta. *CL # 548.*
    Miss Savory: surely not Hester Savory, the Quaker maid of Lamb's poem, sister of one of his colleagues at the East India House?

1857 9.8   Written large and extravagantly, horizontally across the long way of the page.
    The date must be before 1863, which is written around 1858–1862; i.e. 26–28 Jan. The lines are much in the manner of many a *War Song* or *Ode to the Volunteers of Britain on the Prospect of Invasion* in the ephemeral publications of the day. Two poems with the above titles, typical examples, are to be found in *The Poetical Register and Re-pository of Fugitive Poetry for 1802* (2nd ed 1803), in which Coleridge's own unbelligerent poems, *The Picture* and *Chamouny, A Hymn* (308–11), also appeared. Wordsworth's patriotic sonnet *Anticipation:* "Shout for a mighty victory is won!", in more warlike vein, appeared in the next volume, for 1803. But no source has been found for these lines, and it must be admitted that the appearance of the MS with the re-ordering of stanzas arouses the suspicion of original composition.

1858 9.9   Referring with irony to his call on Mackintosh re-corded in 1855? Cf *CL # 540.*

1859 9.10   This and the next entry probably refer to conversa-tion with Davy, with whom he dined 26 Jan. *CL # 540.*
    Wordsworth in the 1805 *Prelude* refers to the statue of Newton "with his Prism and silent Face". The famous lines, "The marble index of a mind for ever/Voyaging through strange seas of thought,

alone" (III 62–3), came later; according to de Selincourt, after 1830. *Prelude* (1926) xlvi; also *Prelude* (1959) lix.

1860 9.11   *Sugar of Lead:* acetate of lead, a poison, used as a mordant. Sugar and sugar of lead were used frequently by Coleridge as an example of the need for desynonymizing, e.g. in *Phil Lects* 152.

1861 9.12   *AP* 53, there dated Dec 1803, incorrectly in view of 1854.

1862 9.13   *Anger . . . the reaction of the living Power:* a reference to Descartes *On the Passions?* Cf *Inq Sp* §52.
      Segur's Coffee House: i.e. Waghorn's Coffee House, "next door to the House of Lords—a quiet domestic place, kept by Betsy Segur's Mother". *CL* # 537. See also 1854n.

1863 9.14   This entry—the yawning, bad dreams, hysteria, difficulties in breathing, optical disturbances—and the nausea referred to in the next, suggest symptoms of withdrawal from opium-taking. See Schneider 60–1.

1864 9.15   Greenough's name is here written with particular precision. The illegible word is blotted out with heavy ink; it might be "Sara!"
      The dreadful Dinner Illness: described in several letters, *CL* # 543, 544, 545, 546.
      Catania & Mount Ætna from Greenough's recommendation: see 447n and *CL* # 548; also 1883–1889 and 2175.
      In reading [?Gown/Gourd], one bears in mind the later reference, in 2366, to a "Struggle in London, 1804—Jan.—".

1866 9.17   Names that came into Greenough's talk at the Sunday breakfast? Monte Pellegrino is a conspicuous limestone headland to the north of Palermo, Sicily; Monte Catalfano is another one to the south. Monte San Giuliano, known to the ancients as Mount Eryx, sanctuary of Aphrodite, is near Trapani.

1867 9.1   These appear to be addresses jotted down during the Jan–March London stay, on the leaf pasted on the inside front cover; they are now barely legible, and some are quite lost; the difficulty of reading them with any certainty as to the order of writing is increased by their being written into and around the advertisement label of Hall & Co, the manufacturers of the notebook. The price, 2/–, was written by the shopkeeper in the upper left-hand corner. No names have been found to attach to any of these addresses in 1804, except the "N°/6 Northumberland Street", which according to Boyle's *Court Guide* was occupied by: Mr Davies, *agent;* A. King Baily; Wm. Braid; John Baker; Henry Wm. Eske; Sam. Felton, attorney; Dunkie McDougall, Navy agent; I. T. Whiteside; Christ. Fred Eley; Chas. Cummins; Robt. Marshall; C. Harrison, attorney. It is just possible, in the light of this list, to suggest that with due allowance for bad writing, "N°1" and the undeciphered word after it could be read "Navy agent", which would point to Dunkie Mc-Dougall as Coleridge's man. In view of the complete disorder of the jottings, however, this plausibility must be eyed with reserve.

1868 9.2   The illegible name in the first line was crossed out and re-written and is now very faint. Possibly the entry refers to a subject for an article in the *Courier.* Stuart had given up the *M Post* a few months earlier, leaving it to be conducted by Nicholas Byrne.

1869 9.3   Is this a remedy for "a something cutaneous—a something neither scrofulous nor scorbutic absolutely, & yet partaking of both", as he described his ailment to his wife in a letter of [25] Jan 1804? *CL #* 537.

1870 9.4   Written on the perpendicular and close to the inner margin, the entry is very faint; the reading of the date is made the more doubtful by the fact that there was no Friday on the 5th, or 15th, or 25th of any month in the period 26 Jan–27 March 1804 of this entry.
     It is possible that the first part of 1868 belongs with this entry, i.e. perhaps Coleridge first wrote "Ease of Taxation . . . &c", then inscribed "Tue [corrected to Thursday], ½ 4°clock/—Mr . . ." above, and the engagement with Ward on the inner margin. 5 April was a Thursday; the two engagements could be one, the "Friday" having not been crossed out. But while the arrangement on the page makes this sequence of events and notes barely possible, the order in which the entries are shown here seems to be a rather more natural interpretation of the appearance of the MS.
     Ward is probably George Ward, printer and bookseller, at this

time at 27 Paternoster Row. See 1764n. There was talk at this time of his publishing Coleridge's projected "Comforts and Consolations". See *CL* # 545 and 536.

1871 9.143   *Boyle's City Guide* for 1803 gives this address for Dr Aikin, probably Dr John Aikin, editor of the *Monthly Magazine;* see 1848n.

1872 9.144   Entries 1945–1948 are written at right angles over this one.
   Coleridge saw so much of Rickman and Davy at this time, 26 Jan–27 March, that it is difficult to fix a date with certainty. Possibly this refers to the later engagement for Monday dinner, 15 Feb, cancelled when Coleridge could not get back to London, there being no Monday coach. *CL* # 554. This would date this entry before Coleridge went to Dunmow 7 Feb 1804.

1873 9.145   This may have been the address of Grosvenor Bedford, referred to in 252 and n, though it looks like a wrong number, as no number 28 Gerrard St is to be found in the London street guides or directories for this period. Presumably the entry was made before 29 Jan, when Coleridge in a letter refers to this as Bedford's street, though he mentions no number. *CL* # 543. Is *28* a date?

1874 9.146   On 1 Feb 1804 Coleridge asked Sarah to send him "a little inventory of the clothes I have with me/". *CL* # 548.

1875 9.18   *AP* 66 variatim. "1803" is evidently written by mistake for 1804. The intended apology was possibly for "the dreadful Rumpus with poor Godwin", at Lamb's supper the evening of 2 Feb. See 1890 and n.

1876 9.19   *AP* 66. On Thomas Holcroft cf 1659 and n, and *CL* # 75.
   Mrs Wolstonecroft: Mary Wollstonecraft Godwin died in 1797, but apparently the story was new to Coleridge and possibly came from Godwin himself.

1877 9.20   The sixth year of the reign of King John was June 1204–July 1205, when apparently the sons of the late King of North Wales were still disputing the succession.

Coleridge undoubtedly made this memorandum for Southey, who
was working on *Madoc*. Almost on the point of departure for Malta,
Coleridge received extracts from the MS of *Madoc* and copied them
for the Beaumonts; he wrote Southey urging him to go on with the
work. *CL* # 568, 562.

Tr: Patent touching the sixth year of the reign of John [?No.] 10. Safe
conduct for Llywelyn, Prince of North Wales, and Madog son of Gruffydd,
to come to the King at Wygorn near Woodstock on 29th July. Calendar of
Patent Rolls, p. 2.

1878 9.130   This and one other of the entries succeeding on *f55*
(1985), clearly attempts to keep accounts early in 1804, are partly
obscured by Mrs Gillman's note (see 2024n); they were all written
in a crabbed hand and are difficult to read in any case. They run in
part the opposite way of the notebook.

1879 9.55   In ink. It is difficult to assign a date to this entry.
It interrupts the flow of information from Greenough in entries
1883–1952, and probably was entered earlier than the Greenough
entries, preceding some of them on *f16*. If when 1879 was being
written, in ink, the first two or three words of 1880 and 1881 were
inked over, they must have preceded 1879. If all these preceded
1883–1889, they must be dated before 7 Feb, when Coleridge left for
Dunmow. See 1883n.
    There is in N 18 a later entry listing the first fifteen kings of
England, in a discussion of periods of English history not dramatized
by either Shakespeare or Marlowe. Coleridge refers there to his own
earlier resolve to write a play on the reign of Stephen. See 2443n.
Possibly, then, this entry in N 9 was made with the intention of
investigating gaps and dramatic possibilities. The two lists vary
slightly as to dates.
    The N 18 entry is quoted in part, but without the list of monarchs
and their dates, in *ShC* I 139–40.
    The dates for the French Revolution are of some interest: the fall
of the Bastille occurred in 1789, but as it was a contemporary event
Coleridge was less precise about it.

1880 9.48   The first two words are inked over; for the dating
see 1879n.

From the *Cottoni Posthuma: Divers Choice Pieces of that Renowned Antiquary Sir Robert Cotton* ed James Howell. The page-references correspond only to the 1679 edition. In Coleridge's day, Howell's attribution of works in this volume to Sidney and Walsingham was unquestioned.

Coleridge's last phrase is an understatement; the words from "Fortitude, calmness of mind," are in fact his own and not either quotation or summary.

This entry was used in Lect xiv, in the course Jan–March 1818, as an example of "plain sober language but distinguished by talent". *MC* 222 and n.

1881 9.49   The first three words are inked over. This also is from the *Cottoni Posthuma* (1679) 157, from the final sentence summarizing a piece entitled "Twenty-four Arguments concerning Popish practices &c".

Coleridge's fourth word, *right*, reads *good* in the text, and there are other minor variations.

1882 9.50   A recent work by John Wheatley, published in 1803.

1883 9.51   More notes from Greenough about Sicily. See 1864. The reference here is to the stone quarries at Syracuse, which Coleridge later recorded seeing, 2239.

Entries 1883–1886 and 1887–1889 seem to belong together and to the evening when Greenough read aloud from his Etna journal, described by Coleridge in a letter to the Wordsworths 8 Feb 1804 as "an admirable, because most minute, Journal of Sights, Doings, and Done-untos in Sicily". *CL* # 553.

1884 9.52   See the note above.

1885 9.53   Coleridge expected to have a letter of introduction to the "Convent of Benedictines at Catania" from Lord Nelson, and to stay there sometime. *CL* # 553. He almost certainly did visit the Benedictine convent at Nicolosi; see 2176n and *L* ii 485n; the fact is asserted by EHC, confidently but without evidence.

1886 9.54   Was Mazzalia a guide Greenough was recommending for the ascent from Nicolosi of Mt Etna? The geological terms remind us that Greenough was later president of the Royal Geological Society, and author of *A Critical Examination of the First Principles of Geology* (1819) and other geological works. See also 2014.

1887 9.56   The list of a traveller's requirements comes again, surely, from Greenough.

   Portable Soup: This was provided by the Beaumonts. *CL* # 589. The first manufacture on a large scale of a liquid portable soup occurred in France, under Napoleon. C. Appert, credited by the French government with the discovery of a method of preserving foods, and given contracts for the army and navy, suggests that he had been working on the problem since 1800, or earlier, and that he included soups among his preserved foods. *The Book for all Households or The Art of Preserving Animal and Vegetable Substances for Many Years, By Appert* ed K. G. Bitting (Chicago 1920) 6, 33–7. Appert, whose original work appeared in 1810, implies in a footnote that meat essences and bouillon tablets produced by evaporation were in existence at that time but offered "only artificial maintenance, without savor and without taste". Ibid 35n. Coleridge's portable soup was of this pemmican type, a block or slab of hard, tough, cooked, dried, shredded meat, to be boiled in water into something like a thick stew or, more accurately, glue. Capt Cook used it on his voyage around the world in 1772–5, giving his men one ounce boiled with pease three days a week. It was frequently carried among the medicinal supplies of ships and served to sick seamen in place of the common provisions. It had the property of keeping sound indefinitely, so much so that a piece of a cake of "portable soup" believed to have been part of Cook's stores is now in the possession of the Metal Box Company of Baker St, London. *Historic Tinned Foods* (publication No 85, 2nd ed, of the International Tin Research and Development Council) 14–34.

   A pair of strong *Boots:* for walking on lava.

   Eau de Luce: a medicinal compound of ammonia, oil of amber, and alcohol, used *c* 1750–1850 against snake-bite and also as smelling-salts.

1888 9.57   Coleridge's copy of this work is in VCL; the attractive historical and geographical account is full of references to poets who have written about Etna as an experience for the imagination.

1889 9.58   Greenough's summary of the facts of the Etna
countryside, exactly the sort of material in Ferrara's book, reminds
Coleridge of Samuel Rogers's poem, of which the prefatory "Analysis" as well as the poem is full of references to "our attachment to
inanimate objects, . . . love of country", etc.
   Oaks and Chestnuts . . . Moonlight: Coleridge was to recall
Greenough's descriptions in August on Etna; see 2175.
   sublime . . . a true Language: Is Coleridge thinking of Greenough's
description of Etna as confirmation of Wordsworth's view of nature
as "the language of the senses" (*Tintern Abbey*); or, even more,
of his own lines in *Frost at Midnight:* "The lovely shapes and sounds
intelligible/Of that eternal language, which thy God/Utters . . ."?
PW I 242.
   dried up lines—are these beautiful: a renewal of the subject of 1755?
   They are the description of a moonlight scenery by Homer: There is
no "description" in Homer to justify the reference. Coleridge probably refers to a passage in Pope's translation of the *Iliad* VIII 555–9:
"As when the moon, resplendent lamp of light . . .". He discusses
it in *BL* I 26n, referring there to an analysis of it he made in one of his
lectures (in 1811–12). He apparently mixed favourable with unfavourable comment, to the disgust of Crabb Robinson. *CR Books* I
62. But it is worth noticing that the lines he objected to, in the
Biographia and probably in the lecture, were lines VIII 691–2:
"Around her throne the vivid planets roll,/And stars unnumber'd
gild the glowing pole." Whereas the lines that suggested Etna—
perhaps quoted by Greenough?—are the much better lines that
follow: "O'er the dark trees a yellower verdure sheds/And tip with
silver every mountain's head;/Then shine the vales, the rocks in
prospect rise . . .". I suggest that in the lecture there may have
been mingled the association with the application to the Etna
landscape suggested by Greenough's enthusiasm, and the sort of
literary disapproval expressed by Wordsworth in the 1815 Preface.
And there may have been a deeper association still. In one of the
autobiographical letters to Poole, Coleridge recalls how his brother
Francis, in a rare burst of gentleness, read Pope's *Iliad* to him when
he was ill in childhood. *CL* # 208. On the relation to Francis see 1494n.
   by slipping . . . a footing: The account of the shifting sand-like
lava of the cone provided Coleridge with yet another example of
extremes meeting. See 1725 and particularly what he had already
noticed about soap in 1017.

1890 9.21   "The dreadful Rumpus" was described fully in the letter to Southey, *CL* # 562. Godwin apparently attacked Southey and Wordsworth as well as Coleridge himself. Good relations with Godwin were restored soon after the return from Malta.

1892 16.236   John Nichols, printer (1745–1826), compiled *The History and Antiquities of the County of Leicester* in 8 folio volumes (1795–1815). Sir George Beaumont was a Leicestershire man, probably a patron or subscriber.

1893 16.237   See 1731 and n. The reading in both instances is clearly *spurge*, not, as EHC has it, *sponge*. Whether the observation is by Lady Beaumont or applicable to her is not clear. She seems to have been given to reflections of a moral or religious nature; cf *CL* # 558.

1894 16.238   Saffron Walden is in Essex, not far from Dunmow.

1895 16.240   *Sir G. B:* Sir George Beaumont, painter and patron of the arts, who helped to found the National Gallery. At this time Coleridge was visiting the Beaumonts at Stonehall, Dunmow, Essex, the home of Sir George's mother. Beaumont was thinking of repairing his own house at Coleorton, and in 1804 asked George Dance to prepare plans. The park at Coleorton Hall was eventually much decorated with sculpture, as Sara Hutchinson noted. *SH Letters* 307.

1896 16.241   *AP* 163–4. EHC places this late in 1805, but its position and appearance, like 1893–1894 opposite, in the notebook, suggest the visit to the Beaumonts in 1804, and the subject is of a sort likely to be discussed with Lady Beaumont.

1897 16.242   *AP* 164. The acid applied to the entry overleaf has obliterated the two or three words towards the end of this entry. EHC supplies them, which raises the question whether he may have seen them before the acid was used. It cannot be assumed from this, however, that he was the censor; he frequently supplied words, as in the normal course of editing, even where the MS is clear.

1898 16.243   The missing words are again obliterated by the acid used overleaf.

A possible topic with Coleridge at any time, the question of genius undoubtedly arose in conversations with Sir George Beaumont, as it did in Coleridge's references to him in letters of this period, e.g. *CL* # 581.

1899 21.418   These are notes on drawings by Sir George Beaumont in his "Blue Book", and on some oil sketches and paintings by him. On 1 Feb 1804 Coleridge wrote to him, apparently resuming discussion of a plan of the summer of 1803 to do some "Translations from the Drawings", whether into "a moral Descriptive-poem", "an Inscription", or "a Tale". The plan had apparently had a set-back. "But I had taken notes of 21 Drawings from the Blue Book—of which I retain a floating & general recollection of all, but an accurate & detailed Imagery only of three—& by no Industry of Search could I find the Paper of notes, which from some over care or other I have mislayed. I propose therefore, if it should be perfectly convenient to you, to pay you a visit for two or three days at Dunmow—". *CL* # 550. Whether the mislaid notes were hidden in N 21, and only added to on this visit, or whether he began here afresh, we do not know. There is in the MS no obvious break after the twenty-first description. In a letter of the previous September, the "translations" had been proposed and referred to as already begun. *CL* # 521. Some notes on the descriptions of the drawings have been supplied by P. A. Tomory, formerly of the Leicester Art Gallery.

The first twenty-seven are drawings, the twenty-eighth may be an oil sketch, and the remainder are oils.

1. A Welsh landscape with Conway Castle?

2. Note the close similarity to Dorothy Wordsworth's description of Sanwick Church: *DWJ* 9 Nov 1805.

3. Probably Conway Castle again.

The second No 3 is reminiscent of Peel Castle on the Isle of Man; cf No 21.

4. Wales.

5. Lowther Castle? Beaumont often stayed there. Yet would Coleridge not have recognized and named it?

6. Most of Beaumont's works depicting the sea are Welsh scenes.

7. A favourite composition of Beaumont, of which there are numerous examples in the Leicester Art Gallery.

8, 9, & 10. Also typical subjects, unidentified.

9. *Waterslope:* see 804n.

11. The conical hill appears in many of the Welsh drawings.

12. An oil sketch in the Leicester Art Gallery of the river Greta shows some resemblance to this drawing.

13. Lake country? There are yews in the churchyard at Coleorton, but the porch there is undistinguished.

14. Another typical subject.

15. Conway Bay.

16. There are numerous sketches of Conway Castle by Beaumont.

17. Is the second insertion Beaumont's answer to Coleridge's question?

18. Seizincote in Gloucestershire? It was on Beaumont's usual summer route, at this time, to Wales. Or it might be Castle Howard, which he could easily have seen in the summer of 1803 from Keswick.

19. Wales again.

20. Another typical subject.

21. Peel Castle near Barrow-in-Furness, not the Isle of Man one.

22. Coleridge was fascinated by High Bridge. See 1489 *f57^v* and 2177.

23. A typical subject.

   with a grand S[alvator] Rosa-Eye: cf 1495 *f67^v* and n.

24. Unidentified.

25. Again, typical.

26. Unidentified.

27. This drawing of Caister Castle, $16\frac{1}{2}$ x $22\frac{1}{4}$ inches, is in the Leicester Art Gallery. *Beaumont Exhibition* (Leicester 1938) No 84.

28. This might be an oil sketch, colour being introduced into the description here.

   potamoeides Moat: the river-shaped moat.

29. An oil sketch.

30. An oil sketch or painting of Conway Castle; there is a Beaumont painting on this subject in Castle Howard, York.

31. An oil painting, unidentified, possibly of landscape in the vicinity of Ulpha Vale, as Coleridge suggests. Beaumont had been in the district.

In addition to Coleridge's interest in line and colour and composition in general, one notes his kinetic responses—a desire to cross bridges, pass under arches, as in No 29—and his sentimental and narrative inferences as in Nos 7, 18, and 29. It should be recalled that the purpose of the notes was literary. Cf the description of another landscape-painting in 2831.

1900 21.419   Sir George Beaumont saw the letter from Lord
Cadogan to George, Viscount St Asaph, Earl of Ashburnham (1760–
1830), conveying this information, and Coleridge made a note of it
for Tom Wedgwood, doubtless thinking his symptoms similar. He
sent it to him in a letter of 24 March. *CL* # 580.
    Papin's Digester: a seventeenth-century pressure-cooker for soften-
ing bone, etc. It is referred to in William Nicholson *A Journal of
Natural Philosophy, Chemistry and the Arts* vii (March 1804) 161–2,
where possible improvements in it are discussed.

1901 22.150   In pencil. Coleridge sent a copy of Daniel's poems to
Sir George Beaumont 8 March 1804. *CL* # 566. This entry was
perhaps made at Dunmow to remind himself of what he meant to do
when he returned to London.
    It is curious that this is the only entry of this period between
Grasmere and Malta in N 22. It is to be remembered that at that
time the notebook was much thinner than it is now (see N 22 Gen
Note) and was convenient for a pocket.

1902 9.23   The word "park" was omitted after "Maynard's",
as is clear from a letter to the Wordsworths in which this episode is
confessed to. *CL* # 558. Charles, Viscount Maynard, of Easton Lodge,
Essex, was a near neighbour to Sir George Beaumont at Dunmow.
    In 1804, a leap year, this Friday was 10 Feb.

1903 9.24   Johnson's quatrain runs: "If the man who turnip
cries/Cry not when his father dies,/'Tis a proof that he had rather/
Have a turnip than his father." *The Poems of Samuel Johnson* ed
David Nichol Smith and Edward L. McAdam (Oxford 1941) 183.

1904 9.25   Source not traced.

1905 9.26   James Tobin was blind, and sufficiently Spartan
(cf *CL* # 580) to exercise with dumb-bells, but the entry reads rather
more like someone's anecdote than a direct statement.

1906 9.27   Sunday was 12 Feb 1804.
    Coleridge was to remember this remark later in a letter to Lady
Beaumont 1 Aug 1804. *CL* # 605.

1907 9.28   Difficulty with his pen almost gives the name the appearance of "Woolelett". William Woollett (1735–85) made two particularly well-known engravings after the Dutch painter Cornelius Dusart, to either of which Coleridge may be referring here: *The Cottagers* and *The Jocund Peasants*.

Possibly this example is intended as part of the Nature *vs* Art argument with the Wordsworths? Cf 1489n and 1755 and n.

1908 9.29   *poor old King:* possibly Beddoes's assistant and brother-in-law, Dr König; see 734n. Another candidate for help, perhaps even more likely, is a clergyman in or near Ottery St Mary (possibly one of the two successors to Coleridge's father as master of the King's School before George Coleridge took over) whose desolation on being left a widower STC took much to heart in 1793; see *CL* # 30. If he was still alive in 1804, it would be quite characteristic of the Coleridge pattern for the entry to refer to an old family friend. Or could it mean the monarch? Or perhaps most likely of all is Thomas King (1730–1805), the well-known comic actor; he had twice "quitted the stage", in 1792 and again in 1802, and though once highly paid and prosperous he died in poverty from gambling.

This entry appears to support the view that Coleridge was contributing at this time to the *M Post* and the *Courier*.

1909 9.30   Whether a caution to avoid a repetition of the fall in 1902, or a sartorial reference, or a joke remains obscure.

1910 9.31   All but "G. Fricker" and the insert in pointed brackets is in another hand.

Apparently the London address of George Fricker, or the address of a friend of his. Coleridge at this time was trying to find work for his young brother-in-law and apparently enlisted John Rickman in the search. *CL* # 557, 559, 568, 592.

There is another address for George Fricker—120 Goswell St—on the back fly-leaf of the tetraglot edition of Pascal's *Les Provinciales* referred to in 2133n. For the reasons given in that note, it seems likely that either the address here is the address of an acquaintance or George Fricker's difficulties with employment made his address a drifting one. Or, again, Mr Davenport may have been a possible employer to be sought out. The street directories of this date do not help.

Coleridge's paternal interest in the youngest of the Frickers is often forgotten when his paternal inadequacies are remembered, e.g. that George, as well as his mother, lived with the newly married Coleridges for many months.

1911 9.32   Mr A. Welles, 44 Upper Titchfield St, was a medical man or an apothecary, a new acquaintance of this London visit, with whom Coleridge breakfasted and dined 19 Feb 1804, and who invited Coleridge to stay with him. *CL* # 561. About what aspect of the law he was to enquire is not clear. There is some reason to think George Fricker in difficulties with the law.

1912 9.33   The insertion in pointed brackets is later, though probably sometime before 27 March, his sailing date. Sara Hutchinson must have known as well as Coleridge did that any journey in search of his health would be ineffectual unless he resolved the emotional conflict connected with her; apparently she took steps to further the process. It is not irrelevant to notice that Coleridge on 10 March sent her an impersonal letter on a copy of Sir Thomas Browne. *CL* # 567. See 1961n.

1913 9.34   On the projected "Soother of Absence" see 1225 and n and 1541 and n. This appears to be a separate entry, though the relation to the preceding one is clear, and "the wanderings of this Ghost", on the brink of the Malta voyage, suggests recollections of and identifications with *The Ancient Mariner*, which are evident from the Scottish tour onwards. See 1473n.

1914 9.35   The dating of the Cartwright entries in N 9 and N 21 is of tantalizing difficulty. The N 9 entries appear to be the earlier; they come, for one thing, from the first part of the Cartwright volume.
    In N 9, the first excerpts (1914–1919), poems in praise of Cart-wright, run in the same direction as the other notebook entries, i.e. with the long side of the book held vertically; but the Cartwright verses themselves, requiring more space for whole lines across the page, are written horizontally, in entries 1920, 1921, and 1939–1943. These also begin new pages, and could have been written at any time, even perhaps when N 9 was largely full, if these pages had been left blank. They could have been written at sea—if Coleridge had Cart-

wright with him; he may have borrowed Southey's copy (*Southey SC* 547) along with the volume of Pascal (2133n).

Yet the N 21 Cartwright entries 1929–1937 must be dated, I think, between the visit to Dunmow—7–16 Feb (1899–1900)—and the next dated entry in N 21, dated 17 April. Cartwright may have been read at Dunmow, i.e. as early as the second week in February or even as late as mid-April, at sea.

All may belong, as the first of these (1914–1919) seem to from their location in the notebook, to the days after 21 Feb and before *c* 8 March, the London doldrums period when no ship was to be found, when he was ill, at loose ends, and staying in Tobin's cheerless rooms in Barnard's Inn. I think this the most likely time for the Cart-wright reading and therefore so place these excerpts. A fact of uncertain relevance is that in a period in which Cartwright is scarcely mentioned, Godwin owned a copy. *Godwin SC* (1836) 109. Coleridge may well have borrowed it; he certainly used Godwin's library in 1806, when he returned from Malta. See 2928n and 1961n.

The first of the Cartwright entries is a comment on John Berken-head's lines *In Memory of Mr. William Cartwright* 13–14, 17–22. (See 1917.) These lines occur in the midst of 155 pages of adulatory verses, of various authorship, prefixed to the 1651 edition of Cartwright *Comedies, Tragi-Comedies, With other Poems* [p xliii]: "Thy Sense and Reason (Man's two Eyes) would reach/All that lay Prose or Sacred Verse could teach./ . . . The Belgick Floud, which drank down fifty Townes,/At dead-low water shews their humble Crowns:/So, since thy flaming Brain ebb'd down to death,/Small Under-witts do shoot up from beneath."

1915 9.36 Ibid line 29 [p xliii]: "For thy Imperial Muse at once defines/Lawes to arraign and brand their weak strong lines./Un-mask's the Goblin-Verse that fright's a page/As when old time brought Devills on the Stage."

Coleridge used the line for his pun in *Alice du Clos: PW* I 474.

1916 9.37 Cartwright ibid lines 41, 55 [p xlv]: "[The verses of others are] stuft, swoln, ungirt:/but Thine's compact and bound/ . . . No grim-stiff-iron Verse stuck full of Points . . .".

1917 9.38 Ibid lines 141–2 [p xlviii]: "No rotten Phansies in thy Scenes appear;/Nothing but what a Dying man might hear . . .".

1918 9.39   Ibid lines 159–60 [p xlviii]: they refer to the clergy.

1919 9.40   Also a reference to the Cartwright volume, to the verses of Matthew Smallwood *On the Death of Mr. Cartwright, and the Life of his desired Poems* line 31 [p xxxix]: "Bright orient formes live here . . .". Coleridge is remembering Thomas Gray *The Progress of Poesy* line 120: "With orient hues unborrow'd of the Sun".

1920 9.41   For this and the next entry, the notebook is used horizontally.
    Cartwright *Comedies . . . Poems* (1651) 12: *The Lady Errant* I iv. Coleridge has altered the last line, which in Cartwright reads: "Steals by the foot of't without noise". This was printed as Coleridge's in *PW* (JDC) 469.

1921 9.42   Cartwright ibid 14: the last speech, Florina's, in I iv. Coleridge has omitted the last two lines and a half: ". . . towards him/Whom it moves to, and then shalt shortly see/Love bleed, and yet stoop to Philosophy."
    This also was published in *PW* (JDC) 467.

1922 9.43   The notebook is righted to the vertical again, its normal position, maintained up to 1941–1943, which again are horizontal on the page and again Cartwright entries.
    my great Critical Work: a reference to an "Essay on Criticism" projected since 1801, perhaps since the appearance of *LB* (1800) in the autumn of that year, with Wordsworth's preface instead of the one Coleridge had been expected to write. See 892 and n.

1923 9.44   "The general Volunteer Spirit of the Nation" was roused by daily fears of invasion by Napoleon. The Volunteer Consolidation Bill, brought down in the House 8 Feb 1804, made it impossible to resign from enlistment. On Coleridge's Volunteer essays see 1752 and n, 1753n.

1924 9.45   Coleridge wrote to Sotheby at this address, 13 March 1804, asking him for letters to Sir Alexander Ball and Gen W. A. Villettes. He had just decided to go to Malta. *CL* # 569.

1925 9.46   *AP* 67. A story clearly from John Rickman, of whom Coleridge saw a good deal in London at this time. As secretary to the

Speaker, Rickman was in a position to help Coleridge try to find a government or other ship, and as a practical person, calmer than Poole, he was a support to Coleridge in various ways.

On George Dyer see 487 and n. A Christ's Hospital Blue before the days of Lamb and Coleridge, learned and benevolent but vague and embarrassingly awkward, he drew a kind but firm reproof from Coleridge 15 March 1804. *CL* # 573.

Rickman's aunt was a Miss Beaumont, who lived with him. Rickman appears to have been cousin to Sir George Beaumont. *Rickman* 77, 67.

1926 9.47   The *True Briton*, begun in 1793, was shortly to merge (16 April 1804) with the *Daily Advertiser and Oracle*. It was a subsidized governmental anti-Jacobinical sheet, edited by John Heriot.

Cobbett's Tory *Political Register* (founded in 1802) opposed the Addington ministry, but this in itself is not enough to account for Coleridge's always strong animosity to Cobbett; see 1752n. Cobbett's early acquiescence in Malthusian doctrines and his later Burdettite sympathies in the Westminster election of 1807 were alike anathema. His reversal of views roughly corresponded (in the opposite direction) to such of Coleridge's views as changed, so that even Cobbett's later support of the anti-Malthusian camp by publishing Hazlitt's articles in the *Political Register* March–May 1807, although Hazlitt's arguments were Coleridgian enough to read as if they might have been partly Coleridge's own, was not enough to win him over to any appreciation of Cobbett. Possibly, as this entry suggests, it was Cobbett's style that was unforgivable. Yet see 2150n.

1927 21.420   Wilson is probably Richard Wilson, R.A. (1714–82), the artist whom Beaumont regarded as the greatest of English painters, and his own most inspiring teacher. Another possible, though much less likely, candidate is Andrew Wilson, the Edinburgh painter who, if the conjecture in 1471n is correct, enlivened a wet evening for Coleridge in the Trossachs. John Wilson (Christopher North) being but nineteen years old at this date, the anecdote is too early even for his precocity.

1928 21.421   Possibly the product of the enquiry by Mr Welles referred to in 1911.

1929 21.422   Like 1914, from Cartwright *Comedies . . . Poems* (1651) 16: ". . . And that fierce Javelin,/I'd rather see a Plume o'r-shade your back/With a large, generous carelessness . . .". *The Lady Errant* II i.

1930 21.423   Cartwright ibid 24. Coleridge's omission of the lines that follow in the same speech is significant: ". . . so Love, that is/Brighter than Eye, or Sun, if not enlight'ned/By Reason, would so much of Lustre lose/As to become but gross, and fool Desire;/I must refine his Passion; None can wooe/Nobly, but he that hath done Nobly too." II iv.
The lines quoted in the entry were used in *Friend* III 191 as a motto.

1931 21.424   Cartwright ibid 33 variatim; lines 5–6 of the quoted passage read: "Of his inspiring God, and am possess'd/With so much rapture . . .". III ii.

1932 21.425   Cartwright ibid 33 variatim: "*Charistus:* Let me ask thee then/As we do those that do come fresh from Visions,/What saw'st thou there? *Olyndus:* That which I see still, that/Which will not out. . . ." III ii. (Instead of Coleridge's last two words, Cartwright wrote "and Lustre".)

1933 21.426   Cartwright ibid 57: "This his short appearance/Is only as th' appearance . . .". IV iv.

1934 21.427   Cartwright ibid 62: "The Motions which it [Love] feels/Are Fury, Rapture, Extasie, and such/As thrust it out full of Instinct, and Deity,/To meet what it desires." IV vi.

1935 21.428   The first line is Coleridge's; the second and third are Cartwright's, ibid 63. Charistus says, "Love is not perfect till it begins to fear". Coleridge grafts on to his own line some lines from the reply of Eumela: "It is not Jealousie/That ruins Love, but we our selves, who will not/Suffer that fear to strengthen it; Give way/And let it work, 'twill fix the Love it springs from/In a staid Center." IV vi.

1936 21.429   Written (after 1937?) down the inside margin. Cartwright (ibid 68) has either reminded Coleridge of some ancedote or set fancy spinning. In the last act Philenis and Machessa are discuss-

ing the pigmies and their habits. Philenis proposes to imprison rebellious pigmies in bird-cages and cony-coops, "and there feed 'em
up/With Milk and Dazy-roots. I will so yerk/The little Gentlemen." v i.

1937 21.430   *AP* 68; but this also is Cartwright ibid 71: ". . . You
ne'er knew/That I destroy'd true virtuous Loves; it is/A pleasure to
me to perceive their Buddings,/To know their Minutes of Encrease,
their Stealths,/And silent Growings." v ii.
On the "Soother of Absence" see 1225n and 1541n.

1938 9.131   In 1804 Boyle's *Court Guide* gives this as the address
of George Dance (1741–1825), architect and portrait-painter. He was
a close friend of Sir George Beaumont and was at this time designing
alterations for Coleorton Hall made in the following years under him.
Though the address may represent merely a social introduction, it is
possible that Coleridge was asked to convey his own ideas on the subject to Dance. Certainly his remarks to the Beaumonts were well
received, and referred to in a letter of WW to Sir George Beaumont
17 Oct 1805: "Setting out from the distinction made by Coleridge
which you mentioned, that your House will belong to the Country,
and not the Country be an appendage to your House, you cannot be
wrong . . .". *W Letters* (*E*) 523. Was Coleridge to discuss with Dance,
as he had discussed with Beaumont, the improvements to house and
grounds? When Coleridge later stayed at Coleorton with the Wordsworths, 1806–7, they occupied the farm-house, for the interior of the
house was not completed; their participation in the planning lends an
additional association to the Constable drawing reproduced in plate
VIII. See also 2981.
    Another possible reason for Dance's address being in Coleridge's
notebook may be Dance's drawing of Coleridge. Though evidence as
to its date is lacking, Southey had seen it by 11 June 1804, when he
wrote Coleridge first about the Hazlitt and Northcote portraits and
then about Dance's; it had, he said, "that merit at least, that nobody
would ever suspect you of having been the original". *S Life and C* II
291. Is its unrecognizableness perhaps part of the explanation why
it has disappeared?

1939 9.133   Printed as Coleridge's in *PW* (JDC) 468. The lines
come, however, from William Cartwright *A Panegyrick to the most*

Noble Lucy Countesse of Carlisle in his *Comedies . . . Poems* (1651) 185. See 1914n. In the first line here Coleridge altered "we" to "I"; and his third line read in the original: "The Agents alter things, and what does come,/Powerful from these, flows weaker far from some."

1940 9.134   Published as Coleridge's in *PW* II 1018 as an experiment in metre, and in *PW* (JDC) 470. It is again from Cartwright, though considerably altered. His poem *Sadness*, stanza 1, reads: ". . . Let Sadness only wake;/That whiles thick Darkness blots the Light,/My thoughts may cast another Night:/In which double Shade,/By Heav'n, and Me made,/ O let me weep,/And fall asleep,/ And forgotten fade." *Comedies . . . Poems* (1651) 220. Was Coleridge not struck also by the next stanza, the first lines of which must have held reminders of *Christabel* for him? "Heark from yond' hollow Tree/ Sadly sing two Anchoret Owles,/Whiles the Hermit Wolf howls. . . ." Cf *Christabel* lines 1–13: *PW* I 215–16.

1941 9.135   In *PW* I 362 (removed from the reprinted edition of 1957) and *PW* (JDC) 467. Again not Coleridge's, but the second stanza of Cartwright's *To Chloe who wish'd her self young enough for me: Comedies . . . Poems* (1651) 245.

1942 9.136   The lines are from Cartwright's play *The Ordinary* I iii: *Comedies . . . Poems* (1651) 11. Coleridge's insertion in ⟨ ⟩ suggests his intention to apply the lines to the state of Fr[ench] Fin[ance]. Sir Francis d'Ivernois, a royalist *émigré* who received the unusual distinction of an English title, though he remained unnaturalized, was a prolific writer on subjects of political economy and finance. In 1795 his *Coup-d'oeil sur les assignats* was translated as *A Cursory View of the Assignats and remaining resources of the French Finance*, which may be the work Coleridge refers to here.

1943 9.137   *The Siedge or Love's Convert* I i by Cartwright: *Comedies . . . Poems* (1651) 100. In the last line Coleridge has altered *aime* to *name*. He used the passage, as altered, in an article in the *Courier* 7 Dec 1809 (*EOT* II 600) and again in *Friend* II 135; in *Friend* III 327–8 he applied another quotation from this play to the subject of Malta and Sir Alexander Ball.

1944 9.138   The author is Pliny. Except for the first two sentences, this is quoted, *Friend* I 316n, and applied to Wordsworth. In that place the reference cited is simply "Plin. Epist. Lib. 1". Was Coleridge on checking it for publication unable to find it? The reference here to Epistle 17 is an error for 16; in the Cortius and Longolius edition of Pliny (Amsterdam 1734) STC's quotation is from p 65, on which Letter 16 ends, and is followed by the heading of Letter 17, though by none of its text. This or similarly printed editions could easily have led to a slip of the eye.

Pliny is referring to his friend Pompeius Saturninus:

His works are never out of my hands; and whether I sit down to write any thing myself, or to revise what I have already written, or am in a disposition to amuse myself, I constantly take up this same author; and, as often as I do so, he is still new. Let me strongly recommend him to the same degree of intimacy with you; nor be it any prejudice to his merit that he is a contemporary writer. Had he flourished in some distant age, not only his works, but the very pictures and statues of him would have been passionately inquired after; and shall we then, from a sort of satiety, and merely because he is present among us, suffer his talents to languish and fade away unhonoured and unadmired? It is surely a very perverse and envious disposition to look with indifference upon a man worthy of the highest approbation, for no other reason but because we have it in our power to see him, and to converse familiarly with him, and not only to give him our applause, but to receive him into our friendship.—Tr William Melmoth rev W. M. L. Hutchinson (LCL 1915) 57–8.

1945 9.139   This and the next two entries are separated by lines across the page, though all come from *Paradise Lost* Bk ix, lines 227–8, 288–9, 309–12, variatim. Milton has "Eve" for "Maid", no comma after "Compare", and lower-case initial letters for the last two words.

This entry and the next were printed as Coleridge's in *PW* ii 1004 and *PW* (JDC) 461.

1946 9.140   See 1945n. Milton wrote "Adam! misthought of her to thee so dear."

1947 9.141   See 1945n. Milton did not use Coleridge's eighteenth-century capitals for "Looks" and "Strength". Printed as Coleridge's in *PW* ii 999.

1948 9.142   On William Windham see 1428 and n. In 1804 he was M.P. for St Mawes, Cornwall, had opposed the peace of 1802, and was assisting Cobbett with his *Political Register*.

1949 9.147   From Cartwright *The Ordinary* I ii: *Comedies* . . .
Poems (1651) 8. See 1942n. Coleridge has substituted "Orator" for
"Madam", and has italicized "endeavouring".
  This entry, at right angles to the two foregoing, appears to have
been written after them.

1950 9.59   Coleridge's compressed version of a note in Sir
Thomas Browne *Hydriotaphia* Chap III. See 1951, 1961–1962. The
reference to Athenaeus, not located specifically by Browne, is to the
Deipnosophistae IV 155.

1951 9.60   Cf Browne *Hydriotaphia* Chap IV: "That they [the
ancients] sucked in the last breath of their expiring friends was surely
a practice of no medical institution, but a loose opinion that the soul
passed out that way, and a fondnesse of affection from some Pytha-
gorical foundation, that the spirit of one body passed into another;
which they wished might be their own."
  The Latin appears to be Coleridge's: "I have loved—the soul of
my beloved." The passage from Browne has set him punning. *Anima*
= soul, *animus* = breath.

1952 9.61   See 1888 and n.

1953 9.62   Written by Mary Lamb, the verses were sent by
Charles in a letter to Dorothy Wordsworth 2 June 1804. *L Letters* I
371. Coleridge must have copied them into his book, probably in
March in London.

1954 9.63   The torn-off page doubtless had the remainder of
this entry on it. Coleridge was at this time attending Davy's lectures
at the Royal Institution.

1957 9.66   The remainder of *f20* was torn out.

1958 16.4   This and the two entries following appear to belong
to January–March in London. This looks like a laundry list, whereas
1874 appears to be an inventory.

1959 16.5   See 344n. Opposite, at right angles, is written,
apparently at a different time, "No! No! Yes! Yes!"

1960 16.6   The banking firm through which Coleridge drew
his Wedgwood annuity changed its designation in 1803. The new one
was in use from Jan 1804 until 1810, when Johnson dropped out.
Cf the earlier name of the firm, in use 1799–1803, in 465n; the change
in it was doubtless the reason why Coleridge entered it in the notebook; the fuller form of it is in 1986.

1961 9.67   In ink. The passage comes from Chap v of *The Garden of Cyrus,* and occurs at the page cited in *Hydriotaphia . . .
together with the Garden of Cyrus,* in the small octavo first edition of
1658.
     The reference to [page] "200" does not fit the copy bound up with
the *Pseudodoxia Epidemica, Religio Medici,* and *A Discourse of the
Sepulchrall Urnes . . .* in the 1659 folio given by Lamb to Coleridge
10 March 1804, and sent by Coleridge to Sara Hutchinson the same
month; annotated to this effect by Lamb, Coleridge, and Sara
Hutchinson, this copy is now in NYPL; the marginalia appeared
in *Blackwood's* (Nov 1819), *LR* ii 398–416, and in *C 17th C.* Nor does
the page reference fit the 1686 folio edition of Browne's *Works* sold in
the *Gillman SC* 524 as Coleridge's; presumably this folio is the copy
referred to in 2014 *f48* as having been sent to Portsmouth to him by
mistake—a heavy addition to his baggage—and it was this volume
over which he "exulted in having procured the Hydriotaphia, & all
the rest lucro posito" (MS note on the 1659 folio); the small octavo of
this entry, containing only *Hydriotaphia* and *The Garden of Cyrus,*
could hardly be described as "all the rest".
     It seems a reasonable guess that Coleridge was here reading in a
pocket copy belonging to Lamb, or Godwin. A copy of this edition
was in Godwin's library: *Godwin SC* (1836) 81. The enthusiasm
generated, as seen here in the notebook, prompted Lamb to buy the
larger collection for STC on 10 March. Neither the 1658 small octavo
nor the 1686 folio belonging to and/or annotated by Coleridge has
been located.

1962 9.68   A favourite theme with Charles Lamb, and probably
connected in both date and subject-matter with the next entry. See
1963n; also 1713, 1717, 1719, and notes.

1963 9.69   Coleridge called twice on Richard Payne Knight,
6 March and 8 March, and wrote about Knight's collection of

bronzes to Sir George Beaumont. See *CL #* 566, where Knight, however, is not identified as R. P. Knight. Doubtless there was discussion afterwards with Charles Lamb and his brother John, who thought of himself as something of a connoisseur. Coleridge was, or later became, scornful of Knight, to whom he referred in his lectures (*ShC* I 180–3 and *Phil Lects* 207, 419 n 20), and even more bluntly in the privacy of marginalia in the 1806 edition of Knight *An Analytical Inquiry into the Principles of Taste*, the copy annotated by both Wordsworth and Coleridge. See *HEHLQ* I (Oct 1937) 63–99.

Coleridge's principal objection to Knight's position was to his crude associationism, and especially his failure to provide for imagination, aesthetic or moral. The tenor of the argument in *Phil Lects* suggests a possible link between this and the foregoing entry, a likelihood supported also by the similarity of the shape and size of the handwriting in the two entries.

1964 9.70   This list of bedding required for the voyage can be dated 12 March from a letter to Southey in which STC gives it (omitting the last item), saying that Captain Findlay was to buy the lot for him for £3 10s. *CL #* 568.

1965 9.71   The address of William Sotheby. It must be dated after 1964 and on or before 13 March, when Coleridge wrote to him there. He saw Sotheby 8 March at Davy's (*CL #* 566) and probably on other occasions at this time, and borrowed £100 from him on Wordsworth's note. *W Letters* (*E*) 371–2 and *CL #* 614. From Sotheby he also had letters of introduction for use in Malta. See 2101n.

1966 9.72   Nearchus, a naval commander under Alexander the Great, wrote a description of his voyage from the Indian Ocean to the Euphrates; only fragments remain.

White: James White (1775–1820), schoolfellow at Christ's Hospital and friend who (with Lamb?) published the *Original Letters . . . of Sir John Falstaff?* The next entry suggests a link with someone with his French-English interests.

1967 9.73   Much of the material in Jeremy Bentham *The Theory of Legislation* was published first in France, and popularized by Pierre Étienne Louis Dumont as *Traités de législation civile et pénale*

(3 vols Paris 1802). According to the Wordsworth LC, Coleridge owned a copy of this work. Dumont, a member of "The King of Clubs" with R. Payne Knight, Mackintosh, Rogers, Sharp, and others, may have been known to him.

1968 9.74   A leaf was cut out before the last five words, with "N. N. N." written on the stub (*ff23–23ᵛ* are blank). The appearance of the handwriting suggests continuousness here.

Coleridge was a Sabbatarian, as Carlyon amusingly records: Carlyon I 100–2.

1970 9.76   In ink.

Stapelia—or carrion Flower: L. fam. Asclepiadaceae. The common name derives from the scent, and the succulent petals and stem.

The *Flesh fly* is a name often applied to the bluebottle and the domestic fly as well as to the *Sarcophaga carnaria*, of which the larva feeds on decaying flesh.

1971 9.77   Harvey Aston, killed in a duel in 1798, was one of the most notorious duellists in English history. A Capt Best and Thomas Pitt, the second baron Camelford, fought a duel 7 March 1804; Camelford's death in consequence three days later gave rise to Coleridge's indignation. Sir James Mackintosh distinguished himself in 1801 in a Norfolk case in which he successfully defended a clergyman indicted for challenging an officer who had insulted his father. *M Memoirs* I 145. Possibly this led Mackintosh to speak in support of duels in general, or possibly Coleridge refers to this case.

1972 9.78   *AP* 67. Samuel Green (1740–96) is the organ builder, more of whose organs are still in use in English cathedrals than of any other builder. *Grove's Dictionary of Music and Musicians* (3rd ed 1927) II 450.

1973 9.79   *AP* 67 has the second sentence only. The name *Vandervelt* is slurred and difficult to read with any certainty as to Coleridge's spelling. The reference is probably to Willem van de Velde, either father (1611–93) or son (1633–1707), both marine painters employed by Charles II and James II.

Coleridge was staying with the Beaumonts in their London house,

S Audley St, Grosvenor Sq, from 19 March until he left 27 March for Portsmouth and Malta. *CL* # 578.

1974 9.80, 81   From a slight change in the size and shape of the hand, these notes at first seemed to be two entries; they appear to be memoranda made at one of Davy's lectures. From Coleridge's letters it is not clear how many he attended. In one of the 1804 series Davy said, "The appearance of the aurora borealis is probably owing to electrical changes taking place in the air around the poles." *D Works* II 402.

1975 9.82   The Portsmouth coach left in the morning, the mail in the evening. Coleridge's feelings on his departure are described in a letter to Sotheby (*CL* # 579); and less conscious ones in 1991.

1976 9.83   James Northcote, R.A., the portrait-painter, on 26 March showed Joseph Farington "a head of Coleridge which he began yesterday and finished to-day". Farington *Diary* II 210. There was thus one sitting only, and that was cut short by Coleridge's indisposition. *CL* # 581. Cf 174 (6)n. The portrait, now in Jesus College, Cambridge, is well known from engravings by W. Say (1805) and J. Thompson (1819). See plate I.

Southey after seeing the original wrote Coleridge comparing it unfavourably with Hazlitt's portrait, saying it looked "like a grinning idiot: and the worst is, that it is just enough like to pass for a good likeness with those who know your features only imperfectly". *S Life and C* II 291. Yet Coleridge had ordered a copy to be made through Northcote, for his "Friends in the North"; this may be the one now owned by Mr John C. C. Holder, but whether it reached them or whether it went to Keswick or Grasmere is not clear. In June 1805 Wordsworth wrote to Sir George Beaumont acknowledging and criticizing a print of the portrait:

"We think it excellent about the eyes and forehead, which are the finest parts of Coleridge's face, and the general contour of the face is well given; but to my Sister and me, it seems to fail sadly about the middle of the face, particularly at the bottom of the nose. Mrs W. feels this also; and my Sister so much, that, except when she covers the whole middle of the face, it seems to her so entirely to alter the expression, as rather to confound than revive in her mind the remembrance of the original. We think as far as mere likeness goes,

Hazlitt's is better; but the expression in Hazlitt's is quite dolorous and funereal; that in this, is so much more pleasing, though certainly far below what one would wish to see infused into a picture of C." *W Letters* (E) 496–7.

1977 9.84   A difficulty of which he was particularly conscious while sitting for the portrait?

1978 9.85   An anecdote out of Northcote's conversation? Benjamin West, American-born painter, was at this time Sir Joshua Reynolds's successor as president of the Royal Academy.

1979 9.86   The last word, as well as being badly written in the corner of the page, is obscured by the page-number written over it, in what I take to be Mrs Gillman's numerals.

1980 9.87   Again from Northcote?

1981 9.88   Joseph Farington (1747–1821), English landscape-painter, published a folio of *Views of Cities and Towns in England and Wales* (1790). Since he was known as the "autocrat of the Academy", his work may well have called forth derisive adjectives in the Beaumont-Northcote circles. He dined with the Beaumonts 25 March and visited Northcote the next day. See 1976n. For his meetings with Coleridge see his *Diary* II 209–11, 217.

1982 9.89   *James's Powder:* for many decades perhaps the best-known patent medicine, its chief constituent being antimony.
      Bark: Peruvian bark; see 235n.

1983 9.90   Coleridge's way of describing to the Wordsworths the kindness of the Beaumonts is of interest by comparison with the private description here. In a letter of 8 Feb he said, "I was welcomed *almost* as you welcomed me at Racedown/And their solicitude of attention is enough to effeminate one." *CL* # 553. He stayed with them from 19 March until he left for Portsmouth the evening of the 27th.

1984 9.91   Northcote, like Coleridge, was a Devonshire man, but a Londoner since 1771.

1985 9.132   A very faint entry, written on *f55* before the end of
2024, and 1938 on that page, at right angles to them and partly
obliterated by Mrs Gillman's heavy pen. It seems to belong to mid-
March. Coleridge had left a deposit of £20 with the captain of the
Speedwell by 13 March and was calculating his fare and arranging
with Stuart for money for Mrs Coleridge during his absence. *CL*
588. BM Add MS 34,046 shows some figures pertaining to this
entry: on 9 March Southey drew on Stuart for £60 for Mrs Coleridge
(f 22); on 12 March STC drew the £20 to be paid to Findlay (f 23);
before he sailed, STC paid an extra £30 on his Equitable Life Assurance policy for the risk of his Malta voyage; this comes from the
minutes of the meeting of the company directors, 25 April 1804
(f 29). On 29 April Stuart paid £61 11s. 5d. on the policy, a sum that
was to shock Coleridge when he heard of it, from Stuart, about a
year later in Malta. *CL* # 616.

1986 9.92   Coleridge sent Mrs Coleridge, 27 March 1804, this
address of the bankers through whom his Wedgwood annuity was
paid. *CL* # 588. Probably he called on them before leaving London,
and got the more complete address; cf 1960.

1987 9.93   Coleridge was seen off by Charles Lamb, Daniel
Stuart, and James Tobin ("*advising* and *advising* to the last moment"), and Sir George Beaumont's valet. *CL* # 597 (II 1129). At the
Crown he seems to have stayed only two or three nights until offered
hospitality by J. C. Mottley, "a dashing Bookseller", newspaper
proprietor, and Portsmouth correspondent for Daniel Stuart. In the
uncertainties of weather and convoy, he stayed with Mottley almost
a week.

1988 9.94   Coleridge again—cf 174 (18) and n—notices a
military-religious ceremony dedicating the colours of a regiment,
in this case those of the South East Battalion of Isle of Wight Volun-
teers; the account in the issue of the London *Star* he cites describes
how the Colonel's lady, attended by eminent persons, and after a
"most impressive sermon" in Godshill Church, presented a pair of
colours, and the Colonel handed them to the ensigns "after reminding
the battalion of the martial spirit of their ancestors and expressing
his conviction that they would live and die in defence of their God,
their King, and their Country".

1989 9.95   Thomas Hope (1770–1831), novelist, art collector, and interior decorator, housed his large and various collections in two houses, one in Duchess St, near Cavendish Square, the other at Deepdene, near Dorking. Three years after this entry he was to publish his *Household Furniture and Interior Decoration* (f° 1807), for which he designed the plates.

1990 9.96   Horndean is on the main London-Portsmouth road. If Maidlow is the name of a country seat, it has not been discoverable in contemporary records or maps, nor has it any apparent connexion with the preceding entry; possibly it is the name and address of some communicative fellow-traveller.

1991 9.97   The lost or orphan child and the dying or absent mother come too frequently into Coleridge's poems to be insignificant images as he takes his own departure, unembraced by family or close friends. In the emotional letter of 11 May 1808 to his brother George, protesting against the family's attitude towards his separation from Mrs Coleridge and the gossip spread by them, he refers to himself as being, even this late, and with his mother still living, "a deserted Orphan", and "an Orphan Brother". *CL* # 705.

1992 9.98   The first epitaph, with its circumstantial heading, suggests the idle traveller finding entertainment in a Portsmouth graveyard; perhaps it reminded Coleridge (or his companion) of the other two. All three might have come out of some book or article on the humour of epitaphs, all being old journalistic favourites. The second e.g. is found variatim in E. R. Suffling *Epitaphia* (1909) as coming from "one of the London churchyards": "Here lies I/John Fry/Killed by/A sky-/rocket in my/eye-socket."
     The reference to "Priestley's intermediate State" is to *Disquisitions relating to Matter and Spirit* (1782) 279, though Priestley denied the validity of the concept: "After the long prevalence of the doctrine of the *intermediate state*, that of the *sleep of the Soul* has of late years been revived, and gains ground. . . . Upon the whole, the doctrine of an intermediate state is now retained by few who have the character of thinking with freedom and liberality in other respects."

1993 9.99   *f28ᵛ the Speedwell:* a "merchant-brig, 130 Tons", Coleridge said. *CL* # 569. *Steel's Navy List* describes a brig of 14 guns

built in 1796; were there two *Speedwells*? The *Star* of 18 April 1804 in its Nautical Intelligence column announced the arrival at Portsmouth, April 17, of "the Speedwell, brig of war, from a cruize".
ff29ᵛ-30   The Captain was John Findlay, of whom little is known. The other two passengers Coleridge described in very ungenial terms to Southey in a letter in which he expands the cradle simile and bemoans the rocking of the cabin. *CL # 597*.
f30ᵛ   the Start, to our right: Start Point, Devonshire.
   read Italian till breakfast Time: he wrote Southey that he had "done little else than read through the Italian Grammar". *CL # 597*. On Coleridge's study of Italian see Appendix A.
f31   read the Theodicee: cf 1835n, where his "Comforts and Consolations" is described in a letter of 1 Feb 1804 as "a new Theodicee". Leibnitz *Essais de théodicée sur la bonté de Dieu, la liberté de l'homme et l'origine du mal*, of which a copy marked as Coleridge's appears (edition not designated) in Wordsworth LC, was also read by Coleridge in a German translation (Hanover and Leipzig 1763). A copy of this edition, now in Yale University Library, annotated by Coleridge, is said to have been De Quincey's copy. If so, it was not the one Coleridge read at this time, as he had not yet met De Quincey, unless he later gave it to De Quincey. In *BL* 1 195 he quotes from a Latin edition of Leibnitz's works. In the *Phil Lects* he makes references to Leibnitz, possibly one to the *Théodicée*. *Phil Lects* 384, 463 n 24.
   my Consolations: "Comforts and Consolations", a work projected at least from the autumn of 1803 onwards. See 1835n. The earliest reference discovered is in entry 1646. Some of the lines of thought connected with it eventually took the form of "my literary life and opinions", as here and as in 1551, 1835, 2598, and *BL* 1 44, to cite but a few examples. Other aspects of the projected work were incorporated in *The Friend*. In a letter of 15 Jan 1804 to Poole, he describes the work as "Consolations and Comforts from the exercise and right application of the Reason, the Imagination, and the moral Feelings, addressed especially to those in Sickness, Adversity, or Distress of mind, *from speculative gloom*, &c. I put that last phrase, tho' barbarous, for your information/". *CL # 536*. "That last phrase, tho' barbarous" found its way into the *Prospectus* of *The Friend* (1809-10).
   For some notes indicative of the nature of this proposed work see e.g. 2011, 2018, 2026 *f8ᵛ*, 2458, 2541.
   my letters on literary Detraction/or a review of Wordsworth: the earlier intention of an attack on Peter Bayley? Cf 1673n.

1994 9.100   *Waterglasses:* presumably drinking-glasses, but possibly water-clocks; or if the reference is to the water-glasses used by fishermen, buckets with glass bottoms, water-telescopes, this is earlier than the first use cited in the *OED*.

1995 9.101   Developing, in daylight, a night-observation at the start of the earlier ocean voyage to Germany; see 335 *f1ᵛ*.

1996 9.102   The phrases here, obviously reminiscent of *The Ancient Mariner* and the gloss added later, add to the impression from other entries of Coleridge's growing identification with his own Mariner.
  Lullaby . . . rocking Cradle: cf *CN* I 20 and n.
  the Lizard: off the south tip of Cornwall.
  the Clouds now all bright . . . now darting off: The phrase "of foam" after *Clouds*, as described in 335, was surely intended. The phrase here used, "darting off", became the "streamed off free" of the temporary revision referred to in 335n.

1997 9.103   There appear to be double quotation marks before *Rear'd*, but no completing ones. Is there a reminiscence here, half contrast, with Wordsworth's lines (he was thinking about them three days later—2011), ". . . but he had been reared/Among the mountains, and he in his heart/Was half a shepherd on the stormy seas./Oft in the piping shrouds . . .". *The Brothers: WPW* II 2. Cf also Wordsworth's lines addressed to Coleridge: "Thou, my Friend! wert reared/In the great city, mid far other scenes . . .". *Prelude* II 452–3. The personal undertones in the entry are strong. Did the swinging albatross-like load almost set in motion a new poem, the lullaby referred to in 1996? The parallel with II *Henry IV* III i, in which appear the ship-boy, "the high and giddy mast", and the figure of a rocking cradle, may be in mind also.

1998 9.104   *Sir C. Grandison's Lady:* presumably Harriet Byron of Richardson's novel. Sir Philip Sidney's wife was Frances Walsingham.
  For other dreams involving dark passages and/or pursuers, especially female figures, see e.g. 848, 1649, and 1726.
  The escritoire was described to Southey in *CL* # 597.
  Tentacula: ?Tantacula. The reading is not absolute and seems to be

rather a telescoping of Tantalus and tentacles than the Latin word for "attempts".

1999 9.105   *And on the gliding Vessel Heaven & Ocean smil'd:* Wordsworth *The Female Vagrant* line 162: *LB* (1798) 78. From the revised and augmented version of 1842, entitled *Guilt and Sorrow*, this line was omitted. Coleridge's thoughts and associations are the backward-looking ones of the passenger but three days out; besides, he had promised the Wordsworths a daily journal. *CL* # 592.

2000 9.106   *Why an't you here?:* cf 981, 2118, but also 2057.

2001 9.107   SICKLY *Thoughts about M. mort. & W. ÷ Sā + Hydrocarb:* i.e. *unhealthy* thoughts of M[ary Wordsworth] dead and W[illiam] married to Sa[ra Hutchinson]. Hydrocarb is himself? Hydro = water, i.e. dropsical, affected by various accumulations of serous fluid; also, an unstable element; and carbon is potentially both charcoal (black and relatively valueless) and that to which the diamond of poetry and genius may be reduced. Cf 1098n *f28ᵛ*. The entry is an important one for interpreting such later entries as 2998 and 3148.

   road of dim Light?—Light of the Compass & rudderman's Lamp: cf "The stars were dim, and thick the night,/The steersman's face by his lamp gleamed white"; *The Ancient Mariner* 206–7, lines not in the early versions of the poem, but first added in *SL* (1817). It is worth noting, in conjunction with the "Sickly Thoughts" and the looking up at the stars in this entry, the first three lines of the same stanza: "We listened and looked sideways up!/Fear at my heart as at a cup,/My life-blood seemed to sip!" *PW* I 195. These also were new lines added in *SL* (1817), as was most of the stanza preceding. See 2086 and n, 2880 and n.

2002 9.108   Another link with *The Ancient Mariner* appears in the "great Sea-savannah", an association with Bartram's *Travels*. See also 2052 *f22*. See *RX* 8–11, and *CN* I Index I for several references to Bartram in the Gutch notebook.

2003 9.109   The Greek phrase from Hesiod *Works and Days* line 40 means "the half is more than the whole".

   Wyndham to tow Mᵣ Addington: Coleridge, though he wrote in support of the Addington ministry, was aware of its weakness. It fell the next month. See 1289, 1753 and n.

2004 9.110   "The loud-roaring sea" occurs frequently in Homer and Hesiod, e.g. in the *Iliad* 1 34; Coleridge (like Homer) uses the genitive case—for its sound. Cf 2777 and n.

2005 9.111   Another poem projected by inspiration of the sea? Was the sheep "from flat peaceable meadows" [of Devon?] being compared with the hardier north-country flocks, in another personal image? Cf 2016 and "I the sole scabbed Sheep" of 2623.

2006 9.112   *multitude of Sunshine:* cf Coleridge's use of *multitude* in 784.
    Have I not seen masses of plumbago: the lead of the slate quarries of Buttermere? On *slant reflections* see 713 and n.

2008 9.114   *Sir G. B.:* Sir George Beaumont. In 1899 in the note on the third of the Beaumont drawings, Coleridge wrote, "remarkably fine Clouds".

2009 9.115   *the crescent Moon with the old Moon in her Lap:* cf the ballad *Sir Patrick Spens* and *Dejection* line 13: *PW* 1 363.
    $\frac{27}{190}$ *of the Cope:* see 2010n.

2010 9.116   Coleridge was probably on the quarter-deck getting his information from an officer. But if he had a recent number of the *Critical Review* with him on the journey it may well have furthered his readiness to ask questions. Or he may have been reading it or the *Philosophical Transactions of the Royal Society of London for the year 1803* before he left. The first paper in the *Transactions*, reviewed in *Cr Rev* (Feb 1804) 1 28–9, was one by William Hyde Wollaston: "Observations on the Quantity of horizontal Refraction; with a method of measuring the Dip at Sea". It refers to a method of measuring dip in conditions of abnormal refraction, by taking the altitude of a heavenly body from opposite horizons; the excess of the sum over 180° would be approximately twice the dip.

2011 9.117   *In my Consolations:* see 1993n for a description of this projected work.

Lamb can't like the Brothers: cf 2013n. For Lamb's lack of enthusiasm for Wordsworth's poem (and for the second volume of the second edition of *LB* in general) see e.g. *L Letters* I 245–7, a letter of 15 Feb 1801 in which he quotes *The Brothers* disparagingly.

Charles James Fox was known as a great reader, and Wordsworth and Coleridge sent him a complimentary copy of *LB* (1800), for which Wordsworth reports receiving his qualified thanks. "He says that he read the poems with great pleasure especially those in rime, he is not partial to blank verse." *W Letters (E)* 327. Fox's letter was printed in Christopher Wordsworth *Memoirs of William Wordsworth* (1851) I 171.

2012 9.118 *f39 the* Men *on the tops of conical mountains:* like the Astrologer, and the Ancient Woman seated on Helm Crag, in 1419, 1420, and 1803.

f41 this phantom of complete visual wholeness: cf 1973.

f41ᵛ Passion unifies: cf with the remainder of this paragraph the "characteristics of original poetic genius" as described e.g. in Chap xv of *BL*, esp I 16–20.

f42 another Book: probably from N 15, which he was about to use. Except for a brief incursion into N 21, N 9 and N 15 were the pocketbooks of the voyage. No more pocketbooks with the metallic pencils have survived from the Malta-Sicily-Italy journey, a fact of some interest. See the Introduction to this volume.

f42ᵛ the repetition of the *of* comes at the turn of the page.

f43ᵛ a sort of natural Telegraph: A semaphoric system of sending messages over a distance was invented in France in 1792 and used in England shortly afterwards.

2013 9.119 *ff44–44ᵛ* In making Cumberland and Westmorland images out of clouds Coleridge is like Leonard Ewbank of Wordsworth's poem *The Brothers*, referred to in 2011, and like John Wordsworth. Cf *W Letters (E)* 509. The reference to places visited on the Scottish tour is another association with the Wordsworths.

my Heart did indeed leap up: in corroboration of Wordsworth's phrase in "My heart leaps up when I behold/A rainbow in the sky"? *WPW* I 226.

f46ᵛ the Mate is whistling aloft for a wind: Like another ancient nautical superstition, this one caught Coleridge's attention, apparently as it was being put into practice. Cf "The impatient mariner the sail unfurl'd,/And whistling, called the wind that hardly curled/The silent sea." *The Female Vagrant* lines 166–8 *LB* (1798) 78: *WPW* 1 114. Cf the association with this poem two days earlier in 1999.

2014 9.120   *f47ᵛ* The measurements are so inserted as to be difficult to make out, with some confusing marks that may be intended for feet and inches signs, but are not clear; in 2522 Coleridge confuses these signs.

half a dozen Books or more: Leibnitz *Théodicée* (1993), Jeremy Collier's translation of the *Meditations* of Marcus Aurelius (1655n), an Italian dictionary and an Italian grammar (*CL* # 584 n 2), and possibly Pascal *Les Provinciales* (2133 and n) were there, in addition to the Browne and Haüy listed below. So probably was a copy of Dante *La divina commedia . . . con gli argomenti, allegorie, e dichiarazione di Lodovico Dolce . . .* (Venice 1774); it had been given to Coleridge by Beaumont 10 Feb 1804 at Dunmow, so inscribed; it is now in the library of W. H. P. Coleridge.

f48   Sir T. Brown's works, sent down to me to P[ortsmouth] by mistake: see 1961 n. This was probably the 1686 folio edition containing *Vulgar Errors, Religio Medici, Hydriotaphia* and *The Garden of Cyrus,* and *Certain Miscellany Tracts.* Coleridge's copy was sold in Gillman's library sale. *Gillman SC* (524).

Haüy's Mineralogy: Traité de minéralogie (4 vols Paris 1801) by the Abbé René Just Haüy (1743–1822), founder of crystallography. Cf 1886 and n.

The "m[irror]-smooth Lake in the sea" seems to be a happier association for the tag *Imperium in Imperio* than an earlier one; cf 1335 and n.

f48ᵛ   ab infra: from beneath.
f49 For the long letter to Southey in which some of the description in N 9 to this point is used variatim, see *CL* # 597.

2015 9.121   *Phocæ:* seals.
Cape Mondego: on the west coast of Portugal between Oporto and Lisbon.

2016 9.122   μεταφορητικα: presumably a combination of μεταφορη-τός and μεταφορικός, i.e. metaphorically, an invention on the analogy of e.g. *anglice.* The *Sea Phrase* was easily applied by the journalist in Coleridge to Pitt's wavering war policies. At this juncture, although the French fleet was bottled up in Toulon harbour under the eye of Nelson, France was threatening invasion of England, and convoys were necessary.

The image of sails stretched before the wind had been used of Wordsworth in 1803; see 1546 and n. Later Coleridge was to apply it, conversely, to himself, in 2086.

With the *Lag Sheep* of this entry, cf the lines in 2623: "O blessed Flock! I the sole scabbed Sheep!/And even me they love, awake, asleep." The "scabbed" sheep was on board; see 2623n. Cf also 2005.

2017 9.123   There is no hyphen between *blue* and *pierced*, though one suspects from the numerous attempts to describe colour, especially such non-colours as white, black, and moonlight, that this was the intention. See e.g. 2026 *f4*.

2018 9.124   *ff51ᵛ–52* The drafted verses have not been published.

f52ᵛ Consolations: as distinct from *Comforts?* See 1993n, and cf a letter to Sir George Beaumont of 1 Feb 1804 when he says, "The 'Consolations' are addressed to all in adversity, sickness, or distress of mind . . . the 'Comforts' are addressed to the Happy & Prosperous, attempting to open to them new & perhaps better—at all events, more numerous & more various Sources of Enjoyment." *CL # 550* (II 1053).

that Phænomenon of Sleep: cf 1250.

Rickman: John Rickman; see 1856n. Lamb described him enthusiastically (*L Letters* I 220–1), but Coleridge, who admired and was grateful to him, did not find him warm or genial. Southey's description (*S Life and C* III 216–17) suggests that he was not even mildly demonstrative, and more interested in mathematical evidence than in the imaginative and humanly complex. Coleridge had probably smarted under what Rickman and Le Grice had in common, quickness of temper and limited powers of sympathy. *Rickman* 98–108, esp 107–8.

Poor Legrice: possibly Samuel Le Grice, who had died in 1802 (979n), probably C. V., but in any case a Christ's Hospital dream, as in 1726. See 2613 and n. From an unpublished letter of Southey to Anna Seward 23 Oct 1807, a good deal of light is thrown on C. V. Le Grice and STC, which would account for Coleridge's adjective here, if it does apply to him. Southey wrote:

"The Critical Reviewer of Madoc is the same person who has spoken in the same spirit of Wordsworth's late volumes. I have seen neither article. . . . His name is Le Grice; he was a schoolfellow of Coleridge's at Christ's Hospital. Before my acquaintance with Coleridge began I past five days at Cambridge, having walked thither from Oxford with Edmund Seward, to see his brother, the Dr John Seward . . . who is now an inhabitant of some better world than ours. We then met this Le Grice; he was unusually courteous towards me, and I as unusually repulsive towards him, for never had I seen a man whose whole temper of mind appeared to me so thoroughly perverted & mischievous. Everything was made the subject of his ridicule, & he seemed to have laughed himself out of every good principle & every good feeling. Considerable talents he had, but only in this miserable direction. His face was as white as a ghost's, & in this clayey & unexpressive face were set two jet black eyes, forming so strange & hideous a contrast that literally & truly that face was the original from which I described the dead countenance of Donica animated by a devil. From that time I never saw him. He remembers with what unconcealed dislike I turned my back upon his proffered civilities, but what has more weight with him has been a notion that he could wound Coleridge thro' me, & thus pay off some of the scores of an old & rooted envy. This man is now settled at Land's End in Cornwall, where he married an old woman to whose children he went to be tutor . . . Le Grice himself is an unsuccessful author." (From a transcript communicated to me by Bertram R. Davis of Bristol.)

2019 9.125   *abiding Hope:* on these two words, cathectic in Coleridge's usage, see e.g. 1486n; also 2045n.
her Presence: the reference is to Sara Hutchinson.

2021 9.127   This and the next two entries are used in *CL* # 597 (II 1127–8).
which I wished to be Cintra: because of associations with talk about it from Southey? See *S Life and C* II 137. Or had he read the description by Camoëns in the *Lusiads*? The Convention of Cintra was still to come—in 1808.

2022 21.431   Coleridge must have borrowed from an officer a volume of sailing directions for the area. These instructions are to be found in J. F. Dessiou, Master R.N., *Directions for Navigating in and*

Throughout the North Sea . . . (London 1816). No earlier edition has been found, nor any of the various ephemeral volumes of sailing directions in which Coleridge might have read this in 1804. But the substance is in Dessiou as follows:

"Account of the Signals made use of at Bamborough Castle . . . as published by the Trustees of Nathaniel Lord Crewe, with the approbation of the Corporation of Trinity House in Newcastle upon Tyne.

"*Signals* I A gun, (a nine-pounder) is placed at the bottom of the tower to be fired as a signal . . . II In every great storm two men . . . III A large flag . . . IV A bell in the south turret . . . V A large weather cock . . . VI A Large speaking trumpet . . . VII An Observatory or watch tower . . . VIII Master and Commanders of ships in distress. . . .

"*Assistance* &c I Rooms and beds . . . II Cellars for wine . . . III A store house . . . IV Four pair of screws for raising ships . . . V A pair of chains . . . VI Two mooring chains . . . VII Whenever any dead bodies . . .".

M. & Com.: Masters and Commanders.

Coleridge's last sentence is perhaps based on a reflection on how far away he is from Bamborough Castle and England. But the whole is additional evidence of his unremitting interest in how men live, the processes of human dynamics, especially in the context of the elements.

2024 9.129   The entry is written very small, and some indecipherable scribbles were superimposed on it from the other direction. It was the latest entry in this notebook; over the earlier notes on *f55* which it encounters and overruns, Mrs Gillman has written large in black ink, "Now proceed to the large black clasp Book", i.e. to N 15. See 2025. The account of "Mrs Carnosity", however, "once a housekeeper in General Fox's family", was given in *CL* # 597 (II 1127-8), where the "plaintive crying Yawns" are also attributed to her.

2025 15.5   A very rubbed and faint entry. The *April 9th, 1804* is inked over by Mrs Gillman, who added at right angles up the outer edge of the page, "In May 18—1806 Left Rome page 203." She refers to "page 203" of this notebook (*f105*), which she may have paginated, the numerals being in ink, and often superimposed on the pencilled entries at the upper right-hand corner of the page, unlike Coleridge's pagination, which regularly respects the text.

The *red Pocket book* is N 9, now more brown than red, and the ink on the cover is only in part visible to the naked eye; ultra-violet light shows the words "Chronology/Portsmouth to Gib[raltar]", the later-imposed label obscuring the last part of the last word. Following Coleridge's directions, Mrs Gillman on "the last leaf but three" noted its continuation in the "black clasp Book", i.e. N 15. See 2024n.

2026 15.7   *AP* 70–4, in part.

f4 Queen's metal: an alloy of tin, antimony, bismuth, and lead. The earliest reference in the *OED* is dated 1839.

f4ᵛ Privateers & Corsairs: the first would be European, and enemy pirates; the second, African or Asian, in this case Algerians and Tunisians from the Barbary coast.

f6 Caernarvon Castle: Coleridge refers to a visit with Hucks in July 1794. His antipathy to sentimental antiquarianism was strong; see also 2169 and n.

losing myself in the flexures of its Branches: the empathy here exhibited (if such it is) appears elsewhere in relation to trees. See a marginal note on his copy of Law's *Behmen* quoted in "Coleridge Redivivus" in *The Major English Romantic Poets* ed C. D. Thorpe, C. Baker, B. Weaver (Carbondale 1957) 116.

f6ᵛ morti ultro occurrens: going of his own accord to meet death.

f7 pure Action, defecated of all that is material: cf "Whene'er the mist, that stands 'twixt God and thee,/Defecates to a pure transparency,/That intercepts no light and adds no stain—/There Reason is, and then begins her reign!" *Reason: PW* I 487. And see below 2078.

f7ᵛ that will [not] *endure the Co-presence?* i.e. a *not* omitted?

Wordliness: for Worldliness?

f8 the Paradise Lost a task: cf the second of "Satyrane's Letters" —*Friend* (1809–10) No 16; *BL* II 162—where Coleridge charges, ". . . do not Dr. Johnson and other great men tell us, that nobody now reads Milton but as a task?" He refers to the notorious passage on *Paradise Lost* at the end of Johnson's *Life* of Milton. "None ever wished it longer than it is. Its perusal is a duty rather than a pleasure." One hopes that Coleridge's attack "with all *due* severity" was to take cognizance of Johnson's statement earlier in the *Life* that *Paradise Lost* was "a poem which considered with respect to design, may claim the first place, and with respect to performance the second, among the productions of the human mind". But the quarrel Coleridge is picking is not merely or primarily literary. In the context of the last phrases of this entry, one remembers that Johnson is reported by Boswell as saying that one green field is very much like another green field; the quarrel is one between two generations and two temperaments.

f8 Consolations: on the projected "Comforts and Consolations" see 1993n.

2029 15.10   *40ᵐ p. 2:* forty minutes past two.

Grasmere & the Maid of Glencoe: the conjunction was first made by Coleridge as he walked up Glencoe the previous September. See 1487 *f48ᵛ*.

The famous Apes hill—a corruption of M. Abbila: cf 2045 *f15*, where it is similarly spelled.

Coleridge gave his impressions of the arrival at Gibraltar in a letter to Daniel Stuart. *CL # 599*. His attempts in N K to draw the outlines of the rock—see 2038–2041—indicate his interest.

2030 15.11   Names of ships in Gibraltar harbour? Coleridge in a later notebook entry (N 18) took ships' names to have some national significance.

2031 15.12   From this to 2050 the entries clearly are notes made at Gibraltar, with attempts to draw the "cut off" Rock.

2032 21.432   *AP 68–70*, and *CL # 598* verbatim to James Webbe Tobin, who had seen Coleridge off from London. Some of the matter of this protest is in a letter to Southey written 16 April; in this case what first appears in a letter (*CL # 597*) was written up more fully in the notebook three days afterwards, and still later, 19 April, used in the actual letter to Tobin.

Three years earlier, in a letter to Poole, advising against advice, Coleridge wrote, "I was with an acquaintance lately, & we passed by a poor Ideot boy, who exactly answered my description—he Stood in the sun, rocking his sugar-loaf Head,/And staring at a bough from Morn to Sunset/*See-saw'd* his voice in inarticulate Noises./I wonder, says my Companion, what that Ideot means to say.—'To give advice,'

I replied: 'I know not what else an Ideot can do, & any Ideot can do that.' " *CL* # 416.

But the more serious charge against Tobin was a weakness for gossiping, even maliciously; see 1855n.

2033 21.433   It may seem curious to think this a shipboard entry; the opinion, in the absence of other evidence, is based on the appearance and position on the page of the writing, which is like that of 2022 and quite unlike that of 2121. From his own or other books on board did he fall on a quotation from Livy that struck him as applicable to his own plight as described in 2032?

The Loeb text varies in minor pointing and reads "magna . . . momenta". A footnote makes it clear that some manuscripts of the text give Coleridge's reading; it might be possible from this to identify his edition of Livy (or the edition quoted by the author he is reading), but so far this is not known.

Tr: In addition there were what seem small things to mention, but at the same time were highly important in the battle: a harmony in the shouting of the Romans, which consequently was greater in volume and more terrifying; on the other side discordant voices, as was natural from many nations with a confusion of tongues.—Bk xxx §34. Tr F. G. Moore (LCL 1949) VIII 492.

2034 15.13   Cf the letter to Stuart: "A dozen plates by Hogarth from this town!" *CL* # 599.

2035 15.14   *Soother of absence:* see 1225n and 1541n.

On the inadequacy of words, cf 1554: "Without Drawing I feel myself but half invested with Language . . .".

2036 15.15   The notebooks so far have not described any walks in the Lakes with Sara Hutchinson and it is not possible to date the events referred to in this entry. Crummock and Scale Force more probably represent expeditions from Keswick than from Grasmere.

the abstrusest Researches: cf "And haply by abstruse research to steal/From my own nature all the natural man": *Dejection* lines 89–90: *PW* I 367. The context in which the phrase appears in this entry confirms the view that in the poem "abstruse research" is referred to as a means of sublimating the old Adam, the man in love with SH, not, as has sometimes been suggested, the thief of poems and the destroyer of imagination.

2037 15.16   The description and rough sketch here confirm the
rude drawings in N K as being also attempts to capture the shapes
of the Gibraltar rocks.

2038 K.1   Inserted on the inside cover, the outline of the Rock
of Gibraltar, which appears again in a letter to Stuart (*CL* # 599),
seems to be an attempt to convey what words fail to describe in 2037.
      The memorandum (probably to ask Southey to send his German
pocketbooks, one of which has N° 3/2 on the cover) is in the right-
hand upper corner; Coleridge had received them by 4 Aug 1804.
CL # 607.
      In this entry the stroke between the 3 and the 2 is very faint, but it
is barely discernible to an eye looking for it. "32" would make no
sense at all at this time, unless one predicates some 14 notebooks,
now lost, belonging to the period 1794–1804. The flow of notebook
entries reveals no such great gaps.
      Coleridge wished to have his pocketbooks, possibly to try again to
write up his travels in Germany, and probably also for the entries on
metrics. The sound of a new language, whether German or Italian,
clearly stimulated this interest. See 2224 and n.
      The *road-book* may have been H. A. O. Reichard *Guide des voyageurs
en Europe, avec une carte itinéraire de l'Europe, et une carte de la
Suisse* . . . (2 vols Weimar 1793). Coleridge owned a copy by March
1800 (*CL* # 323), but a copy now in VCL bearing his initials shows
few signs of use.

2039–41 K.51–3 Like the outline on the inside front cover, drawings
of the Rock of Gibraltar.

2042 K.2   Entries 2042, 2084, 2065, and 2066 were superimposed
on some other pencilled writing very faint or else deliberately erased.
      Coleridge told Stuart about his difficulty in taking brandy, 21
April. *CL* # 599. This entry appears to be datable from 2045 *ff16ᵛ–17*.

2043 15.17   See also 2122. The irritable disputations of travellers?
But this was an old theme with Coleridge; cf 1107, 1109, 1110, and
notes.

2044 15.18   The entry is written over another attempt, similar to
the drawing in 2037, to outline the Rock.

f11   Prattic: or pratique, permission from the quarantine authorities to disembark, was used later by Coleridge in an interesting metaphor: "Hapless Maxilian! the havens of pleasure have . . . *their* quarantine, and repel with no less aversion the plague of poverty. The *Pratique* boat hails, and where is his bill of health?" "The Historie and Gests of Maxilian", originally published in *Blackwood's Magazine* for Jan 1822: *Miscellanies* 279.

Bumbazine: for *bombasine.* OED gives eight different spellings (one of them Coleridge's) for this silk and worsted material such as is used in academic gowns.

f12   Mr. Frome: a Rev Mr Frome appears in the list of subscribers to the Gibraltar garrison library, and in 1803–4 he was apparently an auditor of the library accounts. He died there late in 1804 in the plague. VCL MS F 14.14.

2045 15.19   Printed in *L* II 477–9n.
f15   Massinissa, Jugurtha, Syphax: ancient Numidian rulers involved in Rome's wars with Carthage.

Abiding: Coleridge does not frequently capitalize adjectives; see 1486 and 2019 and notes.

f15ᵛ   my Tragedy: Osorio (1797), later re-written as *Remorse* (1813); the reference is to "this inhuman cavern" with its "fingers of ice", the setting of the first scene in Act IV of *Osorio: PW* II 562–70. In *Remorse* (*PW* II 858–64) the passage is very little altered, except for the removal of the "Drip! drip! drip! drip!" of which Sheridan had made sport. See 2064n.

f16ᵛ   Mrs Ireland: a passenger.
f17   Major Adye: Ralph Willett Adye, of the Royal Regiment of Artillery, wrote an artillery manual, *The Bombardier, and Pocket-Gunner,* 1798, 1802, &c, long in use as a standard text-book. Adye's death of the plague a few months after this entry, 22 Oct 1804 after a visit to Malta, was a personal shock to Coleridge; and the burning of Adye's effects led to the loss of some of Coleridge's documents and letters home, including his comments on Wordsworth's *The Recluse. CL* # 617.

f17ᵛ   Boding: the word *bodings* is used in *Wallenstein* Pt I, I iii 20: *PW* II 610.

2046 15.20   *that last word: Boding* of the previous entry? Or something in a letter to Sara Hutchinson?

bustles about you: see 2052 *f20ᵛ*n.

wishless from excess of wishing: an instance of how Coleridge's theory of the reconciliation of opposites, or extremes meeting, issues directly from his observation of his own emotional conflicts.

2047 15.6   This page was first left blank, as the *verso* of his title-page of a sort, but four or five days later a thriftier mood prevailed.

2048 15.21   Edridge appears (see 2052 *f21ᵛ*) to have been a ship's officer, and not Henry Edridge (1769–1821) the artist and miniaturist, friend of Sir George Beaumont, who in 1805 was to do a drawing of Wordsworth. *W Letters* (*E*) 418. If the painter had been a fellow-passenger we should surely have heard more about him in letters or the notebooks; moreover, the "three passengers" referred to in 1993 are all that are accounted for on disembarkation at Malta: 2099. No personal relationship is needed to explain how conversation about superstitions among sailors could start up with Coleridge. What one would like to know is whether *The Ancient Mariner* was explicitly mentioned and, if so, by whom first.

2049 15.22   *the last curse of the waning moon:* cf *Zapolya*, Prelude 430: *PW* II 897. See also 2060 and n.

2050 15.23   *more & struck:* more & more struck? The reading is difficult.

D[uke] of Kent . . . a good Serjeant Major: a terse summary of the dislike in which this unimaginative martinet was held by his officers. Though earlier unpopular as commander of a regiment at Gibraltar, and transferred to Canada, he was in March 1802 appointed Governor of Gibraltar. His order closing wine-shops to all but commissioned officers led to a mutiny on Christmas Eve 1802. He was recalled to England, requested a formal inquiry, and was refused it. Whether his "Mishap" had something to do with this is not clear; perhaps the word is ironical. At the time of STC's visit and this entry, Kent was still Governor, but *in absentia*, having been forbidden to return.

2051 15.24   *f19   under weigh:* Coleridge's spelling was in his day an acceptable alternative to *under way.*

f19ᵛ   Hepatic Gas . . . Sulphur: It is characteristic that Coleridge should seize hold of or unconsciously try to divert his misery by a scientific interest in it; cf 2070 and the question for Davy.

Granada appears at first glance to be spelled with two *n*'s, but actually it merely is an indication of the difficulties of shipboard writing in the circumstances described in the text.

2052 15.25   *f20   a dead calm ⟨the Ships how* thin! *Profiles/!—⟩*: i.e. ". . . sails that glance in the Sun,/Like restless gossameres"? And is the exclamation sign for the physical fact or for the several striking instances on this journey of the accuracy of the imagination, corroborated now by observation? See e.g. 2045 *f16*.

cherubic swords of Fire: with *The Ancient Mariner* and nostalgic thoughts of earlier days much in mind on the journey, can there be some distant recollection here, not only of the biblical swords of fire, but of those cherubic ones prominent in Michael Psellus's description of Paradise, referred to in 191n?

Ropes rotted, yet still the Tiller moved not: he observes "the rotting deck" of *The Ancient Mariner* line 242: *PW* i 197.

f20ᵛ   a Glory about my Head: see 258 and n. In view of the personal as well as poetic application of many of the images in Coleridge's mind's eye during this voyage, the later use of the Glory to illustrate the phenomenon of Genius, in *AR* 220, is of interest: "The Beholder [of Genius] either recognizes it as a projected Form of his own Being, that moves before him with a Glory round its head, or recoils from it as from a Spectre." In a MS note quoted by Lowes from the Harvard copy, and also in a copy presented to Daniel Stuart, now in the BM, Coleridge described the spectacle and said he had twice seen it; one of those occasions appears to be recorded in this entry.

In the poem *Constancy to an Ideal Object* (*PW* i 456) there is a revealing concatenation of images associated with the observations in this entry (and in 1996 and 2001), with *The Ancient Mariner*, and with Sara Hutchinson, especially in the last ten lines of the poem. J. Dykes Campbell thought the poem was written in Malta, though he does not cite any evidence. *PW* (JDC) 172n.

Sailor's whole Bustle: bustle is one of Coleridge's words, used with distress. See 1682, 2046, and 2337.

like the Stars . . . flames . . . in the Snow of Foam by the Vessel's side: cf 335.

f21   maximafies: not in *OED*.

f22   making the Billows ⟨& the Breeze, which⟩ it did not find: The inserted phrase gives the link with the lines "It ceased; yet still the sails made on/A pleasant noise till noon,/. . . Till noon we quietly sailed on,/Yet never a breeze did breathe". *PW* I 201. Is 2052 a comment on "the supernatural" in *The Ancient Mariner*?

first Star, like the sonorous Savanna Crane of Bartram: see also 2002. Possibly the connexion between the star and the sonorous cranes in Carolina is less the idea of the music of birds and the spheres than the recollection of Bartram's comparison of the noise of the cranes in flight with the creaking of "the joints or working of a vessel in a tempestuous sea". Coleridge's star was rising to the accompaniment of the "right wrong" east wind. Cf *PW* I 181n and *RX* 513 n 76.

2053 15.26   The question of "sublimity" seems to have been in the forefront of Coleridge's thoughts at this time; possibly it was a subject of London discussion with Beaumont and his circle before Coleridge sailed. See 2093.

2054 15.27   An illustration of what? Of the need of all creatures for a port, a home? Coleridge frequently applied bird analogies to himself; see e.g. "I am a Starling self-incaged, & always in the Moult, & my whole Note is, Tomorrow, & tomorrow, & tomorrow." 22 Jan 1802, *CL* # 432. And cf 2064 and n, 2090, 2368 and n, and 2531.

2055 15.28   *Isulia:* Coleridge coined various disguise-names, as well as the anagram *Asra*, for Sara Hutchinson. And cf 2061 and 2078; the reference to the poem *Phantom*, cited below, seems to put the matter beyond doubt.

the more distressful my Sleep . . . the more distant, & Xst's Hospitalized: another pre-Freudian observation of the painfulness of the depths below consciousness (cf 1649, 1726) and of dreams as involving the "distorted Reflection" of the previous day.

All Look: a reference to the lines "All look and likeness caught from earth . . ." entitled by EHC *Phantom: PW* I 393. On the evidence of 2441 EHC dated the fragment as earlier than 8 Feb 1805; but the reference here indicates an April 1804 *terminus ad quem.*

Jealousies the Chills *of Fever:* such jealousies as expressed in 2001? Coleridge was acutely aware of his jealousy of WW; see e.g. 2001, 2998, 3148, and notes.

2057 15.30   *f24 impossible that I could sustain the* presence *of Sara:* cf 2000.

f24ᵛ   the Recluse: Coleridge was reading in MS the Wordsworth poems (see 2092n and Appendix E) that Sara and Dorothy had prepared for his voyage.

His interest in the question of the ego and egotism showed itself early. See 62 and n, 904 and n. The letter on *The Recluse* has not survived; see 2045n.

2058 15.31   *Duumvirate:* from *duovir*, and paralleling "triumvirate", i.e., as translated by STC, twin despotism.

Of the intimate and even reciprocal relations of pain and pleasure Coleridge was frequently explicitly aware. He is also clear about the will being another term for the self, not a separate faculty. See e.g. 1717, *Inq Sp* §2, and *Phil Lects* 224–5, 364–5.

On the parent-child image see 1991n and the article by David Beres cited at 170n.

2059 15.2   Originally in pencil but later retraced in ink.

Dorothea Jordan (1762–1816), mistress from 1790 of the Duke of Clarence, later William IV, was a famous talker as well as a popular actress. In her early days she played many male-impersonation parts.

2060 15.32   Some words are retraced in ink to offset fading.

f25   Hamburgh packet . . . the Devil: Coleridge has an anecdote in the first of his "Satyrane's Letters" of a "little German tailor and his little wife", and how the latter bullied the former into sharing her bed and giving up his, which arrangement "procured me a bed which otherwise I should not have had". *BL* II 139. There is, however, no suggestion that the captain of the packet therefore regarded the tailor with suspicion as a possible Jonah.

ff25–25ᵛ What follows here seems to refer to Coleridge's Capt Findlay, who had "muster enough" to be the fastest ship in the convoy, i.e. crew enough to trim and set sails frequently, to take fullest advantage of light flawing winds. Is "The Devil has help'd . . . &c" a quotation from him?

Star, that dogged the Crescent: "One after one, by the star-dogged Moon": *The Ancient Mariner* line 212: *PW* I 196, on which see 2880n.

"*Cursed . . . waning moon*": *Zapolya*, Prelude 430: *PW* II 897. See also 2049. This play, rejected by Drury Lane in 1816, "was written at Calne, in Wiltshire, in 1815": *PW* II 883n. Apparently this line, at least, was written much earlier; possibly from an earlier frag-

ment of poem or play it was lifted in 1815 for use in *Zapolya*. It has
no very obvious connexion with the pre-1804 poems as we know them.
The Three Graves is full of curses and some sinister moons, but the
metre would not have served in that poem. For Coleridge on *superstition* at this time see also 2045 *f17ᵛ*.
  f26 Hic Labor hic Opus est: Virgil *Aeneid* VI 129, variatim: "This
is the task, this the toil!" Tr H. R. Fairclough (LCL 1940) I 514. The
last two words have now faded from the MS.

2061 15.33   *f26ᵛ Est quod non est:* "Sense of [the thing] being
what it is not".
  Polyolbiosis: possibly, "manifold blessedness". The second com-
ponent formed on ὄλβιος = "happy" is not in Liddell and Scott and
is presumably Coleridge's manufacture with a debt to Drayton's
Polyolbion ("having many blessings") in the coinage.
  On the mingling of the familiar and the unfamiliar, the associated
and the discrete disassociated in dreams, cf 2078. Coleridge clearly
believed that, in the modern sense, dreams have meaning, a view not
generally held until after *c* 1900. See also e.g. 2542 and 2638, and
many other references.
  f27 Dorothy . . . Red Cottle Book: i.e. N 21; the reference, unless
it is to an entry in which DW is not explicitly referred to, appears to
be to 1250, or possibly to 990.
  f27ᵛ Bulls: cf 1620n.

2062 15.34   There were Italian poems at the end of his Italian
grammar. See 2074n.

2063 15.35   Cf his descriptions of Wordsworth in nautical terms
in 1546; see also 2016, 2086, and, significantly, *BL* Chap 22 (II 131).

2064 15.36   *f28 one deep dose after another: dose* for *doze?*
  *Poet[ically] interesting Thought . . . Alas! how dear do these
Thoughts cost you, Coleridge?:* As the Thursday before May night was
26 April, entry 2051 may fit, but 2046 and 2049 of the Tuesday, a
week before, or 2054 of Saturday 28th, *seem* to have more to do with
poetic inspiration. Is the poetically interesting thought, however,
associated with the small birds fluttering about the mast? Attention is
frequently called in these notes to the personal application of bird-
images. In 1546 WW is compared with a ship in full sail; see the self-
contrast in 2063 and 2086.

f28ᵛ   An Afterpiece: a short dramatic "entertainment" of the sort that frequently followed the play? Throughout his life Coleridge recurrently wished to write for the theatre; this particular plan is exceptional in that the piece is to have a setting drawn from observation. But see 2045 *f15ᵛ*.

2. The present Royal Family: see 2050n on the Duke of Kent.

3. . . . Courtney & Blair: presumably John Courtenay, M.P. (1741–1816), a Whig, and Robert Blair (1741–1811), member of Pitt's government, examples from opposing parties of men influential without eminence?

4. Bonapart . . . one *Hecatomb of Gratitude to Stuart:* a reference to a long-promised article for Stuart. The beginning of the story about it is told in *CL # 523* (II 1007): the *M Post* of March 1800 had promised an article on Bonaparte to follow the one on Pitt; Coleridge's procrastination led an envoy of Bonaparte to inquire for it in such a way as to lead STC to prophesy (privately to Stuart) tyranny from Bonaparte; Stuart complimented Coleridge on his political sagacity. Possibly Coleridge thought of expanding his prophecies to include the threats to Sicily and Russia, and also intended a return of compliments to an astute and forbearing publisher. Relations with Stuart at this time seem to have been cordial on both sides, though Coleridge undoubtedly had felt some degree of resentment over Stuart's toning down of the "Letters to Mr. Fox" in the *M Post* in 1802. He had some reason to think they had been modified at Fox's instigation. *CL # 482, 506.*

5. The injunction *adesso*—attend to this—was not followed, so far as is known. Possibly this was among Coleridge's papers lost at sea; see *CL # 608* and 615.

f29   6. . . . 140 pulses, in poetry: cf also 1610 *f72*, where distance is measured by reciting lines of verse.

7. Fame . . . Rebus in the Ladies' Diary: the underlining of the *likewise* makes the same point about the pretentiousness of contemporary versifiers as is made in *Friend* II 13. See 475 and 1237 and notes. *K:* possibly Southey; *XY:* possibly Wordsworth.

f29ᵛ   8. Stars—their natural Sublimity: as opposed to sublimity by association? Cf 2093 and n.

9. . . . continued Indistinctness of Impressions: semi- or preconscious states and their relation to Imagination were of constantly recurring interest, without a precise vocabulary for them. See a continuation in 2073; and cf 1718, 2080, and 2915.

2065 K.4   The last phrase, applying the natural image to the dissociated character of Mary Lamb's life, was certainly an afterthought, inserted later, but not necessarily much later.

2066 K.5   "We were the best sailing Vessel in the whole convoy; but every day we had to lie by, & wait for the Laggards." *CL* # 600.

2067 K.6   Among the many detailed attempts to describe colour, none is more persistent in the notebooks than the struggle to describe water. Although this entry seems to bear out Lowes's statement, based on insufficient instances, that Coleridge had a particular fondness for greens and blues (*RX* 205n, and see 2070), the subject index now in preparation will show a much more inclusive interest in colours.
È *meglio . . . d'appresso:* "It is better to be friends at a distance than enemies close at hand."

2068 K.7   If the interpretation of the order of entries in N K is correct, Coleridge jotted down here (on deck?) what he noted more fully in N 15 later, possibly in his cabin: 2070 *f31.*

2069 K.8   Cf with this the two foregoing, where Coleridge also displays an interest in technical marine language.

2070 15.37   *f30   the Black Book:* a confusing reference, the only black notebooks other than this N 15 being N 4 and N 5, neither of which he seems to have had with him; at any rate, neither contains the "observations" listed here. Either a black book is lost or, mistakenly thinking he is writing e.g. in N 16, he refers to the book under his hand as if it were another.
    There is a note earlier in this notebook on the colour of bilge-water. See 2051.
    On Gibraltar moonlight, see 2031.
    swarming with insect life, all *busy:* the underlining of *all* seems to point forward to lines said to have been written in 1825: "All Nature seems at work . . ./And I the while, the sole unbusy thing,/Nor honey make, nor pair, nor build, nor sing." *Work without Hope: PW* 1 447.
    f30ᵛ   the Leopard: listed in the Royal Navy list of 1806 (there are no lists for 1800–5) as a 50-gun ship of the line; the convoy was therefore of considerable size.

f31 Futtock Shrouds: small shrouds that secure the lowest dead-
eyes and futtock plates of the topmast rigging to a band around a
lower mast; Coleridge had already noted the term in the small pocketbook, K, at 2068.

2071 15.38   *PW* II 980 variatim.

2072 15.39   Based in part on observation of fellow-passengers?
The kind of face described in the doleful ditty seems to have had a
horrid fascination for Coleridge; see 2917. And in view of 174 (6) it
may not be incorrect to see here also some elements of self-castigation
and self-admonition.

2073 15.40   Cf 2064 (9) and n, and on falling asleep, 1078 and
                 1718 and n.

2074 15.41   In ink.
Coleridge greatly admired Adelung's famous German dictionary
(see 378n), and wrote a long note about its excellences on another
dictionary—his *Vocabolario italiano-latino per uso degli studiosi di
belle lettere nelle regie scuole di Torino . . .* (Giuseppe Rosa Venice
1794). This volume, inscribed by STC in pencil and again in ink,
"Sara Hutchinson/S. T. Coleridge", is now in VCL. The pencil inscription is dated "Jan 23 1805", possibly the date of purchase, possibly only of the joint memorializing of the names.
    Later he made fun of an Italian phrase-book by Cesare Mussolini, a
copy picked up in 1813. But at this point he is learning his Italian
from *A New Method of Learning the Italian Tongue to which are added
I an Italian Vocabulary II Choice Italian Phrases III Familiar
Dialogues IV Entertaining Stories V Italian Proverbs VI Extracts from
the best Italian Poets VII Examples of Ceremonial & Mercantile Letters*
by Trigny (pseud Claude Lancelot) translated "by an Italian Master" (1750). His examples are taken from this grammar-dictionary.
    The final sentence carries one of the earliest hints of what was to
materialize five years later as *The Friend.* See *Friend* App F.

2075 15.42   *T for* [*?G/S*]: Tour for George? The abbreviation is
puzzling. Coleridge intended writing up his tours, the Scottish tour
and the Mediterranean one, for the Beaumonts, probably encouraged

by them, with that delicacy of which he often speaks, as a way of repaying their "loans" of money. Sir George had pressed £100 on Coleridge on his departure for Malta; the Mediterranean "Travels" appear to have been sent to him. *CL* # 612. But Coleridge does not refer to Beaumont in letters or elsewhere except by his title; if the *G* here stands for George it must be accounted for by privacy and brevity. If the reading is *S*, the reference may be to Sally Wedgwood, though he had not been in her company for some time; see 1577 and n. Possibly the likeliest guess is *S* for Sara Hutchinson.

Paradise Lost as a Task: see 2026 *f8*n.

his own "believing Mind": quoting his own *Frost at Midnight* line 24: *PW* I 241. Coleridge, in a sharply ironical marginal note on Scott's *The Pirate*, says that Scott had the opposite of the "believing mind" of, say, Spenser. It is only one of many statements critical of Scott or, at least, indicating his temperamental limitations. It is of interest that in this instance, in attacking Scott by means of the phrase "believing mind", Coleridge should attribute it to Collins (incorrectly, as T. M. Raysor points out) instead of remembering it as his own, applied to himself in *Frost at Midnight*. *MC* 332. For another instance of STC *vis-à-vis* Scott, see *TT* 4 Aug 1833.

Wordsworth's Pedlar: The Ruined Cottage of Racedown and Alfoxden days became "The Pedlar" in Grasmere parlance before it was incorporated in *The Excursion*. Precisely how much of it Coleridge had seen, or how he meant to apply a defence of prolixity to it, is not known, but it is clear from *DWJ* Jan–March 1802 that Wordsworth was working hard on the poem at that time and was discouraged about it. Probably Coleridge intended an encouraging defence of the Wanderer's detailed communications about simple things. There is a note to Bk III of *The Excursion* line 931, taken from William Gilbert's notes to *The Hurricane*, that might be a substitute, perhaps suggested by Coleridge himself, for the intended dissertation referred to here.

2076 15.43   As early as 27 Dec 1799 Coleridge had expressed in the *M Post* similar views, in an article on the French Constitution: *EOT* II 342–8.

the King una cum populo: the King on the side of the people.

2077 15.44   Possibly the reference here dates Coleridge's marginalia on his copy of Jeremy Collier's translation of the *Meditations* of Marcus Aurelius as belonging to the *Speedwell* journey. See 1655n.

The marginalia, profuse and interesting, begin with the general comment, "This Translation is ridiculed by Pope in his Martinus Scriblerus.—It must be confessed, that the Style is often even ludicrous, from its 'colloquial barbarisms'; as Johnson phrases it. Yet there is a Life, a Spirit, a Zest, which makes it more pleasing, say rather, less disgusting to me, than is the pompous enigmatic Jargon of modern Prose, since the publication of the Rambler. I speak however only of the Translation of M. Antonine: for that of 'the Picture of Cebes' is an absolute Dictionary of 'SLANG'. . . .".

Bk 7 §54 reads: "As long as a Man can make use of his Reason and Act in concert with the God's, he need not question the Event. There can be no grounds to suspect Misfortune, provided you stick close to Nature, and manage within the Character of your condition" (ed 1701) 123.

(Coleridge has marked the phrase "stick close" with a ϕ, his sign in these marginalia for "a phrase vulgar or ludicrous from its transiency or dependence on an accidental Fashion—such as, *quizzing*, the Tan, &c, &c.")

There is no "§67 of B.6", apparently a slip for §67 of Bk 7, the whole of which in Coleridge's copy is marked with a line down the margin. In spite of its length, the association established here by Coleridge with his own earlier criticism of Southey (see 1815n) makes it seem advisable to quote it: "Which way are we to conclude that *Socrates* was a better Man in Virtue and Temper than *Telauges*. To make out this, 'tis not enough to say, that he disputed better, and died Bolder. The Austerity and Discipline of his Life; his Bravery in slighting the Orders of the *Thirty Tyrants*, and refusing to apprehend an Innocent Person; the Gravity and Greatness in his Mien and Motion: (Tho the truth of this last particular may be question'd:) All this Glitter won't make the Character shine out. To prove the point, we must examine what sort of Soul *Socrates* carried about him: Could he be contented with the Conscience of an Honest and Pious Man? Did he not Fret and Fume to no purpose at the Knavery, and Wickedness of the Age? Was he govern'd by no Bodies Ignorance? Did he never question the Equity of Providence, grow surpriz'd at his hard Fortune, and sink under the Weight of it? To conclude, did he keep Pain and Pleasure at a due distance, and not dip his Soul too deep in his Senses? These Marks are the only Test of a Great Man; and 'tis to no purpose to pretend to that Character without them" (ed 1701) 127–8.

2078 15.45   *An ever-living Death:* not a remarkable phrase in itself, but gathering some accretions as written by the author of *The Ancient Mariner,* and another indication of identification with the central figure in the poem? See 2086 *f38*ᵛn.

The Latin phrases freely translated by Coleridge are, more literally: *passio purissima,* "purest passivity", *actus purissimus,* "purest action". Cf 1072.

On the figures seen in his dreams, cf 2055 and 2061.

2030 15.47   See also 2191.
polyandria Polygnia: many stamens, many pistils. The plant of his half-waking fantasies is androgynous.

2081 15.48   *The Maidstone,* 32 guns, is listed as in the Mediterranean in 1800, and as repairing at Chatham in 1805. Probably she was in the convoy, and Coleridge in his misery was inquiring the name of an available surgeon. See 2085.

2082 15.49   Below this entry, which is very faint, but distinct from 2080, the page was torn off.

2083 15.50   *Mr. Hastings:* the third passenger.
Over or under this entry in a large hand that may or may not be Coleridge's are some words not now decipherable: [R Extra Colocynth] and below: [?Pisa ne nata]. A medical prescription?

2084 K.3   This small pocketbook was probably the notebook used on deck, N 15 with its fuller notes in the cabin. One detects a certain empathy and immediacy here. Note the more personal application of the image of the dying fish in 2606, 27 June 1805.

2085 15.51   *Speak him* is naval terminology; no word has been omitted.
The *Warning* has no doubt to do with the constipating effects of opium.

2086 15.52   *f38*ᵛ *the Cocks answered each other:* A revision in *The Ancient Mariner* owes something to the experience on this voyage of the sharpness of sounds carried over calm waters. The original of the important stanza "The Sun's rim dips; the stars rush out:/At one stride comes the dark;/With far-heard whisper o'er the sea,/Off shot the spectre bark" read in the third line: "With never a whisper on the main"; the becalmed traveller in convoy on the Mediterranean learned better. Worth noticing, in view of 2078, is the fact that the gloss "Death and Life-in-Death have diced for the ship's crew and she (the latter) winneth the Ancient Mariner" immediately precedes this stanza and "The steersman's face by his lamp gleamed white" (see 2001 and n) is in the stanza that follows it. See also 2880 and n.

f39ᵛ   my Voyage in rough weather from Hamburgh: or/and *to* Hamburg? Cf 335 *f1*.

f40   Royals & Studding Sails & the whole Canvas stretched: an entry of the previous October, 1546, using this image, makes the self-comparison with Wordsworth since the Hamburg journey painfully evident, as do 2016 and 2063.

   the combining Power: an early use of this phrase as a description of the imagination; cf *BL* I 202, II 8, and especially II 12, 15, 16; see also 998n. The phrase appears to be a refinement on the "modifying power" and the "aggregating power" used in a letter a few weeks earlier: see *CL* # 536.

   "may quit the tiresome Sea . . . native Tree": Wordsworth *Prelude* (1805) I 35–8; Wordsworth wrote "wild water", in one MS "pure water", not "wine", as Coleridge has it. Cf the later application of the idea here, to himself, in *A Tombless Epitaph* lines 27–8: *PW* I 413.

   ff40–40ᵛ   Poetry a rationalized dream . . . Selves: again Coleridge's awareness of the unconscious—and of the likeness of artistic creation to dream-work—is another anticipation of later systematic psychology.

2087 15.53   *f40ᵛ   o! dear Friends did you see the crescent with its phantom moon, & the evening Star . . . Tip!:* in other words, did the Wordsworths also think of the old moon in the new moon's lap of *Dejection* lines 9–14, and of the star-dogged moon of *The Ancient Mariner* lines 209–12? *PW* I 363, 196. See also 2009, 2139 and n, and 2880 and n.

f41ᵛ   the whole of
   Sunday, May 13ᵗʰ: The MS suggests Coleridge's attempt at a daily diary, though clearly the account of the two days was written at a sitting; the beginning of a new line here for the new date, though in mid-sentence, well illustrates the uncertainty about the exact ter-

minus of many entries, e.g. 2086 and 2095, each of which may be two entries rather than one.

f42   six knots an hour: in spite of his interest in nautical terminology, Coleridge makes a landsman's common mistake.

2088 15.54   *Cockermouth:* Wordsworth's birthplace. See 535n and 1519n.

2089 15.55   So far as is known, an unrealized poem.

2090 15.56   The exegesis of *The Ancient Mariner* in the last sentence has both critical and autobiographical interest. The gyres of the hawk were to become another personal bird-symbol; see 2531 and 2054 and the end of 2091.

2091 15.57   *Ode to Pleasure . . . as the conditio sine qua non of virtuous activity:* On Coleridge's conception of pleasure as the indispensable condition of virtue, some light is thrown by 1710 and 1717; and perhaps also by recalling Wordsworth's *Ode to Duty.* See 2531n.
For one episode of the pain referred to, see 2085.
Sleep a pandemonium: described in *The Pains of Sleep: PW* I 389–91.
Let me live in Truth: the underlining of *Truth* seems to suggest the recoil from the deceptions involved in opium-taking.
I am very, very weak: cf *CL* # 208, 210. And see above, 2090 and n.

2092 15.58   The MS prepared for Coleridge by Dorothy Wordsworth and Sara Hutchinson of Wordsworth's "Poem on the Formation of his mind", known in the circle as the "Poem to Coleridge", later entitled by Mary Wordsworth *The Prelude,* was probably a part of MS M, now in Dove Cottage; that contained of *The Prelude* Bks I–IV in some form, *The Ruined Cottage* or Bk I of *The Excursion,* and more than seventy shorter poems. See Appendix E.

2093 15.59   *f45 in some one of my pocket books, an Idea from Darwin:* The reference is to a paragraph in the chapter "Of Instinct" in Darwin *Zoonomia* §XVI 10, where Darwin argues that emotions connected with sound, e.g. the feelings of terror or sublimity, are aroused by previous associations. "So if the rumbling of a carriage in the street be for a moment mistaken for thunder, we receive a sublime sensation, which ceases as soon as we know it is the noise of a coach and six." (ed 1794) I 156. Apparently Darwin's chapter "Of Instinct" is much in Coleridge's mind at this period, e.g. in 2325 and 2331.

Coleridge wrote *to prove the dependence*, added *entire*, and marked the necessary transposition.

On the subject of sublimity see also 2045 *f13*, 2053, 2057, 2064 (8).

f45ᵛ   Let that noise be produced by the Chariot Wheels of Salmoneus: "let the Thunder be produced not by a cart, but by the brazen car of the arrogant Salmoneus, son of Aeolus, who presumptuously tried to imitate Zeus by making mock thunder and lightning". *Aeneid* VI 585. Of the various references to Salmoneus, Virgil's seems to be foremost in Coleridge's thoughts.

The last sentence of the entry may have associations with 912.

2096 15.62   *as noted in the dark on the Cover of this Book:* Possibly he refers to the illegible words on the front inside cover, mentioned in 2761n; or possibly the words *No anxious Impatience* of 2505, the back inside cover, are meant.

the nature of my Afternoon Sleeps: cf 2087, where he notes that aperients are essential to him on shipboard, until evening.

2098 K.9   This entry in N K follows 2069, and after it the remainder of the page is blank, suggesting that it may perhaps have been written from the ship (in quarantine?) and may be Coleridge's first and characteristically damaging observation on noise in Malta. Cf 2114, 2614, and notes.

2099 15.64   *Mr. Morrison:* John Morrison, known because, with other businessmen in Malta, he signed a letter to Ball in Aug 1805. CO 158.10

Stoddart, (later Sir) John, H.M. Advocate at the Admiralty Court, Malta, at £1500 a year since *c* 1803. It was he who first suggested Malta to Coleridge by inviting him there (*CL* # 513), though it was Greenough's enthusiasm for Sicily and possibly Sharp's encouragement that seem to have crystallized the plan. *CL* # 548.

the sister: Sarah Stoddart, later Mrs Hazlitt, to whom Mary Lamb had written, commending Coleridge to her kindness.

O ipsissima!: "O her very own self!" He notes the irony of escaping the coldness of one Sarah only to encounter it in another?

2100 10.3   In ink, written at right angles to the early notes underneath (in 652). The entry appears to be a very deliberate attempt to concentrate on first impressions of Malta.

Mrs Gillman drew a heavy line under *April* on *f2*, as shown by her note on *f1ᵛ* opposite: "I think it was *May* 18—1804 ther[e] vide large Black clasp Book N° 15 page 92 A. Gillman." The correction points to her as the first to attempt editorial work on the notebooks.

This entry and the two that follow it should perhaps be read as one; they may all have been written at one time, close to the time of arrival, when he still had the feeling, well known to travellers even now, and how much more likely in days of slow travel, of having completely lost the weeks spent at sea. Hence his *April* for *May*.

This notebook was used because N 15 was being reserved for further travel in Sicily (see 2099) and N 16 and N 21 were probably still not unpacked; N 9 was filled. For some reason, N 10, though really filled, was carried to Malta, perhaps picked up at Lamb's in London and hastily put in a pocket, and therefore available (since the scrawling faint notes of parliamentary speeches were of no account, the pages could be used crosswise) in the unsettled busy days of arrival.

light as a blessed Ghost: "I was so light almost/I thought that I had died in sleep/And was a blessed ghost." *The Ancient Mariner* lines 307–8: *PW* 1 199.

Explosive Cries: cf 2098.

the Faldetto: a black silk gown with a large circular hood held out from the face by a hoop, still worn in Malta; originally said to have been a garment conducive to the privacy of the confessional and religious meditation, the *faldetta* has a certain caste significance.

Much of this was elaborated in Coleridge's first letter to his wife in June. *CL # 600.*

2101 10.4   *f4   Sir A[lexander] Ball:* the Civil Commissioner of Malta who in 1798 commanded the British force which, with the help of the Maltese, had wrested Malta from the French. Coleridge's letter of introduction to him and to General Villettes was from William Sotheby. *CL # 601.*

The entry makes it clear that from the first Coleridge expected to find work to do in Malta. He apparently made a favourable impression on Ball, who by July had appointed him his private secretary and, in Jan 1805, made him Acting Public Secretary, which post he held for nine months. In this latter capacity he held rank on the island second only to Ball in civil administration. See Appendix B.

Coleridge's letters about Ball are enthusiastic: his eulogy of him in the final essays in *Friend* (1818) III 278–375 provides much incidental information about their relationship and Coleridge's life in Malta.

General Valette: William Anne Villettes, since 1801 the military commander in Malta.

a striking room: the throne room of the Palace of the Governor, formerly the Palace of the Grand Master of the Order of St John. *f4ᵛ one by Correggio:* Probably an error; none of the authorities lists a Correggio in Valletta, though records are scant for this date. Coleridge may have seen one of the numerous paintings misattributed to Correggio, or, as seems more likely in this his first reference there to a specific picture, he misheard *Correggio* for Caravaggio, whose famous *Beheading of St John* was painted in Malta in 1608 and is perhaps Malta's most important, certainly most noticed, painting. It hung in 1801, somewhat damaged by smoke, where it hangs now, in the Cathedral oratory; possibly in 1804 it had been transferred to the Palace for safe-keeping.

Alternatively—and, since it hung always in the Palace, probably a better guess—he could be referring to one of the two portraits of the Grand Master of the Order of St John, Alof de Wignacourt, also by Caravaggio and held by many to be his masterpiece. Louis de Boisgelin *Ancient and Modern Malta* (1804) I 89. This painting is no longer in Malta.

one of Cain killing Abel: formerly said to be by Jusepe or José de Ribera, called lo Spagnoletto (*c* 1590–1652), but actually by his pupil, Bartolommeo Passante (1614–56).

f5 Mʳ Lane: the Rev Francis Laing (1773–1861), whose name Coleridge learned to spell correctly later, was Ball's private secretary and tutor to his son.

Sᵗ Antonio: about three miles from Valletta, the Governor's country seat, the Palace of St Anton.

f6 Sᵗ Johns: St John's Co-Cathedral, 1578, the principal monument of the great Maltese architect Gerolamo Cassar, historically the most interesting and artistically the most impressive sight in Malta, is best described by the Chevalier Hannibal Scicluna, in his *The Church of St. John in Valletta, Its History, Architecture, and Monuments, With a brief History of the Order of St. John from its Inception to the present*

Day (privately printed by Casa M. Danesi in Rome for the author, San Martin, Malta, G.C. 1955). If Coleridge made fuller notes, they have disappeared; if he was reduced to a single word, *magnificence* was and is the one apt one.

2102 10.5   *General Valette . . . his Country House:* part of the Barracca Gardens.

The Botanic Garden: a part of Ball's effort to provide work and hot-weather walks for the Maltese, a popular measure that eased tension when the walks in the garrison were denied the inhabitants by military order. CO 158.8.

2103 10.6   At right angles to 652, as are 2104–2106.

The word *Idolatry* comes into more frequent use with Coleridge from Malta onwards. See e.g. *Phil Lects* 90 and fn, 267–8 and n 7; it was connected with his developing anti-clericalism (see ibid 100–1), which gained impetus in Malta at this time. See also e.g. 2738.

His interest in Moravianism went back probably at least to Bristol days; the link here is not clear.

2104 10.7   The un-English experience of cooking on an outdoor fire delighted Coleridge again on the slopes of Etna; see 2174.

The thin disguise of Greek letters for Stoddart's name suggests that he was thought of as a disagreeable warning in this instance, not an example. Coleridge soon found Stoddart unpleasant. See also 2123.

2105 10.8   The physical plight described had its counterpart in the depressed uncertainty of the first month or more in Malta.

2106 10.9   A note written by the stranger in this case?

2107 10.15   Possibly Mr England's "flowers of Oratory" referred to in 2451 as having been "noted down" somewhere. A civil servant in Malta? Perhaps the "low mind" of 2106?

2108 16.244   *Malta* is written large and carefully, as if to mark an occasion. The repetition of the facts of arrival, already noted, may be accounted for if N 16 was to be a travel notebook for his tours. See *CN* 1 N 16 Gen Note.

The next page, on which this entry was completed, is cut out.

His reception by the Stoddarts is described in a letter to Mrs Coleridge, *CL* # 600.

The mistake of April for May in 2102 is repeated.

my Breast plate: the chest-protector referred to in 2101 *f6*?

2109 16.245   In his letter to Mrs Coleridge referring to this incident the month is correctly given as May.

This entry, and those on both sides of the leaf *ff75–75ᵛ*, i.e. 2109–2113, appear to have been written 5 June 1804, after which the notebook was not used again until May 1805.

2110 16.246   *AP* 164 variatim; EHC adds another entry appearing further on in this notebook and probably of later date, which will appear in a subsequent volume.

the totus in omni parte of Truth: "the whole in every part of Truth".

2111 16.247   *AP* 148. Coleridge is fond of the simile of the tired traveller and applies it, very much as here, to British policies with regard to Malta, in *Friend* III 355.

2112 16.248   The first couplet, "The Breeze I see . . .", is from Wordsworth's *The Mad Mother* (*LB*): *Her eyes are wild: WPW* II 108; the second is from Butler's *Hudibras* II ii 31–2. The first is used in *BL* II 123 as an example of Wordsworth's capacity for "meditative pathos", and, for its "fine transition . . . so expressive of the deranged state, in which from the increased sensibility the sufferer's attention is abruptly drawn off by every trifle, and in the same instant plucked back again by the one despotic thought, bringing home with it, by the blending, *fusing* power of Imagination and Passion, the alien object to which it had been so abruptly diverted, no longer an alien but an ally and inmate".

The couplet from *Hudibras* is a favourite example with Coleridge of mere "fancy". See *TT* 23 June 1823 and cf also *TT* 3 July 1833. This entry provides one of the early forms of his distinction between Imagination and Fancy. (See 2211 and n.) The implication that the poet who is also metaphysician is a man "of continuous mind" further underlines the intention to reconcile philosophy and poetry in 383 and n.

Was the entry suggested by the irritating proximity of the "discontinuous" mind of Stoddart? Cf 2472 and 2890 and n.

2113 16.249   Cf 2324. The temporal acquisitions of the Church in
Malta are everywhere evident, and the question of whether the island
should be returned to the Order of the Knights of St John was not by
any means firmly settled at this time; Ball and others still felt it
necessary to persuade a vacillating government at home of the strategic importance of Malta to Britain. See also 2124.

2114 K.24   Pencil; much of the first part of the entry was obscured by the ink of 2133.
    When he arrived in Sicily, did he first realize or conclude that the
noises he found so trying in Malta were, contrary to Godwin's
London speculations, like Italian city noises? Cf 2498, 2284. Coleridge's best disquisition on noises in Malta is in 2614.

2115 K.25   The entry is very faint, and 2133 is written over it.

2116 K.28   The Italian verse from which this metre and these
rhyme-endings were taken has not been discovered.

2117 21.329   *AP* 63.
    Entries 2117–2120 and 2262–2265, on *ff57–58*, left blank when *f67*
onwards to *f99* were being used, are difficult to date precisely. It
appears that the first four, alike in the appearance of the writing,
belong, as 2119 certainly does, (*a*) to Malta and (*b*) to a time previous
to 10 Nov 1804 (the date of 2266), i.e. previous to the departure for
Sicily, probably *c* July–August, when Coleridge frequently walked
between the Stoddarts' country place at St Julian and the palace at
St Anton. See 2119n. The other entries from *The Spanish Rogue*, 2125–
2128, close to July, suggest a July date for all of them.
    The reference is to J. Mabbe's translation of *The Rogve: or The Life
of Gvzman de Alfarache. Written in Spanish by Matheo Aleman, Seruant
to his Catholike Maiestie, and borne in Sevill Printed for Edward
Blount* (London 1623) 71, to an interesting and touching passage at
the end of Chap VIII, in the story of two frustrated lovers, Ozmin and
Daraxa, where the fantasy-thoughts and physical symptoms of love
are described. Ozmin sees her "comming all alone, softly pacing her
steps thorow a spacous Walke, beset all with Myrtles, muske-Roses,
Iesmines, and other Flowers, gathering here & there one, where-with
she adorned her haire. Now by her attire, he would neuer haue known
her, if the true Originall had not well agreed with that liuely couter-

feit, which he had imprinted in his heart: . . . [Daraxa, also agitated by seeing him—both are in disguise garb—falls down in a faint, and] when shee came to herselfe . . . leaning her hand on her rosie cheeke, she called many things to remembrance; wherein, if she should haue insisted vpon euery particular, and perseuered in the recordation of them, she might easily haue beene the authour of her owne death. But she did put them off as well as she could, with another new desire which she had, to intertaine her soule with his sight. . . . She rose, but accompanied with a generall trembling, (her whole body and heart, panting & shiuering with an aguish fit of Loue). . . . It seemed vnto her that she had beene in a dreame, but even shee perceiued that she was awake . . . she was afrayd it was some ghost or Fairy-apparition. But afterwards, when vpon better view she saw it was a man, a very man, and no *Phantasma*, she wished that it might be he, whom she loued. . . . Not being able to abstaine to discouer her particular affection vnto him . . . but his tongue being knit close to the roofe of his mouth with the fullest knot of Loue, hauing not the power to speake a word; and not being able, no not for his life, (so great was his passion,) to answer her with his tongue, he replyed with his eyes, watering the earth with that abundance of teares, which fell guttering downe his cheekes, as if they had flowed from two cleare fountaines. And with this, these two deere and faithful Louers came to haue true knowledge of each other."

It should also be noted that in the first line on this page Daraxa is described as "the ioyfull hauen to his long-indured ship-wracks", surely a reverberating image for Coleridge. See also 2125–2128 for other notes on *The Spanish Rogue*.

In a letter to Southey in 1808, Coleridge praised this work highly. *CL* # 675 (III 57). His copy is listed in Wordsworth LC.

2118 21.330   The reference is of course to Sara Hutchinson, repeating the mood of 2000.

2119 21.331   *Omniana* II 28–9, variatim, refers this episode to Malta and specifically to the road between St Julian and St Anton; July–Aug 1804 is the likely time for it, to judge by *CL* # 605.

2120 21.332   *L[yrical] B[allads] I——X:* The implication is hardly clear. Did someone (Stoddart?) wish to cut up and improve the first ten poems in the *Lyrical Ballads*, and yet Coleridge could remember

how the same person had in "rasend Mut" (i.e. in an angry spirit)
razed Bentley's amended *Milton* to the ground? Or is there an echo
here of Pope's attack on "slashing Bentley with his desp'rate hook"
(*Imitation of the First Epistle of the Second Book of Horace* lines 103-4),
or of "From slashing Bentley down to piddling Tibbalds" from the
Epistle to Dr. Arbuthnot (line 164)? The possibility that Stoddart is
meant is strengthened by 2472 and 2890, and by Lamb's remark years
later that Stoddart, given the MS of *Paradise Lost* itself, would have
"pulled it piecemeal". *CL* # 1105.

There may well be a link also with the mixed review in the *British
Critic* for Feb 1801 of *LB* (1800). Mrs Moorman (*W Life* 1 505)
pointed out that this review (reprinted in Elsie Smith *Estimate of WW*
46-51) was not by Wrangham, as we have believed, but by Stoddart.
The evidence is in some letters of JW in Dove Cottage. JW was
friendly with Stoddart but considered him "a very poor judge of
Poetry" ([27-30] Jan 1801 to WW); 16 Feb 1801 he wrote MW that
Stoddart "is writing in William's praise in the British Critic", and
again, 25 Feb 1801 to MW, "I saw the Review of them . . . and it
did not please me. I thought it too indiscriminately flattering. . . ."
In April he wrote again to MW of Stoddart, on *Michael*, "who at the
same time knew no more of it except to praise it than a goose—I
rather think he praised it because he heard Coleridge think highly
of it".

Though Mrs Moorman regards the review as favourable, I suggest
it was so only superficially, that in fact it takes away with one hand
what it gives with the other, and that JW was rightly worried by it.
It may well have irritated Coleridge, for it is a queer mixture of
flattery and condescension with cautious, pompous doubt-raising, the
last not offset by the trite and equally pompous praise. Perhaps by
1804 the reviewer's flattery was showing chiefly its dark under side.
See especially 2472 and 2890.

2121 21.434   *AP* 74-5; the translation of the Greek word there is
given as "Stoddart, for instance"; more accurately, *stod + cardia*
(heart) = Stoddart. *Philalethie* is clearly written, not *Philaletheia*.

Coleridge had known Stoddart since at least Oct 1800, when he
gave him a copy of *Christabel* in MS. As well as general literary interests, they had in common an interest in Schiller; Stoddart had translated *Fiesco* (1796) and *Don Carlos* (1798) before Coleridge translated
Wallenstein (1800). At one time they shared a sceptical and republi-

can bias; Lamb in 1796 had described Stoddart to Coleridge as "a cold-hearted well-bred conceited disciple of Godwin". *L Letters* 120. Now, as Judge Advocate of the Admiralty Court, Stoddart doubtless held different views. Coleridge is critical of his attempts to excuse or to blame himself for his youthful attitudes or his change of heart; see for a particularly acute statement *Friend* I 58.

2122 21.435   *AP* 75.
Possibly from an argument with Stoddart? Coleridge distrusted many of the usual criteria for legal evidence. See 1109, 1110, and notes, and 2043.

2123 21.436   *horror carnis humanæ:* a dread of human flesh.
a me alienum: a play on Terence *Heautontimorumenos* (*The Self-tormentor*) ᴿ I 25, "homo sum: humani nil a me alienum puto": "I am a man; I hold that what affects another man affects me." Tr John Sargeaunt (LCL 1939). Literally, "I consider that nothing to do with man is alien to me." Cf 2104.

2124 21.437   *AP* 75–6. The trend of thought is probably close to 2113.

2125 21.438   The first nine or ten words are partly scratched out. The entry is a recollection, not an exact quotation, from Blount's *Spanish Rogue*, from the page quoted in 2117n.
This entry and the three that follow, all on *f100ᵛ*, could be earlier than 2117, though that is on *f57ᵛ* (earlier left blank); from the attempts at remembering here, it is quite possible that Coleridge was driven to look up the work and the page to which the reference is given in 2117. On the other hand, that reads like a first note; these are phrases and passages recollected, with no book near for consultation.

2126 21.439   Ibid, Coleridge having substituted *My* for "her" and *ague* for "aguish".

2127 21.440   Ibid 72. Coleridge modifies the text, apparently with some idea of versifying, introducing *innocent* and misremembering *virtuous* for "honest".

2128 21.441   Again a recollection of *The Spanish Rogue*, though much condensed. It is a vivid passage on p 83 describing the effect

on the spectators of Ozmin's prowess in a bull-fight: "Nor was anything else in the mouths of the multitude . . . ; and though they had
all seene how it was, yet everyone spoke thereof a-fresh, and it
seemed to them as a dreame; some in wonder clapping their hands;
others highly extolling his valour; one speakes with his fingers; another stands amazed; a third blesses himself; a fourth lifts up his
arme; a fifth acts it with his hand, all of them having their mouthes
and their eyes full of joy; a sixth bowes downe his body, and suddenly
leapes up againe in the ayre; some bend the browe, & some being
ready to burst with content, make gracefull Matachines, with many
other pretty Antike-gestures". Ed cit 2117n.

2129 21.442   *AP* 76. For Coleridge on candle flame see *RX* index,
and entries 174 (8) and (9), 1024, 1770, 1771, and 2994.

He adverted frequently to the poetic quality of Taylor's prose;
the most interesting of many discussions is that reported by R. E. A.
Willmott in *Conversations at Cambridge* (1836) 239–46, reproduced in
C 17th C 259–63.

2130 21.443   On this subject, cf a MS fragment published in
Inq Sp §46.

Tr: Love is often, I am almost inclined to say always, the work of a moment
[the literal meaning of *Augenblick*, i.e. twinkling of an eye, and the resulting
play on *Blick* must have interested Coleridge]. A glance exchanged, the
clasp of a hand, a word, is often the first, the only *true* bond which binds two
harmonizing souls for ever.

The source has not been traced.

2131 21.444   Tr: Not to die? And you were to be my comforter! Leave
me. Away with you.

The source has not been traced.

2132 21.445   A translation or adaptation from some German
writer? Connected with 2130, 2131? The hand is similar in appearance
also to 2137.

2133 k.26   Ink.
This entry and the next must have been written between the first
and second parts of 2146, 9 May–16 July; the latter is compressed
on the page, from the fact that by 16 July the rest of the page had

been written on. That these entries can be so dated, and before 13
July of 2144, and even more closely, *c* 6 July 1804, is confirmed by
CL # 604 and our knowledge of the source of Coleridge's material
here. In the letter (6 July) he says he is reading French and Italian
and will soon have mastered them; and see below in this note, *f9*.
Here he was drawing his instruction from a tetraglot edition (he
found it among Southey's books at Keswick) of Pascal *Les Provinciales ou lettres escrittes par Louis de Montalte . . . traduites en Latin
. . . en Espagnol . . . et en Italien* (Cologne 1684), now in VCL.
    From a letter of 22 Sept 1803 to the Beaumonts we know that he
first read the preface and the first two Letters on 21 Sept 1803, at
which time he seems to have written the annotations on the volume.
It is clear that he later borrowed the book from Southey for the purpose of learning Italian, and took it to London and Malta with him.
A piece of evidence in this direction is the address "G. Fricker, 120,
Goswell St" on the back fly-leaf, probably the address of Mrs Coleridge's young brother, a family problem in 1803–4. Coleridge made
assiduous efforts in London Jan–April 1804 to find him work, as will
be seen by many references to him in letters. The address was perhaps
noted in Keswick for use on this London visit; it does not belong to
the days of Coleridge's return from Malta, for George's address was
then a different one, as we know from *CL* # 633.
    At the end of Letter I (p 21) he wrote in the margin: "Admirable
Letter"; at the end of Letter II: "At least equal to the first/What
life is given even to a Theological Controversy by the Introduction
of Character & Drama!" To the Beaumonts he had written in the
excitement of first reading them: "They are not only excellent; but
the excellence is altogether of a new kind to me. Wit, Irony, Humour,
Sarcasm, Scholastic Subtilty, & profound Metaphysics all combined—
& this strange combination still more strangely co-existing with
child-like Simplicity, Innocence, unaffected Charity, & the very soul
of Christian Humility.—And the Style is a robe of pure Light."
CL # 521. See also *C&S* 147n.
    As will be seen, he plunged into Letters IV and III in this entry,
and in the next went back to Letters I, II, and III.
    On Coleridge's transcription of the Italian text used in this entry,
see Appendix A.
    Questo silenzio . . . avantaggio: "This very silence is a mystery for
the simple, and the Censorship will derive a singular advantage from
it." Letter III.

Se non . . . for it. Letter III.

La verità . . . verità: "The truth of which is of such delicacy that no matter how little a man may step aside from it, he falls into error: but the error of M. A[rnauld] is of such subtlety that without departing from it one finds oneself in the truth." Letter III.

Mi voltai . . . li suoi libri: "I turned towards my Jansenist, and perceived clearly from his gestures that he believed nothing of it. But as he made no answer at all, I said: I could wish that what you say were true, and that you had some good proofs of it. Do you desire some at this point? He replied to me [this is really a mistranslation from the French into the Italian; it should be: *he replied immediately*]: I am going to find some for you, and those too of the best. Leave it all to me. Saying this he went off to look for his books." Letter IV.

fate conto . . . il mio: "consider that never did the Holy Fathers, the Popes, the Councils, nor Scripture nor any book of piety, even in recent days, speak in this sort; but as for the Casuists and the Scholastics he will bring you them in vast abundance. [It is a] pity! said to me in an under voice my [Jansenist]." Letter IV.

2134 K.27   See note to 2133.

f5ᵛ 1. *cosi . . . que:* "so—as". Letter I.

2. *dove si son resolute . . . fuor d'essempio:* "where there have taken place things so extraordinary and so unparalleled". Letter I.

3. *Ne fanno concepire . . . considerabile:* "They cause to be conceived of it an Idea so great that one cannot but believe that they must had had some more than considerable subject." Letter I.

4. *dove vada . . . fracasso:* "what so great an uproar may end in". Letter I.

5. *Il che vi dirò:* "Which I will tell you". Letter I.

6. *dopo di . . . informato:* "after having perfectly informed myself of it". Letter I.

f6 7. *se il signor . . . lettera:* "whether M. A[rnauld] is rash in having said in his second letter". Letter I.

8. & 9. *Settant'uno . . . defence.* Letter I.

10. *non aver' . . . vi sono:* "he could not [*more lit.*, not having been able to] answer other than that—and that nevertheless he condemns them there if they are there". Letter I.

11. *che e quanto è:* "which is what has passed". Letter I.

12. *da quella banda:* "in that quarter". Letter I.

ff6-6ᵛ 13. *senza di . . . propos:* "without having been willing to examine whether what he had said was true or false, having even declared that the question here was not [one] concerning the truth but only the temerity of his proposition". Letter 1.

14. *Poich'* . . . *interessata:* "Then, my conscience is not concerned whether M. A[rnauld] is rash or not [*there is a misprint in the original Italian, which should read* Poi, che]." Letter 1.

15. *E se* . . . *alla S.:* "And if I were curious to learn whether these propositions are in J[ansen], his book is neither so large nor so rare that [I could not read it] without having recourse to the S[orbonne]." Letter 1.

17. *Di manièra* . . . *cagioni:* "So that I fear that this will cause". Letter 1.

18. & 19. Letter 1.

f7 20. *e come* . . . *che lui:* "and as my curiosity made me almost as eager as he". Letter 1.

21–23. Letter 1.

24. *Come* . . . *egli:* "How, said I to him, is not this your opinion? No, he answered me." Letter 1.

25. Letter 1.

26. *io davo* . . . *loro:* "I gave my word to have it guaranteed to him with their blood." Letter 1.

f7ᵛ 27. *bisogn'esser* . . . *finezza:* "one must be a Theologian to be able to fathom its subtlety". Letter 1.

28. *al quale* . . . *il poter:* "to whom I said immediately after the first compliments—Tell me, I pray you, whether you admit the power [or ability]". Letter 1.

29. Letter 1.

30. *Io l'intendo* . . . *de M.?:* "I understand it in the sense of the Molinists. To which my man replied, To which of the M[olinists]?" Letter 1.

31. *Essendo* . . . *rovinar S.:* "Being all united in the intention of ruining M. [Arnauld]". Letter 1.

f8 Della Crusca Dictionary: first of all the great modern language dictionaries, the *Vocabolario degli accademici della Crusca*, begun in 1591 and published in 1612, was the model for the dictionaries of the Académie Française and the Real Academia Española.

32. *che gli uni* . . . *diversamente:* "which both parties would say in accordance, though they understood it differently". Letter 1.

33. *Ne sarete* . . . *medesimi:* "You will be more certain of it if you hear it from themselves." Letter 1.

34. *Io non . . . l'altro:* "I know neither the one nor the other."
Letter I.

35. *se ne . . . nominò:* "whether you will know some among those
whom I will now name to you. I knew some too among those whom
he named to me." Letter I.

36. *E aver . . . che:* "And to have everything necessary so that
nothing may be lacking to fulfil them—so that he may lack nothing
on God's part. Is not this a playing with words, the saying that [you
are in agreement]?" Letter I.

f8ᵛ 37. *Ma ho . . . altri:* "But I learned later that their visits are
not infrequent, and that they are continually together." Letter I.

38. *rizzandomi per lasciargli:* Letter I.

e se bisognerà . . . frati: "and if it should be necessary we will
summon many friars". Letter I.

di modo che . . . risico: "so that it is only the word without any
sense that is in danger". Letter I.

con tal . . . pretext. Letter I.

Se questo racconto . . . sono: "If this account does not displease
you, I will continue to inform you of whatever happens later. I
remain, etc." Letter I.

f9 Quanto tempo . . . due mesi: "How long have you been speaking
Italian? Not quite two months." This is not in Pascal; but if it is a
personal statement it is direct evidence for the date of this entry.

Nel chiudere la lettera: "As I was closing my letter". Letter II.

con la maggior' . . . curiosità: "the most luckily possible for my
curiosity". Letter II.

Perche supposto che: "Because supposing that". Letter II.

Ell'è . . . satisfied: Letter II.

da pochi giorni . . . portmanteaux: not in Pascal.

f9ᵛ Se voi credete . . . solo: "If you believe that you have written
to me alone". Reply of the Provincial to the First Two Letters.

Vedete . . . prima: "You see what one of the most illustrious of
Academicians, among those men who are all illustrious, writes to me
about it, who as yet had seen only the first [letter]." Reply of the
Provincial.

la quale . . . Card. R.: "which owes so much to the memory of the
late Card[inal] R[ichelieu]". Reply of the Provincial.

In quanto al . . . doubtless: not in Pascal.

già è tanto tempo . . . long-temps: Letter III.

f10 In questo mentre . . . Interim: Letter III.

bisognava . . . heretica: "in order to be necessarily heretical, the Proposition [of Arnauld] must have been [shockingly opposed to the Fathers]". Letter III.

di dove . . . whence: Letter III.

per esser . . . Christ: Letter III.

per cagione di sua freddezza: "on account of his coldness". Letter III.

e prima di lui Santo Chr.: "and prior to him St Chr[ysostom]". Letter III.

è egli possibile . . . Chièsa G. e L.: "is it possible that in his works they have never found anything to oppose except in those three lines which are taken verbatim from the greatest Doctors of the G[reek] and L[atin] Churches?" Letter III.

f10ᵛ Scoperto . . . tenerla che: "When we have discovered the poison, we shall detest it [the proposition]; but as long as we find there [only the sentiments of the Holy Fathers] we cannot hold it otherwise [but in veneration]." Letter III. Coleridge uses *them*, because he thinks the writer is referring to the sentiments rather than to the proposition.

Questo è quello . . . intrigarcene: "This is what grieves them; but they are too penetrating. As for us, who do not understand things so profoundly, let us remain calm, without troubling ourselves about it." Letter III.

E in questo timore . . . pur una: "And in this fear I considered it necessary to consult one of the most learned of those who through policy were neutral in the first dispute, and I begged him to tell me the circumstances of this difference, confessing to him frankly that I did not see there any difference at all." Letter III.

O che voi . . . ve ne sia: "Oh, how simple-minded you are to believe that there exists any there." Letter III.

f11 che . . . qualcheduna: Letter III. Coleridge notices the misprints *s' c'* for "se ce" and *n'* for "ne".

che ei . . . si sia: "they have resolved to [suppress Arnauld's work] at whatever price". Letter III.

senza dir in che ne perche: "without saying in what or why". Letter III.

alla meno parola . . . i principii: "at the least word that escapes from the Molinists against the principles [of the Fathers]". Letter III.

Di maniera che . . . ragioni: "So that after so many proofs of their weakness, they have esteemed it more to the purpose, and more useful to them, to censure than to reply, since it is much easier for them to find monks than reasons." Letter III.

La lor censura . . . ch'ell' e: "Their censorship, censurable as it is, will be known for what it really is." Letter III.

f11ᵛ A loro . . . giorno: "For them that is enough. They live from day to day." Letter III.

si son . . . al presente: "they have maintained themselves until the present". Letter III. Coleridge seems to mistake the reflexive *si* for *sì* meaning *thus.*

da quel . . . learned man: Letter III.

i più dotti . . . nulla: "the most learned among them are those who intrigue much, speak little, and write nothing." Letter III.

sin dal principio: "since the beginning". Letter III.

f12 Li essaminatori . . . bene: "The examiners having tried to step aside slightly from this method did not find themselves well off in doing so." Letter III.

prima che . . . ended: Letter III.

si parla poco . . . avanti: "they speak little for fear of running out too far." Letter III.

2135 K.31   Again from Pascal; see 2133n.

Così è . . . debito: "So it is, I confess it. It fell to me to answer you, and I should have done so to satisfy my own desire no less than my duty." Letter III.

2136 K.32   Ink.
Also from Pascal, written later than and around 2135.

f12 Io conobbi . . . presenza: "I knew you by reputation long before I met you." *V. S.:* Vostra Signoria.

Mettete dunque . . . in riposo: "Then set your mind at rest." Letter III.

e non temete . . . condannata: "and have no fear of being an Heretic in serving yourself or [employing] the condemned propos[ition]." Letter III.

credete al D. Le. Moyne: "believe D[octor] Le Moyne." Letter III.

Questa . . . difenderà: "This proposition would be Catholic in another mouth; the Sorbonne has condemned it only in M. Arnauld. The grace [of St Augustine] will never be the true grace as long as he shall defend it." Letter III.

f12ᵛ Lasciamo . . . themselves: Letter III.
Noi . . . contese: "We, who are not doctors, have nothing to do with their squabbles." Letter III.
Li domandai . . . causa: "I asked him, nevertheless, in order to hear his reasons, for what cause [they had attacked the proposition]." Letter III.

2137 21.446   *A 18 and A [for B?] 35 years old:* Sara Hutchinson was born 1 Jan 1775, and therefore was not 30 years old. And Coleridge has curiously reversed the *A*'s and *B*'s if he meant *A* to refer to her. If the inserted words at the end could be dated as late as 1810, the second *A* could be SH. It is possible, and in contradiction of 2426, there are a few entries scattered through this notebook dated 1808, 1809, and 1812.

2138 21.447   *Goree:* an island off the west coast of Africa adjacent to Dakar.
Major Adye: see 2045 and n.
the Duke: the Duke of Kent; see 2050n.
Buonaparte's Stratagem: The anecdote refers to the episode in the retreat from Acre when Napoleon is said to have scorned to accept a horse for himself, having ordered that all should be used for the wounded, and to have led the retreat on foot.
Maltese Regiments raised by the order: the Order of the Knights of St John. The story is told in Sect 1 Essay v of *The Friend* (II 106–7).

2139 21.448   *AP 76.*
the glorious evening [star]: Reference to 2505 raises the question whether Coleridge was seeing here the "occultation of Mercury" referred to in that entry, where the application of the date is uncertain: but the *Berliner Astronomisches Jahrbuch*, the only almanac available for the area and the year, indicates that Venus was the evening star and appeared very close to the moon on this date. Cf 2087, where a few weeks earlier he was observing another star-dogged moon and thinking of his Grasmere friends. See also 2880n.
Dʳ Sewell: John Sewell (1766?–1833), judge of the Vice-Admiralty Court, Malta, D.C.L., F.R.S., knighted in 1815.

2140 21.449   *Locust Tree:* not the N. American tree, *Robinia pseudoacacia*, but the carob-tree, *Ceratonia siliqua*.

dulcacid: Thomas Blount in his *Glossographia* (1681) defines it as "that which hath a mixt taste of sweet and sowr; the Italians call it dulci-pignanti". As the *OED* considers the word rare or obsolete, possibly Coleridge was either composing from Latin roots or translating from Italian.

Linnæus: Was he reading Linnaeus, or did he later follow up this thought? See 2187.

2141 21.450   These are ruts on the NW coast of Malta, referred to as carriage-wheel marks but of unknown origin. They would be the more readily attributed to carriage-wheels in view of the situation referred to in the *bando* reproduced in plate II and translated in Appendix B.

2142 K.33   Ink.
The source being unknown, it is not clear to what happy events on land the writer refers, nor, *ipso facto,* which side he favours in which war.

Tr: Let that suffice for now of myself and of private affairs. As for our public affairs in Italy, I see what you write about them and what you fear about them. Nevertheless, I cling to my original hopes, and I trust that after so happy an outcome in events on land every anxiety about events at sea is on the point of ceasing. . . . Which may it please God to bring about as soon as possible; and may our Italy learn from the miseries of this war to enjoy all the more from now on the felicity of peace.

2143 K.34   An argument with which to support Ball's case for the English occupation of Sicily? See 2162n; the draft report there referred to contains suggestions of this kind, as might be expected from a naval officer.

2144 K.35, 37   Two entries, separated by the observation and reflection on the banana-tree of 2145, yet apparently written on the same occasion. The second (K.37) is opposite the end of the first (K.35). Cf the entry of 10 Oct 1804 in 2195.

f14 whom I had fascinated: the power of the eye; cf *Christabel* in reverse?

2148 K.38   Another comment on sounds in Malta? Or on the ubiquitous presence of the Church? Cf 2547.

2149 K.39   At right angles to the other entries on the page. A list
of names?

2150 21.451   *AP* 76–7 variatim, where, after *Cobbets*, the next
words, difficult to decipher, were omitted.
Juvernhas: for Juvernas? *Juverna* was the signature over which a
series of articles appeared in *Cobbett's Political Register* in 1803, attacking the government for the failure of the union with England and for
its short-sighted policies towards Ireland in general. Ministerial action
against Cobbett led to two adverse verdicts, and finally to the exposure of *Juverna* as an Irish judge, Robert Johnson, against whom
proceedings were still being taken when this entry was written. The
case was dropped in 1806. Coleridge asked Stuart to send the *Political
Register* to him in Malta. *CL* # 599 (P.S.).

2151 21.452   *AP* 77; cf *CL* # 210 (1 354), the well-known passage in
which Coleridge describes how his father showed him the planets. And
on his desire to reconcile the Many and the One, see, to choose one
instance only, 1561.
God . . . possesses it not, but is it: cf 98 and n.

2152 21.453   *words excite feelings of Touch:* cf a fragment from MS
Egerton 2800 in *Inq Sp* §73; and cf the converse in entry 838.
Ghosts & apparitions: many anecdotes on the subject appear to have
been told in conversation in Malta. See e.g. 2416–2418.

2153 21.454   *AP* 77–8 variatim.
auffassen: to perceive, comprehend.
anerkennen: to recognize the validity of something. The difference
between the two words is qualitative and not merely of degree.
agnized: recognized, acknowledged, apprehended. *OED.*

2154 21.455

Tr: 1. Knowledge. 2. Cognition—knowing what is an individual of any
kind (e.g. *a* sheep); 3. [knowing] what is present from what is not present,
i.e. whether it is a *thing;* or the *recollection* of a thing; or *imagination*—
German metaphysicians assign these three to the *lower* cognitive faculty;
and to the higher cognitive faculty [they assign] knowledge of agreement and
contradiction, dividing it into two notions: calling it *judgement* if [the knowledge is] direct, and conclusion or *deduction* if indirect.

2155 K.14   Before he left for Sicily, did Coleridge jot down the correct official address, and alternative forms of the private address, of Dr John Stoddart, his first host in Malta? He had it already in 2108, and it may seem more reasonable to believe that even here in N K he would have written it at Gibraltar, or on shipboard; this is quite possible. The physical position in the notebook, however, suggests the later date; as he did not plan to take N 16 to Sicily, he entered it again in this small pocket notebook?

2156 K.10   The entries on this page appear to have been written in sequence at more or less the same time, and if "June last" (2157) refers to June 1804 would be of a later date than that. They read like entries made, along with some that follow, e.g. 2162 and 2163, in Sicily. Possibly they are stories from Leckie, who as honorary consul in Syracuse, and Coleridge's host, would doubtless tell anecdotes of diplomatic personages like Sir W. Hamilton; if so, they belong to the first ten days in Syracuse, before Coleridge went off towards Catania and Etna.
    Sicily was under the control of the King of Naples at this time, and the Duke of Gravina had been in 1795, and perhaps still was, one of his counsellors. In 1788 and 1789 two sons of the king died of smallpox. Was the duke reported as suggesting that the disease came from "England & Jamaica, & those cold Climates"?

2157 K.11   The military datum was doubtless noted for Ball, who had employed Coleridge as his private secretary, and for whom Coleridge was doing some investigating on his largely holiday trip to Sicily.

2158 K.12   Sir William Hamilton, until his recall in 1800, had been Ambassador to the Court of Naples. He died in 1803.

2160 K.15   *Mezzo dì:* noon.

2161 K.16   George Noble, a businessman, lived in Naples and later befriended Coleridge there, in return, Coleridge suggests, for kindnesses to his brother and partner, Edmund Noble, in Malta. *CL* # 621. This might be either a Malta or a Sicily entry, and presumably may refer, like 2186, to either brother.

2162 K.17   The significance of this memorandum lies in the fact that both Alexander Ball and G. F. Leckie (on whom see 2193n)

were trying to persuade a reluctant government in England that Sicily should be occupied as a check to French aggressiveness in the Mediterranean, and one of their arguments was that the Sicilian population was favourably disposed. Among the papers Coleridge brought back from Malta, there is what appears to be a draft (in an unknown hand) of a statement on the desirability of the occupation of Sicily. VCL F 14.4.
See also 2234 and 2240.

2163 K.18   Pencil re-traced in ink by Coleridge.
Absentee landlordism and the neglect of peasant interests was another criticism made by Ball in the communications referred to in 2162n. Taxes on corn and bread were among the more flagrant griev-ances, especially as they were said to profit individuals rather than the government.

2164 K.19   Pencil re-traced in ink.
From the use made of John Smith's *Select Discourses* (1660) in several entries that follow, it is clear that Coleridge is not reading Plotinus here, but Smith's "Praefatory Discourse, Concerning the true Way or Method of attaining to Divine Knowledge", where the Greek phrases here are to be found, with sources and translations, scattered on pp 2–4: "and as the Eye cannot behold the Sun, ἡλιοείδης μὴ γινομένος, unless it be *Sunlike*, and hath the form and resemblance of the Sun drawn in it; so neither can the Soul of man behold God, Θεοειδὴς μὴ γινομένη, unless it be *Godlike*, hath God formed in it, and be made partaker of the Divine Nature. . . . [God] is best discerned [not in Books and writings but] νοερᾷ ἐπαφῇ, as Plotinus phraseth it, by an *Intellectual touch* of him. . . .
    "It is but a thin, aiery knowledge that is got by meer Speculation, which is usher'd in by Syllogisms and Demonstrations; but that which springs forth from true Goodness, is θειότερόν τι πάσης ἀποδείξεως, as Ori-gen speaks it, it brings such a Divine light into the Soul, as is more clear and convincing than any Demonstration. The reason why, not-withstanding all our acute reasons and subtile disputes, Truth prevails no more in the world, is, we so often disjoyn *Truth* and true *Goodness*, which in themselves can never be disunited; . . . Those filthy mists that arise from impure and terrene minds, like an *Atmosphere*, per-petually encompass them, that they cannot see that Sun of Divine

Truth that shines *about* them, but never shines *into* any *unpurged* Souls. . . ."

2165 K.20   Pencil re-traced in ink.

Again from Smith *Select Discourses* (1660) 7: "At best, while any inward lust is harboured in the minds of men, it will so weaken them, that they can never bring forth any masculine or generous knowledge; as Ælian observes . . . they become [wind-eggs] and all incubation rendred impotent and ineffectual."

Coleridge's omissions and abbreviations seem to be as significant in this instance as his memorandum.

2166 K.21   Pencil re-traced in ink.

Again suggested by Smith ibid 7, not a translation but a meditation on and poetizing of some of his phrases about ostentatious philoso-phers. "Such as these doe but Spider-like take a great deal of pains to spin a worthless web out of their own bowels, which will not keep them warm. . . . Speculations may be hovering and fluttering up and down about Divinity, but they cannot settle or fix themselves upon it. . . ."

And on p 18 Smith returns to the simile: quoting Plato, he says that earth-bound souls, "though, like the Spider, they may appear some-time moving up and down aloft in the aire, yet they doe but sit on the loome, and move in that web of their own gross fansies, which they fasten and pin to some earthly thing or other."

Cf 1598 for a happier and less personal use of the same image.

2167 K.22   Ink.

The first two phrases come from Smith ibid 20–1: "The true Metaphysical and Contemplative man . . . endeavours the nearest Union with the Divine Essence that may be, κέντρον κέντρῳ συνάψας, as *Plotinus* speaks; knitting his own centre, if he have any, unto the centre of the Divine Being. . . . This Life is nothing else but God's own breath within him, and an *Infant-Christ* (if I may use the ex-pression) formed in his Soul, who is in a sense . . . *the shining forth of the Father's glory*."

The second Greek quotation, from Plutarch, appears in Smith's discourse "Of Atheism", the first work ibid 42–3, and is there trans-lated: "*superstition afforded the principle of Generation to Atheism, and afterwards furnished it with an Apology, which though it be neither true nor lovely, yet wants it not a specious presence"*. The last quotation comes from the same volume, from the "Discourse Concerning the Existence and Nature of God" (p 123); Plotinus again is the source. Smith is demonstrating of God, "not so much . . . *That he is* as What he is. Both which we may best learn from a *Reflexion upon our own Souls*, as *Plotinus* hath well taught us, εἰς ἑαυτὸν ἐπιστρέφων, εἰς ἀρχὴν ἐπιστρέφει, *He which reflects upon himself, reflects upon his own Originall*, and finds the clearest impression of some Eternall Nature and Perfect Being stamp'd upon his own Soul. And therefore *Plato* [Smith's continuation of his argument is of interest in view of Coleridge's frequent diatribes against Roman Catholic images] seems sometimes to reprove the ruder sort of men in his times for their contrivance of Pictures and Images to put themselves in mind of the Θεοὶ or Angelicall Beings, and exhorts them to look into their own Souls. . . ."

This group of entries, alike in the appearance of the writing, may have been written at another date, yet that they are similar entries seems clear from the last one on the same page, 2168. Coleridge in Sicily clearly sought the consolations of Protestant Cambridge Platonism.

2169   1.13   Pencil.
From *f11* onwards, the notebook, except for perhaps three stray jottings, was blank when Coleridge left for Malta. It was not used again, apparently, until the Etna expedition in Aug 1804 to which this and following entries belong. (It will be noticed that the entries in N 15 belonging to the Sicilian visit Aug–Nov 1804 are also frequently in pencil. See N 15 Gen Note.)

Cf on this subject 2026. Was Coleridge here expressing irritation with a naïve companion? Or was he thinking of Scott, with whom he used to contrast himself in this respect? *TT* 4 Aug 1833. Cf 2075 and n.

2170   1.14   Pencil.
The first ascent of Etna was evidently made from the Catania side by way of the Benedictine monastery of Nicolò la Rena or (variously) Nicolò l'Arena at Nicolosi; the monastery offered hospitality to strangers who very frequently arranged to spend the early part of the night there for an ascent in time to see the sunrise at the crater.

M. Ross: Monte Rossi, an old crater close to Nicolosi. The "weari-some road" is very steep.

2171 1.15   Pencil.
A stage farther up Etna, in the woody region. Coleridge's procedure here, taking his bearings in a sweeping view of a landscape, and then (in the next entry) observing closely the detail at his feet, follows a pattern familiar in his descriptions elsewhere. Cf 222 and n and 2688.

2172 1.16   Very faint pencil, possibly part of the foregoing entry; it begins a new page. The first part of the entry refers still to the woody region, but the end possibly to the desert region beyond. The little celandine grows on Etna up to the limit of vegetation, about 6000 feet.
Overleaf from this entry is the one already printed in *CN* I as entry 7: "A subject for a romance—finding out a desert city & dwelling there/—Asia—." This is a not unlikely thought to overtake a climber of the lava cones of Etna, and it may belong here. Yet it is in ink, whereas the surrounding Etna entries are in pencil; the hand looks like that of the 1794 entries in this book, and it runs the same way of the notebook as they do. All the weight of evidence is in favour of the early date, and, yet, perhaps it should at least be noticed as being on the Etna pages, even though, except internally, it does not look like an Etna entry.

2173 1.17   The *Casina*, or cottage, may have been the Casina del Bosco, below Nicolosi, or, alternatively, the hut rebuilt by British troops in 1811, the Casina Inglese. My advisers in Catania were in-clined to the view, based partly on the reference to the inescapable wind, that it was the higher one, about four hours' walk above Nicolosi. This would suggest that Coleridge spent the night of 19–20 Aug, the date of 2170–2172, at the hostel run by the monastery, sug-gested also by 2176n, and that this entry records a meal on the ascent next day.

2174 1.19   In pencil. 20–26 Aug 1804, i.e. on either the first or second ascent.
This entry with the guide and the outdoor meal, and the next, in which Coleridge records that he "re-ascended", provide corroboration

for his statement 12 Dec 1804 (*CL* # 612) that he had been "twice on the Top of Mount Etna". It is perhaps the too-willing suspension of belief in Coleridge's veracity that has beset many of his editors that makes it possible for EHC to say, nevertheless, that Coleridge probably never reached the crater. *L* II 485n. If EHC saw this notebook, as his footnote suggests he did, he perhaps did not read the very faint pencilled notes in their entirety; or if he did so, he may have read them without the local geographical information that supports Coleridge's assertion. In matters of this kind at least, the more closely one tracks Coleridge down, the more one must credit him.

EHC, in fact, paid scant attention to this notebook; he took no excerpts from it for *AP*, and in publishing the fragments of *The Triumph of Loyalty* (*PW* I 423, II 1060–73) he made no reference to the draft of that work in it. See 871 and n. And see 2175n.

With the "good natured Guide" Coleridge had an interesting conversation on one descent or the other. See *TT* 25 July 1831.

2175 1.20   See 2174n. The *Casina* is probably that of 2173, later the Casina Inglese.

The association with Greenough is explained by 1864 and 1883–1889 and notes.

This entry makes impossible EHC's (unsupported) statement that by 24 Aug Coleridge was back in Syracuse (*L* II 485n), another indication that he made little use of this notebook.

2176 1.24   A search for the source of these lines has been unavailing in spite of the co-operation of officials of the Archivio Provinciale in Catania. They searched the lists of the papers of the Benedictine monastery, formerly at Nicolosi, in their possession since the secularization in 1866, but to no avail. Coleridge probably, like most travellers of the period, stayed at this hostel. Edward Boid, in 1824, is only one of many who refer to the normal route as "through Nicolosi, and by the celebrated convent of San Nicolò dell'Arena . . . ; a few lay brethren only are left . . . who occasionally entertain travellers on their road up the mountain; but comfort fled with the Benedictines into Catania, & it is now a most undesirable, wretched place of halt". *Travels through Sicily* (1827) 248–9.

The idea that Coleridge might have found the lines in an album there (see 2170n) is supported by a passage in *The Friend*, at the end of the first number. "Previous to my ascent of Etna, as likewise of the

Brocken in North Germany, I remember to have amused myself with examining the Album or Manuscript presented to Travellers at the first stage of the Mountain, in which on their return the Fore-runners had sometimes left their experience. . . ." *Friend* (1809) 16. The album has eluded search and may easily, with much else in the vicinity of Etna, have been destroyed. If the poem is printed elsewhere, it has not been found.

On the other hand, it may have been an inscription, as line 5 could suggest.

The Abbé Lazzaro Spallanzani in his *Travels in the Two Sicilies*, which was translated, possibly by Thomas Beddoes (4 vols London 1798), records seeing, at the half-ruined Benedictine monastery of Nicolò dell'Arena, various inscriptions memorializing eruptions of Etna, the terrible destruction and the acts of heroism. He does not, however, recite any of these memorials, either prose or verse.

Ferrara (op cit in 1888) says that the monastery was destroyed in 1693 and rebuilt, and was used by all travellers ascending Etna (p 13n). The poem/inscription therefore probably refers to and may be dated later than the eruption of that date.

If the poem was copied by Coleridge in 1804 from a stone tablet, it could have been destroyed in any one of several eruptions since then.

Tr: Whatever stranger wants to know about this shrine, stand still for a little on the threshold and honour the holiness of this place—a holiness unquenched by the changes of time. Here under the black sand the ashes of holy monks are treasured away. Do not marvel. The sterile sand of the saints' bones has in the course of time everywhere turned into lovely fruits, and endowed the fruit-trees with laden branches. And those who, living in the flesh, poured forth the fragrance of the virtues, and are now dissolved into dust, still blossom in flowers, still cast their scent in roses. Restless wanderer, consider that this shrine is restored to life by their life and by their miracles. A hill was laid low by the force of Etna and in the earthquake rose again more lovely from its ruins. So noble a grace has it put on in the garment of cruel fate that you would say that Holiness had fought through a multitude of disasters and triumphed. And so, go your way in peace; and, if you honour the image of the guardian spirit with loyal and fervent devotion, you may confidently promise yourself that all will be well with you, thanks to his favours.

2177 15.65   The difficulty of dating this entry is not lessened by its extreme faintness or by the fact that the writing in the early part of the entry looks as if it might have been done on horseback or in some other equally unscribal position.

Cava Secca [Secchia]: Cava di Spampinato, 13 kilometres from Syracuse. The whole appears to record more than one expedition, one from Syracuse and possibly the return from Catania to Syracuse, 27 Aug 1804.

Village of Comi Gatania: a mishearing of Comi Catania, or of Canicattini?

High-Bridge: in Inverness-shire, Scotland, not, I think, the Somersetshire Highbridge; see 1489 *f57ᵛ*.

Bowder Stone: see *CN* i Index 3.

The Paradise/the Gothic Arches: the Latomia del Paradiso, just outside Syracuse.

The School of Archim[edes] . . . to eat: some tourist anecdote from his guide?

Brittleness of the Or[ange?] Trunks.

2178 15.66   *Dr Paolo Cesareo:* written large and in a rounded Coleridgian hand, the name may or may not be connected with what follows. Was Dr Cesareo author or subject of the rhymes? Among the Wordsworth-Coleridge manuscripts at Cornell University is a *jeu d'esprit* not printed by EHC, a version of this entry. It is the same except for the last lines: "De pettitoes and little feet/De little feet not big/Great Feet belog/to de grunting Hog/Pettitoes to the little Pig. S.T.C."
The lines, not spelt with as much attention to broken English and with "belong" for Coleridge's "belog", thus missing a rhyme, are noticed in *The Oxford Dictionary of Nursery Rhymes* (1951) 348 as having first appeared in J. O. Halliwell *The Nursery Rhymes of England* (1853). Have we here a nursery rhyme older than was supposed, or is this now to be attributed to Coleridge? Probably the first.

2179 15.67   Another Syracuse entry. He had noticed the black *faldetta* in Malta; see 2100 and n.

2180 K.40   Presumably the drawing was done and signed by Leckie; see the next note and 2156n and 2193n. The hand is not Coleridge's.

2181 K.41   A drawing of St Paul's Bay, Malta, showing the

Selmun Palace. Possibly it was drawn by Leckie in Syracuse for the purposes of indicating something to Coleridge; as the annotation quoted in 2208n shows, Coleridge was at this date in Syracuse.

2182 K.42   Ink.
Tutti . . . *sicura:* "All these excesses made me consider their safety desperate. But you teach me that they, i.e. these very excesses, make it secure."

2183 K.43   *Aci:* probably Acireale, on the south-west coast road, about 9 miles from Catania.
L.: presumably Leckie.

2184 K.44   The names of the cast of the touring opera company then at the Syracuse opera-house?
    Cecilia Bertozzi appears in the Coleridge story as the siren of Syracuse from whom he was saved, he said in a later notebook (N 13), by a vision of Sara Hutchinson's face. *Asra* 317. See also 2196. She is variously called Cecilia Bertozzoli (N 13 Oct 1808) and Cecilia Bartolozzi (Chambers 189, in error). From 1809 onwards she was *prima donna* of the Palermo company.
    The ⟨*Ne*⟩, *Tos.*, and ⟨*Sig*⟩ possibly stand for the *dramatis personae* of the opera.

2185 K.45   The two composers, Pietro Alessandro Guglielmi (1728–1804), who visited London in 1767 and was the author of some hundred operas, and Sebastiano Nasolini (*c* 1768–*c* 1806), who wrote about thirty operas, were very popular in the eighteenth century.
    Lines 1, 5, and 7 are probably the first lines or the titles of popular arias from the operas of Guglielmi, line 3 from one of Nasolini. Perhaps Coleridge heard them and wished to remember them, or was told about them by some of the persons listed in 2184.

2186 K.46   Edmund Noble? See 2161n.

2187 K.47   Peter Artedi (1705–35), eminent Swedish naturalist and ichthyologist, whose great work on fishes was edited and first published (1738) by Linnaeus after Artedi died by drowning.

2188 K.48   *Mr Dennison:* William Denison (in 2675) and Robert Dennison (in 2578), the former in Sicily, the latter in Malta, were both known to Coleridge. Presumably "Mr Dennison/Denison" is the elder, Robert the younger. From 2578 one would guess they were merchants or connected with the merchant navy.

Leek: the gun-firing context suggests Capt William Martin Leake of the Artillery; see 2740n for Coleridge's link with him. At this time Leake was visiting Malta on his return from England; he had been shipwrecked while conveying some of the Elgin Marbles from the Piraeus. Later he became Lieut-Col, and a friend of Byron.

2189 K.49   Ink.
Ironically, in pursuit of health Coleridge appears to have found closer access to a source of supply of opium than ever before.

2190 K.50   Roughly the shape of Malta.

2191 21.456   A blank space, never filled in, was left for the exact date. Coleridge spent about three months, Aug–Oct 1804, in Sicily, making Syracuse the headquarters from which he went on various expeditions.

2192 21.457   *AP* 78 variatim. Cf Milton's "Lap me in soft Lydian Aires/Married to immortal verse/Such as the meeting soul may pierce/In notes, with many a winding bout/Of lincked sweetnes long drawn out". *L'Allegro* lines 136–40.
Coleridge probably attended the opera frequently in Syracuse; see also 2196n.

2193 21.8   The emendations at the end of the entry arise from the frayed edge of the page; EHC made these suggestions and he undoubtedly saw the MS in better condition.
AP 79. Cf *BL* I 38–9. Coleridge is referring to the company at Leckie's, probably; see 2156n and 2180 and n. Leckie's firm were Lloyds's agents, and his social gatherings were doubtless various. He was a man of wide general interests, for Coleridge admired some scarce and beautiful books in his library (2236) and Leckie wrote various works on economic and political subjects. In 1808 he published *An Historical Survey of the Foreign Affairs of Great Britain with a view to explain the causes and disasters of the late and present wars.*
Tract 1 in this volume is dated "1 Jan 1806", or just shortly after Coleridge had left in 1805 on his homeward journey. See 2220. I

believe that Coleridge's influence, perhaps hand, even, may be seen in that work. See 2213n, 2215n, 2259n, and 2261n. Yet he was critical of the limited character of Leckie's views; see 2295n.

Harrington was a favourite with Coleridge and may have been much in mind at this time; see 2223 and n.

Condilliac: Coleridge always spelled the name this way. The attitude implied here to English and French empiricism is expounded in *Phil Lects* 363, 458 n 50.

Sint . . . præmia: to every man his due.

2194 21.458   *AP* 78–9. The underlining of *Oct. 5. 1804* seems to suggest a reference to the conversations of that evening (2193) and not necessarily that the entry was written on that date.

Philosophy . . . the Friend of Poetry: This is an important entry, clarifying Coleridge's position with regard to the nature of philosophy and poetry in a way frequently overlooked by his commentators. It appears in various forms early and late in his writings. Cf e.g. 383 and n for an early statement and *Phil Lects* 395 for a later one.

2195 15.68   Published with omissions, additions, and many smaller differences in *L* ii 485n.

f51 Timoleon's: the remains of Timoleon's villa at Tremiglia, a retreat given him by grateful fellow-citizens for his deliverance of them in the 4th century B.C. from the Carthaginians and Dionysius II, and his restoration of peace and order in Sicily.

The Gazæ: the *gaggia* tree answers Coleridge's description.

Above Tremillia Neapolis: Coleridge later corrects it to Tremiglia; Neapolis is the lower part of the city of Syracuse.

the Harbour's name: Ortygia, with on one side the Porto Piccolo and on the other the Porto Grande.

f51ᵛ where Alcibiades & Nicias landed/([? *tho some deny/the same day*] *that Neptune died down there*): again a guide's tale? See also 2217 (a).

Cipallaccid: or Cipollaccid, a marine squill.

Epipolis: for Epipolae.

f52 Manghisi: for Magnisi.

Cava Sechia: see 2177 and n.

He clearly scrambled with much zest and energy over this the highest point of the Epipolae, where the remains of the great 5th-century fortress, built by Dionysius the Elder at Euryalus in the hey-

day of Sicilian military prestige, are still impressive, and the view
"glorious indeed". Whether he had a guide or companion is not certain
but it looks likely; apparently he set out from Leckie's house on the
Porto Piccolo, and went up to "the Castle", i.e. Castello Eurialo.
f52ᵛ gliding darts: the underlining of the words suggests an intent
observation made perhaps "for purposes of poetry"? As often before,
here again Coleridge's eye moves from the wide horizon to the small
things at his feet. It is perhaps noteworthy how frequently he tries to
describe movement of all kinds—water, clouds, animals, &c.

2196 21.459   *AP* 80–1 variatim.
la P. D.: the Prima Donna of the opera company, Cecilia Bertozzi?
Cf 2184 and n.
The distinctions between heat of fermentation and warmth of life,
and between positiveness and certainty, occur in the same order in
N 8. See 1409 and 1410 and notes. And see the application in *LS* 53.
Had he been contending with Leckie? See 2718 and n.

2197 15.69   In Syracuse.

2200 15.72   Among the legion of similar anecdotes of military
corruption in the armies of the king of Naples this one appears to be
impossible to locate precisely.

2201 15.73   Valentino Fioravanti (1764–1837) *Le Cantatrici
villane, ossia Le Virtuose ridicole (The Peasant Singers, or The Ridiculous Virtuose).* This was his most popular work, first performed in
Naples in 1799, later in German translation, under Goethe's direction,
at Weimar in 1807, and in English not until 1842. Coleridge's account
suggests either that he saw a somewhat heightened production or
that he exaggerated it in his own interpretation. The hero fled to
Germany because he had fought a duel, but there is no mention of his
having killed his opponent. The libretto was by Giuseppe Palomba.

2202 15.74   *f53ᵛ* Of the old Roman Forum in Neapolis only the
one column remains in what is now the city gardens.
f54 Schiller's Gotter [Götter]: cf 494.
f54ᵛ beneath the Sea: i.e. mirrored in it.
like a monstrous Raft: = ?more "like a monstrous raft . . . than
like a part of the Land".

wooded: a slip for *wood.*
Bay of Manghisi: a mishearing of Magnisi.
f55   Enchanter's Nightshade: Circaea lutetiana, after Circe, the enchantress. There are several varieties.
f55ᵛ Belvedere: above Euryalus.
from my Lectiga in my journey from Cat[*ania*]: i.e. on his return from the Etna expedition in August; the cavern is perhaps the "Cava Secca" referred to in the all but illegible entry 2177. *Lectiga,* which Coleridge elsewhere gives the more usual spelling, *lettiga,* was the typical Sicilian means of transportation at that time. See 2675n.
of considerable: size omitted, or some such word.
Targita: in 2206 corrected to Targea.
f56   Valley of Stones: near Lynton in Devonshire, the destination of a productive walk in 1797–8.
falling abroad: a west-country expression much in use in Coleridge's native Devonshire.

2203 15.75   *Porto minore:* the small harbour between Ortygia and Achradina.

2204 15.76   *Infamous:* apparently quotation marks are implied. Coleridge frequently was to make a point of the inadequacy of individual analogies in social judgements.

2205 15.77   *men ed*[*ucated*] *in the present system:* Coleridge's charge against his own age, of lack of education in logic, was lifelong. Cf *TT* 4 Jan 1823 and 21 Sept 1830.
    The last phrase appears to refer to a conversation at Lamb's, 23 March 1800. See 711.

2206 15.78   The first sentence refers to 2202.

2207 15.79   *A ghost by day time:* as well as being an interesting commentary on his own intentions in *Christabel,* intentions clarified perhaps by the electric storm over Leckie's house, this remark has an interesting link with two reviews of *Christabel.* In a defence that may not have been printed in Coleridge's lifetime, probably by Coleridge's friend John J. Morgan, the reviewer writes: "We have hitherto seen the mysterious Geraldine shrouded in night; . . . The poet has now to introduce this supernatural being in the light, and joyousness of

day. This difficulty has been overcome with great judgement . . .".
If Coleridge himself encouraged the writing of this review, he may also
have helped to suppress it as being ponderously undiscerning on this
very subject of the "supernatural". For the whole review see *Wordsworth & Coleridge* 173–91. See also *TT* 6 July 1833.

2208 21.460   *AP* 81 variatim. EHC omitted the word "Sleepiness"
from Coleridge's list of life-forces, thus all but losing the very personal
character of this note, an early statement of ideas more impersonally
developed elsewhere. Cf "On Poesy or Art": *BL* II esp 258–60.

   De gustibus non est disputandum: "There is no accounting for
tastes"—a favourite tag with Coleridge.

   jus extrinsecum fortioris: "the external law of the stronger force".
The actual Latin phrase does not appear to have been used by Spinoza.
It is, however, attributed to him by A. W. Rehberg in a footnote to a
work Coleridge annotated "August 29th, Syracuse, 1804", *Ueber das
Verhältniss der Metaphysik zu der Religion* (Berlin 1787) 142. Coleridge called it a "masterly" work; his copy is in the BM. Without
deriving from it, this entry perhaps owes some elements to this work.

2209 21.461   An entry intended for development in the "Soother
of Absence", very much crossed out, probably by Mrs Gillman. The
personal conflict evident in this and surrounding entries appears to be
connected with "the siren of Syracuse" and thoughts of "Asra". With
the image of floating cf 1718; there are also numerous uses of it in the
poems. In a marginal note on Jeremy Taylor's *Dissuasive from Popery* in the *Polemical Discourses* (1674) 298, Coleridge noticed that
certain kinds of painful dreams were always associated for him "with
vast water-scenery". The phrase was omitted from *LR* III 356 and
also from *C 17th C.* Coleridge's copy of this work is in the BM.

2210 21.462   *AP* 81–2.
   That constitution which predisposes to certain Virtues: that divine
afflatus has this fearful penalty in it; cf *AR* 43–4.

2211 21.463   *AP* 82 variatim. This entry, with 2112, appears to be
Coleridge's earliest use of the distinction between copy and imitation
(unless 2274 is earlier); in any case, his distinction antedates by four
years Schelling's *Philosophische Schriften* (Landshut 1809), from
which work he is said to have borrowed it. But see *Phil Lects* 291–2
and esp 442 n 7.

The ancient imitation-copy distinction was revived by Edward Young, among others, in his *Conjectures on Original Composition: Works* (1774–8) v, the volume Coleridge borrowed from the Bristol Library in 1795; see 33n.

Coleridge's fullest exposition of the distinction is to be found in the essay "On Poesy or Art". Shawcross points out in his notes on that essay, quoting Plotinus *Ennead* v 8 1, that the conception of art as a copy of nature is Platonic, the conception of it as imitation is Plotinian. *BL* II 318.

In other words, Coleridge's distinction may derive from classical sources, or from English criticism; it does not come from Schelling.

It may be added that Aristotle's *Poetics* entered into their views in the Preface of *LB* (1800), as Wordsworth and Coleridge both implied: *WPW* II 394 and *BL* II 33 (Chap XVII).

2212 15.80   The word *jaw*, towards the end of the entry, is badly written but no other intention is clear.

Dennison: see 2188n.

Pysma: or Pisma, a narrow winding river, a tributary of the Cyane, and almost filled with papyrus, of which the bulbous roots and the bright green rushes that spring from them are triangular in shape. Coleridge may here be associating the viscous fetid fleshy appearance of the growth with some earlier revulsion. Or is there some less pleasant but more poignant association with such an image? See 2557 and n.

2213 15.81   Coleridge's blank after *Tagliator* was perhaps for the Italian word *tagliatore*, a butcher who cuts up meat.

Ounce: 30 *tarì*, about 12s. 6d. in English money in 1824, a *tarì* being about 5d.

Università: tribunal. The crippling and corrupt taxation of meat and bread was viewed by many observers as the chief internal economic problem in Sicily, e.g. G. F. Leckie in his *Historical Survey* Tract VIII. See 2193n and 2261 and n.

2214 15.82   The Marquis of Sortino in 1824 was one of the temporal peers in the Sicilian parliament.

The Duchess of Floridia was duchess in her own right, having succeeded to her father in 1775; the duke Coleridge refers to must be her husband, Benedetto Grifeo e del Bosco, Duke of Ciminna, after 1802 Prince of Partanna, and Duke of Floridia by courtesy.

Perituri [*paratori*]: Coleridge's spelling of the word for sluice-gates reflects Sicilian pronunciation; the *o* would sound like *u*. The private monopoly of the scarce water supply was another source of public misery in Sicily.

2215 15.83   Leckie discussed the same problem in his *Historical Survey* referred to in 2193n. See 2213n.

2216 15.84   See 143 and n.

2217 15.85(a)   See the earlier reference to the death of Neptune at 2195 *f51ᵛ*. In the wash of Achradina there is the Grotto di Nettuno, but there appears to be no legendary association of Neptune's tomb with Tremiglia.

15.85(b)   *Lucern:* the purple medick, a clover-like weed.

Lupa: a broom-rape, described as a large genus of parasite herbs having a brownish-yellow leafless fleshy stem. *OED.*

2218 21.464   *AP* 82-3.

On *resentment*, cf 1606. The phrase "mood of mind", used earlier in a letter of 1802 to Sotheby (*CL* # 459: I 864), became also Wordsworth's heading for one group of his poems.

Coleridge used the word *madness* in a broad sense; see *Inq Sp* §§10 and 11. Clearly he is aware of what is more recently known as projection.

2219 15.86   The passage is from the preface to the second part of Christian von Wolff's *Theologia naturalis*. The work appears in the second volume of *Institutiones philosophiae wolfianae* (1725). See 905 and n. If Coleridge was reading here from his own copy he may have lost it on the journey; the second volume is now missing from it.

He omits, in the sixth line of this entry, *demonstrare* after *numinis*, in the eighth line writes *aspectabilis* for *adspectabilis*, omits a few words at the end of the sentence, after *derivatur*, and *prorsus* after *suo*.

Wolf remarks well in the Præfatio to his *Theologia naturalis*, that the a priori demonstration of Deity is in reality a posteriori from the fact that it could more properly be said that the existence of God is proved from the contemplation of the soul/—Then after a bitter inquisitorial abuse & atheizing of Spinosa he says—therefore to derive the existence of true divinity from the idea of completely perfect Being is the same thing as to derive it from the contemplation of our soul; thus the proof proceeds no less a posteriori than if it is derived from contemplation of this visible universe. He saw this in virtue of his own extraordinary acumen, because the more mentally acute any man is, the more he is bound to look upwards. For this reason, Divine Thomas asserted that the existence of God cannot be proved a priori.

2220 15.87   On Leckie's interest in economic problems, see 2193n and 2213n. The work referred to here, by the famous controversialist, Rev Richard Price, D.D., is *Observations on Reversionary Payments; on Schemes for providing Annuities for Widows, and for Persons in old Age; on the Method of calculating the Value of Assurances on Lives; and on the National Debt. Also Essays on different Subjects in the Doctrine of Life Annuity and Political Arithmetic* . . . (6th ed 2 vols 1803). This edition was favourably reviewed in *An Rev* II 829–32, an issue we know Coleridge saw, which may well have reminded him of a work, one of the early expositions of life insurance, that had been for some time popular.

2221 15.88   Cf 2235.

2222 15.89   In ink.
The "second letter to M. Chastellux" is dated 24 Jan 1766. Pietro Metastasio *Lettere* in *Opere postume* (3 vols Vienna 1795) II 353–4:

And in fact no one can address an audience and make himself clearly understood without raising, expanding, and sustaining his voice noticeably more than he does in speaking ordinarily. These new evident changes of the voice demand art in regulating its new proportions: otherwise they would produce ill-modulated, unpleasant, often ridiculous, sounds. This very art is nothing else but music; so necessary to anyone who speaks in public that when actors lack that of artists appointed to provide it they are obliged [by nature] to devise a music of their own under the name of declamation.

Th.: Theatres.

2223 22.16   Coleridge is reading and annotating two political tracts by James Harrington, appended to Toland's edition of the *Oceana* (1700). See 639–641, 934, and notes. The references in sequence are, in the first two paragraphs, to *A System of Politics* Chap IV Aphorisms 2–4; in the third to Chap IV Aphorisms 10–12 (Toland

499); in the fourth to Chap v Aphorism 18 (Toland 503), though this has gone through a characteristically Coleridgian sea-change, Harrington's words being, "A Parlament of Poets would never have found out the Circulation of the Blood, nor would a Parlament of Poets have written Virgil's *Æneis.*" In paragraph five the reference to *Oceana, p. 203* is to that passage in which Harrington says that France, Italy, and Spain are "all sick, all corrupted together" and that "The first of these Nations (which, if you stay her leisure, will in my mind be *France*) that recovers the health of antient Prudence, shall certainly govern the World"; Chap vi Aphorism 10 of *A System of Politics* reads as Coleridge, modernizing the spelling, transcribes it. In his *N.B.*, his spelling of the *Edict of Nantz* suggests a confusion between the place and the doubtless more familiar brandy. His sixth paragraph, *A man may devote himself to Death* . . . , is from Chap viii Aphorisms 12–13 (Toland 509); his seventh, *The wisdom of late years* . . . , comes in part from Chap x Aphorism 15, which ends with the sentence: "Aristocratical Monarchy is the true Theatre of Expedientmongers and Stateempirics, or the deep Waters wherein that Leviathan the Minister of State takes his pastime" (Toland 513). The eighth paragraph, *Nemo unquam* . . . , takes its Latin from Harrington's Chap x Aphorism 18, in which the epigram is freely translated: "Usurpation of Government is a Surfeit that converts the best Arts into the worst" (Toland 514). The ninth paragraph, *If the House stands awry* . . . , is from Chap x Aphorism 20. The next two paragraphs are from the *Political Aphorisms,* Aphorism 7 (Toland 515) and Aphorism 35 (Toland 516). The tag from Cicero (*De oratore* II 337) is quoted at the end of Aphorism 104 by Harrington as an equivalent for his statement, "in making a Commonwealth, that it be understood, is of absolute necessity" (Toland 522). The final Latin sentence is quoted and translated in *The Ways and Means of introducing a Commonwealth by the Consent of the People.* "*Aut reges . . . libertas:* either the Kings ought not to have bin driven out, or the People to have their Liberty not in word, but in deed: but that is Heathenism, that's Cicero . . ." (Toland 540). It is from Cicero *De legibus* III 25.

Coleridge's copy of this work is in the BM; it was listed in Wordsworth LC as Coleridge's.

2224 22.15   This entry is an editorial Scylla and Charybdis. One must either make rash guesses at specific dates and fail to show the continuity of this attack on metrical problems or fail in this instance to show the physical discontinuity and juxtapositions of the notebook itself. But as this notebook is really several notebooks combined, and the dating more hazardous than usual, it has seemed more useful to try to preserve as one what Coleridge himself treated as one, by numbering its sections, although it is clearly the product of numerous dates. The whole appearance of ink and pencil, larger and smaller writing, uneven margins, and erratically placed numbering (made uniform here for convenience) confirms the description in N 22 Gen Note.

I do not think the entry as a whole so early as EHC suggested: *PW* II 1014. He asserts that "the greater portion" of this notebook belongs to *c* 1801, at any rate to "a much earlier date" than Malta. This composite entry certainly belongs to various dates, probably beginning *c* 1801, but of the 48 metres discussed and exemplified, several at least could belong only to the Malta period, to Malta or later. Coleridge was clearly collecting material on metres in Malta, possibly for his essay on poetry. Probably he sent for his German notebooks for this reason; certainly he was collecting Latin, English, and even Morlack verses here. His own dates in the MS show that he was working on this in the autumn of 1804, when he had by 18 Oct collected "18 airs". See this entry, *f21*. This parallels his immediate interest in metres when he first went to Germany (see 373); the response to Italian, natural enough in any case, was no doubt quickened by the essay on metre or poetry long at the back of his mind. It was first mentioned as a projected accompaniment to *Christabel* (see 998 and n, 1003 and n) in 1801 and perhaps was thought of even earlier, in disagreement with Wordsworth's handling of the subject of metre in the preface to *LB* (1800). EHC is probably right about some parts of this entry belonging to 1801; the dividing lines are impossible to draw.

But although the dating of 2364 is hypothetical and unproven, and of this entry certainly seriatim, much of it does seem to belong to Malta, possibly Sept–Oct 1804, but before 2363 (21 Dec 1804) and before 2223.

f12   The metrical scheme is written on the upper third of *f13* with Coleridge's direction as to where it belongs; the remainder of the leaf was torn off before he wrote on it, the last two lines being crowded in above the tear.

This is the fifth stanza of Schiller's *Die Bürgschaft*, which appeared first in his *Musenalmanach* for 1799, p 177, and then in his *Gedichte* (1800) I 35:

> And silently his trusty friend embraces him
> And delivers himself up to the tyrant,
> The other takes his departure.
> And before the third dawn reddens the sky
> He has swiftly united his sister to her husband,
> Hastens home, his soul full of care
> Lest he fail the appointed hour.

f12ᵛ 2. The lines are from Schiller *Die Ideale*, first published in his *Musenalmanach* for 1796; but this text follows *Gedichte* (1800) I 43. After lines 2 and 4, Coleridge apparently experiments with a feminine ending for the line, as shown in the pointed brackets. These are clearly metrical, not linguistic, additions. "The echo of my own Life—in inanimate Nature" is Coleridge's rendering of the last two lines; the lines may be translated:

> And sharing the fires of my passion
> Silent [Nature] found a language,
> Returned the kiss of love to me
> And understood the music of my heart;
> Then there woke to life the tree, the rose,
> The streams' silvery falls sang to me;
> Even the Inanimate felt
> The echo of my own life.

3. This is the metrical scheme and the first stanza of another Schiller poem, entitled *Bürgerlied* in the *Musenalmanach* for 1799, p 189, and *Das Eleusische Fest*, its now accepted title, in *Gedichte* (1800) I 78:

> Bind the golden sheaves into garlands
> And weave blue cornflowers amongst them,
> Let each eye gladden with joy,
> For the queen is making her entry—
> She, the restrainer of savage customs
> Who joins man to man in civil concord,
> And into peaceful permanent dwellings
> Transformed the nomads' tent.

f13ᵛ 4. *Dance, merrily dance:* not published as Coleridge's, and not traced to another source. The metrical pattern appears to be an attempt to play with and vary the metre of the lines opposite and numbered the same.

f14 [*4a*]. This is on another torn leaf, between the verse Coleridge has numbered *4*, and the rhyme scheme similarly numbered. It could have been written on the stub-leaf at any time: it is now on a leaf tipped in at what was judged to be the intended place.

Lines 3 and 7 may be translated:

> [3] Alas! bedewing his face with tears
> [7] The more arrogant for neglecting the law.

For the rest, it appears to be doggerel or nonsense, possibly written by STC in illustration of the barbarism of some metrical or rhyme scheme.

f15 address summo Poetæ . . . : "address to the greatest Poet, the best and dearest Friend, W.W.—to receive, avow, support, sustain me, if only love had given Asahara a supremely daring spirit."

Asahara appears in an inscription by STC on the Dove Cottage copy of the "Sheet of Sonnets": "The Editor to Asahara, the Moorish Maid, Dec. 1800 Greta Hall, Keswick". The "Moorish maid" appeared in *Osorio* and in *Remorse*.

5. This is the first stanza of *Frühlingsliebe* by J. H. Voss, published in his *Gedichte* 1 (Hamburg 1785) 333:

> The lark was singing, the sun shone,
> The meadow was growing green,
> And brown bursting buds
> Made bush and tree more beautiful:
> Then I plucked beside the thorny lake
> A nosegay for her, beneath late snow,
> Blue, red, and white clover blossoms:
> The maiden let it adorn her breast
> And nodded thanks in friendly fashion.

6. This is the first stanza of *Die Vögel* by Friedrich von Hagedorn, published in his *Sämmtliche poetische Werke* Pt III (Hamburg 1764) 34:

> In this wood, in these dingles
> Nothing but freedom, joy, and quiet prevails.
> Here we pledge ourselves to love,
> To find each other in the thickest shade:
> There I find you, you find me.

7. This is the first stanza of *Die Empfindung des Frühlings*, also by Hagedorn op cit 68:

> You bloom of motley meadows,
> You newly verdant lea;
> Be ever praised by me,
> You bloom of motley meadows!
> Your finery and Cephisa's
> Comes from Spring and from Nature!
> You bloom of motley meadows!
> You newly verdant lea!

f15ᵛ   8. The last stanza of *An den verlohrnen Schlaf*, also by Hagedorn op cit 63:

> Old Friend, O! Sleep, return to me!
>   How I long for you!
> You son of night, O spread your wings
>   Over me too;
> Forsake instead the usurer, to punish him,
>   Whom deceit overjoys;
> And let this wakeful Codrus sleep
> Who's always rhyming and always translating.

9. The first stanza of *Die Nacht*, again by Hagedorn op cit 110:

> Welcome, sweet Night,
> Enfold in thy shade
> The joys which are matched,
> And blind, O blind, suspicion;
> When true love makes lovers kiss,
> Then will the kiss of love,
> And then will all her passion
> Be blessed by the still of night.

10. The fourth stanza of *Der Kuss* by J. H. Voss *Gedichte* (1785) 337:

> Sunk in thought
>   Through tender green
> I watched the bright cloudlets
>   Trail across the blue sky;
> Then you sprinkled me, you rogue,
>   With your wet nosegay
> And fled like a thief
>   Into the summer-house.

f16 11. The third stanza of *Mailied eines Mädchens* by Voss *Gedichte* (1785) 314:

> Come, playmates, and gambol
> As the nightingale sings,
> For her song invites to the dance!
> O swifter and swifter!
> Round and round like the children:
> Ring a ring o' roses!

12. The German lines are the ninth stanza of Selma's song in Voss's idyll *Der Frühlingsmorgen: Gedichte* (1785) 9; the verse below it is Coleridge's translation.

*f16*ᵛ 13. The first stanza of *Minnelied* by Voss in *Gedichte* II (Königsberg 1795) 151, with Coleridge's adaptation, playing with both metre and content. A literal translation would be:

> To the Gracious Lady
> In constancy
> I sing a glad
> Love-song:
> For the Pure One
> Whom I love
> Waves me her lovely thanks.

14. The first stanza of *Die Spinnerin*, also by Voss *Gedichte* (1795) 149:

> Poor girl that I am
> My little spinning-wheel
>   Will no longer turn
> Since the stranger
> In his white shirt
> Helped us to reap the corn.

15. The first stanza of *Das Landmädchen* by Voss *Gedichte* (1795) 131:

> On my father's hilltop
> There stands a beauteous tree:
> The birds of the forest love singing
> On my father's hilltop
> And sing me many a dream.

16. *Scendi propizia . . . degli Dei:* Metastasio *Epitalamio* II:

Descend propitious in your splendour, O fair Venus, mother of love, O fair Venus, who are alone the pleasure of men and Gods.

f17   17. The first stanza of *Im Grünen* by Voss *Gedichte* (1795) 122:

Welcome to the greensward!
The sky is blue
And the lea full of flowers!
Spring has come!
And sees itself clear
In the brook where zephyrs play
In the greensward.

18. The first stanza of *Heureigen* by Voss *Gedichte* (1795) 118:

In the cool breath of the morning we go
To the green fields,
Our scythes red in the sun, and mow
The meadow in the shining dew.
We mowers, tra, la, la lay!
We mow flowers and hay.
Hooray!

Coleridge's underlining of *ei*, *Heu*, and *hei* indicates an interest in the rhymes, possibly a question whether they represent the phonetic rhymes of dialect speech or imperfect literary rhymes. Cf 1718 and n for the sort of rhyme, and 2835 for a theoretical discussion of the question.

After the numbering of metre 18 on *f17*, the next one, "Drunk with I-dolatry . . .", was not numbered. Then *ff17ᵛ–19* inclusive deal with other matters, and on *f19ᵛ* the collecting of metres begins again, continuing with other unnumbered metres, so that it is curious to have him writing on *f21* "I have now *18* airs", even if *f20* was, as he says, "all . . . one blunder". The anomaly here is not to be explained by any theory that *ff18–20* were filled later. On *f21* he continues the numbering with a series of metres in the abstract, as it were, theoretical metres.

f17   Drunk with I-dolatry: Milton *Samson Agonistes* line 1670.

Sumptuous Dalila: ibid line 1072.

f19ᵛ   Siam passeggier . . . smarrir?: Metastasio *Isacco figura del redentore* Pt 1:

We are travellers wandering amidst winds and storms. Behold our stars, these must we follow. With such aid at hand who can be lost? With so much light before us who can wander astray?

Come il candore . . . La sua Beltà: Metastasio *Alessandro nell'Indie* III 5: *Opere* (Fausto Nicolini 4 vols Bari 1912) I 393:

Like the pure whiteness of untouched snow is the faithfulness of a noble heart: one single mark that it receives robs it of all its beauty.

ff19ᵛ–20   I observe in all the Italian Poets the . . . liberty of using Trochees . . . instead of Iambics: The Italian sections in this long entry on metres show that Coleridge was not familiar with the rules of Italian prosody, which differ somewhat from those of English. English scansion is based on the number of stressed syllables in a line, ordered in relation to the unstressed syllables, Italian on the number of syllables. In the Italian *endecasillabo* (which roughly corresponds to the English iambic pentameter in frequency of usage), examples of which Coleridge gives on *f20*, there must be eleven syllables, with a primary stress on the tenth syllable, a secondary on either the fourth or sixth (to refer only to the *endecasillabo piano*). There may be as many as five stressed syllables in a line, or as few as three, but they need occur in no special order. In the case of the seven-syllable lines that Coleridge quotes on *f21*, the primary stress must fall on the sixth syllable, but the secondary may fall on any one of the first four syllables in the line.

Del gran padre . . . legge: source not traced.

The narrow cave contains within its most hidden recess the wave of great father Ocean—the cave whence the Shepherd of the marine flock reads human destinies upon the brow of Jove.

Della piu calda Zon il cerch' accende: "It Kindles the circles of the hottest Zone." Source not traced.

Downward falling to the bottomless pit: a recollection of ". . . head-long themselvs they threw/Down from the verge of Heav'n, Eternal wrauth/Burnt after them to the bottomless pit". *Paradise Lost* VI 864–6.

f20ᵛ   Sta zitta . . . chi sarà: This is evidently a duet from one of the light operas STC heard in Italy. The numbers, which he put on in order to simplify his commentary, are no longer visible on the frayed outer margin of the page.

Be quiet! Good heavens! will you still oppose me? Larice upon the prow I can easily discern from here. What are you saying? It cannot be! If Don Larice is dead, now how ever can he be returning to this port? But what an obstinate wretch! Lesbin, just look! Alas, from where I stand I cannot see

so far. A most unworthy eye is yours, in truth! Now that the ship draws
near we shall learn who it is.

Dropping balsams, show'ring blisses: apparently Coleridge's invention; see §28 below.
Full of madness full of wine: cf *f17* above.
The 1 & 5 often transposed: he refers to the lines on the page
opposite, probably written first, this comment being fitted into a
space at the bottom of *f20ᵛ*, i.e.:
f21 Vorrei . . . ancor:

I should like him to understand me, but he does not understand me yet.

S'amor . . . ognor:

If love kindles your heart, and makes you ever sad, you will always be the
prey of the most pitiless afflictions.

Per gust'e piacere . . . Balzando mi và:

For rapture, for gladness, for joy and delight, my heart is leaping in my
breast.

the finale of the Primo atto of the V. Cant.: with this reference to the
first act of *Le Cantatrici villane*, cf 2201.
Manfred: The reference is to Vincenza Manfredini *Regole armoniche
o sieno precetti ragionati per apprendere i principj della musica* (Venice
1775). Coleridge is probably suggesting that Manfredini's precepts for
learning music are based on the system of Tartini.
Fair is foul . . . : Macbeth 1 i.
f21ᵛ 19–23. These seem to be line-endings manufactured to
convey long or short, single or double, rhyme-endings, with the ham-
mering out of new or experimental metres in mind.
    After metre 23 other matters came into *ff22–23* (2225), before the
unnumbered Morlack metres.
f23ᵛ   The Morlack Songs as given by Abbé Fortis: These verses, all
from one poem, appeared first in Jean Baptiste (called "Abbé Alberto") Fortis *Viaggio in Dalmazia* (2 vols Venice 1774) 1 98–105, in
the appendix to the second section on the customs of the Morlacchi,
with an Italian translation on the facing pages. In an English translation of the work, *Travels into Dalmatia* (1778), the poem was omitted. Coleridge could have found it in a German edition of this section
of the Abbé Fortis's travels, entitled *Reise zu den Morlacken* (Lau-

sanne 1792) 90–9. Here the Morlack appears with a German translation on the pages opposite. But comparison of the texts establishes
beyond doubt Coleridge's use of the Italian edition. In the second
line of his second quotation, he follows the *Viaggio* in a lower case for
sirotize where the *Reise* has a capital letter. More conclusive is his
reading of the last line, where *govoriaju* corresponds to the *Viaggio*
text, but not to the *Reise*, which reads *govornaju*, probably by a misprint.

The Abbé Fortis was a distinguished geologist, mineralogist, ar-
chaeologist, anthropologist, and naturalist who, to judge by the dedications in the English and Italian versions of his work (varying as to
names of recipients, but not in fulsomeness), achieved a double
patronage for his expeditions. According to the English edition, he
went under the patronage of the Earl of Bute to the Dalmatian coast
primarily to examine "the extensive strata of Fossil Bones in the
Islands of Liburnia and along the Coasts of Dalmatia" (Dedication) iv.

The Abbé Fortis included in this work observations also on the
manners and customs of the peoples he encountered, but only in the
Italian edition did he record the poem of the Morlacchi. A literal
linear translation from the Morlack has kindly been supplied by
Audrey J. Ahmad, Assistant Keeper in the Department of Printed
Books in the British Museum, as follows:

> As he was suffering from his wounds
> And he sent a message to his faithful wife:
> Do not wail for me in the white palace,
> Neither in the palace, nor among my kinsmen.
> When the Lady understood [this] speech
> She became even more miserable at the thought.
> The sound of a horse stopped by the palace:
> And Asan-Agha's wife fled
> To break her neck [by throwing herself] down from the
>   window of the tower.

This is stanza 2, lacking the last three lines. Then follow the last
two lines of stanza 5, and the first four lines of stanza 7, run together
in Coleridge's transcript. They read:

> Lest my poor heart should break
> Beholding my orphan girls [her daughters by Asan-Agha]—
> But when they were [going] past Agha's palace

Her two daughters were looking out of the window.
And her sons came out before her,
And remonstrated with their mother.

The title of the poem is *The Lament of the Noble Bride of Asan-Agha* (in Italian, *Canzone dolente della nobile sposa d'Asan Aga*). Although Coleridge is interested primarily in the metre, it is perhaps of interest to note, having regard to his quick eye for a good poem, that although in discussing them, Fortis, perhaps pandering to his British patron, compares them unfavourably with the poems of Ossian, he adds, "Yet the Morlack poetry is not destitute of merit; and has, at least, the simplicity of Homer's times, and serves to illustrate the manners of the nation", and he refers to Ovid having written verses in the Morlack language. *Travels into Dalmatia* (1792) 84.

f24 24. The first three lines from *Macbeth* I iii; Coleridge's final couplet is his fife-and-drum completion (see §26 below) of the first witch's three lines in *Macbeth* I iii.

25. Like §§19–23, rhyme and metre schemes? It is difficult here to convey in type the eccentricities of the MS.

26. See above, §24.

f24ᵛ 27. An argument, among others, for regarding the rhyme-words above as experimental.

28. Does the reference to the *Hymn on the Morning of Christ's Nativity* (and the verses) suggest that it was to be used as a model for a Pindaric ode?

Coleridge seems to be half-recollecting and transforming for metrical purposes *Paradise Lost* v lines *c* 246–88, the flight of Raphael to earth.

f25 Upon the mountain's Edge: *PW* I 393–4.

29. *PW* I 394 variatim and without the corrections dated 1805; but in a note to the selection he gives of "Metrical Experiments" EHC says, of this and the next item in this entry, "They are dated 1805, in accordance with the dates of Coleridge's own comments or afterthoughts, but it is almost certain that both sets of verses were composed in 1801." *PW* II 1014n. The evidence for this statement is not apparent, possibly no longer extant. On present knowledge, I see no reason for doubting that these are Malta entries. Attention may be called to Coleridge's interest in the themes of sun and light in Malta, natural in that Mediterranean seascape. See e.g. 2052, 2094, 2301, 2603, 2625 *ff99ᵛ–101*.

f25ᵛ 30. *PW* I 394 variatim. After this metre on *f25ᵛ*, and clearly connected with it, is 2647.

The "War-embrace of wrestling Life and Death" was of course always with him, though, again, with particular force in Malta. See entries 2100 *f3*, 2510, 2527, 2557.

f78ᵛ The discussion and collection of metres continue on the leaves with the same watermark at the back of the book. The first watermark begins again at *f74*, but *ff74–78* contain other entries, including some epigrams that are not part of this metrical entry, since, although in verse, they are clearly there for satirical and other purposes, not for any metrical interest, and are not numbered by Coleridge.

read (tho' not scan): referring presumably to the correct scansion, which in the case of *Jussit . . . loqui* would be - ᵕ ᵕ/ - - /r /- ᵕ ᵕ/ - ᵕ/ᵕ -.

[*ipse deus somno dormitos emittere vocem*] *Jussit et invitos facta tegenda loqui:* Tibullus I ix lines 27–8: "Heaven itself has bidden the lips that slumber had sealed to open and to speak unwillingly of deeds that should have lain in the dark." Tr J. P. Postgate . . . *Tibullus* . . . (LCL 1912).

Rideat assiduis is from the same source, line 54: "At te qui puerum donis corrumpere es ausus/Rideat adsiduis uxor inulta dolis": "And then who durst corrupt the boy with thy gifts, may thy wife unpunished make a constant jest of thee by her intrigues." Tr ibid.

Treasures of Gold . . . faith: not located.

f79 31. This is the fourth stanza of Schiller's *Laura am Klavier*, published first in *Anthologie auf das Jahr 1782*, but here from *Gedichte* Pt II (Leipzig 1803) 86, a fact significant for the dating of this entry.

> Now sweetly, as over smooth pebbles,
>   Silver clear the waters trickle,
>   Now in majestic glory,
>   Like the organ roll of thunder,
>   Now storming hence, as from the rocks,
>   Roaring, foaming torrents rage,
>   Now sweetly rustling
>   Blandly gentle
>   As through aspen woods
>   Caressing winds—

32. The entry is clearly and firmly written, as if copied either from print or from an earlier draft. If from the former, the source has not been found.

My secret heart dies away within me and all the time hope maddens me with its unresting torment. O you who foster a quiet mind in the face of unquiet

destiny, take away hope from my afflicted spirit. If my lips were not con-
fronted with the fruit of the tree, and with springs that in their fleeting
course cheat my thirst, part of the torture of Tantalus—O how great a
part—would recede.

f79ᵛ 34. If this is the scheme of published verses, they have not been
traced.

35. *PW* II 1015, entitled *Iambics*.

37. The first stanza of *Der Genius* in *Gedichte der Brüder Christian
und Friedrich Leopold Grafen zu Stolberg* (Leipzig 1779) 16. Coleridge
transposed the first two verbs in the last line.

> The weak pinion is not stirred by the ether,
> But in its rocky nest the eagle feels
> Full of its own power, lifts its wing,
> Soars and swoops, and drinks the sun.

f80 38. The lines, full of Miltonic echoes, are, except for the fourth
line as cited above, not Milton's. In *PW* II 1014–15.

f80ᵛ 41. *Adaptation of M[etre] 25—Trochaics: PW* II 1015, dated
1801.

f81 The two stanzas are a Stolberg poem, *An Röschen: Gedichte*
(1779) 52. There is an interesting change in the third line of the
second stanza, where Coleridge writes *meinem* for *unserm*, possibly a
hint at solitariness, though here not devastating.

> Sweetheart Rosie, see how brightly,
> Among the honeysuckle, this stream
> Flows on through forget-me-nots!
> But there it falls, roaring torrent,
> Where, with thunder's peal
> And the valley's echo,
> It pours itself over rocks and crags.
>
> But to me it is sweeter
> Here, my dearest Rosie,
> For it's like our life together!
> When I see it now, so gentle and clear,
> Gliding in the light of the moon,
> Rosie, then I think of you,
> And tears of joy quiver.

42. *PW* I 409. Whenever they were written in this notebook, the
lines were probably composed earlier than Malta; they read like
1800–2. EHC dates them 1801.

They are an adaptation and translation of the German lines above, numbered metre 6, "In diesem Wald . . ." by Hagedorn.

ff81ᵛ–82ᵛ   43. *PW* I 409–10 variatim, with the addition of two stanzas at the end. EHC suggests, without noticing the contradictions, that the first stanza may have been written at Malta, that stanzas 1–4 may have been drafted in 1801, and that the last two additional stanzas of his version (not in this entry) are not contemporary with the first four, but may belong to 1814–15. At this last date, *Sibylline Leaves*, where the whole poem as he prints it first appeared, was being prepared for publication. He dates the poem, however, 1807—a sufficient illustration of the range of possible dates for these "metrical experiments" in this notebook.

The second stanza on *f82ᵛ*, "No voice as yet had made the air . . .", is crowded in beside the previous one, for which it is clearly a second draft, difficult to read. EHC read, "That asking look? that yearning sigh?/That sense of promise everywhere?"

f83   44. *PW* II 1017, undated.

[*44a*] *Nonsense Verses for the trial of the Metre:* written vertically up the outer margin of the page, later than the others on the same page. The first obliterated word, in line 3, is entirely blotted out; the last part of the last line probably may be construed: "and lust as lust."

45. *PW* II 1017.

f83ᵛ   46. *PW* II 1017.

47. *PW* II 1016; in the third line EHC incorrectly reads "endlessly mighty". On the Mohammed theme, see also 2780n.

48. Unpublished lines; some images appear to be refractions from *The Keepsake* and *The Picture (PW* I 345–6, 369–74).

f85ᵛ   49. The discussion seems to belong with this entry, admittedly composite and impossible to date in all its segments; but unless this memorandum was set about three lines low on a blank page, it followed a long excerpt from Chaucer, which in turn followed a comment on the Wordsworths written after the alienation, probably *c* 1811–12. In other words, though it may belong with the 1804–5 parts of this entry, it could be, along with the Chaucer that precedes it, material for the 1811–12 lectures or an even later entry. The relation of notebook memoranda to the various courses of lectures is a problem probably defying satisfactory elucidation; it is also possible that this part of this entry was related to the lectures of 1818.

The entry could not be continued on *f86* because Jane Burr's epitaph was already there, i.e. 2779.

Daniel's *Epistle to the Lady Margaret, Countess of Cumberland* is in Daniel *Works* (1718) II 352–5, the edition that Coleridge sent to the Beaumonts 8 March 1804 (1901n), and also in *B Poets* IV 204–5; in both works "the Epistle preceding" is the one *To the Lord Henry Howard*, of which the metre is as Coleridge describes it. The metrical scheme of the *Epistle to the Lady Margaret*, as he proposed to vary it, he jotted down at 3210.

2225 22.17   The pages on which this entry was written were left blank, apparently for more metrical examples following 2224 *f21ᵛ*; the entry does not fill up the entire space left. It may therefore be of much later date. On the other hand, when Coleridge was reading Brougham's *Inquiry into the Colonial Policy of the European Powers* (1803), he recalled Gravina and used his arguments, against Brougham, and in the same breath "Lardner's first vol. of his Credibility", a work he had read early. (MS Egerton 2800 ff 106–7). These reading notes are quoted in part in *Inq Sp* §§215 and 267.

The passage is from Giovanni Vincenzo Gravina *De romano imperio liber singularis ad S.P.Q.R.* §§19 and 20; in the edition of the *Opera* (Leipzig 1737) II 499–500, with some omissions and minor changes.

Tr: That was the important issue: to establish an emperor, not a king; because an emperor, once acknowledged, derives his sovereign power from the people, whereas a king deflects power from the people to himself. For when a king is established—a king of the kind set up by the barbarians whose mean subjection the Romans always detested—the whole common power of the people is forthwith conferred upon him: in fact he is, like the King of the Persians, an autocrat accountable to nobody, so that if the people try to get rid of that leader at any time on the grounds that he is disturbing the human and divine law and the lives of others and seizing their goods, they are forced to upset the civil order and alter the public will—in effect found a new state. And so that the citizens should not be subdued in the event that the royal power overturned the people's sovereignty, they would insist that he take an oath on the laws; so that he whose power could not be more fully controlled by the people without overthrowing the kingdom should be restrained by the authority of established law and by [the threat of] divine vengeance. But a Roman emperor, in assuming—or at least absorbing—the sovereignty of the Senate and People of Rome, was able, and always was able, if he abused his authority, and was not beset by military violence, to abdicate from his office or from life, without any change in the civil order or alteration of the state. Therefore when an emperor was to be made, the people did not insist that he take an oath on the laws, because while the people's sovereignty was vested in the People and the Senate, they could always avoid violence at his hands. Certainly kingship exhausts a whole state, in as much as it transfers the whole sovereignty to the person of one man or his successors.

Emperorship, on the other hand, is a concentration of civil offices—&c. So Dion did not clearly understand the idea of "the sovereign People" when he showed surprise at the Roman people for conferring royal power upon an emperor through a number of civil offices and yet rejoicing that they did not have to put up with a king. Admittedly Dion was a senator, but he had a Greek way of looking at things and was not [speaking] altogether in earnest; and the Roman people were weighing up the difference between a king and a magistrate endowed with royal power, and considering whether [it was to be] a civil office like that of the consuls who were established with royal authority and had in fact taken the succession in the place of kings. And so just as the consuls were, so also the emperor was part of the whole state; and under its authority they were, together with the other magistrates, all held in check.

postquam . . . civitatis: "by the validation of time and the confirmation of use and civil agreement".

nefas . . . Voluntates: "it is a crime that the whims of Commodus and Caracalla and of ignorant men should be regarded as laws".

2226 15.90   *Cava Secchia:* see 2177.

2227 15.91   Ink.
The Hospital Amer[ican]: American forces were in the Mediterranean because the United States was at war with Tripoli. They had a naval hospital at their base in Syracuse. See also the next note.

2228 15.92   Ink.
These stories of the Davy Crockett type were apparently preserved for future use, especially the first one with its details of moments of fear none of which seem to have escaped this listener.

Commodore Prebell was Edward Preble (1761–1807), who from 1803 was in command of the third American naval squadron in the war against Tripoli until in Sept 1804 he was superseded. He is said to have been tall, distinguished, naturally irascible, severe, but respected despite his "rough exterior".

Decatur: Stephen Decatur (1779–1820) was altogether a more interesting character. This was his second trip to the Mediterranean, he having been returned home in 1802 for involvement in a duel in which the secretary to the Governor of Malta was killed. Returning to Sicily in 1803, and hearing that the American frigate *Philadelphia* had been captured by the Tripolitans, he stole into the harbour at Tripoli in Feb 1804 and destroyed the ship. The event made a stir; Decatur was given a captain's commission in Sept 1804, and the command of the *Constitution*, then overhauling at Malta. He was perhaps "the most striking figure of the war" (*DAB*) and to him is attributed the phrase "our country, right or wrong".

Presumably he and Preble were on leave at this time, in Sicily. Coleridge quoted Decatur in Malta (*Friend* II 183–4 and *TT* 9 June 1832) as opposing too great expansion of the U. S., such as the annexation of Louisiana, and Canada. It is worth noticing that Coleridge's Malta experiences extended his knowledge of Americans.

2230 15.94   Ink. Presumably an anecdote of the Governor of Sicily and Commodore Preble. Coleridge was to have a dramatic encounter with the same Governor later, in a piratical affair, which he reported in full in no very complimentary terms to Sir Alexander Ball. *CL* # 609 and 610.

2231 15.95   Ink. The question of taxation in Sicily agitated Coleridge all his life as a root cause of Sicilian poverty. See *TT* 16 April 1834. Cf 2213 and n.

2232 15.96   Ink. The journey referred to in 2177?

2233 15.97   Ink. See 2226 for more wild life in this place.

2234 15.98   Ink. There is a Capuchin monastery at Syracuse, beside the Latomia de' Cappuccini. On the Italian desire to be English, see 2162.

2235 15.99   Ink. Cf 2221.

2236 21.465   *pictured Title page:* i.e. an engraved title-page in addition to the elaborate printed title-page. The Greek and Latin titles of the *De venatione* of Arrian and the *Enchiridion* and *Apophthegms* of Epictetus are both set in capitals, each with the first word displayed in a large letter, the following words arranged in an inverted and truncated triangle:

"APPIANOY/TEXNH ΤΑΚΤΙΚΗ, ΕΚΤΑΞΙΣ ΚΑΤ ΑΛΑ-/ΝΩΝ,
ΠΕΡΙΠΛΟΥΣ ΠΟΝΤΟΥ ΕΥΞΕΙ-/ΝΟΥ, ΠΕΡΙΠΛΟΥΣ ΤΗΣ ΕΡΥΘ-
ΡΑΣ ΘΑ-/ΛΑΣΣΗΣ, ΚΥΝΗΓΕΤΙΚΟΣ, ΕΠΙΚΤΗ-/ΤΟΥ ΕΓΧΕΙΡΙΔ-
ΙΟΝ, ΤΟΥ ΑΥΤΟΥ ΑΠΟΦ-/ΘΕΓΜΑΤΑ ΚΑΙ ΑΠΟΣΠΑΣΜΑΤΙΑ,/Α
ΕΝ ΤΩ ΙΩΑΝΝΟΥ ΣΤΟΒΑΙΟΥ ΑΝ-/ΘΟΛΟΓΙΩ, ΚΑΙ ΕΝ ΤΑΙΣ ΑΓ-
ΕΛΛΙΟΥ/ΑΓΡΥΠΝΙΑΙΣ ΑΤΤΙΚΑΙΣ ΣΩΣΟ-/MENA./ ARRIANI/
ARS TACTICA, ACIES CONTRA ALANOS,/PERIPLVS PONTI
EVXINI, PERIPLVS/MARIS ERYTHRAEI, LIBER DE VENA-/
TIONE, EPICTETI ENCHIRIDION,/EJVSDEM APOPTHEG-
MATA ET/FRAGMENTA, QVAE IN JOAN-/NIS STOBAEI
FLORILEGIO, ET/IN AGELLII NOCTIBVS AT-/TICIS SVPER-
SVNT./ Cum Interpretibus Latinis, & Notis./ Ex Recensione &
Museo/NICOLAI BLANCARDI./*AMSTELODAMI*/[long hair-line
rule]/Apud JANSSONIO-WAESBERGIOS. 1683."

The engraved title-page has at the head, within a labelled banner:
"ΑΡΡΙΑΝΟΥ ΤΑΚΤΙΚΑ, ΠΕΡΙ-/ΠΛΟΙ, ΚΥΝΗΓΕΤΙΚΟΣ, ΚΑΙ/ΕΠΙ-
ΚΤΗΤΟΥ ΣΤΟΙΚΟΥ/ΕΓΧΕΙΡΙΔΙΟΝ. [At the foot, within a scalloped
lozenge:] AMSTELODAMI,/Apud JANSSONIO-WAESBERGIOS 1683."

Between these two, the engraved title-page is equally divided into
three horizontal lozenges, with scalloped decoration; the bottom
lozenge divided vertically into two. These contain scenes illustrating
the contents. (*a*) Top. On the left an army of foot-soldiers with spears
and banners held upright; on the right an army of mounted horse-
soldiers with lances and banners held upright; all drawn up in battle
order with a mounted leader in front of each. (*b*) Middle. A hunting
scene in open woodland with two low hills behind; on the left a stag
being brought down by hounds; on the right a boar standing at bay
with hounds attacking, and a woman (?Diana with a crescent) aiming
a spear at the boar. (*c*) Bottom left. Two ancient warships engaging,
both with lateen sail set and oars shipped. (*d*) Bottom right. Epictetus
seated at a table, with a pair of scales in his right hand and a tablet
or scroll supported by his left, holding forth to six aged auditors.

The engraving is signed below (*d*): Joh. van den Avele fecit.

For some account of the Greek types used in this edition see Charles
Enschedé *Fonderies de caractères et leur matériel dans les Pays-Bas
du xve au xixe siècle* (Haarlem 1908) 85–94 and fig 76 (p 89) reproduc-
ing two columns of Greek from this edition of Arrian. These types,
rich in ligatures and contractions, are singularly graceful. Coming
from the Frankfurt Lutheran foundry established in the sixteenth
century, they enjoyed a wide reputation and were supplied to the

celebrated Elzevirs of Leyden, and to almost all the Dutch printers of Greek and Latin texts in the seventeenth century. In 1807–8 Coleridge was still looking for another copy of this work, of which the description above serves to indicate his eye for and interest in fine book-making, and his ability to read and transcribe from an old highly-ligatured Greek type.

L refers to Leckie; see 2193n.

Coleridge follows the 1683 text exactly (though disregarding pointing), with these exceptions:

ƒ106ᵛ   συμβολα *for* ξύμβολα

        χαραπωτατην *for* χαρωποτάτην

        τεταρσιν *for* τέτταρσιν

        ηδε ποτε *for* ἤδη ποτὲ

ƒ107   και *for* καὶ τῷ *before* ασπασμῳ

        φθωνη *for* φωνῇ

        μαγιστι [*for* μάστιγι] (following a typographical error in 1683 text)

        μαγιστα *for* μάστιγα (although the 1683 text is here correct)

        ονομασοντι, υποπτηξασα *for* ὀνομάσαντι, καὶ ὑποπτήξασα

ƒ107ᵛ   αναρραψαι *for* ἀναγράψαι

        απολελειφθαι *for* ἀπολελεῖφται in the 1683 text (correcting the typographical error)

Tr: [He is discussing the points of greyhounds—their eyes.] . . . and last of all, grey: nor are these to be considered bad, nor indicative of bad dogs, provided they are clear, & have a savage look.

[Chap v] For I have myself bred up a hound whose eyes are the greyest of the grey; a swift, hard-working, courageous, sound-footed dog, and, in his prime, a match, at any time, for four hares. He is, moreover, (for while I am writing, he is yet alive), most gentle, and kindly-affectioned; and never before had any dog such regard for myself, and friend & fellow-sportsman, Megithus. For when not actually engaged in coursing, he is never away from one or other of us. But while I am at home he remains in by my side, accompanies me on going abroad, follows me to the gymnasium, and, while I am taking exercize, sits down by me. On my return he runs before me, often looking back to see whether I had turned anywhere out of the road; and as soon as he catches sight of me, showing symptoms of joy, and again trotting on before me. If I am going out on any government business, he remains with my friend, and does exactly the same towards him. He is the constant companion of whichever may be sick; and if he has not seen either of us for only a short time, he jumps up repeatedly by way of salutation, and barks with joy, as a greeting to us. At meets he pats us first with one foot and then with the other, to put us in mind that he is to have his share of food. He has also many tones of speech—more than I ever knew in any other dog—pointing out, in his own language, whatever he wants.

Having been beaten, when a puppy, with a whip, if any one, even at this day, does but mention a whip, he will come up to the speaker cowering and begging, applying his mouth to the man's as if to kiss him, and jumping up, will hang on his neck, and will not let him go until he has appeased his angry threats.

Now really I do not think that I should be ashamed to write even the name of this dog; that it may be left to posterity, that Xenophon the Athenian had a greyhound called Horme, of the greatest speed and intelligence, and altogether supremely excellent.—*Arrian on Coursing. The Cynegeticus of the Younger Xenophon translated by "A Graduate of Medicine"* (London 1831) 78–82.

In a charmingly modest preface, this "graduate of medicine" says that he "does not aim at pleasing the mere literary man" but that he has addressed himself to "the coursing public". In fact, as the above passage shows, William Dansey was an admirable translator.

2237 21.466   The usual error about his birthday; he was born 21 Oct 1772. Cf 6n and 997n.

This is the last of the Sicilian-tour entries in this notebook. There are four leaves cut out after this one; the paginating is uninterrupted and hence must have been done after the excising.

2238 15.100   For Coleridge on dancing cf the references in 415n as well as 2363.

2239 15.101   Coleridge is visiting the latomies or slate quarries known as the Latomia del Paradiso. Like most tourists, he experiments with the extraordinary acoustics in the artificial grotto, the Ear of Dionysius, by making sounds with voice, paper, etc, and marvels at the stalactite-like pillars in the large open cavern in which for generations the rope-makers have made use of the peculiarly suitable atmospheric conditions to make a strong hempen rope.

2240 15.102   On the Sicilian desire to be English, cf 2162 and 2234.

2241 15.103   *Lolium:* darnel; *Lolium perenne* is rye-grass.

2242 15.104   Catacombs about Syracuse are of course numerous;
is he thinking of the old—or of children—so buried? The latter would
be a more characteristic thought.

2244 15.122   The cathedral church of Syracuse, S Maria delle
Colonne, is built on the site of the ancient temple of Minerva, and the
cherubim still look up at the Virgin on the ornate modern front in the
way Coleridge describes. I could not find out in Syracuse that it had
ever been called St Paul's, but the difficulty of finding *any* name to
attach to it seemed to make Coleridge's error intelligible enough.
(There is a St Paul's in Malta.) The calm beauty of the ancient columns, twelve of which are still standing, is in marked contrast with
the early eighteenth-century baroque façade.
   With the *John Nobodies* cf those in 2370.

2245 15.123   The reference to Sara Hutchinson is plain. Cf 472
                and 1549.

2246 15.124   A recollection of a water-image in the rope-makers'
cavern in the Latomia del Paradiso in Syracuse. See 2239.

2247 15.106   Ink. The fig is used for fodder.

2248 15.107   Ink. See 2227 and n.

2249 15.108   Ink. Coleridge was clearly fascinated by this wild,
somewhat weird place. See *CN* II Index 3: Spampinato, Cava di.

2250 15.109   Ink.
consuetudine: according to custom.
salm: a Sicilian measure, not Italian. "The measure of land and the
measure of corn bear the same name (*salma*), a salm of wheat being
the usual quantity allowed for sowing a salm of land. A salm of land
is about equal to four English acres, and a salm of corn to eight
Winchester bushels." G. W. D. Evans *The Classic and Connoisseur
in Italy and Sicily* (London 1835) II 373n.
   William Henry Smyth defines a salm of land as 5½ English acres,
and a *salma generale* as 20 English bushels. *Memoir descriptive of the
Resources, Inhabitants, and Hydrography, of Sicily and the islands,
interspersed with antiquarian and other notices* (London 1824) lxii.

Terragio: he is mishearing the Sicilian pronunciation of *terrazzo*, for *level*.

ounces: onza, Sicilan coinage, about 12s. 6d. in the exchange of the period.

2251 15.110   The entries from here to 2261 belong to the last days of this visit to Syracuse. Coleridge returned to Malta 7 Nov just as he was about to set out for Messina and to circle the island; and he was in Valletta harbour awaiting release from quarantine on the morning of 8 Nov. *CL* # 610.

2252 15.111   *Captn Arden:* an American officer?

2253 15.112   *Capt. Baron* may have been Samuel Barron, who had superseded Edward Preble as Commodore of the American Mediterranean fleet in Sept 1804; but in view of Coleridge's reference to him, still in November, as captain, we may suppose it to be a younger brother, Capt James Barron (1769–1851). He also was active in the war, and in command first of the frigate *Essex* and then of the frigate *President.* In 1820 he was to kill Stephen Decatur in a duel. See 2228n.

2254 15.113   There is no evidence, unless this entry can be so regarded, that Coleridge visited Palermo. That he would naturally go there seems so likely that one speculates about a lost notebook.

2255 15.114   *Restuccia* and *Terriozza* are both local Sicilian words. Only *Maggesi* is standard Italian, for *fallow land.*

2256 15.115   On Mrs Leckie, see 2467n.

2257 15.116   The report of an earthquake at Almería, a town in the south of Spain, possibly came from one of Coleridge's naval acquaintances; the reference to alligators would interest him. See 218 and n; perhaps the alligators in the continuation of *The Wanderings of Cain* came, as EHC suggests, from Bartram's *Travels,* there quoted, or, they may be Almerian alligators, or again, they may be a composite, and the latter may well have been noted because of the earlier reading. The date of the MS fragment of the continuation of *The Wanderings of Cain* is more problematical than EHC suggests. Cf *PW* 1 285n. See 2780 and n.

2258 15.117   A badly written entry, and, at the end, faded and rubbed. The *Pharo*—crossed out—was perhaps the Pharos peninsula and lighthouse at the entrance to the harbour of Alexandria.

2259 15.118   This entry appears to have come out of conversation with Leckie, who as well as being honorary consul was a landowner in Sicily (*CL* # 609) and had also been in India and was interested in Indian agriculture. See Tract III of his *Historical Survey* referred to in 2193n.

2260 15.119   Possibly sea water accounts for the faded difficult readings in this and the preceding entries.
[*?Perrit*]*uri* [? for *paratori*]: possibly, the sluices referred to in 2214 and n.

2261 15.120   Ink. An entry derived partly from Leckie, partly from some local guide-book on history, and partly from observation.
zusammengeschrumpft: shrunk together.
doctissima civitas of Cicero: Cicero was *quaestor* in Sicily in 75 B.C. and uses this phrase of Syracuse—"most learned city"—in the *Tusculan Disputations* v 66.
the Emperor Joseph: Joseph II of Austria carried out a series of restrictions of Church authority both in Austria and in Lombardy. In 1783 he visited Florence, Rome, and Naples; Mrs Piozzi says that he and his brother Leopold, the Grand Duke of Tuscany, attempted to persuade the King of Naples to carry out similar reforms in his own dominions, with very little success. Hester Lynch Piozzi *Observations . . . of a Journey through . . . Italy* (2 vols London 1789) II 26. She fills out the account in Ludwig, Freiherr von Pastor *The History of the Popes* Vol XXXIX tr E. F. Peeler (1952) Chap VIII.
Frederic the Simple: Frederick III, King of Sicily, who married the daughter of the King of Aragon.
Sanphilippo: San Filippo d'Argiro.
Vizini: Vizzini.
Capitano di Giustizia: the magistrate.
The information in the last paragraph is found in Leckie's *Historical Survey* 64, where for "Senate" he writes "the corporation of almost each town", and denounces this law, "the absurdity and barbarity of which is unknown in any other part of the world". Cf 2213n.

2262 21.333   This and the three entries that follow it are in small
writing and seem to belong together either to Malta, July–Aug, or to
Sicily, Aug–Nov 1804. Coleridge might have found his list of Bruno's
works (2264) in Leckie's library, and also the Abbé Fortis's *Viaggio
in Dalmazia* (2265); on the other hand, he associated Bruno with
Malta, and later wanted again a rare volume he had seen there. See
2264n. The Fortis work could have been found, presumably, in either
place.

This anecdote is expanded in *Omniana* II 29. The joke hinges on
two meanings of the Greek word φοῖνιξ: the upper pith or brain of
the palm-tree, and phoenix, the bird. Plutarch refers to the first, STC
with delight seizes on the second.

2263 21.334   A reminiscence of Browne *Pseudodoxia Epidemica*
Bk III Chap XII, this entry was used in *Omniana* II 30, with the addition of an interesting comment on Claudian.

2264 21.335   In a footnote to *The Friend* that appears in all three
editions, Coleridge refers to "eleven works the titles of which are
preserved to us", and says he has seen six. *Friend* (1818) I 194n. This
entry is his list of the eleven, jotted down from memory, with some
slips in the Italian titles. The correct titles of the first editions are as
follows:

1. *De umbris idearum* (Paris 1582)
2. *Camoeracensis acrotismus* (Wittenberg 1588)
3. *De progressu et lampade venatoria logicorum* (Wittenberg 1587)
4. *Articuli centum et sexaginta adversus hujus tempestatis mathema-
ticos atque philosophos* (Prague 1588)
5. *Candelaio. Comedia* (Paris 1582)
6. *Spaccio de la bestia trionfante* (Paris [London] 1584)
7. *La cena dele ceneri* (London 1584)
8. Either *Dialogi idiota triumphans* (Paris 1586) or, more likely,
*Dialogi duo de Fabricii Mordentis Salernitani prope divina adin-
ventione ad perfectam cosmimetriae praxim* (Paris 1586)
9. *De l'infinito universo et mondi* (Venice 1584)
10. *De triplici minimo et mensura* (Frankfurt 1591)
11. *Explicatio triginta sigillorum* refers to the *Ars reminiscendi* or
Recens et completa ars reminiscendi (London 1583)
The titles, with fifteen others, are listed by John Hayward in "The
Location of Copies of the First Editions of Giordano Bruno" *The*

Book Collector v (Summer 1956) 152–7. It is curious that Coleridge forgot to include in his list the *De monade, numero et figurâ liber consequens quinque de minimò magno et mensura* (Frankfurt 1591) or the poem *De immenso* (included in that volume), which he so greatly admired. See 927, 928, 929.

In a later note, *c* 1810 (in N 18), he wishes to see again, to the extent of thinking of sending for it to Malta through official sources, what he calls the *Logica Venatrix* (i.e. 3 above) of Bruno.

See also 927n.

2265 21.336   This is §16, "Della Manna di Coslovaz", from Fortis *Viaggio in Dalmazia* 1 36. (See also 2224 *f23ᵛ* and n.)

Coslovaz (in Dalmatia) is a poor place, like the other hamlets in this country-side; but the woods of the district abound in ash-trees, which give manna in abundance when they are properly tapped. The Morlacks do not know how to tap them, and they did not know of this product. Two years ago someone went there with the permission of the government to make experiments. They did not correspond at once to the hopes he had conceived because the air had become somewhat chilly. The experimenter lost patience, and abandoned the tapped trees. When the warm weather returned they produced a prodigious quantity of manna, which the Morlacks avidly took and ate, finding it sweet. Several of them were brought close to death by violent diarrhoea; the manna after a few days was abandoned to the pigs and turkeys.

2266 21.337   *AP* 87. Coleridge's ship was held in quarantine 8–10 Nov 1804. See *CL* # 610.

2267 21.338   Coleridge is remembering the tractate "On Memory and Recollection", in the *Parva naturalia* (see 973A and n), where the distinction made in the title is discussed throughout. But the passage STC probably has in mind is 453ᵃ: "Recollecting differs from memory not merely in the matter of time, but also because many other living creatures share in memory, but *none of the known so-called animals can recollect except man.* This is because recollecting implies a process of reasoning; for when a man is recollecting he reasons that he has seen or heard or experienced something of the sort before, and the process is a kind of search. This power can only belong by nature to such animals as have a power of deliberation; and deliberation is a process of reasoning." Tr W. S. Hett (LCL 1935).

This work was clearly important to Coleridge, to judge from the
frequent references to it. This entry was used in *Omniana* II 30 and in
a letter of 7 Feb 1808. *CL* # 680. And see 2973 and n.

2268 21.467   Search for this ceiling in Malta was fruitless, the old
Treasury having been much damaged by bombs 1940–43. See 2370.

2269 21.468   The missing word or two was lost when the top half
of the leaf was cut out. Swedenborgianism interested Coleridge very
early. See 165n. On Sir Thomas Browne and the copy of his works
Coleridge took to Malta, see 1961 and 2014n. Of Coleridge's reading
of Thomas More, we know little; there is one reference in *MC* 276
and that of the most general sort.

quod Sanitatem: for health's sake(?).

2271 21.470   *AP* 83–4. See also *Friend* III 294, 318–19, where these
ideas are used in the eulogy of Sir Alexander Ball.

2272 21.339   Presumably Coleridge received this number of the
Courier in November on or soon after his arrival back in Malta 10
Nov 1804. The entry after the words "St. Paul" is a newspaper clip-
ping pasted into the book; the italics are Coleridge's and the "N.B."
The tradition linking St Paul's shipwreck with Malta made the
association inevitable; Coleridge's slant here in the direction of higher
criticism is perhaps a reflection of his Göttingen studies and certainly
a foretaste of his New Testament criticism still to come.

2273 21.340   Source not traced.

2274 21.341   *AP* 87. This appears to be another early expression
by Coleridge of the imitation-copy distinction. See 2211. The date
here is admittedly difficult to determine: EHC assigns the entry to
Nov–Dec 1804, and is probably right in so doing, but an 1808 date is
possible, close to the period of 21.351 (to appear in a later volume) and
the Royal Institution lectures on poetry. Entries 2273–2276 and
2676 could all belong to *c* Feb 1808, but not 2672. To date this present
entry, 2274, in 1808, one must assume in regard to 2578 that Denison
was handed the book open at a blank page for his inscription (there is
evidence, e.g. 2381, pointing to this as Coleridge's practice) and that
Coleridge later, in 1808, added the memorandum about his own

movements, 2676, in the extravagant gap Denison left between his lines. The most telling argument, supported by the evidence from the physical appearance of the pages, for the date here assigned is that the subject-matter of this entry was clearly in Coleridge's thoughts, in just this way, in Oct–Dec 1804. See 2211 and 2382.

sense of the analogy . . . which enables a Symbol to represent: cf Wordsworth's "Analogous, the moon to me was dear". *Prelude* (1805) II 196.

2275 21.342   *AP* 86. The "&c" suggests a quotation, perhaps a self-quotation? Cf "There is a grace that would enable us to take up vipers, and the evil thing shall not hurt us: a spiritual alchemy which can transmute poisons into a panacæa." *SM* 44.

2276 21.343   In a large hand, in pencil.
Commander's Balsam is described in Dr Robert James *Medicinal Dictionary* (1743) as compounded of various herbs steeped in wine, useful for gun-shot or other wounds, bites of venomous animals, toothache, the colic. It was chiefly for external application; but for internal use, five or six drops was the maximum dose suggested. Possibly this overdose contributed to C's illness in the spring of 1805; see *CL* # 616.

2277 21.471   *M. M.:* the reading is not absolutely certain. *His Majesty's Ministers?* Coleridge clearly disliked officialdom. Cf the "flowers of Oratory" in 2451 and 2107.

2278 21.472   *Itaque . . . liberatur:* "And so it comes about that ignorance is absolved even of disgrace." Source not traced.

2279 21.473   *AP* 84 variatim. The name "Sara" is almost obliterated; EHC omitted it from his text.
Soother of Absence: see 1541n.
Joy . . . the gladness of Joy: cf *Dejection: an Ode,* stanza v; and with the "quiet fountain" image, cf *Inscription for a Fountain on a Heath* (*PW* I 381–2) and 980n. See also 921, 1394, 1577, and 1609.

2280 21.474   *AP* 85. Coleridge elsewhere refers to the beauty of the *sparonaras.* See 2400 and 2705 *f94.* They are small boats propelled by fixed oars pushed by a rower facing forwards, and usually from a standing position; they were designed for speed, chiefly to escape pirates.

2281 15.121   This entry at the bottom of *f66* was apparently inserted later than the neighbouring entries. It refers to a village in Malta, seen, with its great dome, from the ramparts of the old city of M'dina. On the Botanical Gardens, see the next note.

2282 15.125   The Argotti Gardens in Floriana are the Botanical Gardens of the university. They were finished, according to Ball, by July 1804; his report said they would soon pay for themselves, that they were begun to pacify discontent when walks in the Garrison were denied to the Maltese by a British military order, and to provide hot weather walks, and work for the Maltese. The same dispatch tells of other public works completed or advocated, e.g. a fish-market, and bathing facilities. CO 158.9.

In the uncultivated area near Luqa, an experimental farm was later founded. This entry may perhaps indicate that the suggestion was made by Coleridge to Ball.

2283 15.126   Withering of plant life? Or—Withering, the botanist? See 863n.

2284 15.127   For whatever reason, this entry was repeated in March 1805 in 2498. Cf 2114 and 2614.

2285 15.128   *No Nob:* presumably in the slang sense, meaning an aristocracy is not possible without the "swells"?

2286 15.129   The story of this episode in the sixth year of the reign of Richard II is told in many places, but Coleridge probably found it in Nicolson and Burn *The History . . . of . . . Westmorland and Cumberland* (1777) II 5, which we know he was reading in Malta. See 2443.

2287 15.130   *the Pietà:* a wharf, a great thoroughfare, repaired in 1804.

Locust Trees: acacia, as in N America.

2288 15.131   Coleridge was inadequately informed. The failure to complete the Birca Cara church was owing to a dispute between factions in the church; the winning side built a large new church in the village of Birca Cara; the old one is now a ruin.

2289 15.132   Largely traced over in ink; the order of the words is confused.

Cactus opuntia: a common Mediterranean shrub; capers are frequently found on the bastions of Valletta.

The last sentence refers to the beauty of Maltese stonework (cf *TT* 18 Aug 1832) and the abundance of good fruit.

2290 15.133   Premonitions were doubtless a subject with naval men. He refers of course to the escapade of Silas Tomkyn Comberbacke with the King's Regiment at Reading in 1793–4; there seems to be telescoped with this runaway episode, the earlier flight, at the age of seven, into the fields near Ottery. See 1416 and *CL* # 210.

2291 21.475   το γελοιον: literally, the "laughable" or "funny" thing. Here, the "ludicrous" or "ridiculous" thing?

2292 21.476   This memorandum occurs more than once, a sign of its having been difficult for him to remember?

2293 21.477   *The evening Gun* comes into at least two MS annotations on *The Ancient Mariner,* noticed by Lowes. The context there is the "No twilight within the courts of the Sun" of the marginal gloss, and though "the evening Gun" is located in the West Indies, the observation of light at this time of day as in this entry, together with talk with naval officers from the West Indies that took place in Malta, may link the gloss with Coleridge's experiences in Malta. See *RX* 165–7 and Bald 14–15.

2294 21.478   Used in a footnote on the economic importance of cotton to Malta, *Friend* III 368n. A letter from Alexander Macaulay, in 1800, in the PRO, refers to one of "the most profitable productions of this Island, which is Cotton both white and red. They manufacture it into coarse Cloth for their own consumption but from the clumsiness of their machinery (the Maltese have not the fingers of the Native of the East) the Cotton Cloth they manufacture is too coarse and too dear for any foreign market but the Coast of Barbary. The exportation of Cotton Wool is very wisely prohibited as the spinning of it is the chief business of industry among the Poor and very necessary for their support, but they annually export into Spain, Cotton-thread to the amount of above half a million sterling. . . ." WO 1.291 ff 368ᵛ-9.

It is clear that cotton-seed was plentiful, and that Coleridge was probably concerned about a better use for it than feeding livestock. See Appendix B, the *Avviso* of 22 March 1805.

2295 21.479   *Tab:* a reference to some government house visitor? Or to Tab[le Talk]? The person quoted could be G. F. Leckie, "the one blemish of importance" in whose work on the state of Sicily, Coleridge said later, was that "he appears too frequently to consider justice and true policy as capable of being contradistinguished". *Friend* III 330n.

2296 21.480   *AP* 85-6. The entry may well have been suggested by the *Select Discourses* of John Smith (quoted in 2164-2167), where all these subjects are discussed, or it may have been aroused by such complacency as Lady Ball's; see 2324 and 2113.

2297 21.481   Bryan Edwards, *The History, Civil and Commercial, of the British Colonies in the West Indies* (3 vols 3rd ed 1801). Coleridge had borrowed the first edition from the Bristol Library in 1795. *Bristol Borrowings* (64).

The passage referred to here at II 108 is referred to in the introduction to Parts III & IV of *The Three Graves*, first printed in *The Friend* (1809); see *PW* I 269. It has to do with the "Myal-men, or those who by means of a narcotick potion, made with the juice of an herb (said to be the branched *Calalue* or species of *Solanum*) which occasions a trance or profound sleep of a certain duration, endeavour to convince the deluded spectators of their power to re-animate dead bodies". Reading on to pp 110 and 111 Coleridge found a general description of what he particularized in *The Three Graves*. Edwards describes how a Negro receives "the fearful news" that an Obi is in pursuit of him, and how "his terrified imagination begins to work" and how "presently he falls into a decline, under the incessant horror of impending calamities. . . . Sleep, appetite, and cheerfulness forsake him, his strength decays, his disturbed imagination is haunted without respite, his features wear the settled gloom of despondency: dirt, or any other unwholesome substance, become his only food, he contracts a morbid habit of body, and gradually sinks into the grave. . . . Those anomalous symptoms which originate from causes deeply rooted in the mind, such as the terrors of Obi, or from poisons, whose operation is slow and intricate, will baffle the skill of the ablest physician." On pp 114–17 there is an account of a malevolent Obeah-woman.

The "foolish business" for which he read the work may have been "Observations on Egypt" (BM Egerton MS 2800 ff 118–26). This was probably either an official report for Ball or a piece intended for the *Courier*. An "Appendix to Observations on Egypt" (VCL MS F 14.3b), apparently by Coleridge and Pasley jointly (see 2449n), refers to the second volume of Edwards's work, but to the second edition. The reasons for suggesting that Pasley co-operated in at least the second of these essays on Egypt lie in a MS Coleridge took back with him from Malta, subscribed "C. Pasley Malta 6 Dec 1804" entitled "Remarks on the Extent of Cultivatable Land in Egypt" (VCL MS F 14.3a), which had been largely incorporated in the "Appendix". In these two MS essays it is argued that Egypt might be cultivated to provide much of the same produce as the West Indies, at less risk in transportation, and that therefore Egypt would be not only a military but an intrinsic asset to Britain, which France should not be allowed to acquire.

The MS "Appendix to Observations on Egypt" also refers to Brougham's *Inquiry into the Colonial Policy of the European Powers* (1803), and his "Assertions" in Vol II are corrected in parallel columns. This may be even more likely as the "foolish business". Possibly it was a review of Brougham, for which MS Egerton 2800 ff 106–7 appears to be rough notes. See 2225n. The two undertakings are not unrelated, for Brougham in his Vol II §§2 and 3 (60–183) discusses the West Indies as a colony, and as a risk.

2298 21.482   Referring to 2293?

2299 21.483   *AP* 89 variatim. EHC spells the name *Reignia*. It could be Capt Peter Rainier, R.N. (*d* 1836).

2300 21.484   Again Coleridge is interested in the dynamics of education and human behaviour, however alien the context.

2301 21.485   *AP* 84–5. The "brassy light" of the sun was noticed in 581 and 1628.

2302 21.486   *AP* 85 variatim. Like Freud, Coleridge writes about "the work of Sleep". (*CL* # 614—2 Feb 1805); his descriptions of his own dreams fully support his generalization here; e.g. in 848, 1403, 1649, 1713, 1718, and of the Malta period, 1998, 2018, 2055, 2061, 2441, 2455, 2457, 2468, 2489, 2539, 2542, 2600, 2613; see further theorizing in 2999.

2303 21.487   Dr John Aikin was editor of the *Monthly Magazine* from the founding in 1796 until 1806, when he quarrelled with Richard Phillips, the owner. Mrs Barbauld, Dr Aikin's sister, was at one time respected by both Coleridge and Wordsworth; but on the Aikin literary "Family Compact", see 1848 and n. Though Coleridge had been a contributor to the *Monthly Magazine* from its inception, he certainly had reservations about both owner and editor: see also 1593n.

2305 21.489   *AP* 85 variatim. On the theme of iconography, cf 2167n.
    Possibly Coleridge had his information about the carved cherry-stone from some travelled visitor to Malta. Such a cherry-stone, with eighty rather than eighty-five heads, carved by Leopold Pronner, or Bronner (*c* 1550–1630), an engraver who used a microtechnique in ivory, wood, silver, nuts, cherry-stones, etc., appears in *Beschreibender Katalog des K. grünen Gewölbes zu Dresden* (1881) VII 114, Wappen-zimmer Nr 32. In *Phil Trans* (1703) XXIII there had been an article on "Some Curiosities in Denmark and Holland" by Dr William Oliver, which made reference to ivory crucifixes carved with "the whole history of our Saviour's passion" and to a cherry-stone (then in London) carved with a hundred and twenty-four heads. The article was reprinted in the *Phil Trans* (*Abr*) v 49 that Coleridge used later but could not have seen at this date, and in any case the varying details suggest a different source. For other carvings by microtech-nique see 2452n.

2306 21.490   *AP* 86 variatim.
    Theop[h]neusty, a noun coined from the Greek adjective meaning *inspired of God*. EHC inserted "say the Harmonists", after *holy ghost;* what theologian Coleridge is quoting, or whether he is simply referring to a line of theological argument, is not certain.

2307 21.491   Another example of extremes meeting, to add to 1725?

2308 21.492   The sources of naval anecdotes in Malta must have been numerous. This one probably refers to Sir Charles Rowley (1770–1845), commander of the *Boadicea* in the spring of 1801, on active service off the coast of Spain. Its boats, along with those of two other vessels, slipped out and captured the Spanish vessel *El Neptuna* under the very batteries of Corunna. No other likely engagement is recorded before the date of this entry. John Marshall *Royal Naval Biography* (London 1823) I 673.

2309 21.493   An example of English revulsion at cruelty to animals and disregard of life? See also 2815.

2310 21.494   *AP* 89 variatim.
Cf 1636 for a similar transliteration of words in Greek characters, and 2121 for another play on Stoddart's name. *Stod* + *sagitta* here = Stod + dart, i.e.: "Mrs Stoddart and S[ara] St[oddart] regarding Noble's cruelty to nephew".
Petrus: the specific allusion—to someone's Uncle Peter?—is lost.
Leidenschaft: passion.

2311 21.495   Francesco Caracciolo (1752–99), Neapolitan admiral and one-time viceroy of Sicily, became something of a legend. Surrounded at sea, and trying to escape in disguise, he was caught, accused of being a traitor, and summarily hanged in June 1799 by a Neapolitan court-martial instigated by Nelson, a highly controversial episode in Nelson's career. Two or three weeks after the burial at sea of Caracciolo's body, which was heavily weighted with shot tied to the legs, a corpse seen floating upright was recognized as Caracciolo's. The King of Naples, on board Nelson's flagship at the time, was said to have been moved with some feeling of superstitious fear that was not allayed by the bitter jest referred to in this entry. The story is told in many lives of Nelson, from J. S. Clarke's (and Robert Southey's) onwards.

2312 21.496   A complaint by an officer commanding Sicilians from Ragusa, 70 miles SW of Syracuse, that Malta would not pass them through quarantine?

2313 21.497   Possibly a reference to the foregoing, though the entry appears to be distinctly separate.

2314 21.498   *Grundkraft:* primary force.
Vervollkommung'sgabe [*Vervollkommnungsgabe*]: the gift for achieving perfection.
seraphic: a word recurrent in comments on Klopstock's poetry.
A form of the idea Coleridge frequently expressed, of art as the reconciler of man and nature, of the particular and the universal, the temporary and the permanent—"the true *Atonement*" of 2208?

2315 21.499   *AP* 87. From the next entry, it is clear that Coleridge was reading a minor work of Kant, probably in the edition of *Vermischte Schriften* (Halle 4 vols 1799) of which he annotated at least three copies, two being now in the British Museum. (When Nidecker published the marginalia in the *Revue de littérature comparée* in 1927 only the last three volumes of the relevant set were available; since that time Vols I and II have been acquired by the British Museum from the late Lord Coleridge's library, clearly from another set. A third incomplete set, Vols I–III of H. Crabb Robinson's copy, annotated in all volumes by Coleridge, is in the library of University College, London.
In this entry Coleridge appears to be commenting on *Über den Gebrauch theologischer Principien in der Philosophie* (1788): *Vermischte Schriften* III 101–44, especially 101–2. Coleridge annotated this work at pp 121–2. See the next note.

2316 21.500   An extract from a footnote in Kant's *Von einem neuerdings erhobenen vornehmen Ton in der Philosophie* (1796): *Vermischte Schriften* III 324, the note running on from 322. See 2315n. Reading in J. H. Green's copy, Coleridge made the following note on this passage in the front and back fly-leaves:
"p. 323—326—viz *the Note.* I do not clearly see by what right Kant *forbids* us to attribute to God Intelligence and Will, because we know by experience no Intelligence or Will but the human Understanding (?), the human Volition (?) and these subsist under relations ⟨and limitations⟩ not attributable to God; while yet he allows us to attribute ⟨to him⟩ the notion of a *Ground*, tho' our experience furnishes no instance of an *infinite* Ground, or an *absolute* Ground, more than of an infinite Understanding or of an absolute Will. —not to mention,

except by the ? affixed, the petitio principii in the confusion of all intelligence with that of the Understanding, of 'Will' (arbitrium) with the faculty of Volition (Voluntas), and of all Will with *human* Volition."

Coleridge's underlining in the first line of *the Note* calls attention to the fact that what was for Kant footnote material was for Coleridge a central question. He picks out Kant's most telling sentence.

On the fly-leaves at the back he makes another comment, possibly at another reading and perhaps at a much later time than the foregoing, and twenty years later than the notebook extract:

"P. 317. In this admirable Essay (but what is there of Kant's not admirable!) I am repeatedly regretting that this illustrious Thinker had not anticipated & enabled me to answer the objection: Well! be it that *theoretically* I cannot arrive at a binding assurance of a given Truth, yet if by any other means it is once effected so that it be effected, what is to prevent me from making use of this assurance? What? Is the Categorical Imperative less imperative on my Reason than the *Phænomenon*, (not which but) the coincidence of which with the forms of the Understanding is the sufficing ground of our assurance of an external World? Do I ask more, than that the Moral Command and *involution* of the Truth should be a Surrogate for the Affection of my physical sensibility, in the eye &c?—

"There is, however, besides this a very suspicious point in Kant's reasoning on the anthropomorphic defect in the attribution of Intelligence & Will to Deity—these implying an Einschränkung or Negation incompatible with the idea of God. Essentially? Yes, says he. No! say I.—

"I have had occasion to notice the same 'two faces under one hood' in Spinoza—& that *he* had deluded himself by the merely formal intuitions of Geometry: It A mathematical Circle is, doubtless, formed by a negation of the Space not contained within the periphery: and in this sense (tho' even here it does not to me seem perfectly accurate) the circumferential line itself may be called a *negation*. But let it be a living & willing Circle-animal and let the circumference be effected by a self-retraction at a given point, not in order to, but in the act & as constituting the act of Self-consciousness: & then the same Circumference is a *Position*, a positive Perfection—an unqualified Reality. So in the note, p. 325, fully sympathizing with Kant's contempt for the affected *quality* tone (*vornehm*) of pseudo-mystics, as a privileged class, persons of distinction that look down with a smile of nausea at your vulgar *Operatives* in Philosophy, I cannot help startling at a *Begriff* von Gott von uns selbst *gemacht*—and I confess, that Kant's, as explained p. 324, is but an insufficing *Mach*werk, a pretence to an xyz belief—the affective reality of which I doubt, whether it be even *possible*. I feel the liveliest conviction that no religious man could retain the distinction between the Divine Will, and the unknown Something which is to answer the purpose of a Will—a non-intelligence that performs the function of an Intelligence—nor do I see wherein this differs from a moral & modest Atheism.—17 Feby 1824.—"

It is to be noted that the late date of this note does not preclude the much earlier tendency to the views expressed.

Mache ich mir vom GRUNDE:

If I am to form any conception of the GROUND of all reality, the *ens realissimum*, then I shall say: God is the being which contains the ground of everything in the world for which we human beings have to postulate an INTELLIGENCE, for example everything in it which betrays purpose. He is the being from which the existence of all earthly beings takes its origin, not from any NECESSITY of its NATURE (*per emanationem*), but in accordance with a relation, for which we human beings have to postulate a FREE WILL, in order to make the possibility of this relation at all conceivable.

2317 21.501   *AP* 89. This is the germ of the poem *Psyche*, in which, by 1807, the theme is given a rather more bitter twist. Cf *PW* I 412 (dated 1808) and *C&SH* 29 (dating it 1806–7).

2318 21.502   This is from Reimarus, loc cit 2319n, but more beautifully and succinctly expressed.

2319 21.503   *AP* 89–90. This entry seems to have been set in motion by a reading of Reimarus and Kant in close conjunction. The footnote from Kant referred to in 2316 points to the very limited sense in which there can be said to be any analogy between God's understanding and will and the practical reason. Reimarus (see 2321, 2323, 2325–2330) discusses and struggles with the word *Analogie*, in his *Allgemeine Betrachtungen über die Triebe der Thiere hauptsächlich über ihre Kunsttriebe* §§15–17 (I 104–10). He makes a similar point about differences in degree and differences in kind, and Coleridge is trying to clarify the expression of it.

See the next entry, and cf 2274, where analogy is discussed.

animadverte quam sit ab improprietate verborum: quoted earlier in this notebook, from Hobbes; see 911 and n.

2320 21.504   See the preceding entry; the point is made by Reimarus, and the example of reading and reckoning is given op cit §16 (I 107). See also 2267 and the reference to Aristotle.

Napier's Tables: the logarithmic tables invented by John Napier (1550–1617).

If there was an ephemeral English publication entitled *The House-keeper's Almanac*, no copy is to be found in the BM. A New York edition of 1862 exists, and other variously entitled works of the sort contain ready-reckoners.

2321 21.505   *AP* 91. H. S. Reimarus was referred to earlier, in N 16; as suggested in the note to 1720, Coleridge may have used an English translation of the *Allgemeine Betrachtungen über die Triebe der Thiere hauptsächlich über ihre Kunsttriebe,* but it is clear from this group of entries, especially from the page reference in 2325, that he was here reading the fourth Hamburg edition of 1798; see 2325n.

The note 1720, however, needs emendation. If there ever was an English translation of this work, as EHC in *AP* 91 suggests, it has disappeared from library catalogues and bibliographies. Nor does Sara Coleridge refer to this work, either translation or original, in her notes to *BL* (1847), which he cites. She refers to a quite different work by the son, J. A. H. Reimarus. EHC, one suspects, confused the Reimaruses and, without bibliographical intent, simply translated a title.

On Tom Wedgwood on memory and perception, see *CN* I Index I and "An Enquiry" there referred to; the passage from it quoted in 1297n is relevant here.

2322 21.506   *AP* 91–2. It is one of the charms of Coleridge's marginalia that he frequently addresses the author of the book he is reading, of whatever age or country, by name, to object to or chide or question or compliment him. His notes thus have a free conversational quality.

2323 21.507   The entry comes from Reimarus, §21 of the work cited in 2321 (I 116–18), where Reimarus discusses whether animals are capable of conceptual thinking.

das wir nicht einmal . . . Begriffe haben . . . : "that we have no conception, not even of single objects, except by means of the similarity we perceive between them and other objects", i.e. by means of general cognition.

2324 21.508   *AP* 92; cf 2113. *Lady Ball* is hardly disguised by the Greek letters. Coleridge protested always against religious and moral inertia. See also 2296 and *The Friend* passim.
Sugar and *Sugar of Lead:* see 1860n.
James's Powders: see 1982n.

2325 21.509   The page reference here and the spellings in 2323 identify the edition of Reimarus cited in 2321n: Pt I 184 §70. *Choice,* italicized, suggests STC's amusement at the exact specification of the number and kinds of vegetables eaten by the various animals.
Describe all the creation thus agitated . . . : the instructions to himself, as well as the ironic comments on Darwin's lack of imagination, suggest that Coleridge may be reading scientific works "for the purposes of Poetry", as in N 14 he was later to adjure himself to do; possibly here for the Soother of Absence. See 1541n.
Darwin's Pain from Milk!: Erasmus Darwin deals with the lactative process at some length in *The Botanic Garden* I iii §10. Coleridge may refer, however, to *Zoonomia* (Sect XIV 8, "Of the Production of Ideas"), where Darwin, referring to mammals, says the females have a "natural inlet of pleasure or pain from the suckling of their offspring" (ed 1794) I 125. In the context a reference to the poem seems more likely, but see 2331 and n.

2326 21.510   *AP* 93. Also suggested by Reimarus (op cit 2321) I 184–208 §§70–84. In fact the division of entries here is more apparent physically than real actually.
the Deus minor in his work: the lesser revelation referred to above, from the material world?

2327 21.511   *AP* 93. Skilfully condensed from Reimarus ibid I 196 §77; Coleridge clearly meant to write "as long again as itself", unless he mistranslates Reimarus's phrase "noch einmal so lang . . . als er selber ist, dass die Hälfte der Höhle vor ihm ledig bleibe."
Hirschkafer [Hirschkäfer]: stag-beetle.

2328 21.512   *AP* 94. Also from Reimarus ibid 1 200–1 §80.

2329 21.513   *AP* 94. A *précis* of Reimarus ibid 1 201–3 §81.

2330 21.514   *AP* 94–5 variatim. Again a condensation, with comments interspersed, of Reimarus ibid 1 221–3 §91. The references in quick succession to Unzer, Beverley, Lyonnet, and Boyle put it beyond doubt that it was Reimarus he was reading, not these authors. The reproduction of the lizard, however, does not appear to be discussed in this work of Reimarus.

every animal a republic in se?: an autonomous republic?

one Breeze of Life: "And what if all of animated nature/Be but organic Harps diversely fram'd,/That tremble into thought, as o'er them sweeps/Plastic and vast, one intellectual breeze,/At once the Soul of each, and God of all?" *The Eolian Harp* lines 44–8: *PW* 1 102.

2331 21.515   *Darwin's story of the Bees in Barbadoes:* In his chapter "Of Instinct" (Sect xvi 16) in the *Zoonomia* Darwin writes: "I am well informed that the bees were carried into Barbadoes, and other western islands, ceased to lay up any honey after the first year, as they found it not useful to them: and are now become very troublesome to the inhabitants of those islands by infesting their sugar-houses; but those in Jamaica continue to make honey, as the cold north winds, or rainy season of that island, confine them at home for several weeks together" (ed 1794) 1 180.

The last point, about the honey-broth for the offspring, is made by Reimarus (op cit 2321), 1 195 §77, just before he discusses the stag-beetle of 2327.

2332 21.516   *AP* 96. Reimarus in the same volume, from §108 onwards, discusses various theories of instinct; he stresses the mysteriousness and continuity of life processes.

2333 21.517   The quotation from Martial (*Epigrams* iii 58 line 11) is applied by Reimarus not to the Irish but to a steer calf. Reimarus ibid 1 262n §106. Coleridge was to use it in an article in the *Courier* in 1811, but of a Scotsman: *EOT* iii 937. Possibly the context in Martial is worth giving: "Fiercely in the deep valley roar the bulls, and the steer with brow unhorned itches for the fray." Tr W. C. A. Ker (LCL 1947).

2334 21.518   Reimarus suggests, ibid 1 263 §106, as proof of the
power of instinct, that an eagle, a duck, and a snake, bred artificially,
will from the first moment fly, swim, and coil, and even if confined
until fully grown will, when given freedom, behave according to their
natures.

2335 21.519   *AP* 96. Coleridge has condensed here about four and
a half pages of Reimarus's laborious argument for design; the reference to Mylius is made in a footnote, ibid 1 284n §113.

2336 21.520   *AP* 97. The tarantula does not appear in this work of
Reimarus referred to in the preceding group of entries; nor does it
seem meant for application to Reimarus's style, although at this
point Coleridge stopped reading, or rather memorandizing, Reimarus
and may well have wearied of the repetitious discussion of instinct. He
was thinking about analogy when he began with Reimarus (see 2319
and n), and the tarantula, a natural association, became a favourite
illustration with him.

2337 21.521   *AP* 97. Coleridge is recalling Lucian's story of
Diogenes the Cynic (*c* 412–*c* 323 B.C.), who lived in Athens in the
greatest austerity and finally took up residence in an earthen jar.
"A report that Philip was marching on the town had thrown all
Corinth into a bustle; one was furbishing his arms, another wheeling
stones, a third patching the wall, a fourth strengthening a battlement,
every one making himself useful somehow or other. Diogenes having
nothing to do—of course no one thought of giving *him* a job—was
moved by the sight to gird up his philosopher's cloak and begin
rolling his tub-dwelling energetically up and down the Craneum; an
acquaintance asked, and got, the explanation: 'I do not want to be
thought the only idler in such a busy multitude; I am rolling my tub
to be like the rest.' " *De historia conscribenda* 3 tr H. W. Fowler and
F. G. Fowler (Oxford 1905).
    The subject of mere action, as opposed to contemplation, was much
on Coleridge's mental horizon at this time; cf 2342 and 2386.

2339 21.523   *AP* 97 variatim and in part only. *The Stranger*,
translated from the German of Kotzebue, was frequently produced
in England between 1798 and 1830; it is perhaps best known by the
parody of it in *The Poetry of the Anti-Jacobin. John Bull, or an*

Englishman's Fireside, by George Colman the younger, was first performed at Covent Garden 5 March 1803. *La Morte di Cleopatra* of Nasolini (see 2185n) was a success in Italy 1791–1817, and Guglielmi also composed an opera on this subject. An *Amleto* by G. Andreozzi, popular from 1792 on, may be Coleridge's *Hamlet* reference.

2340   21.524   *AP* 97.

2341   21.525   Having quickly drawn a line under the preceding entry, Coleridge felt he had been wasteful of space and inserted part of this entry above the line. The geographical facts rule out any suggestion that the rainbow with one foot on the sea, described in the previous entry, was noticed from the Strada S Ursula in Valletta.

2342   21.526   *AP* 97–8. With the reflection here on "To be and to act", cf "A spirit made perfect is a self-ponent act, in which (or whom) the Difference of Being and Doing ceases", part of a marginal note on Tennemann *Geschichte der Philosophie* II 50–5, quoted in *Phil Lects* 409 n 34. See also 2382.
    The Pyramid . . . that base of Stedfastness: cf the symbol used by Coleridge for his seal, and his interpretation of his initials around it as "Punic Greek for 'he hath stood'" in *A Character: PW* I 453.
    nor ever—approaches to the ○*?:* In the marginal note on Tennemann just referred to, Coleridge quoted the "Be ye perfect, even as your heavenly Father is perfect"; the cluster of associated phrases is the same, and the reference to personal inadequacy is as clear as it is common in his personal writing. Cf the ironical treatment of the life of action in 2337 and the quite different note in 2386. See also 3131 [12]; and cf the earlier analogous distinction between *having* and *being*, discussed in 1063 and n.

2343   21.527   *AP* 98–9 variatim. Confusion entered with the insertion of ⟨*or all*⟩; the sense appears to be: *there are no straight lines* [in Nature, or rather] *all straight lines comprehend* [or have] *the soul of curves, from activity. . . .*

2344   21.528   *AP* 100.

2345   21.529   *AP* 100. The curious foliation is explained in 2348: "I had turned over two leaves"; *f118ᵛ*—and perhaps *f119ᵛ*—was

already written on when he turned back to *f117ᵛ* and *f118*, but at
exactly what point he turned back is not clear. The correct sequence
of entries is in doubt, but the dating is not seriously affected.

2346 21.530   *AP* 100–1 variatim, where this entry is attached to
the preceding entry. On the Mediterranean sky, see also 2453.

dim sense of the non ~~differ~~resistence: by writing out *difference* first
and altering the first two syllables, Coleridge has inadvertently mis-
spelled *resistance*.

in the manner of the Old Hamburgh Poet: in the sublime style of
Klopstock's *Odes*, which Coleridge bought in Hamburg after discussing them with the poet. See 339, 340, and notes.

2347 21.531   *AP* 101.

2348 21.532   *AP* 99.
of the flame: i.e. the observation he in 2343 promised himself for
that evening.

2349 21.533   *AP* 99, printed as two entries.
Quisque sui faber: "Everyone the fashioner of himself", a play on
the proverb, *Faber est quisque fortunae suae:* "Everyone is the forger
of his own fortune."

2350 21.534   Coleridge records his having made this aphoristic
remark to Alexander Ball and, playing the candid Boswell to Ball's
Johnson, he further records that Ball came down heavily on him, not
for the distinction admittedly just, but apparently for thinking himself clever in making it in "a puzzle of words". *Friend* III 317n.

2351 21.535   *AP* 100; EHC has corrected and accented Coleridge's
Greek phrase, meaning "inventive or resourceful toiler". Coleridge
omitted the second letter of the second word and inserted it confus-
ingly, but the intention seems to be clear.

2352 21.536   *AP* 95, without the deleted personal reference at the
end. This entry is in a somewhat enlarged hand, like the three that
follow. Cf the image of the baby at the breast in 3107, and see also 838
and n, 867, 924 and n.

2353 21.537   *AP* 96. Coleridge elsewhere refers to a hypothetical satire with these leading characters, but I have not found authority for EHC's suggestion that it was to be a "Medical Romance".

2354 21.538   This new excursion into philology was again inspired by Coleridge's readings in Adelung's dictionary (see 378n), which Coleridge follows closely, in both its accuracies and inaccuracies, but occasionally embroiders.

Country: Gegend, a loan formation from Romance, is, according to Adelung, "der Theil der Erdfläche, welcher *gegen* uns oder einen andern bestimmten Körper, d.i. vor demselben, lieget".

Geard, Guardian, Garden: Geard (Mod. Eng. yard) and *Garden* are etymologically connected, but *Guardian* (Adelung quotes it as a term peculiar to the Franciscans for their prior or abbot) is, as he states, a derivative from the Germanic root *ward*.

Hat, Hüt, Hus, House: The first two words, and possibly also the second pair, are derived from a root meaning "to hide, to cover", but the jest is Coleridge's, from Adelung's description of *der Hut* as "in engerer Bedeutung eine Bedeckung des Hauptes".

Word, Werden . . . worthy: Word and *worthy* have no connexion with each other, nor with *werden*, nor does Adelung suggest one. But he does suggest, under *werden*, that this verb "ist vermutlich ein Abkömmling von dem alten *wara seyn*, wovon noch unser *war* ist . . .", which may have given occasion for Coleridge's statement that *werden* is "that which is".

Rede, Redlich: redlich is derived from the earlier meaning of *Rede* = "account" (cf *zur Rede stellen* = "to call to account") and thus meant "that which can be accounted for". It has only comparatively recently been restricted to moral values and so come to mean "honest". Thus it can scarcely be adduced as evidence for man's pristine innocence in speech.

Tale: This, as Adelung points out under *Thalen* (i.e. *dahlen*, a Low German word meaning "to talk nonsense"), corresponds to the High German form *Zahl* and to the English "tale" and "tell".

Word, wahr, wehr: These are not connected, but Coleridge was misled by Adelung, who suggests, wrongly, that *wahr* is identical with the past tense, *war*, of the verb "to be". What does Coleridge mean by *wehr? Gewähren* = "to warrant" (cf the modern *Währung* = "a guaranteed currency") is cognate with *wesen*, but *wehren* = "to guard against" is not.

truth, troweth, throweth: The first two words are obviously connected, but neither of them with the third. At this point Coleridge
abandons Adelung to follow English sources or to indulge in fantasies
of his own. His speculations on the origins of *hitteth* seem devoid of
any philological basis, nor is there any etymological connexion between "through" and "truth".
Are Coleridge's last two sentences, with their play on "spectre"
and "spectrum", a comment on the connexion he would like to discern between "truth" and "through" or an ironic comment on the
pursuit of etymological connexions in general and of his own fanciful
extensions of them in particular?
Nos hæc novimus esse nihil: "We know these are nothing." Used
by Southey as a motto for his *Metrical Tales* (1805). *S Life and C* II
313.

2355 21.539   *AP* 96. In the *Destiny of Nations* the Protoplast
"Stand[s] beauteous on Confusion's charméd wave". *PW* I 140. See
40n. The entry states the very core of Coleridge's view of poetry and
art as a way of ordering the chaos; cf e.g. with the "poet, described
in *ideal* perfection" in Chap XIV of *BL* (II 12), and the *"rules* of
the IMAGINATION" passage in Chap XVIII (II 64–5).

2356 21.540   *AP* 95–6. Cf with this retrospective entry the earlier
more immediate notes on opera in Sicily, in 2192 and 2211.

2357 21.541   *AP* 101–2 variatim. Allied observations of the state
of feeling are made in 2347 and many other entries; this appears to
be an unusually articulate analysis of his need to *sich entäussern.*

2358 21.542   Coleridge frequently shows an awareness of the uncertain boundary line between the ethical and the psychological. See
in a similar connexion his criticism of moral tales for children, 1713
and n.
marriage concubitus cum pregn[ante]: The reading may be *marriages,*
though the possible *s* appears to be rather an abortive stroke of the
pen. Coleridge seems to assume that one of the more negative interpretations of the much discussed problem in Roman Catholic moral
theology, of the lawfulness or sinfulness of intercourse during pregnancy, is universal Roman doctrine. He has in mind such works as
that of Antonino Diana referred to in 2435.

2359 21.543   The entry is incomplete because part of the leaf was cut out of the notebook, presumably because of the personal nature of what was written on the other side (the entry of which we have the last words in 2362).

The vortex image recurs frequently, from the days of Boyer's "Liber Aureus" onwards; see 1706n, 2336, and even 2313.

2360 21.544   *AP* 102 variatim.

2361 21.545   Coleridge undoubtedly included himself among the men here described; see 1830.

2362 21.546   The beginning of this entry at the bottom of *f119ᵛ* was cut out. The last words here are in rather large writing associated with opium or spirits; see the next entry.

2363 22.12   The end of 2364 is written around this entry; i.e. having been begun in a small space left at the bottom of *f11*, 2364 encountered 2363 when the leaf was turned. 2363 therefore, though it *begins* on a later page than 2364, was written there before it, on or before 21 Dec 1804.

At the end of the German lines of entry 1000F on *f7ᵛ*, Coleridge wrote, in a different ink from the entry, and apparently at some later date, "Vide B". This instruction appears to be in the same ink, considerably blacker than that of 1000F, of *f11ᵛ*, the beginning of 2364. Although one can be far from positive, let alone certain—to use Coleridge's terms—it appears that 1000F and 2363, though they both quote German verses on dancing, belong to different dates. Because 1000F is embedded in entries of *c* 1801, and 2364 can, at least conjecturally, be associated with Malta entries close to it, the latter is assigned to that period. Another example of such a later pursuit of what he found already in the notebook appears in the next entry.

The arguments *against* so late a date for 2363 are that we are ignorant of whether Coleridge had access to or was much interested in books of German poetry in Malta; that the hand could be either early or hurried (but it is difficult to be precise about changes in Coleridge's hand between 1800 and 1805); and that he says he received a parcel from Southey by 4 Aug 1805 containing his "german pocket-books". Was N 22 one of those he referred to, and therefore must we visualize it as consisting at that time of *ff2–26ᵛ*, *74–94* of the 1798 watermark (and possibly *ff27–31ᵛ*), and containing, in addition to the English and Latin entries 937A–I, 973A, 1000A–I, the German poems on *ff7ᵛ*, *11ᵛ*, *12–13*, *15–17*, *79–79ᵛ*, *81?* But was reading some German works in Malta and/or Sicily not an easy possibility in the neighbourhood of libraries such as that of the Knights of Malta, the Governor's library, and with such books as a naval force of occupation of six or seven years would accumulate? The private library he seems to have enjoyed most was that of G. F. Leckie in Syracuse. This contained classical and undoubtedly Italian works, but whether German ones we do not know.

On the other side, and in favour of not considering this one of the German pocketbooks, and of conjecturing the later (Malta) date for this entry and the German parts of 2224, are these facts: the German pocketbooks, in the sense of books that were used in Germany, are N 3 and N 3½; N 21 was also used there, though hardly a pocketbook, but there is no indication whatever that N 22 was in use before 1801; in the latter, the hand on some of the last leaves that at first sight looks early is really a hurried hand, and its size and looseness suggest rather some slight effect of opium or spirits, as comparison of the third entry on *ff88ᵛ–89* (2780) with the dated Malta entries on *f74* and *f25ᵛ* shows.

This entry, then, whether correctly dated 1804 or not, has perhaps a close relation to the collection of metres in 2224 which was in progress over a considerable period; see also its use in 2396.

Coleridge begins by paraphrasing Schiller's poem *Der Tanz*. It was first published in the *Musenalmanach* for 1796, but the fact that after the paraphrase Coleridge copies out the central lines from the revised version in *Gedichte* (1800) 12–14 proves that he was using that text. He ends by giving the gist of Schiller's concluding thoughts.

Tr: [the melody] lifts the ethereal body.
Now, as if seeking by force to break through the chain of the dance,/There, where the throng is most dense, a fair couple begins to whirl./At once a path arises before them, disappears as swiftly behind them,/As if by a magical hand the way is opened and closed./See! now they have vanished from sight; in wild entangled confusion/The delicate structure of this world of movement collapses—./But no! there they come, newly exultant, the knot is unravelled,/ And the rule of the dance is restored—but with a new form of charm./Ever again destroyed, this whirling creation renews itself ever again,/And an unspoken law governs this play of transformations./Tell me, how is it that the figures of dance can be involved in endless change/And that utter repose

still lives in these moving patterns./How is it that each is his own master, free to obey the dictates of his heart,/But as he pursues his swift course, yet finds the sole path he must take?

2364 22.11   Commenting on the entry above it on the page, 1000I, from Henry More, Coleridge tries, characteristically, to combine historical with psychological sense, and to distinguish between ignorance and irrationality.

2365 22.13   *Chabrerta:* for *Chiabrera?* The hurried appearance of the entry supports the obvious conclusion that this is a real slip of the pen. And a slip of memory, too? There is no link with Chiabrera.

The source of this entry is Schiller's poem *Die Theilung der Erde,* which first appeared in *Die Horen* (1795) and then in *Gedichte* Pt I (1800) 30. It represents Coleridge's ironical comment on what Schiller makes his Jupiter say to the poet.

2366 22.14   This refers to "the Pest house of the Henly work house" and to Coleridge's brief career as soldier ten years before, when he nursed a comrade who had smallpox.

"It is a little house of one apartment situated in the midst of a large garden—about a hundred yards from the house—it is four strides in length, and three in breadth—has four windows, which look towards all the winds.—The almost total want of Sleep, the putrid smell and the fatiguing Struggles with my poor Comrade during his delirium are nearly too much for me in my present state—In return, I enjoy external Peace, & kind & respectful behaviour from the People of the Work house." *CL* # 32.

The beautiful girl is not referred to in the letter, nor do we know anything about who she was, her after-fate, nor anything specific of any "struggle" in London in 1804.

On the Soother of Absence, see 1541n.

2367 21.547   In a very large shaky hand; see the next entry. The date may be significant; on the depressing effect of holiday seasons on him, see 2647.

2368 21.548   The letter to Southey may be the fragment *CL* # 611, dated 10 Nov 1804, but as this has been reproduced from a transcript we do not know whether it was "in the sprawling characters of Drunkenness", or indeed whether it was a letter; it may be a transcript from an excised notebook entry.

a serpent around the body & wings of an Eagle: the recurrence of bird-images for himself has been noticed earlier; see 2054 and n. Possibly there is a recollection here of the famous description of "an eagle of lofty flight . . . and in its talons it bore a blood-red, monstrous snake, still alive and struggling, nor was it yet forgetful of combat; for it writhed backward, and smote him that held it on the breast beside the neck, till the eagle, stung with pain, cast it from him to the ground, . . . and himself with a loud cry sped away down the blasts of the wind." *The Iliad* tr A. T. Murray (LCL 1954) xii 200–7. In a letter nearly ten years later Coleridge refers to "the direful guilt [of opium-taking], that . . . crept closer, & yet closer, till it had thrown it's serpent folds round & round me, and I was no longer in my own power!" *CL #* 928.

2369 21.*549*   Three leaves were excised after *f120;* they contained the beginning of this entry. The hand here is similar to the hand in the preceding entry, which was, however, completed on *f120ᵛ*.

2370 21.*550*   *AP* 102–3, the first half of the entry. The hand here is normal and neat.

the one moment *of Hume:* presumably Coleridge is thinking particularly of the *Treatise of Human Nature,* in which, from the outset, "simple ideas and impressions" are discussed as "separable", meaning single, complete, not co-existent in any way to modify one another.

unübersehbar: an untranslatable word, needed in English as Coleridge implies. Literally, un-over-see-able, beyond one's range of sight, boundless, vast. See 2794.

the sky-chamber: his room in the old Treasury in Valletta, destroyed by bombs 1940–43, referred to in 2268.

curly-wigged Nobodies: cf 2244; Coleridge obviously disliked baroque.

introcluded: obs. "to shut within", according to the *OED,* which quotes a usage of 1656.

that is the ceiling at the same [*?time*] *of the winding stone Stair Case:* apparently the reference is to a stair-well with green wainscotting of some sort, and boxed in, as described in 2268, to make a toilet-table.

2371 21.*551*   *AP* 103.

2372 21.552   *AP* 103–4. Did Coleridge's self-description here give rise to Beerbohm's famous cartoon, "Mr. Coleridge Table-Talking"? If the final sentence is a true quotation, the maligner has escaped into oblivion.

2373 21.553   *AP* 104–5. It will be noted that the self-castigation increases from 1804 onwards. Cf the entry about not just dreaming, 2391.

2374 21.554   *AP* 105–6.

2375 21.555   *AP* 106, Tetens being omitted from the list of German authors. The omission is probably accidental, for EHC at one time had in his library Coleridge's copy of J. N. Tetens *Philosophische Versuche* (2 vols Leipzig 1777), which was annotated in Malta. See *Inq Sp* §§2, 16, 244 and notes. How much of Kant Coleridge had read by this date it is impossible to be certain. All his editions of Kant are of 1800 date or earlier, except the later volumes of *Vermischte Schriften*. He had perhaps read or looked into the *Kritik der reinen Vernunft* (5th ed Leipzig 1799), but the only works on the reading of which by this date we have definite information are listed in *CN* I Index I and *CN* II Index I. A complete list of Coleridge's known reading of Kant will be found in George Whalley's forthcoming comprehensive study of Coleridge's reading; an interim list may be found in *Phil Lects* 459.

For the reading of Fichte there is no recorded date as early as this, although in 1801 Coleridge was translating (and ridiculing), in a letter to DW (*CL* # 379), the 49th page of *Ueber den Begriff der Wissenschaftslehre*, of which he then or later owned a copy of the second edition (Jena & Leipzig 1798).

The unlocated or unassigned state of numerous entries explains why Coleridge would have found it difficult to specify his indebtednesses. Apart from the fact that the more recent scholarly vanity *cum* scrupulousness in such matters was not to the taste or standard of his time or temperament, it is clear that he could not with certainty remember which entries were original, and which, and from what source, were quotation. Many entries are a mixture of quotation, paraphrase, comment, and some original tangent therefrom. See e.g. the Kant and Kant-stimulated entries 1705 to 1717.

2376 21.556   Four leaves were cut out of the notebook after *f123*, mutilating this entry. Apparently this excision, unlike most, was made by Coleridge himself, for he himself numbered the pages afterwards.

2377 21.557   This incident, previous to the battle of Marengo, is referred to, without the use of names, *Friend* III 370–1. Henry Edward Fox (1755–1811) was the Governor of Minorca, Viscount Keith (George Keith Elphinstone, 1746–1823) the admiral in the Mediterranean; the Austrian army in Italy, an ally of Naples and England, was trying to stem the Napoleonic tide. Southey in his *Life of Nelson* tells the story of Fox's refusal (Chap VI). Coleridge, who perhaps had it from Ball, tells it in *The Friend* to illustrate the defencelessness of Minorca (the reason for the refusal) relative to the natural impregnability of Malta. Minorca itself, and its restoration to Spain, became a sore question, as Coleridge noticed later, *Friend* III 357; see also *TT* 21 April 1811.

2378 21.558   *AP* 106–7. Is some argument going on here with Stoddart? See 2379 and 2394.

2379 21.559   *AP* 107–8 variatim.
    Distinct means to distinct Ends: see 2394, where the controversy is related to Stoddart.
    Dʳ Sewel[l]: see 2139 and n. EHC's "Dr. Sorel" is calligraphically possible but patently wrong.
    Coleridge's quarrel with Southey over pantisocracy 1795–6 was genuinely patched up; the quarrel with Lloyd, epileptic and disciple-turned-enemy, was made irreparably public by Lloyd's novel *Edmund Oliver* (1798).
    crambe bis cocta: the twice-cooked cabbage, or, proverbially, Tuesday's cabbage.

2380 21½.122   This little table of signs appears several times in the notebooks and in other Coleridge manuscripts. It was written at the top of this page, perhaps after 2381 had been written lower down, but before 2382 was carried on to the page from *f74ᵛ* opposite.

2381 21½.123   In another hand, almost copper-plate. As usual in the case of anyone else writing in a notebook, Coleridge opened it at a blank page, or all but blank, in this case at the back of the book.

This must have been before 27 Dec 1804, the date of the entry that begins opposite and then overruns this, i.e. 2382. By 29 March 1805 the *luogotenenti* of Casal Safi was already known to Coleridge; see 2506 and n.

2382 21½.124   The date was inked over by Mrs Gillman, except the *7* in *27*, which she either missed or considered at the time (*c* 1834) to be clear enough. At first, the accuracy of her *1804* appeared doubtful, even under ultra-violet light, the figures underneath looking almost as much like 1805 or 1815 or 1825 as 1804. But on her side are the facts that there is no top stroke for a 5 (Coleridge wrote 4's or 5's in two strokes), and a faint down-stroke on the right-hand side of the 4 is just discernible under her all-but-obliterating ink. Moreover, the date *Dec. 27 1804* is corroborated by the fact that the cipher entry on the other inside cover of this notebook, 2383, can be dated as approximately (at any rate *before*) 27 Dec 1804, from 2387, where the cipher was used.

Possibly this and the other entries at the back of this notebook should appear in the chronology later than those at the front (2383–2388); the reversal of the conventional order arises here from the suspicion that the cipher of 2383, which is in a largish hand, and the use of it in 2387, which refers to "the nightly", are late night entries, this one perhaps a few hours earlier.

The two notebooks N 21 and N 21½ are linked also as to content. See 2274; Wolff and Kant, perhaps Leibnitz, can be seen in the background in both cases.

f74ᵛ der Grundkraft . . . Vorstellungskraft: "the basis, the only one, is the imagination". The translation assumes an error in the gender of *Kraft* and therefore twice reads *die* for *der;* another possibility is that Coleridge is quoting a phrase in the genitive or dative.

Stahl: G. E. Stahl, the German physician (1660–1734), quoted in *Phil Lects* 356 and there referred to as a "truly great" man.

f75 Psiology: for *Psilology,* i.e. mere logic?

τὸ *perceptum definite:* the clear or specific thing perceived, the image.

2383 21½.2   This first attempt to draw up a cipher system is datable from 2387, where it was used on 27 Dec 1804, Coleridge carefully putting his cipher-alphabet in one notebook and his first use of it in another. Later, in 1807, he designed a rather more complicated cipher-system. See Appendix C.

A label bearing the initials "S.T.C." in another hand is pasted on the page at the bottom of this entry.

2384 21½.6   This entry, written above and below 2385, clearly after that was on the page, is in the nature of a postscript to 2383, presumably to be dated close to it.

2385 21½.7   Machiavelli's *History of Florence* was not in Coleridge's library, and we do not know what edition he quotes from here; the likely contemporary ones do not correspond to his text at all points.

Its imaginative treatment of national life, especially its introspective emphasis on the social organism of the state, rather than the military and political events that were the stock-in-trade of contemporary historians, made this an interesting and perhaps influential work for Coleridge.

Machiavelli is here discussing preceding historians of Florence who did not mention the dissensions between noble families and their role in the changing fortunes of the city:

And if these noble authors were restrained by the fear of wounding the memory of those about whom they had to write, they are deceived and show that they know little of the ambition of men and their desire to perpetuate their ancestors' names and their own. Nor has it occurred to them that many who have not had the opportunity of securing fame by praiseworthy deeds have gained it by infamous ones. Nor have they considered that actions intrinsically great, as are those of government and statecraft, however they may be handled, or to whatever end they may come, seem always to bring more honour than blame to men.—Tr W. K. Marriott *Florentine History* (Everyman 1909) 2–3.

2386 21½.8   Source not traced. Cf 1072 and 1834. Possibly this line and a half belongs later, to the revising of *Osorio*, which went on from the end of 1806 until it was produced as *Remorse* in 1813.

Pasted on this page is the printed official signature, *Segreteria* . . . *Prosegretario*, clipped from a copy of the *bando* reproduced in plate II. This may be the first proclamation signed by Coleridge as Public Secretary. See also Appendix B. Whether this evidence of his having lived, for a period, what he might easily have described as the life of a man of action has any oblique reference to the words in 2386 cannot be known; nor can we be certain Coleridge himself pasted this there.

The same page has an entry, almost a doodle, that appears to be associated with lecture preparations later; it is in fact difficult to be sure about the dates of anything on this page.

2387 21.599   The numerals here represent Coleridge's first, or at least simplest, attempt at cipher; see 2383 and n. Substituting for each numeral the corresponding letter of the alphabet one reads:

no night without its guilt of opium and spirit!

2388 21.598   After this entry about nine lines have been erased, possibly with acid, some of them having been previously obliterated with heavy ink. The last line, largely obliterated but not erased, reads in part: "or if a friend should o'ercome [. . .] nothing".
What follows may belong to this entry.

2389 21.594   In accord with his use of the phrase *ego contemplans* in *BL* I 52n (Chap IV), to mean "personal identity", here he contemplates himself *vis-à-vis* the whole circle—Wordsworth, Dorothy, Mary, Sara Hutchinson, and his own three children: they comprise him, i.e. he is nothing without them. On *Ego* and its "intimate Synthesis with the principle of Co-adunation", see 2057.

2390 21.595   In pencil. It is not clear whether this and the next, also in pencil, should be regarded as one entry.
non s'e veduto: it has not been seen.

2391 21.596   See 2373.

2392 21.597   A repetition, as noted, in the same notebook, of 2292.

2393 21.31   This entry at the bottom of *f4ᵛ* is one of the not very numerous instances of an entry judged largely by the hand to be clearly later than the surrounding early entries. It is conjecturally placed with the other Malta entries in this notebook from its appearance as well as the likelihood of Coleridge's reading maritime law in the Malta period. In his official capacity he participated in many disputes in the Admiralty Court, as various references in the letters and documents in the VCL collection indicate. This excerpt is from

Charles Molloy *De Jure maritimo et navali: or a Treatise of Affairs Maritime, and of Commerce* (2 vols 1676, 9th ed 1769) Bk I Chap II §xvi.

2394 21.560   *fasericht: faserig*, i.e. stringy, fibrous, hairy.
The entry is cut off, with the removal of four leaves and the top of the next leaf. Again the pages were later numbered by Coleridge.

2395 21.561   *Reynolds, Morton, Colman:* These were the popular dramatists of the time. Frederic Reynolds (1764–1841), whose first successful play on the stage was a benefit for Coleridge's friend, Miss Brunton, wrote about a hundred comedies and tragedies, many of them adaptations of old plays to contemporary taste. Thomas Morton (c 1764–1838), another prolific playwright, is best remembered for *Speed the Plough*, in which he created the character of Mrs Grundy. It was being played in London, at the Theatre Royal, Covent Garden, in Feb 1804 in the weeks when Coleridge was waiting to sail to Malta. George Colman (1762–1836), the best known of the three, was to become in 1824 an official censor of plays, in which capacity he rigorously cut out from the plays of others the grossnesses and improprieties of the very sort that had given his own the popularity against which Coleridge is here protesting.
    This is one of the earliest hints of Coleridge's view, developed later in the *Lay Sermons* and *Church and State*, of the necessity of a class he was to call a "clerisy".

2396 21.562   *AP* 108–9 variatim. The top of the page has been cut out, and with it the beginning of the entry. The first five words here are largely gone from the MS now, owing to the binding and mending; they exist in the photographs and in my first transcripts from the originals. The first six lines derive from 2363.
    "*Thus him that over-rul'd* . . . : *Venus and Adonis* line 109, with the variation that Shakespeare wrote *he* for *him*.
    Dr *Geddes:* Alexander Geddes (1737–1802), a Roman Catholic priest who gave up parochial work to make a translation of the Bible, which began to appear in 1792; for its heretical criticism the work was put on the Roman Index. He was noted for a cantankerous quarrelsomeness. It appears from this entry that Coleridge knew him. Note here the extremes of frost and fire meeting, in an image recurrent e.g. in 2398n.

Heri vidi fragilem frangi; hodie mortalem mori: "Yesterday I saw the fragile break; to-day I see the mortal die." Did the ~~moi~~ accidentally imply "the mortal part of me"?

2397 21.563   Cf 2410.

Lady Ball: a certain lack of mutual sympathy is evident also in such different contexts as 2324 and 2517n.

telling the Truth . . . conveying falsehood: In similar phrases Godwin stated the problem in Bk ɪᴠ Chap ᴠɪ of *Political Justice* (3rd ed 1797) ɪ 328. The awareness of this difficulty appears frequently in Coleridge's writing: e.g. see *Friend* ɪ 62–77.

Major Adye: The insertion is made as if to retract the preceding sentences. At the moment of this entry Coleridge could hardly yet have learned of the destruction of his own papers—including his "Travels" addressed to Sir George Beaumont (*CL # 613*)—among Major Adye's plague-contaminated effects. On Adye see 2045n.

2398 21.564   *Inq Sp* §37; cf ibid §18. This passage has not been used thoroughly by biographers, though the interesting analysis of his "wholly imaginative and imaginary Love" for Mary Evans was discussed in an article on *The Ancient Mariner* by David Beres, *International Journal of Psycho-Analysis* xxxɪɪ (1951) ɪɪ 97–116.

Mʳˢ Coleridge's Temper: On account of her general cheerfulness and good nature, and from compassion for the real hardships she must have endured, little notice has been taken of this unpleasant facet of her temperament, which must, however, have presented a major, perhaps an insurmountable, difficulty to the writer of this entry. Coleridge makes numerous references to Mrs Coleridge's explosions, and some of the excised passages in the notebooks have to do with her fiery temper combined with her "coldness"; see e.g. 1577 *f54* and 979. One of the most vivid, and characteristically analogical, descriptions of it as it affected him appears in a notebook of the last year of Coleridge's life; it is now in NYPL: "The Scalds so called from their exposure thro' poetic enthusiasm to the Spray of the Geysers/A cold-blooded Woman's angry passions = Iceland Geysers. Cold, Sir! yea, if Love or warm affections be meant, cold indeed—Diana otherwise called Hecate, She of the Frozen Zone not colder cold?—Yea ~~an~~ very Iceland! but like Iceland with its Hecla, its periodical Rivers of Fire, and its daily Geysers—O had you been within the scalding spray of one of them—then you would have learnt, that Extremes Meet—

Frost and Fire, Solid Flint Rocks vaulting and capering in boiling
Fluid/O had you witnessed one of her Geysers, unscalded & without
a broken Head—". The metaphor is specifically applied to Mrs Coleridge. Cf also 1816.

The most direct statement from a third person comes from Mrs
Coleridge's younger sister (Martha); made to Mrs Gillman, it was
repeated to Washington Allston, that "Coleridge would never be able
to live with her sister [Sarah], for she had the most horrible temper
she had ever known or heard of: that she was both irascible and
implacable, and that when they were girls at a boarding-school they
were glad when the vacations were over, and they were to go back
to school, for her terrible temper made the house so uncomfortable to
them. This she told Mrs. Gillman upon her deathbed, when speaking
of her family and of Mr. Coleridge. She lived with them some time
after their marriage and said that no one could behave better than
Mr. Coleridge to her sister. Mrs. Gillman told this in secret and serious conversation with Mr. Allston." *Allston Life* 356–7. In view of
Mrs Gillman's prejudiced devotion and the advanced age and difficult character of her informant, this opinion must be accepted with
reserve, though it can hardly be totally disregarded, and it does
touch on a neglected aspect of Coleridge's marriage.

stimulants in the fear & prevention of violent Bowel-attacks: If opium,
usually taken in spirits, was considered a "stimulant", this is yet
another explanation of the reason for taking it. But Coleridge seems to
have distinguished clearly between narcotics and stimulants.

the least languor . . . in a Letter from S. H. drives me wild: Was the
"heart-wringing" letter referred to in 1912, then, merely languid?
Probably not, and there may be some recollection of it behind 2397.

On the numerals cipher see 2383; the passage here reads: "eunuchs
—in all degrees even to the full ensheathment and the both at once."

2399 21.565   *ff127–127ᵛ* are now bound out of place, after *f134ᵛ*,
but Coleridge's paging establishes the correct order. This entry is
clearly a continuation from the preceding but with a characteristic
impersonalizing of a painful discussion. On touch and double-touch
see 2402 and earlier 1039 and n.

stimulari (esse sub stimulo): stimulation (that is not exclusively
subject to stimulation from without).

1. mem. vi/Riley. inacts of Essex: The mystification in this description of the erotogenic zones appears to be deliberate. The nu-

meral I seems to refer to his I in line 12 above, *Touch with the sense of immediate power;* and does the use of italic suggest some such interpretation as "virile-y in acts of (Es)sex"? Petronius glosses *virilia* as *membrum virile.*

2400 21.566   *AP* 109 variatim and omitting the last half-sentence. *Planicies* appears to be a Coleridge coinage; it is not in the *OED.* EHC read *Planities;* the inserted phrase is cramped, and his more reasonable reading may be what Coleridge intended but it is not what he wrote.
A leaf is torn out after *f127.*

2401 21.567(a) As the preceding leaf is torn out, the entry is cut off at the beginning. The hand, ink, and general impression of the writing are more like what follows than what precedes. Attention to curiosities or distortions of vision in Coleridge's notes are usually to be associated with opium-taking.

2402 21.567(b) *AP* 112–15 variatim.
f128   On double-touch see 2399 and n.
f128ᵛ *"phantoms of Sublimity":* a phrase from his own lines in 791 and *PW* I 345.
ridge of Hills . . . its motion: cf 2347 and 2370.
f129   *Space ⟨is one of⟩ the Hebrew names for God:* cf 687 and 1771.
f129ᵛ *the old sophism of the Cumulus, or the horse's tail:* the logical puzzle known as *sorites,* or the fallacy of the heap—how many grains make a heap: the addition of one more, or the subtraction, does not make or unmake a heap—and the similar one about how many hairs constitute a horse's tail, are recurrent in the arguments of early Greek philosophers, but probably Coleridge is reminding himself here of Horace, the *Epistle to Augustus,* where both examples appear together. ". . . utor permisso, caudaeque pilos ut equinae/paulatim vello et demo unum, demo etiam unum,/dum cadat elusus ratione ruentis acervi,/qui . . .": "I take what you allow, and like hairs in a horse's tail, first one and then another I pluck and pull away little by little, till after the fashion of the falling heap, he is baffled and thrown down, who . . .". *Epistles* II I 45–7 tr H. R. Fairclough (LCL 1955).
Formication: Coleridge's description corresponds to modern definitions, and probably comes out of his personal experience; cf e.g. the

reference to childhood fears of "Itch in my Blood" in 2398 and the next paragraph here.

araneosis: the state of seeing things in multiple divisions, like spider-webs.

2403 21.568   Thelwall, and even Hazlitt, in Coleridge's view of them as critics and thinkers, could easily be associated with the araneotic states described in the foregoing entry.

2404 21.569   *AP* 115. Cf 2463.

2405 21.570   Of the value of historic to revealed religion Coleridge was to say more and more; also of its limitations, rationally considered. This entry, though the deduction from double-touch was not pursued, throws an early light on Coleridge's maturing post-Unitarian theological views. Cf "All religion is revealed;—revealed religion is, in my judgment, a mere pleonasm." *TT* 31 March 1832.

2406 21.571   The observation on the first half-page, it must be said, is *not* entire nonsense to an editor of Coleridge's own MSS.

2407 21.572   *AP* 115. On Johnson, for some relevantly similar comments see *Inq Sp* §§147–9.

2408 21.573   Alexander Macaulay (*c* 1725–1805), Public Secretary in Malta, was almost beyond doing his official work when Coleridge arrived; Ball very early, therefore, appointed Coleridge his own secretary, and there is good reason to think that Coleridge was writing or drafting dispatches for Ball as early as July 1804.

That Coleridge was not alone in expecting his own temporary appointment to be brief is borne out by the letter from Ball to the Colonial Office in which he announced Macaulay's death. "I expect daily Mr. Chapman from Constantinople whom I shall put into the Office of Public Secretary and Treasurer in conformity to the Orders sent me . . . bearing the date the ninth day of January 1804." CO 158.10.

Chapman: Edmond Francis Chapman (Chambers and *CL* erroneously refer to E. T. Chapman) was, according to Ball's dispatches of 12 Oct 1801 (CO 159.3), "a young gentleman" who had carried out in the previous September a successful corn-buying expedition to the

Black Sea; this not only saved the British government and the people of Malta large sums for bread, according to another dispatch of Ball's, but earned considerable additional sums for the Treasury of Malta, in Ball's conception a granary and distributing centre for the Mediterranean (CO 158.9). From the fact that at Ball's death in 1809 Chapman took over his duties as Governor for more than a year, we have some idea of his—and Coleridge's—standing.

Coleridge continued as Acting Public Secretary (without the treasurership which he declined) until September 1805 (2665). See Appendix B for an account of some of Coleridge's duties in office.

2409 21.574   *Massaniello:* Tommaso Aniello (corrupted into Masaniello), leader of a revolt against Spanish rule in Naples in 1647, archetype of the demagogue, who finally was the victim of the mob he incited.

Coleridge was not applying here Humphry Davy's lectures on oxygen and carbon dioxide so much as half-personalizing, half-poeticizing the single flame. It may or may not be significant that the triangular symbol of his seal is a flame symbol, his preoccupation with candle flame being evident in numerous, and some deeply personal, contexts; see e.g. 14 and n. For other fireplace studies see 2414 and 2475.

2410 21.575   *AP* 115-16; the footnote is compressed, written, it is clear, after the next entry.

2411 21.576   *AP* 116 variatim. Coleridge elsewhere distinguishes between unconscious or subconscious actions and "true accident"; cf e.g. the implications of the discussion of luck, *Friend* III 269–77. From that essay and the succeeding one it appears that "accident" was a subject of conversation between Coleridge and Alexander Ball.

2412 21.577   *Prudence:* Ball, Coleridge said, was the best type of the man of prudence, and in this context he develops the theme of *prudence* distinguished from *principle* as a dynamic. See *Friend* III 330n, 356.

2413 21.578   *AP* 116 variatim. On maxims, see 1722 and n and *Friend* I 197–8 and, compared with principles, *TT* 24 June 1827.

Stoddart, whose intellectual limitations irritated Coleridge, was advocate in the Admiralty Court.

inter Jus et æquitatem: midway between law and equity.

2414 21.579   *AP* 116–17 variatim.

The desire of totalizing, of perfecting is discussed in aesthetic terms and e.g. in 2471 it also has deep personal connotations. See e.g. 1679 and 1680.

agnized ⟨anerkennt⟩: The past participle required by the English syntax here would now be *anerkannt;* Coleridge follows an eighteenth-century usage. His rendering it *agnized* reflects his interest in the force of German prefixes (cf 2431 and n and 3160) and an attempt to use them. For the sake of precision and pregnancy, and to avoid the usual but dulled *recognized,* he goes back to the Latin, *agnosco.*

2415 21.580   The episode here is obscure, but might have had to do with the French invasion of Wales in 1797; Ball spent the winter of 1796–7 with the fleet off Brest, and later off Cadiz. Milford Haven and St David's (in 2416) are both on the coast of Pembrokeshire, a few miles apart, but whether this and the next entry are two unrelated entries, or one entry, is far from clear.

2416 21.581   This is the first of what appear to be three anecdotes about optical or hallucinatory or dream phenomena; see 2418 and n.

2418 21.583   *AP* 117 variatim; EHC's editorial emendations here are numerous and unnecessary and make this entry, which reads like a dinner-table anecdote, into something out of a book. Coleridge was intensely interested in analysing fear, and it must have been one of the more interesting subjects of conversation possible to him in the limited military and naval society of Malta in war-time. For another Malta story about fear of cowardice, see *Friend* III 299–301.

Miss Edgeworth's Tales: Maria Edgeworth *Moral Tales* (1801) or her *Popular Tales* (1804) must be referred to here; cf 1713 and n. In a lecture of 1808 he deplored their influence: *ShC* II 13.

2419 21.584   *AP* 118. The illustration indirectly owes something to Hobbes; cf 912 and n.

2420 21.585   *Pictures being the Books of the Poor:* Like Plato, Coleridge protested against visual representation of what he considered not imageable ideas: it was to become a *bête noire;* cf 2480 and *Phil Lects* 90.

Parma . . . Bipont: The contrast between the great printing-house of the Duke of Parma, under the direction of Giambattista Bodoni (1740–1813), producing the finest things of their kind in Europe at this time, and the Bipont press at Zweibrücken in the latter half of the eighteenth century, producing cheap editions of the classics, is direct enough, if unfair to the best Bipont work. Coleridge's fondness for marginal annotations led him more than once to complain of the bad paper and production of German books; they thus leap to his mind as an example of the shoddy, contrasted with works of art. And cf what he says in another context, in *LR* 1 258–9.

It appears from a report of Ball (CO 158.9) that what he calls the "Foundling and Invalid Hospitals" had been united, not by his order but before his regime.

2421 21.586   Is he noting what men do in enforced idleness and boredom? The subject interested him; cf *Inq Sp* §173.

2422 21.587   *the Boston Gazette 3 Dec. 1804:* The *Boston Gazette* gave on its front page every Monday a table of "Wholesale Prices Current, at Boston. In dollars and cents, carefully revised and corrected every Saturday". The Commodore of the American fleet was in Malta at this time, and various American ships and officers from whom Coleridge could easily see such a paper. His prices for coffee are wrong, presumably from error in translating into sterling the 28 to 30 cents, the listed prices. "Not a berry in the Island" may refer to Malta; the *Boston Gazette* carries no such phrase, though in the "remarks" column it does suggest that no coffee, whalebone, or Malaga wine was being offered for sale. The newsprint being poor, Coleridge misread the wine price, which was 50, not 30 dollars.

2423 21.588   *AP* 118.

2424 21.589   Above this entry, deleted by Coleridge as he drafted the lines, are two other entries heavily blacked out (by a later pen?). The bottom of the page is also cut out, losing perhaps three more lines.

2425 21.591   *AP* 118. Above this entry on *f134ᵛ* of N 21 is a
Ratzeburg entry dated "Oct 10th"; Coleridge has inserted ⟨*1798!!*⟩.
Cf 2430 below.

2426 21.592, 21.7 This divided entry began on *f134ᵛ* and was continued on the front inside cover, *f1ᵛ*, compressed in at the top of the
page (see *CN* 1 plate IV); *f134* is torn off below the part of this entry
on it, presumably to excise the lines overleaf in 2424. The top corner
is now worn away. Coleridge clearly thought this was to be the last
entry in the book; later he found a few empty spaces and used them
for eight entries, which will appear in later volumes.

2427 17.1   The quotation from the Song of Songs (8:1–2 variatim) is directed towards the names at the corners of the notebook
pages. See N 17 Gen Note and 2624 and n. The sexes in the original
are reversed, i.e. *Sister* for *brother*, and instead of *my mother's house*
Coleridge writes *my House*. The double underlining of *The Bible* was
doubtless to emphasize the high source from which the authorization
for the personally applied sentiment is taken. See also 2429.

2428 17.2   The sonnets, 91, 92, 97, 98, 113, 109, 105, and 76, are
either transcribed or written from memory, with variations that seem
to arise chiefly from personal application. The first four lines of
sonnet 92 are added to sonnet 91 (in which *Wealth* and *Birth* are
transposed in the first two lines). In sonnet 113 line 6, *B Poets* reads
lack, a misprint; *snatch* may be a corrective guess for *latch*, the true
reading. In 109 there are more considerable changes: "Or that long
Absence hath my love assess'd" was in Shakespeare's poem, "Though
absence seem'd my flame to qualify", and the lines beginning "As
from my soul" in the original read, "As from my soul which in thy
breast doth lie./That is my home of love; if I have ranged/Like him
that travels I return again/Just to the time, not with the time exchanged,/So that myself bring water for my stain./Never believe
. . .". Coleridge omits three lines and changes the rhymes of three
others to suit himself.
    Coleridge was an enthusiastic admirer of the sonnets; in his lectures
on poetry in 1808 at the Royal Institution, according to Wordsworth,
he "publicly reprehended" George Steevens for his "flippant in-
sensibility" to them. Preface to *W Poems* (1815).

That this was an enthusiasm he may have shared with John Wordsworth is made clear by notes in a copy of *B Poets* II once owned by
JW, given to WW, and now in Dove Cottage; the notes were kindly
drawn to my attention and sent by Miss Darbishire.

At the top of the first page of the sonnets, *B Poets* II 645, is written
in Coleridge's hand:

"I first class of goodness
I 2nd or next higher
Ɨ 3rd or higher still
II 4th or highest. The figures mark how many lines the praise is
meant to extend to. N. B. If the marks be placed on the left, or before
the Number of the Sonnet, the manner or style is praised, if on the
right or behind it, the thoughts or matter: if over the number, both
style and thought:—all according to the feelings and taste of S.T.C."

In addition to the sonnets copied out in the notebook, some thirty
others are marked in one way and another, nearly all for both style
and thought. Of those quoted here, 91 is given the fourth or highest
classification, 92, 97, 113, and 76 the third or next highest, 98, 109,
and 105 the second; of these all are marked for virtues of both style
and thought, except 98, marked "on the left" side and not "over", i.e.
for style chiefly.

(It is possible that the evidence of these notes, possibly pre-Malta,
though not certainly, should be considered as pointing to an earlier
date for this entry and for all first three entries in this notebook; there
is, however, no absolute indication one way or another.)

2429 17.3
    Cf   "Witness thou
        The dear companion of my lonely walk,
        My hope, my joy, my sister and my friend,
        Or something dearer still, if reason knows
        A dearer thought, or in the heart of love
        There be a dearer name." *WPW* v 347, dated 1800–6, "per-
haps intended for *The Recluse*". The presence of the lines here neces-
sitates a date not later than 1804, and perhaps confirms Knight's
statement, "extracted from Dorothy Wordsworth's Grasmere Journal, 1802": *WPW* (Knight) VIII 234.

2430 17.4   Coleridge had for some months been acting as Ball's
private secretary, and as a sort of under-secretary to the aged

Macaulay. See 2408n. It is clear from many statements in letters, now corroborated by this entry, that Coleridge regarded himself as a stop-gap. And yet the phrase in parenthesis—though it confirms his knowledge of the temporary nature of his appointment—carries an undertone of doubt, a hint, possibly half a wish, that the position might be reopened, to wish for a post and to wish to be considered for it being two different things. The "late Ministry" was Addington's, the government was Pitt's, though Hobart continued as Secretary for the Colonies.

Coleridge's description of Alexander Macaulay is substantiated by some documents in Macaulay's hand on Malta matters in the PRO, e.g. a letter, dated 24 June 1800, on the importance of Malta, with a description of its economy, a eulogy of Ball, and a plea that, whatever else happens, the island should not again return to the custody of the Knights of St John of Jerusalem. WO 1 291 ff 365–81.

calm as a sleeping Infant . . . Lightning: see in 2425 the general observation to which this seems to have given rise.

2431   17.5   *AP* 118–20, in part, from *f6* "I cannot admit" to the end. The series of brackets and incompleted brackets, part of Coleridge's attempt to thread his own labyrinth, are here made into round brackets in place of his square ones, so as not in print to confound confusion further.

f3ᵛ   falernian strength: i.e. of the wine of ancient Campania, usually spelled with a capital letter. Coleridge probably had his knowledge of the sound and character of the Spanish language from Southey.

*f5   Burns' description of a Brook: Afton Water? The Banks o' Doon?
res illustrate:* for *res illustrata?* The thing illustrated.

f5ᵛ   end: i.e. end of the "parenthetical parentheses".

f6   Full many a glorious morning have I seen: Shakespeare sonnet 33.
the proud full Sail of his Great Verse: cf the application of the image from sonnet 86 to WW in 1546, and, in reverse, to Coleridge himself in 2086.

f6ᵛ   Ein Gott ist: the verse from Schiller's poem *Die Worte des Glaubens* was entered earlier in N 21; see 1074 and n. The emphatic EIN in the last line is of course Coleridge's.

f7   C'est ici que la Mort: The monastery of La Grande Chartreuse made a deep impression on Wordsworth. He may have called to Coleridge's attention the famous inscription, here quoted with STC's usual unconcern for accents: "Here it is that Death and Truth raise

their awful torches. It is from this retreat inaccessible to the world
that one passes to Eternal Life."

f7ᵛ   Hamlet or Lear: It is notable here and elsewhere that Coleridge's
anti-Gallicism rests rather on his denial of imagination to the French
than on the more puritanical considerations he sometimes advances.

Some ideas in *ff3ᵛ–4ᵛ* were used later in a footnote in No 18 of *The
Friend* (1809–10) that did not appear in later editions; the text above
the footnote reads: "Klopstock dwelt much on the superior power
which the German Language possessed, of concentrating meaning . . .". The footnote adds: "Klopstock's observation was partly
true and partly erroneous. . . . I have translated some German hexameters into English hexameters, and find, that on the average three
lines English will express four lines German. The reason is evident:
our language abounds in monosyllables and dissyllables. The German
not less than the Greek, is a polysyllabic Language. But in another
point of view the remark was not without foundation. For the German
possessing the same unlimited privilege of forming compounds, both
with prepositions and with epithets as the Greek, it can express the
richest single Greek word in a single German one, and is thus freed
from the necessity of weak or ungraceful paraphrases. I will content
myself with one example at present, viz. the use of the prefixed
particles *ver*, *zer*, *ent*, and *weg*, thus reissen to rend, verreissen to rend
away, zerreissen to rend to pieces, *entreissen* to rend off or out of a
thing, in the active sense: or schmelzen to melt—ver, zer, ent,
schmelzen—and in like manner through all the verbs neuter and
active. If you consider only how much we should feel the loss of the
prefix *be*, as in bedropt, besprinkle, besot, especially in our poetical
Language, and then think that this same mode of composition is
carried through all their simple and compound prepositions, and many
of their adverbs; and that with most of these the Germans have the
same privilege as we have, of dividing them from the verb and placing
them at the end of the sentence; you will have no difficulty in compre-
hending the reality and the cause, of this superior power in the German of condensing meaning, in which it's great Poet exulted. It is
impossible to read half a dozen pages of Wieland without perceiving
that in this respect the German has no rival but the Greek, and yet I
seem to feel that concentration or condensation is not the happiest
mode of expressing this excellence, which seems to consist not so much
in the less time required for conveying an impression, as in the unity
and simultaneousness with which the impression is conveyed. It tends

to make their language more picturesque: it *depictures* images better. We have obtained this power in part by our compound verbs derived from the Latin: and the sense of it's great effect no doubt induced our Milton both to the use and the abuse of Latin derivatives. But still these prefixed particles conveying no separate or separable meaning to the mere English Reader, cannot possibly act on the mind with the force or liveliness of an original and homogeneous language, such as the German is: and besides are confined to certain words." *Friend* (1809–10) 281 n 2.

2432 17.6   The sheriff's duties and status are discussed in Nicolson and Burn *History and Antiquities of the Counties of Westmorland and Cumberland* (1777) I 33n. See 2442, 2443, and notes.

2433 17.7   *AP* 121–3 in part. Cowper's *Lines to Mrs. Unwin* appeared first in Hayley's *Life of Cowper* in 1803. As Coleridge appears to have been reading the *Christian Observer* in Feb 1805 (see 2440), it is relevant to notice that the poem appeared in full in the number for July 1803 (II 419) in a review of Hayley's *Life*.

το καθολον: the whole, the total effect.

sense and sensibility: Jane Austen's novel was at this date written, but under another title, and so far as is known the final title was not given it until publication in 1811; if the conjunction of terms was a commonplace of the times, examples of usage are notably lacking.

2434 17.8   *AP* 124; see 2435n.

The *Queen-bee* metaphor is used of fanaticism (in German *Schwärmerei*) in *BL* I 130; for the Queen-mother-bee image, interestingly developed, see *Friend* III 240–1: "Disturbed as by the obscure quickening of an inward birth; made restless by swarming thoughts, that, like the bees when they first miss the queen and mother of the hive, with vain discursion seek each in the other what is the common need of all; man sallies forth into nature—in nature, as in the shadows and reflections of a clear river, to discover the originals of the forms presented to him in his own intellect." See also *C&S* 71.

2435 17.9   *AP* 124–5, printed with 2434 as one entry.

the music of the adjusted String at the impulse of the Breeze: the Aeolian-harp image again, this time applied to the moral situation.

Diana de digito in maritali fruitione: Antonino Diana (1585–1663), eminent moral theologian, is chiefly known for his *Resolutiones morales*, which went into many editions. In his tractate on marriage, *De sacramento matrimonii*, he discusses the conjugal act in typical casuistical detail. Coleridge may be referring to Resolution 188 of this work, or to some writer discussing it. Coleridge's words are not an exact quotation from Diana, if the elaborate *Index generalis rerum et verborum* of his *Opera omnia* (Venice 1698) is reliably complete.

2436 17.10   On modern plays cf 2395.

the Entertainment: probably either the "afterpiece" in the common double-bill, or possibly refreshments.

Coleridge himself read this note and expanded it considerably in his lectures of 1811–12. See *ShC* II 126–7.

2437 17.11   *Rom.* VIII. *26:* "Likewise the Spirit also helpeth our infirmities: for we know not what we should pray for as we ought: but the Spirit itself maketh intercession for us with groanings which cannot be uttered." The text of the sermon referred to in the next entry is also from the Epistle to the Romans.

quod semper . . . omnibus [creditum est]: This celebrated phrase is from Vincent of Lérins *Commonitorium* II 6, where it appears in a passage describing and defining Catholicism: "[In the Catholic Church we must carefully adhere to] what has been believed everywhere, always, and by all."

2438 17.12   *Latimer's Sermon:* "The Duty of Kings" Pt I is presumably referred to, which takes as its text Rom. 15:4; Latimer says, having built up his argument to it, "For if ye bring it to pass, that the yeomanry be not able to put their sons to school, as indeed Universities do wondrously decay already, . . . I say, ye pluck salvation from the people, and utterly destroy the realm: for by yeomen's sons the faith of Christ is, and hath been maintained chiefly". *Sermons* (London 1788) 104. Coleridge's copy of the 1635 folio, bearing his initials and Derwent's, is recorded in the Wordsworth LC.

Sophosophron, Wisdom-and-Prudence, as Coleridge glosses it, became his private name for Sir Alexander Ball. See the next entry and n. The conjunction is the point; *prudence* was for Coleridge usually, as for Jeremy Taylor, a pejorative word, used in contrast to conscience, or moral idealism. See e.g. *LS* 69–71n.

2439 17.13   *f12ᵛ de se ipso . . . futuro:* "about himself, his past, and his future".

f13 Hæc omnia . . . adjuvante: "I have done all this myself, with intelligence as guide, and luck permitting, or at most being favourable".

Fortune . . . favors . . . fools: this discussion, in fact the whole entry, was used fully in *The Friend*, Landing Place III Essays I and II. *Friend* III 269–88.

f14 (Arbitrium . . . patiar): "Will is myself *acting*, not [the same as] Choice [which] is a modification of myself by something else, and so a submission—in the latter case *I submit*, in the former *I act;* and the distinction remains sacred and steadfast even though there neither is nor can be division, even though of necessity I act by submitting and submit by acting."

f15 δοκεῖ, ου φαίνεται . . . Schein-phænomenon: "it seems, but does not manifest itself, or what the Germans express by their *illusory phenomenon.*"

2440 17.14   The *Christian Observer*, a monthly "conducted by Members of the Established Church" (1802–74), was under the auspices of the evangelicals of the Clapham Sect, which included Wilberforce and Hannah More. Beilby Porteus (1731–1808), bishop of London, was a friend of Hannah More. The *Observer* ran "Miscellaneous, Literary and Historical" sections in which it treated, with dire emphasis, secular as well as theological and ecclesiastical matters.

William Warburton's title, *The Alliance between Church and State, or, the Necessity and Equity of an Established Religion and a Test-Law demonstrated from the essence and end of civil society, upon the fundamental principles of the law of nature and nations* (1736), explains itself. Warburton has a good deal to say about "duties of imperfect obligation which human laws overlook" (p 13), and about the "independency" of the church from the state. The argument is based on the soul-body distinction which Coleridge abhorred equally with the conclusion to which it led, "that the church shall apply all its influence in the service of the state" and vice versa (p 68), making a case for establishment, tythes, and a share in legislative power for the church "in alliance", and for no other church within the state, and therefore for a Test Act. The core is here of ideas controverted throughout Coleridge's life; see especially the idea of the exclusively spiritual power of the church, as expounded in 1830 in *C&S* 150–60. It is worth noticing that the *DNB* article on Warburton gives HNC as authority for the view that Warburton's *Alliance* had "some affinity with the doctrine of Coleridge in his *Church and State*". That this is a misinterpretation of Coleridge's views is clear from this entry; it is not the only instance of the bias of STC's early editors.

2441 17.15   *AP* 120–1, with the important omission "Of Love in Sleep . . . my Lines".
The lines are from his poem *Phantom: PW* 1 393. See 2055n.

2442 17.16   *AP* 123–4, in part. This entry derives from *The First Part of the Institutes of the Lawes of England*, or the work usually known as "Coke on Littleton" (1628) ff 106ᵛ–7 (§156): "Also it is said that in the Marches of Scotland some hold of the King by Cornage that is to say, to winde a horne to give men of the Countrie warning when they heare that the Scots or other enemies are come, or will enter in to England, which service is grand Seriantie. But if any tenant-hold of any other Lord then of the King by such service of Cornage, this is not grand Seriantie, but it is Knight Service. And it draweth to it Ward and Marriage, for none may hold by grand Seriantie, but of the King only." But here no mention is made of the possibility of paying substitutes to do this service, though it could be inferred. Blackstone adds this point, and refers to the service as "personal"; *Commentaries on the Laws of England* II (1766) 74–5: "Tenure by *cornage*, which was, to wind a horn when the Scots or other enemies entered the land, in order to warn the king's subjects, was (like other services of the same nature) a species of grand serjeanty. These services, both of chivalry and grand serjeanty, were all personal. . . . But, the personal attendance in knight-service growing troublesome and inconvenient in many respects, the tenants found means of compounding for it, first by sending others in their stead, and in process of time making a pecuniary satisfaction to their lords in lieu of it. This pecuniary satisfaction at last came to be levied . . . and therefore this kind of tenure was called *scutagium* in Latin, or *servitium scuti*; *scutum* being then a well-known denomination of money: and in like manner it was called in our Norman French, *escuage*; . . . personal attendance fell quite into disuse. . . . Hence . . . from this period, when our kings went to war, they levied scutages on their tenants . . .".
But for all this, Coleridge was not referring to Blackstone probably,

but to Nicolson and Burn *Westmorland and Cumberland* I 14–19, where the elements here—*cornage, serjeanty* or Knight's Service, and the etymological references to *"scutage,* or *escuage;* from the latin word *scutum,* a shield"—are present. See also 2443 and n.

In view of the implausibility of deductions based on a theory of Coleridge having access to Nicolson and Burn in Malta, it is fortunate that the facts are clear from Coleridge's inscriptions in his copy, now in the BM. On the fly-leaf of Vol II he wrote: "S. T. Coleridge/7, Barnard's Inn/Holborn/at/J. Tobin's Esqre/March 13, 1804/bought at/Mʳ Ryan's/353 Oxford St/". On the verso there is a note dated "29 Aug 1805", which proves that he took these two heavy quartos to Malta; for this note see 2637n.

Seven annotations in Vol I deal chiefly with etymological questions and speculations along the lines of this entry; the entry is in fact a longer continuation of them. Apart from a few marks and brief comments on the Grasmere section, and in Vol II an attempt to render a Latin phrase into Italian, and a considerable note on the proper way to build up cathedral libraries, there are no other marginalia of importance.

With regard to Coleridge's etymological speculations here, it may be said that *Lore* is cognate with *Lehre,* and *shy* with *scheu; eschew* seems to be derived from the Old French *eschever,* itself from the German *scheuen,* "to fight shy of". But there is no connexion between this German root and the Latin *scutum,* from which, through Old French *escuchon,* "escutcheon" is derived.

2443 17.17   This strange list of names may all be traced to Nicolson and Burn; see the previous note.

Ucthred of Northumberland (d 1016): Nicolson and Burn I 27; Uhtred or Uchtred, Earl of Northumbria, a great warrior, ruthless in war, finally tricked to his death by King Canute. *DNB.*

Ranulph de Glanvil (d 1190): ibid I 27, i.e. Ranulf de Glanville, an active leader in the wars of Henry II against the Scots, sheriff of Yorkshire and Westmorland, chief justice of England, and "the king's right-hand man". *DNB.*

Robert de Broy: ibid I 27.

Renfred de Deepdale: Adam de Deepdale appears ibid I 27, followed immediately by Gilbert, son of Reinfred.

Ada de Morvil: she was the grandmother of Hugh de Morville *(d* 1204), one of the murderers of Becket (ibid II 95), and was said herself to be a "licentious and treacherous" woman. *DNB.* See also 771. Hugh de Morville's eldest daughter was also an Ada de Morville: Nicolson and Burn II 95.

Idonea: ibid I 17, and used by Wordsworth for a character in *The Borderers.*

Evo de Johnby: ibid I 28.

Philip Escrope: ibid I 28.

Ivo [de Talebois]: ibid I 29.

Helwise = Heloise: ibid I 29; one was married to Gilbert, son of Roger Fitz-Reinfred, and another (on the same page) to Peter de Brus.

Mary de Brus. Aeiparthen (ever-virgin): Margaret de Brus is referred to at I 29, though no Mary; the adjective appears to be Coleridge's, and not necessarily to be connected with this lady.

For other appearances of Nicolson and Burn in this notebook see 2432, 2493, and 2494.

Possibly the entry is to be linked with preparation for a continuation of *Christabel.* On the other hand, the selection of names mostly north country, all more or less of a period, points to a plan described in a later entry in N 18: "In my happier days, while I had yet Hope and onward-looking Thought, I planned an Historical Drama, of King Stephen on the plan of Shakespeare's Historical Dramas. Indeed it would be desirable that some man of dramatic Genius, ⟨to which I have no pretensions⟩ should dramatize all those omitted by Shakespeare, as far down as Henry the 7th inclusive." After a page of further discussion he gives a list of monarchs and dates, calculating that eleven reigns are left, the first two "unpromising". "All the rest are glorious Subjects; especially Henry the First (struggle between the men of arms & of Letters, Becket) Stephen, Richard I, Edward II & Henry VII." It seems fairly clear that this entry was spadework for the projected play. Coleridge was considering writing plays in Malta (2064 *f28ᵛ*), and on his return to England he very soon set about revising *Osorio* (2928n).

2444 17.18   The first phrase in quotation marks comes from Samuel Horsley *A Charge delivered to the Clergy of the Archdeaconry of St. Albans* (1783) 54: "But lest the relation of primigeniture [*sic*] should lead to the notion of a proper physical generation, which would sink the Sin into the rank of a creature (for generation is only a particular way in which certain things are made) he [Athenagoras] says, that the birth or generation of the Sin, is not to be understood as if he were something that had been ever made: as if his Being had commenced, at any certain time, by the inducement of a form upon a praeexisting material. For that is the general notion of a making; although in common speech it is usual to say of these things only that they are made, to which the form is given at once by the hand of the artist. When the form is gradually brought on by the plastic powers of nature, the secret process is called Generation; which is therefore but a sort of making, and differs from that which is usually called a Making, in the means only by which the end is compassed." It is less Athenagoras than Horsley's interpretation and addenda to which Coleridge objects. His reading of Horsley at this time is a return to an old dislike, perhaps in search for support for evolving Trinitarian views; he had referred to Horsley's *Charge* in *Theol Lects* (1795). See 53n.

With the first part of the discussion in this entry it is interesting to note the close parallel in the essay "On Poesy or Art", where the creative process of the artist is described in terms similar to those used for the life process here. And later still, a similar objection to organization *ab extra* is raised in *TL* 43.

In calling Priestley a *Christologist* Coleridge antedates any use of the word given in *OED* (first date 1855) as distinguishing between Unitarian and Trinitarian views. The close of the entry appears to be his first recorded explicit statement of Trinitarianism as having supplanted his earlier Unitarianism.

2445 17.19   *The Platonic Fathers . . . as quoted by Horsley:* Horsley in his *Charge* (see the previous note) quotes the Greek words in a footnote, giving a reference to "Theoph. ad Autol. lib 2. p. 106. Oxon 1684", and in the text (p 60) he paraphrases: " 'The three days', says Theophilus 'which preceded the creation of the luminaries, were types of the Trinity; of God, and of his Word, and of his Wisdom'."

In what follows in this entry Coleridge is supporting Theophilus (and Horsley) against Priestley's charge of obscurity in the words *God*, the *Word*, and *Wisdom*.

Horsley says (p 68): "The error of the later Platonists was, that they warped the genuine doctrine of the original tradition, . . . to a form in which it might be in friendship with the popular idolatry." Coleridge has this sentence in mind apparently also in 2448.

Πατηρ . . . Ανθρωπος: "Father, Son, and Holy Spirit . . . God, His Word, His Wisdom, Man."
ενεργημα θεοπαραδοτον: energy given by God.
Ου αλογον: a reasonless thing.
Verba significant phænomena . . . : "Words represent phenomena, and phenomena are, as it were, words of thoughts."
ab initio: from the beginning.
It will be seen that Coleridge's return to orthodox Christianity is through the Logos, not the Gospels, a metaphysical rather than a historical approach.

2446 17.20   *AP* 128.

2447 17.21   The attitude expressed here to Platonism, e.g. as found in such later Platonists as Plotinus and Proclus, is one Coleridge maintained later against Tennemann and at various points in the *Philosophical Lectures.* See especially *Phil Lects* 165 and 425–8 n 20.
He is still debating with Horsley; see 2445 and n. As well as to *A Charge,* Coleridge is probably referring to Letter xiii of Horsley's *Letters* referred to in 2448n, in which Horsley, though arguing that the later Platonists did not discard the idea of the eternity of the Logos when converted to Christianity, is negative in discussing their views and Plato's on the eternity of the world. This question, too, was to be discussed in 1819: *Phil Lects* 229–30.

2448 17.22   *Horsley's Letters in Rep. to Dr P.: Letters from the Archdeacon of Saint Albans in reply to Dr. Priestley* (1784) esp Letters xi, xii, and xvi. The list is headed: *The Unitarian doctrine not well calculated for the conversion of Jews, Mahometans, or Infidels of any description.*
the remark of Horsley: "Your device of bringing them to believe Christianity, by giving the name of Christianity to what they already believe, in principle exactly resembles the strategem of a certain missionary of the Jesuits . . . who, in his zeal for the conversion of an Indian chief, . . . told him that Christ had been a valiant and successful warrior, who in the space of three years had scalped men women and children without number. . . ." Letter xvi 150.

2449 17.23   *Lieut. Pasley:* Charles William Pasley (1780–1861), an army officer, and an authority on fortifications, later distinguished himself at the siege of Flushing in Aug 1809. Coleridge maintained a connexion with him and, according to Godwin's MS diary, had Pasley and Godwin to breakfast on 2 May 1807; he corresponded with him in 1809 (CL # 775 and 792) and had confidence in his military opinions and general insights. See 2297n and 2627. In 1810 Pasley produced *An Essay on the Military Policy and Institutions of the British Empire*, which drew from Wordsworth a long and revealing reply. *W Letters (M)* 430–40.

The view from the Cotenera [Cotonera] Lines: the second "view" was presumably from the Hompesch Gate.

To which "Pocket-book" does he refer? In K, the only small note-book in this category (except possibly N 1), there were four blank pages left. There is extant no pocketbook of the type of N 4–N 10, which were used in pre-Malta travelling and to which sort he returned in 1806–8, N 11–N 14. If he did make notes on this magnificent view they have not survived. See Introduction xvi–xviii.

Pri[ckly] Pear Trees: usually *Cactus opuntia;* see 2289.

2450 17.24   *Aleph:* the first letter of the Hebrew alphabet; it means "ox".

2451 17.25   *Mʳ England whose flowers of Oratory I had noted down:* in N 10? See 2107.

"This Gemman" has not been identified.

Chabots: probably Mr Chabot of the firm Vallin and Chabot, merchants, who signed the letter referred to in 2099n.

2452 17.26   *Boverick:* Sobieski Boverick advertised his astonishing carvings in handbills, of which one was published in 1745 as follows:

"*To be seen at Mr. Boverick's, Watchmaker, at the DIAL, near the New Exchange, in the Strand, at One Shilling each Person.*

"The little furniture of a dining room; consisting of a dining-table, with a cloth laid, two figures seated as at dinner; a footman waiting; a card table, which opens with a drawer in it; frame and castors; look-ing glass; two dozen of dishes, twenty dozen of plates, thirty dozen of spoons; and twelve skeleton-back chairs with claw feet.—All the above particulars are contained in a cherry-stone.

"A landau which opens and shuts by springs, hanging on braces, with four persons sitting therein; a crane-neck carriage, the wheels turning on their axles, coachman's box, etc. of ivory; together with six horses and their furniture; a coachman on the box, a dog between his legs, the reins in one hand, and whip in the other; two footmen behind, and a postillion on the leading horse, in their proper liveries: all so minute as to be drawn by a flea.—It has been shewn to the Royal Society, and several persons of distinction.

"The curious little four-wheel open chaise, with the figure of a man in it; all made of ivory, drawn by a flea, which performs all the offices of a large chaise, as running of the wheels, locking etc.; weighing but one grain.—Shewn to the Royal Family, and several of the Nobility and Gentry.

". . . To be seen from nine in the morning till eight at night; and those that please to see them at their house may be waited upon, on Thursdays, at the same hours." R. S. Kirby *The Wonderful and Scientific Museum, or Magazine of Remarkable Characters; including all the curiosities of nature and art, from the remotest period to the present time. Drawn from every authentic source* (6 vols London 1803–20) I 101. Boverick went to Edinburgh, where he advertised, in addition to the aforementioned curiosities, that he "works family hair with a needle", and where he was admitted to membership in the Lodge of St David in 1768. John Smith *Old Scottish Clockmakers from 1453 to 1850* (2nd ed Edinburgh 1921) 50. The latest date for him so far discovered is 1785, when he went to Newcastle.

Coleridge's entry suggests that he had seen either the handbill itself, or Kirby's account of it, or some review of Kirby or some similar work in which it is presented. The last possibility appears likely, i.e. some source that mentions Boverick and Oswald Neringer together. Admittedly no such review has been found in the likely periodicals known to have been read by Coleridge at this period; nor has Oswald Neringer been discovered anywhere. Cf the cherry-stone carvings in 2305.

With reference to the *Wheel-animalcule*, cf 2538.

2453 17.27   *AP* 27, down to "more a Feeling than a Sight", dated by EHC 2 March, inexplicably unless he mistook the hour for the date. On the deep blue of the Mediterranean, cf 2400.

the melting away and entire union of Feeling & Sight: cf 1050 and 1099.

no power, (*and . . . less* strength): In his last letter to Davy before leaving England, Coleridge had written, "There *is* a something, an essential something wanting in me. I feel it, *I know* it—tho' what it is, I can but guess. . . . I seem to myself to distinguish power from strength & to have only the power". *CL* # 581. See also *Inq Sp* §18.

2454 17.28   *Why will ye die?:* the militant language of Jer. 27:13 is less likely in Coleridge's thoughts than the despairing mood of Ezek. 18:31 and 33:11.

The phrase "blasphemous despair" is used in *Osorio* III 207: *PW* II 558.

Those lines (composed in Ottery Church, or at Walthamstow?) of the cold speck: either the lines are lost or the description conceals rather than reveals them.

"In Ottery Church" would go back at least to Sept 1799, his last visit there up to this time. Walthamstow is about six miles NE of Liverpool St Station, virtually on his road from London to Dunmow. The church, like the collegiate church of Ottery St Mary, was "a stately structure on an eminence", and perhaps an association with the Beaumonts led to a parental-filial "breeze of feeling" that confused it with Ottery.

2455 17.29   *AP* 161–2, in part.
T'Aγαθον: the Creation.

2456 17.30   A recording of the quantities that led to the next entry?

2458 17.32   In another notebook entry Coleridge suggested that making memoranda hindered rather than helped recollection; "It rids the mind of it." See also 2474. The quotation marks are probably part of the same faint device as the insertion at the end, "Dramatic Hints these for Characters . . .".

On prayer and his appreciation of its difficulties see e.g. *Inq Sp* §288 and *Phil Lects* 225 and n 43.

clinging to some Passion: again and again he consistently thinks not of the external act but of the inner situation, the clue to his psychological prescience?

Thus ends the Day: source not traced.

The words at the end in pointed brackets are in different ink and compressed in the writing—an afterthought introduced for concealment? In any case, the word *Dramatic*, in the sense of referring to some fictional *dramatis personae* in the proposed "Comforts and Consolations", is a blind; on that work see 1993n.

2459 17.33   The lines by Vincenzo Littara were used by Charles
Wilkinson as an epigraph for his *Epitome of the History of Malta and
Gozo* (London 1804), a likely place for Coleridge to find them. See
also 2460n.

In No 22 of *The Friend* (1809–10) 354, Coleridge quoted and translated these lines: "An island small in size but great by illustrious ex-
ploits, the joint neighbour of Africa, Europe, and Asia, the hospitable
entertainer of St. Paul, and the delightful nurse of the Nobles of the
White Cross." Reprinted in 1812, this was omitted from later editions.

2460 17.34   The rough dimensions of Malta are precisely as given
in Wilkinson's *Epitome* 80, the circumference being an unusual meas-
urement in geographical descriptions of Malta, and the other figures
round rather than close; this seems to support the guess that Coleridge found his quotation in 2459 there. Wilkinson, however, does not
quote Diodorus Siculus, and Coleridge may have been reading something that Wilkinson used for source material which quotes both
Vincenzo Littara and Diodorus Siculus Bk v. Or perhaps Coleridge,
collecting opinions from ancient times onwards, on the economical
and military usefulness of Malta, is going back to originals. The
coincidence of two or three elements in these two entries, however,
suggests a secondary source.

In the quotation from Diodorus Siculus, Bk v §12, according to the
text of the edition *Bibliotheca historica* (2 vols Amsterdam 1746) 1 339,
the parenthetical words (*situs et commoditus portuum*) are carried
forward from the previous sentence:

And this is the reason why (in this place of commodious harbours), the
inhabitants of this island, since they received assistance in many respects
through the sea-merchants, shot up quickly in their manner of living and
increased in renown.—Tr C. H. Oldfather (LCL 1939).

2461 17.35   The clearly constant intention to write, and thoughts
of how to write, as seen in the notebooks, serve as both pathetic
commentary on and evidence of the power-without-strength of 2453.

2462 17.36   I.e. in the Governor's Palace, Valletta, an observation of refracted sunlight presumably related to some attempt to
understand the mathematics of refraction?

2463 17.37   Bellows were another example of Maltese inefficiency
compared with the work of English artisans; see 2404.

2465 17.39   *Li Pomi di terra sono lesti:* "The potatoes are ready".
Io sono lesto: "I am ready."

2466 17.40   A familiar sort of experience to most travellers.

2467 17.41   Either the remark was made by Leckie, or is Coleridge's about Mrs Leckie; the observation is a Coleridgian one, and
there are signs that Coleridge did not find Mrs Leckie quite congenial. She is elsewhere memorialized by him, according to a MS note
by Sara Coleridge now in VCL, as the owner of a lap-dog, "the dainty
beast" of his lines *Rufa: PW* II 960. But as these lines were first published in 1800, before Coleridge had met Mrs Leckie, and were
adapted from Lessing, they could not have been written about her,
though they may easily have been applied to her in conversation in
his later years.

2468 17.42   *AP* 126–7, variatim and in part.
    Souter: a George Suter is referred to in the Malta documents (Ad-
miralty 201), in July 1804, as a public auctioneer who sold captured
ships, i.e. "Prizes".
    I have two or three times felt a horrid touch: cf 848 and n, 1649, and
1726 *f37ᵛ*.
    Quam nihil ad genium, Papiliane, tuum!: the motto of *LB* (1800)
(1802)(1805), variatim; for *Papiliane* it reads *Papiniane.*
    Shawcross in a note in *BL* I 228–9, citing as evidence this entry as
published in *AP*, suggests that "Mackintosh was in all probability
the 'Papinianus' of the motto of the *Lyrical Ballads*".
    The motto, as Thomas Hutchinson, editor of the facsimile edition
of the *Lyrical Ballads* (1898), was the first to point out, came from
the "Address to the Reader from the Author of the Illustrations"
[John Selden] prefixed to Drayton's *Polyolbion* (1613 etc). Hutchinson
says, "Coleridge found the line in Anderson's *British Poets* vol. iii.
p. 238", an assertion probably true, but not inevitably, since Coleridge undoubtedly had other access to Drayton. Hutchinson felici-
tously translates the motto: "How absolutely *not* after your liking,
O learned jurist!" pointing it at Mackintosh. *LB* (1898) lix. Papinianus was a prominent jurist under Septimius Severus, and was
finally beheaded by Caracalla. Mackintosh was also a lawyer, a rival

talker and oracle *vis-à-vis* Coleridge, especially with the Wedgwoods. Is the variant here, *Papiliane*, a deliberate or an unconscious slip, a portmanteau name, in which *papilio*, for butterfly or moth, also applied to Mackintosh, plays a part? Entries like 609, 947, and 634 and n suggest a view of Mackintosh compatible with such an interpretation. His qualities and limitations are discussed also in *TT* 22 April 1823.

I cried out early, like a scarcely-hurt Child who knows himself within hearing of his Mother: cf *Christabel* line 328: "What if she knew her mother near?" *PW* I 226; also *The Wanderings of Cain*, "Has he no friend, no loving mother near?": *PW* I 287.

"The Dews were falling fast": "The dew was falling fast, the stars began to blink": *The Pet Lamb: WPW* I 245; and cf *Osorio* I 310: *PW* II 532.

the sneering and fiendish malignity of the beautiful creature; cf 1250. The relation of such dream-creatures to *Christabel* is discussed in an interesting article by E. E. Bostetter, *"Christabel:* The Vision of Fear" *Philol Q* xxxvi (April 1957) 183–94 and is touched on in my paper, "Coleridge, Wordsworth and the Supernatural" *UTQ* xxii (Jan 1956).

2469 17.43   *The Remark, which escaped my memory:* when he was writing 2440?

Ο Θεος: God.

οι θεοι: the gods.

οι αμφι Αχιληα: Achilles and his train.

Vos, and the Wie befinden sich die Hochdieselben: the upshot of the Greek, Latin, and German farrago seems to be an illustration of how the royal plural can be plural and singular at the same time, as in the polite address to exalted dignitaries: "And how do We do, your Majesty?"

Memory: Coleridge frequently tried to co-relate mental with bodily states, probably from fear that opium addiction was affecting his mind. See also e.g. 1726, 1822.

2470 17.44   *AP* 121. On falling asleep, see 1718 and n, among numerous other observations of hypnagogic phenomena.

2471 17.45   *AP* 166–7 and 127, in part; EHC publishes the words "I confess . . . develope it" at pp 166–7, the P.S. at p 127. There

is no apparent reason for this, unless it lies in the natural confusion
of the Coleridgian editorial desk.

Cottle-book on Envy: N 21; see 1606.

Cottle's & Richardson's . . . points of resemblance: Coleridge at
once shrinks from disloyalty, even in thought, to an old friend, yet
the lines of resemblance between Cottle and Richardson were already laid down in 477 (see 477n), 566, and 1239.

On Fielding and Richardson, Coleridge's classic remark is in *TT*
5 July 1834: "How charming, how wholesome Fielding always is! To
take him up after Richardson, is like emerging from a sick room
heated by stoves, into an open lawn, on a breezy day in May." For
his annotations on Fielding, see *MC* 302–6. What he admired in
Richardson is summarized in a few phrases in *BL* II 183: "the loaded
sensibility, the minute detail, the morbid consciousness of every
thought and feeling in the whole flux and reflux of the mind, in short
the self-involution and dreamlike continuity of Richardson". He had
used some of these phrases of himself, doubtless with a similar mixture
of admiration and disgust.

2472 17.46   The copy of L[yrical?] B[allads?] defaced by Stoddart,
which caused Coleridge frequent distress, has unfortunately not come
to light; see also 2120 and 2890.

2473 17.47   *Dunnage:* the *OED* offers no derivation but suggests
a link with *dün, thin,* and defines it much as Coleridge does here.

Hüt—or Hät-Money: Hutgeld or *Hütgeld* (Adelung gives both spellings) must be in Coleridge's mind, cognate with *hüten,* "to take care
of" or "head". The noun is *die Hut,* identical in form with *der Hut,*
"hat". *Hutgeld* in present-day usage refers to a fee paid for pasturage,
or a herdsman's wages, and does not appear to be applied nautically,
but Adelung's definition of it as money for *Wache* (Watch) might be
so extended. Hat money—or rather a silk top hat—is still ceremoni-
ously presented on the Canadian Great Lakes, to the first skipper who
takes a cargo-laden ship into port after the spring break-up. At
Toronto the hat is regularly (since 1861 at least) put away for future
ceremonies, and money for a more practical hat is given to replace it.

2474 17.48   A return to 2458; one is frequently struck by Coleridge's candour with himself in the notebooks, in contrast to the let-

ters, especially by his awareness of illness in what until recently would have passed for healthy or normal behaviour. See also 1388.

2476 17.50   The Bashaw or Pasha of Tunis at this time was Hamouda. Probably some British representative at Tunis was in Malta, by whom this and the next two anecdotes were reported, probably Oglander; see 2513 and n.

2477 17.51   Again the Bey of Tunis?

2478 17.52   This may also refer to the Bey of Tunis; on the other hand, it is difficult to be specific about attempted assassinations in the Middle East at this time.

2479 17.53   *Bra* appears again in 2487, an unlaid ghost. Possibly O[*ld*] *Bra*[*ve*], i.e. Indian brave?

2480 17.54   *my Room at the Treasury:* Coleridge elsewhere refers with pleasure to his garret, his sky-chamber, in the Treasury; unhappily the room and the picture, possibly a mural, were destroyed by bomb damage 1940–43. Cf 2420, where a similar remark is made about the drunken look of the figures on crucifixes, and about *Picturæ Pauperum Libri:* Pictures the Books of the Poor. They were for Coleridge connected with "idolatry". See e.g. *Phil Lects* 90, the next entry, and 2420.

2481 17.55   See the previous note. Coleridge later was to refer his anti-clericalism largely to his experiences in Malta and Italy, and to contend that his antagonism to Roman Catholicism was based chiefly on what he considered its anti-intellectual anti-educational views. See e.g. *C&S* 153–7, the long footnote.

2482 17.56   *But yesternight I pray'd aloud/In Anguish and in Agony: The Pains of Sleep* (1803): *PW* 1 389. The last line is spontaneous, not in the poem.

2483 17.57   On Hope, see among many diverse references, especially 1552, 1713, 2531, 2549, 2552, 2705.

2484 17.58   *AP* 128.
Cowper's stream "inlaying" *the level vale:* see 513 and n.

Shakespere's shrill-tongued Tapster, answering "shallow wits": a reference to the reiterated "Anon, anon, sir" of Francis in 1 *Henry IV* II iv? Coleridge put quotation marks after *wits*, but none to indicate the beginning of his quotation. Presumably he is telescoping three Shakespeare passages here: *shrill-tongued*, applied to Fulvia in *Antony and Cleopatra* I i 32, "His jest will savour but of shallow wit" from *Henry V* I ii 295, and the re-echoing "Anon" of the tapster.

2485 17.59   *Mr Chapman:* the newly appointed Public Secretary; see 2408n and 2430n. E. K. Chambers here, as at numerous other points in Coleridge's career, slants his remarks in an antagonistic vein not warranted by the full facts. Coleridge, he says, "told his friends that he should start home at the end of February, *and then put it off to the end of May*". Chambers 187, italics mine. This entry makes plain the unavoidable state of affairs, and Coleridge's feelings. And see 2665.

2486 17.60   *AP* 128–9; EHC omits the first sentence.
The full and explicit meaning hidden in the Greek letters remains, from anything we know of the details of Coleridge's Malta days, concealed. Possibly the interpretation depends on a link with the Pauline phrase "O wretched man that I am! who shall deliver me from the body of this death" (Rom. 7:24), i.e. Ομμα, Greek "eye", and the English "am"; the despairing cry appears frequently in Coleridge's writings, especially in later notebooks. In this case, *S.ΣT* may be a reference to himself.

deeply Thinking in a reverie: the phrase is arresting, as qualifying, in the direction of giving more weight to the rational element, Coleridge's ordinary use of the word *reverie;* some discussion of this word is to be found in Bald 37–40. Perhaps the statement should read from the opposite direction, i.e. possibly the entry suggests rather his awareness of subrational factors in cerebral processes.

2487 17.61   Another American story about the Brave of 2479?

2488 17.62   *AP* 128–9 variatim. Is Coleridge, tired of loneliness in the company of "practical" men in the naval, commercial, and civil-service atmosphere of Malta, making a reference that reeks of the good, useless, speculative talk of the Salutation and the Cat days with Lamb? Cf Lamb's "Drinking egg-hot and smoking Oronooko (associated circumstances, which ever forcibly recall to my mind our evenings and nights at the Salutation)", in an early letter to Coleridge. *L Letters* 1 29-30.

2489 17.63   In view of the speculation in the last note, it may be worth noticing that Coleridge sometimes relied on Lamb for a supply of pens, and received from him "a hundred or so of Pens" just before he sailed for Malta. *CL* # 572.

2490 17.64   *Difficilitate:* dated 1611 in *OED* and obsolete before 1700. Playfulness with words in a context of deep personal interest is revealing. Until 1857, divorce in England, unless obtained by special act of Parliament, was a matter for the ecclesiastical courts.

2491 17.65   *Campieri:* guards. A story about the cheapness of life?

2492 17.66   On Decatur see 2228.

2493 17.67   Again (see 2442 and 2443) Coleridge appears to be reading Nicolson and Burn. Of Warcop in Westmorland, near Appleby, this work says: "The church is dedicated to *St. Columbe;* by contraction *St. Combe.* Thus in the year 1380, Thomas de Sandford bequeathed according to the custom of those times, to the vicar of Warcop 20 s (which kind of legacy afterwards obtained the name of *mortuary*) for his forgotten tithes, and his body to be buried in the churchyard of *St. Columbe.*" 1 600. And see the next entry.

2494 17.68   *AP* 129. The source, Nicolson and Burn op cit further down on the same page as 2493, explains: "This saint [St. Columbe] is not in the Kalendar of saints in the Romish Church, having never been canonized at Rome. He was the apostle of the Picts, and settled in one of the Hebrides islands in the sixth century."

2495 17.69   *f38   Mss σε'τκο9:* the last letter, the numeral *9*, is a clearer reading than σε'τκοο, which, however, may be the intention. *M[i]ss Sehtkonine,* an anagram for some name? Or *Mss* = hands, *sehtkoo* = she took? The concealment has not been deciphered. *f38ᵛ   H.N.:* Human Nature.
    narcissine: Coleridge's use is not in *OED* and appears to be original; see also 1746n.

ff39–39ᵛ   Hercules . . . the Cart . . . out of the . . . Rut: the reference is to Aesop's fable of Hercules and the Carter.
f41   a fountain with unwrinkled surface: an image associated with
the Grasmere circle and pursued further here on *f41ᵛ;* see 980 and n.
f41ᵛ   The quoted phrase is from the *Inscription for a Fountain on a
Heath: PW* 1 382.
   Happiness is a Fountain of intellectual activity: cf *Dejection: an Ode,*
especially stanzas IV–VI.
f42   cowardice of pain: a frequent self-accusation, as in 2368.
   The footnote, and the earlier passage it annotates, surely suggest
an attempt to articulate an intuition close to the Freudian concept,
over a hundred years later, of the id, the super-ego, and the ego?

2497 17.71   The obliterated word is probably a first guess at the
name of the Maltese village Luqa or Lucca. Coleridge was much
struck with the stone-walled plots of cultivation, signs of "difficulty
overcome" in Maltese agriculture. See also 2101 and 2283.

2498 17.72   A repetition of 2284; see 2284n.

2500 17.210   There is no possibility of dating this entry precisely.
It is a fragment at the top of *f129ᵛ,* the remainder of the page having
been cut out; the word *hailed* has now disappeared in the repairing
of the notebook. From this page onwards, *ff130–138ᵛ* are blank, except for Coleridge's numbers on the pages and, on *ff133ᵛ, 134,* and
138ᵛ, the names in the corners; *ff139–142ᵛ* appear to have been used
in Malta.
   In the absence of any real evidence as to date, I have placed this
towards the end of March, after a long run of entries in this notebook,
and before 2514, which may refer to it as "at the end [i.e. towards the
end?] of this Book". "That Poem" may have been partly written
here, partly in 2524; what remain of the hints for it in 2514 suggest
that it might have been a poem that would fall foul, as this did, of
the censor.

2501 15.134   See also 2565 and 2787. The simultaneous fruits and
blossoms, striking enough to a northern eye, probably delighted Coleridge especially because he had already written about them—in a
more "shadowy air": "The moon was bright, the air was free,/And
fruits and flowers together grew/On many a shrub and many a tree."

The Wanderings of Cain: PW 1 287. He had recently felt similar pleasure in recalling instances of other verses anticipatory of actual experience, e.g. St Michael's Cave in 2045 already in *Remorse*, and the thin sails and the vessel-made breeze of 2052 already in *The Ancient Mariner*. The connexion with *The Wanderings of Cain*, suggesting that that poem was still being worked on, at some level of Coleridge's mind, may have a bearing on the question of the long span of dates in the composition of that poem.

2502 15.135   Ink. The logically as distinct from the existentially real was to become a frequent subject with Coleridge. At this point he may have had in mind Paley's logic in general, and his *Natural Theology* in particular. The illustration of the equipollent forces [?muscles] keeping a body at rest may come, consciously or unconsciously, from Chap ix "Of the Muscles" of that work.

nihil negativum . . . *irrepresentabile:* a negative nothing, which cannot be presented to the mind [or, which is not even conceivable].

nihil privativum cogitabile: a privative nothing, which is conceivable.

2503 15.136   *Metapothecaries* was Southey's word, Coleridge said in 1801. *CL* # 417.

Coleridge's frequently reiterated defence of the rationality of metaphysics is in reply not only to Southey (as in *Inq Sp* §95), but to the "Worldlings" (as in 2784), and, earlier, to Burke. His rhetorical question in entry 1623, "Is this the metaphysics that bad Spirits in Hell delight in", was discovered, after that entry was published, to be an answer to Burke's attack on intellectual radicals: "Naturally men so formed and finished [by knowledge and talent] are the first gifts of Providence to the World. But when they have once thrown off the fear of God, which was in all ages too often the case, and the fear of man, which is now the case, and when in that state they come to understand one another, and act in corps, a more dreadful calamity cannot arise out of Hell to scourge mankind. Nothing can be conceived more hard than the heart of a thorough bred metaphysician. It comes nearer to the cold malignity of a wicked spirit than to the frailty and passion of man. It is like the principle of Evil himself, incorporeal: pure, unmixed, dephlegmated, defecated, evil." Edmund Burke *A Letter to a Noble Lord* (1st ed 1796) 61. The last three sentences were quoted in the review of this work in the first number of *The Watchman* 19.

2505 15.274   As the scribblings at the top of the page are quite incoherent and the rest of the page only slightly less so, the order and limits of the jottings impossible to determine, and as the date is of uncertain relevance, it has seemed best to show this composite of entries without severing them. Possibly the occultation of Mercury is likeliest for the date, but on the other hand, does the "occultation of Mercury" give a name to the phenomenon of 9 July 1804 described in 2139? Unfortunately the German almanac available for the place and the period records no occultations either in July 1804 or March 1805.

2506 15.138   Possibly this was the occasion referred to in *The Friend* III 321, when the old man "belonging to one of the distant casals" [?Safi] showed him "the sea coombe, where their father Ball . . . first landed; and afterwards pointed out the very place, on which he first stepped on their island", recording the surprise of the inhabitants at so difficult and unexpected a landing. One is able to see from the road, between Maqluba and Zurrieq, "a fine Sea comb," with straight rocky sides which might provide on the coast a difficult landing in any but calm weather. The "good Luogo tenente" was, one suspects, Giuseppe Abdillo, whose Casal Safi address was written at 2381.

Zerrid [*Zurrieq*]: blue, where everyone has blue eyes.

Maccluba [*Maqluba*]: the name means "overturned". The Capuchin Gardens in Syracuse are among rocks upended.

terra rovesciata: "topsy-turvy world".

Krendi [*Qrendi*]: Maqluba is in the village of Qrendi.

escono cattivissimi: "they come out as wicked as possible".

ospizio: the hospice in Floriana for the poor. The conservatory he refers to is there also, and a foundling hospital.

2507 15.139   Carob-trees, with their very shiny leaves; see also 2683.

2508 15.140   The word *Pots* is not a mistake for *Plots*, but descriptive of the small fields enclosed within stone walls, a prominent feature of the Malta landscape.

2509 17.74   The beginning of this entry appears to have been cut out by the excision of the leaf preceding *f43*.

Dimness is a favourite and an emotionally charged word, often associated with growth, change, the unknown processes of life, as well
as with subjective feelings and efforts to explore them. Cf e.g. "By
deep feeling we make our *Ideas dim*" in 921.

Barbouldian pertains to Mrs Letitia Barbauld, aggressive protago-
nist of the Unitarianism Coleridge had abandoned and, for the reason
given in 1848n, anathema at this time. The list of names and the angle
of attack here suggest an important facet of Coleridge's whole op-
position to English empiricism.

2510 17.75   As the footnote sign indicates, this entry was clearly
related to the entry on the excised leaf opposite, referred to in 2509n
but not to 2509 itself.

The projected poem was apparently something other than *The
Suicide's Argument*, dated by EHC as of 1811: *PW* I 419. On suicidal
thoughts in Malta, see also 2100 *f3*, 2527, 2557.

2511 17.76   Had daisies some special significance? See 2778 and n.

2512 17.77   Probably the *29* refers again to 29 March; it is otherwise unexplained. In the lectures of Jan–March 1818 Coleridge
touched on this subject with reference to Boccaccio; see *MC* 22. He
frequently quotes a favourite phrase from the *Della geneologia de gli
Dei*, and owned a copy of that work (see 2737n). He also acquired
at some time a collected edition, *Delle opere di M. Giovanni Boccacci*
(6 vols 8° Florence and Naples 1723–4). Of his copy, four volumes
are now in the library of the Rev A. D. Coleridge.

Of Machiavelli Coleridge quotes *The Prince* in 3015 and *Friend* I
205; and see 2385 for an indication that he knew the *History of
Florence*.

2513 17.78   *Oglander:* Richard Oglander (1783–1857), younger
son of Sir William Oglander 5th bart; he had at this time recently
passed through Malta on his way to Tunis to take up his duties as
Consul-General. His letter of introduction to Ball was dated London
27 Oct 1804. (CO 159.3 f 129.) It may have been from him Coleridge
heard the anecdotes referred to in 2476, 2477, and 2478.

Coleridge deplored British diplomacy, or the lack of it, in the
Barbary States: *Friend* III 354, 367, 372; he was horrified, too, at the
type of official being appointed as consul. *CL* # 601.

2514 17.79   This is the end of an entry largely lost with the excision of three leaves preceding *f44*.

If my dating of this entry is correct, and it does seem to fall clearly between 29 March (2513) and the "Saturday Night" of 2515, which I take to be the Saturday preceding 1 April of 2516, i.e. 30 March 1805, then this entry is a resolve to write the poem of which there are fragments dated 4 April 1805 on the inside cover of this notebook; see 2500 and 2524.

2515 17.80   Again a report of uncongenial conversation in Malta. Coleridge later makes his own explicit statement on national *vs* human loyalties. "I, for one, do not call the sod under my feet my country. But language, religion, laws, government, blood—identity in these makes men of one country." *TT* 28 May 1830.

2516 17.81   *AP* 153-4 variatim. Coleridge misdated this and the succeeding entry 1 April; when he corrected himself in 2517 he simply forgot to do so here.

Variety . . . Uniformity: there appears to be the germ here of the well-known description of the poet in *BL* Chap XIV (II 12).

Hatred of Vacancy . . . love of Rest: in a manuscript fragment this state is associated with reading light novels: *Inq Sp* §173.

Edwin and Angelina: the ballad by Goldsmith (1764); it appears in *The Vicar of Wakefield* Chap VIII.

how beautiful would not the first other man appear: a recollection and adaptation of Miranda's reception of Ferdinand? *The Tempest* I ii: "I might call him/A thing divine; for nothing natural/I ever saw so noble."

2517 17.82   The account of how Coleridge received the news of the death by drowning of Wordsworth's brother John in the sinking of his ship the *Abergavenny* 5 Feb 1805 corresponds to his accounts in his letters (cf 2518 and n), except that here he does not refer to a fall "in a convulsive hysteric Fit", though that accords well enough with his being led home by the sergeant-at-arms, and with the implications of Lady Ball's note (*f46*) to him (when I first saw N 17, pasted in at this page):

"Dear Sir
    I was very sorry I could not send you the news paper but Sir Alex^r had just lent it to Capt Vivian, but as soon as it comes

home I will send it you. had I known the Captain had been a
friend of yours, I certainly wou'd not have been the bearer of ill
news. Your strong feelings are too great for your health. I hope
you will soon recover your spirits.
Your obliged
M.B. [Lady Ball]

[From Lady Ball, April 1 1805. Sunday Evening]"

The endorsements (here given square brackets) are Coleridge's, in
pencil.

Dr *Sewel:* see 2139 and n.

Sara . . . in my imagination . . . connected with him: There is a
family tradition that JW first wished to marry Mary Hutchinson—
borne out by his letter to her quoted in *W Letters* (*E*) 309—and then,
with characteristic self-effacement, on hearing of WW's intentions,
gracefully yielded. "John was the first", Mary wrote later, "who led
me to everything I love in the neighbourhood." *W Letters* (*E*) 474n;
see also ibid 468.

Coleridge elsewhere refers to his "hope" that John would marry
Sara, and complete the circle. See *SH Letters* xxvi, quoting a letter to
Daniel Stuart from BM Add MSS 34,046 ff 61–2; and *W Life* 1 473–4.

The references to the Wordsworths at the close of the entry, exaggerated as they may seem to the conventions of grief a hundred and
fifty years later, are given substance by WW's remark that only Coleridge would know the depth of their distress at John's death. *W
Letters* (*E*) 463.

The entry is here unfinished because the two leaves that follow
were cut out of the notebook.

2518 15.141   Possibly seen from a window, but 2521 makes it clear
that he was not confined to bed, as he later recounted in a letter of
21 July 1805. *CL* # 618. In a letter of 30 April to Daniel Stuart there
is a reference, however, to a recent general worsening of health to
which JW's death was, he says, a contributing factor. *CL* # 615.

2520 15.143   *Civita Vecchia:* Città Vecchia, the old city of M'dina.
   A comment on the reconciliation of opposites, the military and the
domestic, the practical and the decorative?

2521 15.144   *the grand Houses at Bristol left unfinished:* About 1790
the imposing Royal York Crescent was begun, but owing to the

financial disasters of the period of the French Revolution, the unfinished row was offered for sale in 1800, then proposed for barracks
in 1803, and was still unfinished and on the market in 1809. Other
similar misfortunes were evident in Bristol, but this was the most
striking one.

Morrison: John Morrison, the rich merchant of 2099.

Faldettos: see 2100n.

Sulla: a pink vetch resembling red clover, large and profuse in
Malta.

2522 15.145   Aside from the interest shown here in a preoccupation
more Continental than English, it is to be noted that Coleridge uses
the inches sign for feet; see 2014 and n.

2523 17.226   The British Museum has opened and silk-gauzed
two back leaves once stuck together with five blobs of sealing-wax
(? by STC). The pages, though written on with ink, have suffered so
much in the sticking and the severing that little is legible. There are
the names in the corners usual in this notebook. Both pages are full of
draft lines, mostly crossed through, for verses, the first of which, in
this entry, seem to be part of a "doleful [?Ditty/Daughter] dialogue/
Twixt a [?pompous/lumpish] Dutchman [and . . . .]".
(This comes from two lines running perpendicularly up the gutter
margin of the page.)
    The product of boredom in the Admiralty Court?

2524 17.227   See the note above.
    The poem referred to in 2514? See also 2500 and n.
    The lines here are sometimes merely rhyme-endings.
    With "So looks the hawk's wing double", cf an observation Cole-
ridge made in 1803: 1668 and n.

2525 17.83   The beginning of the entry is lost on the excised
leaves referred to in 2517n. On negative judgements, cf 2598.

2526 17.84   *AP* 129–30 variatim. In *Friend* III 297 the substance
of the last three sentences in defence of book-knowledge, more for-
mally expressed, is attributed to a remark of Alexander Ball.

2527 17.85   The references to the visualized event of the sinking
of John Wordsworth's ship suggest that Coleridge had seen Lady

Ball's newspaper, or some of the newspaper accounts that did not spare their readers any of the harrowing details. See Appendix D.

2528 17.86   This semi-coherent entry is written in a firm enough hand. The M^r is written above *Macky!*; I suggest, for concealment; between, whether intentionally over the *ack* or under the M^r is not evident, there is a sign $\doteq$, or what looks like a sign. $\doteq$ reversed ($\div$) is used in the cryptogram once, in 3202, for *M*, but the link seems remote.

Macky = Make ye? I.e. [opium] "does not make you chearful! or comfortable! even for the moment". *Macky* could perhaps also refer to the Mr Mackenzie who later travelled with Coleridge in Sicily, referred to in 2680.

drums: not *dreams,* at first sight more likely.

2529 17.87   Nine lines are heavily deleted at the end of this entry. Coleridge's feelings of depression, brought on by John Wordsworth's death, were added to, he tells Daniel Stuart in a letter at the end of this month, by the loss of letters and newspaper articles sent to England, the entire absence of any letters from Mrs Coleridge or Southey, and only one from the Wordsworths of Sept 1804 date, together with repeated disappointments in not being able to return to England because Ball could not release him. *CL* # 615. He had as well his usual financial worries, *CL* # 616.

2530 17.88   "And haply by abstruse research to steal/From my own nature all the natural man"? *Dejection: an Ode: PW* I 367. If the *confession* was written it has disappeared.

Miserere mei, Domine!: "Lord have mercy upon me!"

2531 17.89   *AP* 130–1, with important deletions.

Did I not particularly notice . . . on my first arrival at Malta: If he means he made a note of it in a notebook, this has been lost; no such memorandum appears in the extant notebooks.

Ode to Duty: Coleridge's letter has not survived in *CL,* but the reference to it proves that in some form Wordsworth's poem was written before April 1804, when Coleridge sailed; his reference suggests a not-recent poem or letter, not so recent as his one letter from the Wordsworths in Malta written Sept 1804. The earliest date assigned to the poem by E. de Selincourt was simply "1804" (*WPW*

IV 83), but in a note he suggests that it was in the MS Wordsworth poems, transcribed by SH and DW, that Coleridge took to Malta: *WPW* IV 418. See 2092n and Appendix E. See also on the *Ode to Duty* 2091 and n, 2556 and n, 3026 and n.

Selfness: presumably as compared with the self-extension or extra-identification discussed in the previous entry. The reference at the end to repeated washing is the only one Coleridge makes to this, though the quick reversal, in the suggestion that anxiety may have its uses, is typical of a pattern in his thought when it touches deeply on personal matters. See 2541.

at every Gyre its wings beat against the personal Self: on Coleridge's frequent use of the bird-image for himself, especially the restricted, encaged, or even the comic bird, see *AP* 193, *A Character: PW* I 451, and the poetic partridges and wild ducks *vs* the prose metaphysical bustard in *CL* # 445 (II 814).

2532 17.90   *PW* II 1000, without the last two words or any indication that the poem is incomplete because five leaves have been cut out of the notebook, *ff54–58;* the leaves had been written on, but no whole words remain on the cropped edges.

2533 17.91   The entry is crowded in between the names on the corners of the page and may have been written after the next two entries. Cf H. W. Fowler *Modern English Usage* in support of Coleridge's view.

2534 17.92   *indefinite sensations of comfort:* as in 1718, 2495?

Spera una delusione, Loda un inganno: "He hopes for a delusion and praises a deception."

cerebelline Tint: cf the next entry. *OED* gives *cerebellar,* or *cerebellic;* C is coining a word for *illusory, in the mind only.*

2535 17.93   *AP* 131–2 variatim, and incomplete, the Greek words at the end having been omitted.

The entry is cut short by the excision of *f60.*

The Greek letters transliterated read like a fragment from the Tower of Babel:

Πανηγυριζε Ξτ* ein *α*γ*ε* Inganno + tintserebel uber νυκτα spegliato [*for* svegliato] in cons. des morgens phruh [*for* fruh], e tallora per μη restare sphegliante [*for* svegliante] ελπις eina Delusione—Then anxiety, stiphlin[g]—αθμη.

The passage may be translated:

He praises a deception and cerebelline fantasies through the night; awakening into cons[ciousness] in the morning early, and sometimes so as not to remain awake, he hopes for a delusion—Then anxiety, stifling—breath.

2536 17.94   The beginning of this entry is missing with *f6o.*
by all sweet images conveying to her *understanding:* the passage recalls 984.

Lord Nelson is pursuing the French Fleet: The French fleet had broken the English blockade of Toulon and Rochefort, 30 March, and though thought to be heading for Egypt was actually making for the West Indies; Nelson at this date was in pursuit from Sicily, trying to intercept a landing in Egypt. Apparently an engagement in the Mediterranean, a deterrent to travel, was thought of as an imminent possibility; it did not take place until the autumn, 21 Oct—in fact, Trafalgar.

Yet if I go, whither am I to go?: a phrase to be taken into consideration in any view of his uncertain movements and delays on his return to England, Aug–Oct 1806.

2537 17.95   *AP* 132–3.
the Concern: the Dove Cottage circle, including SH, as in 980 and n.
the brilliant action with Linois: JW was with the East India fleet 15 Feb 1804 returning from China when it successfully battled a larger French force, under Admiral Linois. Coleridge was in Malta; presumably the one letter he had from the Wordsworths dated Sept 1804 must have told him of it.
"I have done my Duty! let her go!": This is a strange paraphrase, if that is what it is; cf the available accounts of the sinking of the *Abergavenny;* the account in *Il Cartaginese* was not published until about a fortnight after this entry. See Appendix D.

2538 17.96   *AP* 134–6 variatim.
bethrong ⟨and bemurmur⟩: putting in practice his theory of the value of German prefixes.
the wheel Insect: the rotifer or wheel-animalcule? Not insects, but microscopic animals. See also 2452.
the net: presumably spiders.
the Gun: possibly the bombardier beetles (*Brachinus*), which expel with a faint bang and a minute cloud of yellowish vapour an acrid

secretion. Or possibly one of the *Cephalopoda*, molluscs which discharge a secretion under water.

the galvanic eel: or electric eel; see *Inq Sp* §30 and n. On Hartley Coleridge's interest in natural history, and Coleridge's belief in its educational values, see 959 and n.

2539 17.97   *Middleton:* Thomas Fanshaw Middleton, later Bishop of Calcutta, of whose "alienation" from Coleridge when he was at Pembroke, and Coleridge at Jesus College, Cambridge, there is no record, called on Coleridge in London 10 Feb 1808, when feelings seem to have been very friendly on both sides. See *CL* # 679.

On the absence of surprise in sleep Coleridge had commented before. See 1250n. For other Christ's Hospital dreams see 848n, 1176, 1649, 1726. In a record of some of his dreams (BM Add MS 47,887), Southey said (7 June 1805), "Westminster often makes a part of my dreams which are always uncomfortable."

2540 17.98   *AP* 133–4.
Fenelon & Madame Guyon . . . the Worship of Saints: Coleridge's attitude towards these writers (and Pascal) is as to exceptions that tend to prove his anti-Gallican rule. Of Fénelon he read an essay "On Charity", whether in the original or in translation and in what edition are now not known; his annotations on this work, not related to this subject, are generally adverse (*LR* II 368–9); yet cf the delineation of Fénelon "a mystic, an Enthusiast of a nobler breed" in *AR* 381–6. Possibly he is referring here to *Maxims of the Saints Explained.* Fénelon and Mme Guyon, close friends, shared a kind of Neoplatonic Christian mysticism. Of Coleridge's reading of her works there is no record. He may well have known some of them, including the hymns, in Cowper's translations, of which Wordsworth owned a copy, according to the Wordsworth LC.

2541 17.99   The entry is incomplete, two or three leaves having been cut out after they were written on.
Hints and Notes de Consolatione: presumably his "Comforts and Consolations" discussed in 1993n; this particular "hint" may be the one about "Selfness"; see 2531 and n.

2542 17.100   *AP* 134; the entry confirms the account of the loss of his papers in *CL* # 615, and is itself confirmed by an account of the

capture of the *Arrow* 3 Feb 1805 by the French, *An Reg* (1805) 524–6.
The names to which his dreams attached themselves are not
without interest. Marcus Terentius Varro (116–27 B.C.) is the Roman
antiquarian and voluminous man of letters, Gerhard Johann Vossius
(1577–1649), the German classicist and theologian.

Most interesting of all is Coleridge's Freudian observation here of
the fact of the recurrence in sleep of the impressions immediately
preceding, the day-residue.

2543 17.101   One of the most searching of his attempts in the notebooks to analyse varying degrees of consciousness.

outward Forms and Sounds, the Sanctifiers: The notebooks are full
of examples of deliberate use of the external world as a stabilizer; see
e.g. 3026 and also 2550.

dim sense of . . . a Person: cf 1250.

υλη = *confusio . . . efformans:* Matter is the same thing as disorder, which is the same as passivity, which is the same as dissolution
[or death], and these are opposed to Reason, Action, self-determinate
Form.

2544 17.102   He appears to be recalling Blumenbach *Handbuch
der Naturgeschichte* (cf 1748), and Reimarus *Allgemeine Betrachtungen
über die Triebe der Thiere* of more recent reading (see 2325). In the
latter (1 180 §73) Reimarus makes a general observation on insects
laying their eggs on the soft membranes of living animals, but he is
not so specific as this entry; his remark has perhaps recalled to Coleridge's mind the detail from elsewhere, possibly from conversation
with Blumenbach; see 1738n and *Inq Sp* §189 for other word-of-
mouth information from him.

2546 17.104   *AP* 136–7; cf 2375. And cf House 29.

2547 17.105   In his hypersensitivity to sound Coleridge seems not
to have realized the influence of a semi-tropical climate in causing
windows and doors to be left open and life to pour out on to the
streets. The antipathy here is surely heightened by his discomfort
over holidays in general, as discussed in 2647 and n.

2548 17.106   *AP* 138. The footnote sign and what it designates are
in another hand, possibly Edward Coleridge's.

2549 17.107 · *AP* 137. The reference to Wordsworth's *Michael* is to lines 142–8: ". . . but to Michael's heart/This son of his old age was yet more dear—/Less from instinctive tenderness, the same/Fond spirit that blindly works in the blood of all—/Than that a child, more than all other gifts/That earth can offer to declining man,/Brings hope with it, and forward-looking thoughts. . . ." *WPW* II 85.

One of the ends of the state, Coleridge was to say later, was "To secure to each of its members THE HOPE of bettering his own condition or that of his children": *LS* 115.

2550 17.108 *AP* 138.

the forma efformans: see 2543n.

Things without . . . images within: see 2543 and n.

"The Lord said unto my Lord, Sit thou on my right hand, till I make thine enemies thy footstool." Matt. 22:44; also in Mark 12:36, Luke 20:42, Acts 2:34, all quoting Ps. 110:1.

2551 17.109 *AP* 138–9. With the first sentence, cf 15.

2552 17.110 *AP* 139; cf the letter to Mrs Coleridge 21 July 1805. *CL* # 618. And see Appendix B on Coleridge's "official tasks". On the importance of Hope to freedom of thought, see 2086 *ff39ᵛ–40*, 2531.

2553 17.111 *AP* 139.

A rude outline: i.e. his simile in the sentence above for the place of feeling in the intellectual process. The wires on the black resin-plate probably harks back to demonstrations at Humphry Davy's lectures, of experiments with coloured iron filings or wires on electrically charged plates.

2554 17.112 *AP* 139–40. John Tobin died 7 Dec 1804, soon after the successful production of his *The Honey Moon;* for earlier references to him see 590n, 598n.

Robert Allen: see 161[*f*]n, 1726n; he was also a friend of Stoddart, had accompanied Stoddart on his tour of Scotland in Oct 1802 (*L Letters* I 323), and may have called on Coleridge at Keswick then. He was on duty as an army surgeon in Portugal at the time of his death.

the Bell-man's or Clerk's Verses subjoined: e.g. Cowper refers to being a "dirge writer" and reluctantly composing verses to be printed annually at the foot of Bills of Mortality. Cowper to Hayley 2[5] Nov 1792, in Hayley's *Life and . . . [Letters] of William Cowper Esq*

(1803) II 99. Some of these are printed in *The Poetical Works of William Cowper* ed H. S. Milford (Oxford 1950) 365–70. Doubtless most such verses were usually more "commonplace" and by less distinguished versifiers.

2555 17.113   On Coleridge on pre-Darwin evolutionary theories see A. D. Snyder *Logic* 16–23.

2556 17.114   *AP* 140–2, in two separate entries, with important deletions and a significant addition. The last five words of this entry are no longer visible except in the photographs, having disappeared in the rebinding. The entry is cut short in mid-sentence by the excision of the leaf referred to below. EHC's editing elicits comment at this point.

The first gap, not noticed by EHC, is here indicated by the ⌐ . . . . ⌐ on *f74ᵛ* and represents two and a half lines heavily inked over. The second gap, on *f75*, is the consequence of a third of the leaf having been cut out; it will be noted that at this point EHC in *AP* supplies the excised words, after *or else:* "a mere translation or wordy paraphrase,—but the state of that person who, in order to enjoy his nature in the highest manifestation of conscious *feeling* has no need of doing. . . ." EHC refers to Gillman's *Life* 176–9, without disclosing that Gillman also quoted the second group of words now no longer in the notebook. Possibly EHC obtained them from Gillman, and, if so, this would point to Mrs Gillman as the censor, unless EHC himself performed the excisions, simply observing the fact that the passage had already been quoted by Gillman; he noticed Gillman's use of 2546, where no such question is involved. But the evidence, such as it is, goes against Mrs Gillman. It seems unlikely to have been EHC. He, for all his work on the notebooks, left scarcely a mark on them; oddly enough, one on this entry, in pencil: "Thus far copied", he writes, after *Enjoyment* on *f75ᵛ*, and draws a pencil line that marks the end of his use in *AP* of this entry. Mrs Gillman, on the other hand, with more sentiment than judgement, did not hesitate to write her own comments on STC's pages, and her directions to those she was assisting, which in some cases obscured what STC had written (see 2024n); the ink used for these purposes is frequently the same in colour and penmanship as the obliterations scattered throughout the notebooks. It is not difficult to suppose that when ink seemed inadequate to protect STC's reputation she used scissors. This resource is less to be wondered at in the years after his death, especially in the heated controversies that took place between Cottle and the Coleridge circle in 1836–8—be it noted, the years between Cottle's indiscretions, as they regarded them, and Gillman's defensive first (and only) volume of his biography of STC.

The last paragraph of the entry is in neither *AP* nor Gillman. *f73* Coleridge first inserted ⟨*or with Desire objectless*⟩ and then indicated transposition.

Is Coleridge conceivably arguing here with Wordsworth and his *Ode to Duty*? It would be natural, with JW's last words in his mind. See also 2531 and n.

The discussion of *Worth, Duty,* and *Pleasure* here harks back to the arguments against Kant, in 1705 and directly or by implication throughout the entries to 1717. In view of Wordsworth's sentiments in that poem, it seems reasonable to suppose that Coleridge's criticism of it would bear resemblances to his objections to Kant: broadly speaking, to the insufficiently positive role allowed to emotion, and the inadequate view of the self; in Wordsworth's case, a dereliction, in Coleridge's view, from an earlier attitude, e.g. in *Tintern Abbey*. See 2091 and n, 2531 and n, 3026 and n.

f75ᵛ *two Birds of Passage:* the bird-image has doubled; of many examples, see especially 2054 and n, 2531 and n. And cf Wordsworth *The Recluse* 1 161: *WPW* v 319.

2557 17.115 The entry is decapitated (from the cutting of *f75ᵛ* referred to in 2556n) and has suffered two other deletions: the first is a line and a half blotted out with ink; the second consists of about two-thirds of another page (*f77*) cut out, the entry appearing to continue overleaf. The long interpolation on *f76* is in very faint red ink, written in between the lines; it may perhaps be datable from 3041 as *c* May 1807. See 3041n.

AP 143, from "Thought and Reality" (bottom of *f76*) to "Ideas and Impressions", with no indication of the missing words.

f76 *Henderson:* see 174(5)n. Henderson's friends pled with him to leave off opium and spirits and to these attributed his early death. Coleridge probably identified himself at times with him as well as with the others in his list.

Collins: William Collins (1721–59) the poet, also a disappointment to his family. His dissoluteness Coleridge rather overstates: he was at times unbalanced and died insane.

Boyce: Samuel Boyse (1708–49), son of a clergyman, and a gifted, procrastinating, dissipated poet, lived in a way that perpetually "exposed him to the inconveniences of indigence", according to the biographical account prefixed to his poems in *B Poets* x 327–50. His name on the title-page of this volume is spelled *Boyce*, and this is probably Coleridge's source of information about his life and work. Some of his poems, e.g. *Deity*, may have interested Coleridge at an early date. See also 2737n.

I raise my limbs, "like lifeless Tools": Coleridge inserted the final but not the introductory quotation marks, a point of some interest here, in view of the alteration, for personal applicability, of *The Ancient Mariner* line 339: "They raised their limbs like lifeless tools": *PW* I 200.

On the idea of suicide, see also, 2100 *f3*, 2510, 2527, and 2866. *f76ᵛ Fountain or natural Well at Upper Stowey:* cf *This Lime Tree Bower: PW* I 179 and n 2, 981 and n, and *CL* # 522 (II 1000).

f77 Thoughts and Things . . . Ideas and Impressions: the hint here is developed in a letter to Thomas Clarkson 13 Oct 1806 (*CL* # 634: II 1194–5) in a manner that well illustrates Coleridge's mental procedures, going from images and personal experience to theory rather than vice versa.

f77ᵛ Talent as opposed to Genius: to the references given in 669n to Coleridge's frequent use of this distinction may be added another in *C&S* 80.

2558 17.116   The date on this obliterated and fragmented entry, valuable for the dating of the neighbouring entries, has disappeared in the rebinding and repairing of this notebook. The entry is curtailed from the cutting of *f77* referred to in 2557n.

2559 17.117   This may be a complete entry, but it may also be the end of an entry begun on the bottom of *f77ᵛ* now cut out. On the importance of obscure ideas, see e.g. 921 and 2509n.

2560 17.118   *So hard have I worked lately:* see Appendix B.
the Lamp: did STC always sleep with a night-light?

2561 17.119   *AP* 143–4. Cf, in similar vein, 2481, 2547, and his reflections later in Rome, 2827.

2562 17.120   Of the *dramatis personae* as little is known, except for Ball, as of the episode. Millar is probably the Capt Millar RN who in 1800 commanded the *Minerva*. Possibly Coleridge's ready sense of the ludicrous on formal official occasions (cf also Mr England's flowers of oratory, 1432) was not always helpful to him as Public Secretary. See e.g. 2451.

2563 15.146   *St Elmo:* on a promontory, with two harbours. *Civita Vecchia:* after Valletta was built, M'dina was called "the old city".

2564 15.147   *brightest-blue dial-plate:* unidentified.
The *dear Flower in England* is the forget-me-not; see 863n and 3131[23].
The *Lark-spur leafed Flower:* probably *Adonis annuus* L, common in Malta.
the *Stone-crop: Sedum caeruleum Vahl*, a stonecrop much seen in Malta, with fleshy leaves usually ruddy or red, and starry blue flowers as drawn by Coleridge; the carpels at the centre of the flower become red with age.
For Coleridge on his lifelong love of flowers, see 1610 *f72*.

2565 15.148   The reference in the last sentence is to 2501. See also 2787.

2566 15.149   See 2288n.

2567 15.150   He is in St Antonio, the pivot of three villages, of which Balzan is one.
the *Order:* he refers to the Venerable Order of the Knights of St John of Jerusalem, who built the Cathedral and other churches in Malta.

2569 15.152   *Calicé:* caleche or calash, in Italian *calesse*, an error of hearing?

2570 15.153   For other examples of identification with the lesser creation see e.g. 2005, 2016, 2054, 2531, and notes.

2571 15.154   The political uncertainties surrounding Malta at this time led to innumerable intrigues, rumours, and gossip, strong advocates being at work for control of the island by the French or the Order; both of these naturally opposed British occupation. The context may be more personal; Coleridge is said to have hated gossip, and to have left his company, on occasion, because of it.

2572 16.406   As late as 15 Oct Coleridge still expected to take some such route homewards, *via* Trieste. See 2700. But the plan was formed several months earlier. *CL* # 616.

2573 16.407   This entry resembles the preceding one in the appearance of the hand and is therefore dated with it. Otherwise its source, and the reference to the matter of it in 2443n (the excerpt from N 18), might suggest a pre-Malta date.

The "wild history of England" is Thomas Gent's *Historia compendiosa Anglicana: or, A Compendious History of England* (2 vols York 1741). After the *History of England* and a *Succinct History of Rome* also described as "comprehensive" had been dealt with, the local pride of T. G., Printer, filled out the second volume with "An Appendix, relating to YORK . . ." and "A further historical Account of *Pontefract*, and its once stupendous Castle, . . ." and much else "proper to entertain the learned and ingenious Reader".

Coleridge was undoubtedly entertained. What he refers to in this entry is a footnote in Book II Chap IV, "The History of the Life of King Stephen". The text (I 167) reads: "Not long after, in 1153, the King . . . concluded a Peace with Duke Henry; and, on Condition of enjoying the Crown during Life, with some Advantages to his Posterity, adopted him as a Son, (14)." Footnote (14) reads: "*He might well do so, if the following Story be true: That the Empress went to him just as the Armies were going to engage on Egelaw-Heath, and, remembering him of a Love-amour with her a little before her last Marriage, thus added,* In what a miserable, unnatural Conflict are you going to engage! Is it fitting, think you, that the Father should imbrue his Hands in the Blood of his Child; or the Son stain his spear in the reeking Gore of his Father? For Heav'n's Sake, renouned Prince! lay the Instrument of Vengeance aside; and consider, what you may know for certain, that *my* Son, Henry, is *there* also. *Then giving the wondering* Prince some private Tokens, he suspended the Battle, and consented to a Peace."

The Milton parallel in which "Such fatal consequence unites us three", the meeting of Sin and Death with Satan when "Triumphal with Triumphal act have met,/. . . and made one realm/Hell and this World . . .", is in *Paradise Lost* x 364, 390–2.

2574 16.408   This may be Coleridge writing down the full name of the servant who attended him when he stayed with Ball; see 2610.

2575 15.155   Coleridge has confused two episodes here. Jean François Dorel/Daurel/Dorrail, one of the four jurats of the Commune of M'dina up to 1798, was pro-French and considered a traitor to the Maltese cause; he drew up and delivered personally to Napoleon an offer of terms to the French. But it was a Commandant Masson who was killed by the mob. He had been put in charge of a detachment of French soldiers delegated to sell church property; incensed, the Maltese crowds tried to obstruct them. Masson struck one of a party of boys across the face with his sword, was pursued, and was killed by being thrown by a mob from a balcony into the street.

2577 15.157   *Boschetto:* literally a small wood, a public park not far from M'dina.

2578 15.158   *Dennison:* see 2188n.
    For Coleridge's attitude to Cobbett see 1752 and n. Cobbett had entered into Maltese affairs by referring sympathetically in his *Political Register* (7 May 1802) to the petition of the Maltese to the British government and their "Remonstrances" against being returned to the Order of St John. See William Hardman *A History of Malta* (1909) 487. Ball, who had lived through the diplomatic difficulties of 1802-3, would doubtless remember this to Cobbett's credit.

2579 15.159   After the celebration of a youthful indiscretion in 1793 in the poem *To Fortune* (PW I 55), there is no real evidence that Coleridge went in for lotteries; there are some curious mathematics on the front fly-leaf of his copy of Maass *Versuch über die Einbildungskraft* (Halle and Leipzig 1797) in the BM. After some play with figures that looks like a calculation of probabilities:

$$1,406$$
$$3,882$$
$$2\overline{)5,288}/2644/1762\tfrac{3}{10}$$

and another group of figures: 4544
$$3882$$
$$1406$$
$$3\overline{)9832}/3277\tfrac{3}{10}/2/4916$$

there is this note: Numbers for the next Lottery
$$2644$$
$$\underline{4916}$$

He was horrified by the lotteries in Naples (2753) and later by the
gambling at Newmarket (2893). And see 2330.

2580 15.160   *Hydnora Africana:* Coleridge's description is correct,
his source unknown. This parasitic plant grows principally on the
roots of *Euphorbia mauritanica*, a widely distributed shrub in South
Africa.

2581 15.161   *Epidendrum* Flos Aeris . . . *in multos annos . . .
germinet:* "lasts for many years, grows, flowers, and germinates." J.
de Loureiro, in *Flora Cochinchinensis* (Lisbon 1790) II 55, is the
originator of the Latin phrase describing the species *Aërides odorata*
of Genus IX *Aërides*. Coleridge appears to be quoting someone who
used Loureiro. Either Coleridge or his source confused the *Aërides
odorata* with another epiphytic orchid, *Epidendrum Flos aeris*, now
known as *Arachnis flos-aeris* (L.) Rehb.f. These orchids, widespread
in tropical Asia, grow on the branches of trees, a dry habitat, and have
a spongy covering on their aerial roots that enables them to take
moisture from the atmosphere. These spectacular plants were an
object of search for many travellers, in the accounts of some one of
whom Coleridge undoubtedly came across this information. Several
reports have been found, but none corresponding in sufficient detail
to be taken as his source for this, and probably also for the previous
entry.

2582 15.162   Cf the metre in 2806 and 2926. A poem appears to be
germinating. The "a metaphor" is again probably an attempt at a
blind.

2583 17.175   *AP* 144–7.
f104   Mᵣ Dennison: see 2188n.
f104ᵛ   like a Face in a clear Stream: as celebrated in *The Picture*
lines 83–5: *PW* I 371?
f105   Capᵗⁿ Pasley: see 2449n.
    I once told a Lady . . . why I did not believe in . . . Ghosts: used
with a good deal of this entry in *Friend* I 247–9.
f106   outward wooden room: a slip for wooden *frame?*
f106ᵛ   Peter Bell: Peter Bell was not yet published, but Coleridge had
it among the poems of Wordsworth transcribed for him by Dorothy
and Sara Hutchinson, for he read it to Sir Alexander and Lady Ball.

See *Friend* (III 296 and n). (It is now part of MS M at Dove Cottage and has the appearance of having been bound in after the rest. It may well have been sent separately, on account of its length.) He refers here to lines 501–20: *WPW* II 353–4.

2584 17.176   *AP* 152–3

Luthers, Miltons, Leibnitzs, Bernouillis, Bonnets, Shakesperes: The two names that perhaps require comment in this curious list are the fourth and fifth. *Bernouilli* is probably Jean Bernoulli (1667–1748), who corresponded with Leibnitz and shared his mathematical and philosophical interests, but there were at least seven other eminent mathematician-philosophers in the family, in exile in Switzerland for their strong anti-clerical convictions. *Bonnet* is Charles Bonnet (1720–93), the Swiss naturalist and philosopher, also persecuted for reformist views. His most popular work, *Contemplation de la nature*, was much in vogue in English translation and advanced rather confused "Great Chain of Being" theories, which Coleridge seems to have in mind here. Presumably what links these persons together for Coleridge is the common denominator of belief in human liberty and, in theory and practice, their contributions, under protestant banners, at critical moments in cultural history, to humane studies.

Make out such a Dream: a wished-for dream?

2585 16.250   *AP* 149 variatim. The word *only* appears to have been omitted after *you not.*

The preceding entry in this notebook was made in June 1804, when Coleridge was still living with the Stoddarts at N° 4 Strada de' Forni. He was there from the day he landed in Malta, 18 May 1804, to 6 July 1804 (*CL* # 601). The MS shows a change of ink at this point, and the long gap in the use of the notebook probably reflects yet another instance of a notebook being neglected in a writing-desk, drawer, or travelling-case until some circumstance brought it to light many months later.

2586 16.251   Coleridge occasionally uses the double colon sign (: :) to suggest parallels for comparison.

2588 16.253   *AP* 109–10 variatim.

It seems possible, in lieu of any evident direct source, to question whether this elaboration on the blinding-of-Cupid theme may have been instigated by Bacon *De sapientia veterum*, the section on Cupid.

See also 2729 and 2737 and notes. Or does it owe anything to Boccaccio's telling of the story of Cupid and Psyche in *Della geneologia
de gli Dei* Bk v §22? See 2512n.

Emmeline is the name given the beloved lady in *The Keepsake*, a
poem indubitably associated with SH: *PW* i 345.

2589 16.254   Spanish and Moorish themes appear so frequently in
early nineteenth-century literature as to preclude documentation; and
in Malta Coleridge may well have encountered men who had had
military adventures in Spain. Southey also knew Spain and Spanish
literature well. But as evidence of Coleridge's Spanish bent one may
recall that *Osorio* is set in Granada in the reign of Philip II, just at
the close of the wars against the Moors; see 210 and n. *The Triumph
of Loyalty* also has a Spanish setting, perhaps indirectly through
Lessing; see 869n and 871n.

It may or may not be relevant to notice that Frederick Augustus
Fischer *Travels in Spain in 1797 and 1798* was reviewed in the first
number of the *Annual Review* (see 1848n); Coleridge bought the
second number second-hand in Malta in Feb 1805 (*CL* # 614: ii 1161).

But 2617 raises an entirely different question. Is the reference here
geographical or personal, i.e. is this Andalusia *Andalusia D.?*

2590 16.255   The poem by M. Hieronymus Vida in the *Carmina
illustrium poetarum Italorum* (Florence 1726) xi 177–9 is *De divis
coelitibus:*
        "Adeste mecum virgines, & integri
        Pueri, & puellae, & omnis aetas, maxime
        Casti, & pudicae conjuges adhuc viris
        Junctae, aut solutae vinculis jugalibus.
        Neque non vocamus quos juventae nequitet
        Piget peractae, admissa poenitentiâ
        Ex corde, ab imo diluentes pectore.
        Adeste mecum laudibus sustollite,
        Quos praeterivimus, beatos aetheris
        Sublimioris, generis omnis, incolas.
        Non unus omnes prosequi ego versu queam.
        Favete linguis, saltem eos silentio
        Taciti simul veneremur innumerabiles.
        Miremur omnium perennes laureas,
        Claros triumphis inclytasque glorias,

Eos & omneis advocemus sedulo,
Nobis ut alto opem ferant ab aethere
Periculis in omnibus neque nos sinant,
Quoad valebunt, cedere obrutos malis.
Non quod suapte vi, sua aut potentia
Queant juvare hominem, & opem impartirier:
Divi neque bona, neque ulla dant cuiquam mala.
Est unus omnium bonorum publicus
Disseminator, ille coeli praepotens
Regnator, orbis conditor, hominum sator,
Cui omnia famulantur, omnia subjacent
Obnoxia, unus omnibus ubique imperat,
Unusque quos vult eligit, quos ope juvet,
Nullius ipse externae opis porro indigus.
Quos vero habet neglectui, praeceps sinit
Ruere misellos, ac malis prorsum omnibus
Circumvenit, dans cuique pro merito, ut lubet:
Ultor severus criminum, mortalibus
Perterrefaciens conscia intus pectora,
Coelum trisulcis cum coruscat ignibus,
Tonitruque templa concutit coelestia.
Nobiscum enim persaepe agatur saeviter,
Nobis nisi ejus praesto ubique Filius
Adesset advocatus, & se opponeret
Caro Parenti, is dum parat nos funditus
Vertete, malisque quae meremur perdere:
Cui detegit quae passus est olim volens
Vulnera peremtus pro salute publica.
Hunc supplices homines in omnibus adeunt
Discriminibus, & advocatum unum admovent.
Verum quia plerumque suppuder reos
Adire recta regium Gnatum unicum,
Hunc deprecatorem ut sibi illico parent,
Neve alloquantur eum sine internuntio,
Prius adhibent de civium numero aliquos,
Et advocatum qui precentur, advocant,
Seu sint adhuc nos inter hic superstites.
Sive in supernam jam advolarint curiam.
Est tutius vero advocare quos scias
Intra receptos jam aetheris domicilia.

Neque est verendum ne advocati exaudiant,
Quod oppido remoti ab iis habitent plagis,
Humusque ab astris absier quamplurimum.
Vident piorum animae ac volucres spiritus
Semper beati humana facta, & audiunt:
Sed non suapte acie, suove lumine:
His omnia representat ante oculos sua ·
In luce Soboles cuncta cernentis Dei,
Rerum fideles suggerens imagines.
Hunc intuentes intuentur omnia,
Quaecumque opus, vel quae haud Pater eis abnuit,
Itidem audiunt omnia vocati coelites.
Et obsecrati pro obsecrantibus obsecrant.
Est ille speculum, est unus idem Echo omnibus.
Ob id tamen mortalium ipsi mentibus
Haud inseruntur, solus illapsu Deus
Adest, & animis influit praesentiâ,
Solusque propitio fovet nos numine;
Nulli creato est numen aut divinitas.
Vult ipse post se nos tamen venerarier
Honore proximo Quirites aetheris,
Et supplicabundos sepulcra visere,
Et quidquid eorum apud nos reliquum est
Nec tura eis negare, nec crocum, aut rosam.
Quare agite mecum adeste cuncti, & aet heris
Onerate votis universam curiam,
Nobis benevolum ut advocatum sedulo
Reddant, suaque coelites nos evehant
Qua plurima pollent apud eum gratia.
Is dehinc Parentem propitium nobis dabit,
[A quo, perenni in fonte cuncta fluunt bona.]"

Coleridge's copy of this edition of the *Carmina* is in the Dyce Collection in the Victoria and Albert Museum; like all other copies, it lacks
the last line of the poem. The one annotation on the volume is irrelevant and undated.

2591 16.256   The very large polished cone-shaped candle-extin-
               guisher?

2592 16.257   Information from Mr Dennison/Denison; see 2604.

2593 16.258   On the subject of consciousness see also 1554, 1763, 1827.

2594 17.121   This entry appears to refer to the incident noticed more precisely in 2646. Neither the court records in Malta for the period nor documents pertaining to Malta in the PRO reveal any such persecution. Mr Cecil Roth's article in the *Transactions of the Jewish Historical Society of England* XII (1931) 187–251 on "The Jews in Malta" has no details for the first decade of the century and suggests rather, after accounts of acute sufferings under earlier occupations, that from the British possession onwards the lot of the Jews greatly improved, with the result that the Jewish population by 1810 was beginning to increase.

But if the particular incident that stirred Coleridge's feelings has not been found, the type of situation, and possibly an incident that set in motion a series of actions and re-actions of which this was one, is described in MS 430 Vol II in the Royal Malta Library, one of the *avvisi* referred to in Appendix B. A translation reads:

NOTICE

Fortunata Tagliana of the city of Notabile, calling one of the French prisoners quartered in the Boschetto who had entered the house of a neighbour of hers with whom she was on bad terms, a Jew, had him pursued and stoned by two or three ruffians who came running at her cries.

Francesco Borg of the same village, awakened by the noise hastened to the scene also, but far from following the example of the others he undeceived the pursuers and saved the pursued.

Fortunata Tagliana is banished in perpetuity to Gozo, where with no opportunity of meeting Jews she will be able with the change of air to find a cure for her fanaticism.

Francesco Borg is awarded 25 scudi for his good conduct in such a situation.

His Excellency is grieved to be obliged to punish Fortunata Tagliana for the abuse of popular prejudice which she has attempted to create; and he is even more grieved to be obliged to reward as a particular merit the act of duty performed by the aforesaid Francesco Borg. But H. E. hopes that when a stop has been put to the vain pleasure of inventing slanderous stories, and when the people have realized this folly and self-damaging credulity, the Nation, despite those who envy its prosperity, will regain its disturbed tranquillity, the necessity for punishment will cease, and rewards will be reserved for better titles and greater merits.

The Office of the Government
25 March 1805
S. T. Coleridge, Public Secretary to the High Commissioner.

2596 17.123   At the upper left-hand corner of this entry appears
the "d" for copied, fairly frequent in the notebooks, but here with
the addition, "Mr. G", possibly one of the scribes employed by HNC
and others, possibly Mr Gillman?
    AP 147. In *BL* Chap xii Coleridge quoted the words of Leibnitz he
had in mind: "J'ai trouvé que la plupart des sectes ont raison dans une
bonne partie de ce qu'elles avancent, mais non pas tant en ce qu'elles
nient." *BL* i 170. They are from Leibnitz's first of *Trois lettres à*
M. Remond de Mont-Mort: Opera (ed J. E. Erdmann 2 vols Berlin
1840) ii 701–2; Coleridge's edition we do not know.
    See also 1551 on the same point.

2597 17.124   *PW* ii 999, reading in the second line *beamest* for
becom'st; PW (JDC) 461 reads *became.* Neither gives the Italian
phrases, which mean: "in charming mortal spoils", "a most beautiful
soul!"

2598 17.125   *AP* 150–2.
    Schiller . . . deserts from Shakespere: is Coleridge referring to
Schiller's parody *Shakespeare's Schalten* in *Gedichte* (Leipzig 1800)
275–6?
    furr it over: with parasitic growth, or the coating of lime inside a
kettle? Darwin is Erasmus Darwin. Hayley, though Coleridge disliked his views, e.g. on Milton (*MC* 165–70, *Phil Lects* 444 n 18), does
not elsewhere call forth precisely this sort of criticism from Coleridge.
For these and all the other names referred to in this entry, except
Cervantes and Molière, see *CN* i Index i and ii Index i. For Cervantes Coleridge's lifelong enthusiasm was crystallized in Lecture viii of
the Jan–March 1818 lectures. *MC* 98–110. On Molière little that
Coleridge had to say has survived, and that of the most general
nature. See *ShC* ii 145, 204; *MC* 286.

2599 17.159   Some thirty-four entries between this one and 2598
appear to belong to 1808–10, with a good many other entries of those
and later years in the second half of this notebook. This entry *may*
also belong to a later volume. The arguments for placing it somewhere towards the close of 1805 are based partly on the hand, the
colour of the ink, and the impression (from the careful way in which
the entry is neatly written, beginning a fresh page, as if to preserve

these Italian poems carefully for future use in England) that there was a special reason behind the peculiarly isolated position in the notebook. They are also partly based on Coleridge's remarks in *BL* Chap XVI, where he introduces nine of these poems of Strozzi, "As I do not remember to have seen either the poems or their author mentioned in any English work, or have found them in any of the common collections of Italian poetry; and as the little work is of rare occurrence; I will transcribe a few specimens." Coleridge is rather more likely to have stumbled on this rare little work in Italy or Sicily than in England. Besides, he showed there a marked interest in sixteenth- and seventeenth-century Italian poetry. See Appendix A.

A similar problem of dating arises in the case of the long Marino excerpts in 2625, and has been decided the same way for similar reasons. Moreover, it adds considerable point to Coleridge's distress over the loss of his book boxes on his return from Malta, if these entries were already in the notebooks, especially in view of his projected lectures on "the Principles common to all the Fine Arts", referred to 16 Sept 1806 (*CL* # 625) and agreed to by 9 Oct 1806 (*CL* # 632). Furthermore, numerous leaves were left blank after this entry, with good intentions of further transcribing?

f89ᵛ Madrigals . . . Strozzi: This comes from the title-page, except the charming addition of "1 May" drawn from the end of the dedication.

in his diction and metre . . . careless (W. Scott): Coleridge valued Scott much more highly as novelist than as poet. See *MC* 285, 340. His most devastating and detailed comment on Scott's poetry comes in a later notebook entry. At this time, *The Lay of the Last Minstrel* was a new poem, published in Jan 1805; apparently its great success had carried it to Malta by the summer of 1805, even in war-time.

f90 With the unfavourable comparison of contemporary with older landscape-painters (and poets) cf Coleridge's description of Allston's landscape, in 2831, in which the virtues described in this entry are implicit.

the polished elder poets . . . of Italy: from here onwards the entry, in more finished and expanded form, and with interesting changes in the personal reference, was used in *BL* II 23–7.

f90ᵛ Alonzo & Imogen: see 1128 and n.

Hohenlinden: Thomas Campbell's well-known poem had appeared in 1802.

Of the poems Coleridge transcribed, he used in *BL* the second, third, seventh, eleventh, fourteenth, sixteenth, twentieth (variatim), twenty-first, and twenty-sixth.

A translation of the poems follows:

MADRIGALS OF STROZZI.

[I] *p.2.* Either a new star or the Sun, I know not which, descended from Heaven to earth in the form of a rustic Shepherdess to wage war upon me; and her dart and torch were her sweet laugh, and her fair gentle glance: she has no other arms than these; I have no other shield than my grief and tears.

[II] *p.7.* Love showed me his chill stream, clear and tranquil, in summer-time at noonday; the woods were burning, the slopes, the hills were burning. So I, who in the coldest frost burn and sparkle, at once hastened to it; but I saw it flowing on so pure and fair that I did not wish to sully it; I only mirrored myself within it, and on its sweet and shady bank I rested, intent upon the murmuring of its wave.

[III] *p.8.* Breezes, gentle comfort of my tormented life, and so sweet that no longer does burning or death seem grievous to me, but rather desire alone; pray, drive far away the ice, the clouds, the evil weather, now that the clear wave and the shade, no less dear, entice Festivity and Merriment to sport and sing through their groves and meadows.

[IV] *p.9.* Troop of bright breezes, friendly troop, ever the companion and escort of purple lovely Spring, who brings us fair calm and a fair serene sky, waken, open the door of the fair gilded crystal, and through this meadow and that, this wood and that, sport and play sweetly, flying before the lash of Love.

[V] *p.10.* Breezes, ever garlanded with flowers and rays, born indeed at one birth with the golden-haired Loves, with Sport, Play, and Pleasure (it is indeed time), rise up, come forth with gracious April; let Earth show itself like to Heaven, and Heaven, if not to my fair Sun, to her fair veil.

[VI] *p.11.* Goddesses rise up from your fair kindly rose-gardens, beyond the serene realms of light, where the Sun never sets nor is ever clouded; pitying Breezes, ah may Pity lead you to these shadowy vales; and may all Stars, Graces, Muses, and Holy Nymphs accompany you.

[VII] *p.12.* Oh breezes, peaceful, yet often at amorous war with the flowers and grass, advance softly your green standards of the lily and the rose against the immature season; so that I may find truce or rest, if not peace: and I know well where. Oh charming mild glance, oh ambrosian lips, oh gay laughter!

[viii] *p.12.* Breezes, lucent veil of the fair serene, of the purple plumes, and of the fair locks of gold which give light to the Sky and all the World, return to us once more, so that the harsh fog may yield place (and indeed 'tis time) to sweet weather, and so that the violet and the lily with all lovely colours may return from exile.

[ix] *p.14.* Return, gentle little breeze, with your fair Sun, to these eyes of mine, return, and bring day to my gloomy heart, clothed once more in roses and violets! Love does not always desire tears and grief, but sometimes song and laughter, to which he was accustomed in Paradise, his sweet nest, before he dwelt within your holy rays.

[x] *p.15.* This impious wretch had no mercy on her children, and do you to-day madly nest in her bosom? And do you foolishly entrust to her these unfortunate children of yours? Flee the pitiless marble! and hang your sweet nests in some forest. The Sea holds no monster, the Earth no beast, so cruel!

[xi] *p.17.* Now she stands fixed like a Rock, now like a River she glides away, now she roars like a savage Bear, now sings like a pitying Angel; but into what does she not transform herself? And into what does she not transform me, Stones or Streams, wild beasts or Gods, this my fair—I know not whether Nymph or Enchantress, whether Lady or Goddess, whether sweet or pitiless?

[xii] *p.21.* Every night Love dwelled within my heart, his ancient seat, and my faithful Friend spoke to me of his state and my own. But now no longer, no; for his mortal enemy, Anger, ever drives him away; nor does he threaten him alone, but every one of the charming shy thoughts which harbour there flies forth from its nest like a little bird wakened by a harsh cry.

[xiii] *p.25.* Sweetly return, oh Love, courteous and pitying, to that angelic face from which Anger (oh cruel Anger!) has banished you to my great wrong; and pray lead back with you, oh Lord, the wonted laugh and the bright glance; so that the cruel pain which I endure may not bring me to death (if this indeed be life).

[xiv] *p.25.* Weeping you kissed me, and laughing you refused; in grief I found you pitiful, in pleasure I found you cruel; joy was born of weeping, suffering from laughter. Oh wretched lovers, may you always find together Fear and Hope.

[xv] *p.35.* No star shines so sweetly at midnight in a cloudless sky as the fair flower which I saw there upon that bank; around it the fresh new grass is kindled, and it sports and laughs, vieing with the breezes and the waves, and

seems to rain forth as much sweetness as Heaven itself. Love, who is seated there, swears that he has never yet seen so lovely a flower even in the bosom of the vermilion Aurora.

[xvi] *p.36.* Fair flower, you recall to me the dewy cheek of that fair face, and so truly do you resemble it that often I gaze upon you as though upon her: and, blind though I am, contemplate now her charming laugh, now her calm glance. But how lightly, oh Rose, does the morning flee? And who dissolves you like snow, and with you my heart and my very life?

[xvii] *p.36.* Now would I were a light-winged bee, if not a trembling fugitive breeze; for I, still flying from bank to bank in pursuit of my desire, would at last enclose myself within my fragrant white Flower, giving it, amidst a thousand and a thousand sighs, a thousand and a thousand holy kisses of Love, within and without: oh how sweetly would I suck it? There indeed would I gladly die.

[xviii] *p.37.* Now would I were a light-winged bee, for I should go from fair flower to fair flower over vale and hill, until this very day I found myself thus hidden in my Phyllis's bosom. And I would give thee too a thousand warm kisses of Love, oh tender Snow, which dost make her heart so hard: and I would suck from thee as well a sweet pure milk; but alas, let her not indeed find burdensome my pitiful light murmuring alone.

[xix] *p.45.* Return, Zephyr, return, kindly vital breath of our being, which is the wretched victim now of Auster, now of Eurus! each wind which assails us overcomes us. Return! And guiding them aid both our life and that languid frail spirit of mine; not for myself, indeed, do I seek life, but only for her who draws such life from my sighs.

[xx] *p.49.* My Phyllis, sweet Phyllis, oh cadence ever fresh and ever brighter, what sweetness do I feel only in saying Phyllis? I endeavour indeed, but neither here among us nor in the heavens can I find any harmony which is sweeter than her fair name: Heaven, Love, the Echo of my Heart, plays no other tune.

[xxi] *p.57.* Now that the mead and wood grow dim, beneath your shadowy calm sky move forth, lofty Repose! Ah let me rest one single night, one hour! The wild beasts, the birds, every living thing has sometimes some peace, but I, alas, when do I not wander on, nor weep, nor cry out? and indeed how loudly? But since he does not hear, hear me thou, oh Death.

[xxii] *p.59.* Halt, gentle friend, whom the ignorant mad world calls Death, open, oh open the doors of your abode, so dear, so much desired! and may I

no longer be borne along by fear or hope, but through these weary eyes which can watch no more may your eternal sleep pass into my heart!

[xxiii] *p.60.* Behold the dawn! Alas, what a new field for labours and for tears do I see? And who teaches me any defence, any refuge from my tears, except Death? Ah, Day, oh cruel Day, depart, fly far away with my grief! You, my true delight, return, but return for ever, oh my kindly evening!

[xxiv] *p.60.* Our last evening, that prolonged repose which will know no awakening, pray come to us, hear us now; so that I may perish once and for all, not a thousand and a thousand times as this cruel thing desires which the world calls Life; which the world loves so dearly. Oh blind world, I am weary, nor do I desire to wander with you any longer!

[xxv] *p.111.* Oh blessed gentle thought of mine, which never leaves me; and which so lightly transports me, now beyond those mountains, now above the Sky; you ever converse of and with her who consumes me with pleasure, and you bring me peace which is like no other, oh blessed gentle Thought of mine!

[xxvi] *p.89.* At the appearance of fragrant May, the clouds and frost flee; and behold every little bush and stem flowering in the new ray; the Earth and Heaven laugh, all about us, the Night laughs and the Day; how much more sweetly laughs sweet Love within my Heart, and in that fair and lovely breast which is his dear delight and his abode!

[xxvii] *p.152.* I laughed and wept with Love, yet never did I write except in flame, in water, or in wind; often I found cruel mercy; ever dead to myself, I lived in another; now I rose from the darkest Abyss to Heaven, now I fell down from it again; wearied at last, here have I made my close.

The End

2600 17.211   At the top of the page above this entry the word *Malta* is inserted beside Coleridge's page number, in Mrs Gillman's hand. The deletion at the foot of *f139* is Coleridge's. Does the italicizing of *In a Dream*, like the insertions and dramatizations in 2458 and 2582, suggest an attempt to disclaim the personal import of the facts stated?

The entry belongs to 1805, but whether close to *c* Feb, and similar observations in 2441, or to June, and 2606, is not certain.

the power of Feelings over Images: cf 921 and n, 2638, and, less explicit, 2583.

2601 17.212   *AP* 156 variatim, omitting from the "pseudo-poets" the almost-obliterated *Cottle*. Coleridge is often occupied with the subject of bad or second-rate poetry; see also 477 and n, 1239 and n. The reference to the "moral characters" of these men appears to be to *moral* in a broad sense—vanity, egotism, etc.

His heart burnt within him, and he spake: cf Ps. 39:3: "My heart was hot within me, while I was musing the fire burned: then spake I with my tongue."

2602 18.192   The first part of this entry is missing, the preceding leaf having been cut out. The pencilled writing is very hurried, some of it both faint and tortured.

a Fenestra . . . miserabile: from window to window? Literally "to a window through a window/very miserable—".

canestra is Italian for basket; *dixit:* he/she said.

The next word is uncertain, and what the "ideotic plan" was, and what the fragmented words in Greek characters signify, have so far defied elucidation. The first letter of the second could be the digraph for *ov*. The last *κεˣ* could be an erratic *ket* (?basket) or even *Act*.

2603 18.193   In pencil.

Possibly he is half-remembering one of his favourite passages in Plotinus (*Ennead* v 5 8), quoted in *BL* I 167 (see 209 and n and 1678 and n); Coleridge's thoughts had apparently recurred to it in Malta as recently as the latter part of 1804; see 2164.

The De *crescent:* As he observes the waxing moon (like the letter D—see 2766 and n), and the unseen rising sun, he finds an image for the emergence of ideas—systems—poems—religions.

Cf "Reason and Religion are their own evidence. The natural Sun is in this respect a symbol of the spiritual. Ere he is fully arisen, and while his glories are still under veil, he calls up the breeze to chase away the usurping vapours of the night-season, and thus converts the air itself into the minister of its own purification: not surely in proof or elucidation of the light from heaven, but to prevent its interception." *SM* 12; see also ibid 60 and ibid App (C) xiv–xv. See also 327 and n. Cf also "All great and bold ideas in their first conception, in their *very* nature are TOO GREAT FOR utterANCE. [The dawn of an Idea] . . . is a glow without light in which light gradually forms itself." *Phil Lects* 166. See also the final sentences of the *Biographia: BL* II 218.

2604 18.194   In pencil, as far as *Dennison* traced over in ink. The legend about the Negroes consoling themselves with their white wounds was referred to earlier; see 2592.

permanent Principles of Beauty vs *Association or the Agreeable:* the theme is developed in the essay "On the Principles of Genial Criticism Concerning the Fine Arts" (1813) and in "On Poesy or Art" (*c* 1818) esp *BL* II 257. Coleridge is arguing here against such writers as Alison and Knight (1963n).

2605 17.213   The ink is similar to that of the next entry; *Baldwin's Journal* was received in Malta six weeks or more after publication.

2606 17.214   The lines are not in *PW* or in any of the collected fragmentary remains. The "glittering mud" image applied to himself, as but the silt of a Pierian spring, is clear enough; for the dying fish elsewhere associated with another personal image (sails), see 2084.

2607 17.215   Coleridge as usual did not complete the quotation marks, and the true position of them is doubtful; I assume he is quoting an accusation made by someone intimate with him. Cf 2391.

2608 17.216   gr 20 = 1 scruple; 3 scruples = 1 dram; 8 drams = 1 oz. Coleridge uses *drachma*, a quantity almost the same as the dram; he could have extracted this information from the work cited in the next note, from the Appendix on Weights and Measures. He appears to have confused the apothecary's symbols; that he may have had difficulty in remembering them is suggested by their appearance, irrelevantly, in other MSS, i.e. on the front fly-leaf of vol 3 of his copy of Kant *Vermischte Schriften* (Halle 1799) in the BM.

2609 17.217   Difficult to date, this entry is preceded and followed by a part-blank page; *ff143–162ᵛ* are blank, except for Coleridge's pagination and, on *ff143ᵛ–144* and *154ᵛ–155*, the names in the corners.

Coleridge is using *The Edinburgh New Dispensatory* ed Andrew Duncan Jr, probably the second edition (Edinburgh 1804) 133–72. This work combined the most recent pharmacopoeia of London, Dublin, and Edinburgh, and was therefore the most up-to-date authority. Certain peculiarities in the terms used for herbs, symptoms, and instructions, as well as places and persons mentioned (e.g. Anton von Stoerck, 1731–1803, distinguished Viennese internist; Thomas Sydenham, 1624–89, influential London medical reformer; Nils Rosen von

Rosenstein, 1752–1824, famous Swedish specialist in the diseases of children), put the identification, supplied by Dr F. N. L. Poynter of the Wellcome Historical Medical Library, beyond doubt. Coleridge looked first at the uses of the herbs, then at the doses, and altered the order of information; his italicized *watchfully* is a considerable condensation, also his *revulsive* and *anthelmintic*. Between Aconitum and Allium, sections on Alcohol, both Fortius and Dilutius, invited no memoranda.

2610 16.259   The last paragraph is in ink, like the next two entries. In a letter to Mrs Coleridge of 21 Aug 1805 in which the earthquake is reported, though incorrectly dated, the "strong arm" has become "a Giant's Arm". *CL* # 619.

a new-moon . . . silver Thread was not there: cf "For lo! the New-moon winter-bright!/And overspread with phantom light,/(With swimming phantom light o'erspread/But rimmed and circled by a silver thread)/I see the old Moon in her lap, foretelling/The coming on of rain and squally blast." *Dejection: an Ode* lines 9–14: *PW* I 363.

& its color was reddish smoke-color: the night sky in *Dejection* had of course "its peculiar tint of yellow green".

the Stars were bold & mighty that could abide her Presence: a link with the gloss on *The Ancient Mariner* (quoted in 1473n) is evident, as pointed out in Bald 14.

Gioseppe: see 2574.

2612 16.261   By *Festuca* (which is not aromatic) Coleridge probably means sweet-grass, *Hierochloë odorata.*

[?Relham/Relhan]. The first word is not botanically intelligible in this context. If the second is the correct reading, a reference to Richard Relhan, a contemporary botanist, may be involved. He had published *Flora Cantabrigiensis*, 1785–93, and a second edition in 1802. He had been chaplain of King's College, Cambridge, but before Coleridge's Cambridge day. Possibly something was then locally called "Relhan" in Cambridge; he was especially noted for work on flowerless plants; at this date Coleridge cannot be referring to the few species of South African *Compositae* later named after him. Admittedly the reference remains obscure. A conversation with Relhan?

Coleridge's view of marriage as a sacrament, for him precluding divorce, was surely one of his deepest, most sorely tested convictions.

2613 18.195   Coleridge frequently observes the intimate connexion of anger and fear, e.g. see the fragmentary "Essay on the Passions" in *Inq Sp* §52, esp pp 66–7.

Le Grice probably refers to C. V. Le Grice, his desk-mate at Christ's Hospital, and the subject of a monograph by Edmund Blunden, *Coleridge's Fellow-Grecian. Some Account of Charles Valentine Le Grice* (Hong Kong 1956); see 2018 and n.

2614 18.196   *Hearing, in toto:* Hearing with my whole body?

I am obnoxious to: liable, subject, exposed, open (to anything harmful). Formerly the prevailing use. *OED.*

Tympanum auditorium: stretched drum-head of hearing.

the Verum . . . scarcely verisimile: the real thing scarcely true (or credible).

This is Coleridge's longest diatribe on Malta noises; see also 2114, 2148, and cf 2284 and 2547; cf *TT* (ed 1835 only) 16 April 1834.

The entry is quoted in *L* II 483n.

After this entry, *ff*95ᵛ–96ᵛ were apparently left blank; they were used on Coleridge's return to this notebook *c* 1809–10.

2615 18.197   The phrase is from Seneca *Epistles* cxv, in which context *bracteata*, according to Lewis and Short, means "shining only externally, gilded, delusive".

2616 17.177   The May date of the publication suggests a July date for the entry, close to the entries from 2619 onwards; the papers probably arrived in one of the July convoys.

Coleridge was interested in the assumptions underlying the wording of casual statements, advertisements, public memorials, and whatever reflected the presence or absence of a point of view. The significance of his first excerpt lies in the italics, which are his, as well as the exclamation mark; of the second excerpt the point lies in his quotation marks.

2617 17.178   *Andalusia D.:* see 2589; the lady remains unidentified.

2618 17.179   *Mackintosh:* perhaps Coleridge's severest comment on Mackintosh, whose smile he obviously found unendurable; in 2468 Mackintosh is damned as having "a Scotch Smile".

Paisley: presumably C. Pasley of 2449 and other entries.

Scotch, Scottish: Literary usage in the twentieth century appears to be with Coleridge, but his contemporaries apparently were not. Burns and Scott used *Scotch* happily enough.

2619 17.180   *Reynell:* see 241n, which now may be amplified and corrected at one point. The Major Reynell in 241 is James Reynell; the Reynell here is Richard, probably of the same Devonshire family. But until 1825 there was no family relation, as suggested in 241n, between them and the Coleridges.

Merrick: probably Thomas Merrick (*b c* 1772), who, according to Christ's Hospital records, kindly searched by the present Clerk, was at the school Dec 1782–July 1787. Coleridge and Merrick were therefore fifteen years old when last they had seen each other.

Jenny Edwards: Jane Edwards was undoubtedly the daughter (*b* 1770) of Mrs Mary Edwards, Christ's Hospital nurse from 1776 onwards, who had a daughter, Jane. She apparently helped her mother unofficially in the sick-ward, although there is no confirmation of this in the school records. More interesting than Le Grice's practical joke, and probably what helped to fix her in Coleridge's memory, is the fact that she was the original of Genevieve in Coleridge's youthful poem. In a note (*PW* I 19n) EHC refers to the Christ's Hospital tradition that the lines "were inspired by his 'Nurse's Daughter' ", a tradition now confirmed by Coleridge's train of associations recorded here. (EHC's reference in the same note to another Christ's Hospital nurse is a red herring.)

Le Grice: see 2018n and 2613n.

the Face in S^t [? Mary's] church-yard: the episode appears to be lost. St Mary Redcliffe, in Bristol? Ottery St Mary?

2620 17.181   The force of the last word is not clear, but the story may be thought of as an allegory for the concept of *invention* as opposed to *discovery;* see 387n and 930n. Or is the whole labelled an invention?

2621 17.182   *wie man will:* as you will. The *Quicumque-vult* (whosoever wilt) of the Creed in the Book of Common Prayer is given ridiculously irreverent association with "The ladyes of Lubricity that live in the Bordello" of *Panegyrick Verses* in *Coryat's Crudities* (1611 etc).

Possibly Coleridge needed no help in remembering *Coryat's Crudities*, but if he did, Vol IV of *B Poets*, which he may have had with him in Malta (see 2654n), would have given it. Donne's poems come first in that volume, the last one being his lines *Upon Mr. Tho. Coryat's Crudities: B Poets* IV 106. Daniel's poems, quoted in 2654, immediately follow.

2622 17.183   If Coleridge is here adapting some one else's lines, the source has not been found.

2623 18.1   The bracketing of the names is done with deliberate precision. *Sara* without the *h* means, as the verses suggest, Sara Hutchinson. The verses are a later insertion, after the names, and the prose comment appears to be later still, possibly Dec 1807, or even after 1810.

The first sixteen entries in this notebook, judged by themselves, on internal and external evidence, might plausibly be dated in several periods between 1804 and 1816. But I believe their dates may be predicated with one degree more of probability if the broader hypotheses as to the use of the notebook as a whole are correct. See N 18 Gen Note.

With the otherwise trite sheep analogy, cf the self-identifying description of the sheep with its scabbed knees on board the *Speedwell* in 2005 and the "Lag Sheep of the Flock" [or Convoy] in 2016.

Ενοπεντας: five in one; another term for "the Concern" of 2537? And cf 980 and n.

2624 18.2   The framing of the pages with the names of the Grasmere circle continues throughout the notebook, and seems usually to have been done when the pages were blank, possibly a considerable number at one time. It has seemed wise, for the sake of clarity, to call attention to these as a separate entry, but to give the comprehensive description of them in N 18 Gen Note. See also plate III.

2625 18.200   The dating of this entry is uncertain. It appears to have been in the book before the series of entries 2637–2639 were entered; if this is the case, it would fit the theory that this notebook was intended for either a commonplace-book of Italian poems or a travel-book, or both. The entry begins a fresh page and is written with unusual care. See the arguments for a similar situation in 2599.

The pencilled note running vertically up the outside margin of *f98ᵛ* cannot, however, be said to date this as a Malta entry. It consists of the lower part of Coleridge's signature, "S. T. Coleridge", and below that, "At the Treasury". Clearly (the pages not having been cropped) the signature and address ran on to the page from something else; practically, it is difficult to see how, for whatever was being written on must have been behind, or else very precisely flush with the notebook page, to allow the words to overrun the fore-edge. Some awkward arrangement of supporting book, notebook, and another piece of paper on which a note was being written suggests itself. It is tempting to think that the book was an edition of Marino or some collection of Italian poems and that in the midst of transcribing those in this entry Coleridge was interrupted by a messenger requiring a note, the signature of which ran on to this page.

Whether the accidental pencilling or the ink entry was on the page first is not absolutely certain. It looks now as if the page was blank where the pencil overran it, the ink being superimposed. But the page may have been one-third filled when this happened. There is in fact a very slight, scarcely noticeable change of slope of the hand about this distance down the page.

The whole question would be unimportant except that a solution would make it possible to date this entry more confidently. As it stands, one can say only that the notebook was open in Coleridge's hands, at this page, in the Treasury, Malta.

I conclude, rather on general evidence than on this point only, that these sonnets were transcribed and commented on sometime between Coleridge's first bringing out this notebook for use in July 1805 and his packing it away for the homeward journey, either when he left Malta or in Sicily, depending on one's view of the date; cf 2691. It seems natural that on the eve of departure from the scene of his Italian studies Coleridge should collect poems from scarce Italian books.

The edition of Giovanni Battista Marino, or Marini, he used is not known. In Vol xli of the *Parnaso italiano* of Andrea Rubbi (Venice 1789) the poems appear in the order in which Coleridge transcribed them, though the textual variants are too numerous to make this the plausible source.

f97   red-ochring the rose: an adaptation of "To gild refined gold, to paint the lily . . .". *King John* iv ii 11? In *BL* Chap iv Coleridge later referred to "the seductive faults, the dulcia vitia" of Marino. *BL* i 54.

f97ᵛ   A Sonnet often imitated: Among the better known imitations by the Italian *secentisti* are the poem *Infelicità*, beginning "Piange l'uomo infelice", by Girolamo Fontanella (1612–43/44), and *Infelicità della vita umana*, beginning "Dieci lustri di vita o poco meno", by Tommaso Gaudiosi (dates unknown).

  Franciosini: Lorenzo Franciosini (*fl* 1622), grammarian and lexicographer, and translator of *Don Quixote*. The dictionary to which Coleridge refers is the *Vocabolario italiano, e spagnolo*, which ran to several editions from 1620 onwards. A copy (Geneva 1636) appears in *Wordsworth SC* (446).

f98   The three lines of Italian crossed out with diagonal lines are an attempt at a correction (inserted at the bottom of the opposite page, *f97ᵛ*) of lines 6 & 7 of the third Sonnet, "Apre l'uomo infelice . . .".

  dark with excess of light: a favourite quotation from *Paradise Lost;* see 1725n.

f98ᵛ   Argo . . . in an address to the metaphysical God of Reason and purest Christianity: Surely Coleridge is mistaken in thus interpreting a merely occasional piece. The interest of his comment lies in the fact that it suggests he may have been reading from some collection in which the sub-headings of the sonnets were missing. And more important, it indicates his readiness for symbolic interpretation, especially when the natural elements come into play, a point of considerable cogency in interpreting his intentions in his own poems.

  cieco e losco . . . blind and short-sighted: losco has the double sense of purblind and short-sighted.

  a bull: see 2630 and n.

f99   one steps into a hole . . . expecting to place the foot on a stair higher: The metaphor is used with a difference in *BL* Chap xviii, in the discussion of the need for diction to keep pace with feeling. "Where, therefore, correspondent food and appropriate matter are not provided for the attention and feelings thus roused, there must needs be a disappointment felt; like that of leaping in the dark from the last step of a stair-case, when we had prepared our muscles for a leap of three or four." *BL* ii 51.

  The term "sinking" was used in the same work, for what Coleridge thought one of Wordsworth's obvious defects: *BL* ii 38, 110.

f100   Dowlas: a coarse linen. Is he remembering Falstaff's deprecation of Hotspur's gift of shirts, in 1 *Henry IV* iii iii? "Dowlas, filthy Dowlas."

*f96*ᵛ [I] *Sonetto alla Principessa di Stigliano che va in barca per la Riviera di Posilippo* from "Versi d'occasione": *Sonnet to the Princess of Stigliano as she travels by boat along the shore of Posilippo.*

When erstwhile Cytherea came forth from the Aegean flood near the Cyprian coast upon her wheeling shell, with an assembled band of the Graces and Loves, she never appeared as fair as did the nymph or goddess, I know not which, whom I saw seated upon the rich poop,—her luxuriant fair locks, loosed by the light Zephyrs, seemed the golden fleece on the bark of Argos. The winds sighed, and the very waters at the radiance of the new Aurora were decked with amorous sparks; and the sea, curving beneath the prow, seemed to say with hoarse murmur: And I too bow to reverence her.

f97 [II] *Il rossignuol cantante* from "Sonetti amorosi": *The singing nightingale.*

By the bank of a bright pure stream a musical nightingale poured forth so sweet a song that he seemed to have a thousand voices, a thousand birds, in his breast. Echo, who joyed to listen to him, rendered back exactly the notes as he sang: and he warbled all the more, because he believed that she was some other fair small bird who was emulating him. But as he redoubled ever more sweetly the tenor of his lovely harmony, he by chance perceived his own image in the fleeting silver. The nymphs laughed, and he, who then perceived himself to be mocked by the waters, or rather by the wind, flew off in haste to hide among the branches.

*f97*ᵛ [III] *Miserie della vita umana* from "Versi morali e sacri": *Miseries of human life.*

Unhappy man when he is born into this life full of miseries opens his eyes to weeping rather than to the Sun; and, scarcely born, is made the prisoner of constricting swaddling-bands. Next, as a boy whose food is no longer milk, he spends his days beneath the severe rod. Then in an age more sure and more serene, he dies and is reborn between love and fortune. Later, sad and poor, how many labours and deaths does he endure, until, bent and weary, he supports his ancient body with a weak staff? At last a narrow stone seals in his remains so swiftly that sighing I say: From the cradle to the grave is but a short step.

f98 [IV] From "Sonetti morali". The words translated by Coleridge in his commentary are indicated by quotation marks.

Beneath deep gloomy shadows "buried in light inaccessible", amongst "thick and obscure storm-clouds of silence", the eternal Mind conceals his secrets. And if anyone spies out through these impure mists his judgements, wrapped in a black veil, he dazzles with his lightning and stuns with his thunder that rash and foolish human intelligence. Oh invisible Sun, who dost conceal thyself from us within a "luminous dark" abyss, and dost veil thyself with thine own rays; make me another Argos, blind and ignorant though I be, in my night reveal thy splendour; the less I understand thee, the more I know thee.

In the crossed-out passage on *f98* Coleridge is trying to amend Sonnet III according to his suggestions in the commentary. Tr: "Then in a more secure and sometimes sunny age."

2626 17.184 *AP* 154. The fable of the rain that induced madness to the third generation in those on whom it fell is told by Michael Drayton in his poem *The Moone-Calf*; it is in the same volume (II) with the *Polyolbion* in the 1753 edition, and both poems are in *B Poets* III.

Benedict Fay's . . . Lucretian Poem on the Newtonian System: In the first number of *The Friend* (1809–10), there was a reference (not in later editions) to *Philosophiae recentioris a Benedicto Stay* (2 vols Rome 1755), for the fable of the maddening rain, "a fable or allegory", Coleridge wrote, "which I read during my Freshman's Term in Cambridge, in a modern Latin Poet: and if I mistake not, in one of the philosophical poems of B. Stay, which are honoured with the prose Commentary of the illustrious Boscovich." *Friend* (1809–10) 28. In the notebook the reading is clearly (and erroneously) *Fay*. The fable itself is retained in *The Friend* in later editions: *Friend* (1818) 2–6.

2627 17.185 *AP* 154; see also 2634. I assume that Coleridge here forgot he had jotted down the observation the night before, or else he wished to expand it with his own after-reflections.

Pasley: Charles Pasley; see 2297n and 2449n.

Erastians: loosely, those in whose view the state enjoys political supremacy over the church.

2628 17.186 *Captn Lamb:* unidentified. He may be a John Lamb to whom two letters, written by his brother, Robert Lamb, from Gibraltar in Oct and Nov 1804, describing the plague there, were addressed in Malta. Transcripts of them by Coleridge are among his Malta papers in VCL. According to Coleridge's postscript to his transcript, John Lamb was "a clerk in the Dockyard—to Commissioner Otway—". Robert Lamb's list of their friends who had died

Coleridge refers to but does not transcribe, mentioning from it, however, Mr and Mrs Frome (2044 and n) and Major Adye. John Lamb
perhaps allowed Coleridge to copy the letters as material for his
projected account of his Mediterranean experiences, or for journalistic
purposes; but the identification with "Captn Lamb" is of course
doubtful.

2629 17.187   *AP* 155 variatim.

Apuleian is clear enough; *Apollonarian* (clearly enough the reading)
for the more usual terms *Apollinarian* or *Apollonian?*

Apuleian, Apollonarian, &c &c Corruptions of Style: corruptions by
confusion, by mixing the heterogeneous, by extravagance, by a substitution of fancy for intellection?

Does Coleridge think that the word *envy* should be reserved for
feelings of sheer hostility, its original sense? (See his long discussion of
envy in 1606.) The *OED* quotes various writers respected by Coleridge
who from Shakespeare's time onwards have used it in the sense he
objects to here; the concept of deprivation is his addition. If it is
based on a specific use by Johnson, the instance has not been found in
his works or in his *Dictionary.*

This is among the first of Coleridge's several discussions of the importance of "desynonymizing" words; see e.g. *Phil Lects* 173–4.

2630 17.188   *AP* 156. For Coleridge on bulls of thought and speech,
see 915n, 1620n, 1643n, 1645n, and *Omniana* I 219–21. 2663 shows
how deep the concept went with him.

2631 17.189   *AP* 155.

2632 15.163   The seal (though the evidence is mislaid) was a
present from Sara Hutchinson; for its impress see the half-titles of
these volumes.

2633 15.164   The anecdote appears to refer to one Frith, some
minor official, who, pretending to translate the title-page of Sannazaro's *Piscatoria*, was confused by the genitive case. For Coleridge's
contempt for officious incapacity as he saw it in his career as civil
servant, see *TT* 8 April 1833.

Coleridge's copy of Sannazaro *Opera omnia* (Frankfurt 1709) is
now in HEHL.

The Greek characters at the end may be transliterated: *strangury*, now usually referred to as acute retention.

2634 15.165   Cf 2627, where this observation is attributed to Capt Pasley as a remark of 2 Aug 1805; presumably Coleridge forgot he had already made a note of it, or could not thread his own labyrinth.

2635 15.166   Is he noting a potency in moonlight for some poetical purpose? Whereas the sun is the giver of life, in hot countries the moon revives life? Cf the more prosaic 2641.

2636 15.167   Citing a linguistic hotchpotch? *Ha bibi:* my friend, my child. *Himshi!* (or *Imxi* in Malta) is still known to the British army as a fairly strong expression for "Be off!" *Nichts [?push/pish] la:* German, Maltese, and Italian?

2637 18.189   The notebook here was used in a curious and unusual way; the entry begins two-thirds of the way down the otherwise blank *f90; f87* opposite is also blank, before which two leaves are missing. As may be seen in the table for N 18, entries 2637 18.189–2625 18.200 run in an erratic time order.

A possible explanation is that on 24 June 1805 Coleridge desperately scribbled 2602 (in pencil), only part of which was allowed to survive; and 2603 and 2604, in the same sort of quick pencil, followed; then a month later 2613–2615. A page and a third were evidently then left unused, because when on 14 Aug he wished to write at some length in the notebook, that space was not enough, and, 2625 having already filled *ff96ᵛ–100ᵛ*, he went back to the blank pages immediately before this cluster of entries (still keeping most of the notebook blank) and entered the entries of 14 Aug (2637–2639); as he was reserving this notebook for a special purpose, he did not wish to back up on the blank pages any further than necessary.

f90ᵛ   inlayed: cf 513 and n, and 2484.

f91   a breath of air on the surface of Tranquillity: the surface-tension and undercurrent of the cone-of-sand image, inverted? Cf 980 and n.

the Ship streaked it with a transverse bar: cf "And straight the sun was flecked with bars . . .". *The Ancient Mariner* line 177: *PW* I 193. Cf Coleridge's note on his copy of Nicolson and Burn (referred to in 2442n): "As often when the *S*un rises in sand- or brass-colored Vapor, we see him only by the greater Brightness of his *Shekinah*, not by any definite form—so in the Battle—there where the Fight was most

vehement, there was the General/S.T.C. 29 Aug 1805—or of suspect-
ing from that greater blaze, & by little & little detecting = *bringing
out* the melting Outline of the orb." Note on a front fly-leaf of Vol II.

2638 18.190   In Greek characters on the outer margin *Sara
Hutchinson* is written; on the inner margin *Coleridge and Sara.*

an epileptic dream: presumably a comatose state accompanied by
muscular spasms.

στιμυλος = *stimulos*, transliterated from the Latin for "stimulants".
There is no such Greek word.

my "Consolations": see 2018n.

carry on the Dream in his waking Thoughts: cf the cipher passage
2535. The questions Coleridge asks out of his own experience—the
relation of dreams to bodily feelings, the relation to waking thoughts,
the persistence of dream feelings into the waking state—all appear in
Freud *The Interpretation of Dreams.* See also 2600 and 2583.

2639 18.191   The primary material here is better organized, though
perhaps not more illuminating and articulate, in 2866. With the use
of the word *Shekinah* (Glory) here, cf the use, close to this date probably, quoted in 2637n.

2640 22.127   Writing to Southey in 1802 Coleridge said, "Before
the time of Grotius's de Veritate Christianâ no *stress* was lay'd on the
judicial, law-cant kind of evidence for Christianity which has been
since so much in Fashion/& Lessing very sensibly considers Grotius
as the greatest Enemy that Xtianity ever had." *CL* # 458 (II 861).

Hugo Grotius (1583–1645), the eminent Dutch jurist, in his popular
and much translated *De veritate religionis Christianae*, applied secular
arguments, based rather on grammar than on theology, to scriptural
evidence. In a regretful MS note on Richard Baxter *Reliquiae Baxte-
rianae* (1696) 116 Coleridge addresses Baxter as the one "who didst
first introduce into England the Grotian *ab extra* mode of defending
Christianity which leads either to this conclusion [miracles as the
cornerstone of faith] or to Socinianism". In *Eng Div* II 8–9.

Of the later theologians that Coleridge sometimes referred to as
"pseudo-rationalists" (see 1187) Paley is the best representative; his
A View of the Evidences of Christianity is what Coleridge has chiefly
in mind here. That work begins with "Preparatory Considerations—
Of the antecedent credibility of miracles", and pursues the argument

for a Christian revelation from historical evidence, and for the authenticity of miracles and the historical interpretation of the New Testament, to the final chapters.

With this entry, cf a long letter in which the entry is quoted at length, 4 Oct 1806, to George Fricker. *CL #* 631.

2641 22.128   In point of time this entry should either precede or follow 2224, the comments on *f25ᵛ* after metre 30. In this case, owing to the multiple character of that entry and the problems of serialization in general, the serial order makes it appear that there was a greater distance in time between them than there actually was; consultation of the tables is advisable here.

2642 22.129   H. W. Fowler *Modern English Usage* (1934) under "me", in agreement with Coleridge as to the tolerableness of "it is me", gives no such lucid defence.

2643 22.130   The dating of this entry is based chiefly on its proximity to 2641 and 2642 and its general appearance of having been written at the same time or close to them.

probata sunt: they have been tried/thoroughly tested.

the blessedness of Certainty . . . the Bubble-bubble of Positiveness: cf 2196 and n.

W[illiam] T[aylor] of Norwich: About William Taylor of Norwich Coleridge as early as 1799 had written to Southey, of "his all-half believing Doubtingness of all". *CL #* 292. In Feb 1805, again to Southey, he said, "W. Taylor grows worse and worse". *CL #* 614 (II 1162). They had not met personally at this time, if this is a Malta entry. I believe it is, especially in the light of Coleridge's way, of which countless examples could be given, of dramatizing his discussions with the writer he is reading. Taylor in 1805 was writing and reviewing on a wide variety of subjects for *Mon Mag* and *An Rev.*

On the other hand, if this is a reference to a *viva voce* discussion, the entry would necessarily be dated early 1808 or later. In a letter dated 9 Feb 1808 to Southey, Coleridge reports on his first acquaintance with Taylor, who had called on him that day; it is certainly possible that Coleridge's phrase "in some better moment" may have reference to his being ill in bed. "Mr. W. Taylor called again this morning—I regretted, that I was quite incapable of seeing any body, being in great pain with sickness. He seems very amiable—and it would [be] a twofold Sin of Impudence & Uncharitableness to [have] presumed to have gaged a man's understanding in a first conversation, of little more than half an hour. All I dare to say, is that I had anticipated more subtlety, less of the Trot Trot on the beaten road of Hartley & explanations of every thing by nothing—or what is much the same—by the word association. But I doubt not, he would rise rapidly in my opinion if I were with him for any length of Time." *CL # 675.*

Yet the "some better moment by his Fire Side" more probably means, "some one of *his* [Taylor's] better states of mind and feeling".

2644 22.131   The lines, if the initials mean that they are by him, or not merely about him, are not published in *PW*.

2645 22.132   The quotation is from Sir John Davies *Nosce teipsum, Of the Immortality of the Soul* §xxx "That the Soul is immortal, proved by several Reasons" stanza 6: "Yet though these men against their conscience strive,/There are some sparkles in their flinty breasts,/ Which cannot be extinct but still revive;/That though they would, they cannot quite be beasts." This is in *B Poets* II 698.

Coleridge's enthusiasm for Davies is reflected in the use made of some other lines from the same poem to help define Imagination in *BL* II 12–13, and earlier in the lectures of 1811–12. *ShC* II 98–9.

2646 22.133   The date that appears in the entry is not the date of writing it down, but a confirmation later of a date about which Coleridge was not precisely certain in 2594; that this is certainly a retrospective entry, later than 16 Aug, is clear from the physical facts of the pages between 2641 and this entry. See at 2648 the explanation of reasons for thinking the group of entries preceding this one Aug 1805. And see the next note. The hand of this one is different (larger) from what precedes and what follows. It may have been written any time between Aug and Nov 1805.

On the little information available about the persecution of Jews in Malta at this time, see 2594n; the date of the *avviso* there translated, 25 March 1805, together with the notebook references, suggest that the government was aware, at least between March and June 1805, of a persecution problem and anti-Jewish feeling; see also 2668.

Whether in relation to this or another incident, a statement made by Coleridge in an unpublished letter of 4 Jan 1820, shown to me by

Professor Griggs, receives a context. He was writing to his friend Hyman Hurwitz. "At Malta, & at the time when the God of your Fathers vouchsafed to make me the poor instrument of preventing an intended Massacre of your (& my) unoffending Brethren, I read the eleventh Chap—of Paul to the Rom—to the chief Criminal Judge, translating it literally into Italian. He . . . was convinced that I had been reading out of some *heretical* Book . . .".

That Coleridge was deeply shocked by the persecution of the Jews, as suggested by his repetition of references to it in Malta, is also evident earlier in a letter from Germany, 12 March 1799: "The Jews are horribly, unnaturally oppressed & persecuted all throughout Germany." *CL* # 272 (1 473).

2647 22.18   This entry follows 2224 (metre 30) on *f25ᵛ* (dated 16 Aug 1805) and is clearly associated with it in thought. (The separation in the serial order is owing to the span of 2224.)

even when I was a Child . . . at Christ-Hospital: see 1176 and n. The very first of his poems in *PW* 1 1–2, on *Easter Holidays*, derivative as it is, and trite, in the moralistic convention of Boyer's "Liber Aureus", is an ironically prescient commentary (*aet* 14/15) on this entry. See also the lines "O Christmas Day! Oh happy day!" entitled by JDC "Homeless", and dated by him [?1810] and by EHC 1826: *PW* 1 460.

Frank: Francis Syndercombe Coleridge, the brother immediately older, handsome and a general favourite, and associated with unhappy and vividly remembered incidents in Coleridge's early childhood. See 1494n.

2648 22.19   The entries on this last page of the first half of the original notebook (see N 22 Gen Note) are probably to be dated close to 2640, the first entry on the first page of the second gathering. They may have preceded them, i.e. they may have been entered *before* additional leaves were inserted in the middle of the first gathering, *f26ᵛ* and *f74* being then the facing pages of the centre leaves. Whatever the order of entries 2647–2649 and 2640–2646, they all appear to belong to *c* Aug 1805. But see 2646n.

my Comforts & Consolations: see 1993n.

2649 22.20   Whether Coleridge is quoting or observing here, the ideas expressed on the value of a clerical hierarchy and of the importance of a learned laity, a "national clerisy", were to be developed much later in the "pamphlet" (as it was modestly called in the first edition in 1830) *On the Constitution of the Church and State*. This influential work ran to an expanded second edition in 1830; see esp pp 53–7, 157–61.

2650 15.168   The employment of women was a subject of interest among the enlightened of the period, e.g. Dr Thomas Beddoes and Mary Lamb. See 1355 and n.

2651 15.169   Cf for similar sentiments Coleridge's statement "This is not a logical age . . ." in *Inq Sp* §89.

Dr Dodd: Dr William Dodd (1729–77), the fashionable clergyman who was hanged for forgery in spite of the efforts of Dr Johnson and others. He was a *cause célèbre* when Coleridge was a small boy.

Jane Gibbs: The London newspapers of Sept 1799 were full of tales of the tactics of this over-clever street-walker who, if her power to attract attention failed, as it frequently did, she being "an ill-favoured disgusting figure", used to charge with assault and battery those she had engaged in conversation.

Hatfield: see 1395 and n and 1432.

Mors omnibus communis: "Death the lot of all men".

Melita: Malta.

Holkar Welleslio devictus: "Holkar vanquished by Wellesley", i.e. Holkar, ruler of Indore, in 1802 came rather close to defeating Arthur Wellesley, Commander of the Army, later the Duke of Wellington; Richard Wellesley, his brother, was then Governor-General of India; the subject may have calculated ironical overtones.

2652 17.222   *a Doubloon:* a Spanish gold coin, originally 2 pistoles, or 33–36 shillings.

2653 17.223   The lines from Caius Valerius Flaccus *Argonautica* Bk 1 lines 29–31 appear to follow the Leyden edition of 1724. They were applied in *BL* Chap x to the shooting of the Duc d'Enghien by Napoleon.

Moreover, above all the great renown of the hero himself weighed upon his mind, and prowess never welcome to a tyrant. Wherefore he sought to forestall his fears and to destroy the son. . . .—Tr J. H. Mozley (LCL 1934).

2654 17.224   From the first of Daniel's sonnets *To Delia* lines 5–8: *B Poets* IV 218. Coleridge in June 1804 was "haunted by the Thought" that he had lost, among other books, the first four or five volumes of *B Poets* between Keswick and Malta. *CL* # 600 (II 1139). Whether he in fact had taken them, or whether, if lost, they were recovered in Malta, is not clear. See also 2621n.

2656 15.170   This misfortune was referred to later by Coleridge. The question arises whether Coleridge a few years later did not telescope this incident with his collapse on hearing of John Wordsworth's death. In 1808 he referred in a letter to Matilda Betham to "a contusion" received from a fall on that occasion which is not recorded by him at the time. The interest of it is that he has seemed to exaggerate in reporting his reception of the bad news; perhaps he did, and perhaps by this very common sort of slip. See *House of Letters* 107–8.

2657 15.171   There being several eighteenth-century masters of Trinity College, Cambridge, famous for gluttony, the author of these last words has not proved traceable.

2658 15.172   Tr: "*Connelino*, diminutive of that shameful part of women of which the name cannot be written." It will be noted that both word and definition are in Italian.

2659 16.262   *AP* 149.

2660 16.263   Coleridge records one visit to the Valletta hospital, and probably in the course of his duties went there a good many times. An image for a sick poet?

2661 16.264   *AP* 150. Suggested by the experience of the sunrise described in 2637 or, even more likely, the one referred to in the note? Coleridge was fond of the same simile for language, i.e. as a philosopher, going by the sun, but as citizen, by the town clock. See *TT* 1 Sept 1832.

2662 16.265   This entry perhaps dates an anecdote told by Coleridge to Allston of a fellow-passenger in a stage-coach who professed himself an enthusiastic reader of Coleridge's poems, "especially a dialogue which he pronounced capital. 'I don't remember any dia-

logue among them,' said Coleridge. 'Oh, yes,' said the man, 'it was between Strophe (pronounced in one syllable) and Anti Strophe. It was capital, but to tell the truth, I think Strophe had it, all hollow!' "
Allston Life 358.

2663 16.266   Five pages are cut out preceding this entry, which appears to be the last few lines of a personal memorandum. Underneath them Coleridge has drawn a line of half-loops, an unusual indication of restraint?—or inarticulateness?

Sbagli: plural of *sbaglio*, a mistake. This truncated fragment is perhaps to be associated with other entries recording the delusions of sleep or the half-waking state, as e.g. 2535. On bulls, see 2630 and n.

2664 16.267   *f82 St Teresa:* An entry in N 18 states that Coleridge "began to read the Life & Works of Ste Teresa" 25 June 1810. See also *Phil Lects* 314–16, 447–8. The phrases here used of her suggest rather a recollection of Crashaw's verses than more detailed study that came nearly five years later. Crashaw's *A Hymn to the Name and Honour of the Admirable Saint Teresa* is in *B Poets* IV 720–1; see 3102 and n.

Comparison . . . of the Mosaic and Romish Ceremonies: Coleridge appears to be thinking of a work to parallel and complete the aims of Conyers Middleton in *A Letter from Rome* (see 2729), to which, as early as 1796, he referred in *The Watchman* (*EOT* I 121). Middleton, in the words of his sub-title, attempts to prove "an exact Conformity between Popery and Paganism: or, the Religion of the Present Romans to be derived entirely from that of their Heathen Ancestors". Coleridge obviously had in mind a contrast, unfavourable to Roman Catholicism, with ancient Jewish rites.

The question of sacerdotal orders was much under discussion in Malta at this time, with particular reference to the political status and authority of the Order of the Knights of Malta in the island. Having as an ally of the King of Naples driven the French out, with the help of some factions in the Order as well as of the Maltese, Britain faced intrigue, within and without the Order, for control of the life of the island. The growing awareness of British officials like Ball, Macaulay, and Coleridge of the strategic and economic importance of Malta led to much controversy and confused discussion, one aspect of which turned on the nature and political and social *rôle* of Roman Catholicism. Some of this is reflected in Coleridge's notes.

NOTES

f83   symbols of Noumena: Coleridge's earliest use of that phrase? The *OED* gives the first use of *noumenon* in English to William Taylor of Norwich, *Mon Rev* 1798, the first use of *noumenal* to Coleridge in a letter of 1830: *L* II 755. As J. Isaacs pointed out in a valuable paper on "Coleridge's Critical Terminology", the noumenon-phenomenon distinction, established by Kant, and used first in England by Taylor, was introduced into literary criticism by Coleridge. He cites a marginal note on *All's Well That Ends Well* (see *ShC* I 113) which is probably later than this entry. *Essays and Studies* XXI (1935) 94.

Völkslehrer [Volkslehrer]: teacher of the masses.

2665 16.268   *Mr Chapman:* Edmond F. Chapman, the permanent Public Secretary, whose arrival released Coleridge and made it possible for him to leave. See 2408n and 2485n.

2666 16.269   An anniversary? 7 Sept is close to the time of composition of *The Pains of Sleep* in Edinburgh in 1803; and possibly there is here a thinking back to the Sept of 1800 and the struggle to finish *Christabel*, or even to the summer of 1798, the still not quite discarded date for *Kubla Khan*.

The remorseful *Pain from having* cursed *a gnat* suggests a more notable curse, and, on the Coleridgian principle of extremes meeting, that other remorseful relation to the creatures that led to the blessing of the water-snakes in *The Ancient Mariner*.

2667 16.270   Cf the reference to the conjunction of the rosary and the stiletto in *Friend* II 232.

On Coleridge's ambivalent view of Richardson see 2471 and n.

2668 15.173   Naphtali Busnack had from the Dey of Algiers a monopoly of the grain trade there. As chief minister and broker to the Dey, and therefore chief extortionist of the poor, he was hated in proportion to his power. He was killed at the gate of the Dey's palace by a janissary on 28 June 1805, according to a letter to Alexander Ball from Richard Cartwright, the British consul in Algiers; a mob massacre of Busnack's countrymen followed. It is interesting that Coleridge, who must have seen the July–Aug diplomatic correspondence about this event, records of its many aspects only the suffering of the Jews. (It is significant, in view of his secretaryship, that in Ball's letters the name is *Busnak*, as Coleridge spells it once here; elsewhere it is more frequently Busnack, Busnach, or Busnash.) But to judge from the official correspondence that survives, Coleridge must have obtained additional information from other sources. Some further developments were made clear in the consul's letter. "This country was heretofore in the French Interest whereas the English are now all in all." Immediately after this event the Dey and Prime Minister "entreated" barley and wheat from Malta. CO 158.10 ff 233–5. Ball in reply referred to "the fate of Busnak and his unfortunate sect", and made the releasing of Maltese slaves by the Dey (already long agreed to but not carried out) a condition of sending the grain. Ibid f 239.

2669 15.174   An illustration of a civil servant escaping from office on a small island—and fearing—to die?

2670 15.175   *f79ᵛ   1. was taught this hour:* for *one* [of them] *was taught this hour* &c, not, as it appears in print, the beginning of an enumerated list.

f80   Politian: Angiolo Poliziano (1454–94), Tuscan classical scholar and poet in Greek and Latin as well as Italian, under Lorenzo the Magnificent, a Neoplatonist.

psycho-analytical: the earliest use of *psychoanalyse* cited in the *OED* is dated 1906.

a Labyrinth of Parentheses: cf 2431 *ff5ᵛ–6.*

f80ᵛ   The lines here are found in the same volume of the same edition of Ariosto cited in 2770n (IV 652). As this entry is of unmistakable date, the quotation here tends to support the later rather than the earlier date for entries 2770–2773. Any assumption, however, of a single reading of Ariosto would be absurd. If the Ariosto entries in N 15 (2670) and those in N 22 (2770) were from the same copy of Ariosto, then either Coleridge took Wordsworth's copy of Ariosto Vol IV to Malta or, alternatively, the copy in *Wordsworth SC* (2770n) was once Coleridge's.

Tr: I shall conceal neither the year nor the place where I was captured: and at the same time I shall speak of the other trophies which you took then, such that in comparison your conquest of me was a trifle. I say that since the celestial King had sent his seed into the closed womb, the swift steeds of Achilles's bright Slayer had one thousand five hundred and thirteen times renewed that Day in midsummer sacred to the Baptist.

The whole subject of this entry engaged Coleridge deeply and is discussed by him from various angles; see e.g. 2729, 2737, 2738, and 2664. There is also more along these lines in his annotation on a copy of Boccaccio: "Boccaccio from a sense possibly of poetic justice; herein followed by a goodly company of poetic sons—Ariosto, Camoens etc.—reversed the scheme of the early Church and the Fathers of the First Century—they, namely transferred the functions and attributes of the Pagan Godlings & Goddesses & Nymphs to deified Bishops, Monks & Nuns. Boccaccio the functions and histories of Hebrew Prophets & Prophetesses and of Christian Saints and Apostles —nay the highest mysteries and most aweful objects of Christian Faith to the names & drapery of Greek & Roman Mythology." MS note on *Il Filocolo* on the last leaf of Vol I of Boccaccio *Opere* (Florence 1723–4). Quoted in H. G. Wright *Boccaccio in England* (1957) 340–1.

2671 15.176   The entry is puzzling in at least two respects. Why the thought of not returning was uppermost is difficult to understand, since Coleridge's successor as Public Secretary, or rather Alexander Macaulay's successor, had arrived on 6 Sept (see 2665); and in fact Coleridge did leave Malta 21 Sept. Perhaps there was some doubt, even so late as this, about the departure of a convoy or about accommodation for him on a ship. He may have hoped to leave for England, or for Italy and the overland route, instead of for Sicily.

the careless attack on the Scotch by Mackenzie: some horrifying blunder of a military—or conversational—sort? See also 2789. Capt Charles William Pasley was a Scot, on whom see 2449n.

2672 16.271   The dots near the end of the entry represent three and a half lines blotted out by acid.

the Prima Donna: Cecilia Bertozzi? See 2184 and n.

left Malta: Coleridge was on his way home to England. He hoped to go overland, as an official courier from Naples. But he may also have thought to obtain help, possibly a ship, through Mr Leckie at Syracuse, who as well as being the (honorary) British consul was an agent for Lloyd's.

On "man's . . . unconscious . . . *dependence* on some thing *out of* him", see e.g. 3026 and n.

2673 16.272   21 Sept 1805 was a Saturday, and Monday therefore 23 Sept. Does the entry mean that on the roughly 100-mile voyage from Malta to Sicily he did not go to bed? Or that it took 24 hours?

2674 16.273   *Rōōah:* for *Ruach? Ruach hakodesch* is the Hebrew phrase for "Holy Ghost".

A *lettiga* was described by Emily Lowe in 1859: "A perfect lettiga, beautifully painted, was found with mules so plump, they must have been fed surreptitiously. . . . The construction of the vehicle was like the body of a *vis-à-vis* raised on two horizontal poles, a peasant and his son, in long caps, held a bar of wood on which we stepped and sprung through the narrow door; the mules, harnessed between the poles were covered with trappings like war-horses, and if the bells were not of silver, they tingled as such in our ears. Thus rode the ancients, thus ride the moderns in Sicily, particularly ladies when they journey: pleasant enough is the movement when one is wrapped in dreams of classic beauty; but so to pace round the island at the rate, at the most, of eighteen miles a day, through a country whose rains are inundations, whose beauty is that of colouring, and luxuriousness that of the desert . . . is a proposition to which the traveler must tightly close his ears. . . ." (She does not say that the mule-borne litter was led on foot by the driver.) *Unprotected Females in Sicily, Calabria, and on the Top of Mount Etna* (London 1859) 70–1.

2675 21.348, 350   A farewell entry, like an earlier one written in N 3. See 446. It is in what appears to be Denison's autograph, and he left so much space after his name that Coleridge used it a few days later (2676); this made 2675 look at first like two entries.

Lu suderi . . . Ciceri: "The sweat streamed down my forehead. Chick-peas. Chick-peas."

The last two Italian words (the first sentence being Sicilian) are connected with the Sicilian Vespers (1282) and seem to record an anecdote of that time. The Italians would ask any stranger of whom they were suspicious to pronounce the word *ciceri*. If he said *siseri* they knew him for French and put him to death. The meaning of the anecdote referred to here, or its bond for Denison and Coleridge, is not known.

2677 22.134   The hand changes for smaller after the entry preceding this on *f76* (2646), and the events here must refer to events after 20 April 1805, i.e. to the second stay in Sicily Sept–Nov 1805.

Il Cartaginese, which Coleridge has written confusedly, is the title of a Malta periodical, *Il Cartaginese. Giornale Politico* (Edizione terza Filadelfia [Valletta] 1804–5). It is dedicated by the editor, V. Barzoni, "Alla Nazione Inglese/Se conoscessi una Naziona più libera della Nazione Inglese, le dedicherei quest'Opera": "To the English Nation —if I knew a freer Nation than the English Nation, I would dedicate this Work to it."

The interest of this paper, and the relation of its editor to Coleridge, are discussed in Appendix D, where the account of "the Death & Wreck of I[ohn] W[ordsworth]" and his ship the *Abergavenny* is translated. It appeared in No 15 of the third edition, 20 April 1805, which gives at least a *terminus a quo* for this entry.

One more fact is pertinent to Coleridge's seeing an old mariner on the dead lava in Sicily with a copy of this paper. Its method of distribution was extraordinary, a war-time method for propagandist purposes; the English threw it in bundles on the shores of the kingdom of Naples. Napoleon countered by offering a bounty for every copy turned in to the authorities, and sailors and fishermen therefore found it a profitable catch. But Coleridge's phrasing suggests that perhaps what interested him here was less the successful propaganda-device than the conjunctions: the once violent, now dead lava, and the violent events of the sinking, now petrified in the newspaper account; the old Italian mariner, and the lost young English sailors; and perhaps also the incongruities of geography, the distance between the event and the reading about it.

2679 16.274   *Upas Tree:* see 37 and n.

The writing in this and the preceding entry is rather larger and less co-ordinated than usual, possibly from the motion of the *lettiga* or from the effects of spirits or opium. Is the "de-humanizing *Spell*" &c a reference to his having seen signs of considerable drug addiction among the Sicilians, making them, like himself, pilgrims from the poison-tree?

2680 16.275   *Mackenzie:* not identified, and difficult to relate to 2671; probably the Mackenzie of 2789. On the *lettiga* see 2675n.

2681 16.276   Coleridge is again interested in local economy. Salt was an important product of the Syracuse area and constituted the wealth of some towns, e.g. Trapani.

2682 16.277   Valverde may have been reached on a short expedition on the south-eastern slopes of Etna from Catania or Acireale, or it may simply have been visited *en route* from Catania to Taormina, by an excursion from the main coast road. It may have been included in one of the two ascents of Etna referred to in *CL* # 612; the other way—*via* Nicolosi—was certainly the more usual. (See 2170 and n.) Possibly he took both ways. It would be natural for him to stop off almost anywhere on this coastal route for inland explorations, perhaps especially at Acireale because of its medicinal baths.

2683 16.278   The carob-tree, with its hornlike pods used for fodder, is notable in the Levant. See also 2507.

2685 16.280   An exclamation at picturesqueness? Cf 2682. Aci S Antonio is just north of Acireale, towards Taormina. *Gialli:* yellows; *Strada:* road. Possibly a reminder of a road on which many varieties of yellow had struck Coleridge as interesting—grain, rock, dust, clouds, flowers, etc.

2686 16.282   The words are written at right angles on the page, below the rough attempt to draw the lines of the hills at Taormina, on the lower ridge of which lies Taormina itself, and on the higher sky-line, Castel Mola. See 2688.

2687 16.283   The words that appear to be inserted at the beginning of this entry are, I believe, a traveller's practical note to himself as he anticipates his journey. They may constitute a quite separate entry, yet the whole was written before Taormina, i.e. before 2688, which begins on the opposite page and continues around it. However, the advice to beware the landlord of the Lion does not apply to Giardini, where there never was an inn so named, but to Catania, and Coleridge may have been memorializing after the event. Incredible as it may seem, Goethe in 1787 noticed on the façade of the Fondaco Cuba an inscription in English which read: "O traveller, whoever you are, beware in Catania the hotel the Golden Lion; it is worse than to fall into the clutches of the Cyclops or the Syrens or the Scylla." *Italienische Reise*—first published 1816–17—under the date 1 May 1787: *Werke* (133 vols Weimar 1887–1918) XXXI 182. Is it too much to believe that Coleridge saw the same inscription or the same landlord eighteen years later?

It is possible that Coleridge noted down "Giardini below Taormina" as the name of the place where he was to abandon the coast road and mount higher for the sake of the view, and that this was already on the page, when the description of the landlord was written as he left Catania on Friday morning. The distance from Catania to Messina is 60 miles—Giardini to Messina is about 38 miles. Coleridge lengthened his route considerably in distance, and still more in time and difficulty, by his ascent at Taormina described in the next entry.

2688 16.284   Overleaf Coleridge attempted an outline of the hill on which the ancient Greek theatre is so magnificently situated at Taormina, and the "proud Cone", i.e. of Castel Mola, above. See 2686.

as we were entering Giardini: from Catania, or from a descent of Etna? Cf 2685.

An immensely steep *steep road:* The fact that he elected this long climb, instead of the more normal and easy coast road, reminds one of his earlier fell-climbing in the Lakes and the Scottish tour; the taste for "difficulties overcome" appears again at Terni. See 2849n.

Cactus opuntium, the Linnaean name, now *Opuntia vulgaris,* is a common plant in the Mediterranean region; it bears a white blossom. Coleridge's tendency to observe the small detail along with the panoramic has been noticed earlier. See e.g. 222n and 2172.

Island Rock-Hill: Isola Bella.

a high savage Promontory: Capo Sant'Andrea.

2690 16.286   *Candelasia:* Castel Mola? The geographical location is indubitable, but Coleridge's name for it is unknown on Sicilian maps.

about 9 or 10 miles from Giardini: Coleridge's description makes it clear that instead of proceeding to Messina by the easier coast road he mounted straight up, through Taormina, past the "ruined Tower" of the Castello di Taormina and the Church of the Madonna della Rocca to Castel Mola.

cheosi remains unexplained, unless he means *chiuse:* enclosed fields.

2691 18.7   Possibly the whole entry was written in after the other entries were on the page, and the reference to *Taurominum* may be retrospective. Or, alternatively, it appears possible that the first two lines and the name *Taurominum* were written when the page was empty except for the names in the corners to which it refers, and that the second couplet was written later, after 2692. See N 18 Gen Note and 2694n.

In *PW* I 392 the lines are dated 1805.

2692 18.8   *Schinchimurra* is an invented word used by Boccaccio (*Decameron* VIII 9) to induce amusement and wonder.

The reason for including this entry at this date is chiefly the difficulty otherwise of explaining the crowded appearance of the preceding entry. There is also the undoubted fact that Coleridge had been thinking about pot-boiler romances ever since the Bristol days when he and Southey thought they could "toss off" a novel together. The reference here, if to one of those abortive plans, could have been written among the first entries in the notebook. On the other hand, his earliest and only reference to this title so far come to light is in a letter to Byron of Oct 1815: "Laugh till you lose him—a dramatic Romance—. Putting all merit out of the Question, it is in the scheme more analogous to the Tempest than any other. The Songs, & one act written." *CL* # 982. One is perhaps too much inclined to think of this, in 1815, as probably arising from the impetus of the success of *Remorse;* it must be observed that in the same postscript Coleridge refers to *The Triumph of Loyalty*, which goes back to 1801, and "An entertainment . . . the Scene in Arabia—".

The latter, to which he refers elsewhere as "Diadestè" (1723n), is not, I think, the work meant here. A sketch of it exists (VCL MS), and there is a scene or two in a much corrected and clearly experimental MS in BM Add MS 34,225 ff 36–45, both datable after 1812.

But in the same Add MS 34,225 ff 81–3 there is part of a fictional prose work in which the speaker appears to be clownlike and in which there are references to such characters as Lady Aroma Sniff, Mr O'Gourmand, Dr Hyphen, and other such possible *dramatis personae* for a romance. The water-mark of these leaves is dated 1821.

In the list of projected works drawn up in Nov 1803 (1646), the second and third items are "Christabel—or the Dramas". The fifth item, a composite, had as its first part "Romances".

Precise dating of this entry is difficult in the light of Coleridge's incurable lifelong desire to write comic entertainments.

2693 18.9   In pencil. Henry Smeathman read his paper "Some Account of the Termites, which are found in Africa and other hot climates" before the Royal Society 15 Feb 1781. It was published in that year as a pamphlet and also in *Phil Trans* (1781) LXXI 192; Smeathman was long accepted as an authority on ants. He describes chiefly three species, the large African fighting ants, the tree or wood ants, and, largest of all, the marching ants, their social classes and organization and particularly the architecture of their dwellings. His plates also would stir the imagination.

In *Phil Trans* (1771) LXI 182–94 Coleridge may have found "Observations on the Aphides of Linnaeus" by William Richardson, and if he did not read the paper to the end, but only the first seven pages, he might easily have left it with the impression that the author believed all aphides to be female with "a very numerous progeny, and that without having intercourse with any male insect", a view later in the paper denied. But the source of this phrase is not certain; it is not in Smeathman.

2694 18.10   In pencil. This and the two foregoing entries seem to belong to the Malta period. Had they not been on the page, 2691 would not have been crowded in to a limited space.

2695 16.287   6 Oct 1805 was a Sunday; if the dates are correct, he arrived in Messina on Friday, 4 Oct.

2696 16.288   It is no longer possible to see the landscape as Coleridge saw it; Messina was almost totally destroyed by the earthquake of 1908.

2697 16.289   The decline of the ruble owing to the war-time dislocation of trade would concern Coleridge as a prospective government agent for buying wheat in the Black Sea area; see 2740n.

2698 16.290   Salvatore Campolo has not survived in the story— possibly a chance acquaintance; he appears again in 2705.
[*?Gravitell's/Gravitelli*]: this does not appear on any available map; possibly it was destroyed in later eruptions; it may have referred to a house or an estate. See 2705.

2699 16.291   Mr Broadbent, whether on official or private business in Malta, was in the confidence of Ball in the corn-buying manoeuvres. CO 158.110. How he was moistening the air above plants to avoid overwatering is not clear.

2700 16.292   The obliterated passage, seven and a half lines, was deleted with some sort of acid.

The original plan was to return home overland *via* Trieste; see 2572n. However, the entry illustrates the war-time uncertainties to which Coleridge and other travellers were subject, for on this same day the plan must have been altered. Five days later he was still in Messina—see 2705.

2701 16.281   The deleted words are in an unco-ordinated writing probably to be associated here with opium or the spirits Coleridge frequently took at night to forestall sleep. The remainder of the entry, in a large but firmer hand, may have been written the next day. It was written in Messina, and after 2686, which it overruns on *f87*.

2702 16.293   The entry is partly obliterated by the acid used overleaf, referred to in 2700n; what remains is not very clear in intent.

Ferdinand IV of Naples (1751–1825) was also King of Sicily. The inscription or proclamation therefore appears to be a contemporary one, probably on the Strada Ferdinanda, which (one of the principal streets of Messina in 1805) was destroyed, like the streets referred to in 2708, by the great earthquake of 1908. In view of Ferdinand's reputation for anything but authority and courage, as witness even the one episode of Caracciolo referred to by Coleridge himself, in 2311 (see note), this memorandum may well have been made in an ironic or comic spirit.

It reads, with a large element of conjecture, lacking the key words:

For the honour of forcing the hand of fate to foster the Peace and Security of the people, and extend the Ferdinand Way, Ferdinand IV, King, in as much as his rule . . . Sicily . . . and bestows.

2703 16.294   Cf 997 and n, 1604 and n.

2704 16.295   Presumably attempts were being made, from England and from the court of Naples, to rally the Sicilian population to the support of Naples and defiance of Bonaparte.

2705 16.296   On *Gravitelli* see 2698n. Coleridge describes some one of the *fiumare* or defiles on which at picturesque points country villas were built.

f93ᵛ He sees the Faro, and possibly Castellaccio and Gonzaga, referred to in 2706, possibly identified after he returned from his walk.

2706 16.297   *Castellaccio* is a dismantled fortress near Messina. *Castello di Gonzaga* was erected in 1540, and is south of Castellaccio.

2707 16.298   A mishearing of "Braccio di San Ranieri", the narrow arm of land stretching out from the southern tip of Messina, sickle-shaped, to the north, forming the port of Messina?

2708 16.299   *quatro Fontane:* "From this piazza [del Duomo], the street of the Quattro Fontane* intersects the town [Messina] . . . *so called from the four fountains that adorn the angles. . . ." [Edward Boid] *Travels through Sicily and the Lipari Islands* (London 1827) 279. This area also was laid waste in 1908.

2709 16.300   This proposed tour, planned from a large-scale map, was to run from Messina to Syracuse, cross-country southwards *via* Bronte, and to the west of Etna. Although we do not know the map Coleridge used, many of his out-dated spellings and names can be justified by comparing them with those on Capt J. B. M. Chauchard *General Map of Sicily* (London 1800).

2711 16.302   *AP* 149; cf 2724, where the figure of the many-headed source of the Nile, of frequent occurrence in Coleridge's prose writings, is repeated, variatim. On the importance of relating correctly metaphor and reality, see 1675, 2402, and 2724 and n.

2712 16.303   *AP* 163, with variations that are minor except for the last word, altered to "thine!" Empedocles (*c* 490–*c* 430 B.C.), the Greek humanist philosopher and statesman, was a natural association in the presence of Etna, where according to legend he committed suicide by hurling himself into the crater. Simonides of Ceos (*c* 556–469 B.C.), the eminent Greek lyrical poet, celebrated in elegy, epigram, and ode many of the important events of his time. Coleridge appears more than once to have entertained suicidal thoughts, if not actual resolves, on the Malta journey (see 1913, 2100, 2510, and 2557); the Messina period, before embarking for Italy and the clear turn homewards, was presumably a critical time.

The conjunction here of Simonides and Empedocles may be merely the obvious one of poet and philosopher. If it represents more detailed thoughts about the two men it may also carry overtones of Empedocles's passionate appeals for justice for the poor, and a selfless devotion to intellectual problems; and of Simonides as the professional poet, with a strong conviction of his own worth, or at least a willingness to accept as true his public reputation for virtue and wisdom. Coleridge's wish appears, from the ending, to be for a union not only of minds but of temperaments.

2713 16.304   The story is told by Dr John Moore in Letter xiv of his *A View of Society and Manners in Italy with anecdotes relating to some eminent characters* (6th ed 1795) I 135–42. Coleridge's version is very condensed and at points more dramatic than his source. "Sent back a *Corse/*—his Father's & Mother's Darling" are Coleridge's phrases, the first considerably sharpening Moore's ". . . a vessel arrived from Candia with tidings, that the miserable youth had expired in prison a short time after his return". The second phrase is a summary of implications, but nothing of the sort is specifically stated by Moore.
    That Moore was the source is put beyond doubt by Coleridge's adoption of his anglicized spelling of the names, and by the contiguity of this anecdote with the next. See 2714n.

2714 16.305   Ibid Letter xiii I 120–7. Moore tells the story with much moral unction, making a contrast in favour of Charles I. It appears frequently in later histories and travels.

2715 16.306   Names of characters for a farce, or some projected satire?

2716 16.307   No source has been found. Copied as examples of comically bad verses? Or an attempt at a translation of the same?

2717 16.308   Used in a lecture of 5 Feb 1808, according to reports quoted in *ShC* II 8, and a MS note in Egerton 2800 f 15. "Here the Anecdote of the mountebank—at Naples—": *ShC* I 189–90.
    Hor . . . a la Priapo: whore . . . in the way that Priapus, god of fertility, is commonly represented.

2718 16.309 *sustente:* The reading is difficult because the word was loosely and carelessly written. Possibly for *sustent,* an obsolete form of *sustinent.*

Λεχι: G. F. Leckie. See 2156n and 2193n. The suggestion here that Leckie tended to be agnostic may give a direction to the argument, or at least an opponent, in such entries as 2196.

2719 16.310 *Sharpians, or Moorists—both bad:* Samuel Sharp, a surgeon, wrote a vigorous, somewhat Smelfungian travel-book, *Letters from Italy* (1766), which called forth controversy and was followed shortly by his further comments, even more highly critical of Italian manners, entitled *A View of the Customs, Manners, Drama &c of Italy* (1768). Dr John Moore (1729–1802), the author of *Zeluco,* wrote numerous personal and amiable travel-books, several of which were generally popular. (See 2713n.)

Coleridge seems to mean that both sorts were bad from their lack of objectivity. Sharp's books were at least specifically critical and cautionary, written for future travellers, and Moore's full of personal experiences and misadventures, travellers' tales; neither was adequate on the geographical or historical or social side. Perhaps the explanation for Coleridge's desire to defend Sharp is to be found not only in his own difficulties as an English traveller in Italy at this time, but in the attacks on Sharp by Joseph Baretti, which had, according to Chalmers *Biographical Dictionary* (1812), "destroyed the reputation of Sharp's work".

2720 16.311 Coleridge could have seen minor eruptions of Vesuvius Nov–Dec 1805; cf 2749. With the heading later inserted, cf a paragraph on perception and logic from the MS Logic, reproduced in *Logic* 116–18.

2721 16.312 *A[lbergo] di Sole:* in Naples; see 2717.

2722 16.313 *AP* 149.

2723 16.314 Cf ". . . the truth of passion, and the *dramatic* propriety of those figures and metaphors in the original poets, which, stripped of their justifying reasons, and converted into mere artifices of connection or ornament, constitute the characteristic falsity in the poetic style of the moderns . . .". *BL* II 28 (Chap XVII).

2724 16.315   See 2711 and n.

2725 16.316   *AP* 149–50. There are numerous references in Virgil *Aeneid* Bk v to caestuses. The stiletto and the rosary in one pocket became an example of similar treachery for Coleridge; see 2667 and n.

2726 16.317   *AP* 158. A pencil entry traced in ink by another hand, perhaps by Mrs Gillman.
Lamb's remark about Coleridge having gone to see "his god Wordsworth", even allowing for some personal heat, seems to corroborate Coleridge's self-castigation here. As do some of Coleridge's own letters.

2727 16.318   *AP* 159. *Martial . . . Domitian/Dryden . . . Milton:* i.e. Dryden and Martial were approximately on a level, Martial's numerous compliments to his patron, the Emperor Domitian, being like many of Dryden's, fulsome but not venal flattery; Milton was above this practice, but Martial and Dryden are not therefore to be categorized as bad men. Besides, they can be excused from having but the partial view of contemporaries. In the light of later events and more distant focus their compliments appear exaggerated; yet we also in our "fixedness" (*The Ancient Mariner* gloss on line 263: *PW* I 197) distort reality by our own fictions.
Coleridge's opinion of Martial, and indeed his view of Dryden, may be unsupported by modern criticism, but not his protest against misplaced moral judgements.

2728 16.319   *AP* 165. Of Claudian Coleridge was later to express more favourable views: *TT* 18 Aug 1833, 2 Sept 1833.
no perspective: cf *BL* II 44 (Chap XVIII), where a similar point is made about the uneducated mind.

2729 16.320   *the Tale out of Burton:* in 680 and n?
a wild story of Ceres's loss of Proserpine: The cave through which Pluto was supposed to have carried off Proserpine to his own domain is on the side of Etna, and doubtless Coleridge, within earshot of much fantastic local mythology, was spurred to invention. Or possibly this tale, too, may have had its origin in Bacon *De sapientia veterum*, the section on Proserpine. See 2737n.
Conyers Middleton *A Letter from Rome* (see 2664n) has much to say

about the adaptation of pagan altars, images, and customs to Christian or, as he argues, anti-Christian use. In his reports of how statues of pagan deities were given new drapery and new names, still standing on the old pedestals and still receiving religious homage, Middleton quotes a description of the "converting the profane worship of the Gentiles to the pure and sacred worship of the Church" (4th ed 1741) 168; Coleridge's underlining of the word *converted* may indicate a re-reading or a recollection as well as an ironical interpretation. The underlining of *Mars* at this time scarcely needs comment.

If Coleridge used the most recent edition of this work available to him, cited above, he found the "Post-Script" attacking Warburton which fixed the lines of theological controversy for decades. Coleridge remained throughout his life an anti-Warburtonian.

2730 16.321   If Pasley (see 2449 and n) was in Italy with Coleridge at this time, there is no other indication of it, but there is no doubt that Coleridge maintained an intimacy with him beyond any other Malta connexion, and he may well have been along on part of Coleridge's homeward journey.

2731 16.322   *Virgil's Tomb:* a grotto, thought to have been an ancient Roman columbarium, on Mt Pausilippo near Naples, popularly known as the Tomb of Virgil, and bearing, in 1326 and again after 1554, an inscription to this effect. From this point there is a magnificent view of the whole city and Bay of Naples.

È un pecccato . . . severo: "It is a sin/I am very unfortunate in having a somewhat severe confessor".

Non o Sento: a mishearing for "non lo sento"? i.e. "I do not hear him or it", or, "I do not feel it".

Noi tutti: all of us.

2732 16.323   *Thrasybulus, Demosthenes:* Coleridge is referring to the meaning of these names as compound epithets: $\theta\rho\alpha\sigma\acute{v}s$ + $\beta o v\lambda\acute{\eta}$ = bold in counsel, $\delta\hat{\eta}\mu os$ + $\sigma\theta\acute{\epsilon}vos$ = strength of the people.

His interest in what he called the "agglutination" of language is frequently evident; see *TT* 2 Sept 1833 for a comment on Latin and Greek in this respect; and 2431 and n.

2733 16.324   Hugh Elliot (1752–1830) was minister to the court of Naples from 1803 until a few months after this entry, when he was recalled. He had three daughters living at the time of his death, of whom this one could be Emma (d 1866) or Harriet Agnes (d 1845).

Coleridge's letter of introduction from Alexander Ball is of some interest; see Appendix B.

2734 16.325   Fantasy-play with creatures less or larger than normal is not common in Coleridge's writings. But on *minitude* see 2784, on *minimism* 2890n, and on Lilliputian feelings 2402 *f128ᵛ*.

2735 16.326   A generalized comment on the type of experience more intimately described in 3202.

2736 16.327   This appears to be a reference to the legend of the Empress Helena with twenty ships putting into Corfu in search of the True Cross. On finding it, the Cypriot sailors received one of the three nails found in it; the Cross itself was then used as a talisman which on being thrown into the Adriatic in rough weather calmed the waters. C. Gregg is unknown.

2737 16.328   *History of Heath[en] Gods wanting:* Coleridge, though he knew of Samuel Boyse (see 2557 and n), apparently did not know his *A New Pantheon, or, Fabulous History of the Heathen Gods, Heroes, Goddesses &c; explained in a manner entirely new, and adorned with figures depicted from ancient paintings, . . . To which is added, a Discourse on the Theology of the Ancients . . .* (1772), though it had run to five editions by 1777. Andrew Tooke's *The Pantheon* (29 editions by 1793) he certainly knew, probably from school-days; he referred to it in a letter of Jan 1804. See *CL # 540* and *L* II 455n.

Boccac[c]io Genealogia: see 1649n; support for the view that the copy of the edition there cited, listed in the *Green SC* (247), was Coleridge's is to be found in 2512n and in the MS catalogue of Wordsworth's library now in the Houghton Library.

Bacon: Francis Bacon *De sapientia veterum.* See 2588n.

On Middleton's *Letter from Rome* see 2729n.

On this subject in general see 2670 and n.

2738 16.329   See 2729 and n.

2739 16.330   An interesting indication of how a history of heathen gods (2737 above) would have read had Coleridge written it, Pan having to be treated e.g. in the light of the *Lines composed above Tintern Abbey.* Yet the story of Pan's desire for Syrinx, and marriage to Echo, could, like the story of Cupid and Psyche in 2588, and Proserpine in 2729, have been found in Bacon *De sapientia veterum;* given Coleridgian latitude, the last half of the entry could be a selective interpretation of Bacon's material.

2740 15.177   The price of wheat was the crucial question for the economy of both Malta and Sicily. It was also a subject involving Ball's methods and administration when private (and foreign?) interests were trying to discredit him and to restore the corn-buying to private interests rather than the agents he recommended. In Sicily, the grain trade was a monopoly and its maladministration the main cause of poverty. See e.g. G. F. Leckie *An Historical Survey* Tract VIII.

Ball's difficulties are clear in his correspondence with the Colonial Secretary (CO 158.9,10), e.g. in Aug 1804, when he was asking for a capital of £210,000 to be invested, and the following September, when he reports a successful buying mission to the Black Sea by E. F. Chapman, as a result of which the advantageously bought grain will be stored and sold at a profit to the government of £20,000 and at the same time bread will be cheaper than in Sicily, Spain, or the Barbary States. Coleridge was interested in the general problem, but he at one moment had a close personal connexion, when he was on the point of being sent with Capt Leake, a proposed replacement for Chapman, to the Black Sea on a similar errand. But Chapman continued to do the work, and Leake and Coleridge remained in Malta. In Feb 1805 Ball was still battling against such suggestions as that the government *entrepreneur* should be appointed by the consul-general of Russia; he protests against this as folly, and repeats that the Maltese have had grain below the market price of Italy and Sicily since he has "had the direction of the Corn concern".

Trouble was brewing for Ball. It came to a head about 1807–8 through the intrigues of a would-be agent named William Eton, who published *Authentic Materials for a History of the People of Malta* "by William Eton, Superintendant General of the Quarantine and Public Health Department in Malta" (4 pts: 1802, 1805, 1807). In pt IV there is a section, entitled "Cause of the Discontent in Malta", attacking Ball.

Coleridge is collecting material in Ball's defence, strong evidence that there was no foundation for the malicious story that they "parted

on the worst terms, on a mutual notorious hatred of each other".
Rickman 151. The notebook entries about Ball support the essays in
the third volume of *The Friend* already cited. See also Appendix B.

2741 15.178   *a spacious Town:* probably Boscotrecase.

  Troops were reviewed: British troops, by the King of Naples, 30 Nov
1805, two days before the battle of Austerlitz. Charles Boothby, a
captain of the Royal Engineers, refers to "the wintry sun" on "our
brass plates and steely muskets, which Coleridge, who dined with us
afterwards, called 'a beautiful accident' ". *Under England's Flag from
1804 to 1809. The memoirs, diary, and correspondence of Charles
Boothby* (1900) 36.

2742 15.179   Coleridge makes several observations on feminine
dress; see e.g. 335 *f3*ᵛ.

2743 15.180   This may be part of the same trip described in 2744.
At any rate Coleridge must have left Naples not later than 2 Dec
1805, for on that day the news of Trafalgar and Nelson's death
reached Naples, and he did not know of it until his return. See 2744n.

2744 18.318   Four blank pages immediately precede this entry,
and the last entry before the blank leaves was dated by EHC as
c 1811–12 (*AP* 254, on the paper-money controversy). In other words,
there were probably fewer than a score of entries in the notebook when
this one was made; see N 18 Gen Note. It appears to belong to the
period after the first and before the second stay in Naples. See 2743
and 2745.

  It describes a curious journey from Naples, not "to Messina, along
the Coast", but from Naples overland *via* Cassano, to a fairly obscure
point beyond Cariati on the south coast of the Gulf of Taranto. The
account scarcely reads like that of a mere walking trip, and at this
troubled period after the collapse of the allied armies at Ulm, when
the French were carrying all before them and the English not highly
popular in Italy, such a tour was not likely to be undertaken for
pleasure. It reads, too, like a diary of experience and not like a second-
hand report. We know nothing of Coleridge's expedition into Calabria
except that it took place, and that he speaks of it as of an episode,
distinct and of itself an event in his Italian experiences.

  It was made memorable for him later by the fact that it was on his return from Calabria that he first heard of Trafalgar and Nelson's death. *Friend* III 363.

It seems possible to surmise that he may have been sent, by Hugh Elliot (see 2733n) or some military officer, to investigate a possible indirect route for the Neapolitan royal family, and/or the English community, should further military disasters occur. Or was he investigating the extent of pro-British feeling in Calabria? The news of Austerlitz reached Naples on Christmas-day, but even before that there were advocates of an English retirement from their indefensible position in Italy to Sicily, which Sir Alexander Ball had long wished to garrison and occupy. The position of the English, in particular diplomatically, was deteriorating daily at the court of Naples, and it may well have seemed advisable to find friends and possible hospitality along a back-door route of exit. In early February the King of Naples, and a few days later the Queen, did flee to Palermo, the latter accompanied by the British ambassador.

Could this be someone else's report of a tour in Calabria? If so, the entry has no counterpart in the notebooks of this kind of direct reportage (except perhaps 236). And such expressions as "a Priest, Bruinher, received us with hospitality" and various exclamatory comments seem to be personal observations, not hearsay.

If the role of advance courier seems too incongruous to connect with Coleridge, one may recall the nature of his duties in Malta (see Appendix B), that he had an introduction from Ball to the ambassador, and that he had expected to be franked home as a bearer of dispatches. In the exigencies of the time, an ex-civil servant may well have been given such a temporary official or semi-official assignment.

It has further been suggested that the expedition here may have had some link with the successful battle of Maida some months later. This is perhaps not impossible, but on the face of it, geographically and otherwise, it seems less likely. That Coleridge was, however, deeply interested in the battle of Maida, and later obtained some inside information about it, will appear in a later volume.

f160ᵛ holding up the Dæmon Outis *in terrorem plebis:* Outis = Οὖτις = Nobody: "holding up the Daemon Nobody to frighten the people". Οὖτις is the name Ulysses used to hide his identity from Polyphemus.

f161ᵛ a digression ex diverticulo igitur in viam: a digression "from the Inn; therefore, to the Road".

∧ *signifies:* ∧ signifies steep or mountainous.

2745 16.331   The first lodging was 20–30 Nov (2743) at the Albergo del Sole (2717). This second lodging was taken presumably after his "return from Calabria". *Friend* III 363.

2746 16.332   A comparison of the cultivation of the ruling classes in Renaissance Italy with the Italy of 1805, and particularly as reflected in the patronage of men of learning? Ficino's numerous prefaces and dedications to the several members of the Medici family are variations on two themes chiefly: the learning of his patrons, and their generosity and integrity in assuming the social responsibility of patronage. See also Coleridge's later comparison with the situation in England: "The darkest despotisms on the Continent have done more for the growth and elevation of the fine arts than the English government." *TT* 7 July 1831.

As a professional writer, Coleridge was deeply interested in the general question of patronage. (Possibly the verses in 293 are his own.) In 1825 he wrote an article on the subject for *News of Literature* (10 Dec 1825); it is published in Thomas Constable *Archibald Constable and his Literary Correspondents* (3 vols Edinburgh 1873) 479–82, and may be safely assigned to STC. Not only does it begin with six lines of verse signed with his initials and not at that date published (Epigram 74: *PW* II 973); but the language and scope of the essay is thoroughly Coleridgian. In it, as is appropriate to an obituary reference to Archibald Constable, the emphasis is less on the decline of the noble patron—"A literary man of the present day would as soon think of seeking patronage from the Emperor of Austria, or setting forth the talents and the virtues of the Spanish Ferdinand, as of placing his hopes of a hearing with the public upon the foremost nobleman in the land . . ."—than on the development of a reading public as patron, and the increasing prestige of publishers as a result. "This change has brought the publishers of books into an attitude of the greatest importance and honour; it has made them the connecting link between the people of England, and that which has made, is making, and shall continue to make, the people of England superior to the people of every land where intellect has not the same unbounded scope." The whole article is a most sympathetic and interesting appreciation of the responsibilities and functions of publishers.

2748 16.334   Published in Gillman 179n, omitting the parenthetical sigh after "Keswick".

2749 16.335   In a letter of Dec 1804 Coleridge had lamented having narrowly missed seeing an eruption in November of that year (*CL* # 612). Here he apparently describes some minor disturbance. In Aug 1805 there was a violent eruption that at one moment threatened Naples, and there was another in the following May; presumably Vesuvius was not entirely quiescent during Coleridge's visit in Nov–Dec 1805. See also 2720.

2750 16.336   The reference to Martial is merely to the phrase *Rex meus*, which may also be translated, "my Patron", clearly not Coleridge's anxious intention here. The intention of the revision to the perfect tense and the substitution of *usque* for *ecce* in the last line seems to be to pour salt on the wound of his long self-abasement before Wordsworth.

The lines are as difficult to decipher as to interpret, and even more difficult to date correctly. They are here placed in the run of entries on these pages, in what appears to be their normal sequence: possibly they belong earlier or later. One entry in this notebook that must be dated after the 1810 quarrel with Wordsworth—the only one—is the postscript referred to in 1723n. Entry 1723, dated Dec 1803, could, in its subject-matter, be a starting-point for these bitter accusations of moral pride and "tyranny"; so could the postscript that belongs to *c* 1811–15. This entry could emanate also from the period of *The Friend* (1809–10) and its attendant frictions. There is nothing impossible about the expression of this feeling any time after the Scottish tour of 1803, though it would be a very fleeting mood until 1807. A free translation follows:

Modest respect? No, by God, this is tyranny!
You certainly will deny that I toady to anybody
Nor will you fail to deny that I am not wise. And so,
William, are you going to pronounce, as long as you live,
On points of morals, wisdom, and the sacred Muses, by one authority?
I ask you, why and by what law does your "veto" restrain me?
I have come to recognize you as a prophet, seer, and my most honoured
    friend,
Lo, even to this day, with pleasure, but *not* as the final Judge.

2751 16.337   Cf a MS note by STC on his copy, later Gillman's, of *Omniana*, now in the BM: "The Pun may be traced from its Minimum, in which it exists only in the violent intention and desire of the Punster to make one. This is the fluxion or pre-nascent Quantity, the Infinitesimal first Moment, or Differential, of a Pun—as that of the man who hearing Lincoln mentioned, grumbling most gutturally, shaking his head, and writhing his nose, muttered—'*Linc*-oln, indeed! Lɪɴᴄ-oln! LINC-coln! You may well call it *Link* coln!—a pause.—I was never so bit with Bugs in a place, in my whole Life before!'—Here the reason for vindictive anger striving to ease itself by Contempt—the most frequent origin of Puns, next to that of scornful Triumph exulting and insulting and see Parad. Lost, VI/or cause of the impulse of itch to let a pun was substituted for the Pun itself, which the man's wit could not light on. This therefore is the Minim. At the other extreme lies the Pun polysyllabic—of which accept the following as a specimen: Two Nobles in *Madrid* were straddling side by side,/Both shamefully diseased: espying whom, I cried—/What *figures* these men make! The Wight, that Euclid cons,/ sees plainly that they are—Parallel o'—*pippy*—Dons! S.T.C." *Omniana* I 103–5, printed variatim and in part in *TT* (Ashe) 347–8.

2752 15.181   Coleridge appears to be inquiring of one of those door-step family gatherings in Italy their Christian and family names.

2753 15.182   The journalist thinking of his articles? See also 2579n.

2754 15.183   *Pudel*, German for poodle, of which the first English use appears to have been made in 1825.

2755 15.184   The abusive epithets are those hurled by Alcaeus (Alcaeus 37B) against Pittacus: they are found in Diogenes Laërtius I 81. The order in which Coleridge groups them is his own, and not that of any text, but the cancelled word indicates Diogenes Laërtius as the source. The epithets are all in the accusative case, taken from sentences of some such structure as, "Alcaeus calls Pittacus the Blink-eyed one." The words, recalling the names of the *Batrachomyo-machia* frogs that delighted Coleridge earlier (1149), mean: "Alcaeus [calls] Pittacus Blink-eyed, Split-foot, Drag-foot or Club-foot, Pot-gut, Pot-belly, Self-puffed."

2756 15.185   The text is here given "with all faults", most of which are those of an Italian printer slipping into Italian for French words (*per* for *pour*, *e* for *et*, *ancore* for *encore*, etc), or failing to heed genders and accents, or simply using eighteenth-century spellings, like *connoissances;* some of the eccentricities may be Coleridge's own slips, though when he sets out to make a deliberate copy, as distinct from a quick memorandum for future use, he is an accurate copyist.

Mola di Gaeta: presumably where Coleridge found the map on Boxing-day 1805, having journeyed from Naples to the neighbourhood of Rome in two days. On this *New World Map* "dedicated to the progress of our knowledge", and divided into the "water hemisphere" and the "land hemisphere", the advertisement reads:

A New World Map dedicated to the progress of our knowledge.
Water Hemisphere/Land Hemisphere.
We offer this New World Map as being useful for the study of Geography and for the Theory of the Earth, bringing as it does within one single scope the four parts of the world, which have been kept separate until now although Nature has re-grouped them in one single Hemisphere, and leaving in the other only an oddly broken-up tip of America; and the unending seas sprinkled with a few islands and with isolated land masses of no great size compared with our own.

The regularity or even the sort of predilection with which the great continents of America and Asia hug the circle which separates them from the seas of the opposite Hemisphere is such that it can scarcely be looked upon as a pure result of Chance, but rather as a rational provision of some Physical Law, and of some of the facts of Nature of which we are ignorant. Thus it is a new problem in the Earth Theory which this World Map presents to the physicists of our times, the solution of which cannot fail to be very interesting.

Another very great peculiarity is that it is only under the Paris meridian and in a plane between the Equator and the Earth's Axis that our Globe is capable of affording us such varied spectacles. This property is a kind of pre-eminence which must in the future cause it to be looked upon as the First meridian, failing which the Arc is not in our imagination, is not, so to speak, in Nature.

The translation assumes the insertion in the last sentence, after "le Premier meridien, sans", of some such word as *quoi* or *lui*, as a minimal correction of the sentence. The fault may clearly lie in one or more other places, or a whole line may have been omitted.

2757 15.186   *Sad. from St John's:* Saddleback from St John's Vale, Cumberland.
The end of the entry is lost, rubbed off at the bottom of a faint page. Fondi is about 70 miles from Rome.

2758 15.187   A retrospective noting down of his route, through
Aversa, 12½ miles from Naples, a junction for Rome, and through
Capua, 127½ miles from Rome, and apparently through Fondi.

2759 15.188   Coleridge apparently visited S Trinità de' Monti with
one of the Vasi guide-books in his hand; the particular edition,
whether of Giuseppe or Mariano Vasi, to which his page references
should be a clue, has not been found available anywhere.

The *Descent from the Cross* of Daniele Ricciarelli, known as da
Volterra (1509–66), is not quite so despoiled as the other Volterras in
the same church, and is the most remarkable painting there, certainly
the most dramatic. The central naked figure on the cross is light-grey
and white against a sombre ground, the originality in the treatment of
the subject being the three ladders reaching up to the cross, eight male
figures on them, four female figures below, the whole giving an impression of movement, concentration, and tenderness.

It is of some interest to note the kind of painting that commanded
Coleridge's respectful attention here, and in 2786, in contrast to the
Parmigianino commented on in 2853.

This entry corrects Chambers, who, following Gillman, dated
Coleridge's arrival in Rome "the end of January 1806". Chambers
190.

2760 15.189   The Cloisters of the S Trinità de' Monti are referred
to. The church was originally the site of a church and monastery of
the Order of Minims founded by St Francis of Paula. The Latin
inscription, "the night of his birth was celebrated by the splendour of
the heavens—A.D. 1116" (correctly 1416), is now gone, oval opening,
kitchen, and all. But the murals Coleridge refers to are still to be seen
in varying states of preservation.

2761 15.1   See 371n. The word here is in ink, the same as that of
the retracing of 2059. There are some pencilled figures above and
around the word, and some words written very small in pencil now
faded and/or accidentally obliterated.

2762 15.3   This entry is on a loose leaf, part torn off, and may
belong anywhere in this notebook. The entry, suggesting criticism of
methods of estimating the quantity of e.g. grain in the holds of ships
and the duty on it, deals with a problem much under discussion in

Malta. Coleridge's memorandum may have had to do with his official duties, or with his intention of writing articles and reports on his return home.

2763 15.4   The entry at the top of the page is crowded in, possibly a late entry in the book. Nasturtium was a favourite flower: see *Cornell Studies* XXXII (1942) L. N. Broughton 104.

2764 16.409   This entry and entries 1820, 2574, and 2765–2768 are a fine olla podrida on the verso of the last leaf and the inside back cover of N 16. The dating of 2574 is approximate and of 1820 is given. The others appear to be later, but one can scarcely say more than that. Why Coleridge scribbled them into the small blank spaces here, or wrote them, as he did this entry and 2766 and 2767, across what was already written, when *ff123–125ᵛ* were blank (they bear entries dated or datable in 1812, 1821, 1824), there is no telling. Apparently these seven entries were regarded either as (*a*) trivia or (*b*) desirable to have readily accessible, not submerged in the internal chaos of the notebook.

2766 16.412   A mnemonic for waxing and waning moon? Cf 2603 and the old tag, "C for crescendo/D for diminuendo/and the other way round because the Moon is feminine."

2767 16.413   Cf 2042. Difficulty in breathing, noticed frequently in letters and notebooks, was endemic to Coleridge's physical condition, as revealed by the report of the post-mortem examination, published in *C at Highgate* 29.

2768 16.414   Johann Heinrich Bartels *Briefe über Kalabrien und Sizilien* (3 vols Göttingen 1787–92). There is no evidence that Coleridge read this work, but there was a copy in the *Green SC* (22) not marked as his.

2769 22.136   The entry is approximately transliterated from Greek to English letters in 2771. In line 5, a Greek γ appears to have been written for a roman *y*, *yet*.

2770 22.137   Coleridge may have found this charade in Ariosto *Opere in versi* (Venice 1741) IV 897, where it appears with the solution in the title, *Castanea*, and the note, "Ex Italicae Linguae Flore Angeli Monosini". But this does not mean that Ariosto translated it from an

Italian original by Monosini, as Coleridge, oddly reading *Flore* as the genitive of a Christian name, interprets it; it states rather that the lines first appeared in Monosini *Floris italicae linguae* (Venice 1604) as a distich "circumfertur nomine Ludovici Areosti".

There was a copy of this edition of Ariosto *Opere in versi* in *Wordsworth SC* 458; possibly this entry and those around it—2769, 2771–2773—were pre-Malta. See esp 2773n. But on the other hand see also 2670n.

Tr: There is a tree in the wood which is written in eight letters. Take off the last three, and you will scarcely see one in a thousand.

2771 22.138   See 2769 for what was probably the first setting down of the lines of the first quatrain. As epigrams 32 and 33, these are both in *PW* II 961, dated "?1800"; in the absence of whatever evidence EHC based his guess on, such a date appears to be too early. He may have been thinking of the epigrams and light verses of e.g. 625; but Coleridge wrote light verse and nonsense verses all his life. Whether he was reading Ariosto (entry 2770 clearly precedes this) before 1804–5 is not known.

2772 22.139   Unpublished, and a rare example of the macabre in Coleridge.

2773 22.140   Another version was published 9 Oct 1802 in the *Morning Post: PW* II 967. It now appears that this entry is probably pre-Malta (see 2770n and 2771n); certainly the original lines were *composed c* 1802 or earlier; as to when this variant version was entered in this notebook there are, from the surrounding entries, grounds for uncertainty.

2774 22.141   Is Coleridge interesting himself here in the designing of Italian mosaic pavements? Or noting (incompletely) some formula for drawing in linear perspective?

Tr: 3. Raise a perpendicular. 4. Draw a perfect square. 5. Then as you desire select your point of view. 6. . . . . —they diminish—they make the diminishing perspective.

2775 22.142   This, with 2776–2778, follows a part of 2224 that can be dated 1807 and the return to Stowey after eight years' absence.

See 2224 [43] and note that the last three stanzas of the verses are written after 2775-2778, on the other side of the page, the lower half of which had been torn out.

Kitchenist: goes back to 1618, for one who is employed in a kitchen (*OED*).

Salamanders: Possibly the heating-iron or -plate in kitchen use, or if in the first three of his terms Coleridge is thinking of their human application, has he in mind the fiery red kitchen face, e.g. as in Falstaff's description of Bardolph's? "I have maintained that Sallamander of yours with fire any time this two and thirty years. . . ." 1 *Henry IV* III iii.

Swallows: again, if human, great swallowers or gulpers, those remarkable for voracious appetites? Alternatively, sinks?

2776 22.143   The old prefix *good-man* frequent before the designation of occupations, together with *tell-clock*—idler? a watchman?—suggests a similar date for this entry and 2775. If there is a common source it has not been found.

2777 22.144, 145   Apparently the Greek phrase translated by Coleridge was written first, the lines that follow having reminded him of the Homeric epithet for the sea (*Iliad* I 34). Cf "Behold the Iliad and the Odysee/Rise to the swelling of the voiceful sea." *Fancy in Nubibus: PW* I 435. EHC records that the last lines are borrowed from Stolberg's *An das Meer*. (See *PW* II 1134 Appendices.) But in the Stolberg poem as quoted by STC there is no "voiceful sea" phrase—nor anything so compact. And as Coleridge's Greek reminds us here, Homer is himself the originator of the metaphor neatly applied to him in Coleridge's poem.

The lines in the second part of the entry are from Song III (not IV) Bk II of William Browne's *Britannia's Pastorals*; it appears in *B Poets* IV 320. The italicizing of *voiceful* is Coleridge's. Possibly in reading Homer he remembered the lines of his old countryman—and, he claimed, distant relative—whose sentiments about Devonshire and the river Tavy would be full of childhood associations for him. See also *CL* # 614 (II 1161).

In view of Coleridge's interest in the word *voiceful* here, it may be noticed that he earlier copied a passage from Livy about concerted and confused roaring of voices, in 2033.

2778 22.146   Ibid Song III Bk II: *B Poets* IV 317; written on the
same page as metre 48 in 2224. The lines appear in a long descriptive
passage dealing with the legendary significance of various flowers; the
Daisy is not printed in small capitals in *B Poets*, and therefore one
deduces some special point in Coleridge's double underlining. The
daisies in Malta suggested a poem to him; 2511. Traditionally the
daisy is associated with cheerfulness and innocence, the double daisy
with participation or mutuality, the ox-eye with a token, coloured
daisies with (sometimes unconscious) beauty. Mrs Thomas Monkhouse's sister, Mary Horrocks, was nicknamed by the Wordsworth
circle "the Daisy", but this was much later. *SH Letters* 449.

More likely associations are some of Wordsworth's several poems
To the Daisy and (if the date is later rather than earlier) possibly the
verses so entitled that celebrate the planting of that flower on John
Wordsworth's grave: *WPW* IV 260–2.

2779 22.149   In the early months of 1805 dispatches from General
Villettes and Alexander Ball both referred to the Gibraltar fever or the
plague, of which many persons (Coleridge's friend Major Adye for
one) had died. Malta congratulated itself on escaping the scourge,
though the necessarily close naval relations between the two strong-
holds in war-time had caused apprehension in Malta. For all his other
anxieties, Coleridge expresses no fear from the threat of the plague;
perhaps this drafting of a ridiculous epitaph is the obverse of the same
coin.

Although the entry is not confidently dated 1805, the deletion of
Gibraltar and the reference to New York suggest this period. Coleridge occasionally saw American newspapers in Malta and Sicily
through his association with naval officers in both places. (See 2422n.)
There were severe epidemics (of yellow fever) in New York in the
summer and autumn of 1803, and again in 1805; a more than reasonable search of pertinent records, and of the various lines of Burrs, in
Charles Burr Todd *A General History of the Burr Family* (4th ed New
York 1902), revealed nothing about a Jane Burr who died in such
circumstances, and therefore produced no firm date.

2780 22.162   A draft for a continuation of *The Wanderings of Cain*,
possibly for the third canto? According to his own note attached to it
in *Poems* (1828), Coleridge worked on this prose-poem first in 1798,
then "years afterwards" (?1805–16), when "adverse gales" arose, and

then again in 1825, when he included a few lines in *AR* 383. They were, he said, recovered "from the palimpsest tablet of my memory" going back to the period of *The Ancient Mariner* and *Christabel* Pt I (*PW* I 287). One may reasonably speculate as to whether, when *Christabel* was being prepared for publication, there was any notion of completing *The Wanderings of Cain*, in certain respects a companion-piece. If such was the case, 1815–16 would be a credible date for this draft of what looks like a possible third "canto" of the prose poem.

The hand here might be taken for fairly early, but there is no doubt that this entry was written after 1901 on the same page, *f88* (datable 7–16 Feb 1804); it was written in part over that pencilled memorandum, but not in total disregard of it. On *f89*, it begins under 937H 22.159 and 22.160. 937H is probably April–Nov 1801; 22.160 appears to have been written later in an accidental space, and can be dated with confidence 1821. The entry here could be, from the appearance of the page, later than that, but the possibility of an earlier date, perhaps connected with attempts to continue *The Wanderings of Cain* (cf *PW* I 285n, esp the verses on I 287) or with the writing of *Zapolya* (esp I i 438 and Pt II I i), is supported by the subject-matter. *Zapolya* first appeared in 1817, but as has been shown in 2049n, part of it at least must be dated much earlier, before April 1804. It seems wise therefore to think of a wide span of possible dates for this entry. The child in the desert seems to live in the lonely night atmosphere of the "lovely Boy" of *The Wanderings of Cain*, as recorded in *PW* I 287; but at what point between the initial composition and the recovery this entry was written is difficult to deduce. See 2501n.

The link with *Zapolya* may seem far-fetched, yet the general theme of the salvation of a race by its neglected, ostensibly orphaned, child is a large part of the *Zapolya* theme. Had that work first been intended as a prose-poem, or a poem rather than a poetic drama, the entry might well have adumbrated an ending for it.

But there is another child in a desert in "The Flight and Return of Mohammed", a work so referred to in N 25 (*c* early 1808?) but projected by Southey and Coleridge in 1799; see *CL* # 292 and n and 2224 (47). There is a rough outline of it in an undated and untitled MS, now in the Mitchell Library (Sydney, Australia), recently published by Warren U. Ober in *N&Q* (Oct 1958) NS v 448. It is partly in Coleridge's hand, partly in Southey's, the transition being made at a most interesting point.

In Coleridge's hand:

1st Book

The Deathbed of Abu Taleb—herein we develope the character
of Mohammed—After the Death of Abu Taleb the Tumult, &
his escape by the heroism of Ali.

2nd Book

Mohammed & Abubehi in the Cavern. ⟨Fatima & Ali⟩—resolves
~~to~~ by conquest—3. Journey thro' the Desert—the Arab—an
exposed Infant ⟨Hagar & Ishmaël⟩ Convent. ⟨Mary⟩—

4 ~~3~~rd Book

Arrival at Medina.

In Southey's hand (together with the preceding inserts in ⟨ ⟩):

~~4~~ 5
⟨Jew⟩ intrigues to expel him. When a Son accuses his father.
Mary.

~~4~~th 6
Battle of Beder—attempt to assassinate him when sleeping.

~~6~~ 7
Defeat of Mount Ohud— ~~conversion of Caled~~. Hamza slain.

~~7~~ ~~8~~
~~Fatima~~
~~Capture of Mecca~~
~~Exultation of the Koraish~~

The elements here extend in interest beyond the limits of this note,
but the links suggested do not render the date of this entry much less
problematical. They do countenance a wider range of dates for this
entry than a first glance at the notebook might suggest.

2781 18.4   In pencil, and very faint. It is included at this point
because the hand looks very like other entries in this notebook close
to this time, i.e. 2639.

2782 18.5   Also in pencil, this entry was written at the same time
as the last. It comes from Ps. 139:14.

2783 18.6   The entry seems to me undatable, and might be
earlier or later than 2781 and 2782. On the cover opposite, the figures

$\frac{27}{4}$ seem to provide a key to this "mystery": $27 \times 4 = 108 + 3 = 111$.

108

The arithmetic is less clear than the logic as Coleridge scores an old point about reasoning with mere ciphers, as e.g. in 912.

2784   16.338   Σωμα ψυχοπλαστον: Body soul-shaped.
Ψυχη σωμαπλαττουσα: Soul body-shaping.

Reo = reor . . . res: cf Lewis and Short (1922) on *res:* "etymology dubious; perhaps root *ra-* of *reor, ratus;* cf. German *Ding;* English *thing,* from denken, to think; properly, that which is thought of; cf. also λόγος, Liddell and Scott, 9."

Tank: the German is *Tank* for reservoir, a word not of German origin, but Anglo-Indian, from Portuguese. And while the German *denken* and *Dank* (the thought of a kindness) are connected, there is no connexion, according to Kluge (1957), between *denken* and *das Ding;* that would invalidate part of the statement of Lewis and Short under *Reo* above.

To Ov: neuter singular of the participle of εἰμί, for which there is no exact English equivalent; *being* is perhaps nearest (not to be confused with *the One*).

Ο Λογος, η Σοφια: "the Word [and] Wisdom", with New Testament rather than classical overtones.

Radii, Ακτίνες = *Res:* another pun, ἀκτίνες = rays.

Αγω *(acta)*: the Greek verb, I act, I do, is strangely glossed with the Latin noun.

εν θητα *(or Tau)*: "in theta" (as in "= Res in Theta").

Here he is contrasting the form of the capital theta, with its central point, symbolically for the idea of synthesis, with the delta and tau, which in shape suggest, on the one hand, the pyramid and stability, as in STC's seal; and on the other, the *radii,* the *actines,* rays, the out-ward-moving thought.

Minitude: not in the *OED;* cf 2734, as an illustration of mental grooves.

The spider spinning (political) notions out of his own interior occurred early—in 1800. See *EOT* I 226. And Southey, among subjects for "poemlings", noticed that the spider was a metaphysician, in contrast to the silkworm that feeds first and spins afterwards. *SCB* IV 20. Coleridge says he "scoffs at metaphysics" (and see *Inq Sp* §95). Had someone used the image against Coleridge himself as metaphysician, someone here being condemned as a "worldling" taking a superficial view of metaphysics?

gesunder Menschenverstand: sound human understanding, sound horse-sense. This reference to practical men and worldlings in conflict with metaphysicians reaches back into the *Watchman* period and Coleridge's reading of Burke's *Letter to a Noble Lord*. See 24n. 1623 seems to be a direct answer to Burke's attack (1796 1st ed) 61; see 2503n.

In any case the statement here, of the centrality of the self, in various degrees of consciousness, in any attempt to solve the problem of the unity of thought and the diversity of things, ornamented though it is with etymological and pictorial play, is basic in Coleridge's philosophy to the end.

2785 15.190   The story of Coleridge's departure from Rome has acquired various forms, e.g. that he escaped from Napoleon's personal animosity by information sent by the Pope through a noble Benedictine, or that he left, disguised as an attaché, in Cardinal Fesch's carriage (Chambers 190); this second story derives from the *Journals* of Caroline Fox 27 Feb 1840, as narrated by John Sterling, i.e. it is third hand at least, and appears to have apocryphal elements and downright errors. (Caroline Fox was born thirteen years after the time of the events she described.) Then there is Coleridge's own version, that he was warned both "directly" by the Prussian ambassador von Humboldt and by Cardinal Fesch through his secretary. *BL* I 145. This entry introduces a third person. *Mr Jackson* was probably Thomas Jackson, British minister plenipotentiary to the court of Naples, 1799–1806. If he was in Rome at this time, he would undoubtedly be informed of the peace treaty signed by France and Austria 29 Dec 1805, and aware of the imminence of invasion. Warnings might easily have come from him, or through him from the Cardinal's secretary, and from von Humboldt also.

The departure was not sudden, however, as we see from the next entry, except in the sense that it may well have been on too short notice to make arrangements for luggage, especially in the popular excitement of invasion. Coleridge's response to the warnings appears to have been to go about 30 miles outside Rome to Olevano Romano and Washington Allston's hospitable house; actually he finally left Rome in May, as described in 2848.

2786 15.191   The painting of the Franciscan monk is still to be seen in the S Maria Maggiore in Rome, the painter not certainly known, the subject thought to be St Francis himself.

The painting may be less interesting than the Volterra Coleridge noticed in 2759, but again he seems to have been attracted by a fine conception. Probably, too, by the conjunction of elements: the pale face of the monk-saint, luminous and ethereal in old age, and the rough very material bunion on the left toe; the view of the Apennines through the window, and other realistic earthy details, with the vision and feeling in the saint's face and the fiddling angel in the clouds.

2787 15.192   On blossoms and fruit seen together, see 2501 and 2565.

shagren: or shagreen, a kind of leather, or silk, so frequently green that the word is often used to mean *green*.

2788 15.193   For his collection of extremes meeting. See 1725.

2789 15.194   Was the Mackenzie of 2680 (in Sicily) still with Coleridge in Italy? The facts are not known.

2790 15.195   Source not traced.

a lightning-flash of bliss from God's throne through my being when I saw her again.

2791 15.196   This is what appears to be the first draft of a translation and adaptation of Ludwig Tieck's poem *Herbstlied*, which Coleridge could have known from Schiller's *Musenalmanach* (1799) 26. The only other appearances of the poem in print before the date of this entry were in the play *Prinz Zerbino*, twice published in 1799, once as part of *Romantische Dichtungen* (Jena 1799) and, again, bound with *Der getreue Eckart* (Leipzig and Jena 1799). Of these the *Musenalmanach* seems the more likely source, and we know Coleridge had probably used it earlier; see 1128n. But the most likely source of all at this time is Tieck himself, who was kind to Coleridge in Rome and with whom acquaintance was to ripen years later, in 1817, when Tieck visited England. *CL* # 1060, 1065, 1067, 1069.

   This entry was published as "a prose version of Glycine's Song [*Zapolya* II i 65–80], probably a translation from the German", in *PW* II 1109–10; the *Song*, the best-known part of *Zapolya*, is published separately as a lyric in *PW* I 426.

2792 15.197   "It is said that Piero de' Medici [son of Lorenzo il Magnifico] having long been intimate with Michelagnolo, used often to send for him when he wished to buy antiques, such as cameos and other carved stones. One winter, when much snow fell in Florence, he caused him to make in his courtyard a statue of snow, which was very beautiful; and he honoured Michelagnolo on account of his talents in such a manner, that his father, beginning to see that he was esteemed among the great, clothed him much more honourably than he had been wont to do." Vasari *Lives of the . . . Painters* tr Gaston du C. de Vere (London Medici Society 1912–15) IX 10–11.

2793 15.198   Extremes meeting again, as in 2788.

2794 16.339   A second writing of *Allston* (at the end of this entry), amending Coleridge's spelling, is in another hand.

Washington Allston, the American painter (1779–1843), was the most congenial spirit Coleridge found in Rome and, indeed, on the whole of his Malta journey. Allston had been in London in 1801, studying with Benjamin West, Fuseli, and Opie, where he developed an inherent taste for "the sublime". By the time he met Coleridge in Rome he had already painted subjects that indicate their common interests, e.g. several from Schiller's *The Robbers*, from *The Mysteries of Udolpho* of Mrs Radcliffe, from *Paradise Lost*, from the Bible (a *Head of Judas*, and *Head of St Peter When He Heard the Cock Crow*). In Jan 1806 his latest large canvas was *Diana and Her Nymphs in the Chase*, described by Coleridge in 2831 and reproduced in plate v.

When Coleridge was faced with the dilemma as to what to do in the event of the French descent on Rome, Allston invited him to his house at Olevano Romano, some 30 miles from Rome in country that has always attracted painters. Coleridge describes it in 2796 below. Allston and Coleridge formed a firm friendship (e.g. Allston was one of the very few persons with whom Coleridge discussed his marital difficulties); it lasted until Allston left England for good in Sept 1818, and from then onwards in happy recollections.

If, as this entry and a few others suggest, Coleridge learned something about art from Allston, his influence on Allston's views is a matter of record. Years later Allston wrote to a friend:

"To no other man whom I have known, do I owe so much intellectually, as to Mr. Coleridge, with whom I became acquainted in Rome, and who has honored me with his friendship for more than five and twenty years. He used to call Rome the *silent* city; but I never could think of it as such, while with him; for, meet him when, or where I would, the fountain of his mind was never dry, but like the far-reaching acqueducts that once supplied this mistress of the world, its living streams seemed specially to flow for every classic ruin over which we wandered. And when I recall some of our walks under the pines of the Villa Borghese, I am almost tempted to dream that I once listened to Plato, in the groves of the Academy. It was there he taught me this golden rule: *never to judge of any work of art by its defects;* a rule as wise as benevolent; and one that while it has spared me much pain, has widened my sphere of pleasure." From the *Diary of William Dunlap* (3 vols New York 1931) quoted by E. P. Richardson in *Washington Allston* (Chicago 1948) 75. Allston's lectures, some of which are in *Lectures on Art and Poems* (1850), others in rough drafts in the archives of the Massachusetts Historical Society, are full of echoes of Coleridge: the *idea* of art, primary and secondary originality, the distinction between imitation and copy, fame and reputation, stress on the harmony of parts and whole, on the rules for art being in the mind of the artist, all others being expedient fictions only —even his very illustrations and quotations—"Nothing is rarer than a solitary lie; for lies breed like Surinam toads . . .".

"Nothing in nature can be fragmentary, except in the seeming, and then, too, to the understanding only—to the feelings never. For a grain of sand, no less than a plant, being an essential part of the mighty whole which we call the universe, cannot be separated from the idea of the world without a positive act of the reflective faculties, an act of volition. But until then even a grain of sand cannot cease to imply it." Richardson quoting Allston, ibid 70.

As the quotations and Allston's paintings indicate, a study of the intellectual contribution of Coleridge to American romantic art would perhaps be worth making.

One more link. William Ellery Channing, Allston's lifelong friend and brother-in-law, introduced to Coleridge by Allston, was one of the forerunners of that New England transcendentalism through which Coleridge's teaching was filtered westwards, sometimes with distortions, in the middle quarters of the last century.

On *übersehen* see 2370 and n.

2795 16.340   Trajan Mortimer Wallis (1795–after 1847), son of George Augustus Wallis (1770–1847), English painter who lived much in Italy, painting Italian landscapes, also portraits. Coleridge was staying with the father in Rome in May 1806. See 2838. The noting of the son's age is probably pertinent to facts discussed in 2816n.

2796 16.341   *Olevano:* or Olevano Romano, where Allston's house is sometimes pointed out uncertainly as now an *albergo* in the village. This entry suggests, however, another building, "about a quarter of a mile from the Town . . . on a level Ridge a little lower than it", a house in 1954 occupied by a priest, from the terrace of which the view more nearly corresponds to Coleridge's description here. Looking at it with this memorandum in the hand, one is struck again with the accuracy of Coleridge's verbalization of the pictorial, both panoramically and in detail.

f107ᵛ Mʳ Alston . . . his Swiss Landskip: see 2831.

   quam qui non amat . . . : "whoever does not like it must be hated by all the Muses and Loves." This was used, variatim, with *Virtutes* for *Musæ et Veneres,* of Charles Danvers, in Coleridge's inscription in a copy, given him by Danvers, of Burnet *Telluris theoria sacra* (2 vols 1689), now in VCL. He also used it in an enthusiastic early letter praising Southey's poems (*CL # 74*).

f108 Civitella: now called Bellegra.

   Pagliano: Paliano.

   Avita: San Vito.

   See also the further attempts to write reminders to himself of this landscape in 2817, 2818, and 2821.

2798 16.343   These lines, variatim, appeared first (undated) in *The Amulet* for 1833, with the title *A Thought suggested by a View of Saddleback,* with *Blencartha* in the first line and *winds* in the plural. They then appeared in *Friendship's Offering* for 1834, with the addition of Coleridge's note: "The following stanza (it may not arrogate the name of poem) or versified reflection, was versified while the author was gazing on *three* parallel *Forces,* on a moonlight night, at the foot of the Saddleback Fell—S.T.C." The lines follow: "On stern Blencarthur's perilous height/The wind is tyrannous and strong:/And flashing forth unsteady light/From stern Blencarthur's skiey height/As loud the torrents throng!/Beneath the moon in gentle weather/They bind the Earth and Sky together:/But O! the Sky, and all *its* forms, how quiet!/The things that seek the Earth, how full of noise and riot!" These were reprinted with minor changes from one another in *EOT*

III 997; *PW* (JDC) 175, dated in the notes "Olevano, March 8, 1806"; and again by EHC in *PW* I 347, but dated 1800. The three later editors appear to have followed *The Amulet* text. JDC suggested that the "reflection" took place in the Lakes, the versification at Olevano later. But Lowes's guess that the lines in this notebook version (not actually dated 8 March 1806 except by inference) were a recollection of much earlier lines (two borrowed and the rest composed) is probably correct; this would explain the variants.

As pointed out by Lowes (*RX* 604k), the first two lines of verse appear to derive from lines of Isaac Ritson quoted in William Hutchinson *The History of . . . Cumberland* (Carlisle 1794) I 336n: "The winds upon Blenkarthur's head,/Are often loud and strong;/And many a tempest o'er his cliffs/Careering sweeps along./Like him, Helvellyn swells on high/In sullen misty pride;/And low'ring o'er his subject hills,/Surveys the world so wide. . . ." Coleridge was reading this work in 1800–2. See *CN* I Index I.

Lowes discusses at some length the question of whether Coleridge borrowed from Wordsworth or Wordsworth from Coleridge the phrase "tyrannous and strong". More interesting than priorities is the fact that in March 1806 in Olevano Romano Coleridge appears to be experiencing a "breeze of feeling" that recalls the Kirkstone storm of Jan 1803 which he described in a letter to Tom Wedgwood at the time (*CL* # 483), comparing the wind then to a huge stream of lava and Kirkstone to a volcano. Now in volcanic regions, he reverses the image-process. The word "perilous" of the earlier version, which occurs also in the letter to Tom Wedgwood, is omitted here, but it may, nevertheless, have been part of the associated emotions. Perils of another sort are uppermost in the next entry, and the next day there is a nostalgic reference to Keswick, in 2817.

2799 16.344   *PW* II 998, dated "?1803", and with minor differences in punctuation. If the MS from which the lines were published there is this notebook, the dating is unaccountable. Interestingly, EHC gives the lines an even earlier association by entitling them "The Night-mare Death in Life". Other links seem to me, especially in view of the proximity to 2798, to be clear; with "Is no one near?" is recalled "Has he no friend, no loving mother near" of *The Wanderings of Cain* (1798): *PW* I 287. And with "Will no one hear these stifled groans, & wake me?" cf a similar personal experience of the autumn of 1800 in 848; see also 1619 and 1649.

2800 16.345   *PW* II 1000.

2801 15.199   The excellent wine of Affile, not far from Olevano Romano. He twice makes a note of it.

2802 15.200   *Torre nuovo* [*Nuova*]: a farm that belonged to Prince Borghese.
Monte Porcio [*Porzio*]: in the Alban Hills; *Colonna*, one of the Castelli Romani.
3 Capanne: 3 huts. The reading of the next two words, the last on the page, is difficult, perhaps dubious.

2803 15.201   Overleaf from 2801.

2804 15.202   The entry is difficult to interpret correctly, compressed as it is into the upper right-hand corner of the page, after 2805 was written there.
The "Cones" are perhaps the volcanic cones in the neighbourhood of Olevano Romano. "Palatana" is more difficult; *Palatina*, a tippet?
On the cones, cf the remarks of a traveller in the 1830's: "Beyond Albano are these venerable cones which, in contradiction to Livy, usually pass for the tombs of the Horatii. Of these cones there were originally five, on a square basement, corresponding with the number of those to fall in the memorable battle between the Horatii and Curiatii, but only two now remain." G. W. D. Evans *The Classic and Connoisseur in Italy and Sicily* (London 1835) II 108–9.

2806 15.204   In the MS Coleridge first wrote "power and beauty" in the second line, then transposed them. The lines, metrically, in subject-matter, and in the personal overtones of despair and loneliness, are easily associated with the lines in 2582 and 2926. Possibly all are related to a germinating poem that was not written.

2807 15.205   *An History of Fools & Jesters:* The reference may be to C. F. Flögel *Geschichte der komischen Litteratur* (4 vols Liegnitz & Leipzig 1784), which fits Coleridge's description. Southey's copy contained marginalia by Coleridge dated *c* 1813: these were printed, with some bowderlizing, by Buxton Forman in *Cosmopolis* (London and New York 1898) IX 635–48, X 52–67.
A Panorama of Fables, chronologically, as before, &c: the intention

of *as before* is not clear, though the general purpose is plain. There are a few remarks on fable *vs* allegory from the Jan 1818 lectures in *MC* 28–32.

a true Pantheon of Heathen Mythology: see 2737n. Coleridge's interest in the subject was apparently quickened in Malta and Italy.

2808 15.206   The drawing has not been identified. Coleridge was living in the Allston circle of artists at this time, and it might be of any one of many arches in and about Rome by any one of them.

2809 15.207   Palestrina is about 24 miles from Rome *via* the Porta Maggiore, Olevano 6 miles further; the account suggests a stop at Genazzano for a meal.
Another account? Mileage?

2810 15.208   The drawing here looks as if it had been done by Coleridge himself. The words are written at right angles, i.e. at the perpendicular, the drawing extending around them and occupying the page opposite.

2811 15.209   Cf 1166; did Coleridge in Rome receive confirmation of a metaphor? Or had he in 1802 already heard what he here noted down? It was in 1802 that Canova was ordered to Paris to make sketches for his enormous statue of Napoleon, in which Napoleon has in his hand, not Archimedes's lever, but the winged figure of Victory, and without Archimedes's motto quoted in 1166.

2812 15.210   Elsewhere Coleridge discusses Italian speech, particularly feminine speech; see 2174, 2862. In the broader educational effects of language he was greatly interested; see e.g. *Friend* 1 25–6.

2813 15.211   Coleridge's interest in the theme of the cultural importance of printing is seen as far back as *c* 1795–6 (see 128); and cf also "The limited sphere of mental activity in artist" in 77. Later in N 25 in this connexion he referred also to Michelangelo and Raphael. See *ShC* 11 69, 139. He brought back reproductions of Raphael cartoons from Italy. *CL* # 632. He seems here to propose writing a threnody (*threnic* is a Coleridgian word-coinage) on the perishability of paintings, admitting that some writing disappears also when left in manuscript.

W. Alston's large Landscape: Diana and Her Nymphs in the Chase, referred to in 2796 as the "Swiss Landskip", is described in 2831. Doubtless Allston's latest large canvas at this time, it had just been painted, in 1805. It is now in the Fogg Museum, Cambridge, Mass. See plate v.

Apelles, Protogenes: famous painters of antiquity whose works are lost.

Spenser . . . vi *last Books, & his Comedies:* As one likely source of Coleridge's information, apart from general knowledge, *B Poets* ii 4–5 mentions, in the brief biography of him, the nine lost comedies attributed to Spenser.

2814 15.212   Coleridge's derivation from *Esel*, ass, is confirmed by the *OED*.

2815 15.213   On cruelty to animals, see also e.g. 2090.
manus frictoria in pudendis vaccæ: frictoria for *frictura?* i.e. "by a fricative hand on the pudenda of a cow".

2816 16.346   See also 2795n.
It is probably Trajan Wallis to whom Hazlitt refers in his story in the *Table Talk* of "the son of an English artist . . . who had wandered all over the Campagna with him [Coleridge] whose talents he assured us were the admiration of all Rome, and whose early designs had almost all the grace and purity of Raphael's". *H Works* viii 295. The remark quoted in the entry, "It isn't the art for him", might be noted as the dictum of a precocious ten-year-old. Or about him. Trajan Wallis later became a portrait-painter who painted *inter alia* the family of Walter Savage Landor. R. H. Super *Walter Savage Landor* (New York 1954) 179.

2818 16.348   A second attempt to capture in words the landscape of Olevano; see 2796.

2819 16.349   Cf "Thicker than raindrops on November thorn", which comes in a notebook later: *PW* ii 1010.

2820 16.350   There is no record of Coleridge's having gone to Genoa. If Robert Sloane is the Sloane of 2827, he apparently lived in Rome.

2821 16.351   See 2796 and 2818.

2822 16.352   *AP* 110, dated 1804, possibly from the similarity to the outdoor fire on Etna described in 2173; the position in the notebook makes that date impossible.

It appears from Allston's own writings that his companionship may have encouraged the moralistic tone of such a reflection.

2823 16.353   Catullus Frag 11 line 1. Coleridge does not translate *consecroque*, being concerned rather with the metrical pattern of the English line than with an exact translation, which would be: "This inclosure I dedicate and consecrate to thee, O Priapus." Tr F. W. Cornish (LCL 1928).

2824 16.354   Possibly it is unwarrantable to connect this incident with Dr William Hunter (1718–83), elder bachelor brother of the more famous Dr John Hunter; he was eminent as anatomist and obstetrician. Another Dr William Hunter (1755–1812) was from 1794–1806 surgeon to the marines, and Coleridge at this time may easily have heard anecdotes about him; on the other hand, this Hunter was primarily an orientalist and spent most of his life in the East.

2825 16.355   *Go call a coach . . . &c:* Henry Carey's comedy *Chrononhotonthologos* II iv. "Go call a coach, and let a coach be called;/And let the man who calleth be the caller;/And in his calling let him nothing call/But Coach! Coach! Coach! Oh for a coach, ye Gods!"

Is Coleridge suggesting a parallel with (or a parody of) the *Pervigilium Veneris*?

The first line of that poem and the refrain after every stanza is: "Cras amet qui nunquam amavit quique amavit cras amet": "To-morrow shall be love for the loveless, and for the lover to-morrow shall be love." Tr J. W. Mackail . . . *Pervigilium Veneris* (LCL 1912).

In view of the references to Catullus preceding and following this entry—in 2823 and 2826—it is natural to suppose that Coleridge was reading some edition of Catullus in which, as frequently is the case, *The Eve of St Venus* was printed, and sometimes also attributed to Catullus.

2826 16.356   *AP* 165–6.
omnibus trutinatis: when everything is weighed up.

In discussing the difficulties of writing poems on the subtleties of certain human topics, Coleridge takes his phrases from *Carmina* LXXVI of Catullus. The poem indicates so well the kind of theme he has in mind, and something more personal to boot, and the Latin phrases he cites are so embedded in it, that it seems necessary to quote (Coleridge's phrases are in italics) the first fourteen lines:

> "Sique recordanti benefacta priora voluptas
>   est homini, cum se cogitat esse pium,
> nec sanctam violasse fidem, nec foedere in ullo
>   divum ad fallendos *numine abusum homines*,
> multa parata manent in longa aetate, Catulle,
>   ex hoc ingrato gaudia amore tibi.
> nam quaecumque homines bene cuiquam aut dicere possunt
>   *aut facere, haec a te dictaque factaque sunt;*
> omnia quae ingratae perierunt credita menti.
>   quare cur tu te iam amplius *excrucies?*
> quin tu animum offirmas atque istinc teque reducis,
>   et dis invitis desinis esse miser?
> difficilest longum subito deponere amorem.
>   difficilest, verum hoc qualubet *efficias.*"

If a man can take any pleasure in recalling the thought of kindnesses done, when he thinks that he has been a true friend; and that he has not broken sacred faith, nor in any compact has used the majesty of the gods in order to deceive men, then there are many joys in a long life for you, Catullus, earned from this thankless love. For whatever kindness man can show to man by word or deed has been said and done by you. All this was entrusted to an ungrateful heart, and is lost: why then should you torment yourself now any more? Why do you not settle your mind firmly, and draw back, and cease to be miserable, in despite of the gods? It is difficult suddenly to lay aside a long-cherished love. It is difficult, but you should accomplish it, one way or another.—Tr F. W. Cornish (LCL 1928).

N.B. Metastasio: Coleridge knew at least some libretti of Metastasio (*BL* II 98), which he praised for taste as distinct from poetic genius.

in Pope: cf *BL* I 26n, II 21; although the tenor of thought expressed here is similar to the prefaces to *LB* (1798) and *LB* (1800), the open attack on Pope came in Wordsworth's Essay supplementary to the Preface, *Poems* (1815): "Having wandered from humanity in his Eclogues with boyish inexperience, the praise, which these compositions obtained, tempted him into a belief that Nature was not to be trusted, at least in pastoral Poetry." Nowell C. Smith *Wordsworth's Literary Criticism* (1905) 183.

2827 15.214   Maundy Thursday in 1806 was 3 April.
    Sloane: Robert Sloane of 2820 presumably, but of him nothing is known.
    Ranelagh: The best characterization up to this time of the eighteenth-century palace of pleasure is possibly in Fanny Burney *Evelina* Letter xvi. If Coleridge had this in mind he could hardly have made a more disrespectful association. The after-adventure with the child is lost.

2828 15.215   *Ideal:* "The ideal consists in the happy balance of the generic with the individual", Coleridge said in *BL* Chap xxiii (ii 187).
    Pathognomic: Coleridge appears to be reviving an old word. It is of interest to note that the earliest use of *pathognomy* (1793) is attributed by the *OED* to Coleridge's acquaintance Thomas Holcroft in his (abridged) translation of J. C. Lavater's *Essays on Physiognomy;* Coleridge may well have known this work.
    Opie-ism: John Opie (1761–1807), a self-taught painter, the popular portraitist whose reputation was temporarily on the wane at this time, partly from his attacks on sentiment and spiritual qualities in painting. Marie Vigée-Le Brun (1755–1842) painted sweet, pretty, neo-classical insipidities still reproduced on postcards.
    despairing Woman at the bottom of the Last Judgment: It would be of interest to know more specifically what Coleridge meant by "the true Ideal" in painting, by knowing which figure he meant. Michelangelo's mural when Coleridge saw it in the Sistine Chapel (possibly in the company of Allston, who by March 1805 had written a *Sonnet on a "Falling Group" in the Last Judgment of Michael Angelo*) was brighter and clearer than it is now, but in a mural full of despairing figures, not always very distinct sexually, there are at least two or three possibilities. See plate iv. Possibly he means the Savonarola-like figure "at the bottom", beneath the right arm of the figure looking upwards; or does he refer to the figure emerging from behind the huge, reclining one on the left of the big rocks in the foreground, centre, crowded in between the raised left arm of a figure looking upwards and the one with snakes around its feet being lifted by another? But all this is, as Professor Panofsky advises, "extremely uncertain".
    And cf *TT* 24 July 1831:

"Italian masters differ from the Dutch in this—that in their pictures ages are perfectly ideal. The infant that Raffael's Madonna holds in her arms cannot be guessed of any particular age; it is Humanity in infancy. The babe in a manger in a Dutch painting is a fac-simile of some real new-born bantling; it is just like the little rabbits we fathers have all seen with some dismay at first brush." And in the same day's further conversation: "Portraits by the old masters . . . are pictures of men and women . . . they represent individuals, but individuals as types of a species. Modern portraits —a few by Jackson and Owen perhaps excepted—give you not the man, not the inward humanity, but merely the external mark, that in which Tom is different from Bill."

The same view is applied to poetry. "It is for the Biographer, not the Poet, to give the *accidents* of *individual* Life." *CL* # 969. But see *BL* II 33 and Shawcross's note II 273–4.

2829 15.216   In part Coleridge carried out the struggle to "desynonymize" the words for *beauty* in the essay "On the Principles of Genial Criticism Concerning the Fine Arts": *BL* II esp 228–46.

2830 15.217   Cf 2193.

2831 15.218   The painting is reproduced in plate v. Coleridge refers to it in the essay "On the Principles of Genial Criticism . . ." as being "the occasion of my first acquaintance with him [Allston] in Rome." *BL* II 237. See 2813 for the evidence that a poem on the picture was intended, for which purpose these notes were probably made.

The kinetic response to this as to the Beaumont drawings in 1899 will be noted.

On the Bowder Stone see *CN* I Index 3.

2832 15.219   Noticed of waterfalls in the Lakes, as in 1426. Cf also 2793.

2833 15.220   *Magazzino* . . . *Tabacchi:* "Shop for brandy, rosolio, spirits and tobaccos", etc.

The image of the deserted or desert city is recurrent; cf 7 and n.

2834 15.221   The interior of an artist's (Allston's?) studio?

2835 15.222   The matter under consideration is the effect of pronunciation on prosody. Golden Greek poetry, hieratic as distinct from
popular, combined accent by stress and by pitch. W. W. Goodwin
A Greek Grammar (1924) §107: "The Greek accent was not simply a
stress accent (like ours), but it raised the musical *pitch* or *tone* of the
syllable on which it fell. . . . As the language declined, the musical
accent gradually changed to a stress accent, which is now its only
representative in Greek as in other languages." And §1625: "It is very
difficult for us to appreciate the ease with which the Greeks distinguished and reconciled the stress of voice which constituted the ictus
and the raising of tone which constituted the word-accent. Any combination of the two is now very difficult, and for most persons impossible, because we have only stress of voice to represent both accent
and ictus." By the fifth century A.D. the older pitch-accent had become—or was tending to become—the modern stress-accent, the
change being clearly confirmed in the Byzantine πολιτικοὶ στίχοι.

   Tertullian's Poems: a reference to some of Tertullian's no longer
extant early poems (in Greek)? Cave in his *Scriptorum ecclesiasticorum
historia literaria* (1740)—see 1070n—gives, in a list of Tertullian's
supposititious works, some *Poemata*, and some were printed in collections almost to Coleridge's day.

   Coleridge at this time and in the following months shows a special
interest in Pindar's versification. See 2881–2883, 2887, 2900, and
2911–2913. It is as if exposure to a foreign modern language drives
him back on the classics. Cf e.g. what happened in Germany, in 373
and 375.

2836 15.226   A few days later, Coleridge left Rome 18 May 1806
with Mr Thomas Russell of Exeter, an art student in Rome. See *L* II
500n and 2848.

   4 Doppios and four Sequins: a *doppio* (more commonly *doppia*) was
a double *scudo d'oro*, which was worth about 10s at this time; a
sequin (Italian *zecchino*) was also a gold coin, worth about the same,
the value varying slightly from state to state.

   The entry perhaps represents a pathetic attempt to be business-like
about debts. Farington's account of Coleridge's relation to Russell
must be sifted with allowances for Farington's love of gossip and un-
enthusiastic attitude to Coleridge, Wordsworth, and contemporary
poetry (and also for Russell's obvious vanity); but it bears an im-
print of recognizable Coleridgian misery:

"Mr. Russell told me . . . Whilst He was at Rome Coleridge arrived there from Malta, in a destitute condition, His money being
expended. Mr. Russell became His friend and protector, & relieved
[him] from His difficulties, which had reduced His mind to such a
state as to cause Him to pass much of his time in bed in a kind of
despairing state. From Rome Mr. Russell accompanied Him to Leghorn, and from thence to England, which was a great sacrifice on the
part of Mr. Russell, who otherwise wd. have passed through Swisser-
land with two gentlemen of that country with whom he was acquainted." Joseph Farington *Diary* for 2 Nov 1810, where Russell is
described in the index as a banker of Exeter. That Coleridge maintained his friendly acquaintance with Russell is attested to by a letter
from Russell to Coleridge *c* 1809, about subscribers to *The Friend*,
now in Dove Cottage. See also *CL* # 726.

2838 15.228   On Wallis see 2795n.

2839 15.229   The entry ends abruptly because two leaves that had
been written on were cut out, i.e. *f103* and *f104*. On the outer margin
of *f102ᵛ* Mrs Gillman has written, "Most affecting. A.G."
      usury against myself: various forms of this phrase became a euphe-
mism for opium.
      Coleridge gives, as in the *Dejection Ode*, not only a remarkable
piece of self-observation at the very moment when he laments the loss
of his powers, but he also adumbrates once more, and again from
personal experience rather than theory, his knowledge of how intellect and emotion, and pleasure and guilt, are for him inextricably
fused in human life, and how his hopes and fears are transformed into
each other.

2840 15.230   The collection of Frederick Augustus Hervey, the
fourth Earl of Bristol (1730–1803), who spent much of his life in
Naples, was perhaps taken to Rome after his death. Coleridge may
have seen it there before it was plundered by the French. If its location was Rome, Coleridge must have seen it on one of the first two
Mondays in May, for he left on Sunday the 18th. The entry is clearly
retrospective, probably about the same date as 2848, 18 May.

2841 15.231   Said in justification of such collections as referred to
in the previous entry? Or relevant to an Allston landscape? See 2813.

But here the risks of destruction are clearly not only the physical ones of war-time.

2842 15.233   On the S[oother] of A[bsence] see 1225n and 1541n; and on "sots", 2557.

2843 15.234   Mr Baker is not identified.

2844 15.235   [?*Opulence*/*Hence*]: The outer margin is very faint and thumbed at this point; the first reading was *Hence*, but there are suggestions of and space for *Opulence*.

    Possibly the contention here is merely against widespread opinion; it may, however, have reference to Northcote's views, perhaps expressed to Coleridge as he sat for his portrait. See Hazlitt's report of Northcote's *Conversations* (No 18): *H Works* XI 290: "The Church was the foster-mother of the Fine Arts . . . The genius of Italian art was nothing but the genius of Popery."

    The subject of the importance of patronage of the arts is expanded in *TT* 7 July 1831. And see 2746 and n in regard to literary patronage.

2845 15.236   Francesco de Geronimo was beatified by Pope Pius VII 2 May 1806 (*Enciclopedia cattolica*); this was a Friday. Coleridge must have attended the special service the Sunday following.

2846 15.237   These partly unintelligible verses Coleridge must have seen in an inn, perhaps hanging on the wall as a warning to the customers that they need expect no credit. As far as it is decipherable it may be translated:

Listen, my friends! I give no more credit, for my books are full of debtors, and to accommodate other people I have lost both money and customers. I can find no more such endurance in myself, for my own creditors do not behave so. Rather, they would take from my pocket . . . So I say to anyone who refuses to pay me . . . and who wants to drink or eat without money, Go away far from me, depart.

2847 15.238   Coleridge was perhaps reminded of another blind man and another river; cf 572.

2848 15.232   This entry began on *f105* and then two leaves (*ff105ᵛ– 106*) were found to have been already filled. The remainder of *f107ᵛ* (most of it) was left blank, presumably for more notes on the journey from Rome to Terni. Coleridge is travelling from Rome to Florence, *via* Bracciano (and Baccano), Monterosso, Nepi, Borghetto, and Terni. Cf *L* II 498n. He had been in Rome since 31 Dec 1805.

2849 15.239   *f109*   The forked river-bed and the rocks that formed the *narrow plunge* and the *broad aprons* are to-day still witness to the detailed accuracy of Coleridge's description, but the water is largely diverted to the largest hydro-electric power station in Italy.

One interesting fact revealed by reading this entry on the spot is that the steep hillside, over the precipice of which the Falls of Terni descend, now marked off by barbed wire, was apparently climbed by Coleridge (see *ff109–109ᵛ*), a scramble that local people now consider something of a feat.

f110ᵛ   *Futura in rus:* the future for the country, or, at least, in the country.

dram-drinking: i.e. whisky or gin.

Acqua Vita: for *acquavite*, Italian for brandy or gin.

4 miles to Castanea: en route to Florence *via* Perugia.

2850 15.240   This was written in a space left beside the angular drawing in 2849.

2851 15.241(a) In spite of apparent *non sequiturs* and the fact that lines 2 and 4 of this entry are written larger, this seems to be one entry.

Ossaia was repeated because at first writing it was not clear.

Dogana di Ossaia: Custom-house at Ossaia, a frontier village between the Papal States and Tuscany.

una bella ragazza: a pretty girl.

I suggest that Coleridge spent his time there—possibly a stop charmingly prolonged in the Italian fashion—observing a pretty girl and making schoolboy jingles about sparkling conches and more sparkling conchoids.

2852 15.241(b) Did Coleridge think he was noticing an Italian translation of an English name, or was he remarking on evidence of the influence of the English colony in Florence, even at this date?

2853 15.271   *Florence Gallery* means the Uffizi and the picture is *La Santa Famiglia* of Parmegianino or Parmigianino (Girolamo Francesca Maria Mazzola). See plate VI.

umarbeitet into the Puck of Sir J[oshua] Reynolds & again into his Muscipula: Reynolds's *Puck* or *Robin Goodfellow* (see plate VII A) was exhibited in the Royal Academy in 1789 and was reproduced in various engravings and as one of Boydell's Shakespeare Gallery. *Muscipula* or *The Mouse-Trap Girl* (see plate VII B) was also variously engraved, or may have been seen by Coleridge in Holland House.

It is difficult to say in the direction of which painter the *umarbeitet* (worked over, recast) is intended to be more derogatory. For Coleridge on Reynolds as occasionally "affected and meretricious" compared with the old masters, see *TT* 24 July 1831.

It is also difficult to believe that, of all the pictures in the Uffizi, on this Parmigianino alone Coleridge made a note. See Introduction xvi–xviii.

2854 15.272   Is the transliteration of *mendicant friars* and the word *Poison* into Greek letters a sign of war-time precautions?

2855 15.273   The margin has been much thumbed and is faded; two words, *at* and *their*, now not visible, were once to be seen.

2856 15.270   The entry stops abruptly; it may have continued on another leaf, not the succeeding but the preceding one in the notebook, which has been excised. When Coleridge reached the bottom of the page and turned over the leaf he found the next pages filled with 2853–2855.

EHC quoted part of this entry in *L* II 499 n 2; he does not give enough to make it clear whether the entry was longer when he saw it. He thought it could be dated 19 June 1806 from the same letter, now *CL* # 620. But there were two trips to Pisa from Florence, and if this was 19 June it must have been the last visit before Coleridge sailed from Leghorn 23 June; it reads, on the other hand, like a record of first impressions, and possibly comes from a May visit.

The hospitals are a famous and ancient foundation, and Coleridge's pleasure in them was doubtless contrasted with his horror at the hospital in Malta; see 2420 and n.

2857 15.223   In another, probably an Italian, hand, this is a list of the painters to whom the frescoes in the Campo Santo at Pisa were then ascribed. As given by Vasari the names are:
Benozzo Gozzoli (1420–97)
Buonamico Buffalmacco (*d* 1340)

Giotto di Bondone (*c* 1266–1337)
Andrea Orcagna (*c* 1308–*c* 68)
Pietro Laurati, now Lorenzetti (*c* 1280–*c* 1348)
Antonio Veneziano (1319–83)
Simone Martini (*c* 1283–1344)
Murray's Guide to the Campo Santo (1856) ascribes the frescoes on
the north wall to the first two, those on the south to Coleridge's next
three, among other artists mentioned. The order suggests an entry
made as he was looking at the wall, perhaps asking his guide or com-
panion to jot down the names for him. See also 2858.

For Coleridge "these grand drawings" were an important experience. See *TT* 25 June 1830 and *Phil Lects* 167–8, 193.

2858 15.224   This was also noted probably in the Campo Santo at
Pisa; it is the inscription on the tomb of Benozzo Gozzoli there,
copied verbatim except for changes in capitalization, and the date on
the tomb is 20 years later and in Roman numerals. Space was left
under this entry, presumably for more notes of this kind.

Tr: This is the tomb of Benotius the Florentine, who lately painted
these stories; the culture of the people of Pisa made her [Pisa] a present
of him.

2859 15.225   This entry at the bottom of the page follows a gap
that was left, perhaps for additions to the list of Italian painters.
Presumably it arose from his difficulties in understanding or being
understood when he tried to use Latin for communication.

2860 16.357   Part of this is quoted in *L* II 499n, a footnote to a
letter to Allston, written ten days after this entry, in which there is
a similar reference to thoughts of suicide, dismissed for the sake of
his children. *CL* # 620.

of Sara Hutchinson/that is passed: more important as an indication
of wishes rather than of fact, this reference supports the view that
Coleridge's journey to Malta was taken with this hope in mind, i.e.
for reasons of emotional as well as physical health. See 1608n.

His difficulty in opening letters was a constant source of worry to
himself and his friends; see e.g., among many instances that might be
cited, 901, 1517.

The state of despair described here was prolonged; see 2866.

2861 16.358   *John Wordsworth:* This is confirmation of the statement made to Stuart later, that he had expected John to marry Sara. See 2517n and *SH Letters* xxvi. But as to whether this was in John's mind, or Sara's, there is no real evidence. See *W Life* 473–4.

2862 16.359   On the speech of Italian women, cf 2812.

Hazlitt gave it as Coleridge's remark that the women in the streets of Rome "look to this hour as if they had walked out of Raphael's pictures". Hazlitt's review in Feb 1822 "On the Elgin Marbles": *H Works* xviii 157.

2863 16.360   This and the two entries that follow are in a brownish ink and are written with a finer pen, a different ink from that in 2862. They might be from English newspapers seen in Florence or Leghorn. From here onwards in this notebook the dating is uncertain. But if, as seems likely, this practically-filled notebook was packed up for the journey (see N 16 Gen Note), these entries were probably made shortly before embarking.

From a copy of this issue of *Baldwin's London Weekly Journal* kindly made available by the City Librarian, Bristol, it may be seen that Coleridge here skilfully condensed the report in the "Assizes" column. The italics for *Banker* and *compelled* are his. The only other interesting change is his *Within an hour;* this is not in the court account, but only a reference to the young woman's body having been found "the same evening". *Robert Hanford* has not been traced.

Presumably Coleridge was interested in a story so like Poole's of John Walford: *Poole* ii 234–7.

2864 16.361   William Windham (see 1428n) held the War and Colonial Secretaryships in Lord Grenville's ministry until he was dismissed in March 1807.

no confidence in fact: i.e. in the *observable* fact. Coleridge's own "confidence in fact" is part of his skill as an observer, as has been noticed, e.g. by Humphry House; see 1766, 1767 and n, and House 48. This is not to gainsay his distrust of what he called "mere facts", as in 2122. Does he mean here that politicians are deceived by their own rhetoric and will not trust the man-on-the-spot, e.g. the Sir Alexander Balls?

2865 16.362   *Wyndham (loud laugh):* the phrase should be in the quotation marks Coleridge has in mind as an irritatingly frequent

occurrence in the parliamentary reports in the press of the day. Cf
Friend i 182. On political language, see also the previous entry. On
Windham see 1428 and n.

Joe Millerisms: i.e. hackneyed and possibly coarse, at any rate professional rather than spontaneous humour. Joseph Miller (1684–1738)
was a low comedian known as the Father of Jests, chiefly because of
Joe Miller's Jests: or the Wit's Vade Mecum compiled for the benefit
of his family after his death by John Mottley. It ran into numerous
editions.

2866 15.242   Published in *L* ii 499n; the quatrain is also in *PW*
ii 1001, where EHC calls attention to the reminiscence in these lines
of the ballad, "Martin'mas wind, when wilt thou blow/And shake
the green leaves off the tree?/O gentle Death, when wilt thou come?/
For of my life I am wearie."

There is no doubt from numerous hints in the notebooks of the
latter half of the Malta period that Coleridge's thoughts frequently
turned on death at this time, even suicidal thoughts. See 2712n. In
Italy the conflicting anxieties about the delays and dangers of the
journey home, the desirability and dread of the return and especially
the horror of the prospect of returning worsened in health, must have
been acute. This entry is his final comment on his Mediterranean
journey. The next day he sailed from Leghorn.

The germ of the lightning-flash metaphor goes back some years in
Coleridge's thoughts. Cf "Till Frenzy, frantic Child of moping Pain,/
Darts his hot lightning-flash athwart the brain!" *Lines on a Friend
who died in a Frenzy Fever*, sent in letters to Southey and George Coleridge Nov 1794 (*CL* # 68 and 69). They were written before Francis
Coleridge died by his own hand "in a frenzy fever" in 1799 (see 1494n)
but meaning must have accrued to them from the later event. If there
is a link here, it would be strengthened by the parallel in their situa-
tions, both being alone, ill, and desperate, in a foreign country in
war-time.

2867 15.248   *Fornacetti:* Fornacette; see 2868n.

Coleridge was always alert to the difficulties of the common man in
obtaining the necessaries of life.

2868 15.249   *For[nacette] to Castel di Bosco:* Fornacette is a little
off the main road between Leghorn and Pisa. There was an inn there

of good repute, and Coleridge may have stayed overnight on one of his trips to Leghorn in search of passage home.

Salisbury & the good coachman: an unsolved enigma.

2869 11.1   The first new pocketbook after the return from Malta begins with what appears to be an attempt to analyse and control the use of opium by describing the stages of the experience of taking it.
   1. *Uncomfortab[leness]*. If the word was completed, it ran on to the Hall & Co label, and the end is now invisible.
   2. *O[pium]* + *B[randy]?*
   3. *increased N[ervous] E[nergy]?*
   5. *Remorse.* The word is frequently used by Coleridge, but it is interesting to have in mind here that revision of *Osorio*, later to become *Remorse*, was about to begin. See 2928 and n.
   The Greek word (self-tormentor) and the illegible words that follow refer to morbid self-generated fears; the sense is obscured not only by the difficulty in reading what is badly written (on the rough inside cover), but partly by the amorphous (or deliberately cryptic) character of the observations. There seems to be a special concern to leave off the brandy in which the opium was frequently taken: see also 2042 and n and 2767.

2870 11.2   "1806" is inked over, probably later by Mrs Gillman.

2871 11.3   G. B. Guarini *Cristiana compunzione*, from the *Rime*. The selection of these lines for transcription is surely not unrelated to the resolution in regard to SH in 2860.

Tr: Father of Heaven, if once I wept with such mad folly that the end of my weeping is nought but weeping, pray give me now, I beseech thee, tears worthy of thee. I loved, I deny it not, fleeting and fragile beauty, and abandoned that which is immortal. Heal, oh Lord, with loving affection, my fault of love! Listen to my prayers; Thou who art a Father, do not deny me pity.

2872 11.4   In ink, and separated from the last entry, although also by G. B. Guarini, on the same subject, and also from the *Rime*, *Nel medesimo soggetto:*

O Lord, who dost desire the death of the sin, not of the sinner, pray behold with what fallacious guidance my blind desire has brought me to death. Behold thy strayed sheep, call it back to thee, its very life. Cause it to bewail its ill, bewail its error, as bitterly as once it wept for love.

2873 11.5   See 1355 and n; an old plan revived at this time by Mary Lamb's prodding?

2874 11.6   Capt James Burney, Lamb's friend and Fanny Burney's brother, was with Capt Cook on his third and last voyage and brought the *Discovery* home after Cook's untimely end. He was of course an authority on Otaheite. In this year, the second volume (1806) of his *A Chronological History of the Discoveries in the South Sea or Pacific Ocean* (5 vols 1803–17) was published.

Omai, brought to England by Cook, taken to see the king, painted by Reynolds, was from 1774–6, i.e. in Coleridge's childhood, something of a legendary figure. Burney was his interpreter.

2875 11.7   Mr Thomas Russell of Exeter, with whom Coleridge travelled from Rome to Florence. See 2836 and n.

2877 11.9   A story from Burney? The incredibly arduous experiences of Mme Godin des Odonais were not geographically appropriate to the work cited in 2874n, but Burney had very likely heard her story. Surviving her seven companions, she alone, after various misadventures, several nearly fatal, and after hundreds of miles in the Amazon jungle (Oct 1769–July 1770), reached safety and was reunited, after twenty years, to her husband. The most accessible contemporary account was later published in J. Pinkerton *A General Collection of . . . Voyages and Travels* xiv (1813) 259–69, reported by C. M. de La Condamine.

2878 11.10   The entry reads, with the four preceding, as if connected with an evening's conversation at Lamb's. But in view of Coleridge's use of Nicholson's *Journal* (3111n–3116n) and his acute interest in this subject, it is worth noticing that the Nov 1803 issue of the *Journal* (vi 161–79) had as its second article "A Memoir on the Appearance of Spectres or Phantoms occasioned by Disease, with Psychological Remarks. Read by Nicolai to the Royal Society of Berlin, on the 28th February, 1799". The article begins with the problem of knowing "where the corporeal essence in man ceases, and where the mental begins", arguing further that apparitions are the result of nervous excitement. "The phantasms appeared to me in every case involuntarily as if they had been presented externally, like the phenomena in nature, though they certainly had their origin internally and at the same time I was able to distinguish with the greatest precision phantasms from phenomena." Nicolai is expansive on the absence of terror or horror from the phantasms; they were often agreeable. "Had I not been able to distinguish phantasms from phenomena, I must have been insane. Had I been a fanatic or superstitious, I should have been terrified at my own phantasms. . . ." He attacks Fichte's exaggerated subjectivism in applying Kantian idealistic theories (note Coleridge's "Ghost-seer"), as having "degenerated into the gross enthusiastic idealism which is found in Fichte's writings". Towards the close of the article he uses phrases that Coleridge could have recognized as his own. "I find myself frequently in a state between sleeping and waking, in which a number of pictures of every description, often the sharpest forms, shew themselves, change and vanish." There is no direct evidence that Coleridge read this article at this time; he may have done so in 1807, when he was going through several volumes of Nicholson's *Journal*. The attitude was close to his own on a subject of perennial interest to him.

2879 11.11   Source not found. On talent *vs* genius, cf 2557 and n.

Tr: So talent dies, unless tokens of talent (say rather, of Genius) guarantee continuous life.

2880 11.12   In ink. Although this revision of *The Ancient Mariner*, and the two following entries, which are also in ink and also concerned with poetry, are not given a precise date, they do appear to belong to the first six months of Coleridge's return to England. The date of this and 2881 and 2882, all in ink, might be placed, taken by themselves, between 5 Oct 1806 and 25 Nov 1810, the dates of the pencil entries that flank them in the pocketbook. From the fact that 2986, also about Pindar (like 2882) and also in ink, must be dated before 2892, the last part of which it obstructs, a reasonable date for all of these seems to be 5–12 Oct 1806. Probably this entry is connected with Longman's offer in the spring of 1807 to publish Coleridge's poems in two volumes and represents preparations made towards eliciting that offer. *CL* # 647.
    In these lines, several experiences of the Malta journey are fused.
    With never a whisper: cf 2086.
    The Helmsman's Face by his lamp gleam'd bright: cf 2001.
    the star-dogg'd moon: the star within the nether tip of the moon appeared in the first version of *The Ancient Mariner*, and a recollection of it in 2139 along with the fact but not the adjective of this phrase. In a note to this line R. H. Shepherd, the editor of *PW* (1877), re-

corded a MS annotation in which Coleridge said, "It is a common superstition among sailors that something evil is about to happen whenever a star dogs the moon." Also in *PW* (JDC) 598. One wonders whether the phrase was a product of the Malta journey; see another star close to the moon in the voyage out (in an entry in which "the Signal light shone bright" also—2087), and note the discussions of sailor superstitions in 2060, where "the Star, that dogged the Crescent" appears again, precisely in this context.

2881 11.13   Of these seven Greek words, all except the second are to be found in the *Odes* of Pindar in the forms here chosen: (1) *Olympian* III 3; (3) ibid III 1; (4) ibid III 3; (5) ibid III 8; (6) *Pythian* x 30; (7) *Olympian* VI 15. The correct form for (7), however, is Ταλαϊονίδας. Word (2) appears not to occur in Pindar but is to be found in Stobaeus *Anthologium* IV 56 24.

Coleridge appears to have chosen these words as examples of the dactylo-epitritic metre—which works upon an ambiguity between dactyl - ∪ ∪ and epitrite —∪ ∪, is usually rapidly moving, and gives the impression of a sprung rhythm basically dactylic but at times suggesting trochaic (- ∪) movement by the elision of the first short into the long (—∪). Whether by a slip of the pen or by design, word (7) becomes logaoedic.

The source of this entry is probably Schmied's edition of Pindar, demonstrably in use in 2887. See also 2882n.

2882 11.14   In ink, like the other Pindar excerpts in this pocket-book, 2881, 2887, 2911, 2912, 2986, and like them based on Schmied's edition. Coleridge's references here agree with Schmied's running head-lines and line-numbering (though for convenience the lineation of modern texts is referred to in these notes). See 2887 and n.

The reference to *Olympian* III, strophe and second antistrophe, is to the passage (lines 16–25) in which Heracles, the founder of the Olympian festival, brings the olive from the banks of the Ister (an episode that Coleridge's note dramatizes and develops as Pindar does not). "With loyal heart was he entreating for the hospitable precinct of Zeus, the gift of a tree, whose shade should be for all men, and whose leaves should be a crown of prowess. For already had the altars been consecrated in his father's honour, *and in the midst of the month the Moon with her car of gold had at eventide kindled before him the full orb of her light,* and he had ordained on the hallowed banks of Alphaeus the impartial award of the great games, together with the quadrennial festival. But that plot of ground, sacred to Pelops, was not, as yet, flourishing with trees in its valleys below the hill of Cronus. He deemed that his demesne, being bare of such trees, lay beneath the power of the keen rays of the sun. Then it was that his spirit prompted him to journey to the land of the Ister, where he had once been welcomed by Leto's daughter . . .". (The underlined words represent Coleridge's quotation.) Tr Sir John Sandys (LCL 1927) 35.

From *Olympian* VI, the passage he refers to runs from the second epode (line 39) to the third strophe (line 47); he quotes the first and last words to which he refers. "Meanwhile she laid down her crimson zone and her silver pitcher, and 'neath the blue brake was about to bear a boy inspired of heaven; and the Lord of the golden hair sent to her aid the gentle goddess of birth, and the Fates; and from her womb, and amid sweet sorrow, forthwith came Iamus to the light of day. And she, though sore distressed, was fain to leave him there upon the ground; but by the will of the gods, two grey-eyed serpents tended the babe with the bane, the harmless bane, of the honey-bees." Tr Sandys 59.

The third passage referred to, the third antistrophe of the same ode (lines 6–9), refers to the hiding-place where the babe, born five days before, "had been hidden among the rushes and in the boundless brake, with its dainty form steeped in the golden and the deep-purple light of pansies; therefore it was that his mother declared that he should be called for all time by the undying name of Iamus." Tr Sandys 59–60.

It will be noted that the folds and gyves of the serpent, the slant ray of light, on the face of the child, the weak mother with reverted face full of maternal yearning, are Coleridgian additions. Further, that the factors common to the two odes are a hero-son of a god and, as is natural in Olympian odes, the river Alphaeus. Lucina and the Parcae—the minor goddess associated with child-birth, "who makes the child see the light of day" (*OCD*), and the Fates, who are "sometimes present at birth" (ibid)—are also Coleridgian additions to Pindar's story.

It is impossible to avoid sensing here a mysterious conjunction of *Christabel–Kubla Khan* images. Lowes speculated on Coleridge's acquaintance with the Alphaeus as the original sacred river Alph. *RX* 393–6. Aside from the general critical significance of Coleridge's several references to Pindar in this period of revising his poems for a projected two volumes (see 2880 and n), is it possible that this excerpt is to be linked specifically with an attempt to continue *Kubla Khan*?

2883 11.21   This page was used before he left for the north (see
the next note), though possibly the expense account represents some
part of the northward journey, or an estimate for it.

The list of luggage, etc on the right-hand side appears to be a list
of what Coleridge was claiming from the Customs, or from Capt
Derkheim; the story of his trying experiences in this connexion is told
in *CL* # 627–33. For Chesterfield I know no explanation.

2884 11.22   In another—Mr Austwick's?—clerkly hand. Coleridge wrote George Fricker, 9 Oct 1806, that a "Clerk at Russel's
Waggon Office" at the Bell Inn, Friday St, Cheapside, had undertaken
to rescue a trunk of Russell's, containing some of Coleridge's possessions.

2885 11.23   Great St Helen's is a London address, but city guides
of the period throw no light on this entry.

2886 11.114   *AP* 168. In ink.

2887 11.115   This entry is based on, and is part quotation from, an
appendix to the heavily annotated edition of Pindar of Erasmus
Schmied (Wittenberg 1616) 249. Coleridge's copy is now in the
Wisbech Museum and Literary Institute, Wisbech, Cambridge. Of his
marginal notes, all but one are on the *Olympian Odes*. The entry gives
the clue to the source of Coleridge's entry about Pindaric metres in
2881, and was probably used for all the Pindar entries referred to in
2882n.

In this edition, after the index, there is a disquisition *De dithyrambis*
(referred to on the title-page) in which a candidate for examination
in the subject, in the year 1607, makes the statement Coleridge quotes
in this entry:

Dithyramb = father Liber, and of this word different etymologists have
given different accounts, as that class of men usually do for sport or pastime.

2888 11.116   Ink. The back and forth use of these pages suggests
either that Coleridge found but few blank pages left in the notebook,
or that he accidentally skipped a leaf and therefore went back to it.
The date appears to be close to that of surrounding entries; i.e. see
2893n.

The text of articles III, VI, VIII, XIII, XVIII, XIX, XX, XXI, and XXIII
is as follows:

"III. *Of the going down of Christ into Hell.*

"As Christ died for us, and was buried, so also is it to be believed, that he went down into Hell."

"VI. *Of the Sufficiency of the Holy Scriptures for salvation.*

"Holy Scripture containeth all things necessary to salvation: so that whatsoever is not read therein, nor may be proved thereby, is not to be required of any man, that it should be believed as an article of the Faith, or be thought requisite or necessary to salvation. In the name of the Holy Scripture we do understand those Canonical Books of the Old and New Testament, of whose authority was never any doubt in the Church.

"Of the Names and Number of the Canonical Books

Genesis,	The First Book of Chronicles,
Exodus,	The Second Book of Chronicles,
Leviticus,	The First Book of Esdras,
Numbers,	The Second Book of Esdras,
Deuteronomy,	The Book of Esther,
Joshua,	The Book of Job,
Judges,	The Psalms,
Ruth,	The Proverbs,
The First Book of Samuel,	Ecclesiastes or Preacher,
The Second Book of Samuel,	Cantica, or Songs of Solomon,
The First Book of Kings,	Four Prophets the greater,
The Second Book of Kings,	Twelve Prophets the less.

And the other Books (as *Hierome* saith) the Church doth read for example of life and instruction of manners; but yet doth it not apply them to establish any doctrine; such are these following:

The Third Book of Esdras,	Baruch the Prophet,
The Fourth Book of Esdras,	The Song of the Three Children,
The Book of Tobias,	The Story of Susanna,
The Book of Judith,	Of Bel and the Dragon,
The rest of the Book of Esther,	The Prayer of Manasses,
The Book of Wisdom,	The First Book of Maccabees,
Jesus the Son of Sirach,	The Second Book of Maccabees.

"All the Books of the New Testament, as they are commonly received, we do receive, and account them Canonical."

"VIII. *Of the Three Creeds.*

"The Three Creeds, *Nicene* Creed, *Athanasius's* Creed, and that which is commonly called the *Apostles'* Creed, ought thoroughly to be received and believed: for they may be proved by most certain warrants of Holy Scripture."

"XIII. *Of Works before Justification.*

"Works done before the grace of Christ, and the Inspiration of his Spirit, are not pleasant to God, forasmuch as they spring not of faith in Jesus Christ, neither do they make men meet to receive grace, or (as the School-authors say) deserve grace of congruity: yea rather, for that they are not done as God hath willed and commanded them to be done, we doubt not but they have the nature of sin."

"XVIII. *Of obtaining eternal Salvation only by the Name of Christ.*

"They also are to be had accursed that presume to say, That every man shall be saved by the Law or Sect which he professeth, so that he be diligent to frame his life according to that Law, and the light of Nature. For Holy Scripture doth set out unto us only the Name of Jesus Christ, whereby men must be saved."

"XIX. *Of the Church.*

"The visible Church of Christ is a congregation of faithful men, in the which the pure Word of God is preached, and the Sacraments be duly ministered according to Christ's ordinance in all those things that of necessity are requisite to the same.

"As the Church of *Jerusalem*, *Alexandria*, and *Antioch*, have erred; so also the Church of *Rome* hath erred, not only in their living and manner of Ceremonies, but also in matters of Faith."

"XX. *Of the Authority of the Church.*

"The Church hath power to decree Rites or Ceremonies, and authority in Controversies of Faith: And yet it is not lawful for the Church to ordain any thing that is contrary to God's Word written, neither may it so expound one place of Scripture, that it be repugnant to another. Wherefore, although the Church be a witness and a keeper of Holy Writ, yet, as it ought not to decree any thing against the same, so besides the same ought it not to enforce any thing to be believed for necessity of Salvation."

"XXI. *Of the Authority of General Councils.*

"General Councils may not be gathered together without the commandment and will of Princes. And when they be gathered together, (forasmuch as they be an assembly of men, whereof all be not governed with the Spirit and Word of God,) they may err, and sometimes have erred, even in things pertaining unto God. Wherefore things ordained by them as necessary to salvation have neither strength nor authority, unless it may be declared that they be taken out of Holy Scripture."

"XXIII. *Of Ministering in the Congregation.*

"It is not lawful for any man to take upon him the office of publick preaching, or ministering the Sacraments in the Congregation, before he be lawfully called, and sent to execute the same. And those we ought to judge lawfully called and sent, which be chosen and called to this work by men who have publick authority given unto them in the Congregation, to call and send Ministers into the Lord's vineyard."

2889 11.109   Eric Partridge in *Name into Word* (New York 1950) suggests that the word *tallboy*, in the 17th century a drinking-glass, in the 18th–20th a high chest of drawers, is "a jocosity: tall boy. But probably the choice of the term was in part suggested by the surname Tallboys, from French *taillebois*, 'a hewer of wood'."

The reference to Hesiod, for which Coleridge gives a Latin adaptation of the Greek, is to the *Carmina, The Shield of Heracles* line 19: "a monument [*the villages* in Hesiod] of the heroes, the Taphians and Teleboans". Zeus had ordained that Amphitryon must avenge "the death of his great-hearted brothers" and burn the villages of the Taphians and Teleboans before he could form a liaison with Alcmena; hence the reference by "a learned Chaplain" to a putative survivor from the wrath of Amphitryon.

The source appears to have been in part a printed one, untraced, perhaps partly an etymological fantasy original with Coleridge.

2890 11.110   *AP* 167. The letter *d* is clearly inserted with a caret mark; otherwise *Strt* might be mistaken, presumably even by himself, for someone else, *Stuart* or *Street*. An earlier reference to this irritating habit of Stoddart appears in a Malta entry in N 17; see 2120 and n and 2472.

The image of the disproportionately annoying night-fly as a simile for "minimism" in criticism was used years later by Coleridge in an article in *Blackwood's*, "Letter to Peter Morris, M.D. on the sorts and uses of literary praise": ". . . critical minimism, when the attempt . . . made to read the poem, too impatient to wait even for the next semicolon, might remind one of those tiny night-flies, that as they hurry across one's book, contrive, with self and shadow, to cover a word at a time." *Blackwood's* VII (1820) 629–31.

2892 II.112   *AP* 167–8. Coleridge 9–10 Oct visited the Clarksons, who were staying with William Smith at Parndon in Essex (*CL* # 633), and accompanied Mrs Clarkson to Bury St Edmunds, where he stayed until he went to Cambridge 16 Oct (*CL* # 632).

Dr Price: Dr Richard Price (1723–91), the famous rationalist dissenting clergyman. The social and theological factors conjoined in this anecdote convey in a nutshell Coleridge's reaction against his former position.

2893 II.113   *AP* 168 variatim. Written after 2892, with 2886 already on the facing page; Coleridge therefore when he came to the bottom of *f48ᵛ*, and turned back to the preceding page, wrote there, "from overleaf".

2894 II.108   Coleridge's first return to Cambridge since student days; see 2892n.

Brooks: Jonathan Brooks (1774–1855) was a friend of undergraduate days, a member of Trinity College. Coleridge and Hucks met him on their walking tour in Wales in 1794. See *CL* # 52.

Caldwell: George Caldwell (*c* 1773–1848), an undergraduate friend at Jesus College, at this time a Fellow. He and Coleridge had both been associated with Francis Wrangham's *Poems* (1795), where Caldwell's translation of one of Wrangham's Latin poems and Coleridge's of another (*Hendecasyllabi ad Brutonam*) had both appeared.

Mr Jones: If this was Thomas Jones (1756–1807), Tutor and Fellow of Trinity College 1787–1807, Coleridge was renewing another association of his youth. At the famous college trial of William Frend, during which Coleridge distinguished himself by obstructively noisy applause, Thomas Jones showed his sympathy in the more dignified way appropriate to the principal tutor of Trinity, by sitting at the table with Frend throughout the ordeal.

Possibly Robert Jones (1787–1835), Wordsworth's friend, is meant; the Welsh data in 2889 could perhaps have come from either one.

Porson: the great classical scholar, Richard Porson, a Fellow in Coleridge's day, who was now apparently past remembering even an exhibitioner and scholar who had won a gold medal for a Greek Sapphic *Ode on the Slave Trade* in 1792 and whom he had possibly introduced to Godwin in 1794. See B. R. Schneider *Wordsworth's Cambridge Education* (1957) 221. The Greek types used in this edition of the notebooks are based on Porson's handwriting.

Mr Costobody: Jacob de Costobadie (1758–1828), Fellow of Jesus College (1781–96). It is amusing to notice that Mr Costobadie lectured on mathematics, of which Coleridge always lamented that he had learned so little at Cambridge. Here he appears to be discharging an old debt to Costobadie by paying Tiggin's widow Costobadie's debt for bell-ringing. It may be added that in the Frend controversy referred to above, Costobadie was on the wrong side, in Coleridge's undergraduate view, which fact might help to account for his neglect of mathematics. The double underlining of BELL-RINGING may signify memories of bells unheeded, for Costobadie was probably the "excellent Mathematical Tutor" referred to in a remorseful note on the first volume of Coleridge's copy of Law's *Behmen*, now in the BM:

"To H. C. and D. C.

"I shall be obliged to take as my motto §§8, 9, 10, 11, 12, 13 ⌐ p. 219 of the Aurora ⌐ but o! with what bitter regret, and in the conscience of such glorious opportunities, both at School under the famous Mathematician, WALES, the companion of Cook in his circumnavigation, and at Jesus College, Cambridge, under an excellent Mathematical Tutor, Newton all *neglected*, with still greater *remorse*! O be assured, my dear Sons! that Pythagoras, Plato, Speusippus, had abundant reason for excluding from all philosophy and theology not merely practical those who were ignorant of Mathematics. Mη δεις αγεομετρητος εισιτω—the common inscription over all the Portals of all true knowlege. I cannot say—for I know the contrary, and the §§'s above referred to express the conviction—that it *cannot* be *acquired* without the *technical* knowlege of Geometry and Algebra—but never can it without them be adequately *communicated* to others—and o! with what toil must the essential knowlege be *anguished-out* without the assistance of the technical!—   S. T. Coleridge."

2895 11.18   The London-Carlisle coach, taking Coleridge to Penrith, went through Stamford.

2896 11.19   Adrien Quentin Buée wrote a comparison of the theories of Romé de l'Isle and René Just Haüy, of which an English translation by Robert Clifford was published in the *Philosophical*

Magazine in 1804, entitled "Parallel of Romé de l'Isle's and the Abbé Haüy's Theories of Crystallography".

Coleridge's spelling of Romé de l'Isle's (or de Lisle's) name suggests that he took it down from a verbal rather than a printed reference. On the other hand, in Nicholson's *Journal* IX (Sept 1804) 26–39 and (Oct 1804) 78–88 we find the spelling *de Lisle* in "Outlines of the Mineralogical Systems of Romé de Lisle and the Abbé Haüy; with Observations. By the Abbé Buée. Communicated by the Hon. Robert Clifford". More important than the source, although that perhaps affects the argument for the possible use of the *Journal* in 2878, is Coleridge's interest in the comparison of two sorts of scientific work. De Lisle made the study of crystallography more exact by the precision and classification of his observations. Haüy (see 2014 and n) went further than observation, insisting on physical, chemical, and geometrical analysis and on taking into account electric and magnetic phenomena; his excellence lay in combining particulars and finding a law. When Coleridge wrote on this distinction between methods in *Friend* III 165–75 he may have had de Lisle and Haüy in mind; he was not merely generalizing.

2897 11.24   The borders of the palpable-visual, especially in darkness or half-lights, are a recurrent preoccupation, earlier associated with Tom Wedgwood's interest in perception.

2898 11.25   A stage-coach companion? Possibly noted out of a lively prescience of his need of medical help.

2899 11.20   *"Few" come to mean "Many"*: as in the phrase "quite a few".

Ferry Bridge: a coaching-stop beyond Stamford.

2900 11.26   *Christabel*, still in MS, was at this time under discussion in the circle of Coleridge's friends who had read it; Scott's *Lay of the Last Minstrel*, published in 1805, so closely echoed it metrically, in the opinion of Southey, Dorothy Wordsworth, and others, as to be potentially detrimental to Coleridge's poem. See *CL* # 632 and n, and Coleridge's 1811 letter that ended the niggling gossip and took the whole affair to much higher levels. *ShC* II 231–9 and *CL* # 845.

In the reference to Aeschylus *Prometheus vinctus* Coleridge has in mind a three-fold form of considerable intricacy:

His Strophe A = *PV* (Strophe α) 399–406 (8 lines) + (Strophe β) 415–19 (5 lines).

Antistrophe *B* = *PV* (Antistrophe α) 407–14 (8 lines) + (Antistrophe β) 420–24 (5 lines).

Epode   = *PV* 286–99 (14 lines).

(The differences in line numbers is to be accounted for by differences in arrangement of text. In the Loeb text quoted, in which the formal divisions are clearly shown, the Greek words at the end of the entry are the first and last two words of the Epode.)

Strophe and Antistrophe α are in identical form, being sung to the same tune; Strophe and Antistrophe β are in identical form—though different from α—being sung to their same tune. The metrical form of Aeschylus's Strophe α and Strophe β only are given below since Antistrophe α will match Strophe α, and Antistrophe β will match Strophe β.

In this form there would be not only a contrast of mass between

A = 8 + 5 lines   B = 8 + 5 lines   Epode = 14 lines

but also three variations of a tetrametric line, and marked rhythmic contrast between the first and second parts of A and B, and between both those and Epode. The prosodic scheme shows vividly that Coleridge's Strophe and Antistrophe would both start with a light rapidly moving metre, with its double anacrusis at the beginning of all but first line; that the second 5-line part has no anacrusis and will be more deliberate in movement. The Epode, though more varied internally than either of the others, and capable of movement, would probably be solemn and liturgical, and with the additional contrast of over-reaving (like Milton's or Wordsworth's paragraphing) because it abandons the cadential *ritenuto* at line-ends that characterizes both sections of Coleridge's Strophe and Antistrophe.

The scansion is given from Aeschylus:

Strophe A (lines 399–406)

ᴗ / - ᴗ / ∟ / ⁔ ᴗ / - ᴗ / - ᴗ / - >
ᴠᴠ / ∟ / ⁔ ᴗ / - >
ᴠᴠ / ∟ / ⁔ ᴗ / - ᴗ / - >
ᴠᴠ / - ᴗ / - ᴗ / - >
ᴠᴠ / - ᴗ / - ᴗ / - >
ᴠᴠ / - ᴗ / - ᴗ / - >
ᴠᴠ / - ᴗ / - ᴗ / - >
ᴠᴠ / ∟ / ⁔ ᴗ / - >

Strophe B (lines 414–418)

- ∪ / - ∪ / - ∪ / - >
- ∪ / - ∪ / - ∪ / - >
- ∪ / - ∪ / - ∪ / - >
- ∪ / - ∪ / —∪ ∪ /∟ [- ∪ / —∪ ∪ / - ∪ / < in Ant. B]
—∪ ∪ / - ∪ / - >

Epode (lines 286–300)

- - / ∪ ∪ - / - ⌣́∪ / - -
∪ ∪ - / ∪ ∪ - / - ⌣́∪ / - -
- ⌣́∪ / - - / - - / - -
- - / ∪ ∪ - / ∪ ∪ - / - -
- - / ∪ ∪ - / - ⌣́∪ / - -
∪ ∪ - / ∪ ∪ - / - ⌣́∪ / - -
∪ ∪ - / - -
- - / ∪ ∪ - / - - / ∪ ∪ -
- ⌣́∪ / - - / - - / - -
- - / ∪ ∪ - / ∪ ∪ - / ∪ ∪ -
- ⌣́∪ / - - / ∪ ∪ - / ∪ ∪ -
- - / ∪ ∪ - / - - / - -
- - / ∪ ∪ - / - - / ∪ ∪ -
∪ ∪ - / ∪ ∪ - / ∪ ∪ - / - ∧

Possibly Coleridge here still has in mind the essay on metre that he once thought of attaching to the publication of *Christabel* (*CL* # 387, 391); possibly the talk about Scott's having stolen his metrical thunder roused him to thoughts of trying once more to complete and publish it in the projected two volumes of his poems. See 2880n and 2882n.

2901 11.27   Mr Petch, whose address seems, at least temporarily, to have been the Angel, the chief hotel in Catterick, Yorkshire, is unknown.

2902 11.28   This appears to be a separate entry, though perhaps with some mathematical relation to 2903.

2903 11.29   *Quicks:* cuttings for a quickset hedge.
    Probably the reference is to Mr Cookson of Kendal; it was with these Cooksons (no relation to the William Cooksons related to

Wordsworth) Sara Hutchinson frequently stayed, and probably it was there Coleridge found her when, having discovered she had just left Penrith a few hours before he arrived, he followed her to Kendal.

Magnum Bonum: a large yellow cooking-plum.

2904 11.124   On the inside back cover, this entry runs into the ridge of the binding under the pasted-down end-paper.

At midnight, when W[ordsworth]'s watch said 12 o'clock, Coleridge's said 11:52. At 11 the next day, by W[ordsworth]'s watch, Coleridge's said 10:38, having lost 14 minutes in 11 hours.

2905 11.30   The underlining of the date may be nothing more than a division between entries; it looks rather more deliberate, perhaps a smiting of conscience. He had landed in England 17 Aug 1806, after delays connected with retrieving his luggage from the ship and the customs shed, and trying to get journalistic or other work. Much has been made of the evident procrastination behind his return to Keswick, and perhaps too little of practical matters, including even the embarrassment, to one penniless, of the fare itself. But see also 2935 and n.

2906 11.31   From the Apocrypha: Wisd. of Sol. 1:4, the Vulgate version; it is quoted in translation in *Friend* III 204: "Truth . . . will not enter a malevolent spirit."

In Chap XXI of *BL* this was quoted to "dismiss the criticism" of the *Edinburgh* and the *Quarterly* reviews of Wordsworth: *BL* II 91.

2907 11.117   *AP* 168-9. In ink, like 2908.

2908 11.118   In ink.

In the contemporary editions of the Book of Common Prayer there was "A Form of Prayer with Fasting, to be used yearly on the thirtieth day of January, being the day of the martyrdom of the blessed king Charles I". In the Order for Morning Prayer, "Instead of the *Venite exultemus*" another cento of verses out of the Old Testament was suggested, of which the sixteenth to the eighteenth raised the question in Coleridge's mind: *"For the sins of the people, and the iniquities of the priests: they shed the blood of the just in the midst of Jerusalem. (Lam. iv.13)*.

"O my soul, come not thou into their secret; unto their assembly, mine honour, be not thou united; for in their anger they slew a man; *Genesis* xlix.17.

"*Even the man of thy right hand: the Son of man, whom thou hadst made so strong for thine own self. Psalm* lxxx.17."

2909   11.119   *AP* 169. As he apprehensively nears Grasmere, it is of interest to see Coleridge recalling his intimacy with Allston, which seems at times to have presented some conflict, or at least some feelings associated with his friendship with Wordsworth. See e.g. the close of *CL* # 620 and 2830 and n.

2910   11.120   Did Mrs W[ordsworth] and Sir G[eorge] B[eaumont] represent callous and anxious affection? Cf the fragment on duty in *Inq Sp* §302. That the Beaumonts epitomized affectionate care and kindness we know from entry 1983. And that neither the Wordsworths nor Coleridge could have found association easy after the return from Malta is clear from the tensions of the Coleorton visit. See 2975, 2998, among others. This entry (and the group 2904–2908) may belong to that period two months later. But see 2912n, with the link with early November.

2911   11.121   Pindar *Olympian Odes* iv 26–8:

Even young men full often find their hair growing grey, even before the fitting time of life.—Tr Sir John Sandys (LCL 1927) 45.

See 2887 and n.

2912   11.122   *D*^r *Hutton:* Dr James Hutton (1726–97), the great geologist and collector, who wrote *The Theory of the Earth* (2 vols Edinburgh 1795), and whose *Principles of Knowledge* (3 vols 1794) Coleridge owned. See 243n. The fact that EHC found in Coleridge's copy of this work, at I 271, a letter from Wordsworth dated 7 Nov 1806 suggests, together with this entry, that Coleridge was re-reading Hutton, or went to his work for some purpose, at this time. *UL* I 348n (reading Hukon for Hutton).

The applicability to Hutton of the quotation lies in Hutton's theory that the earth surfaces were produced through the action of subterraneous heat operating below the ocean beds to raise up land bodies, and that changes in the earth's surface always had taken place and always would take place. If the *locus* of Coleridge's letter means anything, it may be of interest that at I 271 Hutton is beginning a *résumé* of theories of the earth, beginning with that of Thomas Burnet.

Pindar *Olympian Odes* VII strophe 4 lines 62–4: the story being told is of how, when the earth was being divided among the gods, the absent Sun-god was overlooked. When Zeus was about to order a new casting of lots, the Sun-god brushed the offer aside.

For, as he said, he could see a plot of land rising from the bottom of the foaming main, a plot that was destined to prove rich in substance for men, and kindly for pasture. . . .—Tr Sir John Sandys (LCL 1927) 77.

On Coleridge's copy of Pindar, see 2887n.

2913 11.123   Coleridge's note shows one variant from the usual text: the second line normally reads παραινεῖν.

On 6 Nov 1817 Coleridge returned to H. F. Cary a copy of the edition of Aeschylus *Prometheus vinctus* (1810) and the *Persae* (1814) by C. J. Blomfield. The reading represented by this entry seems to have been earlier, and the variant referred to does not correspond with Blomfield's text. Coleridge's reading may, of course, be a slip; and pencilled entries on the inside covers and fly-leaves of pocketbooks may be of almost any date, though there is no evidence of N 11 being used so late as 1817.

This may be mentally directed at Southey, during the early November misery at Keswick when Coleridge was deciding to separate from Mrs Coleridge. See 1815 and n, 2935 and n, and 2950.

Tr: Tis easy for him who keeps his foot free from harm to counsel and admonish him who is in misery. Myself I knew all this the while. Of mine own will, aye, of mine own will I erred—gainsay it I cannot.—Aeschylus *Prometheus Bound* lines 265–8 tr H. W. Smyth (LCL 1926).

2914 16.363   *AP* 164–5. Coleridge returns to the use of pencil again here. From the hand, this and the next seven entries appear to belong to one date. As 2918 is datable in the period of Coleridge's reading of Fulke Greville, the whole cluster of entries may be dated probably Oct–Nov 1806; see 2918n.

Swift's well-known remark hardly needs tracing in Coleridge's reading. It is, however, to be found in Edward Young's *Conjectures on*

Original Composition, as a remark made to him by Swift in Dublin. "Pointing at it [an elm-tree] he said, 'I shall be like that tree: I shall die at the top.'—He was then but fifty." If Coleridge had it from this source, he could have read it in Young *Works* v 117, the volume he took from the Bristol Library in 1795. See 33n–36n and 2211n. The "hooks-and-eyes" of memory being what they are, it may be relevant to notice that in this part of N 16 the upas-tree (see the next entry) follows hard upon the recollection of Young (if it is Young), as it does in the Gutch book, 33–37.

2915 16.364   Memory bears a suspicious resemblance here to the persecuting hags of Coleridge's dreams, and indeed the various images and phrases weave an intensely personal fabric: *gazing—snatches of the eye—annihilate the one thought—Being . . . absorbed—fluttering off— bitter fruits—Tree of Life—a seal* [stigma]—*phantom-head—wan & supernatural—numb—the eye alone—a rock in a rain-mist—palpability by influent recollections of Touch.* Into this, dreams, *Christabel*, the upas-tree of the Gutch notebook, the Book of Revelation, ghost stories, *The Ancient Mariner*, natural observations in the Lakes, and Tom Wedgwood on touch, all enter.

That this, the earliest recorded use of the word *subconsciousness*, was not a chance or isolated application of a prefix to an accepted word, is borne out by other discussions in the notebooks of the relation of conscious to unconscious processes:

6: "depths of Being below, & radicative of, all Consciousness."

1554: "Man . . . how much lies *below* his own Consciousness."

1575: "Viewed in all moods, consciously, uncons[ciously], semi-consc[iously]".

1798: "he added to the Consciousness hidden worlds within worlds."

2073: "we being semi-demi-conscious".

2086: "Poetry a rationalized dream dealing [?about] to manifold Forms our own Feelings, that never perhaps were attached by us consciously to our own personal Selves."

2999: "A consciousness within a Consciousness".

These are but a few examples from many, and subsequent volumes will provide more.

It is interesting to note that the first use of *subconscious* (1832–4) and *subconsciously* (1823) is attributed by the *OED* to De Quincey. *Subconsciousness* did not appear until 1879.

2917 16.366   Cf 2067.

Was Coleridge, having so recently parted from Allston, proposing
a subject for a painting out of his reading of Fulke Greville? In
Alaham II iv Mahomet says: "Caine! weigh thy course: „ Ambitions
gilded spheres/Are like to painted hells, which please the eyes,/Euen
while they shew the heart where horror lies." *Workes* (1633) 33.
See the next entry.

2918 16.367   According to a note by EHC in the *Athenaeum*
No 3939 (25 April 1903) 531, Coleridge read *Certaine Learned and
Elegant Workes of the Right Honourable Fulke, Lord Brooke* (1633) in
Charles Lamb's copy, Aug–Sept 1806, on his return to London. A
few of the notes were quoted in an article in the *Athenaeum* No 3436
(2 Sept 1893) 322. The "note in the waste Leaf" to which Coleridge
refers is not quoted, an unfortunate omission since the copy has
disappeared. H. S. Young pointed out, ibid No 3437 (9 Sept 1893) 356,
that Coleridge's poem *Farewell to Love*, inscribed in this copy of
Greville, was modelled on Sonnet LXXXIV of Greville's *Coelica*. See
PW I 402 and n. The notes given in the *Athenaeum* are reprinted in
MC 242–3.

Coleridge sent *Farewell to Love* to the *Courier*, where it was published 27 Sept 1806, from which fact EHC dates Coleridge's reading
of Greville. It is possible that this and the other Greville entries here
ought to be dated as early as August–September also. However, as
there is no evidence of this notebook having been used on shipboard,
and the practical considerations point to its having been packed up
among Coleridge's belongings, I suggest that, although Coleridge was
reading Greville at least as early as September, these entries were not
made in this notebook before October, i.e. before 9 Oct, when he
finally extracted his effects from Derkheim's carelessness and the
custom-house. Thereafter he was on the move with the Clarksons, to
Bury and Cambridge, and later in the month went on to Penrith,
Kendal, and Keswick, where he arrived 30 Oct. Greville's *Workes* may
have been a book of the journey.

There is a reference at the close of Lamb's essay "Two Races of
Men" to "those abstruser cogitations of the Greville, now alas!
Wandering in Pagan lands." But this refers, apparently, to the other
Greville, Robert, the second baron, and to his *The Nature of Truth;*
and, indeed, there is no clear suggestion that Lamb's wistful reference
to his lost book is in any way associated with Coleridge.

The line "Time fashions mindes . . ." (the lines are unnumbered) is on p 3 of the 1633 edition of *Alaham*, which appears with a new pagination following *A Treatie of Humane Learning, An Inquisition upon Fame and Honour*, and *A Treatie of Warres*. The corroboration for the use of the 1633 edition of Greville's *Workes* later comes from entries in N 18, where the page references are all to that edition. Those entries, made at Keswick or Grasmere 1808–10, may have been from Southey's copy, sold with his library.

2919 16.368   *AP* 163. Possibly suggested by the description of corruptions and furies in the Prologue to *Alaham*. See the previous note. And cf 2915; Death = Memory?

2920 16.369   From *Alaham* 1 i, in which the old king is dethroned by his son Alaham: "He (passion-ledd) could loue, and trust but one./ . . . /Enuy wrought more in me, and made me know,/This passion in the King . . ./Had counter-passions . . .". Greville *Workes* (1633) 7.

2921 16.370, 371   This part-prose, part-verse entry was first, with hesitation, considered two, yet the appearance of ink and hand certainly suggests one time of writing, and in view of other instances of prose and verse tending to flow in and out of each other in the notebooks (as e.g. in 3231), the conjunction seems more significant than the division. It has therefore appeared desirable to treat this material as one entry, additionally so because JDC and EHC treated them separately without showing the contiguity.

The prose first part is in *AP* 162, dated 1805; the first four lines of verse are printed in *PW* (JDC) 469, undated, and in *PW* II 998, dated 1803. The demonstrable links with Greville's *Alaham*, had they been evident to EHC, would have altered his view of their date. It is not absolutely clear that he derived the four lines of verse from this MS, nor that JDC did.

The prose paragraph and the lines that follow are again suggested by *Alaham*, by the first chorus of spirits:

"And what is that but Man? A crazed soule, vnfix'd;/Made good, yet fall'n, not to extremes; but to a meane betwixt:/Where (like a cloud) with winds he toss'd is here, and there,/We kindling good hope in his flesh; they quenching it with feare./We with our abstract formes, and substance bodilesse,/Image by glaunces into him our glories, their distresse,/And in prospectiue Maps make ille farre off appeare,/Lest it should worke with too great power, when it approacheth neare./Beauties againe of Truth (which those old spirits conceale)/with Opticke glasse we reflect on man to kindle scale./But whether idle man, exceeding orders frame,/(As out of heauen justly cast) must Vulcan-like goe lame;/Or that those euill spirits so dazle humane eyes,/As they thinke foule forbidden things more beautifull, more wise;/Wee see, though they want power to change our reall frame,/Yet in the world they strive to gaine by changing of our shame:/Calling the Goodnesse weake; . . ./So while the o'reswoll'n pride of this Mahumetan,/By wounding of his Princely race, playes false with God and man;/He in it doth disperse those clouds of reuerence,/Which betweene man, and Monarchs Seate keep sweet intelligence;/And while he would be lord of order, nature, right,/ Brings in disorder, that deuouring enemy of might,/Which with her many hands unweaues what time had wrought,/And proues, what power obtaines by wrong, is euer dearly bought." *Workes* (1633) 20-2. *f119 Whispers voyaging from far:* this, if nothing else, would date these lines after the Malta voyage; see 2086 and the revision of *The Ancient Mariner* referred to in that note.

like prattling rill . . . to the roots: cf the personal use of this image, with a difference, in N 25: *AP* 167.

2922 16.372   *AP* 62, dated 1803; but this entry must, from the MS, be dated after 2921. Mrs Gillman has written at the top of it: "Read this".

The personal allusion is not certain in the despondency of the autumn of 1806.

2923 16.373   Cf Greville's *Alaham*, the end of the first chorus: "So in mans muddy soule, the meane doth not content/Nor equally the two extremes; but that which fits his bent./This makes some soare, and burne; some stoope and wet their wings . . .". *Workes* (1633) 23.

2924 16.374   Surrounded by excerpts from *Alaham* as this entry is, and dealing like that play with guilt, uncertainty, love, treachery, and conflict, one would expect to find it there. But it is not there. Rather it seems to be a versification in the manner of Greville of the feelings in 2922.

2925 16.375   The excerpts are all from *Alaham*, variatim: II iii
(p 31); III ii (p 45); "Christian Starre—Divines", III v (p 52); III v
(pp 52–3); IV i (p 59); IV ii (p 62). As Coleridge says, the second scene
in Act IV is an excellent one; possibly it also had special significance
for him in all the uncertainty of mind in which he returned from
Malta. It begins with the dispossessed brother returning home.
"Where am I now? All things are silent here./What shall I doe? Goe
on from place, to place,/Not knowing what to trust, or whom to
feare?/Yet what should I not feare . . .". *Workes* (1633) 62. But
many lines would strike home, full as they are of the recognition of
emotional extremes meeting.

2926 15.243   The entry is in ink like the four that follow it. Below
it Mrs Gillman has written, "Is it not himself? A. G." The top of
f113 was torn out, accounting for the incompleteness of the first line
on it.

Published in *PW* II 1005–6. EHC dates these lines 1810, perhaps on
the theory that after 2866 the notebook was packed away, and that
the ink of this and succeeding entries indicates a break in the use
of the notebook. Possibly, too, he associates some of the neighbouring
entries with the later period. But, the latest date in the notebook is
1808; and there are reasons for thinking the break here not so long.
In 2928 STC is revising *Osorio*, in 2931–2932 he is reading Beaumont
and Fletcher and Fulke Greville. All these may reasonably be dated
c autumn 1806. And 2938, dated 28 Nov 1806, must have been written
after the above, a conclusive argument for an 1806 date.

Like N 16, this notebook does not appear to have been used on the
voyage; I suggest a similar course for it. See 2918n.

2927 15.244   In ink. Possibly suggested by the old king and his
daughter Coelica in Fulke Greville's *Alaham*, particularly in Act IV
scene i; see 2932n.

2928 15.245   In ink. This entry is in part obliterated by accidentally spilled red ink; as red ink appears frequently in EHC's transcripts, the blots may well be his. It is made difficult to read also for
the reason that it was written with too dry a pen.

It appears to be connected on the one hand with *Osorio*, discovered
in Godwin's library (*CL* # 646), which was revised in the fall of 1806 in

the hope of making some money by it, and on the other, biographi-
cally, with the conflict at that same time, about returning to Greta
Hall, Mrs Coleridge's temper, and Southey's "Virtuousness".

That *Osorio* was a name associated with Southey (perhaps a play on
his name—Ro. So-io?) is suggested by a MS note now in the Hunting-
ton Library; it may be argued from it, bearing in mind Coleridge's
various descriptions of Southey (e.g. see especially 1815 and n), that
Southey sat for the portrait of Osorio. The MS is a transcript of a
rough draft of *Osorio* (in the hand of Mrs Coleridge?) corrected by
Coleridge and interleaved with annotations by R. H. Shepherd,
presumably a copy used in preparing his edition of *Osorio* in 1873.
The MS on f 1ᵛ has this interesting note by Coleridge:

"In the character of Osorio I wished to represent a Man who from
his childhood had mistaken constitutional abstinence from vices for
strength of character—thro' his pride duped into guilt—& the en-
deavoring to shield himself from the reproaches of his own mind by
misanthropy."

In the revision, Osorio became Ordonio, and Albert, Alvar. If
Osorio approximates Southey, the Albert/Coleridge identification is
at least better than specious. Albert is the one with dreams and guilt;
and Coleridge's first *Morning Post* poem was signed *Albert* in the
issue of 7 Dec 1797.

2929 15.246   In ink.
L. Grenv. or Wynd.: Lord Grenville or William Wyndham/Wind-
ham? William Wyndham, Baron Grenville (1759–1834), formed the
"Ministry of All the Talents" 11 Feb 1806; its life was brief, and
calamitous. Negotiations with France failed, foreign expeditions were
unsuccessful, Fox died in September, and the Ministry fell in March
1807.

If ambiguity is part of Coleridge's intention, he could mean either
Lord Grenville *or* the other William Windham (1750–1810), who led
Grenville's party in the House of Commons and was War and Colo-
nial Secretary until the Government fell in March 1807.

2930 15.247   In ink. The pre-Freud Freudian interpretation of
Medea as acting from unconscious motives is stated less succinctly
and penetratingly in the 1802 discussion of the subject of Medea in a
letter to Sotheby (*CL* # 457). A comparison of the letter with this
entry is of interest, showing that although always concerned with the

psychology behind the action of the play, Coleridge has now become
more articulate about its delusional aspects.

2931 15.250   In ink. A continuation (from 2930) of the subject of
character, and what lies below the surface?

   Thierry & Theodoret: a five-act tragedy in Beaumont and Fletcher
Fifty Comedies and Tragedies (London 1689) 450–68. Charles Lamb's
copy, annotated by Coleridge, is in the BM, though with no Coleridge
annotations on this play. Nor are there any Coleridge marginalia on
the play as it appears in Stockdale's edition of *The Dramatic Works of
B[en] J[onson] and Beaumont and Fletcher* (4 vols 1811), Coleridge's
copy of which is also in the BM. The story is one of unnatural relations between a licentious woman who destroys her two sons and then
herself chokes to death.

   Alaham: by Fulke Greville; see 2917–2925 and the next entry.
This is a story of a son who deposes his father, whom he blinds, blinds
also his elder brother, and finally puts father, brother, and sister all to
death. His stoic remorse at the somewhat confused close of the play
does not assuage the ire of his wife nor calm the political tempest.

   The "Hints" from these two plays, in which the struggle for power,
an inherent wickedness tending to tyranny, vicious relations between
parents and children, the suffering of the innocent and virtuous at the
hands of the strong and cruel, and a certain retribution at the end
seem to be the common factors, appear to have been connected with
thoughts of a new play on the Medea theme referred to in 2930.

2932 15.251   *Bid winds . . . mind:* "Call vp the dead; awake the
blinde;/Turne backe the time; bid windes tell whence they come;/As
vainly strength speakes to a broken minde./Fly from me *Coelica!* hate
all I doe . . .". Fulke Greville *Alaham* IV i: *Workes* (1633) 60.
Published as Coleridge's in *PW* II 1001, not exactly as here, but as in
Poole II 195.

   Let Eagles . . . soar: this also is in *PW* II 1001. Both entries are
there dated 1807.

2933 15.252   In ink.

2934 11.32   Of the same date as 2935 (possibly a later hour), and
an interesting, if surprising, subject for so momentous a night. It
should, however, be remembered that the real separation in spirit had

taken place for Coleridge years before, and he had long urged a decision in favour of it as a practical measure. I suggest, too, that the candle flame and preoccupation with it is associated for him, almost symbolically, with solitude, or singleness, and inversely with the unfulfilled wish for a marriage of souls. E.g. "The flames of two Candles joined . . . Picture of Hymen" of entry 13 is apposite.

2935 11.125   The resolution, taken before he returned to Keswick, was to separate from Mrs Coleridge, the difficulty of persuading her to accept the realities of the situation having been finally surmounted. See DW to Mrs Clarkson *W Letters* (*M*) 68–70, and Coleridge's letter to the Wordsworths written a few days after this entry. *CL* # 635. Coleridge's next letter to Mrs Coleridge that survives was not different in tone from many that preceded it, and signed "anxiously & for ever/Your sincere Friend, S. T. Coleridge." *CL* # 638.

2936 15.253   The application—to some unresponsive contemporary?—can merely be speculative.

2937 15.254   Cf the spelling *Æolian* in *Dejection* line 7: *PW* 1 363; and var *Eolian* in *The Eolian Harp* (1803) line 12: *PW* 1 100. Coleridge here adds another to the considerable list of uses of the Aeolian harp as romantic metaphor. See Geoffrey Grigson *The Harp of Aeolus* (1948) 24–46.

2938 15.255   *Elpizomene:* i.e. the hoped-for one, Sara Hutchinson. Coleridge is at Keswick, Sara with the Wordsworths at Coleorton, where he was to join them in late December. The entry scarcely bears out the "of Sara Hutchinson/that is *passed*" of 2860. Apparently the meeting 26–9 Oct in Kendal had renewed the bond. See *W Letters* (*M*) 68–70 and *C&SH* 61–3, where this is treated as two separate entries.

2939 11.33   This is not from Laberius but from Publilius Syrus; it appears in fragmentary *Sententiae* collected from various sources in O. Ribbeck *Comicorum latinorum . . . reliquiae* (1855) line 50. No authority cited by Ribbeck ascribes the epigram to Laberius; nor is it in the fragments of Laberius collected by Ribbeck. Coleridge may be using some quoter who attributed the epigram to Laberius; or is he possibly applying it to himself? He used *Laberius* as a signature for at least five poems 1797–9, four in *PW* I 211–13, 237–40, II 953, 977.

Tr: By giving in a worthy spirit, he received benefit from the giving.

2940   11.34   The source is not known.

I used to love France (as far and as much as France can be loved by a true Englishman)—France, or whatever she gave us in that name: but now I pursue her, in that very same name, with hatred.

2941   11.35   Tr: The most Stoic of the Stoics.

2942   11.36   From the preface of Thomas Farnaby (*c* 1575–1647) to his edition of Juvenal; the editions of 1633 and 1642 have the preface, which does not appear in the first edition (1612):

I have written for you—a host of good men—who look to enrichment, not for those few evil men who look to malice: for you who have hearts, who are mindful of rites, manners, events; not for those eye-men, who "see, understand, know" nothing but what is in front of their eyes. In short, I have addressed the soul, not the senses—
          Farnaby to his Readers in his edition of Juvenal—

2943   11.37   In ink. *AP* 170. Coleridge is anticipating Bagehot's "cake of custom" metaphor in *Physics and Politics* (1872).

2944   11.38   In ink. On fear, cf 2398. The references to opium-taking become more explicit from late 1806 onwards.

2945   11.39   *Decivism:* not in the *OED*. De-civism?
the mirrors of Archimedes & Proclus: traditionally used to burn enemy ships.
Anthemius: a Greek mathematician and architect (*fl* A.D. 532) who is said to have produced artificial earthquakes by means of compressed steam. Possibly the "Powder" was his means of creating thunder and lightning, also attributed to him.
vivaparæ of the African Sands: for viviparae, the born-alive or mammalian creatures.
oviparæ . . . of Peru: born as an egg.
Deiparæ of Palestine: born as a god.
The contrast between "regular Government" and government by

monsters was an old one for Coleridge. See 686 and, a later use, *Inq Sp* §248.

2946 11.98   The reversal of normal foliation in entries 2946–2955 is owing to the pocketbook having been turned around for the use of *ff46–43ᵛ*. Whether these entries were written before or after the visit to Cambridge (2894) is not clear from the physical facts of the pages; on internal evidence, especially the reference to Southey and the Soother of Absence in 2950, the likely period seems to be after the return to Keswick 30 Oct and before the Coleorton visit and the temporary strain of 27 Dec 1806; in other words, Nov–Dec 1806.

The equation, unless it is allegorical and not chemical, makes no sense, platinum being no compound but an element. H. Davy until *c* 1812 appears to have used the older form *platina*, at least in his writings; *platinum*, however, had been adopted by the Swedish chemist Bergman and others long before.

2947 11.99   *Aftergame* is a second game intended to reverse the fortunes of the first one. *OED*. Cowper used it in *The Task* II 762. Is this, with the next, personally applied?

2948 11.100   Coleridge referred to himself as a library "cormorant" in *The Devil's Thoughts:* "For I sat myself, like a cormorant once/ Hard by the Tree of Knowledge." *PW* I 321. The floating aspect here describes the period of his return from Malta. The personal use of bird-images in e.g. 2531 and 2556 has been pointed out.

2949 11.101   In ink. This may derive from a conversation with Blumenbach referred to in one of Coleridge's marginal notes on Gilbert White's *Selborne:* "Blumenbach told me, that the abcission of the Horns of the Stag and Male Deer had the effect of castration." *Inq Sp* §189.

2950 11.102   In ink. On the Rock of Names see 1163n. What Australis (Southey) said to arouse Coleridge's indignation is difficult to state specifically, but not to imagine generally. The names on the rock, or rather the initials, were those of the Wordsworths—Dorothy, John, Mary, and William—Sara Hutchinson, and Coleridge. Is there a link here with 2928?

2951 11.103   In ink. The second and third lines are deleted also by diagonal strokes. In *PW* II 1013, from the fourth line.

2952 11.104   From the *De linguarum orientalium, praesertim Hebraicae, Chaldaicae, Syriacae, Arabicae, et Samaritanae praestantia, necessitate et utilitate quam et theologis praestant et philosophis* (1658) by William Beveridge (1637–1708), Bishop of St Asaph. The first passage is on p 15:

It is too majestic, too divine a thing not to slip somewhere into a mistake.

The second is on pp 18–19:

Day teaches day, and what was hidden yesterday from the more learned man, today is known to the more ignorant.

2953 11.105   On the pleasures of sleep cf especially 1718 and n; one remembers also that Coleridge wrote *The Pains of Sleep*.
    cum amatâ: with the beloved.

2954 11.106   Clearly self-observation in the self-troubled mood of the Coleorton days. In the notebooks, at least, Coleridge can blame himself.

2955 11.107   In ink. *AP* 174. On the subject of social rights and duties see also *Friend* (1818) I 283–4, *EOT* III 688–9, 693–4, 699–70.
    Burdett-Mob: Sir Francis Burdett's vigorous efforts towards electoral reform were at their height about the close of 1806, culminating in the successful Westminster election of 1807 after which he was chaired in the streets. Coleridge was less unsympathetic to him as a prison reformer. See 767n.
    Sᵗ Monday: "used with reference to the practice among workmen of being idle on Monday, as a consequence of drunkenness on the Sunday". *OED*. Coleridge so uses it in *TT* 8 June 1833.

2956 11.40   *AP* 170–1, printed with 2957 as one entry, with a note by EHC saying this was written "when S.T.C. was staying with Wordsworth at the Hall Farm, Coleorton."
    The MS suggests two entries, the hand in the second being looser and larger than in the first. As the second one reads *Decemb. 1806*, and Coleridge did not arrive at Coleorton until Sunday 21 Dec (*CL* # 638), there was but one Saturday left in December, the "dreadful Saturday

Morning" of 2975. This entry could belong to that date; but for this one and the next the mathematical probability, the position in the pocketbook, and the internal evidence (2957 is an afternoon or evening entry) point to a December date before he left Keswick, 6 or 13 Dec.

2957 11.41   See 2956n.

2959 11.43   *Walton, in the Dale:* now Walton-le-Dale on the river Ribble near Preston, Lancashire. The entry is in a shaky hand as if written in a coach on the move—not the large unco-ordinated shakiness of opium or alcoholic writing.

2960 16.379   Jan 1804–June 1806.
The dating is difficult, but from appearances there is a break between 1725, also on this page, and 2960–2964. The names here, and the pun in the next, could have been entered by Coleridge at almost any time up to Oct 1810. See also 2962n.

2961 16.380   The phrase is from a play attributed to George Wilkins. *The Miseries of Inforced Marriage* 1 i: "Clara, I must leave thee, with what unwillingness,/Witness this dwelling kiss upon thy lip . . .". Dodsley's *Old Plays* (ed J. P. Collier 1825) v 16. See 2964n.
The evidence that Coleridge read it in some edition of Dodsley's *Old Plays* is to be found in 2964n.

2962 16.381   *AP* 163. This entry and 2963 and 2964 are difficult to date. It may be that their place is immediately after 1725 and written on the same occasion. Going back to the MS I find the forced break perhaps too arbitrary. EHC dates this entry late in 1805, i.e. in Malta. Yet there is argument for dating it and the next two entries, 2963 and 2964, as late as 1806.
The words are the very theme of *The Miseries of Inforced Marriage* quoted in the entry above; Coleridge is concentrating the whole play into a metaphor, echoing Act v (ed cit p 84), where the unhappy father addresses his children, "As dropping leaves in Autumn you look all . . .".

2963 16.382   The idea comes from the play quoted in 2961. Possibly it was also fortified by a contemporary event—the factual description of a forced marriage in the London paper of 22 March 1806, which Coleridge, to judge from the surrounding entries, saw in Italy in June 1806; see 2863n. In the dearth of evidence for dating these entries a straw may indicate the wind.

2964 16.383   The phrase comes from the second play in the Dodsley collection of *Old Plays* cited in 2961: *Lingua: or the Combat of the Tongue and the Five Senses for Superiority* I i: "The learned Greek rich in fit epithets,/Blest in the lovely marriage of pure words" (ed cit p 107). The use in successive entries of phrases from two plays in the same volume, plays not easily come by, seems to be sufficient evidence that Coleridge was using Dodsley.

This entry is quoted, variatim and unidentified, in *BL* Chap x (II 69 fn); it appears also, with the extra preceding line given above, in the Shakespeare lectures of 1811–12 as reported by J. Payne Collier, who traced it to its source; see *ShC* II 119n.

The description of the Greek language as "the happy marriage of sweet words" was used a few months later in a letter to SH on the fly-leaves of a present of Chapman's *Homer*, together with an example, "*joy-in-the-heart-of-man-infusing* wine". *LR* I 259.

2965 16.384   Coleridge has tried with special punctiliousness to reproduce exactly the title-page of this 14-page pamphlet. His quotation, also exact even to the "&c", comes from p 5.

Anno Salutis . . . Anglia: "Year of Grace 1666, & the first year of the Restoration of the Roman Religion in England".

2966 16.385   This entry appears to be linked in the appearance of the hand as well as in type of material with the entries that precede and follow it, yet no connexion has been discovered.

Ego . . . Conscientiarum: "I am a King of People, not of Consciences." Stephen appears to be Stephen Báthory, King of Poland from 1576, who reconquered Lithuania from Russia and in other ways was a powerful ruler who brought advantages to his countrymen. He died in 1586.

2967 16.386   The quotation is from the beginning of the pamphlet *The Horrid Sin of Man-Catching. The Second Part or Further Discoveries and Arguments to prove, that there is no Protestant Plot . . .* (London 1681).

2968 16.387   The reference is to Cicero *De oratore* 1 §198. Coleridge omits an *est* from the first line.

He who . . . was described by the greatest of poets [Ennius] as follows: Notably wise and shrewd among men there was Cato Aelius Sextus.—Tr E. W. Sutton and H. Rackham (LCL 1942).

2969 16.388   Ovid *Epistulae ex Ponto* III ix 23–4: "To Brutus". Coleridge omits *ut* after *corrigere;* and the notation "El. 11" is strange, and untraced.

[While writing the very toil gives pleasure and itself is lessened, and the glowing work glows along with the writer's heart. But] to emend—even as it is a thing as much harder as great Homer was greater than Aristarchus[, so it wears down the mind with a slow chill of worry, curbing the steed all eager for the race.]—Tr A. L. Wheeler (LCL 1924).

2970 15.256   In ink. The geological terms and definitions appear to come from Richard Kirwan *Elements of Mineralogy* (2nd ed 1794) 1 338–49, 361–2, or from an abstract of that work. The terms, as far as the heading *Calcareous Stones*, appear on the pages cited, in the same order and with the same spelling; after that STC, or the writer of the abstract or article based on Kirwan, departed considerably from the text.

2971 15.257   In ink. This entry and 3010 provide the basis for the Earl of Egmont's suggestion in 3170n.

2972 15.258   In ink. Cf 2866 and n, and the description of Alexander Macaulay's death in 2408.

2973 15.259   *Antipho:* Coleridge appears to be referring to the Antiphon or Antipheron whose case was used as an illustration by Aristotle in the essay "On Memory and Recollection" that interested Coleridge in 1801 (973A) and to which he referred in 2267. See 2267n. The relevant passage indicates much about the nature of Coleridge's interest in the essay: ". . . they [Antipheron and other lunatics] spoke of their mental pictures as if they had actually taken place, and as if they actually remembered them. Now this happens when one regards as a portrait [other translations sometimes read "likeness"] what is not a portrait: but practice preserves the memory by the process of recollection. This is nothing but the repeated contemplation of an object as an image, and not as existent in itself." Aristotle *Parva naturalia* Bk I §1 451a tr W. S. Hett (LCL 1935) 291–2.

2974 15.269   The entry is impossible to date, but probably belongs after the return to England 1806–8.

2975 11.44   *The Epoch* is written large and centred, in ink. The date, *Coleorton Church*, and the hour are traced over in ink. Three leaves are cut out after the last word at the bottom of the page.

The episode is further hinted at in 3148 *ff45–45ᵛ*, and made more specific in an entry of probably *c* 1808 in N 21½ *f14ᵛ*:

"O that miserable Saturday morning! The thunder-cloud had long been gathering, and I had been now gazing, and now averting my eyes, from it, with anxious fears, ⟨of which⟩ I scarcely dared be conscious. But *then* was the first Thunder-Peal!

"But a minute and a half with ME—and all that time evidently *restless* & *going*—An hour and more with kk.θκkk.θυ [Wordsworth] *in bed*—O agony!—& yet even ⌈. . . . .⌉."

Whatever happened at the Queen's Head fostered Coleridge's jealous fears of SH's intimacy with WW. A memorandum made in later life, in which he tells himself that the interpretation of the whole episode was a product of his own miserable fancies, is an important one to consider in this context:

"Strange Self-power in the Imagination, when painful sensations have made it their Interpreter, or returning Gladsomeness from convalescence, gastric and visceral, have made its chilled and evanished Figures & Landscape bud, blossom, & live in scarlet, and green, & snowy white, (like the Fire screen inscribed with the nitrate & muriate of Cobalt)—strange power to represent the events & circumstances, even to the anguish or the triumph of the *quasi*-credent Soul, while the necessary conditions, the only possible causes of such contingencies are known to be impossible or hopeless, yea, when the pure mind would recoil from the very ⟨eve-lengthened⟩ shadow of an an approaching hope, as from a crime—Yet the effect shall have *place* & *Substance* & *living energy*, & in on a blue Islet of Ether in a whole Sky of blackest Cloudage shine, like a firstling of creation.—That dreadful Saturday Morning, at [Coleorton; *enciphered incorrectly as* Colorin], did I *believe* it? Did I not even *know*, that it *was* not so, *could* not be so? Would it not have been the sin against the Holy Ghost, against my own spirit, that would have absolutely destroyed the good principle in my conscience, if I had dared to believe it conscientiously, & intellectually! Yes! Yes! I *knew* the horrid phantasm to be a mere phantasm: and yet what anguish, what gnawings of despair, what throbbings and lancinations of positive Jealousy!—even to this day the undying worm of distempered Sleep or morbid Day-dreams—" Notebook L *ff22ᵛ-23.*

2976 11.45   In ink. No clue has been found as to source, application, or the intention of this entry.

2977 11.46   The line is not published as Coleridge's by EHC, nor has any other source been found.

2978 11.47   The first word is in large capital letters, the whole in ink. Above this entry, between this and 2977, four lines in pencil have been heavily obliterated with ink, perhaps Coleridge's own doing. The first Sunday in Jan 1807 was on 4 Jan. This entry is perhaps, therefore, retrospective.

2979 11.48   The coati-mundi or -mondi is described by Buffon; in Smellie's 9-vol translation (3rd ed 1791) v 55 the passage reads: "This circumstance [tail-eating] gave rise to a general conclusion that, in very long members, the extremities of which are, of course, removed to a great distance from the centre of sensation, the feeling is weak . . .". Coleridge said in the lectures of 1808 that he could not think of Buffon without horror. Report of H. Crabb Robinson in *ShC* II 16.

2980 11.49   Coleridge's awareness, particularly of Hartley's sensibilities and affections—and Hartley was at this time with him at Coleorton—comes out clearly e.g. in 617 and in *CL* # 638. On the Soother of Absence see 1225n, 1541n, and *CN* II Index 1.

2981 11.50   DW and WW were at this time planning for Sir George Beaumont the winter garden at Coleorton. Coleridge wanted *birches* added somewhere "on account of the richness of the colour of the naked twigs in winter". *W Letters* (M) I 100. Knight (*Coleorton* I 212) also read *birches*. Possibly Coleridge is simply noting here, in addition to Dorothy's remarks on the "rich purple" of birch twigs, the "lurid" blue of beech. In any case, the reading is clear.

2982 11.51   Ashby Church Yard, given this date, is undoubtedly Ashby-de-la-Zouch, Leicestershire, from which Coleorton is two miles away, and for which it was the coach town.

Once more Coleridge is interested in epitaphs in a churchyard and the contrasts presented; cf 1267 and n.

2983 11.52   The words *in as much as* are inked over and the marked re-forming of the letters suggests the hand of J. H. Green; he would no doubt have been interested, from his Calvinist view-point, in underlining the qualification implied in the phrase.

2984 11.53   Cf the lines called *Desire*, of uncertain date: "Where true Love burns Desire is Love's pure flame . . .". *PW* 1 485. The conflict appears frequently in Coleridge's MSS; see e.g. 1421.

2986 11.55   In ink; see 2882, 2887, 2911, and 2912 for the other Pindar entries in this notebook. The lines are from the *Isthmian Odes* VIII, and except for the insertion of ἐν as the third word in line 7, two omitted accents, and ω for ο in the last word in the penultimate line, Coleridge is following the text of Erasmus Schmied, referred to in 2887n. As the line-divisions in Pindar vary from edition to edition, these as well as the form of the citation help to indicate the source, the Wittenberg edition of 1616.

Therefore, I also, though stricken sorely at heart, am bidden to invoke the golden Muse. Yet, now that we are set free from mighty woes, let us not fall into any lack of festal garlands, nor do thou brood over sorrows, but ceasing to dwell on unavailing ills, we shall delight the people with some strain of sweetness, even after toil. . . .—Tr Sir John Sandys (LCL 1927) 499.

2987 11.56   In ink.

2988 11.57   Also in ink, the division from the foregoing entry being suggested both by a line across the page and by a slight change in the slope and size of the hand. *AP* 171.

Coleridge is articulating one of those split-second experiences familiar perhaps only to those who know thick woods at night. Shakespeare of course knew that "in the night, imagining some fear,/How easy is a bush supposed a bear." *A Midsummer Night's Dream* v i 22–3.

2989 11.58   *AP* 172.

2990 11.59   In ink. The addition at the end may be a separate
entry, a line of verse, as EHC published it in *PW* II 1002; equally it
may have been a deliberate juxtaposition inserted in wry contrast.
Two lines drawn across the page do not make the intention any
clearer; the words *Habit . . . delight*, comprising one line on the page,
have a line above and a line below them. The first appears to have
been drawn in error, the second *after* the word *Habit* was written, not
before, leaving an obvious, marked-off gap. The addition, as I think
it is, is in a smaller finer hand, to fit it in.

2991 11.60   In ink. The observation on which the lines are based
appears in a pocketbook of 1802; see 1168 and n. The lines are published in *PW* II 1002, with minor variations. EHC gave the earlier
note the same date as the versified fragment.

2992 11.61   In ink.

2993 11.62   In ink.

2994 11.63   In ink. *AP* 172, omitting the last two words; cf en-
                 try 13.

2995 11.64   In ink. *PW* II 1002, omitting the last phrase, which
may in fact be a separate entry.

2996 11.65   In ink. In *PW* II 1002 and *AP* 173, printed with 2997
as one entry. EHC's texts vary from each other, the *PW* text being
on the whole, but not entirely, more accurate.

2997 11.66   In ink. See 2996n.

2998 11.67   In ink.
        Pασα: Asra: Sara Hutchinson.
        Veol: love
•   *W͟:* the letter has been heavily re-inked, not, I think, by Coleridge.
        like the Exeter Cathedral Organ: the illustration first appears in N 9
(see 1972); the phrase "Sister pipe" appears, however, only with the
SH context. The entry illustrates Coleridge's readiness to associate
SH with earlier periods of his life, before they met, as e.g. in *Recollec-
tions of Love* (*PW* I 409–10), and the Quantocks lines in 3003. See also
C&SH 135–6 on this point.

a dream of painful fancies overshining the taper-light of Reason: a retraction of sorts, to himself, of his accusations about the "dreadful Saturday Morning"? See 2975 and n.

2999 11.68   In ink. In the penultimate sentence, the third word from the end is obviously a slip, *the* for *that*.

A consciousness within a Consciousness: Coleridge's interest and acuteness in articulating the multiplicity of consciousness is referred to and illustrated in 2915n. See also, on the experiences of the moments of falling asleep, 1032 and n and 1718 and n.

This entry may throw light on the famous conversation recorded by Keats as taking place in 1819 when he and Coleridge walked along together in Millfield Lane, Highgate. Coleridge ran through a remarkable series of topics, including "Different genera and species of Dreams—Nightmare—a dream accompanied by a sense of touch—single and double touch—A dream related—First and second consciousness—the difference explained between will and Volition—so many metaphysicians from a want of smoking the second consciousness—Monsters—the Kraken . . .". *The Letters of John Keats* ed Hyder E. Rollins (1958) II 88–9.

3000 11.69   In ink.

3001 11.70   Originally in pencil, some words are inked over in Coleridge's hand. The footnote is in ink.

Lines of Motion: cf in landscapes on a larger scale in 1771, 2347, and 2357.

3003 11.72   Cf the third stanza of *Recollections of Love* (*PW* I 410): "No voice as yet had made the air/Be music with your name . . .". The entry seems to support EHC's date for the poem, from internal evidence, of July 1807.

A similar thought, but applied to himself, had occurred on the Scottish tour in 1803; see 1463.

3004 11.73   In ink. The first two stanzas are crossed out with a vertical line.

The second version is in *PW* II 1001.

3005 11.74   In ink. The entry appears to be a telescoping, by some secondary source, of two accounts of ascents of the Pike of Teneriffe, one *c* 1650–2, the other 13 Aug 1715. They appear in *A New General Collection of Voyages & Travels* . . . *Published by His Majesty's Authority* (London 1745) in a chapter entitled "Description of the Canary Islands", of which §iv is comprised of "Three Journies to the Top of the Pike of Teneriffe". The first journey is not relevant; in the account of the second journey (1650 or 1652) we find (i 551 col 1), "So soon as the Sun appeared, the Shadow of the *Pico* seemed to cover, not only the whole Island of *Teneriffe* and the Grand *Canaries*, but even the Sea to the very Horizon, where the Top of the *Sugar-Loaf*, or Pico, distinctly appeared to turn-up, and cast its Shade in to the Air itself." The account of the third journey makes no reference to the shadow being horizon-wide, but it names Gomera (i 554 col 1): "A little after Sun-rising, they saw the Shadow of the *Pike* upon the Sea, reaching over the Island of Gomera; and the Shadow of the Upper Part, or Sugar-Loaf, they saw imprinted like another Pike in the sky itself."

The first of these accounts was first published by Sprat in his *History of the Royal Society*, Sprat (1743) 200–13, the second in *Phil Trans* xxix (Sept–Oct 1715) 317–25 and in the *Abridgement* (1792–1809) vi 177. See the two following entries, both from travel diaries.

3006 11.75   In ink. In *A New General Collection of Voyages & Travels*, referred to in 3005n, there is "An Account of the Discovery of the Kingdom of Bambûk, and its Gold Mines, in 1716", by Sieur Compagnon (ii 145–58). Again, Coleridge or his source is not quoting this account exactly, but the verbal similarities are so close as to point to a user of this material or else a common source. At ii 151–2 the account reads: "The second Gold-Mine discovered by the Sieur *Compagnon* is to the East of the River *Falemé*, twenty-five Leagues from its Confluence with the *Niger*, and about five Leagues, Inland, between the Villages of Sambanûra and Dalli Mûlet. . . .

"The neighbourhood of *Segalla*, and Village five hundred Paces to the Right of the Falemé as you go-up, and fifty Leagues from its Mouth. . . . The Mines of Ghinghi-faranna lie five Leagues higher. This Place is sowed with Gold-Veins. . . .

"The village of *Nian Sabana* on the River Sannon. . . . The richest Mine . . . is near the Centre of the Country of *Bambûk*, between the Villages of *Tamba-awra* and Netteko . . . on the same River. . . . Ghingan means Golden Earth. . . . There are two Mines of Gold at Naye."

3007 11.76   The material of the first sentence here may be found again in *A New General Collection of Voyages* II 182, in one of the "Voyages & Travels along the Western Coast of Africa", i.e. "Capt. Richard Jobson's Voyage of Discovery . . . in the year 1620 & 1621": "Not far from Jaye there were a people who would not be seen. . . . It is said, the Reason why these negros will not be seen is their having Lips of an unnatural Size, hanging down half-way over their Breast: which being raw would putrefy with the Heat of the Sun, did they not keep continually salting them."

For Coleridge on William Windham see 1428 and 2865 and notes. He seems to have been especially irritated by Windham's "plentiful lack of wit", i.e. of *sal atticum.*

3008 11.77   In ink. In the MS, *weather-fending* originally came after *Rocks*, and was then transposed; *Snug* as a noun is a word long in nautical use.

3009 24.1   Repeated at the back of the book on *f60*. Probably a temporary London address for Dr Peter Crompton, with whom Coleridge stayed several times. See 742n and 1849. Crompton called on Coleridge early in 1808 when he was ill (*CL # 679*); this memorandum, made twice in this notebook, could be of that date. Dr Crompton lived at Eton Hall, near Liverpool.

3010 24.2   Possibly a much later entry; the next one on the page is clearly 1819 or later. But the hand differs, and the Bristol example here may suggest the earlier period. Moreover, the subject under review is raised at this time, e.g. in 3170n and 3132. St Paul's Church, Portland Sq, opened in 1794, was 110 feet long and 60 feet wide, with "spacious galleries on three sides", according to *The Bristol Guide* of 1815, a large, relatively new building in 1806.

3011 24.4   A leaf has been torn out preceding this entry, presumably containing the beginning of it, and perhaps a date. On the dating of entries 3011–3014 see 3014n.

Coleridge is using a Latin-Italian version of the *De vulgari eloquentia*. In view of the identification of his edition of Dante from 3014 as the *Opere* (5 vols Gatti Venice 1793), we can assume that he was using the same one here, where this work appears in the same (fifth) volume

with the verses in 3012, 3013, and 3014. Further confirmation is supplied from his copying the misprint *dittamente* for *drittamente* in line 6
of the entry (Gatti v 58). See also 3013n, 3014n.

In the first of his quotations STC has paraphrased the beginning of
the first sentence, which in the original reads: "ma perchè (se ben ci
ricordiamo) già è provato, che le cose somme sono degne de le somme,
e questo stile, che chiamiamo tragico, pare essere il sommo de i stili;
però quelle cose che avemo già distinte, doversi sommamente cantare,
sono da essere in questo solo stil cantate; cioè la Salute", etc.

Worthy of the highest style are the highest things, such as Safety, Love, and
Virtue, and those other things, our conceptions of which arise from these;
provided that they be not degraded by any accident.

Let everyone therefore beware and discern what we say; and when he
purposes to sing of these three subjects simply, or of those things which
directly and simply follow after them, let him first drink of Helicon, and
then, after adjusting the strings, boldly take up his *plectrum* and begin to
ply it. But it is in the exercise of the needful caution and discernment that the
real difficulty lies; for this can never be attained to without strenuous efforts
of genius, constant practice in the art, and the habit of the sciences. And it is
those so equipped whom the poet in the sixth book of the *Aeneid* describes as
beloved of God, raised by glowing virtue to the sky, and sons of the Gods,
though he is speaking figuratively. And therefore let those who, innocent of
art and science, and trusting to genius alone, rush forward to sing of the
highest subjects in the highest style, confess their folly and cease from such
presumption; and if in their natural sluggishness they are but geese, let them
abstain from imitating the eagle soaring to the stars.

As for the lines of an even number of syllables, we use them but rarely,
because of their rudeness; for they retain the nature of their numbers, which
are subject to the odd numbers as matter to form.—*De vulgari eloquentia*
Bk II Chap IV tr A. G. Ferrers Howell *Latin Works of Dante* (1904).

And because, if we remember rightly, it has already been proved that the
highest things are worthy of the highest, and because the style which we call
tragic appears to be the highest style, those things which we have distinguished as being worthy of the highest song are to be sung in that style
alone, namely, Safety, etc.—Ibid Bk II Chap V.

3012 24.5   These are from Dante's *Opere* (Gatti 1793) v 158, 162,
where they are similarly numbered; see 3014n. (A copy not marked
as STC's appeared in the *Green SC* 187.) The first of these, like the
poems in 3017 and 3018, is not by Dante, but was associated with
him in the Giuntina edition of *Sonetti e canzoni di diversi antichi autori*

Toscani (Giunta Florence 1527) and in some subsequent collections and editions of Dante.

III

This lady, who with thought clouds all my ways,
Bears on her countenance the power of Love,
Which wakens in the chambers of the heart
The generous spirit that lay there concealed.
So fearful hath she made me, since I saw
Within her eyes my sweet and sovereign lord,
Enthroned in all the glory of his might,
That I approach, yet tremble to regard her.
And if perchance upon those eyes I gaze,
The place I then discern where safety lies;
But want intelligence that place to reach.
Then all my faculties are so subdued,
That the consenting soul, which moves my sighs,
Prepares itself to part from her for ever.

XI

Into thy hands, sweet lady of my soul,
The spirit which is dying I commend;
In grief so sad it takes its leave, that Love
Views it with pity while dismissing it.
By thee to his dominion it was chained
So firmly, that no power it hath retained
To call him aught except its sovereign lord;
For whatsoe'er thou wilt, thy will is mine.
I know that every wrong displeaseth thee;
Therefore stern Death, whom I have never served,
Enters my heart with far more bitterness:
O noble lady, then, whilst life remains,
That I may die in peace, my mind consoled,
Vouchsafe to be less dear unto these eyes.

—*The Canzoniere of Dante Alighieri, including the Poems of the Vita Nuova and Convito: Italian and English* tr Charles Lyell, Esq., of Kinnordy, North Britain (1840).

3013 24.6   This also comes from *De vulgari eloquentia* (Gatti 1793) v 66. Coleridge borrows his two polysyllabic words from Bk II Chap 7 and invents a sentence (beginning with an elaborate fourteenth-century periphrasis for a simple conjunction) in which they might be used. His own translation follows.

The couplet, from Dante's Canzone "Doglia mi reca . . ." (Gatti v 192), reads:

> Man from himself hath virtue far removed;
> Not man, indeed, but beast resembling man.

—Tr Charles Lyell op cit 3012n.

3014 24.7 In *AP* 293, where EHC gave the introductory sentences here (and the note of 1819 below), but did not quote the Italian stanzas, he questions the 1806 date. It must be said that it looks distinctly strange, written with a dry pen, with the unusual "A.D." before it, though it is not crowded in in such a way as to justify assuming it a later insertion.

At the end of this entry Coleridge wrote some years later, "2 Sept. 1819. Ramsgate. I *begin* to understand the above poem: after an interval from 1805, during which no year passed in which I did not reperuse, I might say construe, *parse*, and spell it, 12 times at least, such a fascination had it, spite of its obscurity! A good instance, by the bye, of that soul of *universal* significance in a true poet's compositions in addition to the specific meaning. S.T.C.

"P.S. After the 4 first lines the Hand writing is that of my old, dear, and honored Friend, Mr. Wade of Bristol."

The year 1807, which EHC suggests instead of 1806, is a more likely time for Josiah Wade of Bristol to be copying into Coleridge's notebook, though of course we do not know that Wade was *not* in London in 1806. But Coleridge stayed with Wade *c* May 1807; see 3062n, and 3060 which proves a May visit to Bristol. From *CL* # 649 it appears Coleridge left London for Bristol early in May. In April he had given his brother Wade's address (*CL* # 642), and in March Mrs Coleridge had left Keswick to join him in Bristol. When or how the arrangement for him to stay with Wade was made we do not know. Between the May visit in Bristol and the October–November one with the Morgans Coleridge was mostly with Poole at Nether Stowey, but numerous trips could have been made to Bristol from there. The date of these entries is therefore very uncertain, but *c* May 1807 appears likely. See also 3041n.

The page reference identifies Coleridge's (or Wade's?) edition as a scarce one (not in the BM, Bodleian or Cambridge University libraries): *Opere di Dante Alighieri* col comento del M. R. P. Pompeo Venturi della Compagnia di Gesù (5 vols Gatti Venice 1793).

Three ladies have retreated to my heart,
And on its threshold sit,
For Love sits there within,
Who in his sovereignty commands my life.
Great is their beauty, nor their virtue less;
But he, the mighty lord,
Whose seat is in my heart,
Scarce condescends to speak or think of them.
Each spiritless and mournful seems,
Like banished wanderer weary of the way,
Whom all the world forsakes,
And nobleness and virtue nought avail.
In days of old they were
(If we may trust their speech) mankind's delight,
But now by all are hated and are shunned.
These ladies, thus forlorn,
Are come as to the mansion of a friend;
For well they know that he I have named dwells there.
In many a piteous note one vents her grief,
Her head reposes on her hand,
Like rose divided from the stem;
Her naked arm the pillar is of woe,
And feels the watery gem the eye lets fall;
The other hand conceals
A face distorted by tears;
Unshod, unzoned, lady in look alone.
Soon as Love's eye through tattered gown espied
Some lineaments which it were wrong to name,
Wicked and yet compassionate,
He questions asked of her and of her sorrows.
O thou who bounteous art to few,
She said in voice oft broken by her sighs,
The claim of kindred sends us here to thee.
I, who in sorrow suffer most,
Am Rectitude, the sister of thy mother;
My poverty these robes and zone declare.
When thus her name and state were full disclosed,
My sovereign felt abashed
With grief and shame, and begged
To know who might her two companions be:
And she, whose sorrow was so rife in tears,
No longer heard his words,
Than, fired with greater grief,
She said: Now weep'st thou not who seest these eyes?

Then added: As thou well must know, the Nile,
Springing from fountain, flows a gentle stream,
In land where heaven's great light
Plunders the earth of every leafy plant:
Beside that virgin wave,
Her I brought forth who sits here at my side,
And with her golden tresses dries herself:
She, my fair offspring,
Herself admiring in the fountain pure,
That other, who more distant sits, brought forth.
Love paused awhile, his speech repressed by sighs;
And then, with eyes suffused,
Which late so playful were,
His relatives disconsolate saluted:
Next from the quiver took of darts each kind,
And said: Look up, be cheerful;
Behold the arms I need;
Now dull you see with rust, through want of use.
Beauty and Temperance and the daughters fair,
Allied to us by blood, in beggary stray:
But though we note the ill,
No eye should weep, nor tongue lament, but man's,
On whom the mischief lights,
And whom the beam of bounteous heaven might bless;
Not we, who heirs of the eternal city are;
For though sore wounded now,
Yet still shall we endure, and yet shall find
A race, through whom this dart shall shine again.
I then, who hear the strain divine, and mark
The consolation and the grief
Of exiles great as these,
Henceforth my banishment an honour deem:
And though a judgement, or the force of fate,
Decree this fickle world shall change
The flowers white to black,
To fall among the good is worthy praise:
And if the beauteous star which guides these eyes
Were not by distance taken from my view,
When by its beams inflamed,
Light should I count each burden I endure:
But so the fire within
Each bone and vital organ hath consumed,
That Death upon my breast hath placed the key.
Should fault then have been mine,

Months hath the sun revolved since 't was redeemed;
If guilt expire when man sincere repents.
My Song, forbid that man should touch thy robes,
Or dare to spy what beauteous dame conceals:
Suffice the features now exposed;
To all refuse the sweet and envied fruit
For which each hand is stretched;
And should it ever happen that thou find
A friend of virtue, and he thee entreat,
Array thyself in colours new;
Then show thyself to him, and cause
The flower whose outward beauty is so fair
To be desired by each amorous heart.
—Tr Charles Lyell op cit 3012n.

3015 24.9   Coleridge's edition of Machiavelli's *The Prince* has
not been traced. The references from Chaps 3–22 suggest a substantial
reading of a text, not a quotation from a secondary source. The last
paragraph is quoted in *SM* 15n.

It is truly very natural and common to desire to gain; and when men do it
who are strong enough to succeed, they will always be praised and not
blamed; but when they do not have power and all the same set out to gain
territory, that is an error and worthy of blame. [Chap 3.]

And if someone says that the King yielded in order to avoid a war, I answer
by repeating what I have already said, that one should not let a disorder
take its course in order to avoid a war, because it is not avoided, but deferred
to your disadvantage. [Chap 3.]

A prince needs only to conquer and to maintain his position. The means
he has used will always be judged honorable and will be praised by everybody,
because the crowd is always caught by appearance and by the outcome of
events, and the crowd is all there is in the world. [Chap 18.]

There are three types of brain. One understands things for itself. The
second discerns what others understand. The third neither understands for
itself nor appreciates others. [Chap 22.]—Niccolò Machiavelli *The Prince and
Other Works* tr Alan H. Gilbert (Chicago 1941) 102, 103, 150, 168.

3016 24.10   A source has not been found.

3017 24.11   The words in cipher (at the top of *f7ᵛ* and *f8* opposite)
appear to contrast Coleridge's feelings with those of the Italian poet;
on Italian love-poems see 2062 and on the projected work, *Soother of
Absence,* 1225n, 1541n, and *CN* II Index I.

The first passage in cipher reads:

> In the Soother of Absence introduce
> love singing the ordinary song of
> desire from beauty as for instance
> th[a]t of Dante:

The verses are the first seventeen lines of the spurious Canzone xv from the *Rime* of Dante *Opere* (Gatti 1793) v 198.

In line 8 the misprint *solesca* for *sol esca* appears in the original text from which Coleridge was copying. The italicizing of line 12 is his own.

> Those curled and flaxen tresses I admire,
> Of which with strings of pearls and scattered flowers,
> Hath Love contrived a net for me his prey,
> To take me; and I find the lure succeed.
> And chief, those beauteous eyes attract my gaze,
> Which pass through mine and penetrate the heart,
> With rays so animating and so bright,
> That from the sun itself they seem to flow.
> Virtue still growing is in them displayed;
> Hence I, who contemplate their charms so rare,
> Thus commune with myself amid my sighs:
> Alas, why cannot I be placed
> Alone, unseen, with her where I would wish?
> So that with those fair tresses I might play,
> And separate them wave by wave;
> And of her beauteous eyes, which shine supreme,
> Might form two mirrors for delight of mine.

—Tr Charles Lyell op cit 3012n.

The second cipher passage reads:

> & then to describe myself unaffected
> uninfluenced t[i]ll the soul within through
> the face & form declares a primary
> sympathy

3018 24.12   At the top of *f9* the vowels of the cipher system are repeated, written there before Wade (whose hand appears again here from line 3 onwards) began to transcribe. These spurious poems are attributed to Dante in the *Opere* (Gatti 1793), where they appear in Vol v 202–3:

XVII

Since in these evil days
In expectation of still worse I live,
I know not how I can
Find consolation ever, if from God
Succour relieve me not
Through death, for which I earnestly entreat.
The wretched such as I
He ever scorns, as now I see and prove.
Of her who is the cause I'll not complain;
For peace I shall expect
From her the moment when life's warfare ends;
Because, alas! I hope
To serve her by my death,
Whom living I but injure and displease.
O would that I through Love
Had fallen dead the instant that I saw her!
Then censure of the wrong
Had honour brought to both, to her and me:
So is my life disgraced
Because I do not die, and such my shame,
That greater pain I feel than from the grief
By which from loving many I deter:
For love is one thing, Fortune is another,
Which nature overrules,
The one by habit, the other by its force,
And me they both enthral;
Whence, as a lesser ill,
I nature's will oppose and wish to die.
This fierce desire of mine
Prompts with such violence, that many times,
The power of another to promote,
Death to my heart it willingly would give;
But pity for my soul,
Alas! lest it should perish, nor to God
Return the same it was,
Lest it not die, but heavily it mourns.
Not that I deem it possible to hold
My purpose to the end,
So that desire through excess may not
Call for compassion new:
Then shall perhaps some pity show
My sovereign, who my wretched state beholds.
My Song, thy company I shall retain,

That I may weep with thee;
For I have no safe refuge where to go:
My sufferings are the sport
Of every one and joy.
Stay, for thou shalt not any one offend.

Note: the last line but one of the Italian should read: "Ciaschedun altro ha gioia", according to the edition used by Lyell (op cit 3012n), and so he has translated it; Coleridge's Gatti 1793 text reads: "A ciascun' altra gioja", which might be translated: "To every other joy", or, if *altra* is a misprint for *altro*, "a joy to every one else".

3019 24.13   In Coleridge's own hand again. The cipher at the beginning (used for practice? or to mislead?) suggests that some translations from Italian may have been intended for the two volumes for Longman (2880n). It reads:

> The 2 following sonnets we
> insert for their singularity.

The sonnets are Dante's: *Opere* (Gatti 1793) v 168; see 3014n.

A noble troop of ladies met my view
On All Saints' feast, just past the other day;
And one preeminent advanced as chief,
And at her right hand Love she led along.
She darted from her brilliant eyes a light
Which seemed a glorious spirit all of fire:
Emboldened, on her countenance I gazed,
And there depicted saw an angel form.
Then calmly and benign her eyes she turned
On all who worthy were, and health conferred,
And each with virtuous inspirations filled.
Of heavenly birth I deem this sovereign maid,
And come for our salvation to the earth:
Then blessed is the soul that near her dwells.

One day came Melancholy to my cell,
And said, With you I wish to abide awhile;
Methought too that she seemed to lead with her
Sorrow and Hate, to bear her company.
Instant I cried to her, Avaunt! begone!
And she, like subtle Greek, made smooth reply;
Then, while she leisurely conversed with me,
I looked, and Love I saw advance towards us.

Full strangely was he clad in weeds of black,
And on his head a curious hat he wore,
And certainly in right good earnest wept.
Poor little rogue, I said, what ails thee now?
He answered me: I pensive am and sad,
For, sweet my brother, our loved lady dies.
—Tr Charles Lyell op cit 3012n.

3020 11.78   Henry Home, Lord Kames (1696–1782), in the first of his *Sketches of the History of Man* (1774) propounds a doctrine of "Diversity of Men and Languages", arguing from the evidence of the rest of the animal creation, climate, languages, etc "that were all men of one species, there could never have existed, without a miracle, different kinds such as exist at present." (Dublin 4 vols 1775) I 34.
   ad internecionem: to extermination.

3022 11.80   *anthropotheist:* not in *OED;* one who makes man his God.
   theanthropist: The *OED* cites Coleridge as the originator of the expression (*LR* I 394); it defines theanthropism as "The doctrine of the union of the divine and human natures, or of the manifestation of God as man, in Christ."
   miranda . . . labuit . . . grandchildren: "[to whom] marvels immediately turn into miracles, and everything unknown into marvels/ The region of expanded ignorance spread to the size of Terra incognita [as it was] to Noah's grandchildren".
   In a letter to George Fricker of [4 Oct 1806] Coleridge clearly stated his general position on miracles. "I only say, the miracles are extra essential; I by no means deny their importance, much less hold them useless, or superfluous. Even as Christ did, so would I teach; that is, build the miracle on the faith, not the faith on the miracle." *CL* # 631. A similar statement appears in a marginal note on Edward Stillingfleet *Origines sacrae* (*C 17th C* 376), and there are several discussions of the subject throughout Coleridge's works, all critical of mystery-mongering. See e.g. 3132 and 3137 below, and *Friend* III 104–8. In a postscript to *CL* # 1093 he gives an interesting definition of the term *miracle.*

3023 11.81   In ink. *AP* 173.

3024 11.82   Noted as an example of an Irish bull?

3025 11.83   In ink. A self-portrait, part of a Coleorton conversa-
tion-piece?

3026 11.84   In ink. *Duty as Inclination:* The thesis has been developing at least since entries 1705, 1710–1711, and was naturally
brought into conflict with Wordsworth's *Ode to Duty;* see 2091, 2531,
2556 and notes.
   The further struggle here, to describe his own consciousness of his
need to feel himself as real, and to be reassured of his own identity by
means of objects, including love-objects and symbols, as well as providing an addition to the argument in the debate with Wordsworth
referred to above provides a piece of self-analysis perhaps unmatched
for acuity in the period.
   hic est, ille non est: "this exists, that does not exist".

3027 11.85   In ink. At the end of the entry in Mrs Gillman's hand,
"Alas! Alas!" is written.

3028 11.86   In 1806 the city guides show this firm of chemists at
7 Poultry (a continuation of Cheapside).

3029 11.87   In another hand, in ink. It may be the hand of Mr
Pipers (or Piper) himself. The page and most of the page facing were
blank. Directories do not throw any light on this entry.

3030 11.88   In ink.
   The two sentences from Gregory Nazianzen read: "Whatever I
actually am, this I remain—maligned and admired." "My tragedy
is comedy to my enemies."
   And from Tertullian *Of the Body of Christ:* "There is a danger that
everything, through misnaming, will be misunderstood."

3031 11.89   In ink.
   The *De nugis curialium* of Walter Map existed, in Coleridge's day,
only in one MS in the Bodleian Library; it was first transcribed in
1850. The preface to the modern edition of M. R. James (Oxford 1914)
makes it clear that Coleridge must be using some learned writer who
worked from the MS; Camden, Archbishop Ussher, Thomas Tanner,
Anthony à Wood, all refer to it.
   According to the M. R. James text, Coleridge's reference is wrong,

and should be to Bk I Chap 22 (not 12) lines 29-30; his text reads *quod* for Coleridge's *quae*.

The story itself tells of how Reginald Fitz Jocelin, son of Jocelin de Bohun, bishop of Salisbury from 1141-84, was consecrated bishop of Bath 23 June 1174. To quote James's translation: "Jocelin, bishop of Sarum, made this answer to his son, Reginald of Bath, who had been elected by violence to the See, but was refused consecration by Canterbury, and was complaining: 'Fool, be off quick to the Pope, bold, without a flinch. Give him a good smack with a heavy purse, and he will tumble which way you like.' He went: one smote; the other tumbled. Down fell the Pope, up rose the bishop, and straightway wrote a lie to God at the head of every one of his briefs; for where there should have stood 'by the Grace of the Purse,' he said 'by the Grace of God.'" Coleridge's quotation comes from the beginning of the next paragraph.

But yet may our lady and mother Rome be a stick in the water that seems broken, and may we not have to believe what we see!—Tr M. R. James issued by the Honourable Society of Cymmrodorion (1923).

The story of the ecclesiastics runs true to a type; what is of special interest in Coleridge's excerpt from it is his eye for the metaphorical quality of the bent-stick image, perhaps even a personal preoccupation with it, as indicated by 1473 and discussed in 1473n.

3032 11.90   In ink. Source not traced. Cf *BL* Chap XII (I 202).
a principiis speciei . . . a principiis individui: "derive from the species . . . derive from the individual".

3033 11.91   In ink. From the Vulgate: Ecclus. 14:5.

A man who is worthless to himself—to whom is he good?

3034 11.92   The alternating iambic-trochaic metre, presumably with alternating rhyme, is not found in any of Coleridge's lists of metrical patterns. Did he note it down from a song?

3035 11.93   In ink.

3036 11.94   In ink.

3037 11.95   In ink.

3038 11.96   In ink.

3039 11.97   In ink. *AP* 173-4.
vollendeter Sündhaftigkeit: of consummate wickedness.

3040 19.1   The date "1807" appears on this inside cover, not in
STC's (in Mrs Gillman's?) hand. The first part of the familiar *Pac-
chiaretti* (see 371n) has been covered by a clumsy repair of the cover.

3041 19.2   In pale red (?ink). Or, can it be, his gout medicine?
In writing to the Beaumonts 1 Oct 1803 (*CL # 522*) he said that a few
lines were written with his gout medicine; the MS is in PML and
does bear some resemblance in color to this entry.
    The cipher reads:

> As usual even the epoch of a po[c]ket
> book must be marked with agitati[-]
> on Mrs Coleridge this morning
> first planted in Hartley's mind the pang
> of divided duty/& left
> me stormy and miserable.—
> The same day received the second
> letter from Sara.

Coleridge was at Josiah Wade's, Queen's Square, Bristol, where he
met Mrs Coleridge before going on to Stowey, but not, as he hoped,
to Ottery.
    Does the cipher passage mean that Mrs Coleridge objected to the
expense of a new notebook? Or to the notebooks being kept private—
hence the outbreak of cipher at this point? And this may be an additional argument for dating the Dante entries in N 24, i.e. 3011–3019,
among which are some cipher passages, at approximately this time.

3042 19.3   In red (?ink).
    The cipher reads:

> For a suppression of the menses from
> cold

3043 19.4   In red (?ink). The page was cut, removing the lower
half. See a variant of this entry in 3223.
    The cipher reads, disregarding a smooth breathing:

> Common minds = the stream/the heirs
> of fame = the larger and smaller
> [? . . . float] [?down] upon

3044 19.5   The ink is now black. This is the vowel scheme of the
cipher system; see Appendix C. He is giving variants for vowels;
the insert is lower down on the page, and overleaf at the top of the
page the vowels are repeated, this time with the first two characters
in each case reversed.

3045 19.6   It may be that the first part of this entry was cut
away with the lower half of $f1^v$.
    The cipher reads:

> Thought becomes a thing when it acts
> at once on your more [?conscious/consciousness]
> i.e. [?conscience/conscientiousness] therefore I
> dread to tell my whole & true case
> it seems to make a substantial
> reality/I want it to remain
> a thought in which I may be deceived
> whole [?wholly]

    The passage, though not clear either graphically or cryptographi-
cally, is one of Coleridge's clearest indications of self-awareness and
revulsion at his own deceptions and self-deceptions; but see also e.g.
3078.

3046 19.7   *PW* II 1002; EHC reads: *Cushat*, doubtless what is
meant, i.e. a dove. The MS, however, is clearly in accord with the demands of rhyme.

3047 19.8   The cipher reads:

> Auch du blickest vergebens nach
> mir. Noch schlagen die Herzen
> *für* einander doch, ach! anein[-]
> ander nicht mehr.

    These lines are from Goethe *Alexis und Dora* lines 13–14, which
appeared in Schiller's *Musenalmanach* (1797) 1–16. In enciphering
Coleridge has omitted *nun* after *ach!*, and he has not preserved the
lineation.

Tr: And your gaze, too, follows me in vain; our hearts still beat *for* each other, but alas! not any more against each other.

3048 19.9   The line of cipher at the top of *f2ᵛ* in pointed brackets is the vowel key; Coleridge is apparently reminding himself of it. The cipher reads:

> My love blazeth in presence/
> in absence it glows with a deep
> melancholy consuming flame. The
> walls the window panes, the
> chairs the very *air* seem to sympathize
> with it!

With the substance of the entry compare a parallel statement in 1718.

3049 19.10   The cipher reads:

> I see a lovely woman & am plea[-]
> sed/then perplexed but the moment
> of love is a flash. Even so a
> *riddle* in sweet verse & beau[-]
> tiful images. Love = a riddle

On the spontaneous and inexplicable aspects of love Coleridge frequently commented; see e.g. a late fragment from MS Egerton 2801 f 106 published in *Inq Sp* §46.

3050 19.11   This is one of the *Tabulae votivae* in the *Musenalmanach* for 1797 (32). See 3131 and n.

Tr: The best form of government.
I can recognize as such only one that makes it easy for every one to think aright, but never requires that he should 'think that way.

3051 19.12   Cf the "verses trivocular" in *PW* II 985: *Jeu d'esprit* 16.

3052 19.13   The cipher reads:

> The anger with a beloved object
> mingling with a yearning
> after & anticipation of a
> deeper love from reconciliation

>   & the angry struggles of
>   the head at its own duplicity

On the contradictions and "extremes meeting" in love, cf e.g. "Jealousies the *Chills* of Fever" in 2055.

3053 19.14   The cipher reads:

>   Hanging downward his unpropped
>   head yet still with an eye that
>   looked dimly onward as not
>   down in despair but seeing nothing
>   yet gazing aided the action of
>   thought, half-objectless, by an object[-]
>   less action of vision—
>   His lax hand watching at his
>   languid heart

The last line does not appear in any of Coleridge's poems; possibly it is to be linked with the embryonic poem in 3056.

3054 19.15   The cipher reads:

>   Love a grief that marred all
>   joy & made the grief of all
>   other grief/yet could be purchased
>   to no other bliss.

3055 19.16   The cipher reads:

>   Influence of images unconnected
>   inward belief in exciting
>   anger or jealousy in lovers

3056 19.17   The cipher reads (italics used for words not in cipher):

>   *Who* fain would wish yet *cannot*
>   wish to die *Because he* yearns & cannot choose
>   but yearn *And ever frets and feeds his own* d[e]sp[ai]r
>   with the deep yearnings of his stricken
>   heart.

This entry was not as it stands used in a poem, but many of the phrases appear in conjunction in a fragment associated with *The Pang more Sharp than All*, a poem which EHC says belongs to *c* 1826. Cf e.g. "To live and yearn and languish incomplete/. . . A Blank my Heart, and Hope is dead and buried,/Yet the deep yearning will not die; but Love/Clings on . . .". *PW* I 457n. With this fragment 3075 is also closely associated; and cf metrically the last line of 3053 with the last line of this entry. If *The Pang more Sharp* is correctly dated as late as EHC suggests, in 1826, it was germinating a very long time.

3057 12.1   Below the words on the inside front cover of N 12 is written "a/t   3/6" in some other hand. If this was the stationer's price of this small pocketbook, it was high enough. The other figures are a rough working out of the multiplication at the foot of *f11ᵛ* (3111), i.e. 363 oaks per acre at £25 for each oak would realize £9075 per acre.

3058 12.2   *Susan Ashby:* unknown to fame.

3059 12.3   Possibly related to 3111.

3060 12.4   *AP* 175; the words in square brackets, now illegible, were read or suggested by EHC. His other suggestion, that this entry, or this and other entries on p 175 of *AP*, were to be used in the Soother of Absence seems less reasonable.
  At this date Coleridge was probably staying with Wade; see 3041n and 3062n.

3061 12.5   From the *Asceticων* of Alteserra, cited in 3065. The passage runs "ait *Trithemius* Abbas de viris illustribus Ordinis sancti Benedicti cap. 8. Peperit . . . suffocavit", from Bk I Chap XIV entitled "Lapsus Monachismi, ac ejusdem variae causae & remedia" ed cit 99: Coleridge substitutes a semicolon for Tritheim's comma.

Once upon a time Religion begat Riches; but now the daughter has strangled the mother.

3062 12.6   In ink. Instructions on proof-correction symbols were close at hand, for Coleridge was either staying at or in touch with Agg's Printing Office, St Augustin's Back, Bristol, Wade's address, which he had given to George Coleridge in April. *CL* # 642.

3063 12.7   Various transliterations of Wordsworth's name in Greek (see also 3231n):

[ϝ is *digamma* = *W*]
Wordsworthe   Hordshorthe
Hourdsherthe   Axiologos
Epaxios Wiliamos
Willelmos

3064 12.8   *AP* 175. This is the first explicit statement of his awareness of colour relationships, that colours change one another.

3065 12.9   From Bk 1 Chap xiv of Antonio Dadino Alteserra *Asceticωv sive originum rei monasticae* ed Christ. Frid. Glück (Halle 1782); see also 3061. Coleridge quotes with variations that are minor except the omission after *Franciscanæ* of the words "cujus unum propositum fuit humilitatis & paupertatis Evangelicae studium" and the substitution in the second sentence of *suos* for *nos*.

But the peculiar harm done by the Franciscan Order was in treating the study of letters as though it were hostile to the calling of the Order. Francis wanted us to pray rather than to read. He sensed some danger to the Order when he heard that a school of letters had been founded at Bologna by John, Priest General of the Order: and so he uttered a curse upon him, and refused to remit the curse even when John besought him with his dying breath, declaring that it was of heavenly origin, and that he would rather have his brothers pray than read.

3066 12.10   There are reminiscences here, perhaps deliberate adaptation, of Virgil *Georgics* 1 201: "Non aliter, quam qui adverso vix flumina lembum/Remigiis subigit, si brachia forte remisit,/Atque illum in praeceps prono rapit alveus amni."
    Coleridge's words read:

Like one who drives a boat against an adverse current, if he relax for an instant at the oars, begins quickly to give way to the stream—So I feel the ground lost in the slightest relaxation [of effort]—alas! how great a loss.

3067 19.18   Late in life, Coleridge made one of his finest personal statements on the importance of Hope. It is part of a note on the blank last page of a pamphlet by John James Park, *Conservative Reform. A Letter addressed to Sir William Betham* (1832). After discussing the first two offices of friendship—first, compassionate understanding, and, second, candour—he adds: "Thirdly, and the holiest office of Friendship. *Hope* even against Hope for the sustentation of Hope in our poor self-condemning Friend. O try to save him from despairing of himself. In the Duck-and-Drake projection across the Stream of Error and Misery let the Friend be as the elastic force of the Water, giving a new bound to the Stone, & preventing its touch of the stream from being its submersion.—O how much can Hope & the Infusion of Hope from a kind Friend effect for a right principled Soul, groaning under the sense even more bitterly than under the consequences of its error & frailty. My Disease is—Impatient Cowardice of Pain & the desperation of outwearied Hope. S. T. Coleridge."

The word *Hope*, frequently with a capital letter, appears 223 times in *C Concordance*.

3068 19.19   The entry is again in the red ink; the leaf following it, also written on in red, has been cut out. The cipher reads in Italian:

E'l mio speme la giu e mia gioia Sara

A pun is suggested by the word order:

My hope and my joy on earth is Sara

or,   she is my hope on earth and she will be my joy.

3069 19.20   The entry begins in mid-sentence because of the excision of the leaf preceding. It is in red-brown ink.

3070 19.21   In red ink almost to the bottom of *f4;* with the words *greater progress* black ink begins, a rather pale black. Was it at this point Coleridge irritated Poole by demanding ink? See 3094.

supervivance: clearly the reading, not *supervivence*, possibly by false analogy with *survival?*

Supersto and *supervivo* may both be translated "I survive", but they are not quite synonyms. *Supersto = superstites esse; supervivo = supersum.*

Genius with the inverted Torch: The ancient death-symbol is here contrasted aesthetically with the death's-head, as the ancient cremation rites are compared, also favourably, with contemporary funerals. In other words, in spite of the modern emphasis on survival of the body as well as the soul, and the difficulties in obtaining bodies for dissection, the science of anatomy, *mirabile dictu*, progresses. Is there an association here with Schiller *Der Genius mit der umgekehrten Fackel?* (*Musenalmanach* 1797) 87.

3071 19.22   That Coleridge annotated Thomas Poole's copy of
the *Transactions* abridged by Hutton, Shaw, and Pearson (1792–1809)
is known from a miscellaneous Sotheby sale catalogue of 18 Dec 1908,
when a set was sold to Dobell for a guinea and has not since then been
recorded. A note in the catalogue reads: "This interesting copy was
formerly in the library of Thos. Poole of Nether-Stowey a friend of
Coleridge, the latter having been given unlimited access to the library
of its owner. Several of the volumes contain profuse pencil notes, in
the margins, in the handwriting of Coleridge dating from 1796 onwards until his leaving the village." The 1796 date is perhaps dubious,
but the statement is generally true and corroborative of the dating of
much of this notebook during the 1807 visit to Poole.
      Coleridge transcribes verbatim from the *Abridgement*. The italics
are his.
      Liber Vetus . . . et inutilis: "an old book . . . and unusable".
      liber novus . . . &c: "a new book . . . clean, elegantly written,
and easy to read, &c".

3072 19.23   *Phil Trans (Abr)* v 294–5n; Coleridge has misread a
small unclear 5 as a 3.
      He was reading "Observations of the Solar Eclipse, May 1–12,
1706, at the Royal Observatory at Greenwich, &c.", by the Rev
Mr John Flamsteed, in which Abraham Sharp is referred to and
commented on in the footnote that Coleridge took to heart in this
entry to an extent that makes it seem worth quoting extensively:
"Mr. Sharp, by private study, became an eminent astronomer, mathematician, and mechanist. He was descended of an ancient family at
Little Horton, near Bradford, Yorkshire, where he was born in 1651
or 1652, and where he died in 1742 in the 91st year of his age. Becoming very early acquainted with Mr. Flamsteed, and being an exceed-
ingly accurate engraver and ingenious operator with all kinds of
tools, he remained a considerable time with him, to assist in con-
triving, adapting, and fitting up the astronomical apparatus in the
Royal Observatory at Greenwich . . . where with his own hands, he
constructed, divided, and set up the large brass mural quadrant of
$79\frac{1}{2}$ or 80 inches radius. With this instrument he continued sometime
in making these various astronomical observations, and assisting
Mr. F. in settling the places and catalogue of 3,000 fixed stars. But
the fatigue of continually making such observations at night, and in a
cold thin air, impaired his constitution, which was naturally delicate;

so that he was obliged to quit this favourite situation, and retire to his family estate at Little Bradford, worth about 200£. a year, and which had devolved on him. Here he resided the rest of a long life, spent in close study and calculations, and ingenious mechanical devices. Here he furnished an observatory with instruments of his own construction entirely, as telescopes, quadrants, &c. and these of the very best kinds; here he filled a workshop with delicate tools of his own making, for various mechanical operations, as those of joiners, clockmakers, turners, opticians, mathematical instrument makers, &c. In this retreat also it was that he still continued to assist Mr. Flamsteed. . . . Here also he kept up a correspondence with the principal mathematicians in and about London; as Newton, Halley, Wallis, Hodgson, Sherwin, &c. to whom he was the common resource in many nice and troublesome calculations. Though Mr. Sharp wrote and calculated so much for others, he published but little himself . . .". The indications of Coleridge's wishful thoughts, about working (a) privately, (b) with the hands as well as the head, (c) for another older person or persons, (d) at cataloguing the heavens and especially the *fixed* stars, (e) successfully against ill-health, and (f) in the haven of the old family estate—all suggest that the attraction, as hinted in the entry, went deep.

3073 19.24   The precise Greek-Latin version of the Sibylline oracles being quoted has not been found; possibly Coleridge was noting a quotation from the oracles by another.

Samos shall become a desert, Delos unknown, and Rome a hamlet.

The three-fold pun passes away in both Latin and English.

3074 19.25   As Coleridge was certainly reading in Vol v of the *Phil Trans (Abr)* about this time (see 3071–3072), one must notice, without necessarily drawing any firm inferences about his use of it here, an article on pp 681–4 entitled "Observations on the Subterraneous Trees in Dagenham, and other marshes, bordering on the River Thames, in the County of Essex" by the Rev Mr W. Derham. Coleridge admired Derham's work, and might have been attracted by his vivid account of a submerged forest, where the trees lay thick "upon or near each other;" some "remaining in the very same posture in which they grew, with their roots running some down, some branching and spreading about in the earth, as trees growing in the earth commonly do".

3075 19.26   This entry follows four dated with certainty post-1809; those were written presumably on a blank page and a half, for it appears that entries 3075–3186 inclusively were probably 1807 entries. See e.g. 3078, which was necessarily written before Dec 1808 yet after this entry. See also 3079n.

Many phrases here are to be found in *The Pang more Sharp than All: PW* 1 457; see 3056n.

3076 19.27   Untraced.

3077 19.28   Untraced.

3078 19.29   *Dr B.*: probably Dr Thomas Beddoes, long a friend, whose death in Dec 1808, Coleridge said, took "more hope out of my Life than any former Event". *CL* # 743.

If "Dr B." is Dr Beddoes, about which there is little doubt, this entry is datable before Dec 1808, and, from its position in the note-book, after 3075. And 1807–8 was a period when Coleridge's serious physical apprehensions led him, after Beddoes's death, to lay his case before Dr Daniel.

The repetition of A̲s̲r̲a̲, A̲s̲r̲a̲ in cipher at the end of the entry is also confirmation of the likelihood of an 1807 date; 1807 was the period when the cipher was chiefly used.

Mrs Gillman wrote at the foot of this entry, "How very affecting —nay heart rending!"

3079 19.30   This is from Sir Walter Ralegh *History of the World* (1677), the Preface. That this was the edition Coleridge was using is proved by the lines in 3087. See 3087n.

Ralegh translates the quotation from Casaubon: "A day, an houre, a moment is enough to over turne the things, that seemed to have beene founded and rooted in Adamant." Preface B₂ᵛ.

On the same page Ralegh says: "Of whom [Henry VI] it *may truly be said which a counsellor of his own spake* to Henry *the third* of France, Qu' il estoit . . . temps: that he [sic] was a very gentle Prince; but his Reigne happened in a verie unfortunate Season."

3080 19.31   Ibid Preface C₂.

3081 19.32   Ibid Preface C₂ᵛ–C₃, with numerous interesting additions as indicated in the text by the use of bold type. There are also
minor changes in spelling, capitalization, and wording; a few other
significant additions and variations in phrasing are worth noting.
f7 For Coleridge's *sheep*, Ralegh reads *negligent.*
f7ᵛ For Coleridge's *let the Politician . . . faith*, Ralegh reads *the
Politicians all gross that cannot merchandize their faith.*
    For Coleridge's *and exact vengeance*, Ralegh reads *and pay us to the
uttermost for all the pleasing passages of our lives past.*
f8ᵛ For Coleridge's *as to delivering the oppressed, how can I confess
myself to have been unjust?*, Ralegh reads *and confess myself to have
been unjust . . . if I deliver the oppressed.*
    For Coleridge's *Hopers*, Ralegh reads *wise wordlings.*
    For Coleridge's *devotees*, Ralegh reads *devout lovers.*
f9 For Coleridge's *transient*, Ralegh reads *dureless.*
    For Coleridge's *Rivals*, Ralegh reads *opposites.*
    For Coleridge's inserted *like clouds . . . shadows*, Ralegh has *beat
but upon shadows.*
    For Coleridge's *blind valor* Ralegh reads *Giant-like.*
    For Coleridge's *Judgment of the Omnipotent* Ralegh reads *terrible
judgements of the All-Powerful God.*

3082 19.33   Ibid Preface C₃: "So, as whosoever he be, to whom
Fortune hath been a servant, and the Time a friend; let him but take
the accompt of his memory . . . and truly examine what he hath
reserved; either of Beauty and Youth, or fore-gone delights; what it
hath saved, that it might last, of his dearest affections, or of whatever
else the amorous Spring-time gave his thoughts of contentment, then
invaluable . . .".

3083 19.34   Ibid 2: Bk 1 Chap 11 §1: "For, Truth (saith S. Am-
brose) by whomsoever uttered, is of the Holy Ghost; Veritas, . . .
Sancto est: and lastly, let those kind of men learne this rule; Quae
. . . non sunt; Nothing is prophane, that serveth to the use of Holy
Things." These quotations are used in MS Egerton 2801 f 3.

3084 19.35   Ibid Preface C₃ᵛ with variation and addition; Ralegh
reads: "But for my self, I shall never be perswaded, that God hath

shut up all the light of Learning within the lanthorn of *Aristotle's* brains."

3085 19.36   Ibid Preface D₂ᵛ. The word *Travels* perhaps refers not to Ralegh's but to Coleridge's "Travels", still a projected work. Ralegh in closing his Preface says, "It will be said by many, That I might have been more pleasing to the Reader, if I had written the Story of mine own Times. . . . To this I answer, That whoever in writing a modern History, shall follow Truth too near the heels, it may haply strike out his Teeth." This was used variatim in *TT* 7 June 1830.

3086 19.37   Ibid Preface D₂ᵛ. "Seneca hath said it, and so do I . . . and to the same effect, Epicurus, Hoc . . . tibi."

3087 19.38   Ibid ("The Life of Sir Walter Raleigh") 54.
    This entry establishes beyond doubt that Coleridge's edition, or the one he was reading, was the 1677 edition, which contains these verses by John Shirley omitted in other editions.

3088 19.39   The first phrase appears to be Coleridge's summary of Ralegh Bk 1 Chap 1 §1: "by this visible World is God perceived of Men. . . . The World universall, is nothing else but God exprest" (p 2). The Latin phrase comes from ibid 3: Bk 1 Chap 1 §4: "Fecisti mundum (saith S. Augustine) de materia informi; quam fecisti de nulla re, pene nullam rem: That is, thou hast made the World of a Matter without Form; which matter thou madest of Nothing, & being made, it was little other than Nothing."

3089 19.40   An echo from Ralegh also? Cf ibid 7: Bk 1 Chap 1 §13: "Memory of the Past, Knowledge of the Present, & Care of the Future: and we ourselves account such a Man for provident, as, re-membering things past, and observing things present, can by judg-ment . . . provide for the future."

3090 19.41   Ibid 8: Bk 1 Chap 1 §14: "I will answer with *Gregory*, who saith, Qui in factis Dei rationem non videt, infirmitatem suam considerans, cur non videat, rationem videt; He that seeth no reason in the Actions of God, by consideration of his own infirmity per-ceiveth the reason of his blindness."

idque is written with what appears to be rather an accidental jab of the pen after the *d* than a meaningless *e* or *i*.

3091 19.42   Ibid 9: Bk I Chap I §15. Ralegh translates Ovid: "While Fury gallops on the way,/Let no Man Fury's gallop stay."

3092 19.43   Crowded at the foot of *f10*, the corrections in this entry indicate the importance to Coleridge of the precise wording. The fruit of this struggle appears e.g. in the essay "On Poesy or Art": *BL* II 253–63. On the heat of life and the light of intellect, cf 467 and 1233.

3093 19.44   The quotation marks at the beginning are not closed, no written source having been discovered; possibly they should be completed after "form". The remainder of the entry could well have its roots in Coleridge's feelings late in 1807 (e.g. about the Brent sisters?).
      The word *preattuned* is attributed in *OED*, quoting a letter of 1794, to Coleridge.

3094 19.45   This is written with the notebook reversed; it probably belongs to the period of Coleridge's domestication with Poole, May–Sept 1807.

3095 19.46   *fermenting . . . positiveness:* cf 1409 and 1410, where the image first appears, and 2196; it was used in No I of *The Friend* (1809–10) 4 and, though deleted from later editions, reappeared in *Phil Lects* 204. Among Coleridge's numerous observations on love being known not by proofs but by recognition, see e.g. *The Improvisatore: PW* I esp 464; and on its distinctness from kindred emotions, see *TT* 27 Sept 1830.

3096 19.47   Published as Coleridge's in *PW* II 1011. Actually another excerpt from Ralegh *History of the World* (1677) 22 (Bk I Chap III §3): "Of which Ovid *Eurus ad Auroram, Nabathaeq: regna recessit, Persidaque, & radiis juga subdita matutinis.*
      The East Wind with *Aurora* hath abiding
      Among th' *Arabian* and the Persian Hills.
      Whom Phoebus first salutes at his first rising."

3097 19.48   Again from Ralegh *History of the World* (1677) 107 (Bk I Chap IX §3): "But they . . . account the Times injurious and Iron."

3098 19.49   Comparison with the Migne text of St Hilary *De Trinitate* Bk VII §38 lines 6–8 suggests that Coleridge, or the author he was reading who was quoting St Hilary, omitted in the first two lines *praeter* after *alius*. The other two passages, if they come from St Hilary, have not been located. The third one, shifting syntax as it does (*duco, fecit*) and incomplete, reads rather like a Coleridgian adaptation, perhaps of St Hilary or some other.

[1] Human language has been left with no other choice than to express the things of God in the words of God.—Tr Stephen MacKenna *Saint Hilary of Poitiers: The Trinity* (Fathers of the Church, New York 1954) 266.
[2] Even what we say in behalf of religion we ought to say with great fear and restraint.
[3] Though crushed by very great afflictions of my whole body, with a doubtful hope of life, I draw my breath in misery, nevertheless my supreme and lasting judgement concerning you has somehow made me break through these tortures until I may perform this last literary service for you. Go therefore where . . . you through—

3099 19.50   Undoubtedly copied into the notebook as an example of that kind of ridiculous improbability in romances to which Coleridge had taken objection in his early reviews of them. See Garland Greever *A Wiltshire Parson and His Friends* 168–9, 185–6, 191–5.

3100 19.51   Crashaw's poem from Marino *Sospetto d' Herode* Bk I (*B Poets* IV 714–19) contains all the elements here, in the eight lines of stanza xvii; see 3102–3105 and notes. Is Coleridge enjoying an exercise in compression? Or is there a blending here of Crashaw and Ralegh op cit 3079? Cf Ralegh ed cit 23 (Bk I Chap III §3): "*All the Trees of Eden which were the Garden of God, envied him*".

3101 19.52   Source not known.

3102 19.53   From Crashaw's *Hymn to . . . Saint Teresa: B Poets* IV 720–2. (In the first line Coleridge's *meet* is a slip for *greet*.) Coleridge's notes on two sets of *B Poets* bearing in Vol IV his annotations on Crashaw are in *MC* 277–9. Later (*c* 1810) he read and annotated

(*LR* IV 65–71) Southey's copy of *The Life [and Works] of . . . St Teresa . . . Translated into English* (1675); the prefatory matter does not contain the lines quoted here.

3103 19.54   With fewer capitals and minor differences in spelling, in Crashaw *An Apology for the Precedent Hymn: B Poets* IV 722; see the previous note.

3104 19.55   Also from Crashaw, the final couplet of *On a Treatise of Charity: B Poets* IV 723.
   Malthus *Letter on the Poor Laws* appeared in April 1807, in which the aim was to discourage private and public aid to the poor, as pressure towards self-support and a check on untoward increases in population. The date of this work perhaps is additional evidence on the side of an 1807 date for this and neighbouring entries, although the remark here is one that Coleridge might have applied to Malthus at almost any time from 1803 onwards.

3105 19.56   No exact reference has been found, but perhaps it is no coincidence that in another poem by Crashaw in *B Poets* IV 730, *To the Queen, upon her numerous Progeny. A Panegyric*, the expression "sweet supernumerary star" occurs twice in a dozen lines.

3106 19.57   The last line could be a separate entry; the situation is not clear. Below this, five lines are effectively blacked out with ink.

3107 19.58   EHC printed the last eleven lines in *PW* I 486, with no indication of those preceding, which are, however, undoubtedly connected with them. Coleridge's note at the end, describing the verses as an imitation of du Bartas, was an afterthought compressed into small space after the subsequent entries, 3185 and 3186 (first part), were written.
   An imitation is strictly correct as a description of these lines; in Sylvester's manner and on a cognate theme, they are not a copy, not quite a parody, of the First Day of the First Week in *Du Bartas His Devine Weekes and Workes* tr Josuah Sylvester.
   The image of the spider-web (cf 24n and many other places), the babe at the mother's breast as a simile for his love (cf 1718 and n), and the seeing of letters of the alphabet in the sky, especially *M* and *W* as referred to later in N 18, all mark these as intensely personal

lines. See also *PW* ii 1111 for another "fount where Streams of Nectar flow", and another use of the spider-web image.

At the same time it is probable, in view of other Crashaw references, that "The Heavens one large black Letter" comes from Crashaw's lines *In the Glorious Epiphany of our Lord God, a Hymn:* "It was their weakness woo'd his beauty,/But it shall be/Their wisdom now as well as duty/T' enjoy his blot; and as a large black letter/Use to spell thy beauties better,/And make the night itself their torch to thee." *B Poets* iv 741.

3108 12.11   *AP* 175. The hayfield with the fresh-cut hay suggests July.

3109 12.12   Eight miles from Taunton and nine from Bridgwater, on the main Taunton-Bridgwater road, seems to refer to the vicinity of Aisholt, a village in the heart of the Quantocks where Coleridge's friends the Brices lived. He visited them during this summer. See *SC Memoir* i 8.

3110 12.13   *AP* 175. On Washington Allston see 2794 and n. Allston treated numerous historical subjects, and was clearly interested in their emotional aspects.

Coleridge frequently referred to the sixteenth-century astronomer Tycho Brahe, the teacher of Kepler (e.g. *Friend* iii 200, 314, and *Phil Lects* 336). His information about the voluble and oracular dwarf Seppe, or Sep, who was supposed to be endowed with second sight, was presumably general knowledge, yet one wonders whether he was back in the Bristol Library, having another look at William Coxe *Travels into Poland* (3 vols 1784–90). He may have seen it years before, or heard of it from Southey, who had the first two volumes out in Aug–Sept 1794. *Bristol Borrowings* (23) (24). The story of Sep is told in Vol iii 64–5:

"While he lived at Uranienburgh [Tycho Brahe] had a fool, whose name was Sep, who was accustomed during dinner to sit at his feet, and whom he used to feed with his own hand. This man was continually uttering incoherent expressions, which Tycho observed and noted down, from a persuasion that the mind, in a state of emotion, was capable of predicting future events; and he even believed, if any inhabitant of the island was taken ill, that this mad-man could predict whether he should live or die."

3111 12.14   There is no doubt that Coleridge found the practical information on *ff8–10* of this entry in William Nicholson *A Journal of Natural Philosophy, Chemistry & the Arts* VII (Jan 1804) 17–23, in an article entitled "Observations on the Cultivation and Growth of Oak Timber" by the Rev Richard Yates, F.R.S. Nicholson's *Journal* was comprised largely of articles condensed from many journals, scientific or pseudo-scientific, submitted by interested readers and contributors. See e.g. 3129 and n, where, as in this case, Coleridge reorganized the information as he extracted it.

At least part of Coleridge's interest in Nicholson's *Journal* came from Davy's contributions to it, and part from the fact that Nicholson had been and perhaps still was employed by the Wedgwoods. As early as 1801 Coleridge had said he was going to give up the *B Critic* and take in Nicholson's. *CL* # 401. There is, however, no sign of his use of it until this time. Vol VII he quoted later for an illustration of the difficulty of precise theories even in physics. *Friend* Sect II Essay VI (1818): III 184n.

f10ᵛ John Tomlet: This is unexplained by anything we know of the Wordsworth children. John was born in 1803, Thomas in 1806; Thomas was loved with particular affection by Coleridge. John Tomlet = John and Thomas, i.e. the only sons at this time?

f11ᵛ some amabilis insania . . . arithmetica: "some amiable madness or rather some damnable hallucination and arithmetical blindness (or diarrhoea)". See 3057 and n.

f12ᵛ Sic transit gloria Somnii: a play on a famous phrase. "So passes away the glory of the Dream."

3112 12.15   *AP* 175. Also from Nicholson's *Journal* VII (Feb 1804) 128–9, from an article "On the Cultivation of the Sun-Flower, and its Advantages". Coleridge's entry is a neat *précis* of the article.

3113 12.16   *AP* 176. We here see the author of *Christabel* pursuing through two volumes of Nicholson's *Journal* "A Memoir concerning the Fascinating Faculty which has been ascribed to the Rattle-Snake and other American Serpents" by Benjamin Smith Barton, M.D. The article begins in Vol VII (April 1804) 270–85, and refers to Bartram, Blumenbach, and other Coleridge favourites; it continues in Vol VIII (May 1804) 58–62 and (June 1804) 100–14, quoting in a footnote (VIII 108n) Horace *Epodes* I 20, which Coleridge quotes here: "He fears the gliding approach of snakes".

The article would interest Coleridge not only for the author's attempt to discredit the view that snakes fascinate by power of eye, enchantment, or some other hypnotic device, but for his attack on superstitious credulity in general, and also for an engaging personal modesty. He confesses, for instance (VIII 101), that he suffers miserably from the fact that although he knows well that the fear of snakes is irrational, "it is the only prejudice which I think I have not the strength to subdue". The writer's evident sense of "power without strength", as Coleridge described his own state, must have struck a responsive chord generally, and specifically in connexion with snakes. See e.g. *C Concordance* under *snakes*.

On the advocacy of prefixes and suffixes cf 3160.

3114 12.17   This advice is given in Nicholson's *Journal* VIII (Aug 1804) 237, in an article "On Spontaneous Inflammations" by G. C. Bartholdi, continued from the July number. Again Coleridge's entry is an achievement in condensation.

3115 12.18   The phrase has not been found in Nicholson's *Journal*, although related subjects are much discussed there. But cf: "For Discovery of Coal, they first search for the Crop". *Phil Trans (Abr)* VI 401. As Coleridge was reading and making notes on *Phil Trans (Abr)* Vols II and V in this notebook and in N 19 (and in Poole's copy), it seems altogether likely that his eye was caught by this sentence there, especially as the article in question associated outcroppings of coal with an area "near Stowy". Seeing the new word, he then asked and got the definition he wrote down here?

3116 12.19   A fairly exhaustive search in *Phil Trans*, in the original as well as the abridged edition (see 3115, 3161, 3162, 3163, and notes, and other entries of this period in N 19). has not, for all the numerous Newtonian and anti-Newtonian discussions of light and colours along these lines, uncovered the source of this entry. It seems likely to be Coleridge's own developing argument out of an abridgement entitled "Mr. Isaac Newton's Answer to some Considerations on his Doctrine of Light and Colours". In this, as admittedly in diverse places, Newton speaks of "the corporeity of light", of colours as "qualities of light without us", not "modes of sensation excited in the mind by various motions, figures, . . . making various mechanical impressions on the organ of sense", how "the rays of several colours, which are blended together in light, must be parted from one another by refraction, and so cause the phaenomena of prisms and other refracting substances"; and that the length of vibrations making red and yellow are longer than those that make blue and violet.

He also asks and answers the question in Coleridge's last sentence, "Whether the unequal refractions made without respect to any inequality of incidence, be caused by the different refrangibility of several rays; or by the splitting, breaking or dissipating the same ray into two sorts of colours?" *Phil Trans (Abr)* II 13–17. Coleridge seems in fact to be fortifying, as well as explaining for himself, Newton's argument.

3117 12.20   In ink. This passage appears as a footnote in Algernon Sidney, the work cited in 3118n, p 91. Coleridge omits from Sidney's quotation the καὶ before φασιν, writes παραδυσαντα for παραδωσονται, and omits a breathing (Sidney omits others) on the penultimate word.

This King (Theopompus), they say, on being reviled by his wife because the royal power, when he handed it over to his sons, would be less than when he received it, said: "Nay, but greater, in that it will last longer."—"Lycurgus" §7: *Plutarch's Lives* tr B. Perrin (LCL 1914).

3118 12.21   In ink. After this entry someone wrote "Done" in pencil—probably a transcriber working for Derwent Coleridge or HNC, or someone helping them.

The sentence comes from Algernon Sidney *Discourses Concerning Government* Chap II §xviii (*Works* 1772) 154, where Sidney is opposing the abolition of capital punishment. Coleridge's annotated copy of this edition of Sidney's *Works* was once in the library of G. H. B. Coleridge and is now at Indiana University. The annotations were published in *Notes Theol* 189–93; there is no further discussion there of this passage.

3119 23.6   In addition to the fact that Coleridge was an inveterate memorializer of personal occasions, there may be a supplementary reason for entries such as this in Mrs Coleridge's attitude, especially if the first guess about it in 3041n has any foundation. Mrs Coleridge set off for the Lakes "toward the end of October". *Minnow Among Tritons* 8.

3120 23.7   Possibly this in a larger than usual hand, written with care as for a title, was the first entry in the book. Entry 23.5, which probably belongs to the lecturing of May 1808, was written around this. *Religious Musings* was of course an old title with Coleridge, and what may be called *Moral Mournings* intermittently depressed his prose writings throughout his life, from the 1795 Bristol lectures to *Church and State* (1830).

3121 12.76   In ink.
Psilosophy: BL I 49n, quoted by *OED* as the earliest use of this word, which it defines as "would-be or pretended" philosophy, or "shallow" philosophy, is close to this note. Coleridge used the term frequently to distinguish mere cerebration from a full and complex appraisal of philosophical problems. In his view it usually implies a rejection of idealism in any form, and a refusal to recognize the legitimacy and importance of the imagination in the intellectual process. See 3158 and a later reference, *CL* # 1181.

Tr: Pseudo-philosopher, or rather, to speak accurately, psilosopher—
      French Psilosophy
      //German philosophy

3122 12.77   In ink. The phrase, in the accusative case suggesting a quotation, has not been precisely located, though it is reminiscent of Xenophon. The first word means a love-potion; the third word is the bird, wryneck. It was used as a love-charm by being tied, legs and wings, to the spokes of a wheel, which was revolved continuously in one direction during an incantation. In Xenophon *Memorabilia* III xi 17 Socrates says: "I assure you these things don't happen without the help of many potions and spells and magic wheels". Tr E. C. Marchant (LCL 1923). STC means something like "the potion and magic spell (or twists and turns?) of diction". It could have a reference to the preceding entry.

3123 12.78   If this is not Coleridge's, the source has not been
                traced.

3124 12.79   In ink.
tanquam gemitus Columbæ: "like the moanings of doves".

3125 12.80   In ink. The address has not proved referable to any-
                one.

3126 12.81   In ink. There are some scribbled numerals under this entry. It is a curiosity that Coleridge repeats this simple self-instruction several times in the notebooks.

3127 12.82   *Jiffle* is a seventeenth-century word for shuffle or fidget—"Now dialect". *OED.*

3128 12.83   The entry may be evidence that Coleridge had thoughts in the summer of 1807 of moving his family south. It is true it hardly coincides with his "finally resolved" separation from Mrs Coleridge. Yet when he met her in Bristol in May, for the purpose of going to Ottery to separate, officially, with the family blessing, he must scarcely have known whether he most wished to fly from her incompatibility or from the now painful insecurity with the Wordsworths and Sara Hutchinson. Southey was firmly established as the tenant of Greta Hall, and doubtless there were desperate moods on the one hand, and euphoric bursts of energy on the other, when Coleridge may have thought of setting himself up again in his native south, near Poole and Stowey, in just such a cottage in the valley of Taunton.

Another possibility is that he was scouting for a place for himself and the Morgans; we do not know exactly when his "domestication" with them was broached. See *CL # 667.*
f54ᵛ G[ood] Stables?

3129 12.84   On Coleridge's use of Nicholson's *Journal* at this period see 3111n. The interest here, however, is that the *Mem.* led him to transcribe the article in Nicholson VII 148–57: "Prognostics of the Weather, established by long, continued Observations upon the Conduct and Appearances of Birds, Beasts, Insects, Plants, Meteors, the Heavenly Bodies, Minerals, &c. Communicated by a Correspondent." Signed "(R. B.)". It is perhaps irrelevant to notice what Coleridge did not, that "R. B." was condensing Theophrastus; cf *Theophrastus on Winds and Weather Signs* ed G. J. Symons (1894).

Coleridge reorganized the material into a reordered *précis* (MS Egerton 2800 ff 152–4) that seems worth quoting *in extenso;* see Appendix F.

Did he still think of writing his Hymns to the Elements, possibly for Longman's proposed two volumes of poems? It is difficult to believe that the considerable task of this manuscript was not for some literary purpose. Is it gratuitous to point out that the mechanical tabulating of this material may suggest a flagging confidence in imagination?

3130 12.85   *AP* 188. This is from the *Memoirs* of the life of Sir William Jones by Lord Teignmouth prefixed to the *Works of Sir William Jones* (1807) II 307n, being the translation of a note in Sanskrit written to Jones by a venerable pundit employed by him to superintend his compilation of Hindu law: "Trivédi Servoru Sarman, who depends on you alone for support, presents his humble duty, with a hundred benedictions.
                                    Verses.
To you there are many like me; yet to me there is none like you, but yourself; there are numerous groves of night flowers; yet the night flower sees nothing like the moon, but the moon."

   Coleridge's improvements in course of transcribing suggest the possibility of a poem in embryo, perhaps another for the Soother of Absence. See 3017n.

3131 12.46   The entry is written in a very small hand with little differentiation of spacing between some of the distichs: a few are separated by a short line. On moving on to *f34*, Coleridge turned the notebook sideways so as to have the longer way of the page for these long lines.

   He is here copying from Schiller's *Musenalmanach* for 1797, distichs published as the joint work of Goethe and Schiller and signed "G. und S." Many, though not all, were subsequently printed in the works of each poet separately. Following their example of using initials for some titles, Coleridge applies distich [1] to Cumberland and [22] to Rogers. In the translations the titles of the originals are supplied, though Coleridge's omission of them (with a few exceptions) suggests, perhaps, as do the names Cumberland and Rogers, that he thought of them in other contexts of his own.

   The first nine distichs are from the *Xenien: Musenalmanach* 203-79.

   The verses numbered editorially [10]-[22] are from the *Tabulae votivae* or *Votiftafeln: Musenalmanach* 153-78.

   Verses 1-5 and [23]-[28] are from the groups *Vielen* (To the Many) and *Einer* (To the One [feminine]) in the *Musenalmanach* 187-95. In editions of the poetical works of each poet subsequently, these were entitled *Frühling* and *Sommer* in the collection *Vier Jahreszeiten* (Four Seasons). Here Coleridge himself has provided the numbers 1–5; he supplied his own title to the whole group.

[1] *Cumberland:* the German verse applied to Richard Cumberland the dramatist? Coleridge had his *Observer: Being a Collection of Moral, Literary and Familiar Essays* (1786–90) I and v from the Bristol Library in May–June 1796: *Bristol Borrowings* (78). But the reference here is more likely to Cumberland's popular comedies. *A Hint to Husbands* was being performed in London 1806–7, and Cumberland's *Memoirs* had just been published in 1806.

In the following translations, although prose has been adopted, it has sometimes been possible to preserve the line-endings.

[*Der Kunstgriff,* lit., The Trick; better, Tricks of the Trade]
[1] Would you please worldlings and godly alike? Then
     Lust is the thing to portray—but paint the Devil in too.

The Prophet
[2] A pity that Nature made but one man of you.
     There was material there for a good man and a rogue.

[*Das Amalgama:* The Amalgam]
[3] Nature blends everything so uniquely and intimately; but here,
     alas! she has blended nobility and cunning all too intimately.

For a Change
[4] Some shoot up like glittering balls and others ignite, some we
     just throw as in play to delight the eye.

[*Der Zeitpunkt:* The Historical Moment]
[5] The century has given birth to a great epoch, but the great moment encounters an insignificant generation.

[*Manso von den Grazien:* Manso on the Graces]
[6] Witches can be conjured by uttering wretched spells.
     The Graces only appear in response to the call of the Graces.

Philosophical Dialogue.
[7] One of them, as you can hear, is speaking *after* the other, but neither speaks *to* the other: who would call two monologues a discussion?

[*Der treue Spiegel:* The Faithful Mirror]

[8]   Pure stream, you do not distort the pebble, you bring it nearer the
      eye; thus I see the world when W— describes it. [The dubious
      word/title is faint, and may have been deleted.]

[The *Musenalmanach* had three stars where Coleridge writes "W—". An
intended compliment to Wordsworth?]

[*Griechheit:* Greekness]

[9]   An attempt to render in a distich of his own a comment on
"Griechheit, was war sie? Verstand und Mass und Klarheit! Drum
dächt ich,/Etwas Geduld noch, ihr Herrn, eh' ihr von Griechheit uns
sprecht." Literally: "Greekness, what was it? Plain sense, measure,
clearness! Wherefore I would have thought, a little patience, gentlemen, before you start talking of Greece!" *Dignity* and *Grace*, here, are
Coleridge's additions, interesting in view of his admiration for Schiller's essay *Über Anmut und Würde* (On Grace and Dignity).

[*Das Belebende:* The Life-Giving]

[10] Only at the peak of life, the flower, is new life kindled in the organic
      world, *and* in the world of feeling.

[*Zweyerley Wirkungsarten:* Two Ways of Having Effect]

[11] Do good, and you nourish the divine plant of humanity,
      Make beauty, and you scatter germs of the divine abroad.

[*Unterschied der Stände:* Class-Distinctions]

[12] In the moral world too there's nobility: vulgar natures pay with
      what they *do*, beauteous ones with what they *are*.

Here follows in the *Musenalmanach* the first of the distichs in 1063.
See 1063n on the distinction between *having* and *being*. The distinction
here is between *doing* and *being*.

[*Die Übereinstimmung:* Correspondences]
[The second couplet of this quatrain]

[13] If the eye is sound, it encounters the Creator outside it; if the heart
      is sound, it must mirror within it the world.

[*Mein Glaube:* My Faith]

[14] "Which Faith do I confess?" Not one you can name me. "And why
      not?" For reasons of faith.

[*Theophagen:* Theophagists]

[15] Everything's their meat. They gobble ideas and take a knife and fork with them even into the kingdom of heaven.

[*Das irdische Bündel:* This Mortal Pack]

[16] They would love to fly heavenwards; but the body too has its attractions. And so it gets neatly packed on to the seraph's back.

Light and Colour

[17] Dwell, thou eternally One, there with the Eternal Oneness! Colour, thou changeful one, descend graciously to Man!

[*Das eigne Ideal:* Your Own Ideal]

[18] What you *think* belongs to all; your own is only what you *feel*. If He is to be really your own, then *feel* the God which you think.

[*Der Vorzug:* Preference]

[19] To triumph *over* the heart is great; I *honour* such bravery. But I think more of him who triumphs *through* his heart.

[*Der Nachahmer und der Genius:* Imitator and Genius]
[The last line of this quatrain]

[20] Even what is already shaped is but raw material to the shaping spirit.

[*Wahl:* Choice]

[21] If you cannot please *everyone* with your deeds and your works [of art], then aim at pleasing *the few*. To please the many is bad.

Here follows in the *Musenalmanach* the third distich in 1063.

[22]   Rogers
[*Dilettant:* Dilettante]
Just because you bring off one line in a language which is itself a finely-tuned instrument,
Which thinks and composes for you, you think you're a *poet!*

The underlining of *Dichter* is Coleridge's. The hit at Rogers is clear enough (and see 1434n), but the one line [or poem?] to which Coleridge refers is less apparent.

Here follow *Vielen*—Coleridge's *Blumen moralische:* "Moral garland"? "Flowers-moral"?

[*L.B.*]
1. Rosebud, you are dedicated to the blossoming maiden,
Who is the most lovely and at the same time the most modest.

[*L.D.*]
2. One I knew—she was slender as the lily, and her pride was
Innocence—None more glorious did even Solomon see.

[*A.L.*]
3. Night-scenting dame's violet, in the glare of the daylight people
pass you by;
But when the nightingale sings, you breathe your precious essence.

Tuber rose
4. Among the crowd you shine, you give delight in the open;
But stay away from my head, stay away from my heart.

[*M.R.*]
5. Say, what fills the room with fragrance? Mignonette.
Colourless, without form, quiet and delicate plant.

[23]   [*C.F.*] *Vergiss mein nicht:* Forget-me-not
[This is Coleridge's title; see also 2564.]
Your lovely smallness, your gracious eye, they keep on saying:
Forget me not, forget not thou me.

[24] An attempt at rendering lines 5, 6 *Einer?* "Wie im Winter die
Saat nur langsam keimet, im Frühling/Lebhaft treibet und schosst,
so war die Neigung zu dir." Literally: "As in winter the seed germinates but slowly, in spring is busy sending forth shoots, thus was my
love for you."

[25] [The underlining of *du* is Coleridge's.] Field and wood and crag and
gardens were always to me nothing but space, and *you*, Beloved,
make them into a place.

[26] I would wish to possess everything, in order to share it with her;
I would gladly surrender it all, were she, the Only One, mine.

[27] Why am I transient, O Zeus? asked Beauty.
Because, said the god, it was only the transient that made you
beautiful.

[28]   And Love, Flowers, Dew and Youth heard it,
        And they all turned, weeping, from Jupiter's throne.

3132 12.47   It is clear that in 1806–7, on his return from his first experience of countries officially Roman Catholic, Coleridge gave considerable thought to the conflict between rational and mysterious elements in religion and in religions. One may deduce something about his conversation on the subject, e.g. from Lord Egmont's suggestion (see 3170n); possibly this entry is linked with that proposal.

Anti-mysterii: those who deny the mystery.

Lipo-mysterii: those who ignore the mystery.

the intellectual philo-mysterii: those who (intellectually) love the mystery.

3133 12.48   *AP* 179, attached to 3134; although the entries look alike, being in pencil, this one appears to deal with religious belief, the other with personal relationships. This same passage is quoted in MS Egerton 2801 f 260 independent of this context. (In Migne's *Patrologia* this sermon from *De verbis Domini* is numbered 139 of *Sermones de scripturis.*)

EHC *AP* 179 provides a translation:

So receive, so believe [divine ideas] that ye may earn the right to understand them. For faith should go before understanding, in order that understanding may be the reward of faith.

3134 12.49   *AP* 179. With this clear reference to Wordsworth's attitude towards Coleridge's relation to Sara Hutchinson, see also 3146.

3135 12.50   In ink. This also seems to point, like 3132, to Lord Egmont's proposal of a history of Christianity, referred to in 3170n.

f37ᵛ per fas et nefas: justly or unjustly.

f38 Thus Newcome Cappe: It is interesting to find Coleridge still in 1807 reading a Unitarian divine on the Christian miracles. The passage he quotes comes from Cappe *Critical Remarks on Many Important Passages of Scripture* (2 vols York 1802) II 414. It is difficult to believe that Coleridge read through the two volumes of this dull work to extract the sentences almost at the end of it, yet it may be over-sceptical to suggest that he turned at once to the end, to a collection of short passages entitled "Christian Principles deduced from Scripture", where he found this passage in the 17th of them.

ff38ᵛ–39   On the familiar Grotius-Paley charge see e.g. 2640 and n.

3136 12.51   In ink. *AP* 179. The quotation from Strabo's *Geography* is from Bk x Chap 3 §9:

And secondly the religious frenzy seems to afford a kind of divine inspiration and to be very like that of the soothsayer.—Tr H. L. Jones (LCL 1917).

Coleridge in *rekindles* immediately translates the Greek word he has just used; possibly he used it with some associated feeling for the use of the word by Aristotle (*De spiritu* 484a 7), or some other; it appears frequently in a spiritual sense.

On the MS at the end of this entry Mrs Gillman has written: "Alas! Alas!"

3137 12.52   In ink. The reference is not in the work of Cappe quoted in 3135; Coleridge frequently referred to Maimonides, and is perhaps thinking of, or quoting someone's paraphrase of passages in, *The Guide to the Perplexed* Pt II, e.g. Chaps XXXVI, XLVII.

Prophetic truth is not corroborated by miracles.

3138 12.53   In ink. A reference to the Ephesian Diana (Artemis), whose image in the temple of Ephesus was many-breasted.

Earth is the Great Mother, many-breasted Diana.

3139 12.54   Fall ploughing appears to provide a west-country setting and help with the dating (together with 3148) of this group of entries.

3140 12.55   In ink.

3141 12.56   In ink. Dr *Stock & his uxor Tyranna* are referred to in a letter to RS in Feb 1808, Stock having been "cock-pecked [by STC] into an opinion of Wordsworth's merit as a Poet" but "hen-pecked out of it again" next morning. "Tho' I laughed, yet inwardly I had a sick pang . . .". *CL* # 679. The anecdote of Stock and his tyrant wife is reported as referring to an episode in the past, in Bristol.

3142 12.57   In ink. No link connecting this entry with intelligi-
bility has been found. The deliberate jingle of "7" more than half
points, in spite of the assurance in "8", to the fantasy at work in the
next entry.

3143 12.58   The *Zahuris* have not been tracked to their native
country; possibly they spring full-blown out of the head of STC. His
interest in subterranean dwarfs and their eccentricities was shown in
the Kobolds, *Phil Lects* 322. Creatures "always born on Good Friday"
have their counterpart in one of his marginal notes where one would
hardly expect it, the single comment on his copy of the *Codice di
Napoleone il grande pel regno d'Italia* (Florence 1806). Coleridge's
note, on the fly-leaf, refers to §§25 and 64, both ordinances concerned
with marriage, on which he writes, "If there lurk any Truth in As-
trology, i.e. in Times and Seasons, something curious might result
from a Nation of 40 Millions all wedding and bedding on Wednesdays
—and only on Wednesdays." (In the BM.)

3144 12.59   Ἀγνος: the chaste-tree, the branches of which were
strewed by matrons on their beds at the Thesmophoria. The Linnaean
name is *Vitex agnus castus:* and *agnus castus* is also found in Pliny
Natural History Bk xxiv §38.
     Liddell and Scott notes that ἄγνος was "associated with the notion
of chastity from the likeness of its name to ἁγνός". So the pun was
already present in the mind of the Greeks. STC, who was often careless of Greek breathings, may have assumed that "Botanists" suffered from ignorance of Greek. But the Latin name *agnus castus* uses
the word *castus* as a gloss on the pun; for ἄγνος—λύγος was another
name for the same tree—was a tree-name in its own right.
     Ορος is Greek for Mountain: so Mons Oros = Mount Mountain.
Botanists giving a chaste-tree the name of "chaste chaste-tree" is the
same as if geographers or local authorities called a mountain "Mt
Mountain".

3145 12.60   *Tacitus:* Thomas Gordon, an eminent Unitarian
clergyman, produced a translation and commentary on Tacitus that
ran to several editions; the latest available at this date would have
been one of 1753.
     John Barclay's *A[rgenis]* and his *Eup[hormio's Satyricon]*. Cole-
ridge's annotated copy of the *Argenis* (Amsterdam 1659) is in HUL;

he also annotated Southey's copy (1629) now in the BM. A copy of
the *Euphormionis Satyricon* in the Wordsworth LC was marked as
Coleridge's.

Stockdale's Shakespere: Coleridge and Wordsworth favoured this
editor, and Coleridge annotated two copies, one of the two-volume
edition of 1807, which is in the BM with his notes, reproduced in *ShC*
I *passim;* the other (1784) is in HUL, the notes on which have been
published in an article by Professor Sylvan Barnet in the *Harvard
Library Bulletin* XII No 2 (1958) 210–19.

Sh[akespeare]'s poems: We do not know Coleridge's edition.

*Butler's An. & Serm: The Analogy of Religion, Natural and Re-
vealed, to the Constitution and Course of Nature* (1736) and the *Sermons*
of Joseph Butler, Bishop of Durham, both of which Coleridge admired. Butler's *Works* were first collected in 1804 and again in 1807.
But Coleridge had known the *Analogy* as early as Feb 1798, when he
offered to assist Estlin with an edition of it. *CL* # 232. The *Sermons* he
owned, again according to the Wordsworth LC, where the edition is
not identified, possibly the Glasgow 1769 edition in 2 vols.

Paley's *Horae Paulinae* had just been republished, in 1807. The
latest edition of the *Natural Theology* (5th) would have been 1804.
There is of course no guarantee that Coleridge would buy the latest
edition, though of a modern work it would be the most likely to be
available; the dates are suggested here only as being of possible use,
speculatively in relation to other factors, were one trying to deduce
Coleridge's editions.

3146 12.61   Cf 3134 and 3148 below.

3147 12.62   Coleridge owned a copy of *Catulli Tibulli Propertii
Opera* (1774 12°), now in the possession of A. H. B. Coleridge. The
Tibullus citation is thus an understandable error for Propertius
Elegies Bk II vi 25–6:

What profits it for maids to found temples in honour of Chastity, if every
bride is permitted to be whate'er she will?—Tr H. E. Butler (LCL 1912).

The next entry suggests a bitter personal implication.

3148 12.63   The entry is in pencil, from the middle of *f44ᵛ* inked
over.

f44ᵛ Self in me derives its sense of Being from having this one absolute Object: cf 1679 *f45.*

f45 that Saturday Morning: 27 Dec 1806. See 2975.

ff45–45ᵛ See 2975n.

f47 The⌈ *Sara!—   Sara!* ⌉represents STC's own attempt to conceal by writing random letters over the words; this is not the obliterating of some other censor.

On Coleridge's awareness of the diseased, involuntary aspect of jealousy, see 2001, 2055, 2998.

3149 12.64   In ink. Cf "My sole sensuality was *not* to be in pain!" of 2368.

3150 12.65   In ink. Source not found.

Never before did the *angel Spring* descend in such glorious vestment of blossom. Never such a thrill through marrow and limbs—How? —— Not that —— First you had to prepare in me, beloved, a place for the *angel.*

3151 12.66   In ink. *AP* 184; repeated variatim in a MS fragment in MS Egerton 2801 published in *Inq Sp* §301. One recalls the projected Hymns to the Elements (see also 3129n and 174 [16] and n) and the frequent concatenation in Coleridge's thoughts of frost or ice and fire; see 3156 and 3157.

3152 12.67   To Ἑν: the One.
          Λογος: the Word.

Wirkung: In the version of this entry in MS Egerton 2801 f 260 (see N 12 Gen Note) Coleridge translates this as *product.* The Egerton MS version is different in wording: "Life knows only its product & beholds itself only as far as it is visible in its offspring. Therefore, yea the Ground & Cause of All comprehends itself only because the Logos is co-eternal, its Offspring, its Product, is at the same time its Adequate Idea. No Word, No God—". The fragment (watermark 1820) goes on to deplore the "Spirit locum tenens of Unitarianism in the Church = the dregs of Grotianism—as in D'Oyley, Mant,—Magee, in short, all the Prigs of Preferment—far worse than Unitarianism itself . . .".

The logic here appears to be of the sort that accounts for such observations as the one in entry 80.

3153 12.68   For another and grosser *matted mass, & witch-lock of confusion*, see the reference to *Plica Polonica* in 1380 and n. It is relevant to note, because of the speculation about Tycho Brahe's dwarf, Sep, in 3110, and in support of it, that if Coleridge was reading Coxe's *Travels into Poland* at this time, he could have found *Plica Polonica* there, at I 234–6.

3154 12.69   In ink. *AP* 187–8 variatim. Cf 3148.
verschiedene Eine: i.e., to some unique One [the form is feminine] of our own kind, who is yet different from our self.

3155 12.70   The source of the quotation has not been found. With the last part of the German, cf 2453. For Coleridge on Bürger see 340 and n and 787n. This appears to be the earliest reference to J. J. W. Heinse's *Ardinghello* (1787, 1794).

No tree falls at one blow: let alone a cedar, which has stood for so many centuries, from the beginning of recorded time, and with its verdant top defies every storm.
    —in which one is rapt away from earth's turmoil into the serenity of the ethereal blue, and in the unfathomable vault of heaven can breathe free of all bonds.

3156 12.71   In ink. In part in *AP* 185.
Time, Space . . . : partly used in *BL* I 162–3.
The reference to the importance of early admirations, whether in poetry or philosophy, is in keeping with what Coleridge says auto-biographically in *BL* Chap I. And with the same pages cf the *Morning Star-Sun* image here: "The great works of past ages seem to a young man things of another race, in respect to which his faculties must remain passive and submiss, even as to the stars and mountains. But the writings of a contemporary . . . possess a *reality* for him . . .". *BL* I 7.
Extremes meet: see 1725 and n.
the living moving Ocean . . . : see 3151 and n.
blinde Fenster . . . *die schönste Aussicht seyn sollte:* "[like one who?] merely for the sake of order tolerates blind windows in a building just at those points where the best light should enter and the fairest view should be."
Potentia fit Actus: "Power becomes Act".

3157 12.72   In ink. The first paragraph is in *AP* 185. The entry
with its rapid and free movements among the elements raises a question as to whether Coleridge may not have been revolving in his mind
the long-projected Hymns to the Elements, possibly for Longman's
two volumes of his poems. This is supported by the Darwin reference
below, going back to the same period. And see above 3151, 3156.

Bigness for Greatness: The metaphor here comes (by natural association with Darwin's pretentiously bulky tomes?) from *The Botanic
Garden* i i, the note to line 105. Lines 103–8 read: "LET THERE BE
LIGHT! proclaim'd the ALMIGHTY LORD,/Astonish'd Chaos heard the
potent word;/Through all his realms the kindling Ether runs,/And
the mass starts into a million suns;/Earths round each sun with quick
explosions burst,/And second planets issue from the first." Darwin's
note reads: "It may be objected that if the stars had been projected
from a Chaos by explosions, they must have returned again with it
from the known laws of gravitation; this however would not happen,
if the whole of Chaos, like grains of gun-powder was exploded at the
same time, and dispersed through infinite space at once . . ." (ed
1795) 9.

Possibly all this harks back even farther—to childhood; see the
autobiographical letter *CL* # 210.

3158 12.73   *AP* 186–7. See also 3121 and n.

Thought elaborates Essence into Existence: in a passage useful to set
beside this one, in Chap xviii of *BL*, he defines *Essence* as (a) "the
principle of *individuation*", and (b) "the point or ground of contra-
distinction between two modifications of the same substance or subject". *BL* ii 47. But see 3159 and n.

Outis, Esqre: the Greek word for Nobody; cf 2744.

3159 12.74   Down to "submissive Gaze" in *AP* 187; EHC deletes
all the word-play and makes of the final sentence a detached entry,
thus losing a characteristically Coleridgian train of thought.

zerflossenes Eins: suffused oneness.

The Greek and Latin terms can perhaps best be dealt with in their
context, i.e. this spontaneous effort to show that *Thought* [is] *formed
not fixed.* By analysis and combination of word-elements Coleridge
wishes to discern the intellectual process of arriving at the Logos from
the starting-point of phenomenal existence (*Logos ab Ente*). This is
scarcely intended as a serious etymological exercise but is a use of

etymology as a "suggestive analogy" which will provide him with a vivid series of word-symbols. We are (so to speak) familiar with the words and the implications of the words when compounded; but when we consider what has been compounded, and how, we see both the process of combination and an extension of that process in heuristic thinking.

Est, Idea, Ideatio: Existence (i.e. it is, it exists, or a thing exists), Idea, Ideation.

Id—inde, ʜoc *et illud: Id*—hence, this thing and that thing. Does this imply the two lowest terms in a hierarchic or dynamic structure? *Hoc* and *illud* are the bottom terms representing "this particular phenomenal thing" and "that particular phenomenal thing". Above these is *Id,* a *thing* which has made a notable step in the direction of *Idea*—if only because etymologically it will become *Idea. Id* is no longer a phenomenal thing but a significant thing—perhaps a symbol. He goes on: *Idea* minus *actio* = *Id.* That is, looking at *Id* from "above" one sees it to be on the way to, but lacking the generative force (*actio*) of, Idea. *Id*-in-itself has now been established in respect both of the terms below and the term above.

iterum, ⟨*Hoc + Id, & then*⟩ *Id + Ea* . . . *= Idea:* Again (i.e. looking at this another way), when *Id* is brought into conjunction with *Hoc* (a particular phenomenal thing) and then with *Ea* (things in general—on the assumption that *Ea* is neuter plural and not feminine singular) you get *Idea.* And since he has glossed the nature of the conjunction as "the coadunation of the individual with the universal through love" we see how the energetic nature of *Idea,* which *Id*-in-itself lacks, is imparted to *Id.* But in the same way that *Id* was derived from *Idea* by the withdrawal of *actio,* so *Idea* itself needs the addition of *actio* to bring it to the highest term—*Ideatio;* the energy (*actio*) of *Idea,* like the potential of *Id,* is latent.

Idea + actio = Ideatio: Idea-in-action is Ideation (Contemplation: Thought?). Ideation is immediately glossed as "holy spirit, which being transelemented into we are mystically united with the *Am*—I ᴀᴍ". The importance of *Est* in the opening formula is now clear, and another dimension has been added: for the transition that has now been effected from *Est* to *Eimi (Sum)* is a transition from the pronoun *it* to *I,* and from thing to person.

Finally, the whole process is rendered by repeating the earlier scheme of *Idea*—*Hoc* added to *Id* and then *Id* multiplied into *Ea*—and adding on *Actio* is the same as *Ideatio*—being now glossed as "the holy spirit of the Unity".

This seems to show in highly condensed form five modes of transition in thought:

(*a*) From existence to creative Word (the object of the exercise);

(*b*) From thing to symbol to Idea;

(*c*) From thing to person;

(*d*) From contemplation of a thing or symbol to contemplation of Idea and then to transelementation into spirit;

(*e*) From scrutiny of the world to mystical union with God.

The whole implies Coleridge's belief in the inherence of the Word in the world as shaping Spirit. But the demonstration is remarkable for the way it proceeds from "bottom" to "top" instead of (as one would expect of a Platonist) from "top" to "bottom".

The related matters in 2784 become more than mere word-play; cf 886–921, and see also 2274 and 2323.

3160 12.75   In ink. Except for the German first sentence, the entry is in *AP* 187–8. On the virtues of compounded words see also 2431n; *CL* # 679 (the P.S.); "Satyrane's Letters" III; *Friend* (1809–10) No 18n, reprinted *BL* II 172n.

He who is most inwardly alive to the beauties of Nature, feels her most secret stirrings, cannot bear her flaws, and does all in his power to rectify them: he is putting into practice the essential truth and the essential holiness of all religions.

Source not found.

3161 12.22   The original of this entry is an article in *Phil Trans* IX (1674) 149; Coleridge's source for it was very probably the abridged edition (1792–1809), where it appears as a subsection, "Laudanum Helmontii Junioris", of an "Account of the two sorts of the Helmontian Laudanum, communicated to the Editor by the Hon. Robert Boyle; with the Way of Baron F. M. Van Helmont of preparing his Laudanum". *Phil Trans* (*Abr*) II 155–7. For the evidence of Coleridge's use at this time of *Phil Trans* (*Abr*) see 3071–3072. The expression "a walme or two" comes from the article, the quotation marks being Coleridge's: i.e. a bubble or two, to the boiling-point.

3162 12.23   In ink. This entry comes from an article entitled "Experiments and Observations on the Motion of Sound &c", by William Derham, originally in *Phil Trans* XXVI (1708) but read by Coleridge in *Phil Trans* (*Abr*) V 380–95. It is given as a line of "verse", for the use of "echometricians" as an example of sounds too prolonged to be completely reproduced in an echo. The meaning of the words is not relevant, but they mean:

Arx: castle, in Rome the Capitol.
Tridens: trident.
rostris: rostrum.
præster: protector, guardian.
torrida: parched, torrid.
seps: serpent.
strix: screech-owl.

3163 12.24   A pencilled entry, traced over in ink by a later hand —Mrs Gillman? It seems highly probable that this entry arose out of the footnote referred to in 3072 from *Phil Trans (Abr)* v 294–5, and out of Coleridge's own reflections on it. It may owe something, too, to an earlier article in the same volume, "An Instrument, for seeing the Sun, Moon, or Stars, pass the Meridian of any Place: useful for setting Watches in all Parts of the World with the greatest Exactness; to correct Sun-Dials; to assist in the Discovery of the Longitude of Places, &c." Again by William Derham. Ibid v 129–33.

3164 12.25   In ink.

3165 12.26   In ink. *AP* 176.
Another version of this note (BM MS Egerton 2801 f 260: *Inq Sp* §38) states that the idea of separate individual atmospheres originated in the observation on shadows in 3171: "A shadow, that subsists in shaped and definite Non-entity. It has often suggested to me the fancy of a Planet without any common atmosphere, but where each Individual has an atmosphere of his own, like a travel-warmed Horse in a winter morning—to receive & communicate, one joins his atmosphere to that of another, and according to the symp- or anti-pathy of their nature, the refractions & aberrations are less or greater —their Thoughts more or less reciprocally intelligible." The watermark is 1820, not, as stated in *Inq Sp*, 1800; Coleridge was perhaps selecting materials from his notebooks for some work—*C&S*?
Cf 10n, on the moon having no atmosphere; that entry probably owes something, as this one may do also, to Swedenborg, and the English translation of his *De telluribus: Concerning the earths in our Solar System, which are called planets . . . together with an account of their*

inhabitants . . . (tr J. Clowes 1787) 31, the section "Concerning the Spirits and Inhabitants of the Moon": "It was perceived . . . that the Inhabitants of the Moon do not speak from the Lungs, like the Inhabitants of other Earths, but from the Abdomen, and thus from a certain Quantity of Air there collected, by Reason that the Moon is not encompassed with an Atmosphere like that of other Earths."

3166 12.27   In ink. *AP* 176–7, where EHC suggests that Coleridge refers to De Quincey and himself. See 3168. If he was thinking of a poem with "And a confusion of countenance" as the last line, it apparently was never written. With *a greater trouble, a fear, and darkness of the mind* cf Ordonio's "dark perturbed countenance" in *Remorse* IV ii 69: *PW* II 866. Here also two countenances are compared, though of course with a very different context and direction.

3167 12.28   This sentiment was expressed by William Pitt in introducing a famous motion—"Lord Chatham's motion to withdraw the troops from Boston" in the House of Lords, 20 Jan 1775: ". . . But it is not repealing this or that act of Parliament, it is not repealing a *piece of parchment*, that can restore America to our bosom: you must repeal her fears and her resentments; and you may then hope for her love and her gratitude." *Speeches of the Earl of Chatham* (London 1848) 137. The speech was reprinted variatim in 1775; Coleridge's version may owe something to his own elaboration in paraphrasing.

3168 12.29   Coleridge and De Quincey met first in Bridgwater in Aug 1807, and continued to meet until about December in Bristol. The address is a sociable one, in the centre of things at the Hot Wells, near the Rooms. De Quincey's famous report of the first encounter is in his *Reminiscences: De Q Works* II 140, 150. He had begun taking opium in 1803. See also 3166 and n.

3169 12.30   *Tincture of Hops:* a solution in alcohol.
Extract of Hops: a concentrated solution in any solvent. A substitute for, possibly to wean one away from, opium? From De Quincey?

3170 12.31   Enmore Castle was the seat of John James Perceval, third earl of Egmont, elder half-brother of Spencer Perceval, who was at this time a highly influential minister in the government. Coleridge visited Lord Egmont in the summer of 1807 and, if De Quincey's account is correct, excited high admiration; it is of some interest to note the impression Coleridge could make at this low ebb-time in his affairs and hopes, at least on a complete stranger, when none of the emotional ties that obstructed communication with his friends was present.

"Lord Egmont called upon Mr. Poole, with a present for Coleridge: it was a canister of peculiarly fine snuff, which Coleridge now took profusely. Lord Egmont, on this occasion, spoke of Coleridge in the terms of excessive admiration, and urged Mr. Poole to put him upon undertaking some great monumental work, that might furnish a sufficient arena for the display of his various and rare accomplishments; for his multiform erudition on the one hand, for his splendid power of theorizing and combining large and remote notices of facts on the other. And he suggested, judiciously enough, as one theme which offered a field at once large enough and indefinite enough to suit a mind that could not show its full compass of power unless upon very plastic materials—a History of Christianity, in its progress and in its chief divarications into Church and Sect, with a continual reference to the relations subsisting between Christianity and the current philosophy; their occasional connexions or approaches, and their constant mutual repulsions. 'But, at any rate, let him do something,' said Lord Egmont; 'for at present he talks very much like an angel, and does nothing at all.' Lord Egmont I understood from everybody to be a truly good and benevolent man; and on this occasion he spoke with an earnestness which agreed with my previous impression. Coleridge, he said, was now in the prime of his powers—uniting something of youthful vigour with sufficient experience of life; having the benefit, beside, of vast meditation, and of reading unusually discursive. No man had ever been better qualified to revive the heroic period of literature in England, and to give a character of weight to the philosophic erudition of the country upon the Continent. 'And what a pity,' he added, 'If this man were, after all, to vanish like an apparition, and you, I, and a few others, who have witnessed his grand *bravuras* of display, were to have the usual fortune of ghostseers, in meeting no credit for any statements that we might vouch on his behalf!'

"On this occasion we learned, for the first time, that Lord Egmont's carriage had, some days before, conveyed Coleridge to Bridgewater, with a purpose of staying one single day at that place, and then returning to Mr. Poole's. From the sort of laugh with which Lord Egmont taxed his own simplicity, in having confided at all in the stability of any Coleridgian plan, I now gather that procrastination in excess was, or had become, a marking feature in Coleridge's daily life." *Reminiscences: De Q Works* II 148-9.

3171 12.32   *AP* 177. The same note variatim is to be found among the Egerton MS 2801 fragments, f 260; see 3165n.

3172 12.33   *AP* 176. Traced over in ink (by Mrs Gillman?). An adaptation of the first part of Isa. 30:20: "And though the Lord give you the bread of adversity, and the water of affliction, yet shall not thy Teachers be removed into a corner any more, but thine eyes shall see thy teachers."

3173 12.34   In ink. Coleridge is reading *Observations on the Utility and Administration of Purgative Medicines in Several Diseases* by James Hamilton, M.D. It is clear from comparing his notes with the first two editions that he is using the second edition, Edinburgh 1806.
ff19ᵛ-22 He is extracting prescriptions to be found in Hamilton beginning at p 151.
f22   Aqua acetitis . . . : Having finished with the enemas, he turns back to p 130 to the second table given of *materia medica*, selecting what interests him. (His list includes items to be found in the second and not in the first edition.)
ff22ᵛ-23ᵛ   1. Injicitur Enema domesticum . . . : He is here reading about cases of typhus, p 156 onwards. He follows the case history, omitting the description of symptoms, but recording the doses, though these are not complete. On *f23ᵛ* the words in parenthesis are Coleridge's, derived from p 152, to which he clearly turned back for this purpose; it is of interest that he uses instead of "tincture of opium" here, "laudanum".
ff23ᵛ-26ᵛ   Marasmus . . . : He passes over scarlatina cases to p 210, again selecting, abbreviating, omitting the symptoms, many of which he recognized as similar to his own, e.g. dilated pupils, frequent waking with screams during the night. Was it for emphasis he translated (*f26*) "N.B. Throughout the whole 4 ounces of Port wine a day"?
f26ᵛ   Four Grains of Calomel . . . *laxative:* For this sentence he turned back to the beginning of the work (p 12), using his own words, e.g. the clarifying and cautioning (*either of them*), though the sense is Hamilton's.

f27 J.D. . . . : He now turns ahead, skipping a number of diseases uninteresting to him—chlorosis, haematemesis, chorea, hysteria, tetanus—until he comes to "Chronic Diseases" on p 347, and
the case of Jean Macdonald. He notes her early symptoms apparently as far as he recognizes them as his own, omitting more as the
account proceeds. The "N.B." on *f28ᵛ* is his.

Coleridge was probably more inclined than most to be his own
diagnostician, but such notes remind us, as do e.g. *SH Letters*, of the
amateurism of much of the contemporary medicine. Such works as
Hamilton's were written less for the profession than for the public.

3174 12.35   In ink. The first six words are in pencil; the remainder
is in ink. Parts of this entry, given as separate memoranda, are in *AP*
176–7.

Coleridge is reading the ten-volume octavo edition of Bacon published by J. Johnson in 1803. The first Greek phrase ("water is most
excellent") introduces the passage; he then implies that what follows
are sentiments of Francis Bacon interpreted by S. T. Coleridge.

f29 If Kings are Gods . . . : not the words of Bacon's essay "Of a
King" (II 393), but suggested by them. "A King is a mortal God on
earth, unto whom the living God hath lent his own name as a great
honour; but withal told him, he should be like a man . . .".

Ora tu, tu lege . . . labora: "Pray thou, choose thou, protect thou,
labour thou."

Minos, Lycurgus, Solon . . . : with minor variations, the passage
is as cited, and gives the clue to the edition Coleridge was using.

f29ᵛ The place Coleridge could not find again (one suspects that a
considerable number of quotations and paraphrases written in the
notebooks led to similar uncertainties) was ibid IV 446, at the end of
"The Charge of Owen, Indicted of High Treason, in the King's Bench.
By Sir Francis Bacon, Knight. Her Majesty's Attorney General".
Coleridge quotes verbatim, though he inserts an extra *c* in "Luca".

Non illos homicidas arbitramur . . . : "We do not regard as murderers those who, burning with zeal for the Mother Church against
the excommunicated, have happened to put some of them to death."

Parisatis . . . unhurt: IV 475, in Bacon's "Charge . . . against
Robert, Earl of Somerset, concerning the poisoning of Overbury".
Coleridge paraphrases, and adds the possible application.

f30 "I confess . . . cunctative": IV 493, from Bacon's "Speech on
Taking his Place in Chancery".

Heu! quam miserum [est] *ab illo lædi, de quo non possis queri:* Thus far, the Latin is one of the *Sententiae* of Publilius Syrus, some of which were published in various collected editions of Bacon's works, under the title he gave them in his commonplace books, *Ornamenta rationalia* (II 465); the addition appears to be Coleridge's: "O! what a misery it is to be hurt by one of whom it is impossible to complain—alas, how utterly miserable is it to suffer from one of whom it is impossible to complain because of one's love."

Keeps his wounds green: versified from Bacon's "A man that studieth revenge, keeps his wounds green, which otherwise would heal and do well." "Of Revenge" (II 262).

Things . . . Fortune: from the essay "Of Counsel" (II 300), with slight variants, including the substitution of "Council" for "counsel".

Of Sheridan's many speeches on Irish affairs, the most likely one to which Coleridge was referring here seems to be the long one in the closing session of Parliament 13 Aug 1807, in which Sheridan unsuccessfully moved for an inquiry into the state of Ireland, hoping in this way to reverse discussion of such recent legislation as the Irish Arms Bill, which passed its third reading, nevertheless, 17 Aug 1807. This speech is reproduced in *Speeches of the Right Honourable Richard Brinsley Sheridan* (3 vols 1842) III 522–43.

f30ᵛ Death of an Immortal: This first phrase is Coleridge's, and comparison with Bacon's exact words is of some interest. "Nor in my own thoughts, can I compare men more fitly to any thing than to the Indian fig-tree, which being ripened to his full height, is said to decline his branches down to the earth; whereof she conceives again, and they become roots in their own stock." It is from "An Essay on Death" attributed to Bacon (ed cit II 475).

I ought . . . mutinies against it: cf ibid II 476, "Death arrives graciously only to those who sit in darkness . . . to those whose fortune runs back, and whose spirit mutinies; unto such death is a redeemer . . .".

The remainder is from the same edition, as Coleridge cites it.

3175 12.36   In ink. *AP* 178.

3176 12.37   In ink. *AP* 178; cf 2173.

3177 12.38   *AP* 178. The Greek words mean: Of Love, regarding Love.
With *works abstruse* cf *Dejection: an Ode* lines 89–90 (*PW* I 367):

"And haply by abstruse research to steal/From my own nature all the natural man—".

The frequency of the child-parent metaphor in morally painful contexts is noticeable in Coleridge; see e.g. 1991, 2224 [43], 2780, 2962.

3178 12.39   Henry N. and George Sealy are listed in *Gore's Liverpool Directory* for 1805 and 1807 as Merchants at 3 Great George Street, Liverpool.

The name of Annie Sealy is connected with a happy fantasy of the youthful Hartley C; see 617.

3179 12.40   In ink. The first enciphered word reads "Sara's"; in the second Coleridge makes the slip "*lived* her" for "*loved* her".

3180 12.41   In ink. Coleridge is returning to an old interest in *Samson Agonistes* for metrical ideas. Possibly the reading of Hayley's *Life of Milton* (1796) about this time (Poole's copy now in HEHL), as well as the preparation of his poems for Longman, and the imminent course of lectures on poetry for the Royal Institution, were all contributing factors.

The first passage appears to refer to lines 80–114, beginning: "O dark, dark, dark, amid the blaze of noon"; but by mistake in the 11th and 12th lines of the passage, STC calls line 24 line 25. The second passage, the Chorus, is lines 115–50: "This, this is he . . .".

3181 12.42   *my poems:* referring again to Longman's offer in 1807 to publish two volumes.

Abstine, Sus! non tibi spiro: In *Friend* I 59n he transfers this to another herb: "I was always pleased with the motto placed under the figure of Rosemary in old Herbals", and he quotes it, "Sus, apage! Haud tibi spiro." T. Hutchinson in his introduction to *LB* (1898) lix compares it with the *LB* (1800) motto, *Quam nihil ad genium, Papiniane, tuum!* Translating *that* motto, "How absolutely *not* after your liking, O learned jurist!" he adds, "It was a polite way of saying, 'Sus . . . spiro!'" i.e. "Hold off, pig! I do not blow for you."

A marjoram: Gerard makes no reference to the antipathy of swine to this herb or to rosemary either, but of "Bastard Marjoreme" or wild marjoram he does say that it "cureth them that haue drunk *Opium*, or the juyce of blacke Poppy, or hemlockes, especially if it be giuen with wine and raisons of the sunne." John Gerard *The Herball* (ed Thomas Johnson 1636) 667 (Chap 218). The explanation of Coleridge's change from marjoram to rosemary in *The Friend* is perhaps not far to seek.

3182 12.43   *AP* 178. That this was his image of himself at this time is borne out by his suggestion later that the peacock might be used in the design for his seal, probably one he was commissioning from Matilda Betham *c* 1808. Another bird-image; see 2054, 2556, and notes.

3183 12.44   Cf 1708 and n. The numerous Friendly Societies of the day, many being very small, local, and unsoundly administered, were under frequent criticism in this period, to the point of parliamentary investigations.

3184 12.45   *AP* 178. Half a page is torn out after this entry.

3185 19.59   The cipher reads:

A mother with anticipated glee.

It is puzzling to know why this had to be written in cipher, unless for practice, as one suspects in the case of e.g. 3019.

3186 19.60   The later insert is written up under 3107; after 3186 part of the page was torn off. The impression persists, though difficult to assign to references, that talk with *C.B.* was freer and more flippant than the serious talk of Coleridge's circles heretofore, and perhaps was sought at this wretched period for that reason.

Charlotte Brent was the sister of Mary Morgan, the wife of John Morgan, a west-country lawyer. Of him little is known except that he went through some severe financial embarrassments and that if it had not been for him the *Biographia Literaria* might never have reached paper.

3187 15.260   Coleridge read Massinger in at least two editions; Mason's (4 vols 1779) he borrowed from the Bristol Library in 1797–8: *Bristol Borrowings* (95); and Gifford's (4 vols 1805 or 1813) he used for the lectures of 1818: *MC* 94n, 96. It is not certain which

edition he is referring to here, as his spellings and capital letters do
not follow either of these exactly.

Although there is no physical evidence in the MS the facts seem
to assign this 17 Nov entry to 1807. On his return from Malta Coleridge first heard of Tom Wedgwood's death. The "O me" paragraph
may contain a *double entendre*. He seems to be thinking partly of Tom
and Josiah, inseparable in their friendship with each other and also
with him, and of their joint gift to him of the annuity; but he is also
thinking of attributing to Josiah the divisive feelings denied in the
quotation. Wedgwood had made it plain to Poole, Wordsworth, and
others that he thought that Coleridge not only was neglecting him,
and had done so ever since leaving for Malta, but also, what cut
Coleridge to the quick, that Coleridge had neglected Tom in his fatal
illness. Coleridge had not heard all this in Nov 1806, and by the
spring of 1808 the tension had largely abated. The entry belongs
to the west-country days of 1807. On 27 June 1807, by Poole's in-
sistence, Coleridge wrote an explanatory letter to Josiah Wedgwood
(Meteyard 324–8; *CL* # 650), but in [Aug] 1807 he was still apprehen-
sive about losing his annuity. *CL* # 653. The exact date of the restoration of the old relation with J. Wedgwood, referred to in *UL*
I 381n, is not clear, if it ever was entirely restored.

3188 15.261   Cf 2984, 2998, entries earlier in 1807 that draw attention to SH's attitude and Coleridge's difficulties.

The Greek phrase may be translated: "and chaste caresses".

3189 15.262   Suggested by Massinger *The Maid of Honour*? See
3187. In Act III scene i Bertoldo, who has been refused marriage by
Camiola, the Maid of Honour, says: ". . . And tell the cruel King
that I will wear/These fetters till my flesh and they are one/Incor-
porated substance." The entry pursues the mood of 1807, as well as
the interest in the elements; the dating of the next entry in this notebook on 24 March 1808 probably indicates that there was a gap in
time between them.

3190 18.329   The entry is in the hand of Dr Callcott himself (on
whom see 3218n).

Below the entry, much later, when the notebook was full or nearly
so (*c* 1816 or 1819), Coleridge wrote his comment on the titles of
these songs: "Dr C. has never returned my Music: and alas! what a

prophetic, and ominous motto to this volume has the crazy Musician's Hand unintentionally placed here!—What has all my Existence been since then but an Amo te solo accompanied by

Teneri miei sospiri! senza gioia, senza speme? [My tender sighs!
    without joy, without hope.]
Complain'd of, complaining, there shov'd & here shoving,
Every One blaming me, never a one loving!"
Amo te solo: "I love thee alone".

This is a soprano aria from the libretto *La Clemenza di Tito* (1 7) of Pietro Metastasio; the composer involved here is unknown, several composers having written operas based on this text. Possibly Coleridge took back with him from Sicily a sheet of music that had moved him, as apposite to his thoughts, poignantly so if he heard it sung, as he probably did, by Cecilia Bertozzi; see 2184n.

The words of the whole aria are as follows:

Amo te solo
Te solo amai;
Tu fosti il primo
Tu pur sarai
L'ultimo oggetto
Che adorerò
Quando sincero
Nasce in un core
Ne ottien l'impero,
Mai più non muore
Quel primo affetto
Che si provò.

Tr: "I love thee alone, thee alone have I loved; thou wert the first, thou shalt also be the last object that I adore. The first affection that is experienced, when it is born sincere within a heart obtains sway over it and never dies."

3191 19.61   There were quarrels with the Morgans; see e.g., though later (1811), *CL* # 831, 832. Was this "peevish mood, a tedious time" referred to as explained by the same cause—disappointed love—in *The Improvisatore* lines 35–48? *PW* I 467–8. On the Soother of Absence see 1225n, 1541n.

From here onwards, half a page is blank and the next ink much darker, and the internal evidence of several entries points to a use of this notebook in 1808 and later, except for entry 3195, which is notes made of some case, possibly one in which John Morgan was interested. See 3195n.

3192 19.62   Of all Coleridge's suggestions *substrate* is the only one that has been adopted; of it he is credited with the earliest usage (1810) by *OED*.

3193 19.63   The first half-brackets represent half a page excised; the second, part of a line, also cut out.

Coleridge's love of true sociability makes him sensitive to attitudes that nullify it; see also e.g. 2193 and 2830.

3194 19.64   If this is not Coleridge's own, it has not been traced to a source.

3195 19.76   For this long entry the notebook was reversed.

Coleridge's reasons for taking notes on the statement of a west-country lawyer, Wickham, in vindication of his character against the charges of one Champneys are obscure. Possibly John Morgan, as a fellow-lawyer practising in Bristol 1804–8, was interested.

The details are less interesting than the broad fact that Coleridge interested himself in something so remote from his personal bent. The Records of the Court of the King's Bench clarify some points.

Champneys was Thomas Swymmer Champneys of Orchardleigh (not *Orchardhigh*, as Coleridge writes it *f26ᵛ*). That Champneys was very short of money indeed in 1802 is borne out by the fact that in that year six judgements were given against him, three for a total of £7500 and three for other sums (unspecified). In the next year it was three judgements for a total of £790, and in the next, four judgements for a total of £11,400.

William Allard's case was still active in 1804 and was not settled until 1805.

3196 22.21   Here begin the entries on the second gathering in N 22; they appear to be datable, though not necessarily consecutively, not earlier than 1807, probably towards the end of that year or even into 1808. Some of them were probably written with the "Lectures on Poetry" for the Royal Institution in mind. The plans for the lectures were described in a letter to Davy 11 Sept 1807 (*CL # 656*), and the first lecture was delivered 15 Jan 1808 (*CL # 666*). The autumn of

1807 undoubtedly saw some preparation for them, along the lines of the letter to Davy. A year earlier the subject was to have been the Fine Arts (*CL* # 632).

Coleridge may certainly have had access to more than one copy of Cowley's Latin poems, but in *BL* II 209n he refers to seeing a copy in Bristol, *c* 1814; if it was Wade's or Cottle's copy, he could have seen it when he was there in 1807 also. In 1801 he had written two notes on Wordsworth's copy of the *Works* of Cowley (2 pts 1681), on the "Preface to the Miscellanies" (*Wordsworth SC* 508). This edition has *Davideidos* immediately after *Davideis*, but Coleridge's reference in *BL* II 209n to the Italian gentleman running through the Latin of Cowley and Milton *c* 1814 suggests the possibility of some collection, like *B Poets* v or *Eng Poets* vII, in which Cowley and Milton appear together, but not these specifically, as neither of them contains any of Cowley's Latin poems. *Wordsworth SC* shows also (507) a copy of the 1678 edition of Cowley's *Works*.

The lines come from Bk I of the *Davideidos* (lines 499–506 and line 541), translated by Cowley himself in *Davideis* I 441–56:

> Tell me, oh Muse (for Thou, or none cans't tell
> The mystick pow'rs that in blest Numbers dwell,
> Thou their great Nature know'st, nor is it fit
> This noblest Gem of thine own Crown t'omit)
> Tell me from whence these heav'enly charms arise;
> Teach the dull world t'admire what they despise,
> As first a various unform'd Hint we find
> Rise in some god-like Poets fertile Mind,
> Till all the parts and words their places take,
> And with just marches verse and musick make;
> Such was Gods Poem, this Worlds new Essay;
> So wild and rude in its first draught it lay;
> The ungovern'd parts no Correspondence knew,
> An artless war from thwarting Motions grew;
> Till they to Number and fixt rules were brought
> By the aeternal minds Poetick Thought.

The isolated line (541) is: "From thence ['sympathy' with the cosmic harmony] blest Musick's heav'enly charms arise." *Davideis* I 473.

3197 22.22   If Coleridge was here reading Wordsworth's 1681 edition of Cowley, or some other in which *Davideidos* appeared with the English poems, he could have turned from the *Davideidos* (of the foregoing entry), near the end of Bk I, to the "Preface of the Author", in which Cowley uses the words "Reputation" and "Fame", and says, "As for the *Portion* which this [affection to *Poesie*] brings of *Fame*, it is an *Estate* . . . that hardly ever comes in whilst we are *Living* to enjoy it, but it is a *fantastic kind of Reversion to our own selves:* neither ought any man to envy *Poets* this posthumous and imaginary happiness, since they finde commonly so little in the present . . .".

The distinction between *Fame* and *Reputation* became a Coleridgian *cliché*. It follows the pattern of other pairs of terms in opposing something living and dynamic to something having to do with the external and the fixed, e.g. imagination and fancy, wisdom and prudence. See e.g. *CL* # 689; *EOT* III 695–6.

3198 22.23   The inscription from Herodotus II 141 is quoted by Cowley in his n 74 on *Davideis* II and translated by him: "Let him who looks upon me learn to fear God." Coleridge's accents and breathings on the Greek are the same as in the text of Cowley *Works* (3 vols 1707–8) I 388–9.

3199 22.24   From Cowley *Davideis* I n 11; see 3196. It is a note to the lines "No bound controls th' unwearied space, but Hell/Endless as those dire pains that in it dwell." Cowley says these must be taken in a poetical sense, "yet on my conscience, where ere it be, it is not so strait, as that Crowding and sweating should be one of the torments of it, as is pleasantly fancied by Bellarmin. Lessius in his Book *de Morib. Divinis*, as if he had been there to survey it, determines the Diameter to be just a Dutch mile. But Ribera, upon (and out of the Apocalypse) allows Pluto a little more elbow-room, and extends it 1600 furlongs, that is 200 Italian miles . . .".

The last sentence and a half of the entry is Coleridge's.

3200 22.25   STC's *Catalectus* is wrong, probably an incorrect expansion of *Catal*, or some such abbreviation. The first lines are from Virgil *Catalepton* v lines 11–14. The first four lines were used, in part, in the preface to *SL* iii, cited, according to another numeration, as being from Bk VII. They appeared also in No I of *The Friend* (1809–10) 13, not in later editions.

Catalepton v 11–14:

Get ye hence, ye Muses! yea, away now even with you, ye sweet Muses! For the truth we must avow—ye have been sweet. And yet, come ye back to my pages, though with modesty and but seldom!—Tr H. R. Fairclough (LCL 1920).

Culex lines 8–9:

Hereafter shall our Muse speak to thee in deeper tones, when the seasons yield me their fruits in peace.—Tr ibid.

3201 22.26   The latter part of this entry, on *f29*, was already there when 3203 was written around it, i.e. 3201 is clearly earlier, a point possibly relevant to the so-far-unsolved problem of dating Coleridge's reading of the *Convivio* of Dante. This entry is an abridgement of the opening sentences of the fourth book. After his comment on the sentence he quotes first, Coleridge introduces a sentence of his own in Italian, *La connessione . . . uno di più:* "The connexion of love and beauty—in beauty the many are made one, in friendship one is made of many." Then after *Amore* he omits Dante's "as we learn from the concordant opinion of the wise who discourse on it, and as we see by constant experience", and thereafter quotes directly:

Love, as we learn from the concordant opinion of the wise who discourse on it, and as we see by constant experience, is that which joins and unites the lover with the person loved. Whence Pythagoras says that "friendship makes the many one." And because things that are joined together do naturally interchange their qualities insomuch that at times the one is entirely transformed into the nature of the other, it comes to pass that the feelings of the person loved enter into the person who loves, so that the love felt by the one is communicated to the other; and the same holds true of hatred and desire and every other feeling. Wherefore the friends of the one are loved by the other, and the enemies hated.—*Convivio* IV I tr W. W. Jackson (Oxford 1909) 193.

3202 22.27   This cipher entry will be seen to be unique among Coleridge's cipher passages; I am indebted to Col W. F. Friedman for deciphering it, though he must not be held responsible for the last two words or for the various interpretations suggested.

The entry comes at the top of a page and in appearance as well as content seems to be uncompleted. The cipher reads:

in what situati[o]n are we
thelaws of the world are they

> in themselvs, i m considered
> altogether w[ith] referens/reverens

The decisions as to the correct punctuation are difficult to make and fundamental to the interpretation. Should we read:

> In what situation are we? The laws of the world, are they in themselves I.M., considered altogether with reverence

ending with an interrogation mark or leaving the sentence incomplete? Or, in some ways what seems a more authentically Coleridgian reading, should we read:

> In what situation are we the laws of the world? Are they in themselves I M [?I AM] considered altogether with reference/reverence . . . ?

The first line ends with "we"; on the other hand, in the very next word spacing seems insignificant with *thelaws* run together.

In view of *Dejection* lines 47–8 (*PW* I 365): "O Lady! we receive but what we give,/And in our life alone does Nature live", the second interpretation not only seems to make better sense, but to deal with a problem in which Coleridge was deeply interested. The *I M/i m/ I m/* tempts one to a variety of guesses. With reference to the suggested I AM, see 3159 and n, and the numerous references in Coleridge's writings, especially in biblical contexts, to the creator fiat, the divine *I Am.*

Perhaps the most reasonable assumption is that Coleridge here misciphered *im* for *if*, especially as his symbol for *f* is the Greek *m*. There are other instances of slips in ciphering in the notebooks, and such a hypothesis gives an intelligible if incomplete reading.

Or possibly *i m* = im[mutable]?

Both from its position in N 22 and from its nature, I conclude that this is a later development of Coleridge's cipher system; he began wholly with transliteration into Greek characters, used fewer of them in the cipher passages earlier in this volume, and here uses fewer still. This last system, so far as my present knowledge of later notebooks goes, he did not persist in; presumably it was not so easy to remember as the other. See also Appendix C.

3203 22.28   Although nothing is needed to account for Coleridge's interest in allegory, it is worth noticing that he had recently been reading with some thoroughness Cowley's *Davideis* and Cowley's notes to it: see 3196–3199.

Note 77 to Bk II of this work, which could in any edition be on the same or a facing page to n 74 (see 3198), is about the Egyptian worship of the Moon and Sun Calf, which fascinated Coleridge in Drayton. See Essay I *Friend* 3–7. Cowley quotes Ovid frequently, and many sources on Jewish and Greek mythology, in his indications of the parallelisms or metamorphoses of the gods.

Some sentences in the lecture notes drafted for the course Jan–March 1818 reflect and expand the ideas and instances in this entry, especially the idea of the non-sensuous character of allegory, and the examples of the Tablet of Cebes, Apuleius, and Prudentius as a progression in idealization.

"The most beautiful allegory ever composed, the Tale of Cupid and Psyche, tho' composed by a heathen, was subsequent to the general spread of Christianity, and written by one of those philosophers who attempted to Christianize a sort of Oriental and Egyptian Platonism enough to set it up against Christianity; but the first allegory completely modern in its form is the *Psychomachia* or *Battle of the Soul* by Prudentius, a Christian poet of the fifth century—facts that fully explain both the origin and nature of narrative allegory, as a substitute for the mythological imagery of polytheism, and differing from it only in the more obvious and intentional distinction of the sense from the symbol, and the known unreality of the latter—so as to be a kind of intermediate step between actual persons and mere personifications." *MC* 30–1.

Bellay: Joachim du Bellay (*c* 1524–60) in this connexion is referred to probably less for his love poems than for his *Antiquités de Rome*, to be found in *B Poets* II 559–63 (where his name stands as here, without prefix). It is possible Coleridge is recalling, perhaps from some distance of time, Spenser's version.

It is, for instance, noticeable that in his sixteenth stanza Spenser begins three lines with the word *eftsoons*. Of the use of *eftsoons* in *The Ancient Mariner*, Lowes pointed out that the original *eftsones* dropped out in *LB* (1800), to return as *eftsoons* in *SL* (*RX* 337). Lowes did not list Spenser among the users of *eftsoons* (*RX* 335), and so far as I know no one on his list uses it in quite so emphatic a fashion as Spenser in this instance.

3204 22.29   In the reign of Louis XI the territory under the lordship of the comtes de Boulogne was given back to the French crown.

3205 22.30   The entry appears to have been written with a fine, perhaps stiff, rather dry pen; the word *mortar* appears to end in *t* rather than *r*, but it is a graphic sort of slip with the pen; the intention is *mortar*.

The conjunction of elements in this entry, and the spelling of *Dalkaïs*, point, after a search of the primary sources of Irish antiquities and history, and the better known historians who used them and one another, to William Parnell *An Historical Apology for the Irish Catholics* (Dublin 1807) as the work Coleridge was reading when he made these notes. Coleridge's (Poole's) copy of this work and his annotations on it were described in a letter by Alfred Hart from Melbourne, Australia, in *TLS* 9 May 1935. The one note on it is favourable to the work and antagonistic to Scottish reviewers; possibly Coleridge then had not seen the enthusiastic review by Sydney Smith in the *Edinburgh Review* for July 1807. The work must have been published early in 1807, and was well enough received to run to a third edition in London in 1808, facts that support the dating of this entry, otherwise unspecific.

Parnell writes: "Murrogh O'Brien, King of Thomond, swore fealty to Henry VIII, and accepted the title of Earl of Thomond. . . . This is the description the Irish annalists of the time give of it. 'He accepted', they say, 'the title of earl, but gave up the dignity of Dalkaïs, to the astonishment and indignation of the descendants of Heber, Heremon, and Ith' " (p 52). Coleridge's next paragraph refers to pp 76–8, where Parnell is describing the behaviour of the English, "royal and lordly robbers" he calls them, in confiscating Irish property. "The Irish might have replied by the same rule, when they reconquered the lands that had been confiscated (which they had done,) the right derived by the English from confiscation, should merge in superior right of conquest. But unluckily the Irish, according to their own proverb, had to go to law with the devil when the court was held in hell. We find directions from the Queen to escheat granted lands . . ." (p 76); and the commissioners appointed to sit in judgement on the proving of Irish titles to land are described as "Mr. Smith and Mr. Meagle, 'meet men, and apt in the profession of the law' ". The play on words is Coleridge's.

The concluding sentences are also based on Parnell. "And now came the triumph of power. 'The multitude, (as Sir J. Davies informs us) being brayed, as it were in a mortar, with the sword, pestilence, and famine, altogether became admirers of the crown of England.'

. . . The very commanders, with some degree of inconsistency, had to hang a parcel of old women, convicted of being cannibals, after they had reduced them to the necessity of being so. At length Sir Arthur Chichester was eye witness to three children feeding upon the dead body of their mother; and some compunction seems to have arisen in the breasts of the English when they found nature thus outraged by the effect of their measures" (pp 115–16).

In general, Parnell argued, the root cause of trouble in Ireland was not Roman Catholicism, but the disaffection caused by injustice and oppression, of English Catholics within the Pale as well as the Irish outside it. And in the pages immediately after Coleridge's last excerpt he discusses the cause of Irish poverty as owing not only to English rapacity, but to "the peculiar laws of property which were in force under the Irish dynasty", i.e. the custom of gavelkind—the equal distribution of inherited property.

In view of Coleridge's later articles in the *Courier* on Irish affairs (see *EOT* I xxxv–lxxiii, III 891–6, 925–32) it is of some interest to find him here reading a plea for the civil rights of Irish Roman Catholics, and an account of English misrule from the earliest conquests. He expressed views sympathetic to Parnell's as late as 1830 in *C&S* 191–4.

The Greek phrase in line 9 was translated in *Omniana* I 197 as "Tail-horn-hoofed Satan", with the suggestion that Henry More "would have naturalized the word without hesitation".

3206 22.31   The 4 has been made badly, and might be something else, possibly 7. But the date on this entry is probably that of the horrific event, not of the memorandum; a search of the likely periodicals and newspapers has, however, not found it under the Nov 1804/7 date. Was it for the pun he noticed it? Or as a sign of the state of human depravity even as late as A.D. 1804, having come upon it in an old number of some periodical? The date in 1804, against the weight of all the other evidence, does not offset the practical certainty that such entries in the gathering of the second watermark in this notebook are not earlier than 1807. For another example of an entry referring to an episode dated much earlier see 2616.

3207 22.32   *Mommock:* mommet, a doll, telescoped with mammock, a scrap of something? The subject of this portraiture is unknown; for a similar interest in immobility &c cf 995 and n.

3209 22.34   Indubitably about himself, this entry, written at the same time as the two preceding (possibly even one entry with them), suggests that all are autobiographical.

3210 22.35   See 2224 (49); Coleridge is here playing with variants on the metre described there. This seems to be a later return to it. The *Epistle to the Lady Margaret, Countess of Cumberland* is quoted as a motto in *Friend* I 166 (Essay XIV).

3211 22.113   If it were not for the indications in the next entry of Coleridge's reading at this time, the suggestion that he was here adapting and improving on Chapman might seem a wild guess. But cf "Wherein as th' Ocean walks not, with such waves,/The Round of this Realme, as your Wisedomes seas;/Nor, with his great eye, sees; his Marble, saves/Our State, like your Ulysian policies:/So, none like HOMER hath the World enspher'd;/Earth, Seas, & heaven, fixt in his verse, and moving . . .". Dedication sonnet *To the most worthie Earle, Lord Treasurer, and Treasure of our Countrey, the Earle of Salisbury, &c.* among the sonnets to his patrons prefatory to the *Iliad* in Chapman's *Homer* (ed cit 3212) Gg4ᵛ.

3212 22.114   The lines are from the sonnet *To the most honorable restorer of ancient Nobilitie, both in blood and vertue, the Earle of Suffolke, &c.*—in the folio edition of Chapman's *The Whole Works of Homer* (1616), among the sonnets to his patrons prefacing (G4ᵛ) the translation not of the *Odyssey*, as Coleridge states, but of the *Iliad*. This edition Coleridge sent to SH early in 1808 and it is probably the one from which he is quoting here. (*LR* gives an 1807 date for the marginalia; the *Wordsworth SC* 491 refers to a note dated 12 Feb 1808 on the verso of the engraved dedication page.)

3213 22.115   The first Greek phrase is used by George Chapman in the "Epistle Dedicatorie" to the Earl of Somerset of his translation of the *Odyssey:* ed cit A4; see the preceding note. Chapman translates it: "to speake things little, greatly; things commune, rarely; things barren and emptie, fruitfully and fully."
     The second Greek phrase is Coleridge's adaptation and turning of the first: "to treat big things as great, and new things with wonder".
     Do we see here the germ of the well-known words on the purpose of

LB (1798)? See *BL* II 3–4 (Chap XIV). The explicit articulation of the aims of *LB*, at the time of this entry, was still to come.

3214 22.116   *AP* 127–8, with "What then" for "Irene". The question is a recurrent one in Coleridge's notes (see e.g. 892) but is raised in this sequence of entries from Chapman's *Homer* by the "Epistle Dedicatorie" of the *Odyssey*. Chapman is attacking, in his vivid phrases, "this Prozer Dionysius, and the rest of these grave and reputatively learned", and quotes, "*Qui Poeticas ad fores accedit*, &c. (says the Divine Philosopher) he that knocks at the Gates of the Muses; *sine Musarum furore*, is neither to be admitted entrie, nor a touch at their Thresholds. . . . Nor must Poets themselves . . . presume to these doores, without the truly genuine, and peculiar induction." And Chapman continues, in prose and verse, to describe the bad poets, "Such men as sideling ride the ambling *Muse;*/Whose saddle is as frequent as the stuse./Whose raptures are in every Pageant seene;/In euery Wassall rime, and Dancing greene." A4ᵛ–5.

Irene presumably refers to Samuel Johnson's tragedy; see *MC* 439 for an attack on Johnson as poet.

3215 22.117   *I trust, you are very happy in your domestic being:* a phrase from or for a letter to Wordsworth? In view of the link between the Chapman entries before and after this with Wordsworth, probably *to* him.

The secret pang that eats away the Heart: a line of a non-extant Coleridge poem?

the Soul never is . . . *but lives in approaches:* The attempt here to analyse varying states of consciousness is marked by close attention to words and an acute sense of concepts as yet unborn. It may also be something of an attack on Locke, who, in the same book of the *Essay* that Coleridge refers to in 3217 and after considerable discussion of the impossibility of thinking in sleep, denies the possibility of the unconscious. "Can the soul think and not the man? or a man think, and not be conscious of it?" Bk II Chap I §19. (The interpretation is unfair to Locke if he means "consciously reason" by "think", but if so, that is just the point of Coleridge's quarrel with him.)

The Spirits of great Events Stride on before the events: Wallenstein (Pt II) v i 100–1: *PW* II 797. Coleridge quotes his own translation of Schiller's lines from *Wallensteins Tod* (Pt III) v iii, i.e. Wallenstein's last long speech in which he says ". . . so schreiten auch den grossen/

Geschicken ihre Geister schon voran,/Und in dem Heute wandelt
schon das Morgen.''

3216 22.118   *Two kinds of Madness:* again a reference to and part
quotation from Chapman's "Epistle Dedicatorie"; see 3214n. "There
being in Poesie a two fold rapture, or alienation of soule, . . . one
Insania, a disease of the mind, and a meere madnesse, by which the
infected is thrust beneath all degrees of humanitie . . . the other is
Diuinus Furor; by which the sound and diuinely healthful, *supra
hominis naturam erigitur, & in Deum transit.* One a perfection directly
infused from God: the other an infection, obliquely and degenerately
proceeding from man." Op cit A4^v.

   Insania: madness.

   Furor divinus: divine frenzy.

   supra hominis . . . *transit:* lit. "is elevated above human nature
and is transformed into God".

3217 22.119   Possibly it was intended to take more from Chapman
and thus part of *f70* was left blank. After using it, Coleridge found
f70^v partly used for 3216.

   is all memory an anxious act: cf *Inq Sp* §3, from a late notebook,
N 44.

   emptiness & absence . . . *as Spinoza observed whose pocket Mr Locke
picked:* Coleridge is perhaps thinking of that passage in the second
part of the *Ethics* where Spinoza says:

   "Those who think that ideas consist in images which are formed
in us by contact with external bodies persuade themselves that the
ideas of those things, whereof we can form no mental picture, are
not ideas, but only figments which we invent by the free decree of our
will; they thus regard ideas as though they were inanimate pictures
on a panel, and, filled with this misconception, do not see that an
idea, in as much as it is an idea, involves an affirmation or negation."
Ethics Pt II Prop XLIX. The same idea recurs in the *Ethics,* e.g. in
Pt II Prop XVII and Corollary, in Pt III Prop XVIII &c.

   Cf Locke: "The picture of a shadow is a positive thing. Indeed we
have negative names, which stand not directly for positive ideas, but
for their absence, such as insipid, silence, nihil, &c, which words denote positive ideas; v.g. taste, sound, being, with a signification of
their absence." John Locke *Essay Concerning Human Understanding*
Bk II Chap VIII §5.

Vorstellungen: mental representations.

Coleridge's general explanation here of slips in writing finds little support in modern psychology, but his interest in the subject and his search for an understanding of the experience, even his denoting it a class of facts, show an awareness beyond that even of many editors to-day.

3218 22.125   John Wall Callcott (1766–1821), composer and lecturer on music, took Coleridge 13 Jan 1808 to an evening at "a sort of Glee or Catch Club, composed wholly of professional Singers", apparently to Coleridge's delight and theirs. *CL* # 666. From 3190 we know that on 20 Dec 1807 Callcott had borrowed two Italian songs from Coleridge. Presumably the address was noted here Dec 1807–Jan 1808. According to the *DNB*, "the crazy Musician", as Coleridge calls him in N 18 (see 3190n), was living from 1807–12 in an asylum, possibly at this strange address.

On the other hand, Callcott was announced in an interesting list of lectures in the *Courier* of 9 March 1808 as a lecturer at the Royal Institution: "The following Courses of Lectures will be delivered this spring: . . . Mr. Davy on Geology, the Rev. Mr. Dibdin on the History of English Literature, Dr. Smith on Botany, Mr. Coleridge on Poetry, the Rev. Mr. Hewlett on Belles Lettres, Dr. Calcott [*sic*] on Music, Rev. Mr. Crowe, on Architecture." Presumably Coleridge came to know him late in 1807 in this connexion.

3219 22.126   From Dante *Convivio* (or *Convito*) Bk II Canzone I lines 53–55. We do not know what edition Coleridge used. He later quoted these lines variatim and translated them: "O lyric song, there will be few, think I,/Who may thy import understand aright:/Thou art for *them* so arduous and so high!" *BL* II 120; also in *Friend* III 244. The additional line is the first line of the same *canzone:* "Ye who by thought move the third heaven". Tr W. W. Jackson (Oxford, 1909), p 71.

3220 24.14   There are X's opposite lines 1 and 3, put there, I suspect, by EHC when copying the lines for publication; they are quite different from Coleridge's own asterisks on *f10* indicating a line revised.

The first seven lines are an attempt at rendering three distichs of the *Tabulae votivae* of Goethe and Schiller; see 3131 and n. The first is a fairly close translation of *Der berufene Leser:*

> Welchen Leser ich wünsche? den unbefangensten, der mich,
> Sich und die Welt vergisst und in dem Buche nur lebt.

Unbefangen, i.e. unbiased, unprejudiced, impartial, is perhaps attempted in Coleridge's "earnest *impersonal*"; or is he substituting for it a description of the kind of reader he would like? The next two lines are a paraphrase, still quite close, of *Die Unberufenen:*

> Tadeln ist leicht, erschaffen so schwer; ihr Tadler des schwachen,
> Habt ihr das treffliche denn auch zu belohnen das Herz?

With the next three lines Coleridge begins to expand *Die Belohnung:*

> Was belohnet den Meister? der zartantwortende Nachklang,
> Und der reine Reflex aus der begegnenden Brust.

The phrases that stimulated him to more than translation or paraphrase were "Reflex" and "Brust" and their adjectives, which fused with Schiller's *Der Tanz* (in 2363), with Kant, and with his Latin; the psychological association, especially with the adjectives, is plain here and also from the extension of some of the ideas in 3231.

The first four lines are in *PW* II 1000 as Frag 17, dated 1805; this is an error, the water-mark of the notebook being 1806, unless another MS was used. From the fifth line onwards, the lines are in *PW* I 391, entitled *Ad Vilmum Axiologum*, the title given by STC in 3231.

3221 24.15   These are jottings from Goethe's Introduction to the periodical *Die Propyläen*, which he founded in 1798; in the Weimar edition of Goethe's *Werke* (133 vols 1887–1918) the paragraphs appear respectively on XLVII 7, 9–10, 20, 21–2.

In paragraph 2, after *die er sich gleichgesinnt weiss*, the sceptical *oder hofft* is Coleridge's addition. In paragraph 3 he does little more than jot down key sentences. Goethe wrote, "Natürlicherweise hat das Publikum auf die Kunst grossen Einfluss, indem es für seinen Beifall, für sein Geld, ein Werk verlangt das ihm gefalle, ein Werk das unmittelbar zu geniessen sei, und meistens" &c. After *gebildet*, instead of Coleridge's English paraphrase, not wholly clear, Goethe's text reads, ". . . auch er fühlt die gleichen Bedürfnisse, er drängt sich in derselbigen Richtung, und so bewegt er sich glücklich mit der Menge fort, die ihn trägt, und die er belebt.

"Wir sehen auf diese Weise ganze Nationen, ganze Zeitalter von ihren Künstlern entzückt, so wie der Künstler sich in seiner Nation, in seinem Zeitalter bespiegelt, ohne dass beide nur den mindesten Argwohn hätten, ihr Weg könnte vielleicht nicht der rechte, ihr Geschmack wenigstens einseitig, ihre Kunst auf dem Rückwege, und ihr Vordringen nach der falschen Seite gerichtet sein."

In the first line of the last paragraph Coleridge has changed Goethe's *Bild* into *werk. Einbildungsgefühl* is Coleridge's un-German emendation of Goethe's *Einbildungskraft*, whereby he would seem to deny to an inferior work of art the power to engage the imagination, and to suggest that it affects only the feelings.

As the *Einleitung* was not published again until 1830, Coleridge must have taken these excerpts from the periodical itself or from a work quoting it. The 1807 date, conjectured from the relation to other entries in the notebook, seems a not unlikely time for Coleridge to be casting about for just such material on the eve of his lectures on "the principles of poetry" at the Royal Institution, especially in the light of his earliest intention to lecture on the fine arts generally, and on "Taste". Thomas Beddoes seems a likely person to have the work in his library. Or De Quincey; see *CL #* 806.

The second paragraph was used by Coleridge as a motto for *BL* and there translated with some interesting differences from the literal translation given below, e.g.: "Little call as he may have to instruct others, he wishes nevertheless to open out his heart. . . . He wishes to spare the young those circuitous paths, on which he himself had lost his way."

Tr: What can afford us greater confidence in this respect is the harmony in which we find ourselves with many others, is the experience that we are not alone . . . when we find ourselves again in many others. . . .

However little he may be destined to instruct others, he will yet wish to communicate with those whom he knows, or hopes, to be like-minded, whose number, however, are scattered throughout the whole world, he wishes thereby to take up again the relations with his oldest friends, to continue those with new ones and to win, among the youngest generation, still others for the remainder of his days. He wishes to spare youth the roundabout ways on which he himself strayed. . . .

The public . . . demands a work that will please it . . . and mostly the artist will fall in with this demand, for he himself is part of the public, he too was formed in the same age and day. . . .

The worst of works can speak to our sensibility and to our feeling (*not* power) of imagination, by setting it in motion, releasing and liberating it and leaving it to its own devices; the best work of art speaks to our feeling too, but speaks a nobler language, and one which has to be learnt; it engages the feelings and the *power* of imagination, it destroys all our arbitrariness and caprice, we cannot do as we like with what is perfect; we are obliged to give ourselves up to it, in order that we may receive ourselves back from it, exalted and improved.

3222   24.16   This entry invites comparison, especially towards the end, with 1718; and the whole indicates again how personal would have been any Hymn to the Elements. See also e.g. 3151 and n.
   The cipher reads:

> asra Schonthinu
> musaello rita gelocedri

The first line is his anagram for Sara Hutchinson, used in the title (revised) of *The Devil's Thoughts* in "Sara's Poets"; see *C&SH* 20n. The second line is, of course, Samuel Taylor Coleridge.

3223   24.17   *AP* 294. Note the appearance of this, or part of it, in 3043 in cipher.

3224   24.18   The Dampier reference is to Capt William Dampier *A Collection of Voyages &c* (4 vols London 1729) II ii 77, the only discoverable edition with this page reference.

3225   24.19   *AP* 293. This is a paraphrase of the third paragraph copied from the *Propyläen* in 3221.

3226   24.20   Dampier (ed cit in 3224) II ii 89: "And I have particularly observed there, and in other Places, that such as had been well-bred, were generally most careful to improve their time, and would be very industrious and frugal when there was any probability of considerable Gain. But on the contrary, such as had been inur'd to hard Labour, and got their Living by the sweat of their Brows, when they came to a Plenty, would extravagantly squander away their Time and Money in Drinking and making a Bluster."
   The fact that in *Friend* III 293-4 this passage is referred to as if recited to Sir Alexander Ball in Malta does not affect the dating. Coleridge used it there for literary purposes to illustrate a point, probably

similar to one made in conversation with or suitable to the spirit of Ball, not as a scholar giving evidence. The water-mark of this note-book rules out the possibility in any case.

3227 23.1   This specimen of this recurrent entry suggests Coleridge's difficulty in mastering the name; see 371 and n.

3228 23.2   The Greek is Plato (?) *Axiochus* 366c; Coleridge omits an iota subscript in the verb θανατᾳ. His translation is impeccable.

3229 23.3   SυυThνηCκω: *C* is one form of capital *S* in Greek. Hence Συυ Θνῄ Σκω: "I die with [?her]". The capitals STC complete the story, unless there is also an attempt to co-mingle his anagram for Hutchinson, i.e. Schonthinu, with his own initials; note the value of the medial theta in this respect.

Che Sara Sara: The words of the motto of the dukes of Bedford had scarcely the present-day spurious familiarity in Coleridge's time. He wished them used on a seal to be designed *c* May 1808 for him by Matilda Betham. See *CL* # 704.

3230 23.4   On the duty-pleasure conflict cf *inter alia* 2058, 2210, 2556, and 3026. In various forms the subject is much discussed throughout *The Friend*.

3231 24.21   *Ad Vilmum Axiologum.* Under this title the lines in English on *f13*ᵛ are in *PW* I 391–2. As JDC pointed out, WW coined this name for himself, in 1787, by signing his first published poem *Axiologus. PW* (JDC) 614.

f13 See p.30: i.e. of the notebook, *f15*ᵛ, where there is a fair copy of the Latin lines.

*f13*ᵛ The second line of the nine in English was written below the present sixth, the transposition being indicated in the MS.

the Eternal begets the Immortal: cf 3159, suggesting a probing of the deepest levels here.

Passion and order aton'd: cf *BL* (Chap XVIII) II esp 49–50; "On Poesy or Art" ibid II 254.

Be able to will . . . *Being:* a return to the dispute with Wordsworth (as well as Kant) about Duty. For another similar conjunction see 3220n.

f14 I should have no Self: see 3026 and n.

miracles: see 3022.

f14ᵛ   Knowlege as opposed to mere calculating: philosophy *vs* psilosophy, as in 3121 and 3158.

Seven years ago: if this is correct, the date of this entry is
approximately 1807–8, if EHC's dates for the verses (*f15*) "O ye
Hopes . . .", "Jan 1801", is also correct. *PW* I 360.

In this further example of poetry and prose dissolving into each
other, several points seem noteworthy. There is, first, the return to
hexameters directed towards Wordsworth, a poignant reminiscence
of the earlier attempt in Germany. See *PW* I 304–5.

The translation below takes the second version (B) as standard;
variants between the two versions are shown in the following notes
and are indicated by superscript numbers in the translation.

    1. A reads *leni/ . . . fronte:* with a calm brow, i.e. with equanim-
ity.

    2. A reads *Grata . . . grata* (agreeable, pleasing) for *cara . . .
cara* in B; but *grata* could be translated "dear".

    3. A reads *fœdifragam* (perfidious) for *eam falsam* in B.

    4. A has cancelled draft (*a*) *Hancque pati jubes:* and her you bid
[me] endure; (*b*) *Me lucem noctemque pati:* endure light and night.

    5. A reads *falsam* (false) for *vanam* in B.

Tr: Do you command me to abide Asra's neglect? and submit to the sight
of Asra's estranged ¹eyes? and know for certain that she who was—and always
will be—²dear to me is ³false and cruel? And you bid me ⁴endure the daylight
when I am crazily in love with an ⁵empty woman and my whole wide world
quivers and totters? Why not, William, order me—with mock grief—to let
my guts be pierced with a knife? Why not tear out my heart, or my eyes, or
whatever—if possible—is more precious! I shall command my failing spirit
to observe your wish—though I am dying—as long as faith in Asra lingers.
But I have seen the last rites of loyalty, and I am dying. Do you think I shall
be won over by a facile argument—by *Reason?* What sort of man is it can
love without losing his wits! What is [?becoming/good] and what is [?unbe-
coming/bad]—let that be the care of men of sound mind. My life is finished;
yet Asra lives on, heedless of me.

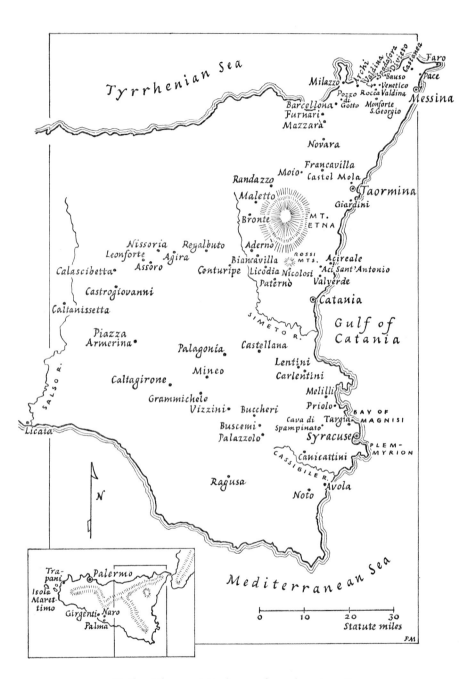

11. Sicily. Places visited or referred to in 1804–5

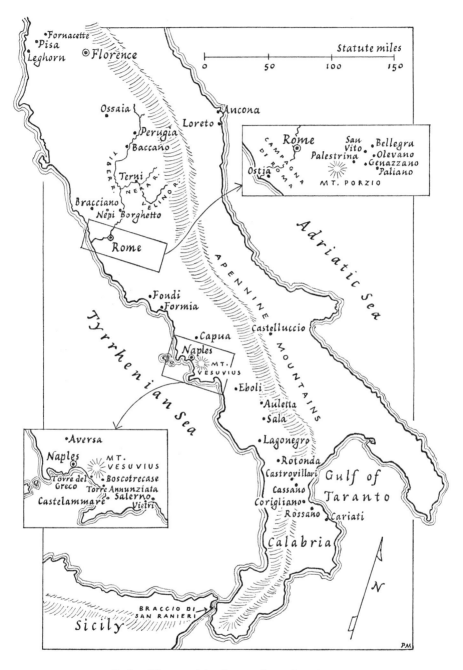

III. Italy. Places visited or referred to in 1805–6

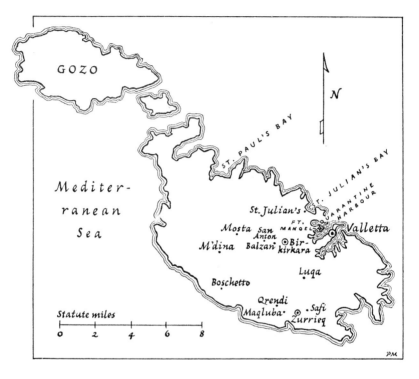

1. Malta. Places visited or referred to in 1804–5

APPENDIXES

Coleridge's Knowledge of Italian

WHEN COLERIDGE was twenty-six years old he visited a peaceful Germany, where he easily found congenial acquaintances who could initiate him into the language and the literature of their country. He went abroad for the second time at the age of thirty-two, in a period of great emotional and physical suffering, and found the Mediterranean countries he visited enduring the upheavals of invasion and internal dissension. Most of his time was spent in Malta, a centre of international ferment, almost completely isolated from Italian culture. In both Malta and Italy he developed an antipathy for Roman Catholicism as the official religion; it was something of a barrier between him and the ordinary people (though it did not necessarily impair his relations with the educated classes), and much in the literary masterpieces of Italy was intolerable to him on moral grounds. These are some of the reasons why, though he acquired an extensive knowledge of Italian literature, he was less in sympathy with it than with German, and why there are fewer references to it in his later work. Yet the beauty of Italy itself, and the charm of Italian poetry, painting, and music, did make a deep impression on him.

Italian was to be the second language Coleridge learned for the purpose of travelling, for when he left England for Malta in April 1804 he intended to make his way to Sicily with only a brief delay. He had with him on the voyage a grammar and dictionary presented to him by Lady Beaumont, which she said were "as portable as could be carried". This particular dictionary has not been identified. His copy of the *Vocabolario italiano-latino* was inscribed and perhaps bought 23 Jan 1805—see 2074n; he refers in 2625 *f97* to an Italian-Spanish dictionary. He also owned the *Dittionario toscano* of Adriano Politi (Venice 1728), now in VCL. The grammar was probably *A New Method of Learning the Italian Tongue* . . . tr "from the French of Messieurs de Port Royal by an Italian

Master" (2074n). He had with him also another work associated with Port-Royal, Pascal's *Lettres provinciales*, a tetraglot copy of which (French, Latin, Italian, and Spanish) he had found among Southey's books in 1803. During the three weeks of the voyage he studied the Italian grammar as diligently as the tempestuous weather and his own ill-health would permit (2074). He also read some "Italian Love-poems", possibly an anthology, possibly Dante's lyric poetry (2062). N K records his interest in Italian syntax and his study of the tetraglot edition of Pascal to find illustrations for some of the more idiomatic usages that have a parallel in French. In Feb 1804 he had mentioned to the Wordsworths his intention of buying "Dante and a dictionary" if his funds permitted. By July 6 he could write to Daniel Stuart that he would soon be able to speak and write both French and Italian.

He looked forward to his trip to Sicily in Aug 1804 as an occasion for perfecting his command of the spoken language, but was somewhat disappointed because he had apparently not anticipated the difference between the Italian spoken there and the Italian he had learned from his grammars. Besides, the vigorous rapidity with which it flowed from Sicilian lips disconcerted him, and he comments very aptly that unless a listener anticipates what his companion is going to say the difficulty of comprehension is doubled (2179). However, he did learn a good deal during his journey in the south, and his letter to Sir Alexander Ball of 8 Nov 1804 shows that he was by then able to understand even rapidly spoken Italian as long as it was distinctly enunciated. His conversations with the English-speaking Barzoni at the beginning of 1805 were sometimes, at least, in Italian; see Appendix D below. But his ear was still not accustomed enough to catch accurately either the name *Barzoni* (which he wrote as *Bassoni* in a book given to him by its author) or the name of the newspaper he edited, *Il Cartaginese* (2677). When he went to Florence in 1806, however, he perceived immediately the harshness of the Tuscan pronunciation as compared with that of Rome. He never reconciled himself to the sound of Italian as spoken by the Italians, although he considered it delightful on English tongues. He found the fiery vehemence of the native speaker distasteful, and even blamed this unsweet "Jargoning" for some of the extremes of the Italian temperament (2812).

His interest in the language extended to the dialect he heard in Sicily, of which he records a phrase (2675) and a few agricultural technicalities, possibly learned from the British Consul, G. F. Leckie (2250). And he was sufficiently interested in dialects to buy, probably during his brief and penniless visit to Florence in 1806, a reprint, newly published there in that year, of Francesco Baldovini's *Lamento di Cecco da Varlungo,* a poem in rustic Tuscan first published in 1694.

Before leaving England Coleridge had almost certainly read very little Italian literature in the original, though he had made a beginning in the language. See 1269. His one quotation from Boccaccio before 1804 (see 1649, 1653) could be from an intermediary source, although we now know from the Wordsworth LC that he owned a copy of the *Geneologia de gli Dei* (2737n). He had read Boyd's translation of Dante's *Inferno* in 1796, and in the same year he spoke disparagingly of Petrarch in his Introduction to "A Sheet of Sonnets": *PW* II 1139. In 1802 he may possibly have heard Wordworth read some stanzas from Ariosto's *Orlando furioso,* which he was then translating. In 1803 he recommended to Southey Machiavelli's political and historical works, "in a good old English translation", professing to prefer him to Tacitus. In Italy he was to read Machiavelli in the original.

When N 22 reached him in Malta in Aug 1804 the German entries already in it probably revived his interest in metres (2224n). It was then that he began to study Italian prosody, and copied out fragments of Metastasio's melodramas and of other operas, probably first heard on his travels in Sicily. It is evident that he enjoyed the opera more uncritically and with greater enthusiasm than any other phase of Italian life. His references to it are frequent and warm (e.g. 2356 and n), and he recalled it with pleasure in later life.

It may have been this renewed interest in versification, as well as his decision early in 1801 to write a series of love poems (possibly the Soother of Absence, which he mentions in connexion with the Italian love poems), that turned his attention to the lyric poets of the sixteenth and seventeenth centuries. In them he found a form of literary art hitherto unknown to him, an art that consisted in expressing trivialities and commonplaces with incomparable craftsmanship. It is this that so interests him in Strozzi and Marino—the exquisite melody that enchants the ear and leaves the mind and heart untouched. He analyses this very acutely for his own future guidance (2599), and expresses his hope some day to unite this perfection of form with sincerity of thought and emotion. Whether he acquired his copy of Girolamo Ruscelli *Del modo di comporre in versi nella lingua italiana* (Venice 1594) at this time is not known, but the few notes on it and the water-stains give it a Mediterranean appearance. It is now in the possession of W. H. P. Coleridge.

It is perhaps not surprising that Coleridge makes hardly any mention of contemporary Italian literature. Malta was isolated and, while he was there, was concerned entirely with politics. When he travelled he went to southern Italy, where the interests of the educated class lay in philosophy, science, and history rather than in letters, and where again politics would be almost the exclusive subject of conversation. He never, of course, visited the literary centre of that era, Milan, which was in the hands of the French, and it was not until the very end of his stay that he went to Florence, and then for but a short time. In Rome he seems to have associated chiefly with artists. Indeed, the only Italian man of letters whom he mentions as an acquaintance during his three years abroad is Vittorio Barzoni, and he was an English scholar, so that it was natural for them to discuss Southey rather than Foscolo, though Barzoni must have known the latter in Venice. It may be noted, too, that Coleridge's residence in Italy coincided with a lull in Italian literary activity. The great figures of the eighteenth century were dead or outmoded, with the exception of Monti, who at that time was the official Francophile laureate. Of the Romantics, only Foscolo had yet made a reputation. Among the few eighteenth-century writers Coleridge mentions in the notebooks are Alfieri, who died the year before Coleridge left England, and Metastasio, whose taste, melody, and judgement please him, though he doubts his poetic genius. He also refers, though not in the notebooks, to Algarotti, Casti, and to Carlo Gozzi, whose death in

1806 he may have heard mentioned while he was still in Italy.

Of the mediaeval authors he had a wide knowledge. Dante of course he now read in the original, and probably Petrarch too (although the notebook references come much later), this time with admiration. Characteristically, he extended his reading to their minor and more erudite writings, and quotes the Latin works of both. It is noteworthy that although the moral tone of much of the *Decameron* was unpleasing to him, his admiration for Boccaccio seems to have increased with time, and flowered in one of the most beautiful of his later poems, *The Garden of Boccaccio,* with its lovely description of the Tuscan countryside he had visited in 1806. It must have made a deep impression on him, and linked itself closely with the garden scenes in the *Decameron.*

Among the major poets of the Renaissance he considered Ariosto the greatest, and though he deplored his "disgusting licentiousness" he once speaks of him, apparently in a spontaneous outburst of affection, as "darling Ariosto" (2670). Though he says that he would praise his poetry rather than his poem, he sets him above Tasso: indeed, he excludes Tasso from what he considers the age of superior truth in the Italian language. He had also read Pulci and Boiardo, and considered the Italian poets supreme in the field of narrative poetry (2431 *f4*"). His interest in satire and burlesque poetry is evident in his reading of Grazzini, Berni, and Salvator Rosa, though at first he found their racy popular vocabulary difficult after the formal Italian with which he was familiar. Among the lyric poets he found Chiabrera incomparable, though Chiabrera belonged to a period that Coleridge elsewhere characterizes as one of decline. His admiration for Strozzi and Marino as artificers has already been mentioned, and Guarini too was among his favourites, though he seems to have read his *Rime* rather than the famous *Pastor Fido.*

Of the historians he read at least Machiavelli (both *The Prince* and *The History of Florence* in Italian), and Lodovico Muratori.

In a separate class because they wrote in Latin must be placed some of the Italian philosophers. Giordano Bruno early won and retained his deepest admiration and sympathy, both as a philosopher and as "an enlightened Christian". He acknowledges the influence of Bruno's "polar logic and dynamic philosophy" on his own thought, and in Sicily or Malta made a list of Bruno's works with the hope of collecting, or at least reading, as many as possible (2264). He had already learned in Germany how rare they were, and it may have been these works, all on the Index and many destroyed by the Inquisition, that he was seeking in Naples and Rome when he discovered the availability of so much prohibited literature. Other Italian philosophers whom he read at various times were Giambattista Vico, Girolamo Cardano, Marsilio Ficino, and Famiano Strada.

Italian poets who wrote in Latin were represented in his library by the *Carmina illustrium poetarum* (11 vols Florence 1719–26); his copy is now Dyce 7644 in the Victoria and Albert Museum, Kensington.

But this brief review gives only a most imperfect idea of the wide range of Coleridge's reading in Italian. What has been said about his interest in the minor works of Dante and Petrarch can be extended to many other writers. He has read Metastasio's letters as well as his plays (2222), and though he may not have read Sannazaro's *Arcadia* he refers to his Latin eclogues and owned his works (2633n). He is familiar not only with Marino, but with Marino's imitators (2625); not only with the principal lyricists of the Renaissance, but with more esoteric poets such as Girolamo Benivieni (referred to later in N 22); and besides the great historians he knew many minor local histories. What he read probably depended to some degree on what was available in the libraries and bookshops of the cities he visited rather than on his own considered choice, but even so he acquired an unusually wide knowledge of Italian literature of various periods.

The result of his study of Italian appears principally in his lectures, in the *Biographia Literaria*, and in *The Friend*. He made use in the lectures of some of the material he had collected on the great mediaeval and Renaissance writers, and he developed in the *Biographia Literaria* the notes he had made on Strozzi in N 17; but he had many other projects, which were unfortunately never realized. In *The Friend* he refers to the desirability of an anthology of translated passages from the treatises and letters of Petrarch. He promises in the prospectus to write essays on the present and past state of Italian literature. He suggests an analysis of contemporary history in the light of Machiavelli's maxims. He had also planned a work on allegory from the time of Dante until its decline (3203), and in 1814 he proposed to Murray a translation of the prose works of Boccaccio with the exception of the *Decameron,* a new edition of which (a reprint of the 1741 translation [by Charles Balguy]) had appeared in 1804. Other unfulfilled hopes were an account of his own travels, a life of Giordano Bruno, some sort of critical work on Ariosto, and, as late as 1819, a drama based on one of Carlo Gozzi's *scenari.*

He completed very few translations; unfortunately, because his version of Guarini's dialogue between Faith, Hope, and Charity is both faithful and felicitous (*PW* 1 427–8). His translation of Marino's "Donna, siam rei di morte" (*Alla sua amica*) is less satisfactory (*PW* 1 392), for though it is plain that he burlesques the conclusion intentionally, he gives no idea of the skilfully contrived flow and check of the first line. His prose translation of a stanza from Chiabrera at the end of Essay VIII of *The Friend* (*Friend* 1 101–2) follows unerringly the intricate construction of the original, whereas his treatment of the same author's seventh epitaph, "Fu ver, che Ambrosio Salinero a torto", is a most ingenious improvisation on a theme, with only a few lines of the original surviving.

The passages of Italian that Coleridge transcribed in the notebooks are generally copied accurately, so much so indeed that they often serve to identify the editions he was using. He is, however, not always careful about accents, and this is particularly noticeable in the fragments of Pascal (2133), where the omission of the accent that distinguishes *è* (is) from *e* (and) is often confusing. This is an early entry, and he may not yet have realized that in Italian the accents, in spite of the frequent carelessness of sixteenth- and seventeenth-century Italian printers, are even more important than in French. In the extracts from Strozzi (2599) and Marino (2625) the substitution of exclamation marks for periods or colons often heightens the emotional quality of the poem. In the Strozzi madrigals, too, he occasionally gives such words as *Albergo, Sera, Giorno,* an initial capital that does not appear in the original. In his faithfulness to his text he seldom corrects a misprint in the edition he is using; one of the few exceptions is his correction of *Ecco* to *Eco* in the last line of the Strozzi madrigal *Filli mia*.

Coleridge in Malta

LITTLE IS KNOWN of Coleridge's Malta period. Such information as we have has come in almost casual references in his works—in the third volume of *The Friend* and in *Table Talk*, a few references in EHC's notes to poems—a few more in the memoirs of other persons, not always accurate. There are only twenty letters written from Malta, and but thirty-nine are extant from May 1804, when he arrived, to the end of 1806, i.e. four months after his return to England. Although illness, and procrastination, and the additional lethargy induced by a warm climate may be held partly responsible for the dearth of communications, there is no doubt whatever that war-time shipping disasters accounted for some gaps, and that the destruction of Coleridge's papers at Gibraltar among Major Adye's plague-infested effects was responsible for considerable losses, possibly a journal written for the Beaumonts and the Wordsworths, and a criticism of some of Wordsworth's poems, notably of *The Recluse*.

In the scarcity of information, therefore, it seems not irrelevant to notice here some materials more or less loosely related to the notebook entries of the period.

In the archives of the Royal Library, Malta, there are bound volumes (MSS 430, 431) of proclamations and notices, of the sort reproduced in plate II and referred to in 2386n and 2594n, many with the printed signature of S. T. Coleridge.*

* I am indebted to Mr Joseph Galea, archivist in the Royal Malta Library, for first showing me these documents; and to Mr Donald Sultana, of the Royal University of Malta, who obtained photostats at my request. Mr Galea's knowledge of the history of Malta, and his personal kindnesses, have put many visitors in his debt. Mr Sultana is the author of several newspaper articles on Coleridge in Malta, in the *Sunday Times of Malta* Oct–Nov 1956; in a later issue, on learning of the existence of the *bandi*, he referred briefly to them in an article "Samuel Taylor Coleridge and the Royal Malta Library" 29 June 1958.

A translation of the one reproduced in plate II is as follows:

PROCLAMATION

His Excellency the Royal Commissioner, taking into consideration the advantage which the existence and maintenance of good Roads affords the Public, because of his solicitude for the furtherance of so important an end, is incapable of neglecting any means which might attain it.

Hence, in consideration of the fact that the wheels of Carriages and Carts as they are at present constructed are the principal cause of the deterioration and destruction of the Roads, he orders and commands that in future such wheels shall be made according to the model which will be supplied to the respective Artisans, and that the nails shall not project from the bands of iron which surround their circumference, on pain of the contumacious Artisans being compelled to pay, on each occasion of contumacy, the penalty of 20 ounces, half of which sum will go to the public treasury, half to the informer.

As His Excellency hopes, then, that the majority of the Owners of Carts and Carriages will, for the sake of his pleasure and their own convenience, have remodelled the wheels of any Carts or Carriages belonging to them, even if already built, from then on the satisfaction may be expected of seeing introduced a system of constructing wheels which besides saving the Roads is also of great advantage to the Owners of Carriages and Carts, since it is very easy to understand that large protruding nailheads, by continually jarring the Carriages and Carts as well as the Persons or goods being conveyed, destroy the Carriage or Cart itself more rapidly, particularly the iron wheel-bands which receive the shock directly; they inconvenience the passenger, damage the goods conveyed, and tire the animal much more quickly, because those projecting nailheads act as so many points of resistance and levers opposed to the action of the moving force.

Secretariat of the Government 29 January 1805.
Samuel T. Coleridge Public Secretary of the Royal Commissioner.
G. N. Zammit Deputy Secretary.

The last sentence (and especially the final clause), unmatched in any of Coleridge's later notices or proclamations, which are more official and perfunctory in tone, strikes one as a typically Coleridgian effort to offer his audience a reasonable explanation of fundamental principles, whether or not they could be expected to understand the physics of the thing. Possibly when he heard this cried by the town-crier of Valletta he realized the unsuitableness of the proclamation as a literary medium for abstract generalizations; the annotation on the proclamation reads:

31st January 1805. It has been read, made public and posted in the usual places in these four cities and Floriana, at the sound of a trumpet in the presence of a great many persons, whence &c

A mere list of the other *bandi* and *avvisi* suggests the variety and incongruity of his official duties, or what he described as "the business, intrigue, form and pomp of a public situation".

Avviso 1 March 1805. Matteo Sacco jailed for extorting money on pretence of procuring pardon for an exile, and the public reminded that the Governor is always ready to hear complaints.

Avviso 8 March 1805. Notice of division of prize money to Maltese soldiers to all ranks who participated in the capture of Valletta; to be carried out by the Lieutenants of their respective villages.

Bando 8 March 1805. An imposition of a tax on wine in consideration of the poverty of the Maltese. The plight of religious institutions and foundations will be considered later.

Avviso 9 March 1805. A warning not to moor boats at a certain floating buoy.

Bando 22 March 1805. An attempt to curb the use of spirits by licensing distilleries.

Avviso 22 March 1805. An inspection of the quality of wine instituted.

Avviso 22 March 1805. The export of cotton forbidden. (See 2294 and n.)

Avviso 22 May 1805. Two men and a boy flogged and banished for spreading false rumours (unspecified).

Avviso 25 May 1805. Fortunata Tagliana punished for instigating an attack on a Jew; and a man rewarded for quieting the mob. The woman is banished to the neighbouring island of Gozo, where there are no Jews. (See 2594n for the full translated text of this notice.)

Avviso 12 June 1805. A warning about counterfeit money.

Avviso 14 June 1805. Aloisia Caruara imprisoned for offering an ounce of gold to the Judge of the Criminal Court of Valletta, and

407

the money confiscated. Let her punishment serve as a warning to others.

Avviso 20 June 1805. A reminder of the penalty for those who take enlistment money and do not join the army.

Avviso 21 June 1805. Regulations to define relations of Naval Lieutenants and Night Watchmen with regard to permits for fishing boats to work at night in the Great Port.

Bando 21 June 1805. An attempt to regulate registration of foreigners and licensing of vehicles.

Avviso 23 June 1805. Formerly emergency certificates of British protection were issued to foreign ships, and respected by the government of Barbary, but these having been abused, passports were issued only to English-owned or Maltese-owned ships. These, too, having been abused, new "Mediterranean passports" on parchment will be issued; should any ships be found sailing under false colours, they will be plundered and the crews enslaved by the Barbary government, nor in such case would the Governor intervene.

Avviso 15 July 1805. A warning to deserters from the Royal Regiment of Malta and to their harbourers, and an offer of rewards to informers.

Bando 5 Aug 1805. A ban on the sale or display of unripe fruit.

Avviso 5 Aug 1805. A reminder that soldiers may not buy anything, even bread.

Avviso 19 Aug 1805. A notice about the distribution of the Royal Bounty [referred to in *Avviso* 8 March 1805] from the Secretary's office, on the basis of reports from the Lieutenants of the villages.

Bando 2 Sept 1805. A second warning to deserters and their harbourers.

Avviso 21 Sept 1805. An announcement of the appointment of Edmond Francis Chapman as successor to Alexander Macaulay in the office of Public Secretary and Treasurer. Signed by Alexander Ball.

Another quite different collection of Malta documents was preserved, apparently by Coleridge himself in the first instance, and then by the family custodians of his library. It is now in VCL, and consists of some twenty-one assorted items. They too indicate, fragmentary though the tales they tell, that Coleridge as a civil servant was certainly deeply involved in the administration of the island, and that his work must often, as e.g. 2552 and many other entries suggest, have taxed energy and patience and tact.

The list of VCL documents is as follows:

F 14.2: Observations relative to the conduct of the Government of Algiers—1804 [EHC's annotation says that the first part is in the hand of Sir A. Ball]. 9ff. The conduct of the Dey of Algiers, 14ff, in an unknown hand, with marginal annotations by STC.

F 14.3a: Remarks on the Extent of Cultivatable Land in Egypt. Signed "C. Pasley." 2ff. (See 2297n and 2449n.)

F 14.3b: Appendix to "Observations on Egypt", in a clerk's hand. 8ff [By STC and C. Pasley].

F 14.4: Thoughts on the occupation of Sicily by the English: a transcript in an unknown hand (6ff) of what could be a report by Ball, Coleridge, or Macaulay. It incorporates many observations found in Coleridge's notebooks.

F 14.5: A letter [c May 1805], in Coleridge's hand, to Lord Camden, drafted for Sir Alexander Ball in defence of Ball's plan to have corn bought by a public official responsible to him, not by commercial agents. (See 2740n.)

F 14.6: Transcripts and abstracts by Coleridge of a correspondence from Corfu beginning 5 Jan 1805 to Lord Harrowby from Mr Morier and Mr Foresti on military tactics, privateering, etc. 8ff.

F 14.7: An attestation dated 15 Oct 1804 by General St André, transcribed by Coleridge, as to the military reputation of the Chevalier Pietro Conte.

F 14.8a: A letter from Nathaniel Taylor to S. Stocker, dated Malta 1 Aug 1805, enclosing a letter purporting to be from S. Stocker to N. Taylor, dated Naval Arsenal, 30 July 1805, challenging Taylor to a duel.

F 14.8b: A deposition in clerkly hand, imputing malpractices in the receipt and disposal of government stores to Mr Stocker, signed by Anthony Kelly with his signature attested by S. T. Coleridge, 28 July 1805.

F 14.9: A pencilled MS fragment by Coleridge, describing the sub-

409

version of the Fountain of Arethusa, Syracuse, to the purposes of women washing clothes.

F 14.10: An incomplete prose fragment by Coleridge touching on popular dislike of the English [in Malta? Sicily?].

F 14.11: A duplicate of a letter from Sir Alexander Ball, 26 Nov 1804, to the Earl of Camden, saying that "Capt Leake . . . is to be sent . . . to purchase corn in the Black Sea and that a Mr. Coleridge will go with him to act as his substitute should Leake have to return"; duplicate. (See 2740n.)

F 14.12: An affidavit by James [Tutroino?] Paymaster, sworn before Coleridge 13 March 1805 and signed by him as Public Secretary to H.M. Civil Commissioner.

F 14.13: A petition from John Ross, & Co., merchants, 13 July 1805, to Sir Alexander Ball to compel payment of a bill of exchange they had accepted on Cadiz and which had come back protested for nonpayment.

F 14.14: A transcript by Coleridge of two letters of Robert Lamb, Oct and Nov 1804, to his brother John Lamb describing the plague in Gibraltar. (See 2044n.)

F 14.15: A list of papyri from Herculaneum made under John Hayter, 25 Jan 1802–30 Nov 1805. In Italian.

F 14.16: A proclamation in Italian by Emanuel, prince de Rohan, Grand Master of the Order of the Knights of St John of Jerusalem (Malta), concerning quarantine of vessels from the Barbary Coast, 1786.

F 14.17: An official visit of inspection to prisoners, Easter 1805. In Italian, in an unknown hand.

F 14.18: In conformity with the regulations of Sir Alexander Ball, Capt Skinner, captain of the British cutter *L'Hirondelle*, makes application (undated) for the booty from the two ships which were captured illegally. In Italian. (See Coleridge's correspondence with Ball on this matter in *CL* # 609, 610, the second letter having been written on board *L'Hirondelle*.)

F 14.19: A MS letter to Sir Joseph Banks from Antonio M. Jacj, dated Messina 9 Oct 1805, concerning a solution for the problem of finding the longitude at sea. In Italian.

F 14.20: A MS letter of T. W. Zamitt, to Coleridge, dated Valletta 21 May 1805, advising that a poem, *La musica*, has nothing in it contrary to the Catholic religion. In Italian.

F 14.21: A list, dated May 1803, of supplies brought to Malta? Cargoes? Government stores? Bills of lading?

It should not escape our attention that the Public Secretary was second in importance to H.M. Civil Commissioner (actually the Governor, though Ball's difficulties with the authorities at home prevented him from receiving the official title). A few years later, when Ball died in 1809, E. F. Chapman (for whom Coleridge had waited long and anxiously in Malta, as the only hope for his release) took over the duties of Governor for most of a year. Such was the prestige of the office of the "Most illustrious Lord, the Public Secretary", as Coleridge told Mrs Coleridge he was hailed in the streets: but as he said, such salutations and "living in a huge Palace all to myself, like a mouse in a Cathedral on a Fair or Market Day . . . are no pleasures to me who have no ambition, & having no *curiosity*, the deal, I see of men & things only tends to tinge my mind with melancholy". *CL* # 619. He hoped to leave by 1 Sept; actually it was 21 Sept (2674). A letter from Ball to Hugh Elliot, British Minister at the court of Naples, dated 23 Oct (see 2733n) is also a manuscript in the VCL collection (F 14.1):

Malta 23 October

My dear Sir

I beg to introduce to your Excellency Mr Coleridge whose literary fame I make no doubt is well known to you: He possesses great genius, a fine imagination and good judgment, and these qualities are made perfect by an excellent heart and good moral character—He has injured his health by intense Study, and He is recommended to travel for its re establishment—You will have much pleasure in his conversation, any attention paid him will be an obligation conferred on My dear Sir

Your most faithful and obedient
Alex^{der} Ball

The letter refutes beyond doubt Rickman's gossip (*Rickman* 151) that relations between Ball and Coleridge were not good by the end of Coleridge's stay in Malta. To the last weeks of his life Coleridge talked enthusiastically about Ball, and also, as the long conversation reported for 16 April 1834 in the *Table Talk* bears witness, with energy, compassion, and interest, of the Maltese.

Coleridge's Cryptogram

A CRYPTOGRAM, "Cryptographina, reveal unto me", was found by EHC among a bundle of Coleridge's letters of the German period, but, he said, "only accidentally placed among them". His statement is undoubtedly correct. The watermark of the paper was 1802, and we know that Coleridge's use of various systems of concealment began with transliteration into Greek characters, as in entry 1636 in 1803, or with 172, perhaps even in school-days. The second stage, the use of numerals for letters of the alphabet, is dated 27 Dec 1804, in entry 2387. It is a sign of the deterioration in his physical and mental health in Malta that on his return to England and to a daily life lived among friends and, briefly, family, he should feel the need of inventing a more complicated system for secrecy; and perhaps it is equally significant that he wrote little of anything dire or dreadful under its cover. The cipher here described originated in 1807.

EHC's transcript of the cryptogram was retranscribed for me by his son, the late Rev G. H. B. Coleridge, whose accompanying note explains why it seems preferable here simply to set forth the key rather than to reproduce exactly the third-hand copy: "I have copied this as accurately as I can. But as this is a copy of a copy, and as my dear Father's handwriting with all the will in the world was not remarkable for its legibility, and as I have perhaps little right to boast a better, there are doubtless signs difficult to decipher. On the whole though, I think it is clear." The cipher alphabet follows, including some additional signs for prepositions, pronouns, and articles, not all of which appear to have been used by STC.

It will be seen that the system is primarily a single-substitution cipher without transposition: that is, each letter of the original text is altered to a corresponding symbol, the order of the symbols in a ciphered passage remaining the same as the order of the original

letters. The symbols are primarily Greek characters; but in providing variants for the vowels, STC has used roman letters, punctuation points, and a few invented symbols. He has also provided
a code for prepositions, conjunctions, pronouns, and other words of
common occurrence; some of these are self-evident (e.g. $\rho = R =$
are); others are self-evident when deciphered (e.g. $\alpha = B =$ be);
others are rendered arbitrarily by numerals and invented symbols.
Not all of these coded elements seem to have been used by STC,
but some appear in cipher passages and in other contexts in various
Coleridge manuscripts. The most interesting of these is the use of
the Hebrew character ש, shin (sh), which sometimes stands for
"she" but more often represents Sara Hutchinson (either through
the initials SH or as the initial character in the anagram [ΑΣΡΑ]
שΟΝΘΙΝΥ).

It is clear that Coleridge constructed his cipher without any
exact cryptographic counsel. Word-units are not concealed; cipher
passages are often introduced by or contain phrases in clear; single
letters sometimes occur in clear in ciphered words and are usually
marked as clear by a point or stroke placed underneath. All these
factors seriously limit security. He evidently recognized the importance of suppressing the identity of letters that occur most frequently, for he provided for some letters at least four variants, but
only for the six vowels, thereby suppressing only four of the eight
highest frequency letters in English.

Vowel key, each vowel having four signs:

$$a = , \; y + f \qquad\qquad o = . \; j \ddagger i$$
$$e = ; \; u \not{+} g \qquad\qquad u = ! \; e \ddagger k$$
$$i = : \; ö \not{\ddagger} h \qquad\qquad y = ? \; æ \maltese £$$

Consonants:

b	$= \alpha$		g	$= \epsilon$
c (hard)	$= \eta$		h	$= \text{'}$
c (soft)	$= \kappa$		j	$= \epsilon$
ch	$= \nu$		k	$= \eta$
d	$= \iota$		l	$= \omega$
f	$= \mu$		m	$= \beta$

n	$= \gamma$		v	$= \mu$
p	$= \zeta$		w	$= kk$
ph	$= \mu$		wr	$= \theta$
qu	$= \eta$		sw	$= F$
r	$= \theta$		wh	$= \phi$
s	$= \kappa$		z	$= o$
t	$= \lambda$			

Below this transcript of the alphabet of the system is a note in quotation marks, presumably by STC himself: "N.B. Greek letters not included in this Cryptogram mean themselves. Cyphers having a dot included mean themselves: thus $6 =$ from, but $6\cdot = 6$. Stops bracketed mean stops: thus $(?) = ?$ $\mathcal{w} =$ she $\mathcal{w}: = ,\kappa\theta$, $\mathcal{w}^c$ in combination *Sh:* $\beta =$ b; and so on with any other letter: thus $\underline{\lambda} =$ L."* There follow, also in quotation marks, two fantastic words: "onorificabilitudinate—sov[r]amagnificentissimamente".†

are $= \rho$		herself $= E$	
be $= a$		her, him $= \Gamma$	
by $= 2$		himself $= \Gamma$	
beside } besides } $= 3$		his $= \Sigma$	
before $= 4$		if $= \cdot\mu$	
behind $= 5$		of $= \mu$	
betwixt $= T$		is $= \sigma$	
between $= T$		the $= ;$	
but $= \underline{B}$		you $= \iota$ or !	
for $= \curlyvee$		thou $= \iota$ or v	
from $= 6$		thee $= i$ or $\dot{v}$	
in, into $= 7$		we $= \frown$	
through $= 8$		us $= \frown$	
to, unto $= 9$		and $= \&$	
her $= P$		me $= \beta$	
		not $= N$	

---

* The Hebrew letter shin (sh) is $\mathcal{\dot{w}}$, with a dot to the right; sin (s) is $\mathcal{\dot{w}}$, with the dot to the left. Coleridge's schoolboy Hebrew would have taught him the pun-potential of these signs; he used the first of them in his anagram for SH in *The Devil's Thoughts* in "Sara's Poets"; see *C&SH* plate opp p 32.

† For the source of these two words and therefore additional authority for the dating of the cipher see 3013 and n. Their mnemonic (?) use here is not clear.

ourselves = A   yourselves = $\wedge$
she = w with = $\sqcup$
tho = δ we = $\frown$
their, themselves = Δ who, which = Φ
yourself = Λ whom, whose = Ψ

It will be noted that e and ϵ, i and ι, k and κ, u and v are not easily distinguished in themselves, and are confused at times by STC himself in using them as well as in the transcript of the transcript of the system. Other uncertainties of a different kind are introduced by Coleridge's addiction to word-play, etymological fantasies, mildly anagrammatical tricks, and especially by his habit of mixing languages. Examples of all of these will be found in this volume.

The last cipher entry in *CN* II (3202) introduces new elements not included in the key found by EHC; Col W. F. Friedman has been kind enough to elucidate its alphabet and to decipher the passage. The alphabet, so far as it is used in the passage, reads:

a   c   d   e   f   g   i   l   m   n   o   r   s t u v w the(y)

Entries like this one, in which punctuation is crucial but not self-evident, and the polyglot entry 2535 are open to more than one interpretation. Possibly 3202 is incomplete, and its ambiguity either may be deliberate or may merely reflect the uncertainties of an incomplete cipher being used more or less experimentally. The difficulties of passages like 2535, on the other hand, which occur also even without encipherment, seem to arise out of the attempt to express an all-but-inarticulable complexity of idea or feeling.

Il Cartaginese on the Sinking of the *Abergavenny*

THIS ACCOUNT of the sinking of Capt John Wordsworth's ship, the *Abergavenny*, is translated from an account in Italian in a political journal, *Il Cartaginese*, published in Malta. *The Carthaginian*, as it defiantly called itself (Napoleon having boasted that Malta was another Carthage to be burned and sacked), was a propagandist sheet published 1804–8, subsidized by the British government.

The editor, commissioned by William Pitt, was Vittorio Barzoni (1767–1843), a highly intelligent Anglophile journalist, to whom Coleridge undoubtedly refers when he writes to Southey in Feb 1805: "I now translate as truly, tho' not as verbally as I can the sense of an observation, which a literary Venetian who resides here as the editor of a political Journal, made to me after having read your review . . .". *CL* # 614. Barzoni presented Coleridge with a copy of his *Rivoluzioni della repubblica Veneta* (Valletta 1804) Vol 1, now in VCL, which, like the letter quoted above, suggests that he and Coleridge found they had some interests in common. In a brief autobiographical sketch written in the third person, Barzoni says: "Barzoni received in Malta frequent marks of attention from important personages stationed in government posts, from the English and Spanish admirals and generals who came ashore, and from various famous men of letters who came there from time to time. He lived on the most intimate terms with Walpole, Colleridge [*sic*], with Lord Byron, and with the famous Sir William Drummond. He also made the acquaintance of the Comte de la Tour, the Duke of Modena, Count Pozzo di Borgo, the Duke of Orleans, the Cavalier d'Azara, Sir Robert Wilson, and with other gentlemen distinguished in letters, arms, or power." He also mentions reading in the British library translations of Greek prose and poetry. *Biografie autografe ed inedite di illustri Italiani di questo secolo* ed D. Diamilla Müller (Cugini Pomba e Comp Turin 1853) 58.

Coleridge was later to use the name Barzoni in *Zapolya*, for a Jewish doctor, about whom the first remark in the play is, "I held him for a spy" (*PW* II 885); certainly it was easy to associate the name with war-time propaganda.

Of the distribution of *Il Cartaginese*, the authority from whom the information about Barzoni is drawn, Alberto Lumbroso, in *Gli scritti anti-Napoleonici di Vittorio Barzoni lonatese* (Modena 1895) 22 fn 1, says: "The English sailed close to the coast of the kingdom of Naples and threw bundles of the journals there. Napoleon ordered five francs to be paid for every copy that was turned over to his police. The fishermen were out at all hours scanning the sea-shores, and let their nets lie idle, intent on a kind of fishing that was less strenuous and more profitable." See 2677 and n.

The question naturally arises whether Coleridge had any finger in the following account of the sinking of the *Abergavenny*. It reads in Italian like a translation out of English, and Coleridge may well have assisted with it: some sentences could easily be his.

The Carthaginian

April 20, 1805   No. 15   Malta Political Journal

Wreck of the Vessel called The Earl of Abergavenny

The great ship of the East India Company called The Earl of Abergavenny, commanded by Captain Wordsworth, left Portsmouth last February bound for the Indies, but a few days after setting sail she was miserably wrecked off the Bill of Portland. She broke on a rock, and sank twelve feet below the surface of the water. As she was laden with an immense quantity of porcelain ware and 27,000 ounces of minted silver she sank with unusual speed, as though dragged down by her own weight. Captain Wordsworth, who commanded her, was regarded by the East India Company as one of their best sailors, and by his comrades as one of the best men ever produced by the human race. This excellent Captain, scorning to survive the precious charge which had been entrusted to him, refused even at the last moment to abandon his employers' property: he perished with his ship. The majority of both passengers and crew were drowned. The fate of the former arouses pity; the heroism of the latter deserves an honoured memory. With the exception of a few, the names of those who survived and of those who perished are unknown to me;

417

but I am well acquainted with the dreadful catastrophe which I shall proceed to relate.

On the first day of February, The Earl of Abergavenny sailed from Portsmouth with the Henry Addington, the Wexford, and the Bombay Castle, under the escort of the frigate Weymouth. These vessels as they passed through the Needles were unfortunately separated from the warship which was accompanying them. The next day that little merchant fleet cast anchor to wait for the Weymouth, but it was not seen to appear. On the third day the wind grew so violent that all the vessels ran for safety to the nearest ports. Captain Wordsworth thought he should find shelter for The Earl of Abergavenny in the Portland Roads. The ship arrived there quite safely about 3.30 P.M., on February 5th. Then the wind grew much less violent, but the tide which was swiftly going out made the ship recede. It appeared exactly as though she were drawing back several paces from the roadstead in order to take a run and go more speedily towards her destruction. The tides rushing impetuously in the opposite direction drove her violently upon the rocks which tower before the Bill of Portland. There she remained almost half an hour, striking repeatedly against the rocks with such violence that at the frightful shocks the sailors could scarcely keep on their feet on deck. Towards four o'clock they managed to extricate the ship from that danger; they even thought they might get her into the Bay of Weymouth, but every effort to use the sails was in vain. The water spouting from the various cracks with which the ship's sides were riddled damaged her so much that the hand of man could no longer manoeuvre her. In this perilous situation a cannon was fired as a distress-signal; twenty shots or more were fired soon after, but unfortunately no one came to the rescue.

The moment was highly critical. The officers, seeing the water pouring in from all sides, took every measure to diminish what had already entered and to prevent the entrance of more. At 5 o'clock they began to use the pumps, but it was of little use. They realized then that the ship was full of holes, even on the bottom, and that it would be very difficult to prevent her from sinking gradually. The harsh lot of the people who were in her became increasingly deplorable as night approached. As 8 o'clock struck, in order to seek aid from some quarter they began to fire the alarm cannon again, this time continuously; but as fate would have it the wind was once more blowing in gusts, and the sea had become so heavy and threatening that no one dared to venture on it. When they saw that neither from the coast nor the sea did there appear a soul to succour them, the unfortunate wretches who were all calling for help in turns took a hand at the pumps to pump out the water, but the constant rushing in of high impetuous waves, following fast upon each other, frustrated all efforts to save the ship.

Then it seemed certain to the sailors that within a few hours they would be swallowed up by the sea, and despite the fearless behaviour of the officers, who used every exertion to encourage the disheartened and to keep the rebellious to their duty, there was confusion and uproar on board. Nevertheless they redoubled their efforts to keep her afloat. Officers, sailors, and passengers, men and women, all toiled with despairing zeal, but all their efforts were in vain. At 10.30 the water was already washing over the bridge. Shipwreck was inevitable, and all the unfortunates on board the vessel, plunged in the fatal examination of their fatal position, recognized that the moment of their death was close at hand. Abandoned as they were to their hard lot, and tortured by cruel anxiety, with staring eyes and dejected hearts, they counted every hour, every instant of that unfortunate night. Every now and then deep sighs were heard, and broken sobs and tearful cries, which mingled with the roaring of the waves and the screams of the sea-gulls flying through the winds.

At 11 the passengers were informed of their desperate situation, so that they might make some attempt to save themselves. Shortly later the officers spoke these terrible words to the sailors: "We and the ship are all about to sink". Three cadets, still only children, when they heard this dreadful sentence went to their little cabin and remained there looking at one another, and not breathing a word. After a little, the youngest broke the horrible silence by exclaiming, "Let us go back to the bridge, there must be something . . .". Two of them did so: Gramshaw (such was the name of the third) remained in the cabin, opened his chest, took out a little money, the certificates of his commissions, and some letters from his mother, then came on deck to seek his companions; he could not find them: they had perished.

The wind was blowing fiercely, the sea was frightfully tempestuous, the ship staggered, and the rising water was hiding her from view. Gramshaw, wishing to gain a height, went up to the top-deck of the poop. As he was climbing the stairs which led to it, an immense column of water sweeping right across the bridge carried the youth away into the whirlpool of the sea. Although in such a disaster he lost all hope, still love for life made him exert extraordinary efforts to keep afloat, but as his clothes were soaked with water it was of little or no avail for him to try to swim. Then his courage abandoned him, and he resigned himself to his Creator's will, patiently awaiting the moment when he would be swallowed up in the whirlpool which the ship would produce as she was engulfed. In that terrible crisis he felt as though something were striking against his back: he thrust out his right hand, and vigorously grasped what he had been led to find: it was a rope hanging from the Verga di Civada. This fortunate coincidence revived his failing courage, he scrambled up the rope so successfully that he was able to climb on board. This child was one of the few people saved from the wreck. His existence is a miracle.

To see a good man struggling in vain against adversity, and finally succumbing beneath a heavy burden of misfortunes, is a spectacle worthy of heaven and earth. Socrates, as though triumphing over his iniquitous destiny, in his last moments consoled his family, gave his disciples memorable lessons, then remained serenely in his prison awaiting death from the fatal hemlock. Captain Wordsworth, after having discharged the duties of his rank during that scene of desolation, and having given the poor passengers all the consolation which the natural goodness of his heart suggested to him, stopped on the quarter-deck to await death with the calm of an impassive being. Midnight strikes: and all at once the first officer of the Abergavenny, Baggot, runs up to him out of breath, and in a voice broken by profound anguish informs him that the ship is sinking rapidly. Wordsworth looks at him fixedly, and stifling the tremendous grief which overwhelms him answers with greatest gentleness, "Let her sink! May the will of God be done!" Such were his last words, and such was the last moment of his life. To hear loud wails, strange piercing voices, cries of grief, accents of despair, to feel the ship submerging, to perceive a turmoil, a tumult of men and women scrambling up the rigging or rushing up the masts to seize the yards, was all the work of one instant.

As a climax of desolation in that moment of calamity, the winds blew more fiercely than ever, and furious waves made the vessel reel from stem to stern with such violence that in a moment it sank more than ten feet, and struck the bottom of the sea. The suddenness of its sinking submerged all those who were close to the water level. The shock which the ship sustained also made many abandon their little anchors of safety. The miserable wretches fell from the masts, from the ropes, from the yards, like withered fruit from a tree shaken by the blast. And this cruel catastrophe took place two miles from the Bay of Weymouth! It is hard to perish, harder still to perish miserably, hardest of all to perish within sight of the shores of one's native land!

The night was extremely dark, extremely cold. Nothing appeared above the surface of the water but swaying masts, ragged ropes, and sailors clinging to them, against whom enormous floods broke, driven by a violent wind. Those miserable men were suspended between the sky and the sea, yet they were forced to struggle at the same time against the rigorous cold, the pounding waves, the exhaustion of desolation, the agonies of life, and the terrors of death. Abandoned to the sport of all those cruel scourges, having lost all hope of aid, they perished one by one. Some were violently carried away by the constant beating of the waves; others were forced by the dreadful cold to let go of the ropes which they were clutching. The few who held fast in these circumstances saw at every instant by the light of the lighthouse of Portland some of their companions in misfortune, floating for a moment on the sea, then, indicating the last moment of their existence with frightful cries, sinking beneath the surface never to reappear.

It was one in the morning: there was a slight lull in the dreadful storm: the profound darkness of the night seemed to melt away, and through enormous masses of black clouds a few stars appeared in the firmament. They seemed to those unhappy men who still survived like stars of good augury, and full of fresh confidence they conceived the hope that they would be snatched from their doom. They were not deceived, Providence had not abandoned them. It was just at that moment that far away there appeared a sloop: it soon drew nearer, and cast anchor near the Abergavenny to assist her. At that sight hurrahs of exultation and tears of joy succeeded the anguish of despair: they blessed heaven, they blessed the kindly hand which was coming to save so many unfortunate men from the abyss over whose edge they hung, and they kissed the miserable ropes which had saved from death those poor survivors of a deplorable wreck. A skiff was at once launched and was rowed towards the wrecked vessel, and in three trips they were able to rescue ninety persons.

Naval discipline did not lose in those cruel circumstances its empire over the English sailors. Though those unhappy men were placed between the hope of life and the terror of an immediate death, they gave at that tremendous moment a stunning proof of their habitual obedience; with the greatest coolness, and without anxiety of any sort, they got into the skiff two by two, as their names were called by the officers and they were ordered to embark. What a sight, to see sailors suspended over the crater of a whirlpool, exhausted with hunger, with thirst, with weariness, benumbed by excessive cold, fainting from terrible sufferings, ready to perish; and yet make no attempt to preserve their lives except in the order laid down for them by their commanding officers! To preserve in the urgency of a perilous instant the behaviour customary in tranquillity, is the height of heroism.

When they thought they had taken on board all those poor patient fellows who had survived the wreck, the sloop set sail to leave. The fourth officer of the Abergavenny, the brave Gilpin, was going away, keeping his eyes fixed on the cordage on and by which he had escaped the peril of drowning; when by chance he perceived a man sheltering in the yards of the top; he shouted to him repeatedly; there was no answer. Once more risking a life which he had ventured so many times that night for the good of others, Gilpin returned to the sunken ship, and found that man, who, because he had for many hours been exposed to cruel cold and the fury of the sea, had lost all his faculties; he carried him to the sloop, gave him all possible aid, left no way untried to reanimate him, but every effort was useless: he perished two hours after he had been taken from the top. This was Sergeant Heart [*sic*].

After this lamentable series of tragic events, the sloop was slowly proceeding towards the Bay of Weymouth when not far away they perceived struggling against the waves a poor wretch who had escaped from the wreck. He was soon recognized as the famous Baggot. This youth who during the wreck had distinguished himself with a display of extraordinary bravery by trying even in that condition to carry out a magnanimous enterprise lost his life. A poor passenger, the young woman Blair, swimming some distance from him thought she could reach safety; but the heavy waves which tossed her about threatened to hurl her into the bosom of eternity. The deplorable situation of this poor woman, her tearful words, her piercing cries, made Baggot's blood leap in his veins. Moved by that sight, although he needed all his strength for his own preservation, he forgets himself, listens only to the magnanimous impulses of his heart, and heeds only the hope of saving that poor creature in some way from the tomb rather than the risk of destroying himself. Just at the moment of her most extreme danger he hastens to her aid, holds her above the water, and draws her towards the sloop: he has almost reached it and is just about to experience the ineffable pleasure of saving both her and himself; all of a sudden an enormous wave overtakes him, completely covers him, exhausts his failing strength and drowns him. This generous youth in whose veins human sensibility ran like a flood sacrificed himself in vain. The unfortunate Blair was swallowed up by the sea a moment later, and was seen no more.

At 3 P.M. the sloop finally reached the port of Weymouth, bearing the bitter news that besides 263 persons one of the largest vessels of the East India Company had perished. After the most terrible of nights the dawn broke, and lighted up that spectacle of horror. A calm sea, two masts, a few fragments of naval equipment, and several corpses floating about on the vast expanse of ocean. The day only revealed how lamentable had been the night preceding it.

APPENDIX E

Contents of Wordsworth MS M

IN VIEW of Coleridge's frequent quoting of Wordsworth's poems, sometimes with variants from the accepted texts that may be either his own or Wordsworth's, it may be useful to give here the titles of the poems he had with him in Malta. This information is based on the assumption that MS M, now in Dove Cottage, is the set of transcripts made for him by the Wordsworth household. Miss Darbishire, who shared this view of Professor de Selincourt, generously provided in her own hand a list of the contents of the manuscript.

It may be noted that although *Peter Bell* appears on paper of a different size and was bound in after the others were there, it must have reached Coleridge before he left London. He read it to Ball in Malta. *Friend* III 296.

MS M

The Ruined Cottage (*The Excursion* Bk I)
Sonnets:
    Anticipation October 1803 (Shout for a mighty Victory . . .)
    How sweet it is . . .
    Where lies the land . . .
    Methought I saw the footsteps . . .
    The world is too much with us . . .
    O gentle sleep . . .
    A flock of sheep . . .
    Ere we had reach'd the wish'd for . . .
    These words were utter'd . . .
    Beloved Vale, I said . . .
    England the time is come . . .
    Vanguard of Liberty . . .
    Six thousand Veterans . . .
    These times touch monied worldlings . . .
    Is it a reed that's shaken . . .

Jones, when from Calais . . .
Toussaint the most unhappy . . .
Festivals have I seen . . .
I griev'd for Buonaparte . . .
We had a Fellow-passenger . . .
Dear Fellow-traveller, here we are . . .
Coleridge! I know not which way I must look . . .
Great men have been among us . . .
It is not to be thought of . . .
When I have borne in memory . . .
One might believe that natural . . .
When looking on the present face . . .
How dolefully O Moore . . .
Whom pure despite of heart . . .
Nuns fret not . . .
There is a trickling water . . .
With ships the sea . . .
Brook that hast been . . .
Fond words have oft . . .
Pelion and Ossa . . .
Calvert it must not be . . .
Beaumont, it was thy wish . . .
I am not one that much or oft . . . (4 Sonnets)
The Sailor's Mother
It is no Spirit who from Heaven hath flown
Motto—for Poems on naming of Places
       Some minds have room alone . . .
To the lesser Celandine—To the same Flower
Up with me, up with me into the clouds . . .
To H. C.
To a Butterfly
To the Cuckoo
My heart leaps up
To the Daisy
The Sparrow's Nest
From Stirling Castle we had seen (*Yarrow Unvisited*)
Among all lovely things . . .

To a Butterfly—Stay near me . . .
Once in a lonely hamlet I sojourn'd (*Emigrant Mother*)
Ode to Duty
This is the spot (*Travelling*)
O Fools that we were we had land . . .
Alice Fell
When first I journey'd hither . . .
There is a flower, the lesser Celandine
Dear native Brooks . . .
I travell'd among unknown men . . .
I have been here in the Moon-light . . .
On seeing a Red-breast chasing a Butterfly
The sun has long been set . . .
Who leads a happy life/If it's not the merry Tinker
These chairs they have no words . . .
The cock is crowing . . .
Stanzas . . . in my Pocket copy of Castle of Indolence
Foresight
The Green Linnet
Farewell thou little nook . . .
She was a phantom . . .
There was a roaring in the wind . . .
She had a tall man's (*Beggars*)
There was a time (*Ode on the Intimations of Immortality* . . .)
Sweet Highland Girl—a very shower . . .
The Owl as if he had learn'd his cheer . . .
Peter Bell
Book the First
[*The Prelude*] Bks I–IV

BM MS Egerton 2800 ff 151–4

See entry 3129 and note

THIS MS has no general heading or title. At the top, inserted probably after the transcribing was under way, are the indications:

"+ unusual, more than usual—
= the same as the last word marked *Italic*".

The article on "Prognostics of the Weather", condensed and revised by Coleridge from Nicholson's *Journal*, follows.

———

Signs of Rain from Birds

Sea and Fresh Water Fowls such as Cormorants, Seagulls, Muir[!] Hens, &c flying from sea or the fresh water, to land, shew bad weather at hand—land fowls flying to water, and these shaking, washing & noisy, especially in the evening, =. Geese, ducks, coots &c picking, shaking, washing, noisy—rooks, and crows in flocks, & disappearing suddenly, pies & jays = & noisy—the raven or hooded crow crying in the morning with an interruption of their notes, or crows very clamorous at eve—the Heron, Bittern and swallow flying very low—birds forsaking their nest and flying nestward[1]— poultry to roostward, pidgeon to dove-cote—tame fowls grubbing in the dusk, and clapping their wings—small Birds seeming to duck, and wash in the sand—the late & early crowing of the Cock, and wing-clapping[2]—the *early* singing of wood-larks— = chirping of sparrows—note of chaffinch *near houses*—the dull appearance of the robin = —peacock, and owls unusually noisy.—

From Beasts.

Asses braying more than usual—Hogs playing, scattering their

[1] The article reads, "to their nests", and similarly for Coleridge's *roostward*, "going to roost"; and see also *hiveward* below, again Coleridge's compression.]
[2] The article reads, "clapping his wings".]

food, carrying straw in their mouths—Oxen snuffing the air, looking south-ward, while lying on their right sides or licking their
Hoofs—cattle gasping for air at noon—calves racing violently &
gamboling—deer, sheep or goats, pushing, leaping, fighting—Cats
washing their face & ears—dogs eagerly scraping up earth, foxes
bark, wolves howl—moles throw up earth + more than usual, rats
& mice more restless +: a grumbling noise in the belly of
Hounds.—

From Insects

Worms in numbers crawling out of earth—spiders falling from
their webs—flies dull and restless—ants haste nestward—bees hiveward—and there keeping close—frogs and toads toward Houses—
frogs croak from ditches—toads *unking* from[3] eminences—gnats
shrilling[4] + − ;—

From the Sun—

Rising dim or waterish— = red with blackish beams mixed among
his rays— = with misty or muddy color— = red & *blackish*—setting under a thick cloud or with a *red* sky in the East—

From the Moon—

Pale in color—horns blunt at first rising—blunt within 2 or 3 days
after change, rain for that quarter/an iris with a S.Wind, rain *next
day*—S.W.3rd night after change, =. S.W., & the M. not seen before the fourth night, rain for the *Month*/full moon in April, new
and full moon in August, rain, for most part—. Mock moons sign
of great rains.—

From the *Stars*.

= a large, dull, pale—twinkling not perceptible, or with irides.[5]—
in summer, when W[ind] is E. and stars seem large, = sudden
rain

[3 The article reads, "crying on".]
[4 The article reads, "singing more than usual".]
[5 The article had the singular, "an iris".]

from Clouds—

in cloudy weather, when wind falls—*clouds* growing bigger, or like rocks or towers settling on the mountains— = coming from the S., often changing their course—/many at N.W. in Even—when black from E., rain at night but from W., next day.—like fleece from W., = for the 2 or 3 next days—lying in ridges about noon in S.W. shew storms of wind & rain nigh.—

From Rainbows—

After long droughts, sudden and heavy Rain—if Green predominant rain, if red, rain & wind—if the Bow be broken, violent storms/if appearing at noon, much rain/—if in the West, great rain with thunder—

From Mists:

If Mists be attracted to the tops of Hills, rain in a day or 2—ascending in dry weather +, sudden r.—mists in the New Moon foretel rain in the old—/—mists in O vice versa—A misty white scare, in a clear sky, in the S.E.—/—rain.

from inanimate Bodies.

Woods swelling, stones sweating—lute or viol strings breaking—painted Canvas, pasted Maps relaxing—salt in deliquium[6]—rivers sink, floods suddenly abate—lamps, candles sparkle + —halo about candle—dryness of the Earth + pools troubled—yellow scum atop stagn. waters—dandelion or pimpernel shutting up—trefoil swelling in stalk, while the leaves sink to sleep[7]———

a dry spring brings a rainy winter—

Signs of Wind from Birds

Sea & fresh W. = gathering in flocks to the Banks, & there sporting, espec. in morn. Wild geese fly high, in flocks, E.ward/coots restless and clamorous—the hoopoe loud—the Halcyon[8] takes to land—rooks dart, shoot in the air, or sport on banks of fresh

[6 The article reads simply, "becoming moist".]
[7 The article reads, "bow down"; the change of image recalls 1718.]
[8 In error for "kingfisher"; Coleridge's eye fell on "halcyon" five lines below.]

Waters—the appearance of the malefigie[9] at Sea a certain fore-runner of viol. Winds or early in the morning denotes *tempest.*

from the Sun.

Rising pale, & setting red, with an iris— = *large* in surface, or with a red sky in the N./setting in blood[10]—or pale, with one or more dark circles, or with red streaks—seeming concave or hollow——seeming divided = great storms—parhelia, mock suns, = tempest.—

from the Moon—

greatly enlarged, of a red color, horns sharp and blackish—if included within a clear & ruddy iris—if the Iris be double. or broken. = storm[11] When the M. at 4 days old, has her horns sharp—storm, unless she have an *entire* circle—then not bad Weather, till next New[12] Moon——

from the Clouds.

flying to & fro—suddenly from the S. or W.—red, or with redness in them, at morn—of a leadish Color, in N.W. single clouds = wind from their quarter—

from inanimate bodies—

Winds shifting to the opposite point—sea calm with a *murmuring*[13]—a murmuring from woods & rocks—leaves and feathers agitated in calm air—high tides in & high thermometer—flames trembling or flexuous—Coal burning white with a murmuring noise ——thunder in morning with a clear sky, or from the N.—

Signs of Fair Weather
from Birds.

[9 Under "malafiges" the *OED* quotes the *Century Dictionary:* "A sailors' name for a small sea-bird supposed to appear before a storm: apparently, the stormy petrel or Mother Carey's chicken".]

[10 The article reads, "blood colour".]

[11 Twice he changes "tempest" to *storm.*]

[12 STC's mistake: the article reads, "full Moon".]

[13 The article reads, "noise"; the italics are Coleridge's.]

Halcyons, Sea ducks, &c flock seaward—Kites, Herons, Bitterns, and swallows fly high & are loud—lapwings restless & loud[14]— Sparrows after Sunrise ditto—and ravens, hawks, & Kestrils d^o— robin redbreast high & loud—& larks = = & Owls hoot with an easy and clear note—bats appear early in the even——.

from insects—[15]

gnats play in open air, hornets, wasps, and glowworms abound in eve—spiders webs float in the air, on grass, or trees—

from the Sun.

rises clear after a clear setting—*rises* while the clouds about him drive Westward—/with an iris about, that wears away gradually on all sides—clear, and not hot—/sets in red. Evening red & morning grey.

Signs of fair Weather from the Moon

Moon exhibits bright spots—a clear Iris with a full moon,/Horns sharp, fourth day—moon clear 3 days after change, or before full—

from Stars

great in number, clear, shooting—

from Clouds—[16]

at sun set, Clouds with golden edges, or diminish in bulk—or when small clouds sink low, or draw against the wind, or appear small or white and scattered in the N.W. when the sun is high (this is called a mackerel sky) fine weather—(yet for the most part rain 3 or 4 days after a mackerel Sky.)—

from the Rainbow.

after long rains—when the colors grow lighter—or the bow VANISHES.

[14 The article reads, "clamorous".]
[15 This is rightly removed from the section on "Rain from Insects".]
[16 From the section "Signs of Wind from Clouds".]

from Mists.

if Mists dissipate suddenly, or *descend* after rain—a general mist before sun rising near the full moon, fair Weather for a fortnight —about sun *set* or *rise*, white mists rise from waters & watered meads—a misty dew on the inside of glass windows—

Signs of Rain ceasing.

The sudden closing of gaps in the earth—the + rising of Springs or Rivers——if the rain begins an hour or so before sun rise, it is like to be fair ere noon—the contrary, if an hour or so after/

of Wind ceasing—

a hasty shower after a gust—water ruckles, and babbles—if the King-fisher attempts the sea during the Storm—or moles come out, or sparrows chirp merrily—fishes rise and flutter on the surface— dolphins *spouting* during the Storm/

Signs of Hail.

Clouds yellowish-white—/—& move heavily in strong winds—if the Eastern Sky before sunrise be pale, & refracted rays appear in thick clouds—/—white clouds in summer—hail—in winter, snow— /—in spring or winter, clouds blueish white, & expanding, small drizzling Hail.

Signs of Thunder—

Meteors shoot—earth chops & cleaves—a sultry air—in summer, or harvest, when the Wind has been S, two or three days, and the thermometer high, and Clouds rise with great white Tops like Towers, as if one were on the top of another, and joined with black on the nether side, expect rain & thunder suddenly./if two such clouds arise, one on either hand, it is then time to look for shelter, as the thunder [is] very nigh.—

Signs of Cold or frosty Weather—

Sea-pies, starlings, fieldfares, with other migratory Birds appearing early, denote a Cold season/the same of small birds in flocks, and of robin redbreasts near houses—sun in harvest after setting in a mist or broader than usual—moon bright with sha[r]p horns after change—sky full of twinkling stars—small Clouds hovering low in the N./Snow falling small, while clouds appear in Heaps, like rocks.—

Signs of Thaw.

Snow falling in large flakes, while wind is S. Cracks in the Ice—sun waterish—Moon horns blunt—stars dull—wind turning Southward —or extremely shifting—

The Hazel Tree flowering denotes a hard winter—and acorns found without insects—

Of the Leech Worm in an 8 ounce Phial, $\frac{3}{4}$ths filled with water, covered with a bit of Linen—N.B. Change the water once a week in summer, once a fortnight in winter—

If the Leech lie motionless at the Bottom in a spiral, fair weather —if crept to the top, rain—if restless, wind—if very restless, & out of the water, thunder—if in winter at bottom, frost—but if in winter it pitch it's dwelling at the mouth of the Phial, Snow.—

THE NOTEBOOK TABLES

NOTEBOOK 1

All entries in N 1 not listed here are in *CN* 1 (entries 1–6, 8, 11, 12, 18, 23, 25, 27) or will appear in later volumes (7, 9, 10, 21, 22, 26, 28).

Series	N Entry	Date	Series	N Entry	Date
2169	13	[19 Aug 1804]	2173	17	20 Aug [1804]
2170	14	19 Aug [1804]	2174	19	[20–26 Aug 1804]
2171	15	[20 Aug 1804]	2175	20	26 Aug [1804]
2172	16	[20 Aug 1804]	2176	24	[19–26 Aug 1804]

NOTEBOOK 9

Series	N Entry	Date	Series	N Entry	Date
1867	1	[26 Jan–27 Mar 1804]	1912	33	21 Feb 1804 + [Mar] 1804
1868	2	[26 Jan–27 Mar 1804]	1913	34	[*c* 21 Feb–*c* 8 Mar 1804]
1869	3	[26 Jan–27 Mar 1804]	1914	35	[*c* 21 Feb–*c* 8 Mar 1804]
1870	4	[26 Jan–27 Mar 1804]	1915	36	[*c* 21 Feb–*c* 8 Mar 1804]
1854	5	26 Jan 1804	1916	37	[*c* 21 Feb–*c* 8 Mar 1804]
1855	6	[26 Jan 1804]	1917	38	[*c* 21 Feb–*c* 8 Mar 1804]
1856	7	[26 Jan 1804]	1918	39	[*c* 21 Feb–*c* 8 Mar 1804]
1857	8	[26–27 Jan 1804]	1919	40	[*c* 21 Feb–*c* 8 Mar 1804]
1858	9	[26–27 Jan 1804]	1920	41	[*c* 21 Feb–*c* 8 Mar 1804]
1859	10	[26–27 Jan 1804]	1921	42	[*c* 21 Feb–*c* 8 Mar 1804]
1860	11	[26–27 Jan 1804]	1922	43	[*c* 21 Feb–*c* 8 Mar 1804]
1861	12	[26–27 Jan 1804]	1923	44	[*c* 21 Feb–*c* 8 Mar 1804]
1862	13	27 Jan [1804]	1924	45	[*c* 21 Feb–*c* 8 Mar 1804]
1863	14	28 Jan [1804]	1925	46	[*c* 21 Feb–*c* 8 Mar 1804]
1864	15	29 Jan [1804]	1926	47	[*c* 21 Feb–*c* 8 Mar 1804]
1865	16	[29 Jan–5 Feb 1804]	1880	48	[26 Jan–7 Feb 1804]
1866	17	[29 Jan–5 Feb 1804]	1881	49	[26 Jan–7 Feb 1804]
1875	18	5 Feb [1804]	1882	50	[26 Jan–7 Feb 1804]
1876	19	[5 Feb 1804]	1883	51	[29 Jan–7 Feb 1804]
1877	20	[5 Feb 1804]	1884	52	[29 Jan–7 Feb 1804]
1890	21	7 Feb 1804	1885	53	[29 Jan–7 Feb 1804]
1891	22	[7–10 Feb 1804]	1886	54	[29 Jan–7 Feb 1804]
1902	23	[10] Feb 1804	1879	55	[26 Jan–7 Feb 1804]
1903	24	[10–12 Feb 1804]	1887	56	[29 Jan–7 Feb 1804]
1904	25	[10–12 Feb 1804]	1888	57	[29 Jan–7 Feb 1804]
1905	26	[10–12 Feb 1804]	1889	58	[29 Jan–7 Feb 1804]
1906	27	[12] Feb 1804	1950	59	[Feb–10 Mar 1804]
1907	28	[13–16 Feb 1804]	1951	60	[Feb–10 Mar 1804]
1908	29	[13–16 Feb 1804]	1952	61	[Feb–Mar 1804]
1909	30	[13–16 Feb 1804]	1953	62	[Feb–Mar 1804]
1910	31	[17–18 Feb 1804]	1954	63	[Feb–Mar 1804]
1911	32	[17–18 Feb 1804]	1955	64	[Feb–Mar 1804]

Series	N Entry	Date	Series	N Entry	Date
1956	65	[Feb–Mar 1804]	2001	107	[12 Apr 1804]
1957	66	[Feb–Mar 1804]	2002	108	13 Apr 1804
1961	67	[9–10 Mar 1804]	2003	109	[13 Apr 1804]
1962	68	[10–12 Mar 1804]	2004	110	[13 Apr 1804]
1963	69	10–[12] Mar [1804]	2005	111	[13 Apr 1804]
1964	70	[12 Mar 1804]	2006	112	[13 Apr 1804]
1965	71	[12–13 Mar 1804]	2007	113	[13 Apr 1804]
1966	72	[13–26 Mar 1804]	2008	114	[13 Apr 1804]
1967	73	[8–24 Mar 1804]	2009	115	[13 Apr 1804]
1968	74	[8–24 Mar 1804]	2010	116	[13 Apr 1804]
1969	75	[8–24 Mar 1804]	2011	117	14 Apr [1804]
1970	76	[8–24 Mar 1804]	2012	118	14 Apr 1804
1971	77	[10–24 Mar 1804]	2013	119	[14 Apr 1804]
1972	78	[10–24 Mar 1804]	2014	120	16 Apr 1804
1973	79	[19–24 Mar 1804]	2015	121	16 Apr [1804]
1974	{ 80 / 81 }	[19–24 Mar 1804]	2016	122	[16 Apr 1804]
			2017	123	[16 Apr 1804]
1975	82	24 Mar 1804	2018	124	17 Apr 1804
1976	83	25 Mar [1804]	2019	125	[17 Apr 1804]
1977	84	[25–26 Mar 1804]	2020	126	[17 Apr 1804]
1978	85	[25–26 Mar 1804]	2021	127	[17 Apr 1804]
1979	86	[25–26 Mar 1804]	2023	128	18 Apr [1804]
1980	87	[25–26 Mar 1804]	2024	129	[18 Apr 1804]
1981	88	[25–26 Mar 1804]	1878	130	[c 6 Feb 1804]
1982	89	[25–26 Mar 1804]	1938	131	[Feb–Mar 1804]
1983	90	[25–26 Mar 1804]	1985	132	[26–27 Mar 1804]
1984	91	[25–26 Mar 1804]	1939	133	[23 Feb–8 Mar 1804]
1986	92	[26–27 Mar 1804]	1940	134	[23 Feb–8 Mar 1804]
1987	93	28 Mar 1804	1941	135	[23 Feb–8 Mar 1804]
1988	94	[28 Mar–8 Apr 1804]	1942	136	[23 Feb–8 Mar 1804]
1989	95	[28 Mar–8 Apr 1804]	1943	137	[23 Feb–8 Mar 1804]
1990	96	[28 Mar–8 Apr 1804]	1944	138	[23 Feb–8 Mar 1804]
1991	97	[28 Mar–8 Apr 1804]	1945	139	[23 Feb–8 Mar 1804]
1992	98	[28 Mar–8 Apr 1804]	1946	140	[23 Feb–8 Mar 1804]
1993	99	10 Apr 1804	1947	141	[23 Feb–8 Mar 1804]
1994	100	[10 Apr 1804]	1948	142	[23 Feb–8 Mar 1804]
1995	101	[10 Apr 1804]	1871	143	[Jan–Feb 1804]
1996	102	10 Apr 1804	1872	144	[Jan–Feb 1804]
1997	103	11 Apr 1804	1873	145	[Jan–Feb 1804]
1998	104	[11 Apr 1804]	1874	146	[Jan–Feb 1804]
1999	105	12 Apr [1804]	1949	147	[23 Feb–8 Mar 1804]
2000	106	[12 Apr 1804]			

NOTEBOOK 10

All other entries in N 10 are in *CN* 1.

Series	N Entry	Date	Series	N Entry	Date
2100	3	[c 23 May] 1804	2104	7	[c 23 May 1804]
2101	4	[c 23 May] 1804	2105	8	[c 23 May 1804]
2102	5	[c 23 May 1804]	2106	9	[c 23 May 1804]
2103	6	[c 23 May 1804]	2107	15	[c 23 May 1804]

NOTEBOOK II

All entries in N 11 not listed here will appear in later volumes.

Series	N Entry	Date	Series	N Entry	Date
2869	1	[6 Sept 1806]	2982	51	6 Feb 1807
2870	2	6 Sept 1806	2983	52	[Feb 1807]
2871	3	25 Sept 1806	2984	53	[Feb 1807]
2872	4	[25 Sept–5 Oct 1806]	2985	54	[Feb 1807]
2873	5	[25 Sept–5 Oct 1806]	2986	55	[Feb 1807]
2874	6	[25 Sept–5 Oct 1806]	2987	56	[Feb 1807]
2875	7	5 Oct 1806]	2988	57	[Feb 1807]
2876	8	[5 Oct 1806]	2989	58	[Feb 1807]
2877	9	[5 Oct 1806]	2990	59	[Feb 1807]
2878	10	[5 Oct 1806]	2991	60	[Feb 1807]
2879	11	[5 Oct 1806]	2992	61	[Feb 1807]
2880	12	[c 5–12 Oct 1806]	2993	62	[Feb 1807]
2881	13	[c 5–12 Oct 1806]	2994	63	[Feb 1807]
2882	14	[c 5–12 Oct 1806]	2995	64	[Feb 1807]
2895	18	23 Oct 1806	2996	65	[Feb 1807]
2896	19	[23–25 Oct 1806]	2997	66	[Feb 1807]
2899	20	25 Oct 1806	2998	67	[Feb 1807]
2883	21	[c 9 Oct 1806]	2999	68	[Feb 1807]
2884	22	[c 9 Oct 1806]	3000	69	[Feb 1807]
2885	23	[c 9 Oct 1806]	3001	70	Feb 1807
2897	24	24 Oct 1806	3002	71	[Feb 1807]
2898	25	[24 Oct 1806]	3003	72	[Feb 1807]
2900	26	[Oct 1806]	3004	73	[Feb 1807]
2901	27	[Oct 1806]	3005	74	[Feb 1807]
2902	28	[Oct 1806]	3006	75	[Feb 1807]
2903	29	[Oct 1806]	3007	76	[Feb 1807]
2905	30	30 Oct 1806	3008	77	[Feb 1807]
2906	31	[30 Oct 1806]	3020	78	[Feb–May 1807]
2934	32	15 Nov 1806	3021	79	[Feb–May 1807]
2939	33	[Nov–Dec 1806]	3022	80	[Feb–May 1807]
2940	34	[Nov–Dec 1806]	3023	81	[Feb–May 1807]
2941	35	[Nov–Dec 1806]	3024	82	[Feb–May 1807]
2942	36	[Nov–Dec 1806]	3025	83	[Feb–May 1807]
2943	37	[Nov–Dec 1806]	3026	84	[Feb–May 1807]
2944	38	[Nov–Dec 1806]	3027	85	[Feb–May 1807]
2945	39	[Nov–Dec 1806]	3028	86	[Feb–May 1807]
2956	40	[6–13 Dec 1806]	3029	87	[Feb–May 1807]
2957	41	[6–13] Dec 1806	3030	88	[Feb–May 1807]
2958	42	[20–21 Dec 1806]	3031	89	[Feb–May 1807]
2959	43	[20–21 Dec 1806]	3032	90	[Feb–May 1807]
2975	44	27 Dec 1806	3033	91	[Feb–May 1807]
2976	45	[1806–1807]	3034	92	[Feb–May 1807]
2977	46	[1806–1807]	3035	93	[Feb–May 1807]
2978	47	[4] Jan [1807]	3036	94	[Feb–May 1807]
2979	48	[4 Jan–6 Feb 1807]	3037	95	[Feb–May 1807]
2980	49	[4 Jan–6 Feb 1807]	3038	96	[Feb–May 1807]
2981	50	[4 Jan–6 Feb 1807]	3039	97	[Feb–May 1807]

Series	N Entry	Date	Series	N Entry	Date
2946	98	[Nov–Dec 1806]	2892	112	[12–16 Oct 1806]
2947	99	[Nov–Dec 1806]	2893	113	[12–16 Oct 1806]
2948	100	[Nov–Dec 1806]	2886	114	[5–12 Oct 1806]
2949	101	[Nov–Dec 1806]	2887	115	[5–12 Oct 1806]
2950	102	[Nov–Dec 1806]	2888	116	[5–12 Oct 1806]
2951	103	[Nov–Dec 1806]	2907	117	[Oct 1806]
2952	104	[Nov–Dec 1806]	2908	118	[Oct 1806]
2953	105	[Nov–Dec 1806]	2909	119	[Oct 1806]
2954	106	[Nov–Dec 1806]	2910	120	[Oct–Nov 1806]
2955	107	[Nov–Dec 1806]	2911	121	[Oct–Nov 1806]
2894	108	16 Oct 1806	2912	122	[Oct–Nov 1806]
2889	109	[12 Oct 1806]	2913	123	[Oct 1806]
2890	110	[12–16 Oct 1806]	2904	124	[Oct 1806]
2891	111	[12–16 Oct 1806]	2935	125	15 Nov 1806

NOTEBOOK 12

All entries in N 12 not listed here will appear in later volumes.

Series	N Entry	Date	Series	N Entry	Date
3057	1	[May 1807]	3172	33	[c Oct 1807]
3058	2	[May 1807]	3173	34	[c Oct 1807]
3059	3	[May 1807]	3174	35	[c Oct 1807]
3060	4	28 May 1807	3175	36	[c Oct 1807]
3061	5	[28 May 1807]	3176	37	[c Oct 1807]
3062	6	[28 May 1807]	3177	38	[c Oct 1807]
3063	7	[28 May 1807]	3178	39	[c Oct 1807]
3064	8	[28 May 1807]	3179	40	[c Oct 1807]
3065	9	[28 May 1807]	3180	41	[c Oct 1807]
3066	10	[28 May 1807]	3181	42	[c Oct 1807]
3108	11	[July 1807]	3182	43	[c Oct 1807]
3109	12	[July–Oct 1807]	3183	44	[c Oct 1807]
3110	13	[July–Oct 1807]	3184	45	[c Oct 1807]
3111	14	[July–Oct 1807]	3131	46	[c Sept 1807]
3112	15	[July–Oct 1807]	3132	47	[c Sept 1807]
3113	16	[July–Oct 1807]	3133	48	[c Sept 1807]
3114	17	[July–Oct 1807]	3134	49	[c Sept 1807]
3115	18	[July–Oct 1807]	3135	50	[c Sept 1807]
3116	19	[July–Oct 1807]	3136	51	[c Sept 1807]
3117	20	[July–Oct 1807]	3137	52	[c Sept 1807]
3118	21	[July–Oct 1807]	3138	53	[c Sept 1807]
3161	22	[c Oct 1807]	3139	54	[c Sept 1807]
3162	23	[c Oct 1807]	3140	55	[c Sept 1807]
3163	24	[c Oct 1807]	3141	56	[c Sept 1807]
3164	25	[c Oct 1807]	3142	57	[c Sept 1807]
3165	26	[c Oct 1807]	3143	58	[c Sept 1807]
3166	27	[c Oct 1807]	3144	59	[c Sept 1807]
3167	28	[c Oct 1807]	3145	60	[Sept 1807]
3168	29	[c Oct 1807]	3146	61	[Sept 1807]
3169	30	[c Oct 1807]	3147	62	[Sept 1807]
3170	31	[c Oct 1807]	3148	63	13 Sept 1807
3171	32	[c Oct 1807]	3149	64	[Sept 1807]

Series	N Entry	Date	Series	N Entry	Date
3150	65	[Sept 1807]	3121	76	[May–Sept 1807]
3151	66	[Sept 1807]	3122	77	[May–Sept 1807]
3152	67	[Sept 1807]	3123	78	[May–Sept 1807]
3153	68	[Sept 1807]	3124	79	[May–Sept 1807]
3154	69	[Sept 1807]	3125	80	[May–Sept 1807]
3155	70	[Sept 1807]	3126	81	[May–Sept 1807]
3156	71	[Sept 1807]	3127	82	[May–Sept 1807]
3157	72	[Sept 1807]	3128	83	[May–Sept 1807]
3158	73	[Sept 1807]	3129	84	[May–Sept 1807]
3159	74	[Sept 1807]	3130	85	[May–Sept 1807]
3160	75	[Sept 1807]			

NOTEBOOK 15

All entries in N 15 not listed here will appear in later volumes.

Series	N Entry	Date	Series	N Entry	Date
2761	1	[c 1805]	2064	36	2 May 1804
2059	2	1 May 1804	2070	37	3 May [1804]
2762	3	[c 1805]	2071	38	4 May 1804
2763	4	[c 1805]	2072	39	[4 May 1804]
2025	5	19 Apr 1804	2073	40	[4 May 1804]
2047	6	24 Apr [1804]	2074	41	[4 May 1804]
2026	7	19 Apr 1804	2075	42	[4 May 1804]
2027	8	[19 Apr 1804]	2076	43	[4 May 1804]
2028	9	[19 Apr 1804]	2077	44	5 May [1804]
2029	10	19 Apr [1804]	2078	45	6 May [1804]
2030	11	[19 Apr 1804]	2079	46	7 May [1804]
2031	12	[19 Apr 1804]	2080	47	8 May [1804]
2034	13	[20 Apr 1804]	2081	48	[8 May 1804]
2035	14	[20 Apr 1804]	2082	49	[8 May 1804]
2036	15	[20 Apr 1804]	2083	50	[8 May 1804]
2037	16	[20 Apr 1804]	2085	51	[10 May 1804]
2043	17	[20–23 Apr 1804]	2086	52	10 May [1804]
2044	18	[20–23 Apr 1804]	2087	53	13 May 1804
2045	19	23 Apr 1804	2088	54	[13 May 1804]
2046	20	24 Apr 1804	2089	55	[13 May 1804]
2048	21	[24 Apr 1804]	2090	56	[13 May 1804]
2049	22	[24 Apr 1804]	2091	57	13 May 1804
2050	23	24 Apr [1804]	2092	58	[14 May 1804]
2051	24	26 Apr [1804]	2093	59	14 May [1804]
2052	25	27 Apr [1804]	2094	60	[14 May 1804]
2053	26	[27 Apr 1804]	2095	61	16 May [1804]
2054	27	[27 Apr 1804]	2096	62	17 May 1804
2055	28	[27 Apr 1804]	2097	63	18 May 1804
2056	29	29 Apr [1804]	2099	64	[18 May 1804]
2057	30	30 Apr [1804]	2177	65	27 Aug [1804]
2058	31	[30 Apr 1804]	2178	66	[27 Aug 1804]
2060	32	1 May 1804	2179	67	[27 Aug 1804]
2061	33	[1 May 1804]	2195	68	10 Oct 1804
2062	34	[1 May 1804]	2197	69	12 Oct [1804]
2063	35	1 May [1804]	2198	70	[12 Oct 1804]

Series	N Entry	Date	Series	N Entry	Date
2199	71	[12 Oct 1804]	2245	123	[5] Nov [1804]
2200	72	[12 Oct 1804]	2246	124	[5 Nov 1804]
2201	73	[12 Oct 1804]	2282	125	[Nov 1804–1805]
2202	74	[12 Oct 1804]	2283	126	[Nov 1804–1805]
2203	75	[12 Oct 1804]	2284	127	[Nov 1804–1805]
2204	76	[12 Oct 1804]	2285	128	[Nov 1804–1805]
2205	77	[12 Oct 1804]	2286	129	[Nov 1804–1805]
2206	78	[12 Oct 1804]	2287	130	[Nov 1804–1805]
2207	79	[13 Oct 1804]	2288	131	[Nov 1804–1805]
2212	80	15 Oct 1804	2289	132	[Nov 1804–1805]
2213	81	[15 Oct 1804]	2290	133	[Nov 1804–1805]
2214	82	[15 Oct 1804]	2501	134	24 Mar 1805
2215	83	[15 Oct 1804]	2502	135	[24–27 Mar 1805]
2216	84	[15 Oct 1804]	2503	136	[24–27 Mar 1805]
2217	85	16 Oct 1804	2504	137	[24–27 Mar 1805]
2219	86	[16–18 Oct 1804]	2506	138	27 Mar [1805]
2220	87	[16–18 Oct 1804]	2507	139	[27 Mar 1805]
2221	88	[16–18 Oct 1804]	2508	140	[27 Mar 1805]
2222	89	[16–18 Oct 1804]	2518	141	2 Apr 1805
2226	90	18 Oct 1804	2519	142	[2 Apr 1805]
2227	91	19 Oct 1804	2520	143	[2 Apr 1805]
2228	92	19 Oct 1804	2521	144	4 Apr [1805]
2229	93	[19 Oct 1804]	2522	145	4 + ⟨6⟩ Apr 1805
2230	94	[19 Oct 1804]	2563	146	[23 Apr 1805]
2231	95	[19 Oct 1804]	2564	147	[23 Apr 1805]
2232	96	[19 Oct 1804]	2565	148	23 Apr [1805]
2233	97	[19 Oct 1804]	2566	149	[c 23 Apr 1805]
2234	98	[19 Oct 1804]	2567	150	[c 23 Apr 1805]
2235	99	[19 Oct 1804]	2568	151	[c 23 Apr 1805]
2238	100	[19–26 Oct 1804]	2569	152	[c 23 Apr 1805]
2239	101	[19–26 Oct 1804]	2570	153	[c 23 Apr 1805]
2240	102	[19–26 Oct 1804]	2571	154	[c 23 Apr 1805]
2241	103	26 Oct 1804	2575	155	4 May [1805]
2242	104	[26 Oct 1804]	2576	156	[4 May 1805]
2243	105	[26 Oct 1804]	2577	157	4 May 1805
2247	106	[6 Nov 1804]	2578	158	11 May 1805
2248	107	[6 Nov 1804]	2579	159	[May 1805]
2249	108	[6 Nov 1804]	2580	160	[May 1805]
2250	109	6 Nov 1804	2581	161	[May 1805]
2251	110	[6 Nov 1804]	2582	162	[May 1805]
2252	111	[6–7 Nov 1804]	2632	163	11 Aug 1805
2253	112	[6–7 Nov 1804]	2633	164	[12 Aug 1805]
2254	113	[6–7 Nov 1804]	2634	165	[12 Aug 1805]
2255	114	[6–7 Nov 1804]	2635	166	12 Aug 1805
2256	115	[6–7 Nov 1804]	2636	167	[12 Aug 1805]
2257	1.16	[6–7 Nov 1804]	2650	168	[c 20 Aug 1805]
2258	117	[6–7 Nov 1804]	2651	169	20 Aug 1805
2259	118	[6–7 Nov 1804]	2656	170	24 Aug 1805
2260	119	[6–7 Nov 1804]	2657	171	26 Aug [1805]
2261	120	[6–7 Nov 1804]	2658	172	[26 Aug 1805]
2281	121	[Nov 1804–1805]	2668	173	[c 15 Sept 1805]
2244	122	[5 Nov 1804]	2669	174	[c 15 Sept 1805]

Series	N Entry	Date	Series	N Entry	Date
2670	175	15 Sept 1805	2857	223	[May–June 1806]
2671	176	15 Sept 1805	2858	224	[May–June 1806]
2740	177	[Sept–Nov 1805]	2859	225	[May–June 1806]
2741	178	[30 Nov 1805]	2836	226	[4 Apr–11 May 1806]
2742	179	[30 Nov 1805]	2837	227	[4 Apr–11 May 1806]
2743	180	[1 Dec 1805]	2838	228	[1–11] May [1806]
2752	181	[1–26 Dec 1805]	2839	229	[1–11 May 1806]
2753	182	[1–26 Dec 1805]	2840	230	[12–18] May [1806]
2754	183	[1–26 Dec 1805]	2841	231	[12–18 May 1806]
2755	184	[1–26 Dec 1805]	2848	232	18 May 1806
2756	185	26 Dec 1805	2842	233	[4–18 May 1806]
2757	186	26 Dec [1805]	2843	234	[4–18 May 1806]
2758	187	[26 Dec 1805]	2844	235	[4–18 May 1806]
2759	188	31 Dec 1805	2845	236	[4–18 May 1806]
2760	189	[31 Dec 1805]	2846	237	[4–18 May 1806]
2785	190	1 Jan 1806	2847	238	[4–18 May 1806]
2786	191	5 Jan 1806	2849	239	[20–21 May 1806]
2787	192	[5 Jan–6 Mar 1806]	2850	240	[20–21 May 1806]
2788	193	[5 Jan–6 Mar 1806]	2851	241(a)	[20–21 May 1806]
2789	194	[5 Jan–6 Mar 1806]	2852	241(b)	[20–21 May 1806]
2790	195	[5 Jan–6 Mar 1806]	2866	242	22 June 1806
2791	196	[5 Jan–6 Mar 1806]	2926	243	[Oct–Nov 1806]
2792	197	[5 Jan–6 Mar 1806]	2927	244	[Oct–Nov 1806]
2793	198	[5 Jan–6 Mar 1806]	2928	245	[Oct–Nov 1806]
2801	199	[6 Mar 1806]	2929	246	[Oct–Nov 1806]
2802	200	6 Mar 1806	2930	247	[Oct–Nov 1806]
2803	201	[6 Mar 1806]	2867	248	[June 1806]
2804	202	[6 Mar 1806]	2868	249	[June 1806]
2805	203	[6 Mar 1806]	2931	250	[Oct–Nov 1806]
2806	204	[6 Mar–3 Apr 1806]	2932	251	[Oct–Nov 1806]
2807	205	[6 Mar–3 Apr 1806]	2933	252	[Oct–Nov 1806]
2808	206	[6 Mar–3 Apr 1806]	2936	253	[28 Nov 1806]
2809	207	[6 Mar–3 Apr 1806]	2937	254	[28 Nov 1806]
2810	208	[6 Mar–3 Apr 1806]	2938	255	28 Nov 1806
2811	209	[6 Mar–3 Apr 1806]	2970	256	[?1806]
2812	210	[6 Mar–3 Apr 1806]	2971	257	[?1806]
2813	211	[6 Mar–3 Apr 1806]	2972	258	[?1806]
2814	212	[6 Mar–3 Apr 1806]	2973	259	[?1806]
2815	213	[6 Mar–3 Apr 1806]	3187	260	17 Nov [1807]
2827	214	3 Apr [1806]	3188	261	[Nov 1807]
2828	215	[3 Apr 1806]	3189	262	[Nov 1807]
2829	216	4 Apr 1806	2974	269	[?1806]
2830	217	[4 Apr–11 May 1806]	2856	270	[May–June 1806]
2831	218	[4 Apr–11 May 1806]	2853	271	[May–June 1806]
2832	219	[4 Apr–11 May 1806]	2854	272	[May–June 1806]
2833	220	[4 Apr–11 May 1806]	2855	273	[May–June 1806]
2834	221	[4 Apr–11 May 1806]	2505	274	[25 Mar 1805]
2835	222	[4 Apr–11 May 1806]			

NOTEBOOK 16

All entries in N 16 not listed here are in *CN* I (entries 1–3, 7–225, 376–378, 410) or will appear in later volumes (389–405).

Series	N Entry	Date	Series	N Entry	Date
1958	4	[Feb–27 Mar 1804]	2666	269	7 Sept 1805
1959	5	[Feb–27 Mar 1804]	2667	270	9 Sept 1805
1960	6	[Feb–27 Mar 1804]	2672	271	27 Sept 1805
1843	226	14 Jan 1804	2673	272	[27 Sept 1805]
1844	227	14 Jan [1804]	2674	273	30 Sept [1805]
1845	228	[15–16 Jan 1804]	2679	274	[30 Sept–3 Oct 1805]
1846	229	[16 Jan 1804]	2680	275	[30 Sept–3 Oct 1805]
1847	230	[16–18 Jan 1804]	2681	276	[30 Sept–3 Oct 1805]
1848	231	[16–18 Jan 1804]	2682	277	3 Oct 1805
1849	232	[19 Jan 1804]	2683	278	[3 Oct 1805]
1850	233	[19 Jan 1804]	2684	279	[3 Oct 1805]
1851	234	20 Jan 1804	2685	280	[3 Oct 1805]
1852	235	[20 Jan–6 Feb 1804]	2701	281	16 Oct 1805
1892	236	[7–16 Feb 1804]	2686	282	[4 Oct 1805]
1893	237	[7–16 Feb 1804]	2687	283	4 Oct 1805
1894	238	[7–16 Feb 1804]	2688	284	[4 Oct 1805]
1853	239	20 Jan 1804	2689	285	[4 Oct 1805]
1895	240	[7–16 Feb 1804]	2690	286	[4 Oct 1805]
1896	241	[7–16 Feb 1804]	2695	287	6 Oct 1805
1897	242	[7–16 Feb 1804]	2696	288	7 Oct [1805]
1898	243	[7–16 Feb 1804]	2697	289	[7–14 Oct 1805]
2108	244	[24–25 May 1804]	2698	290	[7–14 Oct 1805]
2109	245	5 June 1804	2699	291	[15–20 Oct 1805]
2110	246	[5 June 1804]	2700	292	15 Oct 1805
2111	247	[5 June 1804]	2702	293	[15–20 Oct 1805]
2112	248	[5 June 1804]	2703	294	20 Oct 1805
2113	249	[5 June 1804]	2704	295	[20 Oct 1805]
2585	250	24 May 1805	2705	296	20 Oct 1805
2586	251	[May 1805]	2706	297	[20 Oct–20 Nov 1805]
2587	252	[May 1805]	2707	298	[20 Oct–20 Nov 1805]
2588	253	[May 1805]	2708	299	[20 Oct–20 Nov 1805]
2589	254	[May 1805]	2709	300	[20 Oct–20 Nov 1805]
2590	255	[May 1805]	2710	301	[20 Oct–20 Nov 1805]
2591	256	[May–July 1805]	2711	302	[20 Oct–20 Nov 1805]
2592	257	[May–July 1805]	2712	303	[20 Oct–20 Nov 1805]
2593	258	[May–July 1805]	2713	304	[20 Oct–20 Nov 1805]
2610	259	12 July 1805	2714	305	[20 Oct–20 Nov 1805]
2611	260	[12 July 1805]	2715	306	[20 Oct–20 Nov 1805]
2612	261	[12 July 1805]	2716	307	[20 Oct–20 Nov 1805]
2659	262	[July–Sept 1805]	2717	308	20 Nov 1805
2660	263	[July–Sept 1805]	2718	309	[20 Nov–14 Dec 1805]
2661	264	[July–Sept 1805]	2719	310	[20 Nov–14 Dec 1805]
2662	265	[July–Sept 1805]	2720	311	[20 Nov–14 Dec 1805]
2663	266	[July–Sept 1805]	2721	312	[20 Nov–14 Dec 1805]
2664	267	6 Sept 1805	2722	313	[20 Nov–14 Dec 1805]
2665	268	6 Sept 1805	2723	314	[20 Nov–14 Dec 1805]

Series	N Entry	Date	Series	N Entry	Date
2724	315	[20 Nov–14 Dec 1805]	2825	355	[c Mar 1806]
2725	316	[20 Nov–14 Dec 1805]	2826	356	[c Mar 1806]
2726	317	[20 Nov–14 Dec 1805]	2860	357	7 June 1806
2727	318	[20 Nov–14 Dec 1805]	2861	358	[7 June 1806]
2728	319	[20 Nov–14 Dec 1805]	2862	359	[8–17 June 1806]
2729	320	[20 Nov–14 Dec 1805]	2863	360	[8–17 June 1806]
2730	321	[20 Nov–14 Dec 1805]	2864	361	[8–17 June 1806]
2731	322	[20 Nov–14 Dec 1805]	2865	362	[8–17 June 1806]
2732	323	[20 Nov–14 Dec 1805]	2914	363	[Oct–Nov 1806]
2733	324	[20 Nov–14 Dec 1805]	2915	364	[Oct–Nov 1806]
2734	325	[20 Nov–14 Dec 1805]	2916	365	[Oct–Nov 1806]
2735	326	[20 Nov–14 Dec 1805]	2917	366	[Oct–Nov 1806]
2736	327	[20 Nov–14 Dec 1805]	2918	367	[Oct–Nov 1806]
2737	328	[20 Nov–14 Dec 1805]	2919	368	[Oct–Nov 1806]
2738	329	[20 Nov–14 Dec 1805]	2920	369	[Oct–Nov 1806]
2739	330	[20 Nov–14 Dec 1805]	2921	{370 371	[Oct–Nov 1806]
2745	331	14 Dec 1805			
2746	332	[14 Dec 1805]	2922	372	[Oct–Nov 1806]
2747	333	[14 Dec 1805]	2923	373	[Oct–Nov 1806]
2748	334	15 Dec 1805	2924	374	[Oct–Nov 1806]
2749	335	[15 Dec 1805]	2925	375	[Oct–Nov 1806]
2750	336	[15 Dec 1805]	2960	379	[?1806]
2751	337	[15 Dec 1805]	2961	380	[?1806]
2784	338	1 Jan 1806	2962	381	[?1806]
2794	339	15 Feb 1806	2963	382	[?1806]
2795	340	[15 Feb–8 Mar 1806]	2964	383	[?1806]
2796	341	[15 Feb–8 Mar 1806]	2965	384	[?1806]
2797	342	[15 Feb–8 Mar 1806]	2966	385	[?1806]
2798	343	[15 Feb–8 Mar 1806]	2967	386	[?1806]
2799	344	[15 Feb–8 Mar 1806]	2968	387	[?1806]
2800	345	[15 Feb–8 Mar 1806]	2969	388	[?1806]
2816	346	8 Mar 1806	2572	406	[Apr 1805]
2817	347	9 Mar [1806]	2573	407	[Apr 1805]
2818	348	[9 Mar 1806]	2574	408	[Apr 1805]
2819	349	[9 Mar 1806]	2764	409	[?1805]
2820	350	[9 Mar 1806]	2765	411	[?1805]
2821	351	[9 Mar 1806]	2766	412	[?1805]
2822	352	[c Mar 1806]	2767	413	[?1805]
2823	353	[c Mar 1806]	2768	414	[?1805]
2824	354	[c Mar 1806]			

NOTEBOOK 17

All entries in N 17 not listed here will appear in later volumes.

Series	N Entry	Date	Series	N Entry	Date
2427	1	[c 4 Feb 1805]	2433	7	[4–7 Feb 1805]
2428	2	[c 4 Feb 1805]	2434	8	7 Feb 1805
2429	3	[c 4 Feb 1805]	2435	9	[7 Feb 1805]
2430	4	4 Feb 1805	2436	10	8 Feb 1805
2431	5	[4–7 Feb 1805]	2437	11	[8–9 Feb 1805]
2432	6	[4–7 Feb 1805]	2438	12	[8–9 Feb 1805]

443

Series	N Entry	Date	Series	N Entry	Date
2439	13	9 Feb [1805]	2491	65	[17–20 Mar 1805]
2440	14	[9 Feb 1805]	2492	66	[17–20 Mar 1805]
2441	15	[9–10 Feb 1805]	2493	67	[17–20 Mar 1805]
2442	16	[9–10 Feb 1805]	2494	68	[17–20 Mar 1805]
2443	17	[9–10 Feb 1805]	2495	69	21 Mar 1805
2444	18	[9–10 Feb 1805]	2496	70	21 Mar 1805
2445	19	[9–10 Feb 1805]	2497	71	[c 21 Mar 1805]
2446	20	11 Feb 1805	2498	72	[c 21 Mar 1805]
2447	21	12 Feb [1805]	2499	73	[c 21 Mar 1805]
2448	22	12 Feb 1805	2509	74	[c 28 Mar 1805]
2449	23	13 Feb 1805	2510	75	28 Mar [1805]
2450	24	[13 Feb 1805]	2511	76	29 Mar [1805]
2451	25	15 Feb 1805	2512	77	29 [Mar 1805]
2452	26	[15 Feb 1805]	2513	78	29 [Mar 1805]
2453	27	[16 Feb 1805]	2514	79	[29–30 Mar 1805]
2454	28	16 Feb [1805]	2515	80	[30 Mar 1805]
2455	29	[18 Feb 1805]	2516	81	1 Apr 1805
2456	30	18 Feb 1805	2517	82	[1 Apr 1805]
2457	31	[18 Feb 1805]	2525	83	[1–4 Apr 1805]
2458	32	21 Feb 1805	2526	84	5 Apr 1805
2459	33	[21 Feb–3 Mar 1805]	2527	85	6 Apr 1805
2460	34	[21 Feb–3 Mar 1805]	2528	86	6 Apr 1805
2461	35	[21 Feb–3 Mar 1805]	2529	87	[6 Apr 1805]
2462	36	[21 Feb–3 Mar 1805]	2530	88	[6 Apr 1805]
2463	37	[21 Feb–3 Mar 1805]	2531	89	7 Apr 1805
2464	38	[21 Feb–3 Mar 1805]	2532	90	[7 Apr 1805]
2465	39	[21 Feb–3 Mar 1805]	2533	91	[7 Apr 1805]
2466	40	[21 Feb–3 Mar 1805]	2534	92	[7 Apr 1805]
2467	41	[21 Feb–3 Mar 1805]	2535	93	[7 Apr 1805]
2468	42	4 Mar [1805]	2536	94	[7 Apr 1805]
2469	43	[5 Mar 1805]	2537	95	8 Apr 1805
2470	44	[5–8 Mar 1805]	2538	96	[8 Apr 1805]
2471	45	[5–8 Mar 1805]	2539	97	9 Apr [1805]
2472	46	[5–8 Mar 1805]	2540	98	[9 Apr 1805]
2473	47	[5–8 Mar 1805]	2541	99	[9 Apr 1805]
2474	48	[5–8 Mar 1805]	2542	100	[10 Apr 1805]
2475	49	[5–8 Mar 1805]	2543	101	[10 Apr 1805]
2476	50	[5–8 Mar 1805]	2544	102	[13 Apr 1805]
2477	51	[5–8 Mar 1805]	2545	103	[13 Apr 1805]
2478	52	[5–8 Mar 1805]	2546	104	[13]–14 Apr 1805
2479	53	[5–8 Mar 1805]	2547	105	15 Apr [1805]
2480	54	[5–8 Mar 1805]	2548	106	15 Apr 1805
2481	55	[5–8 Mar 1805]	2549	107	15 Apr [1805]
2482	56	8 Mar 1805	2550	108	[17 Apr 1805]
2483	57	[10 Mar] 1805	2551	109	17 Apr 1805
2484	58	16 Mar 1805	2552	110	[17–21 Apr 1805]
2485	59	[16 Mar 1805]	2553	111	[17–21 Apr 1805]
2486	60	17 Mar 1805	2554	112	[17–21 Apr 1805]
2487	61	[17–20 Mar 1805]	2555	113	[17–21 Apr 1805]
2488	62	[17–20 Mar 1805]	2556	114	[17–21 Apr 1805]
2489	63	[17–20 Mar 1805]	2557	115	[17–21 Apr 1805]
2490	64	[17–20 Mar 1805]	2558	116	21 Apr 1805

444

Series	N Entry	Date	Series	N Entry	Date
2559	117	[c Apr 1805]	2627	185	3 Aug 1805
2560	118	[c Apr 1805]	2628	186	3 Aug 1805
2561	119	[c Apr 1805]	2629	187	3 Aug 1805
2562	120	[c Apr 1805]	2630	188	[Aug 1805]
2594	121	[May–June 1805]	2631	189	[Aug 1805]
2595	122	[May–June 1805]	2500	210	[?c Mar 1805]
2596	123	[May–June 1805]	2600	211	[c June 1805]
2597	124	[May–June 1805]	2601	212	[c June 1805]
2598	125	[May–June 1805]	2605	213	[c 27 June 1805]
2599	159	[May–Aug 1805]	2606	214	27 June 1805
2583	175	12–14 May 1805	2607	215	[c 27 June 1805]
2584	176	14 May 1805	2608	216	[c 27 June 1805]
2616	177	[July 1805]	2609	217	[June–Aug 1805]
2617	178	[July 1805]	2652	222	24 Aug 1805
2618	179	[July 1805]	2653	223	[24 Aug 1805]
2619	180	22 July 1805	2654	224	[24 Aug 1805]
2620	181	[July 1805]	2655	225	[Aug 1805]
2621	182	[July 1805]	2523	226	[4 Apr 1805]
2622	183	[July 1805]	2524	227	4 Apr 1805
2626	184	[3 Aug 1805]			

NOTEBOOK 18

All entries in N 18 not listed here will appear in later volumes.

Series	N Entry	Date	Series	N Entry	Date
2623	1	[July–Oct 1805]	2639	191	[14 Aug 1805]
2624	2	[July–Oct 1805]	2602	192	24 June [1805]
2781	4	[1805–1819]	2603	193	[24 June 1805]
2782	5	[1805–1819]	2604	194	[24 June 1805]
2783	6	[1805–1819]	2613	195	20 July 1805
2691	7	[4 Oct 1805]	2614	196	[20 July 1805]
2692	8	[4 Oct 1805]	2615	197	[July 1805]
2693	9	[4 Oct 1805]	2625	200	[?July–Oct 1805]
2694	10	[4 Oct 1805]	2744	318	[Nov–Dec 1805]
2637	189	14 Aug 1805	3190	329	20 Dec 1807
2638	190	14 Aug 1805			

NOTEBOOK 19

All entries in N 19 not listed here will appear in later volumes.

Series	N Entry	Date	Series	N Entry	Date
3040	1	[c 22 May 1807]	3050	11	[May 1807]
3041	2	22 May 1807	3051	12	[May 1807]
3042	3	[May 1807]	3052	13	[May 1807]
3043	4	[May 1807]	3053	14	[May 1807]
3044	5	[May 1807]	3054	15	[May 1807]
3045	6	[May 1807]	3055	16	[May 1807]
3046	7	[May 1807]	3056	17	[May 1807]
3047	8	[May 1807]	3067	18	31 May 1807
3048	9	[May 1807]	3068	19	[31 May 1807]
3049	10	[May 1807]	3069	20	[1807]

445

Series	N Entry	Date	Series	N Entry	Date
3070	21	[1807]	3093	44	[1807]
3071	22	[1807]	3094	45	[1807]
3072	23	[1807]	3095	46	[1807]
3073	24	[1807]	3096	47	[1807]
3074	25	[1807]	3097	48	[1807]
3075	26	[1807]	3098	49	[1807]
3076	27	[1807]	3099	50	[1807]
3077	28	[1807]	3100	51	[1807]
3078	29	[1807]	3101	52	[1807]
3079	30	[1807]	3102	53	[1807]
3080	31	[1807]	3103	54	[1807]
3081	32	[1807]	3104	55	[1807]
3082	33	[1807]	3105	56	[1807]
3083	34	[1807]	3106	57	[1807]
3084	35	[1807]	3107	58	[1807]
3085	36	[1807]	3185	59	[Nov 1807]
3086	37	[1807]	3186	60	5 Nov 1807
3087	38	[1807]	3191	61	24 Dec 1807
3088	39	[1807]	3192	62	[Dec 1807]
3089	40	[1807]	3193	63	[Dec 1807]
3090	41	[1807]	3194	64	[Dec 1807]
3091	42	[1807]	3195	76	[1807]
3092	43	[1807]			

NOTEBOOK 21

All entries in N 21 not listed here are in *CN* 1 (entries 1–6, 9–30, 32–126, 128–287, 289–328, 357–417, 590, 593) or will appear in later volumes (127, 288, 344–347, 351–356).

Series	N Entry	Date	Series	N Entry	Date
2426	{7 / 592	3 Feb 1805	2676	349	[c 30 Sept 1805]
			1899	418	[7–16 Feb 1804]
2193	8	5 Oct 1804	1900	419	[7–16 Feb 1804]
2393	31	[1804–1805]	1927	420	[Feb–Mar 1804]
2117	329	[July 1804]	1928	421	[Feb–Mar 1804]
2118	330	[July 1804]	1929	422	[Feb–Mar 1804]
2119	331	[July 1804]	1930	423	[Feb–Mar 1804]
2120	332	[July 1804]	1931	424	[Feb–Mar 1804]
2262	333	[July–Nov 1804]	1932	425	[Feb–Mar 1804]
2263	334	[July–Nov 1804]	1933	426	[Feb–Mar 1804]
2264	335	[July–Nov 1804]	1934	427	[Feb–Mar 1804]
2265	336	[July–Nov 1804]	1935	428	[Feb–Mar 1804]
2266	337	10 Nov 1804	1936	429	[Feb–Mar 1804]
2267	338	[10 Nov 1804]	1937	430	[Feb–Mar 1804]
2272	339	[Nov 1804]	2022	431	17 Apr 1804
2273	340	[Nov 1804]	2032	432	19 Apr 1804
2274	341	[Nov 1804]	2033	433	[19 Apr 1804]
2275	342	[Nov 1804–?1808]	2121	434	[July 1804]
2276	343	[Nov 1804–?1808]	2122	435	[July 1804]
2675	{348 / 350	30 Sept 1805	2123	436	[July 1804]
			2124	437	[July 1804]

Series	N Entry	Date	Series	N Entry	Date
2125	438	[July 1804]	2306	490	[7–11 Dec 1804]
2126	439	[July 1804]	2307	491	[7–11 Dec 1804]
2127	440	[July 1804]	2308	492	[7–11 Dec 1804]
2128	441	[July 1804]	2309	493	[7–11 Dec 1804]
2129	442	[July 1804]	2310	494	11 Dec [1804]
2130	443	[4 July 1804]	2311	495	[12 Dec 1804]
2131	444	[4 July 1804]	2312	496	[12 Dec 1804]
2132	445	[4 July 1804]	2313	497	[12 Dec 1804]
2137	446	4 July 1804	2314	498	[12 Dec 1804]
2138	447	[4 July 1804]	2315	499	[12 Dec 1804]
2139	448	9 July 1804	2316	500	[12 Dec 1804]
2140	449	[12] July [1804]	2317	501	12 Dec 1804
2141	450	[12 July 1804]	2318	502	[12 Dec 1804]
2150	451	[12 July–3 Aug 1804]	2319	503	12 Dec 1804
2151	452	[12 July–3 Aug 1804]	2320	504	[12–13 Dec 1804]
2152	453	[12 July–3 Aug 1804]	2321	505	[12–13 Dec 1804]
2153	454	3 Aug 1804	2322	506	[12–13 Dec 1804]
2154	455	[3 Aug 1804]	2323	507	[12–13 Dec 1804]
2191	456	[25] Sept 1804	2324	508	[12–13 Dec 1804]
2192	457	27 Sept 1804	2325	509	[12–13 Dec 1804]
2194	458	[5–11] Oct 1804	2326	510	[12–13 Dec 1804]
2196	459	11 Oct 1804	2327	511	[12–13 Dec 1804]
2208	460	13 Oct 1804	2328	512	[12–13 Dec 1804]
2209	461	[13 Oct 1804]	2329	513	[12–13 Dec 1804]
2210	462	14 Oct 1804	2330	514	13 Dec 1804
2211	463	[14 Oct 1804]	2331	515	[13 Dec 1804]
2218	464	17 Oct 1804	2332	516	[13 Dec 1804]
2236	465	[17–21 Oct 1804]	2333	517	[13 Dec 1804]
2237	466	21 Oct 1804	2334	518	[13 Dec 1804]
2268	467	22 Nov 1804	2335	519	[13 Dec 1804]
2269	468	22 Nov 1804	2336	520	[13 Dec 1804]
2270	469	[23 Nov 1804]	2337	521	[13 Dec 1804]
2271	470	23 Nov 1804	2338	522	[13 Dec 1804]
2277	471	[23 Nov 1804]	2339	523	[13 Dec 1804]
2278	472	[23 Nov 1804]	2340	524	15 Dec 1804
2279	473	[23 Nov 1804]	2341	525	[15 Dec 1804]
2280	474	[23 Nov 1804]	2342	526	16 Dec 1804
2291	475	7 Dec 1804	2343	527	17 Dec 1804
2292	476	[7 Dec 1804]	2344	528	[17 Dec 1804]
2293	477	[7 Dec 1804]	2345	529	[17 Dec 1804]
2294	478	[7 Dec 1804]	2346	530	[17 Dec 1804]
2295	479	[7 Dec 1804]	2347	531	[17 Dec 1804]
2296	480	[7 Dec 1804]	2348	532	17 Dec [1804]
2297	481	7 Dec 1804	2349	533	18 Dec [1804]
2298	482	[7 Dec 1804]	2350	534	[18 Dec 1804]
2299	483	[7–11 Dec 1804]	2351	535	[18 Dec 1804]
2300	484	[7–11 Dec 1804]	2352	536	[18–22 Dec 1804]
2301	485	[7–11 Dec 1804]	2353	537	[18–22 Dec 1804]
2302	486	[7–11 Dec 1804]	2354	538	[18–22 Dec 1804]
2303	487	[7–11 Dec 1804]	2355	539	[18–22 Dec 1804]
2304	488	[7–11 Dec 1804]	2356	540	[18–22 Dec 1804]
2305	489	[7–11 Dec 1804]	2357	541	[18–22 Dec 1804]

Series	N Entry	Date	Series	N Entry	Date
2358	542	[18–22 Dec 1804]	2405	570	17 Jan 1805
2359	543	[18–22 Dec 1804]	2406	571	[17 Jan 1805]
2360	544	[18–22 Dec 1804]	2407	572	[17 Jan 1805]
2361	545	[18–22 Dec 1804]	2408	573	18 Jan [1805]
2362	546	[18–22 Dec 1804]	2409	574	[18–19 Jan 1805]
2367	547	22 Dec 1804	2410	575	19 Jan 1805
2368	548	23 Dec [1804]	2411	576	22 Jan 1805
2369	549	[23–24 Dec 1804]	2412	577	23 Jan 1805
2370	550	25 Dec 1804	2413	578	[23 Jan 1805]
2371	551	25 Dec 1804	2414	579	[23 Jan 1805]
2372	552	25 Dec 1804	2415	580	[23–28 Jan 1805]
2373	553	[25 Dec 1804]	2416	581	[23–28 Jan 1805]
2374	554	[25 Dec 1804]	2417	582	[23–28 Jan 1805]
2375	555	[25 Dec 1804]	2418	583	[23–28 Jan 1805]
2376	556	[25 Dec 1804]	2419	584	[23–28 Jan 1805]
2377	557	[25 Dec 1804]	2420	585	28 Jan 1805
2378	558	[25 Dec 1804]	2421	586	[28 Jan–1 Feb 1805]
2379	559	[25 Dec 1804]	2422	587	[28 Jan–1 Feb 1805]
2394	560	9 Jan 1805	2423	588	1 Feb 1805
2395	561	[9–11 Jan 1805]	2424	589	[1 Feb 1805]
2396	562	[9–11 Jan 1805]	2425	591	3 Feb 1805
2397	563	11 Jan 1805	2426	{592 / 7}	3 Feb 1805
2398	564	11 Jan 1805			
2399	565	[11 Jan 1805]	2389	594	[c Dec 1804]
2400	566	[11 Jan 1805]	2390	595	[c Dec 1804]
2401	567(a)	[15 Jan 1805]	2391	596	[c Dec 1804]
2402	567(b)	15 Jan 1805	2392	597	[c Dec 1804]
2403	568	[15–17 Jan 1805]	2388	598	[27 Dec 1804]
2404	569	[15–17 Jan 1805]	2387	599	27 Dec 1804

NOTEBOOK 21½

All entries in N 21½ not listed here will appear in later volumes.

Series	N Entry	Date	Series	N Entry	Date
2383	2	[c 27 Dec 1804]	2380	122	[c 27 Dec 1804]
2384	6	[c 27 Dec 1804]	2381	123	[c 27 Dec 1804]
2385	7	[c 27 Dec 1804]	2382	124	27 Dec 1804
2386	8	[c 27 Dec 1804]			

NOTEBOOK 22

All entries in N 22 not listed here are in *CN* 1 (entries 1–10, 151–157, 159, 161) or will appear in later volumes (120–124, 147, 148, 158, 160).

Series	N Entry	Date	Series	N Entry	Date
2364	11	21 Dec 1804	2647	18	[c Aug 1805]
2363	12	[21 Dec 1804]	2648	19	[c Aug 1805]
2365	13	[21 Dec 1804]	2649	20	[c Aug 1805]
2366	14	[21 Dec 1804]	3196	21	[1807–1808]
2224	15	[?1801]–18 Oct 1804–[?1807]	3197	22	[1807–1808]
2223	16	[before 18 Oct 1804]	3198	23	[1807–1808]
2225	17	[?Oct–Dec 1804]	3199	24	[1807–1808]

Series	N Entry	Date	Series	N Entry	Date
3200	25	[1807–1808]	2642	129	[Aug 1805]
3201	26	[1807–1808]	2643	130	[Aug 1805]
3202	27	[1807–1808]	2644	131	[Aug 1805]
3203	28	[1807–1808]	2645	132	[Aug 1805]
3204	29	[1807–1808]	2646	133	[Aug–Nov] 1805
3205	30	[1807–1808]	2677	134	[Sept–Nov 1805]
3206	31	[1807–1808]	2678	135	[Sept–Nov 1805]
3207	32	[1807–1808]	2769	136	[c 1805]
3208	33	[1807–1808]	2770	137	[c 1805]
3209	34	[1807–1808]	2771	138	[c 1805]
3210	35	[1807–1808]	2772	139	[c 1805]
3211	113	[1807–1808]	2773	140	[c 1805]
3212	114	[1807–1808]	2774	141	[c 1805]
3213	115	[1807–1808]	2775	142	[1805–1807]
3214	116	[1807–1808]	2776	143	[1805–1807]
3215	117	[1807–1808]	2777	144 145	[1805–1807]
3216	118	[1807–1808]			
3217	119	[1807–1808]	2778	146	[1805–1807]
3218	125	[1807–1808]	2779	149	[c 1805]
3219	126	[1807–1808]	1901	150	[c 7–16 Feb 1804]
2640	127	[c Aug 1805]	2780	162	[1805–1816]
2641	128	16 Aug 1805			

NOTEBOOK 23

All entries in N 23 not listed here will appear in later volumes.

Series	N Entry	Date	Series	N Entry	Date
3227	1	[1807–1808]	3230	4	[1807–1808]
3228	2	[1807–1808]	3119	6	Aug 1807
3229	3	[1807–1808]	3120	7	[Aug 1807]

NOTEBOOK 24

All entries in N 24 not listed here will appear in later volumes.

Series	N Entry	Date	Series	N Entry	Date
3009	1	[1806–1808]	3019	13	[c May 1807]
3010	2	[c May 1807]	3220	14	[1807–1808]
3011	4	[c May 1807]	3221	15	[1807–1808]
3012	5	[c May 1807]	3222	16	[1807–1808]
3013	6	[c May 1807]	3223	17	[1807–1808]
3014	7	[c May 1807]	3224	18	[1807–1808]
3015	9	[c May 1807]	3225	19	[1807–1808]
3016	10	[c May 1807]	3226	20	[1807–1808]
3017	11	[c May 1807]	3231	21	[1807–1810]
3018	12	[c May 1807]			

NOTEBOOK K

Series	N Entry	Date	Series	N Entry	Date
2038	1	[c 20 Apr 1804]	2065	4	[2–3 May 1804]
2042	2	[20–23 Apr 1804]	2066	5	[2–3 May 1804]
2084	3	8 May [1804]	2067	6	[2–3 May 1804]

449

Series	N Entry	Date	Series	N Entry	Date
2068	7	[2–3 May 1804]	2135	31	[1–6 July 1804]
2069	8	[2–3 May 1804]	2136	32	[1–6 July 1804]
2098	9	[18 May 1804]	2142	33	[1–13 July 1804]
2156	10	[Aug–Nov 1804]	2143	34	[13 July 1804]
2157	11	[Aug–Nov 1804]	2144	35 / 37	[13 July 1804]
2158	12	[Aug–Nov 1804]			
2159	13	[Aug–Nov 1804]	2145	36	[13 July 1804]
2155	14	[19 Apr–10 Aug 1804]	2148	38	[July 1804]
2160	15	[Aug–Nov 1804]	2149	39	[July 1804]
2161	16	[Aug–Nov 1804]	2180	40	29 Aug 1804
2162	17	[Aug–Nov 1804]	2181	41	[29 Aug 1804]
2163	18	[Aug–Nov 1804]	2182	42	[Aug–Sept 1804]
2164	19	[Aug–Nov 1804]	2183	43	[Aug–Sept 1804]
2165	20	[Aug–Nov 1804]	2184	44	[Aug–Sept 1804]
2166	21	[Aug–Nov 1804]	2185	45	[Aug–Sept 1804]
2167	22	[Aug–Nov 1804]	2186	46	[Aug–Sept 1804]
2168	23	[10 Aug–7 Nov 1804]	2187	47	[Aug–Sept 1804]
2114	24	[May–June 1804]	2188	48	[Aug–Sept 1804]
2115	25	[May–June 1804]	2189	49	[Aug–Sept 1804]
2133	26	[1–6 July 1804]	2190	50	[Aug–Sept 1804]
2134	27	[1–6 July 1804]	2039	51	[c 20 Apr 1804]
2116	28	[May–June 1804]	2040	52	[c 20 Apr 1804]
2146	29	[c 16 July 1804]	2041	53	[c 20 Apr 1804]
2147	30	[c 18 July 1804]			

INDEXES

EDITORIAL NOTE

There are three indexes for each double volume, respectively, of persons, selected titles, and place-names; a subject index to the whole work is being prepared for the final volume.

In the index of persons, which is complete, and the index of selected titles, the cited dates of publications are the dates of the editions used or referred to by Coleridge or in the notes.

References are to the serial numbers of the notebook entries and, in the case of a long entry, to the foliation, e.g. 1098*f21*. A serial number followed by n refers to the relevant editorial note in the Notes volume. The exceptions are: references to preliminary matter in the Text volume, by page numbers, in lower-case roman numerals; references to the General Notes on each notebook, in the Notes volume, of the style N G Gen, N 3 Gen; references to the Appendixes in the Notes volume, of the style App A, App B.

References marked with an asterisk * contain quotations from the author or work under which they are found, "quotation" being broadly rather than narrowly interpreted. References marked with a dagger † designate notebook passages later used in the printed works under which they are found, whether by Coleridge, or Wordsworth, or Southey. Square brackets [ ] indicate that the person or work in question is referred to in the entry or the note but not by name or title. Parentheses around a question mark (?) indicate an uncertain identification.

Names of persons, publications, and places are indexed according to the accepted forms. Where Coleridge's spellings are sufficiently different to make references from them to present-day convention a desirable convenience, such references are made.

Names of Persons

Philosophy, Chemistry and the Arts ed W. Nicholson 1804) 3129, 3129n, App F*
Bacchus 2561, 2842
Bacon, Francis, viscount St Albans (1561–1626) 2193, 2598, 2737
The Works (1803) 3174*ff29–30*ᵛ*, 3174n: "Charge . . . against Robert, Earl of Somerset, concerning the poisoning of Overbury" 3174-*f29*ᵛn; "The Charge of Owen, Indicted of High Treason, in the King's Bench" 3174*f29*ᵛ*, 3174-*f29*ᵛn; "An Essay on Death" 3174-*f30*ᵛn*; "Of Counsel" 3174*f30*, 3174*f30*n; "Of a Digest of Laws" 3174*f29*, 3174*f29*n; "Of a King" 3174*f29*n*; "Of Revenge" 3174-*f30*n*; "Ornamenta rationalia" 3174*f30*, 3174*f30*n; "Speech on Taking his Place in Chancery" 3174*f30**, 3174*f30*n: "Tract on the Pacification of the Church" 3174-*f30*ᵛ
SINGLE WORKS: *De sapientia veterum* 2588n, 2729n, 2737n, 2739n
Badia, Giuseppe Antonio (*fl* 1731) *see* Pasini, G. L. comp *Vocabolario italiano-latino*
Bagehot, Walter (1826–77) *Physics and Politics* (1872) 2943n*
Baggot, 1st officer of the *Abergavenny* (*d* 1805) App D
Baily, A. King (*fl* 1804) 1867n
Baker, Mr 2843, 2843n
Baker, John (*fl* 1804) 1867n
Bald, R(obert) C(ecil) (1901–   ) "Coleridge and *The Ancient Mariner*" (*Nineteenth Century Studies* ed H. Davis, W. C. De Vane, R. C. Bald, Ithaca N. Y. 1940) 2293n, 2486n, 2610n
Baldovini, Francesco (1635–1716) *Lamento di Cecco da Varlungo* (1694) App A
Balguy, Charles (1708–67) *see* Boccaccio, G. *Decameron*

Ball, Sir Alexander John, 1st bart (1757–1809) xvii, 1924n, 1943n, 2099n, 2101*ff4, 4*ᵛ*, 5, 5*ᵛ*, 2101n, 2102n, 2113n, 2137, 2138, 2143n, 2157n, 2162n, 2163n, 2188n, 2228n, 2230n, 2271n, 2282n, 2297n, 2350n, 2377n, 2408n, 2411n, 2412n, 2415, 2415n, 2420n, 2430n, 2438, 2438n, 2439*f12*ᵛ, 2506, 2506n, 2513n, 2517*ff45*ᵛ, 47, 2517n, 2526n, 2529n, 2562, 2562n, 2574n, 2578, 2583n, 2594n, 2664n, 2668n, 2699n, 2733n, 2740, 2740n, 2744n, 2779n, 2864n, 3226n, App A, App B, App E; A letter in Coleridge's hand . . . to Lord Camden (VCL MS F 14.5) App B; attributed author Letter to the Earl of Camden saying that "Capt. Leake . . . is to be sent . . . to purchase corn in the Black Sea and that a Mr. Coleridge will go with him . . ." (VCL MS F 14.11) App B; *see also* Ross, John & Co. (merchants); Skinner, Capt; Tutroino(?), J.
Ball, Mary (Wilson), Lady (*fl* 1804) 2296n, 2324, 2324n, 2397, 2397n, 2517*f45*ᵛ, 2517n*, 2527n, 2583n
Ball, Sir William Keith, 2nd bart (1791–1874) 2101*f5*, 2101n
Banks, Sir Joseph (1743–1820) *see* Jacj, A. M. Letter to Sir Joseph Banks
Banquo (*Macbeth*) 2583*f105*
Barbauld, Anna Letitia (Aikin) (1743–1825) 1848, 1848n, 2303, 2303n, 2509n
Barclay, John (1582–1621) Lusininus Euphormio (pseud) *Argenis* 3145; (1629, Amsterdam 1659) 3145n; *Euphormionis Lusinini Satyricon* 3145, 3145n; *see also* Coleridge, S. T. MSS: Marginalia
Bardolph (1 *Henry* IV) 2775n
Barebones, Praise-God (name) 2732
Baretti, Giuseppe Marc' Antonio (1719–89) 2719n

"Bison, Bubalus, Esqre" *see* Coleridge, S. T. PROJ WORKS: characters

Black Prince *see* Edward, prince of Wales

Blackstone, Sir William (1723–80) *Commentaries on the Laws of England* (1766) 2442n*

Blair, Miss (passenger on the *Abergavenny d* 1805) App D

Blair, Robert (1741–1811) 2064(3), 2064(3)n

Blancardus, Nicolaus *see* Blankaart, Nikolaas

Bland, Sir Thomas (*fl* 1632) 3187

Blankaart, Nikolaas (1624–1703) *see* Arrian . . . *Arriani Ars tactica*

Blomfield, Charles James, bp of London (1786–1857) *see* Aeschylus *Persae, Prometheus vinctus*

Blount, Edward (*fl* 1588–1632) *see* Alemán, Mateo *The Rogve*

Blount, Thomas (1618–79) *Glossographia* (1681) 2140n

Blumenbach, Johann Friedrich (1752–1840) 2544n, 2949n, 3113n; *Handbuch der Naturgeschichte* (Göttingen 1799) 2544n

Blunden, Edmund (Charles) (1896–) *Coleridge's Fellow-Grecian. Some Account of Charles Valentine Le Grice* (Hong Kong 1956) 2613n

Boccaccio, Giovanni (1313–75) 2512, App A

Delle opere (Florence & Naples 1723–4) 2512n: *Il Filocolo* 2670n

SINGLE WORKS: *Decameron* 2692*, 2692n*, App A; tr [C. Balguy] (London 1741, 1804) App A; *Della geneologia de gli Dei* 2512n, 2588n, 2737, 2737n, App A

See also Coleridge, S. T. MSS: Marginalia; POEMS: *The Garden of Boccaccio;* Wright, H. G. *Boccaccio in England*

Bodoni, Giambattista (1740–1813) 2420n

Böhme, Jakob (1575–1624) *The Works of Jacob Behmen . . . To which is prefixed, The Life of the Author. With figures, illustrating his Principles, left by the Reverend William Law* (1764–81) 2026f6n; *see also* Coleridge, S. T. MSS: Marginalia

Boiardo, Matteo Maria, conte di Scandiano (*c* 1441–94) App A

[Boid, Edward] *Travels through Sicily and the Lipari Islands* (1827) 2176n*, 2708n

Boisgelin de Kerdu, Pierre Marie Louis de (1758–1816) *Ancient and Modern Malta . . .* (1804) 2101n

Bonaparte, Napoleon *see* Napoleon I, emperor of the French

Bonnet, Charles (1720–93) 2584, 2584n; *Contemplation de la nature* 2584n

Boothby, Charles (*c* 1786–1846) *Under England's Flag from 1804 to 1809* (1900) 2741n*

Borg, Francesco (*fl* 1804) 2594n

Borghese, Camillo Filippo Ludovico, principe (1775–1832) 2802n

Boscovich, Ruggiero Giuseppe (1711–87) 2626n

Bostetter, Edward E(verett) (1914–) "Christabel: The Vision of Fear" (*Philological Quarterly* 1957) 2468n

Boswell, James (1740–95) 2026f8n, 2350n; *The Life of Samuel Johnson* 2026f8n

Bottari, Giovanni Gaetano (1689–1775) *see* Vida, M. H. *De divis coelitibus*

Boulogne, comtes de 3204n

Boverick, Sobieski (*fl* 1785) 2452, 2452n; *To be seen at Mr. Boverick's, Watchmaker, at the Dial, near the New Exchange, in the Strand, at One Shilling each Person* (1745) [handbill] 2452n*

Boyce, Samuel *see* Boyse, S.

COLERIDGE, SAMUEL TAYLOR (1772–1834)

(Headings: COMPLETE WORKS; COLLECTIONS AND SELEC-
TIONS; POEMS (*including* PLAYS); ADAPTATIONS (*not listed
elsewhere under* COLERIDGE); PROSE; LECTURES; PERI-
ODICALS (*actual, projected, and conjectural contributions*);
MANUSCRIPTS; PROJECTED WORKS.)

lines "On stern Blenkarthur's perilous height" 2798†, 2798n; Martial quoted 2333n*; Middleton's *Letter from Rome* (*Watchman*) 2664n; rights and duties 2955n; spider-web image 2784†, 2784n

Friend, The 2324n

—— (1809–10) Bruno, eleven works of 2264n; certainty *vs* positiveness 3095†, 3095n; Etna poem, at Nicolosi(?) 2176n*; fable of the maddening rain 2626n*; frictions with WW in the period 2750n; German language 2431n*; S. Hutchinson N 18 Gen; Italian studies xix, App A; Littara's lines 2459†, 2459n*; Prospectus of 1993n*, App A; Russell and subscribers 2836n; "Satyrane's Letters" 2026n, 3160n; B. Stay 2626n*; *Three Graves* 2297n; Virgil quoted 3200†, 3200n*

—— (1818) anecdote of Bonaparte and Maltese regiments 2138n; A. Ball eulogized 2101n, 2271n, 2740n; Ball's landing in Malta 2506†, 2506n*; Ball, lines read to 3226n; Ball quoted 2350n*, 2526n; Barbary States 2513n; T. Brahe 3110n; Bruno, eleven works of 2264n; Cartwright 1930†, 1930n, 1943†, 1943n; Chiabrera used App A; cotton seed unsuitable fodder in Malta 2294n; S. Daniel quoted 3210n; Dante quoted 3219†, 3219n*; S. Decatur quoted 2228n; Drayton 3203n; duty *vs* pleasure 3230n; duty *vs* rights 2955n; fable of the maddening rain 2626n; fame 2064n; "fortune . . . favors . . . fools" 2439†, 2439n; ghosts 2583n; Leckie 2295n*; "loud laugh" in parliamentary reports 2865n; Machiavelli quoted 2512n; Malta App B; Malta anecdote of fear of cowardice 2418n; maxims 2413n; method 2896n; Minorca 2377n; motto for rosemary 3181†, 3181n*; mystery-mongering 3022n; Nichol-

son's *Journal* quoted 3111n; prudence 2412n; Queen Bee metaphor 2434n*; *Spectator* at first to be model for 2074n; stiletto and rosary 2667n; tired-traveller simile 2111n; Trafalgar and news of Nelson's death 2744n; "Truth . . . conveying falsehood" 2397n; unconscious *vs* accidental 2411n; Wordsworth's poems read to Ball 2583n, App E n

"Historie and Gests of Maxilian" (*Blackwood's* 1822) 2044n*

Inquiring Spirit; a selection of Coleridge's . . . prose ed K. Coburn (1951) 1862n, 2058n, 2130n, 2152n, 2218n, 2225n, 2375n, 2398†, 2398n, 2407n, 2421n, 2453n, 2458n, 2503n, 2516n, 2538n, 2651n*, 2910n, 2945n, 2949n*, 3049n, 3151†, 3151n, 3165†, 3165n: "Essay on the Passions" 2613n

Lay Sermon, A (1817) 2196n, 2395n, 2438n, 2549n*

Lay Sermon addressed to the Higher Classes of Society, A see *Statesman's Manual, The*

"Letter to Peter Morris, M.D. on the sorts and uses of literary praise" (*Blackwood's* 1820) 2890n*

Literary Remains ed H. N. Coleridge (1836–9) 1961n, 2209n, 2420n, 2540n, 2964n*, 3022n, 3102n, 3212n

Miscellaneous Criticism ed T. M. Raysor (1936) 1880n*, 2075n, 2269n, 2471n, 2512n, 2516n, 2598n, 2599*f89ᵛ*n, 2807n, 2918n, 3102n, 3187n, 3203n*, 3214n

Miscellanies, Aesthetic and Literary; to which is added "The Theory of Life" ed T. Ashe (1885) 2044n*

"Notes marginales . . . en marge de Kant" ed H. Nidecker (*Revue de littérature comparée* 1927) 2315n

Notes on English Divines ed D. Coleridge (1853) 2640n*

MANUSCRIPTS:
Appendix to Observations on Egypt [by S. T. Coleridge and C. Pasley] (VCL MS F 14.3b) 2297n, 2627n, App B
Christabel 2121n
Diadestè (BM Add MS 34,225) 2692n
Fictional prose work (BM Add MS 34,225) 2692n
Flight and Return of Mohammed, The [by S. T. Coleridge and R. Southey] (Sydney MS) 2780n*
Fragment (VCL MS F 14.10) App B
Fragments (BM MS Egerton 2800) 2152n, 2225n, 2297n
Fragments (BM MS Egerton 2801) N 12 Gen, 3049n, 3133n, 3151n, 3152n*, 3165n, 3171n
Letter to the Beaumonts 3041n
Letter to Daniel Stuart (BM Add MS 34,046) 2517n
Letters, etc (BM Add MS 34,046) 1985n
Logic 2720n
Marginalia 2322n: on Adelung 2074n; on Anderson's *British Poets* 3102n; on Barclay 3145n; on Baxter 2640n*; on Beaumont and Fletcher 2931n; on Boccaccio 2670n*; on Böhme 2026*f6*n, 2894n; on F. Greville, 1st baron Brooke 2918, 2918n; on Sir T. Browne 1961n*; on Chapman's *Homer* 2964n*, 3212n; on *Codice di Napoleone* 3143n*; on Collier 2077n*; on Cowley 3196n; on Crashaw 3102n; on Fénelon 2540n; on Flögel 2807n; on Kant 2315n, 2316n*; on R. P. Knight 1963n; on Leibnitz 1993*f31*n; on Malta document (VCL MS F 14.2) App B; on Nicolson and Burn 2442n, 2637*f91*n*; on *Omniana* 2751n*; on Park 3067n*; on W. Parnell 3205n; on Pascal 2133n*; on *Philosophical Transactions of the Royal Society* 3071n; on Pindar 2887n; on Rehberg 2208n*; on The

Rime of the Ancient Mariner 2293n, 2880n*; on Ruscelli App A; on Scott 2075n*; on Shakespeare 2428n*, 2664*f83*n, 3145n; on A. Sidney 3118n; on Stillingfleet 3022n; on J. Taylor 2209n; on Tennemann 2342n*; on St Teresa 3102n; on G. White 2949n*
Note (BM MS Egerton 2800) 2717n*
Observations on Egypt (BM MS Egerton 2800) 2297n
"Prognostics of the Weather" reorganized by Coleridge (BM MS Egerton 2800) 3129n, App F*
Sicily, Fountain of Arethusa (VCL MS F 14.9) App B
Theological Lectures, transcript E. H. Coleridge 2444n
Transcript of a rough draft of *Osorio* 2928n*
Transcripts from the notebooks, E. H. Coleridge 2556n, 2861n, 2928n
Travels 2075n, 2397n
Verses 2178†, 2178n*

PROJECTED WORKS:
Adventures of Dr Hocus & Dr Pocus *see* characters; afterpiece 2064(1), 2064(1)n; allegory from the time of Dante, a work on 3203, 3203n, App A; allegory of an embryo soul 2373; Allston's landscape, address on, poem 2813, 2813n; Andalusia, poem on 2589; Ariosto, critical work on App A;
Beaumont, Sir G., Translations from the Drawings of 1899n; Bonapart 2064(4), 2064(4)n; Browne, Sir T., a character of 1961; Bruno, a life of App A;
characters: Bison, Bubalus, Esqre 2715; Hocus, Dr 2353, 2353n; Hyphen, Dr 2692n; Inert, Strenuous, Esqre 2715; Mammoth, Rev Leviathan 2734; Midge, Minim 2734; O'Gourmand, Mr 2692n; Pocus, Dr 2353, 2353n; Schinchimurra

* * * * * *

don 1873) 3109n; *see also* Coleridge, S. T. PROSE: *Biographia Literaria* (1847)

Coleridge, Sarah (Fricker) Mrs S. T. Coleridge (1770–1845) accounts, name in 2883; Bristol journey (1807) 3014n; brother of 2133n; coldness of 2099n; C's letters to 1869n, 1874n, 2100n, 2108n, 2109n, 2552n, 2610n, App B; initials among others N 18 Gen; letters, none from 2529n; money for 1985n, 1986n; mother of his children 2092; notebooks and 3041, 3041n, 3119n; not in C's dreams 2078; separation from N 11 Gen, 1991n, 2913n, 2935n, 3128n; temper of 2398, 2398n, 2928n; *Minnow Among Tritons; Mrs S. T. Coleridge's Letters to Thomas Poole, 1799–1834* ed S. Potter (London 1934) 3119n*

Coleridge (family) 1991n, 2860, 2860n

Collier, Jeremy (1650–1726) *see* Aurelius Antoninus, M., Roman emperor *The Emperor Marcus Antoninus*

Collier, John Payne (1789–1883) *see* Coleridge, S. T. PROSE: *Seven Lectures on Shakespeare and Milton;* Dodsley, R. ed *A Select Collection of Old Plays*

Collins, William (1721–59) 2075n, 2557, 2557n

Colman, George (1762–1836) 2395, 2395n; *John Bull, or an Englishman's Fireside* 2339, 2339n

Columba, St (521–97) 2493n, 2494, 2494n

Combe, St *see* Columba, St

Comberbacke, Silas Tomkyn (*fl* 1794) 2290n

Commodus, Lucius Aelius Aurelius, Roman emperor (161–192) 2225*f23*, 2225n

Compagnon, P. (*d c* 1750) "An Account of the Discovery of the Kingdom of Bambûk, and its Gold

Mines, in 1716" (*A New General Collection of Voyages & Travels* London 1745) 3006n*

Condé, Louis Antoine Henri de Bourbon, duc d'Enghien *see* Enghien, L. A. H. de Bourbon Condé, duc d'

Condillac, Étienne Bonnot de (1714–80) 2193, 2193n

Constable, Archibald (1774–1827) *see* Constable, T. *Archibald Constable*

Constable, John (1776–1837) 1938n

Constable, Thomas (1812–81) *Archibald Constable and his Literary Correspondents* (Edinburgh 1873) 2746n

Constance, queen consort of Frederick III of Sicily (*fl* 1360) 2261*f65ᵛ*, 2261n

Conte, Chevalier Pietro (*fl c* 1804) *see* St André, General An attestation

Cook, James (1728–79) 1887n, 2874n, 2894n

Cooke, Thomas (1763–1818) "A Practical and Familiar View of the Science of Physiognomy" (*Blackwood's* 1820) 2828n*

Cookson, Mr (Kendal *fl* 1806) 2903, 2903n

Cookson (family of Kendal) 2903n

Cookson (family related to Wordsworth) 2903n

Correggio (Antonio Allegri 1494–1534) 2101*f4ᵛ*, 2101n

Cortius (Gottlieb Kortte 1698–1731) *see* Pliny the Younger *Epistolarum libros decem*

Coryat, Thomas (*c* 1577–1617) *Coryat's crudities* (1611): *Panegyrick verses* 2621*, 2621n*; *see also* Donne, J. *Upon Mr. Tho. Coryat's Crudities*

Costobadie, Jacob de (1758–1828) 2894, 2894n

Costobody, Jacob de *see* Costobadie, J. de

Cottle, Amos (Simon) (*c* 1768–1800) 2471*f32*, 2471n

473

Halley, Edmund (1656–1742) 3072n
Halliwell, James Orchard (1820–89) *The Nursery Rhymes of England* (1853) 2178n
Hamilton, James (1749–1835) *Observations on the Utility and Administration of Purgative Medicines in Several Diseases* (Edinburgh 1806) 3173*, 3173*ff19ᵛ–28ᵛ*n
Hamilton, Sir William (1730–1803) 2156n, 2158, 2158n, 2161
Hamouda, Bey of Tunis (*d* 1814) 2476*, 2476n, 2477(?), 2477n, 2478(?), 2478n
Hamza (The Flight and Return of Mohammed) 2780n
Hanford, Robert 2863, 2863n
Hanover, House of *see* Coleridge, S. T. PROJ WORKS: royal family, the present
Hanrott, Burkitt & Winstanley 3028, 3028n
Hardman, William (of Valletta) *A History of Malta during the period of the French and British occupations, 1798–1815* (1909) 2578n
Hardy, Mr (surgeon of the *Maidstone fl* 1805) 2081
Harrington, James (1611–77) 2193, 2193n, 2598
The Oceana and other Works ed J. Toland (1700) 2223*f18*, 2223n*: *Political Aphorisms* 2223*f19**, 2223n*; *A System of Politics* 2223-*f18**, 2223n*; *The Ways and Means of introducing a Commonwealth by the Consent of the People* 2223*f19**, 2223n*
Harris, Mr 1985
Harrison, C. (*fl* 1804) 1867n
Harrowby, Dudley Ryder, 1st earl of (1762–1847) *see* Morier, Mr Transcripts . . . of a correspondence from Corfu
Hart, Alfred (1870–) [Letter from Melbourne, Australia] (*Times Literary Supplement* London 1935) 3205n

Hartley, David (1705–57) 2382, 2643n
Hasan-Baba, Dey of Algiers (*fl* 1805) 2045, 2668, 2668n, App B
Hastings, Mr (passenger on the *Speedwell fl* 1804) 2083, 2083n
Hatfield, John (*c* 1758–1803) 2651, 2651n
Hauteserre, Antoine Dadin *see* Dadinus Alteserra, Antonius
Haüy, René Just (1743–1822) 2896, 2896n; *Traité de minéralogie* (Paris 1801) 2014*f48*, 2014n; *see also* Buée, A. Q. "Outlines of the Mineralogical Systems of Romé de Lisle and the Abbé Haüy", "Parallel of Romé de l'Isle's and the Abbé Haüy's Theories of Crystallography"
Hay, Lucy (Percy), countess of Carlisle *see* Carlisle, L. (P.) Hay, countess of
Hayley, William (1745–1820) 2598, 2598n; *The Life and posthumous writings* [chiefly *Letters*] *of William Cowper* (1803) 2433n, 2554n*; *The Life of Milton* (1796) 3180n
Hayter, John (1756–1818) [List of Papyri from Herculaneum] (VCL MS F 14.15) App B
Hayward, John (Davy) (1905–) "The Location of Copies of the First Editions of Giordano Bruno" (*The Book Collector* 1956) 2264n
Hazlitt, Sarah (Stoddart) (*d c* 1842) 2099, 2099n, 2297n, 2310, 2310n
Hazlitt, William (1778–1830) articles pub by Cobbett 1926n; C disagreeing with 2403, 2403n; portrait of C 1938n, 1976n; severity of as judge 1850, 1850n
The Complete Works ed P. P. Howe (London 1930–4): *Conversations of James Northcote* 2844n*; "On the Elgin Marbles" 2862n*; *Table Talk* 2816n*
Heart, Sergt (*d* 1805) App D
Heber *see* Eber

See also White, J. *Original Letters of Sir John Falstaff*; Index 2: "Review of Lamb's *John Woodvil*"
Lamb, John (1763–1821) 1963, 1963n
Lamb, John (clerk in Malta *fl* 1804) 2628n; *see also* Lamb, R. [Transcript by S. T. Coleridge of two letters to John Lamb]
Lamb, Mary Ann (1764–1847) 2065, 2065n, 2099n, 2650n, 2873, 2873n; Dialogue between a Mother & Child [MS verse] 1953, 1953n
Lamb, Robert (*fl* 1804) 2044n, 2628n; [Transcript by S. T. Coleridge of two letters to John Lamb] (VCL MS F 14.14) 2628n App B
Lancelot, Claude *see* Trigny, sieur de (pseud)
Landor, Walter Savage (1775–1864) 2816n
Landor (family) 2816n
Lane, Mr *see* Laing, Francis
Lardner, Nathaniel (1684–1768) *The Credibility of the Gospel History* 2225n
Larice, Don (opera) 2224*f20ᵛ*, 2224-*f20ᵛ*n
Latimer, Hugh, bp of Worcester (*c* 1485–1555) *Sermons* 2438; (1635) 2438n; (1788): "The Duty of Kings" 2438n*
La Tour, Charles Antoine Maximilien Baillet, comte de (1737–1806) App D
Laurati *see* Lorenzetti, Pietro
Lavater, Johann Caspar (1741–1801) *Essays on Physiognomy . . . written in the German language by J. C. Lavater, abridged from Mr. Holcroft's translation* (1793) 2828n
Lavoisier, Antoine Laurent (1743–97) 2439*f15*
Law, William (1686–1761) *see* Böhme, J. *The Works*
Leake, William Martin (1777–1860) 2188, 2188n, 2740n; *see also* Ball, Sir A. J., 1st bart attributed author Letter to the Earl of Camden

Le Brun, Marie Louise Élisabeth (Vigée) (1755–1842) 2828, 2828n
Leckie, Gould Francis (*fl* 1805) 2156n, 2162n, 2180, 2180n, 2181n, 2183, 2183n, 2193n, 2195n, 2196, 2196n, 2199, 2207, 2207n, 2213, 2220, 2220n, 2236, 2236n, 2252, 2259n, 2262n, 2295n, 2363n, 2467, 2467n, 2491, 2599n, 2672n, 2676, 2709, 2718, 2718n, App A; *An Historical Survey of the Foreign Affairs of Great Britain with a view to explain the causes and disasters of the late and present wars* (1808) 2193n, 2213n, 2215n, 2259n, 2261n*, 2295n, 2740n
Leckie, Mrs G. F. (*fl* 1805) 2256, 2467n, 2676
Leda 2670*f80ᵛ*
Leek *see* Leake, W. M.
Le Grice, Charles Valentine (1773–1858) 2018(?), 2018n, 2613(?), 2613n, 2619, 2619n; *see also* Blunden, E. (C.) *Coleridge's Fellow-Grecian*
Le Grice, Samuel (1775–1802) 2018(?), 2018n
Leibnitz, Gottfried Wilhelm, Freiherr von (1646–1716) 1993n, 2382-*f74ᵛ*, 2382n, 2442*f18*, 2584, 2584n, 2596, 2598
. . . *Opera philosophica quae exstant latina gallica germanica omnia* ed J. E. Erdmann (Berlin 1839–40): "Trois lettres à M. Rémond de Mont-Mort" 2596n*
SINGLE WORKS: *Essais de théodicée sur la bonté de Dieu, la liberté de l'homme et l'origine du mal* 1993n; . . . *Théodicée* . . . [tr from the French] (Hanover and Leipzig 1763) 1993*f31*, 1993n, 2014n
See also Coleridge, S. T. MSS: Marginalia
Le Moyne, Pierre (1602–72) 2136, 2136n

489

Mary II, queen of England, Scotland, and Ireland (1662–94) 1879
Mary (The Flight and Return of Mohammed) 2780n
Mary de Brus *see* Brus, Mary de
Masaniello (Tommaso Aniello *c* 1622–47) 2409, 2409n
Masinissa, king of Numidia (*c* 238–149 B.C.) 2045*f15*, 2045n
Mason, John Monck (1726–1809) *see* Massinger, P. *The Dramatick Works*
Massaniello *see* Masaniello
Massinger, Philip (1583–1640) *The Dramatick Works* ed J. M. Mason (1779) 3187n; *The Plays* ed W. Gifford (1805) 3187n; *The Maid of Honour* 3187*, 3189n*
Masson, Commandant (*d* 1798) 2575n
Matilda, empress consort of Henry V, Holy Roman emperor (1102–67) 2573, 2573n,
Maud, empress *see* Matilda
Maurice, prince of Orange, stadholder of the Netherlands (1567–1625) 2918
Maurice of Nassau, prince *see* Maurice, prince of Orange
Maynard, Charles Maynard, viscount (1752–1824) 1902*f9*, 1902n
Mazzalia (guide? *fl* 1804) 1886, 1886n
Mazzarese, Salvatore (1755–1847) 2840
Mazzola, Francesco *see* Parmigianino, Il
Meagle, Mr (Elizabethan commissioner) 3205n
Medea 2599*f92*, 2930, 2930n; *see also* Coleridge, S. T. PROJ WORKS: Medea, play on
Medici, Lorenzo de', the Magnificent (1449–92) 2670n, 2792, 2792n
Medici, Piero de' (1471–1503) 2792, 2792n
Medici (family) 2746, 2746n
Megithus (*fl* 2nd cent A.D.) 2236, 2236n

Melmoth, William (1710–99) *see* Pliny the Younger *Letters*
Melville, Henry Dundas, 1st viscount (1742–1811) 2598
Memmi, Simone *see* Martini, Simone
Merrick, Thomas (*b c* 1772) 2619(?), 2619n
Metastasio, Pietro Antonio Domenico Buonaventura (Pietro Trapassi 1698–1782) 2826, 2826n, App A
  Opere ed F. Nicolini (Bari 1912): *Alessandro nell'Indie* 2224*f19*n;
  Opera postume . . . (Vienna 1795) 2222n, App A
  SINGLE WORKS: *Alessandro nell'Indie* 2224*f19v*; *La clemenza di Tito* 3190, 3190n*; *Epitalamio* 2224*f16v*, 2224*f16v*n; *Isacco figura del redentore* 2224*f19v*, 2224*f19v*n; *Letters* 2222*
Meteyard, Eliza (1816–79) *A Group of Englishmen* (1871) 3187n
Michael (Wordsworth *Michael*) 2549n
Michael Angelo *see* Buonarotti, Michelangelo
Middleton, Mr (banker *fl* 1802) 3195*ff26,24v*; *see also* Davison, Noel, Templer, Middleton, Johnson & Wedgwood
Middleton, Conyers (1683–1750) *A Letter from Rome shewing an exact Conformity between Popery and Paganism* 2664n*, 2729, 2737; (1741) 2729n*
Middleton, Thomas Fanshaw, bp of Calcutta (1769–1822) 2539, 2539n
"Midge, Minim" *see* Coleridge, S. T. PROJ WORKS: characters
Migne, Jacques Paul (1800–75) ed *Patrologiae cursus completus: Latina* 3098n, 3133n
Millar, Capt of the *Minerva* (*fl* 1805) 2562, 2562n

Parma, Duke of 2420n

Parmeggiano *see* Parmigianino, Il

Parmigianino, Il (Francesco Mazzola 1503–40) 2759n, 2853, 2853n

Parnell, William (*d* 1821) *An Historical Apology for the Irish Catholics* (Dublin 1807) 3205n*; *see also* Coleridge, S. T. MSS: Marginalia

Partanna, Benedetto Maria Grifeo e del Bosco, principe di (*fl* 1806) 2214, 2214n

Partridge, Eric (1894–   ) *Name into Word* (New York 1950) 2889n

Parysatis (*fl* 401 B.C.) 3174*f29ᵛ*, 3174*f29ᵛ*n

Pascal, Blaise (1623–62) 2540n, 2598, App A; *Les Provinciales* (Cologne 1684) 1910n, 1914n, 2014n, 2133*, 2133n, 2134*, 2134n, 2135*, 2135n, 2136*, 2136n, App A; *see also* Coleridge, S. T. MSS: Marginalia

Pasini, Giuseppe Luca (1687–1770) comp *Vocabolario italiano-latino per uso degli studiosi di belle lettere nelle regie scuole di Torino* [comp G. L. Pasini & G. A. Badia] (Venice 1794) 2074n, App A

Pasley, Sir Charles William (1780–1861) 2449, 2449n, 2583*f105*, 2618, 2618n, 2627*, 2634n, 2671, 2671n, 2730, 2730n; *An Essay on the Military Policy and Institutions of the British Empire* (1810) 2449n; Remarks on the Extent of Cultivatable Land in Egypt (VCL MS F 14.3a) 2297n, App B; *see also* Coleridge, S. T. MSS: Appendix to Observations on Egypt

Passante, Bartolommeo (1614–56) 2101n

Pastor, Ludwig, Freiherr von Campersfelden (1854–1928) *History of the Popes from the close of the Middle Ages* tr E. F. Peeler (1952) 2261n

Paul, St, Apostle 1896, 2272, 2272n, 2326, 2459, 2459n, 2539, 2646n,

2888*f51ᵛ*; *see also* Paley, W. *Horae Paulinae*

Pearson, Richard (1765–1836) *see* Index 2: *Philosophical Transactions of the Royal Society* (London *Abridgement*)

Peatfield, T. (Holbeach *fl* 1804) 2272

Pelops (Pindar) 2882n

Penelope 2351

Perceval, John James, 3rd earl of Egmont *see* Egmont, J. J. Perceval, 3rd earl of

Perceval, Spencer (1762–1812) 3170n

Persius (Aulus Persius Flaccus 34–62) *see* Juvenal *J. Juvenalis et A. Persii Flacci satyrae*

Petch, Mr (*fl* 1806) 2901, 2901n

Peter, St, Apostle 2794n, 3081*f8*

Peter IV, king of Aragon (1319–87) 2261n

Peter de Brus *see* Brus, Peter de

Petrarch (Francesco Petrarca 1304–74) App A

Petronius Arbiter (*d c* 66) 2399n

Petrus, Uncle 2310, 2310n

Philenis (*The Lady Errant*) 1936n

Philip II, king of Macedonia (382–336 B.C.) 2337n

Philip II, king of Spain (1527–98) 2589n, 2918

Phillips, Sir Richard (1767–1840) 2303n

Phoebus 3096n

Phyllis (Strozzi) 2599[XVIII],[XX], 2599[XVIII],[XX]n

Pindar (*c* 522–443 B.C.) 2835, 2835n, 2880n, 2882n, 2886, 3174*f29*
    . . . *Pindari* . . . Ολυμπιονικαι . . . ed E. Schmied (Wittenberg 1616) 2881n, 2882n, 2887n, 2986n; *The Isthmian Odes* 2986*, 2986n; *The Olympian Odes* 2881n, 2882*, 2887n, 2911*, 2912*; *The Pythian Odes* 2881n
    The Odes tr Sir J. Sandys: *The Isthmian Odes* 2986n*; *The Olympian Odes* 2882n*, 2911n*, 2912n*
    See also Coleridge, S. T. MSS:

SOUTHEY, ROBERT (1774–1843)

(Headings: PERSONAL REFERENCES; COLLECTIONS AND
SELECTIONS; POEMS AND PLAYS; PROSE.)

PERSONAL REFERENCES:
books borrowed from 1914n, 2133n,
2807n, 2918n, 3102n, 3145n; Bristol days and 2692n, 3110n; criticism of 2077n; draws on Stuart for
Mrs C 1985n; good 2092n; and
Hazlitt's escapade 1850n;
at Keswick 2946n, 3128n; letters,
none from 2529n; letters of 2018n*;
letters to xvii, 1848n, 1890n,
1964n, 1993$ff29$–30^{v}n, 1998n,
2014$f49$, 2014n, 2032n, 2038n,
2117n, 2368, 2368n, 2640n, 2643n,
2899n, 3141n, App A, App D;
and metaphysics 2503n; metapothecaries his word 2503n; names
for: Australis 2950, 2950n, K
2064(7)(?), 2064(7)n(?), Osorio
2928n; parcel from 2362n; projected work with 2074; quarrel
with 2379, 2379n, 2398; and Scott
2900n; and Spanish 2431n, 2589n;
virtuous and unsympathetic 2913n

COLLECTIONS AND SELECTIONS:
Common-Place Book ed J. W. Warter
(1849–51) 2784n*
Omniana (1812) 2751n; *see also* Coleridge, S. T. PROSE: *Omniana*

POEMS AND PLAYS:
Madoc 1877n, 2018n
Madoc (MS) 1877n
Metrical Tales and Other Poems
(1805) 2354n

PROSE:
BM Add MS 47,887 2539n*
Life and Correspondence ed C. C.
Southey (1849–50) 1938n*, 1976n*,
2018n, 2021n, 2354n
The Life of Nelson 2311n, 2377n

See also Coleridge, S. T. MSS: The
Flight and Return of Mohammed;
PROJ WORKS: The Flight and Return of Mohammed

* * * * * *

Spain, King of *see* Charles IV, king
of Spain
Spallanzani, Lazzaro (1729–99) *Travels in the Two Sicilies* [tr T. Beddoes?] (London 1798) 2176n
Speedwell, Capt of *see* Findlay, John
Spenser, Edmund (*c* 1552–99) 2075,
2075n, 2598, 2813, 2813n, 3197,
3203; *The Faerie Queene* 2813; *The
Ruines of Rome* by Bellay 3203n
Speusippus (*c* 380–339 B.C.) 2894n
Spinoza, Baruch (Benedictus de
Spinoza 1632–77) 2208, 2208n,
2219, 2219n, 2316n, 3217$f71$; *Ethics* 3217n*
Sprat, Thomas, bp of Rochester
(1635–1713) *The History of the
Royal Society of London* 3005n

Stahl, Georg Ernst (1660–1734)
2382, 2382n
Stay, Benedetto (1714–1801) *Philosophiae recentioris a Benedicto Stay*
(Rome 1755) 2626, 2626n
Steevens, George (1736–1800) 2428n
Stephen, king of England (*c* 1097–
1154) 1879, 2443n, 2573, 2573n;
see also Coleridge, S. T. PROJ
WORKS: Stephen, historical drama
of King
Stephen Báthory, king of Poland
(1533–86) 2966*, 2966n
Sterling, John (1806–44) 2785n
Stigliano, Principessa di *see* Marino,
G. B. *Sonnetto alla Principessa di
Stigliano*

505

Memoirs of . . . *Martinus Scriblerus*

Sydenham, Thomas (1624–89) 2609, 2609n

Sylvester, Josuah (1563–1618) 3107n; *see also* Bartas, G. de Saluste, seigneur du *Du Bartas His Devine Weekes and Workes*

Syphax (*d c* 201 B.C.) 2045*f15*, 2045*f15*n

Syracuse, Siren of *see* Bertozzi, C.

Syrinx 2739, 2739n

T

T., J. *see* Tobin, James Webbe

T., W. *see* Taylor, William

Tacitus, Publius Cornelius (*c* 55–*c* 120) App A; *Opera quae extant* 3145; [tr T. Gordon] 3145, 3145n

Tagliana, Fortunata (*fl* 1804) 2594n, App B

Talebois, Ivo de *see* Ivo de Talebois

Tall-boy, David ap 2889

Tallboys (surname) 2889n

Tanner, Thomas, bp of St Asaph (1674–1735) 3031n

Tantalus 1998n, 2224*f79*, 2224*f79*n

Taphians (Hesiod) 2889n

Tartini, Giuseppe (1692–1770) 2224-*f21*, 2224*f21*n

Tasso, Torquato (1544–95) App A

Taylor, Jeremy, bp of Down (1613–67) 2129, 2129n, 2431*f4*, 2438n, 2968; *Polemical Discourses* (1674): *Dissuasive from Popery* 2209n; *see also* Coleridge, S. T. MSS: Marginalia

Taylor, Nathaniel (*fl* 1805) A letter . . . to S. Stocker (VCL MS F 14.8a) App B

Taylor, William (1765–1836) 2643, 2643n, 2664*f83*n

Teignmouth, John Shore, 1st baron (1751–1834) *Memoirs of Sir William Jones* (*The Works of Sir William Jones* 1807) 3130n*

Telauges (*fl* 5th cent B.C.) 2077n

Teleboans (Hesiod) 2889n

Templer *see* Davison, Noel, Templer, Middleton, Johnson & Wedgwood

Temporal, T. (*d* 1806) 2863

Tennemann, Wilhelm Gottlieb (1761–1819) 2447n; *Geschichte der Philosophie* (Leipzig 1798–1819) 2342n; *see also* Coleridge, S. T. MSS: Marginalia

Terence (Publius Terentius Afer *c* 195–159 B.C.) *Heautontimorumenos* 2123n*; tr J. Sargeaunt 2123n*

Teresa, St (1515–82) 2664*f82*, 2664-*f82*n; *The Life [and Works] of* . . . *St. Teresa* (1675) 2664n, 3102n; *see also* Coleridge, S. T. MSS: Marginalia; Crashaw, R. *Hymn to the Name and Honour of* . . . *Saint Teresa*

Tertullian (Quintus Septimius Florens Tertullianus *c* 160–*c* 220) *De carne Christi* 3030*; *Of the Body of Christ* 3030n*; spurious and doubtful works: *Poemata* 2835(?), 2835n

Tetens, Johann Nikolaus (1736–1807) 2375; *Philosophische Versuche* (Leipzig 1777) 2375n

Thelwall, John (1764–1834) 2403, 2403n

Theophilus, St, bp of Antioch (*fl* 2nd cent) . . . *Ad Autolycum* (Oxford 1684) 2445*f20**, 2445n

Theophrastus (*c* 370–*c* 286 B.C.) *Theophrastus of Eresus on Winds and on Weather Signs* tr J. G. Wood ed G. J. Symons (1894) 3129n

Theopompus, king of Sparta (*fl* 8th cent B.C.) 3117*, 3117n*

Thomas à Becket, St, abp of Canterbury (*c* 1118–70) 2443n

Thomas Aquinas, St (*c* 1225–74) 2219, 2219n

Thomond, Murrough O'Brien, 1st earl of (*d* 1551) 3205n

Thompson, John (1785–1866) 1976n

Thrasybulus (name) 2732, 2732n

Thwaites, Mr (*fl* 1666) 2965

WORDSWORTH, WILLIAM (1770–1850)

(Headings: PERSONAL REFERENCES; COMPLETE WORKS;
COLLECTIONS AND SELECTIONS; SINGLE WORKS.)

PERSONAL REFERENCES:
annotated W. P. Knight 1963n; Ariosto, his 2670n, App A; Axiologus (pseud) 3231n; Mrs Barbauld once respected by 2303n; birthplace 2088n; brother John 2517n, 2527, 2531; Coleorton 2956n; in C's dreams 2078; C's jealousy of re SH 2001n, 2009, 2055n, 2975n, 2998, 2998n, 3148n; C's projected essay on 1993, 2064; C's self-contrast with 2086n, 2712, 2750n, 3148; Cornell collection of 2178n; critical of Northcote portrait of C 1976n;

on duty 3231n; Edridge to draw 2048n; England to C 2598; Farrington's dislike of 2836n; gives note for C to Sotheby 1965n; Godwin attacked 1890n; in Grasmere circle 2389, 2389n, 2397, 2517, 2623;

image of ship applied to 2016n, 2063n, 2064n, 2431n; initials in page-corners N 17 Gen, 2624, 2628; R. Jones his friend 2894n; Le Grice reviewed poems of, antagonistically 2018n; lends C books 3196n, 3197n; letter to C 2912n, 3215n(?); literary relations with C 2798n, 2900n;

"mood of mind" used by 2218; name in cipher 3063, 3063n, 3231; no pleasure in transitory 2026; oak-planting suggested to 3111; observing lines of mountains with C 2347; observing reflections in water with C 1844;

Pasley, replies to 2449n; poems alluded to N 9 Gen, 2092, 2906n, 3131, 3131n, App B, App E; poetry of, impassioned and particularized

2431*f5*; quarrel with C N 18 Gen; quotes distinction by C 1938n; recluse, referred to as 2057, 2057n; relations with C N 11 Gen, 2032-*f99*ᵛ, 2193, 2750, 2909n, 3134n; Rock of Names 2950n; "sinking" a defect of his poetry 2625n; in Soother of Absence 2224*f15*; *Spectator* projected with 2074; Dr Stock and W poems 3141, 3141n; Stockdale's *Shakespeare* his favoured ed 3145n;

walked with C to Troutbeck 1843n; watch of C's 2904, 2904n; J. Wedgwood complains of C to 3187n; as XY 2064(7)(?), 2064(7)n(?)

COMPLETE WORKS:
The Poetical Works ed E. de Selincourt and H. Darbishire (1940–9) 2429n, 2531n, App E
The Poetical Works ed W. Knight (1896) 2429n*

COLLECTIONS AND SELECTIONS:
Lyrical Ballads 2120, 2120n, 2121n, 2472(?), 2472n; (1800) 1922n, 2011n, 2211n, 2224n, 2468n, 2826n, 3181n, 3203n; *see also* poems by title under SINGLE WORKS
Lyrical Ballads of William Wordsworth and S. T. Coleridge 1798 ed T. Hutchinson (1898) 2468n, 3181n*
Lyrical Ballads, with a few other Poems (1798) 2826n, 3213n
Poems (1815) 1889n, 2428n*, 2826n*
[Poems transcribed by S. Hutchinson and D. Wordsworth (MS)] 2531n, 2583n
Wordsworth's Literary Criticism ed N. C. Smith (1905) 2826n*

SINGLE WORKS:

Anticipation 1857n*

The Borderers 2443n

The Brothers 1997n*, 2011, 2011n

The Excursion 2075, 2075n

The Female Vagrant 1999*, 1999n, 2013*f46*[v]n*

Guilt and Sorrow 1999n, 2013*f46*[v]n*; see also his *The Female Vagrant*

"Her eyes are wild . . ." *see* his *The Mad Mother*

Lines composed a few miles above Tintern Abbey 1889n*, 2556n, 2739n

The Mad Mother 2112*, 2112n

Michael 2120n, 2549, 2549n*

"My heart leaps up when I behold . . ." 2013n*

Ode to Duty 2091n, 2531, 2531n, 2556n, 2750n, 3026n

"The Pedlar" *see* his *The Excursion*

The Pet Lamb 2468*f29*[v]*, 2468n*

Peter Bell 2583*f106*[v], 2583n

The Prelude 1997n*, 2057, 2057n, 2086*f40**, 2086*f40*n*, 2092n; ed de Selincourt 1859n*, 2274n*

The Recluse 2045n, 2397n, 2429n, 2556n, App B

The Ruined Cottage 2075n, 2092n

"Witness thou/The dear companion of my lonely walk . . ." 2429*, 2429n*

See also for single poems App E

See also Coleridge, S. T. POEMS: *Ad Vilmum Axiologum*; Margoliouth, H. M. *Wordsworth and Coleridge, 1795–1834*; Moorman, M. C. *William Wordsworth; a Biography*; Schneider, B. R. *Wordsworth's Cambridge Education*; Smith, E. ed *An Estimate of William Wordsworth by his Contemporaries*

* * * * * *

Wordsworth (family) xix, N 11 Gen, N 19 Gen, 1849n, 1883n, 1902n, 1907n, 1938n, 1983n, 1999n, 2013n, 2224*f85*[v]n, 2517n, 2529n, 2531n, 2537n, 2860, 2910n, 2935n, 2938n, 3128n, 3146, App A, App B, App E

Wrangham, Francis (1769–1842) *Poems* (1795) 2120n, 2894n: *Hendecasyllabi ad Brutonam* tr S. T. Coleridge 2894n

Wright, Herbert Gladstone (1888–) *Boccaccio in England* (1957) 2670n*

Wyndham *see* Windham

X

Xenophon (*c* 430–*c* 354 B.C.) 2236, 2236n; *Memorabilia* . . . tr E. C. Marchant 3122n*

"Xenophon the Younger" (*fl* 2nd cent A.D.) *see* Arrian

XY *see* Wordsworth, William

Y

Yates, Elizabeth (Brunton) (1799–1860) 2395n; *see also* Wrangham, F. *Hendecasyllabi ad Brutonam* tr S. T. Coleridge

Yates, Richard (1769–1834) "Observations on the Cultivation and Growth of Oak Timber" (*A Journal of Natural Philosophy, Chemistry and the Arts* ed W. Nicholson 1804) 3111n

Young, Edward (1683–1765) *Works* (1774–8): *Conjectures on Original Composition* 2211n, 2914n*

Young, H. S. (*fl* 1893) 2918n

Younge, Mr (butler *fl* 1802) 3195*f29*

Z

Selected Titles

See Index 1 under the name of the author for the following titles not listed here: all works by Samuel Taylor Coleridge; all collected works, autobiographies, essays, letters, sermons, speeches, and collected or single short poems by other authors. For memoirs and lives other than Coleridge's see under the name of the author or of the person who is the subject; for lives of Coleridge see Index 1 under the author or this Index under the title. For explanation of symbols, see the headnote preceding Index 1.

A

"Account of a Journey from the Port of Oratava in the Island of Teneriff, to the top of the Peak in that Island, An" (*Philosophical Transactions of the Royal Society* London 1715) J. Edens 3005n

"Account of the Discovery of the Kingdom of Bambûk, and its Gold Mines, in 1716, An" (*A New General Collection of Voyages & Travels* London 1745) P. Compagnon 3006n*

"Account of the two sorts of the Helmontian Laudanum . . . with the Way of Baron F. M. Van Helmont of preparing his Laudanum . . ." (*Philosophical Transactions of the Royal Society* London *Abridgement* 1792–1809) R. Boyle 3161n

. . . *Ad Autolycum* (Oxford 1684) St Theophilus 2445*f20**, 2445n

Ad Lucilium epistulae morales L. A. Seneca 2615*, 2615n

Aeneid Virgil 2060*f26**, 2093n, 2223n, 2725n, 3011, 3011n; tr H. R. Fairclough (1920) 2060*f26*n*

Alaham F. Greville, 1st baron Brooke, 2917n*, 2918*, 2918n*, 2919n, 2920n*, 2921n*, 2923n*, 2924n, 2925*, 2925n*, 2927n, 2931, 2931n, 2932*, 2932n*

Allegro, L' J. Milton 2192n*

Allgemeine Betrachtungen über die Triebe der Thiere (Hamburg 1798) H. S. Reimarus 2318n, 2319n, 2320n, 2321, 2321n, 2323*, 2323n, 2325, 2325n, 2326n, 2327n*, 2328*, 2328n, 2329n, 2330n, 2331n, 2332n, 2333n, 2334n, 2335n, 2336n, 2544n

Alliance between Church and State, The (1736) W. Warburton 2440-*f16*ᵛ, 2440n*

Alonzo the Brave and the Fair Imogene M. G. Lewis 2599*f90*ᵛ, 2599*f90*ᵛn

Amleto (1792) G. Andreozzi 2339n

Amulet, The (1833) 2798n*

Analogy of Religion, Natural and Revealed, to the Constitution and Course of Nature, The (1736) J. Butler 3145, 3145n

Analytical Inquiry into the Principles of Taste, An (1806) R. P. Knight 1963n

"Anatomizing of Honesty, Ambition and Fortitude" (*Cottoni Posthuma* 1679) F. Walsingham 1880*, 1880n

Place-Names

Alley 2194; Cheapside 2884n, 3028, 3028n; Christ's Hospital 1854n, 1925n, 1966n, 2018n, 2055, 2539n, 2613n, 2619n, 2647*f26*, 2647n, 2859; Clapham 2440n; Covent Garden 1856n, 2339n;

Deptford N K Gen; Drury Lane 2060*f25ᵛ*n; Duchess St 1989n; East India House 1856n; Essex St 3009; Finsbury Sq 3026; Fitzroy Sq 1867; Friday St 2884, 2884n;

Gerrard St 1873, 1873n; Goodge St 1867; Goswell St 1910n, 2133n; Gray's Inn Lane 1910; Great Cumberland Place 2875; Great St Helen's 2885, 2885n; Grosvenor Sq 1973n;

Highgate xviii, N 18 Gen, N $21\frac{1}{2}$ Gen, 2999n; Holborn 2442n; Holland House 2853n; House of Lords 1854, 1862n; Howland St 1867;

Kensington Gravel Pits 3218; King St 1856n; Liverpool St Station 2454n; Lombard St 2194; Marylebone Parish 2605; Millfield Lane 2999n; National Gallery 1895n; Newgate 2578; Northumberland St 1867, 1867n; Oxford St 2442n; Pall Mall N 9 Gen, 1854, 1960, 1986; Paternoster Row 1870n; Pimlico 1867; Poultry 3028n;

Ranelagh 2827, 2827n; Royal Academy 1978n, 2853n; Royal Institution of Great Britain N 23 Gen, 1954n, 2274n, 2428n, 3180n, 3196n, 3218n; Russel's Waggon Office 2884n; St Paul's School 2859; Shakespeare Gallery 2853n; South Audley St 1973n; Strand 2452, 2605; Swinton St 1910; Theatre Royal 2395n; Tottenham Chapel 1867;

Upper Eaton St 1867; Upper Gower St 1938, 1938n; Upper Seymour St 1924; Upper Titchfield St 1911n; Uxbridge Rd 3218; Waghorn's Coffee House 1862,

1862n, 1878; Westminster 1854, 1926n, 2955n; Westminster School 2539n, 2859; Whitehall 1867
Loreto 2848
Loughton 1965
Louisiana 2228n
Lowther Castle 1899(5)n
Lucca *see* Luqa
Luqa 2282n, 2497, 2497n
Lynn *see* King's Lynn
Lynton 2202*f56*n

M

Maccluba *see* Maqluba
Madonna della Rocca, church *see* Taormina, Madonna della Rocca, church
Madrid 2751n
Magnisi, Bay of 2195*f51ᵛ*, 2195*f51ᵛ*n, 2202*f54ᵛ*
Magnisi, peninsula 2195*f52*
Maida 2744n
Maidlow 1990, 1990n
Maio *see* Moio
Malaga 2422
Maletto 2709*f95*
Malta xvi, xvii, xviii, N K Gen, N 11 Gen, N 15 Gen, N 17 Gen, N 18 Gen, N $21\frac{1}{2}$ Gen

Admiralty 2155; Admiralty Court 2379; *Adonis annuus* L in 2564n; Major Adye, his death after visit 2045n, 2397n; almanac 2637*f90ᵛ*; American newspapers in 2779n; anecdotes in 2416n; apricot tarts at 2024;

B Poets in 2621n, 2654n; *Baldwin's Journal* in 2605n; Sir A. Ball in 2101n; barley and wheat from 2668n; *Beheading of St John* painting in 2101n; British Library App D; British policies regarding 2111n; British representative at Tunis in 2476n; British wrested M from French 2101n; Broadbent in 2699n; Buonaparte at 2138;

Cartaginese, Il M periodical

tine 2312n; mameluke Minister at xvii; Manoel, fort 2563; "Melita" 2651, 2651n; men with military adventures in 2589n; military usefulness of 2460n; J. Morrison in 2099n; MS signed C. Pasley, M 2297n;

naval anecdotes in 2308n; naval officers in 2293n; noises 2098, 2098n, 2114, 2114n, 2148, 2148n, 2614, 2614n; nonsense verses 2224-*f25*; notebook used in 2500n;

Oglander, R., passed through 2513n; *Omniana* refers this to 2119n; orange trees in 2501;

papers brought from 2162n; papers returned to xvii–xviii; Pasley, C's intimacy with 2730n; peculiar vapor in 2610$f79^v$; period between Grasmere and 1901n; *Peter Bell* read in App E; *Philosophische Versuche* annotated in 2375n; pinks in 2499; plague and 2779n; pocketbook, used pre-M 2449n; pocketbooks with metallic pencils 2012$f42$n; political uncertainties 2571n; presence of Sara on vessel for 2057; product of M journey 2880n;

Quarantine Harbour 2100, 2266, 2313; quiet of 2284, 2498; quotation applied to 1943n; Ragusae forced to sea from 2312; rain at 2147; Remarks on Cultivatable Land in Egypt signed C. Pasley M 2297n; ruts in NW coast 2141n;

sacerdotal orders 2664n; St Paul's Church 2244n; St Paul's shipwreck linked with 2272n; Sewell, judge of Vice-Admiralty Court 2139n; shape 2190n; Sharp suggested M 1856n; Sicily, distance from M 2673, 2673n; sight of 2097; sky at 3159; Sir J. Stoddart advocate in Admiralty Court 2099n, C's first host in 2155n, suggested M 2099n; S. Stoddart in 2297n; stonecrop 2564, 2564n;

strategic and economic importance of 2664n; Stuart to send *Political Register* to 2150n; sun and light 2224$f25$n; Suter in M documents 2468n;

to mark an occasion 2108n; Tragedy scene Malta 2064(5); vetch in 2521n; W. A. Villettes military commander in 2101n; want of money common in 2288; war-time 2418n; windmills 2568; word *idolatry* 2103n; word *imxi* 2636n; Wordsworth poems C took to 2531n; Wordsworths, letter from 2531n; "wrestling life and death" in 2224$f25^v$n

For Proclamations and Notices of the Government of Malta *see* Index 2 under *Avvisi; Bandi;* and *Proclamations*

* *

Man, Isle of 1899(3)n,(21)n
Manchester, Literary and Philosophical Society 1849n
Manghisi, Bay of *see* Magnisi, Bay of
Manhoel, fort *see* Malta, Manoel, fort
Maqluba 2506, 2506n
Marengo 2377n
Marettimo, island 2095
Maretto *see* Maletto
Maritimo, island *see* Marettimo, island
Marylebone Parish *see* London, Marylebone Parish
Massaria di San Nicola 2709$f95^v$
Mazzara 2709$f95$
M'dina (Notabile) 2281n, 2520, 2520n, 2521, 2563, 2563n, 2575, 2575n, 2577n, 2594n
Mecca 2780n
Medina 2780n
Mediterranean Sea xviii, xix, 2050, 2052$f20^v$n, 2060$f25$, 2075n, 2081n, 2086$f38^v$n, 2162n, 2224$f25$n, 2227n, 2228n, 2253n, 2280, 2289n, 2377n, 2400, 2408n, 2453n, 2536n, 2628n, 2688n, 2705$f94$, 2866n, App A

North Walsham 3125
Northumberland 2022*f98ᵛ*
Northumberland St *see* London,
　Northumberland St
Norwich 2272, 2643, 2643n, 2664*f83*n
Notabile *see* M'dina (Notabile)
Noto xvi, 2709*f95ᵛ*
Novara 2709*f95*

O

Odessa 2697
Ohud, mt *see* Uhud, mt
Olevano 2785n, 2794n, 2796*ff108*,
　108ᵛ, 2796n, 2793n, 2801n, 2804n,
　2809, 2809n, 2816, 2817, 2818,
　2818n, 2821; Castle 2821
Olympus, mt 3203
Oporto 2014*f49*, 2015n
Oran 2668
Orchardhigh *see* Orchardleigh
Orchardleigh 3195*f26ᵛ*, 3195n
Ortegal, cape 2002
Ortygia *see* Syracuse, Ortygia
Ossaia 2851, 2851n
Ostia 2847
Otaheite, island *see* Tahiti, island
Ottery St Mary 1908n, 2290, 2290n,
　3041n; Church 2454, 2454n, 2619n;
　King's School 1908n
Oxford 2018n; University 2651:
　Bodleian Library 3031n
Oxford St *see* London, Oxford St

P

Pace 2709*ff94ᵛ,95*
Pagliano *see* Paliano
Palagonia 2709*f95ᵛ*
Palazzolo 2709*f95ᵛ*
Palermo xvi, xviii, 1866n, 2184n,
　2254, 2254n, 2261*f65ᵛ*, 2744n
Palestine 2945
Palestrina 2809, 2809n
Paliano 2796*f108*, 2796n
Pall Mall *see* London, Pall Mall
Pallas, cape *see* Palos, cape
Pallestrina *see* Palestrina

Palma 2709*f95ᵛ*
Palos, cape 2064*f28*
Papal States 2851n
Papinio 2849*f109ᵛ*
Paraguay 2945
Paris 2264n, 2756, 2756n, 2811n
　Bastille 1879n; Sorbonne 2134-
　f6ᵛ, 2134*f6ᵛ*n, 2136, 2136n; Uni-
　versité *see* Sorbonne
Parma 2420
Parndon 2892n
Paternò 2709*f95*
Paternoster Row *see* London, Pater-
　noster Row
Pauline Chapel *see* Rome, Pauline
　Chapel
Pausilippo, mt 2731n
Peel Castle (near Barrow-in-Furness)
　1899(21)n
Peel Castle (Isle of Man) 1899(3)n,
　(21)n
Pellegrino, mt 1866, 1866n
Peloponnesus *see* Morea, peninsula
Pembroke College *see* Cambridge
　University: Pembroke College
Pembrokeshire 2415n
Pennsylvania 2253
Penrith 2895n, 2903n, 2918n
Perilli, stream 2709*f95*
Peru 2945
Perugia 2849n, 2850
Pharos, peninsula 2258n
Piazza Armerina 2709*f95ᵛ*
Piel Castle *see* Peel Castle (near
　Barrow-in-Furness)
Pillars of Hercules 2045*f15*; *see also*
　Apes' Hill
Pimlico *see* London, Pimlico
Piraeus 2188n
Pisa 2856, 2856n, 2858, 2858n, 2867,
　2868n
　Baptistery 2856; Campanile
　2856; Campo Santo 2856, 2857n,
　2858n; Cathedral 2856; Globe, inn
　2866
Pisma, river 2212, 2212n
Place Fell 2013*f44ᵛ*
Plemmyrion 2195*f51*